R. Gupta's®

Popular Master Guide

IBPS Specialist Officer

Institute of Banking Personnel Selection

Rajbhasha Adhikari Law Officer

Preliminary Exam

- Specialised Study & Practice Material Prepared by Experts
- Solved Multiple Choice Questions
- Solved Previous Year Paper

by

RPH Editorial Board

2027 EDITION

RAMESH PUBLISHING HOUSE, NEW DELHI

Published by
O.P. Gupta *for* Ramesh Publishing House

Admin. Office
12-H, New Daryaganj Road, Opp. Officers' Mess,
New Delhi-110002 ✆ 23275224, 23245124

E-mail: info@rameshpublishinghouse.com
For Online Shopping: www.rameshpublishinghouse.com

Showroom
• Balaji Market, Nai Sarak, Delhi-110006 ✆ 23282525 📱 9354373464
• 4457, Nai Sarak, Delhi-110006

Book Code: R-1942

ISBN: 978-93-86845-82-5

Price: ₹ 430

Printed by : Repro India Ltd.

Contents

SCHEME OF ONLINE PRELIMINARY EXAMINATIONS

The structure of the Examinations which will be conducted online are as follows:

PRELIMINARY EXAMINATION

Sr. No.	Name of Tests	No. of Questions	Maximum Marks	Medium of Exam	Duration
1.	English Language	50	25	English	40 min
2.	Reasoning	50	50	English & Hindi	40 min
3.	General Awareness with Special Reference to Banking Industry	50	50	English & Hindi	40 min
	Total	**150**	**125**		

Note:

- Candidates have to qualify in each of the three tests by securing minimum cut-off marks to be decided by IBPS. Adequate number of candidates in each category as decided by IBPS depending upon requirements, will be shortlisted for Online Main Examination.
- **Penalty for Wrong Answers:** There will be penalty for wrong answers marked in the Objective Tests. For each question for which a wrong answer has been given by the candidate one fourth or 0.25 of the marks assigned to that question will be deducted as penalty to arrive at corrected score. If a question is left blank, *i.e.* no answer is marked by the candidate, there will be no penalty for that question.

Previous Years' Paper

IBPS-SPECIALIST OFFICERS

Rajbhasha Adhikari and Law Officer, 2025*

Preliminary Exam

ENGLISH LANGUAGE

Directions (Qs. No. 1-10): *Read the following passage and answer the given questions.*

When Company X introduced its online game, the market response was immediate and overwhelming. The very next year, the company earned huge profits and quickly gained users across the globe. Reports revealed that the game generated 50 million dollars worldwide, making it one of the most successful digital launches in recent years. This sudden success was seen as a major **hit**, granting Company X recognition and dominance in the industry.

Yet, beneath the shining surface of profits and popularity, a darker picture began to emerge. Parents started to **raise** concerns over the time children were spending on this game. Many young users became addicted, unable to manage their daily schedules, and their studies suffered significantly. Teachers noticed falling grades, a decline in participation, and a visible drop in discipline. At home, the situation worsened as children grew increasingly irritable, spending less time with family and showing signs of inappropriate behavior.

Roommates, on the other hand, reported that their relationships remained smooth only during gaming sessions. Once the console was turned off, interactions were minimal, and genuine conversations reduced. What was marketed as a tool for entertainment and bonding ironically created isolation and dependency. Parents found themselves struggling to establish healthy routines for their children, often entering into conflicts that left family ties strained.

An independent organisation decided to investigate these growing concerns and carried out a largescale survey. The data collected and the report submitted revealed an alarming trend. The impact of the game was largely negative, with cases of extreme dependency, reduced academic achievement, and antisocial tendencies being repeatedly recorded. What initially gave the company a **toe hold** in the international gaming market was now turning into a nationwide social concern.

The report strongly emphasized that while the company's financial growth was undeniable, the cost to society was far greater. Addiction had begun to reshape the daily lives of thousands of children, disturbing family harmony and disrupting the overall learning environment. Based on the overwhelming findings, the organisation recommended that the game should be banned in the country. The conclusion was clear: no amount of profit could justify the erosion of discipline, values, and future prospects of the younger generation.

* Based on Memory.

1. What is the primary irony highlighted by the author regarding Company X's online game?

A. The company's most profitable year was also its most controversial.
B. A game designed for entertainment and bonding ended up fostering addiction and isolation.
C. The company grew financially, but its user base started declining soon after.
D. Parents initially appreciated the game but later demanded it be banned.
E. While profits surged, the company secretly planned to shut down the game.

2. What negative consequences of the game were observed in children, as per the passage?

A. Children began losing interest in digital games and preferred outdoor activities instead.
B. Students became highly disciplined and responsible with their schoolwork and home routines.
C. Many children showed signs of addiction, poor academic performance, irritability, and spent less time with family members.
D. Young users formed better relationships with their teachers but struggled with peer pressure.
E. Children used the game as a stress-relief method and became more independent in their decision-making.

3. What can be inferred about the survey conducted by the independent organisation?

A. It focused solely on academic performance in urban schools.
B. It revealed mild concerns that were largely exaggerated by the media.
C. It showed that most users balanced gaming and daily life efficiently.
D. It confirmed widespread negative impacts, prompting a ban recommendation.
E. It offered technical fixes for the game's issues but no regulatory suggestions.

4. According to the passage, what role did roommates play in revealing the social effects of the game?

A. They actively tried to prevent gaming in their homes.
B. They became addicted and dropped out of college.
C. They used the game as a bonding tool but lacked real interaction otherwise.
D. They encouraged younger players to limit their screen time.
E. They often fought over gaming equipment, causing tension.

5. Why did Company X's game gain global popularity so quickly after its launch?

A. The game was unique and had no competitors in the digital market.
B. The company launched a global advertising campaign supported by educational institutions.
C. The game quickly attracted millions of users and earned substantial profits, establishing the company's position in the gaming industry.
D. Parents and teachers encouraged children to use the game for both fun and learning.
E. The company offered the game free of cost to users during the initial launch phase.

6. How did teachers contribute to the concern about the game's impact?

A. They partnered with the company to create school-safe gaming tools.
B. They observed and reported a consistent decline in student behavior and academic performance.
C. They welcomed the game, saying it helped students with teamwork.
D. They banned the use of computers in classrooms due to gaming.
E. They noticed students becoming physically stronger due to eye-hand coordination practice.

7. Which of the following word/phrase does mean a small or initial position that leads to progress or expansion?
   A. downfall
   B. shortcut
   C. toe hold
   D. decline
   E. conclusion

8. Choose the option that is the closest in meaning to the word "hit" as used in the passage:
   A. Blow
   B. Success
   C. Punch
   D. Trial
   E. Drama

9. Choose the word that is the opposite in meaning to "raise" as used in the passage:
   A. Boost
   B. Improve
   C. Lower
   D. Distribute
   E. Elevate

10. What was the main recommendation made by the independent organisation after analyzing the impact of the game?
   A. The organisation suggested that the game should be modified to include educational content.
   B. The organisation recommended that the game should be banned due to its harmful effects on children and society.
   C. The organisation advised parents to install stricter internet filters to monitor their children's gaming habits.
   D. The organisation proposed that the game be used as a tool for team building and school collaboration.
   E. The organisation recommended offering rewards to children who limit their gaming time.

Directions (Qs. No. 11-16): *In the following question, few sentences are given. Choose and mark the sentence which contains no grammatical or contextual error in it. If all the sentences are grammatically and contextually incorrect, mark "All are incorrect" option as the answer choice.*

11. A. He insisted to go to the market even though he was not feeling well.
   B. She said she would rather stay home than going to the party.
   C. The manager along with his team were present at the conference.
   D. The players were congratulated for their outstanding performance.
   E. All are incorrect.

12. A. If he will call me, I will inform you immediately.
   B. The police is investigating the matter seriously.
   C. The meeting has been rescheduled due to unavoidable circumstances.
   D. Everyone must submitted their reports by tomorrow without fail.
   E. All are incorrect.

13. A. He told me that he is living in Delhi since 2010.
   B. The data show a remarkable increase in productivity this year.
   C. Either the principal or the teachers is responsible for this confusion.
   D. The book that you gave me are very interesting.
   E. All are incorrect.

14. A. He did not attend the meeting, nor he informed anyone about his absence.
   B. The new policy aims at improving efficiency across departments.
   C. She is one of the student who always complete their homework.
   D. The company have decided to expand its operations abroad.
   E. All are incorrect.

15. A. Neither of the brothers were willing to take responsibility for the mistake.
   B. The committee have submitted its report to the higher authorities.
   C. She denied to have taken any money from the locker.
   D. The workers demanded that their wages be increased immediately.
   E. All are incorrect.

16. A. If I was you, I would accept the offer immediately.
B. She congratulated him on his promotion to the post of manager.
C. Each of the boys are responsible for cleaning the classroom.
D. The results of the survey has been published in today's newspaper.
E. All are incorrect.

Directions (Qs. No. 17-22): *In the following question, a passage is provided with few blanks. Choose the most suitable word from the given options to fill the respective blank.*

The nation has recently ___ **(A)** ___ a surge in fake bomb threats targeting trains and flights, creating panic among passengers and disrupting essential travel services. Anonymous calls and messages falsely claimed the ___ **(B)** ___ of explosives, forcing authorities to carry out emergency checks. These incidents led to delays, cancellations, and inconvenience for thousands of travelers.

Union government ministers confirmed that detailed information about the threats had been ___ **(C)** ___ and stressed that such false alarms are treated as serious crimes. They noted that spreading fake information not only causes fear but also ___ **(D)** ___ security resources and diverts attention from genuine concerns.

Investigations are underway to ___ **(E)** ___ the sources of these false alerts. Early indications point to organized attempts to spread chaos. Officials assured that once the responsible organization is identified, strict punishment will be ___ **(F)** ___ under existing laws. The government has also directed railways and aviation authorities to step up security measures and verify all suspicious communications without delay.

While no actual explosives have been discovered, the gravity of the threats cannot be ignored. Passengers are advised to remain calm and cooperate with security checks, as the government reiterated its commitment to ensuring safety and penalizing those spreading fake threats.

17. Which of the following is most suitable to fill the blank A?
A. faced
B. created
C. ignored
D. welcomed
E. imagined

18. Which of the following is most suitable to fill the blank B?
A. growth
B. presence
C. function
D. arrival
E. reason

19. Which of the following is most suitable to fill the blank C?
A. invented
B. ignored
C. delayed
D. destroyed
E. received

20. Which of the following is most suitable to fill the blank D?
A. saves
B. collects
C. wastes
D. builds
E. increases

21. Which of the following is most suitable to fill the blank E?
A. confuse
B. mislead
C. identify
D. replace
E. hide

22. Which of the following is most suitable to fill the blank F?
A. ignored
B. enforced
C. avoided
D. delayed
E. reduced

Directions (Qs. No. 23-25): *In the question given below two sentences are given which are grammatically correct and meaningful. Connect them with the most suitable word given below the statements in the best possible way without changing the intended meaning. Choose the answer accordingly from the options to form a correct coherent sentence.*

23. (I) She saved money for several months;
(II) She finally bought a new laptop.

A. although
B. so
C. however
D. despite
E. moreover

24. (I) He prepared well for the interview;
(II) He did not get selected for the job.

A. yet
B. because
C. therefore
D. moreover
E. hence

25. (I) The shop was closed;
(II) We could not buy any groceries.

A. although
B. therefore
C. yet
D. despite
E. moreover

Directions (Qs. No. 26-27): *Rearrange the following five sentences (A), (B), (C), (D) and (E) in the proper sequence to form a meaningful paragraph.*

26. (A) The development of the electronic computer began in the 20th century, with machines like ENIAC marking a significant leap.
(B) Early computing devices such as the abacus and mechanical calculators laid the foundation for modern machines.
(C) Over time, computers evolved rapidly, moving from bulky machines to compact, powerful personal computers.
(D) In the 19th century, Charles Babbage conceptualized the Analytical Engine, often regarded as the first mechanical computer design.
(E) This evolution continued into the 21st century, leading to innovations like smartphones and cloud computing.

A. BDACE
B. CBADE
C. DCBAE
D. CBEAD
E. DBAEC

27. (A) Glucose, commonly referred to as blood sugar, is the primary source of energy for the body's cells.
(B) When blood sugar levels drop too low, a person may experience dizziness, confusion, and even loss of consciousness.
(C) Such regulation is vital for maintaining stable blood sugar, ensuring overall health and the proper functioning of organs.
(D) Conversely, consistently high blood sugar can lead to serious health issues such as nerve damage, vision problems, and diabetes.
(E) The body carefully regulates these glucose levels through hormones like insulin, which enable cells to absorb sugar from the bloodstream.

A. BCADE
B. ADCBE
C. DBCAE
D. AECBD
E. DACBE

Directions (Qs. No. 28-29): *In the given question, few sentences are given. Also, sentence (D) is fixed as the fourth sentence. Rearrange the remaining four sentences in the proper sequence to form a meaningful paragraph.*

28. (A) Wheat thrives on a cool growing season, followed by a warm, dry period for harvest.
(B) In many parts of the world, wheat is a staple food crop, cultivated extensively for its adaptability and nutritional value.
(C) With the help of modern techniques like mechanized irrigation and improved seed varieties, wheat production has seen significant growth.
(D) After harvesting, the grains are cleaned, stored in dry conditions, and distributed for consumption or further processing.
(E) Given these requirements, farmers select suitable soils and time their sowing to secure a healthy yield.

A. CEADB
B. AEBDC
C. ABCDE
D. AECDB
E. BAEDC

29. (A) Technology has become a defining force of modern life, reshaping domains from communication to healthcare and beyond.

(B) While it brings convenience and efficiency, it also raises concerns about privacy, mental health, and dependency.

(C) As innovations continue to emerge, society must learn to balance technological advancement with human values.

(D) These developments have deeply influenced human behavior, altering habits, routines, and even attention spans.

(E) This rapid pace of change has introduced both opportunities and challenges into daily routines.

A. CEADB B. AEBDC
C. EACDB D. EABDC
E. ACEDB

Directions (Qs. No. 30-32): *In the following question, a word is highlighted in the sentence given. Followed by few sentences are given using that word. Identify the sentences that have use the given word in the same meaning as used in the question statement.*

30. The teacher asked the students to ***show*** their homework notebooks.

(A) They went to see a ***show*** at the theatre.
(B) His paintings are on ***show*** at the gallery.
(C) The wound did not ***show*** any sign of infection.

A. Only B B. Both B and C
C. Only C D. Only A
E. All A,B,C

31. He ate the ***whole*** cake by himself.

(A) The ***whole*** matter was discussed in the meeting.
(B) She is missed terribly and her death has left a ***whole*** in all our lives
(C) The ***whole*** class was present during the lecture.

A. Only B B. Both A and C
C. Only C D. Only A
E. All A, B, C

32. She has a ***firm*** belief in honesty.

(A) He started his own law ***firm*** in the city.
(B) The ground was ***firm*** after the heavy rain.
(C) The manager took a ***firm*** decision against corruption.

A. Only B B. Both A and C
C. Only C D. Only A
E. All A,B,C

Directions (Qs. No. 33-37): *In each of the questions given below, six words have been highlighted. These six words may or may not have been placed in their correct positions. The sentence is then followed by options with the correct combination of words that should replace each other in order to make the sentence grammatically and contextually correct. Find the correct combination of the words that should replace each other. If the sentence is correct as it is, then select option "No interchange required" as your choice.*

33. The manager's **missing (A)** question about the **unexpected (B)** report seemed to abash him **completely (C)**, leaving him **speechless (D)** and visibly **uncomfortable (E)** in front of **colleagues (F)**.

A. B-F B. A-B
C. A-B & C-D D. A-F & B-E
E. No interchange required

34. **After (A)** hours of **relentless (B)** rain, the storm **abate (C)** to **began (D)**, allowing residents to **cautiously (E)** step outside and **assess (F)** the flood damage.

A. C-D B. A-B
C. A-B & C-D D. A-F & B-E
E. No interchange required

35. The monarch **while (A)** to **abdicate (B)** his throne, choosing a **immense (C)** life of service, **decided (D)** his **successor (E)** prepared for **quieter (F)** responsibility.

A. B-F B. A-B
C. A-D & C-F D. C-F & B-E
E. No interchange required

36. The sudden **collapse (A)** of a strong financial **institution (B)** was **considered (C)** an **aberration (D)**, shaking investor **confidence (E)** and disrupting the otherwise **stable (F)** market.

A. B-F　　B. B-D
C. A-B & C-D　　D. A-F & B-E
E. No interchange required

37. Many voters **chose (A)** to **abstain (B)** from the election, citing **participation (C)** with both **candidates (D)**, which significantly **reduced (E)** overall turnout and **dissatisfaction (F)** rates.

A. C-F　　B. D-F
C. A-B & C-D　　D. A-F & B-E
E. No interchange required

Directions (Qs. No. 38-42): *In each of the following sentences, a part of the sentence has been bold. Below are given alternatives to the bold part which may improve the sentence. Choose the correct alternative. Wherever no improvement is needed, choose 'No replacement required' as the answer.*

38. Five years later, **I was eating** this same dish at the same restaurant.

A. will have been eating
B. has been eating
C. am eating
D. had been eating
E. No replacement required

39. **I have been yet** to go to the flower exhibition at Delhi University.

A. have yet being　　B. have yet
C. have yet been　　D. had been yet
E. No replacement required

40. I had **not only helped her by** giving hints but also with providing her links.

A. helped her not only by
B. helped her not by
C. helped her only by
D. helped not only her by
E. No replacement required

41. This secret will remain **between you and I.**

A. between you and me
B. between I and you
C. between you
D. among you and I
E. No replacement required

42. The train **left before I reached** the station.

A. left before I had reached
B. left before I reach
C. left before I have reached
D. had left before I reached
E. No replacement required

Directions (Qs. No. 43-50): *Read the following passage and answer the given questions.*

Lakes are crucial freshwater reserves that support aquatic life, agriculture, and human needs. Their long-term health depends greatly on internal chemical processes. Two significant ones are phosphorus reactions and the chloride + water reaction.

Phosphorus, though essential for growth, becomes harmful when it enters lakes in excess through fertilizers, detergents, or untreated sewage. These phosphorus reactions trigger algal blooms that block sunlight and reduce oxygen. As algae decompose, oxygen levels in the lake **lower**, suffocating fish and disrupting biodiversity. Since phosphorus can remain trapped in sediments for years, its negative effects often persist long after the external supply is reduced.

The chloride + water reaction influences lakes differently. Chloride, introduced through road salts, mining, or industrial effluents, steadily raises salinity. This alters water density and circulation, stressing species adapted to freshwater. Over time, plant diversity declines, fish populations shrink, and the water often acquires a taste unsuitable for drinking or irrigation.

Lake water naturally contains several elements vital for ecological balance. Oxygen is essential for aquatic organisms, calcium supports shell-forming species like mollusks, while sodium and magnesium maintain mineral stability. When levels of elements such as chloride or phosphorus rise unnaturally, however, the lake's chemistry shifts in ways that damage both ecosystems and human use.

Monitoring these chemical reactions helps prevent major damage. Tracking phosphorus levels makes it possible to predict algal blooms, while chloride studies guide alternatives to road salt, such as sand or organic compounds. Establishing buffer zones around farms and improving wastewater treatment can also reduce nutrient flow into lakes.

Yet, implementing such measures often demands high costs or changes in established practices.

Farmers may resist reducing fertilizer use, while cities in snowy regions rely heavily on road salts for safety. Balancing ecological preservation with economic and practical needs remains a challenge.

If ignored, these reactions can leave lakes unsuitable for consumption, raising the risk of dehydration in communities dependent on them. Protecting the chemical balance of lakes is therefore vital not only for biodiversity but also for ensuring safe and reliable freshwater for human survival.

43. Why the effects of phosphorus on lake ecosystems are difficult to reverse?

A. Phosphorus is continually supplied by natural sources like aquatic plants.

B. Phosphorus boosts oxygen production, which leads to microbial overgrowth.

C. Phosphorus reactions are neutralized quickly, masking their long-term impact.

D. Even after external inputs are reduced, phosphorus trapped in sediments continues to affect the ecosystem.

E. Chloride presence intensifies the impact of phosphorus, making it a dual threat to aquatic life.

44. Why is the chloride + water reaction considered particularly disruptive to lake biodiversity?

A. It reduces calcium levels, thereby weakening shell-forming species.

B. It causes rapid pH fluctuations that kill algae and fish.

C. It increases water salinity, which affects circulation and freshwater-adapted species.

D. It directly interacts with oxygen, accelerating eutrophication.

E. It combines with magnesium to form harmful mineral clusters.

45. Which of the following measures is NOT mentioned as a strategy to mitigate chemical imbalance in lakes?

A. Creating buffer zones around farms

B. Improving wastewater treatment systems

C. Substituting road salts with organic alternatives

D. Using oxygenation devices to prevent fish suffocation

E. Monitoring chloride and phosphorus levels regularly

46. Which of the following statements is/are CORRECT based on the passage?

(I) The chloride + water reaction can affect the drinkability of lake water.

(II) High chloride concentration leads to biodiversity decline and poor irrigation quality.

(III) Phosphorus boosts plant diversity in lake ecosystems.

A. Only (I) B. Both (I) and (II)

C. Only (III) D. Both (I) and (III)

E. All (I), (II) and (III)

47. Which of the following statements is INCORRECT according to the passage?

A. Road salts are a significant source of chloride in lakes.

B. Phosphorus comes solely from industrial sources and has no agricultural links.
C. Excess phosphorus can lead to oxygen depletion in water bodies.
D. Freshwater species can suffer due to changing water density.
E. Socioeconomic barriers can impede ecological reforms.

48. Based on the passage, how does the chemical balance in lakes impact the survival of aquatic plants and animals?

A. Species in lakes can adapt quickly to chemical imbalances caused by human intervention.
B. Minor fluctuations in chemicals like chloride or phosphorus help sustain aquatic food chains.
C. Disruptions in chemical balance can cascade through the ecosystem, affecting biodiversity and human utility.
D. Human influence on chemical levels in lakes has negligible impact on species survival.
E. Lakes with higher oxygen and chloride content support a broader range of aquatic species.

49. According to the passage, why is it difficult to protect lakes from harmful chemical changes?

A. Governments lack awareness about freshwater preservation.
B. Road salts have no viable alternatives in snow-heavy regions.
C. Human reluctance and economic dependency hinder ecological practices.
D. Farming practices naturally prevent phosphorus runoff.
E. Chloride has more environmental benefits than drawbacks.

50. Choose the word that is opposite in meaning to "lower" as used in the passage:

A. intensify B. improve
C. raise D. filter
E. enhance

REASONING

Directions (Qs. No. 51-55): *A number and word arrangement machine, when given an input, rearranges the words and the numbers following a particular set of rules. An illustration is given below of it.*

Input: 53 Quashing 59 Crusader 75 Stipulate 48 Enactment 22 Plummet 34 Resentment

Step I: Resentment 53 Quashing 59 Crusader 75 Stipulate 48 Enactment Plummet 34 22

Step II: Plummet Resentment 53 Quashing 59 Crusader Stipulate 48 Enactment 34 22 75

Step III: Enactment Plummet Resentment 53 Quashing 59 Crusader Stipulate 48 22 75 34

Step IV: Crusader Enactment Plummet Resentment 53 Quashing Stipulate 48 22 75 34 59

Step V: Stipulate Crusader Enactment Plummet Resentment 53 Quashing 22 75 34 59 48

Step VI: Quashing Stipulate Crusader Enactment Plummet Resentment 22 75 34 59 48 53

Input: 43 Purview 68 Chronic 73 Dismantle 47 Incumbent 38 Relegating 56 Doughty

51. What is the position of "Incumbent" in Step VI from the left end?

A. Fourth B. Fifth
C. None of these D. Second
E. Third

52. How many numbers are to the left of "Doughty" in Step III?

A. Two B. Three
C. One D. Four
E. None of these

53. Which of the following numbers will be 2nd to the left of the 3rd number from the right end in step V?

A. 38 B. 73
C. 47 D. 68
E. None of these

54. In which of the following step "Purview 68 47" exists in the same order?

A. Step I B. Step II
C. Step III D. Step IV
E. None of these

55. What is the sum of the numbers at the odd position in Step IV from the right end?

A. 118 B. 126
C. 120 D. 134
E. None of these

Directions (Qs. No. 56-58): *Study the following alphanumeric-symbol series carefully and answer the questions based on it.*

F M 9 0 * Y 7 U F G % $ 3 2 O 6 @ N X 4 # L 1 & Z R 6 * V S

56. Which of the following element is fourth to the right of 12th element from the left end?

A. @ B. O
C. X D. 6
E. 2

57. How many such consonants are there each of which is immediately preceded by a symbol and immediately followed by a number?

A. One B. Four
C. Two D. None
E. Five

58. What will be the sum of 3rd odd number from left end and 2nd number from right end?

A. 3 B. 4
C. 8 D. 7
E. 6

Directions (Qs. No. 59-62): *Each of the questions below consists of a question and two statements numbered I and II given below it. You have to decide whether the data provided in the statement are sufficient to answer the question. Read both the statements and Give answer:*

A. If the data in statement I alone are sufficient to answer the question, while the data in statement II alone are not sufficient to answer the question.
B. If the data in statement II alone are sufficient to answer the question, while the data in statement I alone are not sufficient to answer the question.
C. If the data either in statement I alone or in statement II alone are sufficient to answer the question.
D. If the data even in both statements I and II together are not sufficient to answer the question.
E. If the data in both statements I and II together are necessary to answer the question.

59. Seven people-A, B, C, D, E, F and G-live on different floors of a 7-floor building but not necessarily in the same order. The ground floor is numbered 1, the floor just above it is numbered 2, and so on. Who lives three floors below A.

Statement I: A lives on an even-numbered floor. E lives immediately above A. B lives on floor number 4. There are as many persons live above A as below G.

Statement II: D lives on a floor immediately above G. F does not live on the topmost floor. C lives on floor number 5 below A.

60. In a row of children facing North, where does Rajat stand in the row?

Statement I: Jyoti stands 3rd from left end and 2nd to the left of Rajat who stands immediate left of the one who is 10th from the right end of the row.

Statement II: There are 19 children between Rajat and Meena, and Meena is 15th from one of the ends of the row.

61. In four family members, how is Rohan related to Meena?

Statement I: Rohan's father is the only brother of Meena's mother.

Statement II: Meena's mother is the sister of the father of Rohan's sister.

62. Eight boxes—P, Q, R, S, T, U, V, and W—are stacked above each other but not necessarily in the same order.

Statement I: Box P is immediately above box Q. Box S is immediately above box R, which is not at the bottommost position.

Statement II: Box T is above box U but below box V. Box W is at the bottommost position. Box P is not at the topmost position.

Directions (Qs. No. 63-67): *Study the following information carefully and answer the given questions.*

Seven Boxes i.e. A, B, C, D, E, F and G placed one above the other and all are of different colours viz. Yellow, Brown, Pink, Green, Red, Black and Blue but not necessarily in the same order. Each box contains different items i.e., Balls, Pencils, Chocolate, Juice, Berry, Toys and Bottles but not necessarily in the same order.

Box A is placed three places above the brown colour. More than three boxes placed between box B and the box of yellow colour. Blue colour box placed below the box which contains Bottles and placed above the box which contains Balls. The box contains Chocolate placed just above box B. Two boxes placed between box B and box E which contains Juice. Box C is of red colour and placed 2 places above box E. Brown colour box contains Pencil but that is not box B. Box F is placed above the box of yellow colour. Black colour box contains Toy's and placed below box D. Green colour box contains Berry.

63. How many boxes placed between black colour box and green colour box?

A. As many boxes placed below box D
B. As many boxes placed between A and B
C. As many boxes placed above yellow colour box
D. As many boxes placed between D and G
E. None of these

64. Which of the following statement is not true?

A. Box A is placed at the topmost position
B. Box E is of blue colour
C. Box G does not place above box F
D. Box C is placed just below box D
E. All are true

65. If box A and box E interchanged with each other then, how many boxes placed above box A?

A. Four
B. Five
C. Two
D. Three
E. None

66. If box D is related to bottles and box F is related to juice in the same way which of the following box is related to chocolate?

A. G
B. B
C. C
D. D
E. F

67. How many boxes placed above the pink colour box?

A. Six
B. Two
C. None
D. One
E. Three

Directions (Qs. No. 68-71): *Read the given information carefully and answer the questions based on it:*

In a family, D is mother-in-law of N. N's spouse is only paternal aunt of E. P is the mother of E's sibling. V is the grandchild of P's father-in-law. C is father-in-law of V's mother who is U. A is the only nephew of N's spouse. L is paternal grandparent of A whose parent is G. R is parent of L's son-in-law and parent of H. Gender of G and H is same but different to N's child.

68. If R has a daughter, then, how will N's spouse relate to R's daughter?

A. Sister-in-law B. Sister
C. Cousin D. Uncle
E. Brother-in-law

69. What is the relation of H with respect to E's cousin?

A. Father B. Uncle
C. Aunt D. Grandmother
E. None of the above

70. Who among the following is A's mother?

A. H B. G
C. P D. V
E. None of the above

71. If V is married to S, then how will S relate to N?

A. Brother-in-law B. Daughter-in-law
C. Son-in-law D. Sister-in-law
E. Father-in-law

72. 1 million species at risk of extinction: UN. Industrial farming, fishing are factors that threaten to end existence of many species, says report. Relentless pursuit of economic growth, twinned with the impact of climate change, has put an "unprecedented" one million species at risk of extinction.

Which of the following is a course of action for the following statement?

(I) This is the impact of the damage done by modern civilization to the natural world.

(II) Only a wide-ranging transformation of the global economic and financial system could pull ecosystems that are vital to the future of species and human communities worldwide.

(III) The essential, interconnected web of life on Earth is getting smaller and increasingly frayed due to this extinction.

(IV) "This loss is a direct result of human activity and constitutes a direct threat to human well-being in all regions of the world."

A. Only I and II are implicit
B. Only II is implicit
C. Only III and II are implicit
D. All are implicit
E. Only I, II and III are implicit

73. Training and completing a first-time marathon reverse ageing of major blood vessels, according to a study which found that the older and slower runners benefit the most.

Which of the following can be inferred from the given statement?

(I) Only first-time marathon runners will get benefit from it.

(II) Those who run fast gets older earlier than others.

(III) Blood vessels play a major role in ageing of the person.

A. Only I and II are implicit
B. Only III is implicit
C. Only III and II are implicit
D. All are implicit
E. None is implicit

Directions (Qs. No. 74-78): *Study the following information carefully and answer the questions given below:*

Eight persons—A, B, C, D, E, F, G, and H sit around a square-shaped table. Four persons sit at the corners of the table and face inside, while the other four sit at the middle of each side and face outside. Each person is from a different city—Delhi, Mumbai, Kolkata, Chennai, Pune, Jaipur, Hyderabad, and Bengaluru. G sits two places away from the one who is from Pune. The one who sits immediate left of the one who is from Pune doesn't sit on the middle of the sides of the table. The one who is from Delhi sits third to the right of G. One person lives between the ones who are from Delhi and Chennai. A sits immediate right of the one who is from Chennai. No one sits between E and D who sits third to the left of A. C is from Jaipur and sits immediately to the right of B. B doesn't sit at the corners. Three persons sit between the ones who are from Kolkata and Mumbai. The ones who are from Mumbai and Delhi are not immediate neighbours. B and D are not from Bengaluru. F doesn't sit immediate right of A.

74. Who sits second to the left of the person who sits immediate left of the one who is from Hyderabad?

A. E B. G
C. F D. C
E. B

75. If A is related to Mumbai and in the same way E is related to Pune, then F is related to which among the following?

A. Pune B. Delhi
C. Jaipur D. Chennai
E. Hyderabad

76. What is the position of H with respect to the one who is from Delhi?

A. Immediate left
B. Third to the right
C. Second to the left
D. Fourth to the left
E. Third to the left

77. Four of the following five belong to a certain group based on their facing direction. Find the one who does not belong to the group.

A. F
B. The one who is from Hyderabad
C. H
D. The one who is from Mumbai
E. C

78. Who is from Bengaluru?

A. H B. A
C. G D. E
E. F

79. **Statement:** Due to the devastating floods in several states, the government has announced a special relief package for affected farmers.

Which of the following is an assumption implicit in this statement?

A. Farmers are among the worst-affected groups in flood-hit areas.
B. Floods are unlikely to cause damage to urban infrastructure.
C. Only financial relief is sufficient to rebuild the lives of flood victims.
D. Farmers do not have any alternative means to recover losses.
E. None of the above.

80. **Statement:** To reduce increasing air pollution levels in major cities, the government has decided to impose stricter emission norms for vehicles.

Which of the following is an assumption implicit in this decision?

A. Air pollution can be completely eliminated by emission norms.
B. Vehicular emissions are a significant contributor to rising pollution levels.
C. Citizens will willingly adopt cleaner alternatives without resistance.
D. Industrial pollution is not responsible for poor air quality in cities.
E. None of the above.

Directions (Qs. No. 81-83): *Read the given instructions carefully and answer the related questions:*

A certain number of persons sit in a linear row and face north. H sits third to the right of K. B sits five places away from K. At most three persons sit between B and G who is an immediate neighbour of K. The number of persons sit between G and O is two times the number of persons sit between G and B. O sits fourth from the left end of the row. One person sits between O and V. As many persons sits to the left of V as to the right of M who sits immediate left of H. Not more than three person sits to the right of H.

81. How many persons sit between M and O?

A. Ten B. Eleven
C. Twelve D. Nine
E. Eight

82. Who among the following sits seventh to the left of M?

A. V B. O
C. B D. Unknown person
E. G

83. How many persons sit in the row?

A. 15 B. 17
C. 13 D. 19
E. 14

84. If in the given word "CONCEPTUAL", all the letters are arranged in alphabetical order from the right end, then the position of how many letters remain unchanged in the new arrangement?

A. One B. Two
C. None D. Three
E. Four

85. If 'MUD' is written as 'FYS', and 'BAT' is written as 'VEH', then how is 'HAN' written, also the code of "HAN" should be a meaningful word?

A. FEN B. HEN
C. PIG D. PEN
E. PAN

Directions (Qs. No. 86-89): *In this question, the relationship between different elements is shown in the statements. The statements are followed by two conclusions. Study the conclusions based on the given statements and select the appropriate answer:*

86. Statements: $D < H > U \geq E > N \geq P \leq K \leq R < S$

Conclusions:

I. $H > P$

II. $P \leq S$

A. If only conclusion I is true
B. If only conclusion II is true
C. If either conclusion I or II is true
D. If both conclusions I and II are true
E. If neither conclusion I nor II is true

87. Statements: $P \geq M = O < D; R > O = T; R < H$

Conclusions:

I. $H > M$

II. $P \geq T$

A. If only conclusion I is true
B. If only conclusion II is true
C. If either conclusion I or II is true
D. If both conclusions I and II are true
E. If neither conclusion I nor II is true

88. Statements: $S > W \geq T \leq Z; K > R < J = N \geq T$

Conclusions:

I. $Z \geq J$

II. $R < S$

A. If only conclusion I is true
B. If only conclusion II is true
C. If either conclusion I or II is true
D. If both conclusions I and II are true
E. If neither conclusion I nor II is true

89. Statements: $Y = A \geq R < V; I = B \leq V < L$

Conclusions:

I. $A \geq I$

II. $Y < B$

A. If only conclusion I is true
B. If only conclusion II is true
C. If either conclusion I or II is true
D. If both conclusions I and II are true
E. If neither conclusion I nor II is true

90. In the number '435673538', the digit which are less than 6 is subtracted by 2 and rest all the digits are subtracted by 1. Now remove all the repeated digits and then find the difference between sum of odd digits and sum of even digits in the new number formed after rearrangement?

A. 5 B. 4
C. 8 D. 12
E. 3

Directions (Qs. No. 91-95): *Study the following information carefully and answer the questions given below:*

Eight persons—A, B, C, D, E, F, G, and H—live on eight different floors of a building, where the floors are numbered from 1 to 8 (the bottom-most floor is numbered 1 and the top-most floor is numbered 8). Each of them likes a different subject—Philosophy, Chemistry, Biology, Science, English, Physics, Mathematics and Hindi.

Three persons live between H and the one who like English. At least three persons live below H. As many persons live above the one who likes English as below the one who likes Science. G likes Physics and lives on the second floor, immediately below E. More than two persons live between D and the one who likes Science. D doesn't like Philosophy and doesn't live on fourth floor. The one who likes Biology lives two floors above D. Two persons live between the ones who like Biology and Chemistry. The one who likes chemistry live immediately below C and immediately above A. A lives above F who lives three floors below the one who likes Hindi.

91. The number of floors above the floor on which A lives is one more than the number of floors below the floor on which the person who likes _________ lives.

A. Mathematics
B. Chemistry
C. English
D. Biology
E. Science

92. Which subject does F like?

A. Philosophy
B. English
C. Science
D. Hindi
E. Physics

93. Who lives exactly between G and the one who likes Philosophy?

A. B
B. C
C. The one who likes Science
D. F
E. The one who likes Biology

94. Which of the following combination is correct?

A. H - Chemistry
B. A - Biology
C. F - Physics
D. G - Hindi
E. D - Mathematics

95. Which of the following statements is/are false?

I. E lives on floor above D's floor
II. B likes Science
III. No one lives above H

A. Only II
B. Both I and III
C. Only I
D. Only III
E. Both II and III

96. If 'PLAYER' is written as '28', and 'NOISE' is written as '14', then how is 'HOCKEY' written?

A. 30
B. 29
C. 27
D. 33
E. 31

Directions (Qs. No. 97-100): *Study the following information carefully and answer the questions given below:*

Point L is 15 m south of point M. Point N is 13 m west of point L. Point Q is 6 m east of point M. Point R is exactly between Point M and Point Q. Point O is 9 m north of point N. Point S is 6 m south of point R. Point T is 7 m east of point S. Point U is 11 m south of point T.

97. In which direction is point T with respect to point M?

A. North-east
B. North-west
C. South-east
D. South-west
E. North

98. What is the shortest distance between point S and point L?

A. $\sqrt{90}$ m
B. $\sqrt{91}$ m
C. 8 m
D. 12 m
E. 9 m

99. Four of the following five points form a particular pattern in terms of direction and related to a group. Which one does not belong to the group?

A. M and S
B. O and L
C. S and U
D. Q and T
E. O and T

100. What is the total distance from Point R to Point O?

A. 50 m
B. 45 m
C. 41 m
D. 40 m
E. 35 m

GENERAL AWARENESS

101. The Amazon River does not pass through which of the following cities?

A. Iquitos
B. Manaus
C. Santarém
D. Buenos Aires
E. Macapá

102. The Indian Constitution replaced which previous legal framework?

A. Government of India Act, 1919
B. Indian Independence Act, 1947
C. Government of India Act, 1935
D. Regulating Act, 1773
E. Pitts India Act, 1784

103. The Nobel Prize is primarily awarded by which country (for most categories)?

A. Norway
B. Sweden
C. Switzerland
D. United States
E. United Kingdom

104. The 'Ek Ped Maa Ke Naam' scheme is related to:

A. Women Empowerment
B. Girl Child Education
C. Tree Plantation
D. Rural Healthcare
E. Digital Literacy

105. Kargil Vijay Diwas is observed on:

A. 15 August
B. 26 January
C. 26 July
D. 30 January
E. 15 January

106. Which mountain range separates Asia from Europe?

A. Andes
B. Himalayas
C. Rockies
D. Ural Mountains
E. Alps

107. Which Indian state became the first to implement the Uniform Civil Code (UCC)?

A. Gujarat
B. Uttar Pradesh
C. Uttarakhand
D. Himachal Pradesh
E. Goa

108. Which of the following regulatory bodies regulates the insurance sector in India?

A. RBI
B. SEBI
C. IRDAI
D. PFRDA
E. NABARD

109. What is India's rank in the 2025 SDG Index?

A. 85th
B. 92nd
C. 99th
D. 101st
E. 105th

110. Exercise Shakti is conducted between India and:

A. USA
B. Russia
C. Japan
D. France
E. Singapore

111. Which city hosted the SCO Summit 2024?

A. New Delhi
B. Astana
C. Beijing
D. Moscow
E. Tashkent

112. Which UNESCO World Heritage Site was declared India's 44th World Heritage Site?

A. Raigad Fort
B. Shivneri Fort
C. Maratha Military Landscapes of India
D. Sindhudurg Fort
E. Pratapgad Fort

113. What is the NISAR satellite system?

A. Naval defense radar
B. Deep-sea mapping project
C. Joint Earth-observation mission by NASA and ISRO
D. AI surveillance tool
E. Space debris cleanup mission

114. In BIRAC, the letter 'A' stands for:

A. Agency B. Association
C. Assistance D. Authority
E. Administration

115. What is the objective of the MISHTI scheme?

A. Solar power adoption
B. Mangrove plantation
C. Micro-irrigation expansion
D. Skill development
E. Urban housing

116. Which country is NOT a member of the Global Biofuel Alliance?

A. India B. USA
C. Brazil D. China
E. Argentina

117. Khelo India launched which campaign for women equality?

A. ASMITA B. SHAKTI
C. JYOTI D. UDAAN
E. PRAGATI

118. Which Indian cricketer became the first player to score a double century in ODI cricket?

A. Virat Kohli
B. Rohit Sharma
C. Sachin Tendulkar
D. MS Dhoni
E. Yuvraj Singh

119. Which Indian state launched the 'Subhadra Yojana' for women empowerment in 2024?

A. Odisha B. Assam
C. Bihar D. Rajasthan
E. Madhya Pradesh

120. Which body released the latest report on India's chemical industries?

A. NITI Aayog
B. FICCI
C. Ministry of Chemicals and Fertilizers
D. CII
E. RBI

121. Which of the following is NOT an Officially Valid Document (OVD)?

A. Passport B. PAN Card
C. Voter ID D. Driving License
E. Aadhaar Card

122. Which monetary policy tool is used by RBI to absorb excess liquidity from banks?

A. Repo Rate B. Reverse Repo Rate
C. Bank Rate D. CRR
E. SLR

123. What was the theme of the G20 Summit hosted by India?

A. One Earth, One Family, One Future
B. Shaping the Future
C. Global Growth and Stability
D. Prosperity for All
E. Sustainable Development

124. Which is the highest civilian award in India?

A. Padma Shri
B. Padma Bhushan
C. Padma Vibhushan
D. Bharat Ratna
E. Param Vir Chakra

125. What is the full form of STRIPS?

A. Separate Trading of Registered Interest and Principal of Securities
B. Standard Tax Information Reporting Payment System
C. Secured Transfer of Institutional Retail Portfolio Securities
D. System for Targeted Investment and Reporting of Public Securities
E. None of these

126. Sovereign Gold Bonds are issued by:

A. SEBI
B. RBI on behalf of Government of India

C. SBI
D. Ministry of Finance
E. NABARD

127. UPI stands for:
A. Unified Payment Interface
B. Unified Payments Interface
C. Universal Payment Interface
D. Universal Payments Integration
E. Unified Processing Interface

128. Who is the MD & CEO of Federal Bank?
A. Shyam Srinivasan
B. KVS Manian
C. Siddhartha Sengupta
D. Amitabh Chaudhry
E. Sashidhar Jagdishan

129. What is SLR (Statutory Liquidity Ratio)?
A. Reserve ratio maintained by RBI
B. Cash kept by banks with themselves
C. Percentage of NDTL maintained by banks in liquid assets
D. Ratio of gold reserves held by IMF
E. None of these

130. What is the Fintech Repository launched by RBI?
A. Platform for banking job seekers
B. Database of fintech companies
C. Digital payment clearing system
D. Online bank for startups
E. Tax collection portal

131. What is the full form of CASA in banking?
A. Current Account Savings Account
B. Cash and Savings Account
C. Current and Savings Account
D. Cash Account and Savings Account
E. Credit and Savings Account

132. What is the minimum maturity period for an NRE Term Deposit?
A. 6 Months B. 1 Year
C. 2 Years D. 3 Years
E. 5 Years

133. Which financial entities are regulated by RBI?
A. Insurance Companies
B. Mutual Funds
C. Scheduled Commercial Banks
D. Commodity Exchanges
E. Pension Funds

134. Which organization publishes the World Economic Outlook Report?
A. World Bank B. IMF
C. WTO D. UNDP
E. OECD

135. PM SVANidhi Scheme is primarily meant for:
A. Farmers B. Self-Help Groups
C. Street Vendors D. MSMEs
E. Artisans

136. Which Indian state has the longest coastline?
A. Tamil Nadu B. Andhra Pradesh
C. Maharashtra D. Gujarat
E. Odisha

137. What does "M" stand for in MSME?
A. Market B. Manufacturing
C. Medium D. Monetary
E. Management

138. Which Article of the Constitution deals with Fundamental Duties?
A. Article 32 B. Article 51A
C. Article 19 D. Article 356
E. Article 370

139. The headquarters of the World Bank is located in:
A. Geneva
B. Paris
C. Washington, D.C.
D. New York
E. London

140. Which ministry implements the Atal Pension Yojana?
A. Ministry of Labour
B. Ministry of Finance

C. Ministry of Rural Development
D. Ministry of Commerce
E. Ministry of MSME

141. What is the currency of South Korea?

A. Yen B. Yuan
C. Won D. Ringgit
E. Baht

142. Which committee is associated with banking sector reforms in India?

A. Sarkaria Committee
B. Balwant Rai Mehta Committee
C. Narasimham Committee
D. Kelkar Committee
E. Punchhi Committee

143. Which Indian bank launched the YONO digital platform?

A. PNB B. Bank of Baroda
C. SBI D. Canara Bank
E. Union Bank of India

144. What is the full form of IFSC?

A. Indian Financial Security Code
B. Indian Fund Settlement Code
C. Indian Financial System Code
D. International Financial System Code
E. Integrated Financial Service Code

145. Which of the following is a money market instrument?

A. Equity Shares B. Debentures
C. Treasury Bills D. Mutual Funds
E. Preference Shares

146. Which organization manages the RuPay card network?

A. RBI B. NPCI
C. SEBI D. NABARD
E. SIDBI

147. The term NPA in banking stands for:

A. Net Profit Account
B. Non-Performing Asset
C. National Payment Agency
D. New Public Account
E. Net Provision Asset

148. Which institution is known as the "Banker to Banks" in India?

A. SBI B. NABARD
C. RBI D. SEBI
E. SIDBI

149. Which payment system allows real-time fund transfer 24 × 7 in India?

A. ECS B. NEFT
C. RTGS D. IMPS
E. NACH

150. What is the maximum deposit insurance cover provided by DICGC per depositor per bank?

A. ₹ 1 Lakh B. ₹ 2 Lakh
C. ₹ 3 Lakh D. ₹ 5 Lakh
E. ₹ 10 Lakh

EXPLANATORY ANSWERS

1. (B): The primary irony is that the game was promoted as a source of enjoyment and social bonding, but it produced the opposite effects. Children became dependent on it, withdrew from family interaction, and experienced behavioural and academic problems. Even roommates interacted smoothly mainly while gaming and had little genuine conversation after the console was switched off. Thus, a product intended to connect and entertain people ultimately encouraged isolation and addiction.

2. (C): The passage describes children as being unable to control the time spent on the game or organise their daily schedules properly. Their grades, classroom participation, and discipline declined significantly, showing that their academic lives were adversely affected. At home, they became irritable, displayed inappropriate behaviour, and reduced their interaction with family members. These consequences collectively demonstrate the game's harmful influence on children's studies, behaviour, and relationships.

3. **(D):** The independent organisation conducted a large-scale survey rather than examining only a limited group or a single aspect of gaming. Its findings repeatedly recorded extreme dependency, reduced academic achievement, antisocial tendencies, and disruption of family harmony. The evidence showed that the harmful effects were widespread and serious, not mild or exaggerated. Consequently, the organisation recommended banning the game in the country.

4. **(C):** Roommates reported that their relationships appeared smooth while they were actively engaged in gaming sessions. However, after the console was switched off, their communication became minimal and genuine conversations decreased. This showed that the apparent bonding created by the game was temporary and dependent entirely on gaming. Their experience therefore revealed how the game could weaken natural social interaction and encourage emotional isolation.

5. **(C):** The game received an immediate and overwhelming market response after its introduction. Within the following year, it generated 50 million dollars worldwide and rapidly acquired users across the globe. This commercial achievement brought Company X recognition and dominance in the digital gaming industry. Therefore, its rapid user growth and enormous financial success were responsible for its quick global popularity.

6. **(B):** Teachers noticed that students' grades were falling and that their participation in academic activities had declined. They also observed a visible deterioration in discipline, indicating that the effects extended beyond examination results. These classroom observations helped establish a connection between excessive gaming and the children's worsening educational performance and behaviour. Thus, teachers contributed important evidence that strengthened the concerns regarding the game.

7. **(C):** A "toe hold," more conventionally written as "toehold," means a small but secure initial position from which further progress, influence, or expansion can be achieved. In the passage, the game's early commercial success gave Company X an initial position in the international gaming market. That position enabled the company to gain recognition and strengthen its presence in the industry. Therefore, "toe hold" correctly conveys the meaning of an initial advantage or opportunity for future growth.

8. **(B):** In the passage, the game is described as a "major hit" because it generated enormous profits, attracted users worldwide, and gave Company X industry recognition. Here, "hit" does not mean a physical blow or punch. It refers to something that becomes extremely popular or commercially successful. Therefore, "success" is the word closest in meaning to "hit" in the given context.

9. **(C):** The word "raise" in the expression "raise concerns" means to bring forward, increase, or call attention to worries about a matter. Among the given options, "lower" expresses the opposite general sense of reducing rather than increasing or elevating something. "Boost," "improve," and "elevate" all suggest an upward movement and are therefore closer to the meaning of "raise." Hence, "lower" is the most appropriate antonym among the available choices.

10. **(B):** The survey revealed extreme gaming dependency, poor academic achievement, antisocial tendencies, and disruption of family relationships. The organisation concluded that the company's financial gains could not compensate for the serious damage caused to children's discipline, values, and future prospects. It did not merely suggest parental controls, educational modifications, or rewards for limited gaming. Based on the overwhelming negative findings, it specifically recommended banning the game in the country.

11. **(D):** The sentence is grammatically and contextually acceptable because "congratulated for" may be used to state the reason for which praise or congratulations were given. Here, the players received congratulations because of their outstanding performance. Although "congratulated on their outstanding performance" is more idiomatic and commonly preferred, the use of "for" is not grammatically wrong in this context. Therefore, Sentence D is the only error-free option.

12. (C): This sentence is grammatically correct and contextually meaningful. The present perfect passive construction "has been rescheduled" correctly indicates that the schedule was changed and that the change remains relevant at present. Sentence A should use "If he calls me," Sentence B should use "The police are," and Sentence D should use "must submit." Therefore, Sentence C is the only error-free sentence.

13. (B): The plural noun "data" correctly agrees with the plural verb "show," and the sentence conveys a clear and logical meaning. Sentence A should use the present perfect continuous form "has been living" with "since 2010." In Sentence C, the verb should agree with the nearer subject "teachers" and therefore should be "are responsible." Sentence D is incorrect because the singular subject "book" requires the verb "is."

14. (B): The expression "aims at improving" is grammatically correct because "at" is followed by the gerund "improving." The sentence also conveys the logical objective of the new policy clearly. Sentence A requires inversion after "nor" and should read "nor did he inform anyone." Sentence C requires "students," "completes," and appropriate pronoun agreement, while Sentence D requires the singular verb "has decided."

15. (D): This sentence correctly uses the subjunctive construction "demanded that...be increased," which is appropriate after verbs expressing demands or recommendations. Sentence A should use the singular verb "was" because "neither" is treated as singular in formal usage. Sentence B has faulty agreement between the collective noun and the pronoun, and Sentence C should use "denied having taken." Therefore, Sentence D is the only grammatically and contextually correct sentence.

16. (B): The verb "congratulated" is correctly followed by the object "him" and the preposition "on." The phrase "promotion to the post of manager" is also grammatically accurate and contextually suitable. Sentence A should use the subjunctive form "If I were you," Sentence C requires "is responsible," and Sentence D requires "have been published" because the subject "results" is plural. Hence, Sentence B contains no error.

17. (A): The sentence requires a verb showing that the nation has experienced or encountered a sudden increase in fake bomb threats. The expression "has faced a surge" is grammatically correct and naturally conveys that the country has had to deal with this serious problem. "Created" would wrongly suggest that the nation caused the threats, while "ignored," "welcomed," and "imagined" do not fit the context. Therefore, "faced" is the most suitable word for blank A.

18. (B): The anonymous communications falsely claimed that explosives were present in trains and flights. The expression "the presence of explosives" is the standard and contextually appropriate phrase for indicating that explosive materials supposedly existed at particular locations. Words such as "growth," "function," "arrival," and "reason" cannot logically describe explosives in this sentence. Hence, "presence" correctly completes blank B.

19. (E): The sentence indicates that Union government ministers confirmed that detailed information concerning the threats had reached the authorities. The past perfect passive form "had been received" correctly shows that the information was obtained before the ministers made their confirmation. The alternatives "invented," "ignored," "delayed," and "destroyed" contradict the intended meaning of the passage. Therefore, "received" is the most suitable word for blank C.

20. (C): Fake information causes authorities to deploy personnel, equipment, time, and emergency procedures unnecessarily. Thus, it "wastes security resources" and diverts attention from genuine threats that may require immediate action. The singular subject "spreading fake information" also correctly takes the singular verb "wastes." The other options do not express the harmful misuse of limited security resources, so "wastes" best fills blank D.

21. (C): The investigations are being conducted to discover who or what is responsible for issuing the false bomb alerts. The verb "identify" means to establish the identity or source of something and therefore fits both grammatically and contextually after the infinitive marker "to." "Confuse," "mislead," "replace," and "hide" express actions contrary to the purpose of an investigation. Hence, "identify" is the correct choice for blank E.

22. **(B):** The passage states that strict punishment will follow once the responsible organisation is identified. The passive construction "will be enforced under existing laws" means that the prescribed punishment or legal action will be applied through the available legal provisions. The words "ignored," "avoided," "delayed," and "reduced" would weaken or contradict the government's assurance of strict action. Therefore, "enforced" is the most suitable word for blank F.

23. **(B):** The first sentence states that she saved money for several months, and the second sentence presents the result of that action—she was able to buy a new laptop. The conjunction "so" correctly expresses this cause-and-result relationship. The coherent sentence is: "She saved money for several months, so she finally bought a new laptop." Words such as "although" and "however" would incorrectly indicate contrast.

24. **(A):** The first sentence states that he prepared well for the interview, whereas the second states the unexpected result that he was not selected. The coordinating conjunction "yet" appropriately connects two contrasting ideas without changing their intended meaning. The coherent sentence is: "He prepared well for the interview, yet he did not get selected for the job." "Therefore" and "hence" would wrongly suggest that his preparation caused his rejection.

25. **(B):** The closing of the shop was the reason that the speakers could not purchase groceries. The conjunctive adverb "therefore" correctly introduces the result or consequence of the shop being closed. The coherent sentence is: "The shop was closed; therefore, we could not buy any groceries." The other alternatives express contrast or addition and do not convey the required cause-and-effect relationship.

26. **(A):**

B. Early computing devices such as the abacus and mechanical calculators laid the earliest foundation for the development of modern computing machines. These devices logically introduce the historical progression discussed in the paragraph.

D. In the nineteenth century, Charles Babbage designed the concept of the Analytical Engine, which included ideas resembling memory, input, processing, and output. It represents the next major stage after early calculating devices.

A. The development then progressed into the twentieth century, when electronic computers such as ENIAC marked a major technological advancement. The chronological reference to the twentieth century correctly follows Babbage's nineteenth-century contribution.

C. Computers subsequently evolved from enormous, room-sized machines into smaller and more powerful personal computers. This sentence describes the rapid development that followed the arrival of electronic computers.

E. The phrase "This evolution" refers to the continuous development described in Sentence C and extends the account into the twenty-first century. Smartphones and cloud computing appropriately conclude the chronological development of computing technology.

27. **(D):**

A. Glucose is first introduced as blood sugar and as the principal energy source used by the body's cells. This sentence establishes the central subject of the paragraph.

E. The paragraph then explains that hormones such as insulin regulate glucose levels and help body cells absorb sugar from the bloodstream. This naturally follows the introductory description of glucose.

C. The expression "Such regulation" directly refers to the hormonal regulation described in Sentence E. Maintaining stable glucose levels is essential for proper organ function and general health.

B. The paragraph next describes one consequence of failed regulation—abnormally low blood sugar, which may cause dizziness, confusion, or unconsciousness. This provides a specific example of why glucose regulation is necessary.

D. The word "Conversely" introduces the opposite condition of consistently high blood sugar. It completes the paragraph by explaining that excessive glucose levels may cause diabetes, nerve damage, and vision-related complications.

28. (E):

B. The paragraph begins by introducing wheat as a widely cultivated staple crop valued for its adaptability and nutritional importance. This provides the broad subject before discussing its cultivation requirements.

A. Wheat requires a cool growing season and a warm, dry period during harvesting. This sentence explains the climatic conditions needed for successful cultivation.

E. The phrase "Given these requirements" directly refers to the climatic conditions stated in Sentence A. Farmers accordingly select appropriate soil and sowing time to obtain a healthy crop yield.

D. After the crop is harvested, the wheat grains are cleaned, stored under dry conditions, and distributed for consumption or processing. As required in the question, Sentence D correctly occupies the fourth position.

C. The paragraph concludes by explaining how mechanised irrigation and improved seed varieties have increased wheat production. This provides a broader final observation about modern developments in wheat cultivation.

29. (B):

A. The paragraph opens by introducing technology as a powerful feature of modern life that has transformed communication, healthcare, and numerous other fields. It establishes the central theme in a broad and coherent manner.

E. The expression "This rapid pace of change" refers to the technological transformation introduced in Sentence A. It explains that technological development has produced both opportunities and challenges in everyday life.

B. This sentence expands upon those opportunities and challenges by mentioning convenience and efficiency on one side and privacy, dependency, and mental-health concerns on the other. It therefore logically follows Sentence E.

D. The phrase "These developments" refers to the technological changes and their effects described in the preceding sentences. As fixed by the question, it occupies the fourth position and explains their influence on behaviour, habits, routines, and attention spans.

C. The paragraph concludes with the need to balance continuing technological advancement with human values. This is an appropriate concluding statement because it offers a responsible response to the advantages and concerns discussed earlier.

30. (B): In the given sentence, "show" is used as a verb meaning to display, present, or make something visible to another person. In Sentence B, "on show" means being displayed publicly at the gallery, while in Sentence C, "show any sign" means display or reveal evidence of infection. Sentence A uses "show" as a noun meaning a theatrical performance. Therefore, only Sentences B and C use the word in the same essential sense as the given sentence.

31. (B): In the given sentence, "whole" means complete or entire, indicating that no part of the cake was left. Sentence A uses "whole" to mean the entire matter, and Sentence C uses it to mean every member of the class collectively. In Sentence B, "whole" is incorrectly written in place of the noun "hole," which means an empty space or emotional void. Therefore, only Sentences A and C use "whole" in the same meaning as the given sentence.

32. (C): In the given sentence, "firm" means strong, definite, or unwavering, describing a deeply held belief in honesty. Sentence C uses "firm" in the same sense to describe a decisive and resolute decision against corruption. In Sentence A, "firm" means a business organisation, whereas in Sentence B, it means physically solid or hard. Therefore, only Sentence C uses "firm" with the same meaning as in the given sentence.

33. (B): The words "missing" (A) and "unexpected" (B) should be interchanged to form the meaningful sentence: "The manager's unexpected question about the missing report seemed to abash him completely, leaving him speechless and visibly uncomfortable in front of colleagues." A question may be unexpected, whereas a report may be missing. The remaining words are correctly positioned and together describe the person's embarrassment before his colleagues.

34. (A): The words "abate" (C) and "began" (D) should be interchanged to form the correct expression "began to abate." The corrected sentence is: "After hours of relentless rain, the storm began to abate, allowing residents to cautiously step outside and assess the flood damage." The verb "began" must be followed by the infinitive "to abate," meaning that the storm gradually became less intense.

35. (C): The words "while" (A) and "decided" (D), as well as "immense" (C) and "quieter" (F), should be interchanged. The corrected sentence is: "The monarch decided to abdicate his throne, choosing a quieter life of service, while his successor prepared for immense responsibility." The monarch's decision to give up the throne is logically connected with a quieter life, whereas the successor would have to assume immense responsibility.

36. (E): The sentence is grammatically and contextually correct in its original form. The "sudden collapse" of a strong financial institution can appropriately be described as an "aberration," meaning an unusual departure from what is normal or expected. Such an event may shake investor confidence and disturb an otherwise stable market. Therefore, every highlighted word is already placed correctly.

37. (A): The words "participation" (C) and "dissatisfaction" (F) should be interchanged. The corrected sentence is: "Many voters chose to abstain from the election, citing dissatisfaction with both candidates, which significantly reduced overall turnout and participation rates." Voters may abstain because they are dissatisfied with the candidates, and widespread abstention naturally reduces participation. The corrected arrangement is both grammatically accurate and logically coherent.

38. (E): The sentence "Five years later, I was eating this same dish at the same restaurant" is grammatically correct when describing an action that was in progress at a particular time in the past. The past continuous form "was eating" appropriately presents the activity as ongoing at that past moment. The phrase "five years later" can refer to a later point within a past narrative and does not necessarily indicate the future. Therefore, no replacement is needed.

39. (B): The correct sentence is: "I have yet to go to the flower exhibition at Delhi University." The construction "have yet to + base verb" means that an expected or intended action has not happened up to the present time. The word "been" is unnecessary and makes the original expression grammatically incorrect. Therefore, "have yet" is the correct replacement.

40. (A): The corrected sentence is: "I had helped her not only by giving hints but also by providing her links." The correlative construction "not only...but also" requires parallel grammatical structures on both sides. Here, "by giving" must be balanced with "by providing," and placing "not only" immediately before the first prepositional phrase creates proper parallelism. Therefore, "helped her not only by" is the correct improvement.

41. (A): The corrected sentence is: "This secret will remain between you and me." The preposition "between" must be followed by objective-case pronouns, so "me" is required instead of the subject pronoun "I." The word "among" is generally used for relationships involving more than two persons or entities, whereas "between" is appropriate here. Hence, "between you and me" is grammatically correct.

42. (D): The corrected sentence is: "The train had left before I reached the station." The train's departure occurred earlier than the speaker's arrival, and the past perfect tense "had left" clearly marks this earlier completed action. The later action is appropriately expressed in the simple past as "reached." Therefore, "had left before I reached" provides the clearest and most accurate sequence of past events.

43. (D): Phosphorus can accumulate in lake sediments and remain there for several years. It may subsequently be released back into the water, continuing to promote algal blooms even after fertilizers, detergents, or sewage inputs have been controlled. The decomposition of excessive algae consumes dissolved oxygen and harms fish and other aquatic organisms. Therefore, the persistence of phosphorus in sediments makes its ecological effects difficult to reverse.

44. (C): Chloride entering lakes through road salts, mining activities, and industrial effluents gradually increases the salinity of the water. Increased salinity changes water density and interferes with the lake's natural mixing and circulation patterns. Freshwater plants and animals are adapted to low-salinity conditions and may experience physiological stress when chloride levels rise. Consequently, plant diversity declines, fish populations shrink, and the lake's biodiversity is disrupted.

45. (D): The passage mentions monitoring phosphorus and chloride levels, establishing buffer zones around farms, improving wastewater treatment, and replacing road salts with sand or organic compounds. These measures aim to prevent excessive nutrients and salts from entering lakes. However, it does not mention installing mechanical oxygenation or aeration devices to increase dissolved oxygen. Therefore, using oxygenation devices is the strategy not stated in the passage.

46. (B):

(I) The chloride + water reaction can affect the drinkability of lake water — Correct: An increase in chloride concentration raises the salinity of lake water and may give it an unpleasant taste. Such water can eventually become unsuitable for drinking by communities dependent on the lake.

(II) High chloride concentration leads to biodiversity decline and poor irrigation quality — Correct: Elevated chloride levels disturb water density and circulation, stress freshwater species, reduce plant diversity, and shrink fish populations. The resulting saline water may also become unsuitable for agricultural irrigation.

(III) Phosphorus boosts plant diversity in lake ecosystems — Incorrect: Excess phosphorus produces harmful algal blooms rather than improving the diversity of aquatic plants. These blooms block sunlight and reduce oxygen during decomposition, thereby damaging aquatic biodiversity.

47. (B): This statement is incorrect because the passage explicitly identifies fertilizers as an important source of excess phosphorus in lakes. Fertilizer runoff connects phosphorus pollution directly with agricultural activity, while detergents and untreated sewage are additional sources. Excess phosphorus encourages algal blooms, whose decomposition reduces dissolved oxygen and harms aquatic life. Therefore, phosphorus neither comes solely from industrial sources nor lacks agricultural links.

48. (C): Lake organisms depend upon balanced levels of oxygen, calcium, sodium, magnesium, phosphorus, and chloride. When phosphorus rises excessively, algal blooms block sunlight and lower oxygen levels, while excessive chloride increases salinity and disturbs water circulation. These changes reduce plant diversity, shrink fish populations, and damage other freshwater organisms. The same imbalance can also make lake water unsuitable for drinking and irrigation, affecting both ecological survival and human use.

49. (C): Measures for protecting lakes may require substantial expenditure and major changes in established agricultural and urban practices. Farmers may resist reducing fertilizer use because fertilizers support crop production, while cities in snowy regions depend heavily on road salts to keep roads safe. These economic and practical interests make environmental reforms difficult to implement. Thus, balancing ecological protection with human convenience, safety, and livelihood requirements remains a major challenge.

50. (C): In the passage, "lower" is used as a verb in the statement that the decomposition of algae causes oxygen levels in the lake to decrease. The word "raise" means to increase or cause something to move to a higher level, making it the direct opposite of "lower" in this context. "Improve" and "enhance" indicate making something better, while "intensify" means making something stronger. Therefore, "raise" is the most precise antonym.

51. (E): The words are selected according to the alphabetical order of their second letters: Relegating (e), Chronic (h), Dismantle (i), Incumbent (n), Doughty (o), and Purview (u).

As each selected word is successively moved to the extreme left, the final word arrangement in Step VI becomes "Purview Doughty Incumbent Dismantle Chronic Relegating." Counting from the left, Purview is first, Doughty is second, and Incumbent is third. Therefore, "Incumbent" occupies the third position from the left end.

52. **(B): Step III:** Dismantle Chronic Relegating Purview 68 47 Incumbent 56 Doughty 38 73 43

Numbers to the left of "Doughty" = 68, 47 and 56

Total numbers = 3

Therefore, three numbers are positioned to the left of "Doughty."

53. **(A): Step V:** Doughty Incumbent Dismantle Chronic Relegating Purview 56 38 73 43 68 47

Third number from the right end = 43

Second number to the left of 43 = 38

Therefore, the required number is 38.

54. **(C):** Step III is "Dismantle Chronic Relegating Purview 68 47 Incumbent 56 Doughty 38 73 43." In this step, "Purview" is immediately followed by 68 and then by 47. Thus, the sequence "Purview 68 47" exists consecutively and in the same order. Therefore, it occurs in Step III.

55. **(C): Step IV:** Incumbent Dismantle Chronic Relegating Purview 47 56 Doughty 38 73 43 68

The odd numbers occurring at odd positions from the right end are 73 and 47.

Required sum = 73 + 47 = 120

Therefore, the required sum is 120.

56. **(D):** Twelfth element from the left end = $

Fourth element to its right = 12 + 4 = 16th element

The 16th element in the series = 6

Therefore, the element fourth to the right of the twelfth element from the left end is 6.

57. **(C):** A qualifying consonant must be immediately preceded by a symbol and immediately followed by a number. In the sequence "* Y 7," the consonant Y is preceded by * and followed by 7, so it qualifies. Similarly, in "# L 1," the consonant L is preceded by # and followed by 1. No other consonant satisfies both conditions simultaneously; therefore, the total number is two.

58. **(B):** Odd numbers from the left end = 9, 7, 3, 1

Third odd number from the left end = 3

Numbers from the right end begin as 6, 1, 4, 6, 2, 3, 7, 0, 9

Second number from the right end = 1

Required sum = 3 + 1 = 4.

59. **(E):** Statement I permits more than one possible floor arrangement and therefore does not uniquely identify the person living three floors below A. Statement II also fails to determine the complete arrangement independently. On combining both statements, the floors are fixed as F–1, G–2, D–3, B–4, C–5, A–6 and E–7. Thus, D lives three floors below A, and both statements are necessary.

60. **(A):** From Statement I, Jyoti is third from the left and Rajat is two places to her right; therefore, Rajat is fifth from the left end. The additional information that Rajat is immediately left of the child who is tenth from the right is consistent with this position. Statement II does not specify from which end Meena is fifteenth and does not determine Rajat's unique position. Hence, Statement I alone is sufficient.

61. **(C):** In Statement I, Rohan's father is the only brother of Meena's mother; therefore, Rohan and Meena are children of siblings and are cousins. In Statement II, the father of Rohan's sister is Rohan's father, and Meena's mother is his sister. This also establishes independently that Rohan and Meena are cousins. Thus, either statement alone is sufficient.

62. **(D):** Statement I fixes only two consecutive pairs—P immediately above Q and S immediately above R—without determining their exact positions. Statement II establishes the relative order V–T–U, places W at the bottom, and states that P is not topmost. Even after combining both statements, several different arrangements of the eight boxes remain possible. Therefore, the complete stacking order cannot be uniquely determined, and both statements together are not sufficient.

63. (A): The complete order from top to bottom is A, B, C, D, E, F and G. The green box is B at the second position, while the black box is F at the sixth position; therefore, three boxes—C, D and E—are placed between them. Box D occupies the fourth position, and three boxes—E, F and G—are below it. Hence, both quantities are equal.

64. (D): The established order from top to bottom is A, B, C, D, E, F and G. Thus, Box C is immediately above Box D, not immediately below it. Box A is topmost, Box E is blue, and Box G is below Box F, so the other stated relationships are true. Therefore, the statement about Box C being just below Box D is not true.

65. (A): Initially, Box A is at the first position and Box E is at the fifth position from the top. After Box A and Box E interchange their positions, Box A moves to the fifth position. The boxes occupying the first, second, third and fourth positions are then above Box A. Therefore, four boxes are placed above Box A.

66. (B): Box D is related to Bottles because the box containing Bottles, namely Box C, is immediately above Box D. Similarly, Box F is related to Juice because Box E, which contains Juice, is immediately above Box F. Chocolate is contained in Box A, so the box immediately below it is Box B. Therefore, Box B is related to Chocolate in the same way.

67. (C): The pink-coloured box is Box A, which occupies the topmost position in the arrangement. Since no box can be placed above the topmost box, the number of boxes above the pink-coloured box is zero. Hence, "None" is the correct answer.

68. (A): N's spouse is the daughter-in-law of R because N is the child of R. If R has another daughter, that daughter will be N's sister. The relationship of N's spouse with N's sister is that of a sister-in-law. Therefore, N's spouse will be the sister-in-law of R's daughter.

69. (B): N's spouse is the paternal aunt of E, making N's child a cousin of E. H and N are children of R and are therefore siblings. Since H is of the same gender as G, who is male, H is also male. Thus, H is the maternal or paternal uncle of E's cousin, depending upon the connecting parent, and the required relation is "uncle."

70. (C): N's spouse is the only paternal aunt of E, so the father of E is the brother of N's spouse. A is described as the only nephew of N's spouse and is therefore the male child of that brother. P is the mother of E's sibling, and A is that sibling of E. Hence, P is the mother of A.

71. (C): V is the grandchild of P's father-in-law and is identified through the family structure as the child of N and N's spouse. The gender of N's child is different from that of G, who is male; therefore, V is female. If V marries S, S will be the husband of N's daughter. Consequently, S will be N's son-in-law.

72. (B):

(I) This is the impact of the damage done by modern civilization to the natural world — Not a course of action: This statement describes the cause or background of the extinction crisis. It does not suggest any practical step that should be taken to address the problem.

(II) Only a wide-ranging transformation of the global economic and financial system could pull ecosystems that are vital to the future of species and human communities worldwide — Course of action: This statement recommends a broad transformation of economic and financial systems to protect ecosystems. It proposes a definite remedial measure and is therefore the only valid course of action.

(III) The essential, interconnected web of life on Earth is getting smaller and increasingly frayed due to this extinction — Not a course of action: This statement explains a harmful consequence of species extinction. It describes the worsening environmental condition but does not prescribe any corrective action.

(IV) This loss is a direct result of human activity and constitutes a direct threat to human well-being in all regions of the world — Not a course of action: This statement identifies human activity as the cause and explains the threat created by biodiversity loss. It contains no recommendation or practical measure for solving the problem.

73. **(B):**

(I) Only first-time marathon runners will get benefit from it — Not implicit: The study concerns first-time marathon runners, but it does not establish that experienced runners receive no benefit. The word "only" introduces an unsupported restriction that cannot be inferred from the statement.

(II) Those who run fast gets older earlier than others — Not implicit: The finding that older and slower runners benefit the most does not mean that faster runners age earlier. It merely indicates that the improvement observed was greater among older and slower participants.

(III) Blood vessels play a major role in ageing of the person — Implicit: The statement says that marathon training can reverse ageing in major blood vessels. This indicates a meaningful association between the condition of blood vessels and the ageing process. Therefore, Statement III can reasonably be inferred.

74. (B): The fixed arrangement, taken clockwise, is C–G–D–E–F–A–H–B, with the corresponding cities Jaipur–Mumbai–Hyderabad–Bengaluru–Delhi–Kolkata–Chennai–Pune. The person from Hyderabad is D, who sits at a corner and faces inside. The person immediately to D's left is E, and E faces outside because E sits at the middle of a side. The person sitting second to the left of E is G; therefore, G is the required person.

75. (C): In the established arrangement, A sits opposite the person from Mumbai. Similarly, E sits opposite the person from Pune, which explains the two relationships given in the question. Applying the same positional relationship to F, the person sitting opposite F is C. Since C is from Jaipur, F is related to Jaipur in the same way.

76. (C): The person from Delhi is F, who sits at a corner and faces the centre of the table. For a person facing inside, movement towards the left follows the clockwise direction. A sits immediately to the left of F, and H occupies the next position in the same direction. Therefore, H sits second to the left of the person from Delhi.

77. (D): F, H and C sit at the corners of the square table and therefore face inside. The person from Hyderabad is D, who also occupies a corner and faces inside. The person from Mumbai is G, who sits at the middle of a side and faces outside. Therefore, the person from Mumbai does not belong to the group based on facing direction.

78. (D): The complete city arrangement shows that C is from Jaipur, G from Mumbai, D from Hyderabad, E from Bengaluru, F from Delhi, A from Kolkata, H from Chennai and B from Pune. The clues that B and D are not from Bengaluru are also satisfied by this arrangement. Hence, E is the person from Bengaluru.

79. (A): The government's decision to announce a special relief package specifically for farmers presupposes that farmers have suffered serious losses due to the floods. Without such an assumption, there would be no clear basis for providing targeted assistance to them. The statement does not imply that urban infrastructure is unaffected or that financial relief alone is sufficient. Therefore, the implicit assumption is that farmers are among the groups most severely affected.

80. (B): The decision to impose stricter emission norms on vehicles assumes that emissions released by vehicles materially contribute to air pollution in major cities. Otherwise, tightening vehicular standards would not be a relevant measure for reducing pollution. The decision does not assume that emission norms will eliminate pollution completely or that industrial pollution has no role. Hence, vehicular emissions being a significant contributor is the implicit assumption.

81. (D): O sits at position 4, V at position 2, B at position 7, G at position 11, K at position 12, M at position 14, and H at position 15.

Number of persons between M and O

$= 14 - 4 - 1 = 9$

Therefore, nine persons sit between M and O.

82. (C): Position of M from the left end = 14th

Seventh position to the left of M

$= 14 - 7 = 7$th position

B occupies the seventh position; therefore, B sits seventh to the left of M.

83. (A): V occupies the second position, so one person sits to the left of V. The same number of persons must sit to the right of M, placing M second from the right end. Since M occupies the fourteenth position, the total number of persons is 14 + 1 = 15. The condition that H sits immediately to the right of M is also satisfied because H occupies the fifteenth position.

84. (C): The letters of "CONCEPTUAL" arranged alphabetically beginning from the right end produce the left-to-right sequence U, T, P, O, N, L, E, C, C, A. Comparing this sequence with the original arrangement C, O, N, C, E, P, T, U, A, L shows that no letter remains at its original position. Therefore, the position of none of the letters remains unchanged.

85. (D): The coding rule reverses the letters and then moves the first, second, and third reversed letters forward by 2, 4, and 6 places respectively.

HAN → N, A, H

N + 2 = P, A + 4 = E, H + 6 = N

Therefore, "HAN" is coded as the meaningful word "PEN."

86. (D): I. H > P — True:

$H > U \geq E > N \geq P$

The inequalities proceed in the same direction, and the chain contains strict inequalities. Therefore, H is definitely greater than P.

II. P ≤ S—True

$P \leq K \leq R < S \Rightarrow P < S$

Since $P < S$, it necessarily follows that $P \leq S$. The symbol "≤" includes every case in which the first quantity is strictly less than the second; it does not require equality to remain possible. Therefore, both conclusions are true.

87. (D):

I. H > M — True:

$M = O = T,\ R > O,\ H > R$

$H > R > O = M \Rightarrow H > M$

Therefore, Conclusion I is definitely true.

II. P ≥ T

$P \geq M = O = T$

$P \geq T$

Therefore, Conclusion II is also definitely true.

88. (E):

I. Z ≥ J — False:

$Z \geq T \leq N = J$

Both Z and J are related to T, but no definite relationship exists between Z and J. Therefore, Conclusion I does not follow.

II. R < S — False:

$R < J = N \geq T \leq W < S$

The inequality signs change direction, so no definite comparison between R and S can be established. Therefore, Conclusion II also does not follow.

89. (C):

I. $A \geq I$ and II. $Y < B$

Since $Y = A$ and $I = B$, the conclusions become:

I. $A \geq B$

II. $A < B$

These two conclusions form a complementary pair: either $A \geq B$ or $A < B$ must necessarily be true, although the statements do not establish which one individually is true. Therefore, either Conclusion I or Conclusion II is true.

90. (B): 435673538

Digits less than 6: subtract 2; remaining digits: subtract 1.

4→2, 3→1, 5→3, 6→5, 7→6, 3→1, 5→3, 3→1, 8→7

"New sequence" = 2, 1, 3, 5, 6, 1, 3, 1, 7

The digits 1 and 3 occur repeatedly, so all their occurrences are removed:

Remaining digits = 2, 5, 6, 7

Sum of odd digits = 5 + 7 = 12

Sum of even digits = 2 + 6 = 8

Required difference = 12 − 8 = 4

91. (D): A lives on the fifth floor, so the number of floors above A is:

$$8 - 5 = 3$$

This is one more than the number of floors below the required subject-holder:

$$3 - 1 = 2$$

A person having two floors below lives on the third floor, and E, who likes Biology, occupies that floor. Therefore, the required subject is Biology.

92. **(B):** The complete floor arrangement from bottom to top is D–G–E–F–A–B–C–H. The corresponding subjects are Mathematics, Physics, Biology, English, Science, Chemistry, Hindi and Philosophy. F occupies the fourth floor and likes English. Therefore, F's subject is English.

93. **(C):** G lives on the second floor, while the person who likes Philosophy, namely H, lives on the eighth floor. The floor exactly midway between floors 2 and 8 is the fifth floor. A occupies the fifth floor and likes Science. Therefore, the person who likes Science lives exactly between G and the person who likes Philosophy.

94. **(E):** The complete arrangement establishes that D lives on the first floor and likes Mathematics. H likes Philosophy, A likes Science, F likes English, and G likes Physics. Therefore, the only correctly matched person–subject combination among the options is D–Mathematics.

95. **(A):**

I. E lives on floor above D's floor — True: E lives on the third floor, whereas D lives on the first floor. Thus, E definitely lives above D.

II. B likes Science — False: B lives on the sixth floor and likes Chemistry. A, who occupies the fifth floor, likes Science.

III. No one lives above H — True: H occupies the eighth or topmost floor of the building. Therefore, no person lives above H.

96. **(C):** The coding rule is:

Code = position of first letter + position of last letter – number of letters

For PLAYER:

$P + R - 6 = 16 + 18 - 6 = 28$

For NOISE:

$N + E - 5 = 14 + 5 - 5 = 14$

For HOCKEY:

$H + Y - 6 = 8 + 25 - 6 = 27$

Therefore, HOCKEY is written as 27.

97. **(C):** Let M be at (0, 0). Since Q is 6 metres east of M and R is exactly midway between M and Q, R is at (3, 0). S is 6 metres south of R, so S = (3, –6), and T is 7 metres east of S, so T = (10, –6). T is therefore east as well as south of M, placing it in the south-east direction.

98. **(A):** Taking M = (0, 0):

L = (0, –15)

R = (3, 0), S = (3, –6)

Horizontal distance between S and L:

$3 - 0 = 3$ m

Vertical distance:

$-6 - (-15) = 9$ m

$$SL = \sqrt{3^2 + 9^2} = \sqrt{9 + 81} = \sqrt{90} \text{ m}$$

99. **(E):** M lies north-west of S, O lies north-west of L, S lies north-west of U, and Q lies north-west of T. Thus, the first four pairs share the same directional relationship. However, O and T lie on the same horizontal line, with T directly east of O. Therefore, the pair O and T does not belong to the group.

100. **(D):** The route connecting R to O through the given points is R→M→L→N→O. Since R is midway between M and Q and MQ = 6 metres, RM = 3 metres. Also, ML = 15 metres, LN = 13 metres and NO = 9 metres.

Total distance = RM + ML + LN + NO
= 3 + 15 + 13 + 9
= 40 m

101. **(D):** The Amazon River flows across northern South America, principally through Peru, Colombia and Brazil. Iquitos lies on the Amazon in Peru, while Manaus and Santarém are major Brazilian cities situated along the Amazon river system. Macapá is located near the Amazon's northern estuary. Buenos Aires, however, is situated in Argentina on the Río de la Plata and is not traversed by the Amazon River.

102. **(C):** Before the Constitution came into force on 26 January 1950, India's governmental system largely functioned under the Government of India Act, 1935, as adapted after independence. The Constitution replaced this colonial constitutional framework and established India as a sovereign democratic republic. It introduced parliamentary government, fundamental rights, an independent judiciary and a federal structure with a strong Union government.

103. **(B):** Most Nobel Prizes are awarded by Swedish institutions in Stockholm. The prizes in Physics,

Chemistry, Physiology or Medicine, Literature and Economic Sciences are awarded in Sweden. The Nobel Peace Prize is the notable exception, as it is awarded by the Norwegian Nobel Committee in Oslo. Therefore, Sweden is the country primarily associated with awarding most Nobel Prize categories.

104. **(C):** The 'Ek Ped Maa Ke Naam' campaign encourages people to plant a tree as a tribute to their mothers and to Mother Earth. It was launched on World Environment Day in 2024 and promotes mass participation in environmental conservation. Its principal objective is to increase tree plantation while strengthening public responsibility towards nature and ecological protection.

105. **(C):** Kargil Vijay Diwas is observed every year on 26 July to commemorate India's victory in the Kargil War of 1999. On this date, Indian forces successfully completed Operation Vijay and regained strategically important positions occupied by infiltrators. The day honours the courage and sacrifices of the armed forces personnel who participated in the conflict.

106. **(D):** The Ural Mountains form a traditionally recognised geographical boundary between the continents of Europe and Asia. They extend broadly from the Arctic Ocean in the north towards Kazakhstan in the south. Along with the Ural River and other geographical features, this mountain range is commonly used to distinguish European Russia from Asian Russia.

107. **(C):** Uttarakhand became the first Indian state after independence to implement a Uniform Civil Code, which came into force on 27 January 2025. It provides a common framework for personal matters such as marriage, divorce, inheritance and succession. Goa has an older common civil system inherited from Portuguese rule, but Uttarakhand is recognised as the first state in independent India to enact and implement its own UCC.

108. **(C):** The Insurance Regulatory and Development Authority of India regulates and develops the insurance sector in India. It protects policyholders' interests, registers insurance companies and supervises their financial and operational conduct. RBI regulates banking, SEBI regulates the securities market, and PFRDA regulates the pension sector. Therefore, IRDAI is the appropriate regulatory body.

109. **(C):** India ranked 99th among 167 countries in the Sustainable Development Report 2025 SDG Index, with a reported score of 67. This was the first time India entered the top 100 positions in the global SDG ranking. The index evaluates countries' progress towards achieving the 17 Sustainable Development Goals covering social, economic and environmental development.

110. **(D):** Exercise Shakti is a bilateral military exercise conducted between the armies of India and France. It is organised alternately in the two countries and focuses on joint operational capabilities, tactical coordination and interoperability. The exercise also enables the armed forces of both countries to exchange procedures and experience in undertaking coordinated military operations.

111. **(B):** The 24th meeting of the Shanghai Cooperation Organisation Council of Heads of State was held in Astana, Kazakhstan, on 4 July 2024. The summit adopted the Astana Declaration and discussed regional security, economic cooperation and multilateral coordination among member states. Therefore, Astana was the host city of the SCO Summit 2024.

112. **(C):** The Maratha Military Landscapes of India was inscribed on the UNESCO World Heritage List in July 2025 as India's 44th World Heritage Site. It comprises twelve forts, including Raigad, Shivneri, Pratapgad, Sindhudurg and Gingee, representing the strategic military architecture developed under the Marathas. Therefore, the collective property, rather than any single fort listed in the options, is correct.

113. **(C):** NISAR stands for NASA–ISRO Synthetic Aperture Radar and is a joint Earth-observation satellite mission developed by NASA and ISRO. It uses advanced radar technology to monitor changes in land, ice, water, vegetation and the Earth's surface. Its observations support the study of natural hazards, ecosystems, glaciers and groundwater movement.

114. (C): BIRAC stands for Biotechnology Industry Research Assistance Council. It is a public-sector enterprise established by the Department of Biotechnology, Government of India, to encourage biotechnology innovation, research and entrepreneurship. Hence, the letter "A" in BIRAC represents "Assistance."

115. (B): MISHTI stands for Mangrove Initiative for Shoreline Habitats and Tangible Incomes. Its primary objective is to restore, conserve and expand mangrove forests through reforestation and afforestation along India's coastline. The programme also supports shoreline protection, biodiversity conservation and livelihood opportunities for coastal communities.

116. (D): The Global Biofuel Alliance was launched by India along with countries including the United States, Brazil, Argentina, Italy, Singapore, Bangladesh, Mauritius and the United Arab Emirates. India, the USA, Brazil and Argentina were among its participating countries, whereas China was not included among the alliance's founding participants. Therefore, China is the correct answer.

117. (A): ASMITA is the Khelo India initiative designed to increase women's participation in sports through dedicated leagues and competitions. The acronym expands to "Achieving Sports Milestone by Inspiring Women." It aims to identify female sporting talent, create competitive opportunities and address gender imbalance in organised sports.

118. (C): Sachin Tendulkar became the first male cricketer to score a double century in One Day International cricket. He scored an unbeaten 200 against South Africa at Gwalior on 24 February 2010. His innings included 25 fours and three sixes and established a historic milestone in men's ODI cricket.

119. (A): The Subhadra Yojana was launched by the Government of Odisha as a major women-centred empowerment scheme. It provides eligible women with financial assistance over a specified period and promotes economic independence and digital participation. Therefore, Odisha is the state associated with the scheme.

120. (A): NITI Aayog released the report titled Chemical Industry: Powering India's Participation in Global Value Chains in July 2025. The report examines the size, growth potential, competitiveness and global-value-chain opportunities of India's chemical sector. Therefore, NITI Aayog is the body that released the report referred to in the question.

121. (B): Under the current KYC framework, Officially Valid Documents include a passport, driving licence, proof of possession of Aadhaar number, voter identity card, NREGA job card and a National Population Register letter containing address details. A PAN Card is separately required for tax identification but is not classified as an OVD under the current definition. Therefore, PAN Card is the correct answer.

122. (B): Under a reverse repo transaction, the RBI borrows money from commercial banks by providing eligible securities. Banks deposit their surplus funds with the RBI and earn interest, thereby reducing the amount of liquidity available in the banking system. Thus, the reverse repo rate is conventionally used to absorb excess short-term liquidity from banks.

123. (A): The theme of India's G20 Presidency was "Vasudhaiva Kutumbakam," translated as "One Earth, One Family, One Future." It emphasised the interconnectedness of human beings, animals, plants and the wider environment. The theme promoted inclusive, sustainable and human-centred global development.

124. (D): Bharat Ratna is the highest civilian award of India and is conferred in recognition of exceptional service or performance of the highest order in any field of human endeavour. Padma Vibhushan, Padma Bhushan and Padma Shri follow it in the hierarchy of civilian honours. Param Vir Chakra is India's highest military decoration for wartime gallantry and is not a civilian award.

125. (A): STRIPS is a process through which the periodic interest payments and the principal repayment component of an eligible government security are separated and traded individually as zero-coupon securities. This permits investors to purchase distinct cash flows according to their investment requirements. Therefore, STRIPS expands as "Separate Trading of Registered Interest and Principal of Securities."

126. (B): Sovereign Gold Bonds are government securities denominated in grams of gold and issued by the Reserve Bank of India on behalf of the Government of India. Investors receive the market-linked value of gold at redemption along with the prescribed interest on the initial investment. Thus, the RBI acts as the issuing authority on behalf of the Central Government.

127. (B): UPI stands for Unified Payments Interface, a real-time digital payment system developed by the National Payments Corporation of India. It permits instant transfer of money between bank accounts through mobile applications using identifiers such as a UPI ID or linked mobile number. The official expansion uses the plural word "Payments," making Option B correct.

128. (B): KVS Manian is the Managing Director and Chief Executive Officer of Federal Bank. He assumed the position with effect from 23 September 2024, succeeding Shyam Srinivasan. The bank's current key-personnel information also identifies KVS Manian as its MD and CEO.

129. (C): Statutory Liquidity Ratio is the prescribed percentage of a bank's Net Demand and Time Liabilities that must be maintained in specified liquid assets. These assets may include cash, gold and unencumbered approved securities. Unlike CRR, which is maintained as cash with the RBI, SLR assets are maintained by the banks themselves.

130. (B): The RBI's FinTech Repository is designed to capture essential information about fintech entities, including their activities, products and technology applications. It supports better understanding of the fintech ecosystem and facilitates appropriate regulatory and policy formulation. A related EmTech Repository records the adoption of emerging technologies by regulated entities such as banks and NBFCs.

131. (C): CASA is the commonly used banking abbreviation for "Current and Savings Account." It refers collectively to the current-account and savings-account deposits maintained with a bank. These deposits generally provide banks with a comparatively low-cost source of funds, especially because current accounts ordinarily carry no interest. Therefore, the exact expansion matching the given options is "Current and Savings Account."

132. (B): The minimum maturity period prescribed for an NRE term deposit is one year. NRE deposits are rupee-denominated deposits maintained by non-resident Indians, and both the principal and interest are generally repatriable subject to applicable rules. A deposit must remain for the stipulated minimum period to qualify for interest under the relevant banking regulations.

133. (C): The Reserve Bank of India regulates and supervises scheduled commercial banks as part of India's banking system. Insurance companies are regulated by IRDAI, mutual funds by SEBI, commodity derivatives exchanges by SEBI, and pension funds by PFRDA. RBI's responsibilities include banking regulation, monetary policy, currency management and financial stability.

134. (B): The World Economic Outlook is published by the International Monetary Fund, generally twice a year, with interim updates when required. It presents the IMF's assessment of global economic growth, inflation, trade, fiscal conditions and major risks. It also provides country-wise and regional economic projections used by governments and financial institutions.

135. (C): PM SVANidhi, or the Prime Minister Street Vendor's AtmaNirbhar Nidhi, provides collateral-free working-capital loans to eligible street vendors. It was introduced to help vendors restart and strengthen their businesses, particularly after disruptions caused by the COVID-19 pandemic. The scheme also encourages regular repayment and adoption of digital transactions through incentives.

136. (D): Gujarat has the longest coastline among Indian states, extending for about 1,600 kilometres along the Arabian Sea. Its coast includes the Gulf of Kachchh and the Gulf of Khambhat and supports major ports such as Deendayal Port and Mundra. The state's extensive coastline contributes significantly to maritime trade, fisheries, salt production and coastal industries.

137. (C): MSME stands for Micro, Small and Medium Enterprises. These enterprises are classified according to prescribed limits of investment in plant and machinery or equipment and annual turnover. The MSME sector plays an important role in employment generation, manufacturing, exports, entrepreneurship and balanced regional development.

138. (B): Fundamental Duties are contained in Article 51A of Part IVA of the Indian Constitution. They were added by the 42nd Constitutional Amendment Act, 1976, on the recommendation of the Swaran Singh Committee. Originally ten duties were included, and an eleventh duty concerning children's education was later added by the 86th Constitutional Amendment Act, 2002.

139. (C): The headquarters of the World Bank is located at 1818 H Street, Northwest, Washington, D.C., United States. The World Bank Group consists of institutions that provide financial and technical assistance for development and poverty reduction. Its principal lending institutions include the International Bank for Reconstruction and Development and the International Development Association.

140. (B): The Atal Pension Yojana is a Government of India social-security scheme administered under the Ministry of Finance and regulated by the Pension Fund Regulatory and Development Authority. It primarily targets workers in the unorganised sector and provides a guaranteed pension after the age of sixty, subject to prescribed contributions and eligibility conditions. PFRDA oversees the scheme's operational and regulatory framework.

141. (C): The official currency of South Korea is the South Korean won, represented by the symbol ₩ and the international currency code KRW. The Bank of Korea is responsible for issuing and managing the currency. Yen is used in Japan, Yuan in China, Ringgit in Malaysia and Baht in Thailand. Therefore, Won is the correct answer.

142. (C): The Narasimham Committees are associated with major banking-sector reforms in India. The first committee, constituted in 1991, recommended changes relating to statutory pre-emptions, prudential norms, competition and banking autonomy. The second committee, constituted in 1998, focused on strengthening banks, reducing non-performing assets and improving capital adequacy. Therefore, the Narasimham Committee is the correct answer.

143. (C): YONO, meaning "You Only Need One," is the integrated digital banking and lifestyle platform launched by the State Bank of India. It provides facilities such as banking, investments, insurance, loans and online shopping through a unified application. It was introduced to offer SBI customers a comprehensive digital-service platform. Therefore, SBI is the correct answer.

144. (C): IFSC stands for Indian Financial System Code. It is an eleven-character alphanumeric code used to identify individual bank branches participating in electronic payment systems. It facilitates transfers through systems such as NEFT, RTGS and IMPS. Therefore, Indian Financial System Code is the correct expansion.

145. (C): Treasury Bills are short-term money-market instruments issued by the Government of India to meet temporary funding requirements. They are zero-coupon securities issued at a discount and redeemed at face value, commonly with maturities of 91, 182 or 364 days. Equity shares, debentures and preference shares belong mainly to the capital market. Therefore, Treasury Bills are the correct answer.

146. (B): The RuPay card payment network is managed by the National Payments Corporation of India. RuPay provides domestic debit, credit and prepaid card services and enables transactions through ATMs, point-of-sale terminals and online platforms. NPCI also operates payment systems such as UPI and IMPS. Therefore, NPCI is the correct answer.

147. (B): NPA stands for Non-Performing Asset. A loan or advance becomes an NPA when the borrower fails to pay interest or principal for the period prescribed under banking regulations, generally more than 90 days for a term loan. NPAs reduce a bank's income and may require provisioning against potential losses. Therefore, Non-Performing Asset is the correct expansion.

148. (C): The Reserve Bank of India is known as the "Banker to Banks" because commercial banks maintain prescribed reserves and accounts with it. RBI provides settlement facilities, acts as lender of last resort and supports banks during liquidity shortages. It also regulates and supervises the banking system. Therefore, RBI is the correct answer.

149. (D): Immediate Payment Service permits instant inter-bank fund transfers on a real-time basis throughout the day, including weekends and holidays. It is operated by NPCI and is specifically described as a round-the-clock real-time payment service. NEFT also operates continuously but settles transactions in half-hourly batches, while RTGS is mainly intended for high-value real-time transfers. Therefore, IMPS best fits the wording of the question.

150. (D): DICGC insures eligible bank deposits up to a maximum of ₹ 5 lakh per depositor per bank, including both principal and accrued interest. Deposits held in different branches of the same bank are aggregated for calculating this limit, while deposits in different banks receive separate coverage. Therefore, the maximum insurance cover is ₹ 5 lakh.

YOUR SPACE

Previous Years' Paper

IBPS-SPECIALIST OFFICERS

Rajbhasha Adhikari and Law Officer, 2024*

Preliminary Exam

ENGLISH LANGUAGE

Directions (Qs. No. 1 to 4): *In each of the questions given below a sentence is given with three words in bold. Choose the option which gives the correct sequence of these words to make the sentence grammatically and contextually correct.*

1. Despite being in the spotlight, a range of issues in the **unaddressed (A)** remain **development (B)**, such as the delay in shifting of the mofussil bus stand, lack of industrial **constituency (C)**.

A. CBA B. None of these
C. CAB D. BCA
E. ACB

2. Peak summer **interior (A)** is yet to begin but several **season (B)** places are already in the **grip (C)** of a heatwave.

A. CBA B. BAC
C. ACB D. None of these
E. BCA

3. The interns have **indefinitely (A)** to **boycott (B)** work **decided (C)** until their demands were met.

A. None of these B. CAB
C. ABC D. BCA
E. CBA

4. BioNTech-Pfizer said their vaccine showed 100% **efficacy (A)** against the coronavirus in 12- to 15-year-olds, as they eye **adolescents (B)** for **approval (C)** to get the jabs before the next school year.

A. BCA B. ACB
C. CAB D. BAC
E. None of these

Directions (Qs. No. 5 to 7): *Which of the phrase/ word from the options (A), (B), (C) and (D) given below each sentence should replace the phrase printed in bold letters to make the sentence grammatically correct? If the sentence is correct as it is, mark (E) i.e., "No replacement required" as the answer.*

5. High Court directed the Election Commission of India **to forming new policies** to prevent double voting.

A. to reveal the winner
B. conduct elections
C. by take strict actions
D. to take all possible steps
E. No replacement required

6. Last month the government **were announcing the policy** lagged revision in small savings rates.

A. is mandating the
B. has effected a substantial
C. must be controlling inflation
D. will pay heed to many
E. No replacement required

* Based on Memory.

7. In the absence of taxi services, air-passengers **are relying on** private vehicles.

A. cancelling ticket
B. were worried
C. was hiring
D. are believable
E. No replacement required

Directions (Qs. No. 8 to 15): *Read the following passage carefully and answer the questions given below it. Certain words have been printed in bold to help you locate them, while answering some of the questions.*

By the end of May 2021, only 2.1% of Africans had received at least one dose of a COVID-19 vaccine. We need to close the vaccination gap between advanced economies and developing countries to avoid what the World Health Organization (WHO) Director-General, Dr. Tedros Adhanom Ghebreyesu has called "vaccination apartheid". Doing so is both morally right and in everyone's interest. Therefore, we need global multilateral action to increase the production of vaccines and **accelerate** the roll-out worldwide. Since the beginning of the novel coronavirus pandemic, this is the path chosen by the European Union (EU). It is now also the path defined by the G20 leaders at the Global Health Summit in Rome on May 21.

The pandemic is still killing thousands of people every day and at the current pace, the whole world will not be vaccinated before 2023. Yet, a widely vaccinated world population is the only way to end the pandemic; otherwise, the multiplication of variants is likely to **undermine** the effectiveness of existing vaccines. Vaccination is also a prerequisite for lifting the restrictions that are holding back our economies and freedoms. These restrictions penalise the whole world, but they weigh even more heavily on developing countries. Advanced countries can rely more on social mechanisms and economic policy levers to limit the impact of the pandemic on their citizens.

If the vaccination gap persists, it risks reversing the trend in recent decades of declining poverty and global inequalities. Such a negative dynamic would hold back economic activity and increase geopolitical tensions. The cost of inaction would for sure be much higher for advanced economies than what we collectively would have to spend to help vaccinate the whole world. Therefore, the EU welcomes the $50 billion plan proposed by the International Monetary Fund in order to be able to vaccinate 40% of the world population in 2021 and 60% by mid-2022.

To achieve this goal, we need closely coordinated multilateral action. We must resist the threat posed by linking the provision of vaccines to political goals and "vaccine nationalism". The EU has rejected both since the beginning of the pandemic. The EU has been vaccinating its own population, while exporting large volumes of vaccines and contributing **substantially** to the vaccines roll-out in low-income countries. Europeans can be proud of this record. India's "Vaccine Maitri" is another example of global solidarity. In 2020, the EU supported the research and development of vaccines on a large scale and contributed significantly to the new generation of mRNA vaccines. The EU then became a major producer of COVID-19 vaccines with, according to WHO, around 40% of the doses used globally so far. The EU has also exported 240 million doses to 90 countries, which is about as much as we have used within the EU.

8. Why there is a need to increase the pace of production and vaccine drive?

A. because the medication is not enough efficient to fight COVID-19 infection
B. it is imperative both ethically right and for everyone's well being
C. as the government is seeking to give approval to many more vaccine manufacturer companies
D. because an increase in the number of cases has become threefold than before
E. None of these

9. Which of the following will be the consequence of lack of sufficient supply of vaccine?

A. the existing vaccine will not be efficient for an outbreak of new variants of infections.

B. the economic impact of the COVID-19 pandemic in India will be largely disruptive.

C. the perpetuate Covid-19 pandemic will erode all the available necessary resources.

D. enlarging the variant will wear away the efficacy of the available vaccine.

E. None of these

10. Which of the following is/are the contribution(s) of international organizations to fight pandemics?

I. continuous efforts have been put by them in order to provide vaccines throughout the world.

II. financial aid has been given for the coverage of population for vaccine.

III. by ensuring food security to everyone to make sure minimum death due to starvation.

A. Only I B. Both I and II

C. Both I and III D. Only III

E. All are correct

11. Although patriotism is praiseworthy, why it is not like the same in the case according to the passage?

A. global politics during pandemic making it more challenging to control the spread of the virus.

B. nationalism is necessary for national security and cannot be compromised by any nation.

C. promote the interest of own nation only will contradict the idea of vaccination drive for everyone.

D. EU is exporting vaccines to many countries and setting it as an example of global cooperation.

E. None of these

12. Which of the following statements can be concluded from the passage as a solution?

A. more financial aids are required as there is a lack of resources for the manufacturers of the vaccine.

B. Immunisation needs cooperation and is rudimentary for abolishing the international restrictions.

C. the restrictions need to be extended to stop people from gathering and spread of the transmitted virus.

D. the production of vaccines should be increased as its supply is much lesser than the demand.

E. None of these

13. Among the given options, choose the word which can replace the highlighted word in the given passage.

UNDERMINE

A. dawdle

B. cripple

C. supervene

D. draconian

E. None of these

14. Among the given options, choose the word with the most similar meaning of the given word.

ACCELERATE

A. expedite

B. noxious

C. fervent

D. fitful

E. None of these

15. Among the given options, choose the word with the opposite in meaning of the given word.

Substantially

A. flout

B. offensive

C. flawed

D. paltry

E. None of these

Directions (Qs. No. 16 to 20): *In the following questions, a sentence is divided into four parts consisting of a highlighted word in each part. Choose the option reflecting the word which is either misspelt or grammatically incorrect. If all the highlighted words are correct, choose option (E) i.e. "all are correct" as your answer choice.*

16. The Supreme Court has **cautioned (A)** courts against **mechanical (B) granting (C)** bail in heinous **offences (D)**.

A. cautioned B. mechanical
C. granting D. offences
E. All are correct

17. We do not have **adequate (A)** knowledge about the virus and should be very **careful (B)** about **extrapolating (C)** its **behaviour (D)** during the last wave.

A. adequate B. careful
C. extrapolating D. behaviour
E. All are correct

18. The Finance Ministry has put to rest all **spectulation (A)** about the inflation **targeting (B)** framework that will guide the **interest (C)** rate **decisions (D)** of the RBI's Monetary Policy Committee over the five-year.

A. spectulation B. targeting
C. interest D. decisions
E. All are correct

19. The **optimism (A)** that India might have beaten the COVID-19 **pandemic (B)** has given way to **pesimism (C)** from a sharp increase in new cases and deaths from the **disease (D)**.

A. optimism B. pandemic
C. pesimism D. disease
E. All are correct

20. Though the diasporas are always active, it is an international civil society made up of a whole **arrey (A)** of **disparate (B)** groups that **dominate (C)** the **agitational (D)** space of the Human Rights Council.

A. arrey B. disparate
C. dominate D. agitational
E. All are correct

Directions (Qs. No. 21 to 25): *In the following questions, a grammatically correct and meaningful sentence is given which is divided into four parts namely (A), (B), (C) and (D). You have to arrange the four parts to make a contextually and grammatically meaningful sentence. If no such rearrangement is possible mark (E) as your answer i.e. 'No rearrangement required'.*

21. A. a free, open and
B. we are united by our democratic
C. values and our commitment to
D. inclusive Indo-Pacific.
A. DABC
B. BCAD
C. CDAB
D. ADCB
E. No rearrangement required

22. A. the State Election Commission
B. the duty of the State to not interfere
C. with the functioning of
D. under the constitutional mandate, it is
A. ADCB B. BACD
C. CDBA D. DBCA
E. No rearrangement required

23. A. substantial volume of the vaccine
B. the Serum Institute of India
C. has an agreement with
D. Novavax to manufacture a
A. ADCB B. BCDA
C. CDBA D. DABC
E. No rearrangement required

24. A. at the helm will be under scrutiny
B. itself will vote for a chief ministerial
C. For the first time, the constituency
D. candidate, whose stint
A. DACB B. ABDC
C. CBDA D. BCDA
E. No rearrangement is required

25. A. The daughter of a village temple priest,
B. who was murdered along with his son for
C. exposing encroachments on a waterbody district,
D. has decided to take the political plunge

A. ABCD B. CADB
C. DABC D. BACD
E. BDAC

Directions (Qs. No. 26 to 31): *Given below is a paragraph that has blank spaces. Corresponding to each blank, five options are given, out of which only one is appropriate. Choose the option that fits most suitably in the given blank making sentence grammatically and contextually correct.*

If anyone were to peruse the __**(26)**__ newspapers, and listen to the different television channels in the country, one would get an __**(27)**__ that India is approaching a new 'gilded' era. Unfortunately, electoral politics in the country appears to be out of sync with this __**(28)**__. Threats to the conduct of orderly elections are increasing, more so in some States than perhaps in others, and must not be underestimated. Pressing the stop button is not a viable option as of now, as it is a __**(29)**__ of the pervasive decline in political attitudes and behaviour in the nation. Violence, money power, and communal attitudes tend to exercise a disproportionately greater __**(30)**__ on the outcome of elections as of now. A great deal of this is attributable to the prevailing belief that winning elections is the sine qua non of democratic politics, and the raison d'etre for any political party to exist. India's leading political party, which currently holds power at the Centre and a majority of States, has converted this into a fine art, and makes no secret of its __**(31)**__ to pursue this path.

26. A. standard B. numerous
C. preserve D. defection
E. absurdity

27. A. treasure B. insulate
C. combat D. stability
E. impression

28. A. direct B. disqualify
C. contrary D. portrayal
E. reluctant

29. A. delegate B. constitute
C. acceptance D. complex
E. reflection

30. A. accountable B. draft
C. influence D. plunge
E. betrayed

31. A. ostensible B. determination
C. fora D. detrimental
E. executive

Directions (Qs. No. 32 to 35): *There are three sentences given in each question. Find the sentence(s) which is/are grammatically correct and mark your answer choosing the best possible alternative among the five options given below each question. If all the sentences are correct, choose (E) as your answer.*

32. (*i*) The provision was not limited to confidence motions or money bills.
(*ii*) The Court correct observed that there was the possibility of the formation of a new government.
(*iii*) Ambulances and other emergency services are enable to use the roads due to the encroachments.

A. Only (*i*) B. Only (*ii*)
C. Only (*iii*) D. Both (*i*) and (*ii*)
E. All are correct

33. (*i*) The document has been supported by animation to explains that the riots were the part of large-scale conspiracy.
(*ii*) The NIC has suggested a multidisciplinary learn that would included skill enhancement and research.
(*iii*) This article is a brief critique of the recommendations of the Fifteenth Finance Commission with regard to local government.

A. Only (*i*) B. Only (*ii*)
C. Only (*iii*) D. Both (*i*) and (*iii*)
E. All are correct

34. (*i*) If one contributed more then the limit prescribed, they did not get a tax break on the excess contribution.
(*ii*) It is vital to excess the performance of incumbent government.
(*iii*) The legality of the decision was questioned by an opposition politician.
A. Only (*i*) B. Only (*ii*)
C. Only (*iii*) D. Both (*i*) and (*iii*)
E. All are correct

35. (*i*) The Bench issued the directives while disposing of a writ petition filed by Leader.
(*ii*) The accidents not only resulted in damage to property but also led to the loss of precious lives.
(*iii*) For savers, the option with the highest returns at this point is the Sukanya Samriddhi Account Scheme.
A. Only (*i*) B. Only (*ii*)
C. Only (*iii*) D. Both (*i*) and (*iii*)
E. All are correct

Directions (Qs. No. 36 to 42): *In the following questions, a sentence is divided into four parts. Choose the part of the sentence which may contain a grammatical error in it. If all the parts of the sentence are grammatically correct and contextually meaningful, choose option (E) i.e., "no error" as your answer choice.*

36. As a business counsellor, I spend my days (A)/ dolling out advices to entrepreneurs (B)/ and business owners about how to best (C)/ build and maintain their businesses. (D)/ No error (E)
A. As a business counsellor, I spend my days
B. dolling out advices to entrepreneurs
C. and business owners about how to best
D. build and maintain their businesses
E. No error

37. As the billionaire rode to work (A)/ each day, he closed his eyes (B)/ to avoid having the awareness (C)/ of the homeless crisis. (D)/ No error (E)
A. As the billionaire rode to work
B. each day he closed his eyes
C. to avoid having the awareness
D. of the homeless crisis
E. No error

38. Firefox, being open-source, (A)/ build up a following of people (B)/ who liked its independence and its (C)/ vast array of community-built add-ons. (D)/ No error (E)
A. Firefox, being open-source
B. build up a following of people
C. who liked its independence and its
D. vast array of community-built add-ons
E. No error

39. Prohibition aims (A)/ at reducing traffic accidents (B)/ many of which is (C)/ caused by drunkenness. (D)/ No error (E)
A. Prohibition aims
B. at reducing traffic accidents
C. many of which is
D. caused by drunkenness
E. No error

40. More than 50 years ago, (A)/ a Russian psychologist proposed that (B)/ children's thoughts and actions originate from their (C)/ social interactions, particular with parents. (D)/ No error (E)
A. More than 50 years ago
B. a Russian psychologist proposed that
C. children's thoughts and actions originate from their
D. social interactions, particular with parents
E. None of these

41. Because she depended on (A)/ her son to take out the trash, (B)/ Trina was disappointed to see that (C)/ he forgot two times in one week. (D)/ No error (E)
A. Because she depended on
B. her son to take out the trash
C. Trina was disappointed to see that
D. he forgot two times in one week
E. No error

42. The bidding starts (A)/ on eleven o'clock, (B)/ but you can look at the items (C)/ over any time after ten. (D)/ No error (E)

A. The bidding starts
B. on eleven o'clock
C. but you can look at the items
D. over any time after ten
E. No error

Directions (Qs. No. 43 to 50): *Read the passage carefully and answer the questions given below it. Certain words/ phrases are given in bold to help you locate them while answering some of the questions.*

About 20 years ago, Thailand rolled out universal health coverage for its population at a per capita GDP similar to today's India. What made this possible was a three decade-long tradition of investing **gradually** but steadily in public health infrastructure and manpower. This meant that alongside the availability of funds, there also existed robust institutional capacity to assimilate those funds. For India, the lesson of COVID-19 entails setting forth on a steady and incremental path to universal health coverage; not attempting a sudden and giant leap. This is important because enough evidence exists on weak fund-absorbing capacities particularly in the backward States — at times, such unused funds have been to the tune of over half of the State's public health expenditure.

The Union Ministry of Health and Family Welfare budget for 2021-22, viz. ₹ 73,932 crore, saw a 10.2% increase over the Budget estimate (BE) of 2020-21. Also, a corpus of ₹ 64,180 crore over six years has been set aside under the PM Atma Nirbhar Swasth Bharat Yojana, (PMANSBY), and ₹ 13,192 crore has been allocated as a Finance Commission grant. While the allocations still leave a lot to be desired, these could make the first steps of a journey that steadily builds towards sustainable universal health coverage through **incremental** strengthening of grass-root-level institutions and processes.

The BE for the Pradhan Mantri Jan Arogya Yojana (PM-JAY), which covers over 50 crore poor Indians for hospital expenses up to ₹ 5 lakh per annum, has stagnated at ₹ 6,400 crore for the current and the preceding couple of years. And so have the actuals and revised estimates at around 50% of the BEs, which should be a cause for concern. Large expenditure projections and time constraints involved in input-based strengthening of public health care have inspired the shift to the insurance route for achieving universal health coverage.

However, insurance does not provide a magic formula for expanding health care with measly levels of public spending. Available estimates have pegged the costs to be between ₹ 62,000 crore and ₹ 1,08,000 crore for 2021, if PM-JAY is to meet its stated commitments. Given these circumstances, making do with such paltry spending year after year would mean that the scheme benefits are being spread out too narrowly or too thin, implying the inability to afford enough protection against catastrophic health expenses to the poor. Beyond low allocations, poor budget reliability merits attention. Another related issue is the **persistent** and large discrepancies between official coverage figures and survey figures (for e.g. the National Sample Surveys, or NSS, and National Family Health Survey) across Indian States, indicating that official public health insurance coverage fails to translate into actual coverage on the ground. This is particularly intriguing for forward States such as Maharashtra, Gujarat, and Karnataka, where state-level public health insurance schemes have been operational for around a decade. Robust research into the implementational issues responsible for such discrepancies and addressing them is warranted. Without the same, the PM-JAY's quest for universal health coverage is likely to be precarious.

43. Which of the following statements does the author want to convey in the first paragraph of the passage?

A. Thailand is a role model of India for medical infrastructure.
B. Without proper absorption, the availability of funds does not guarantee proper health infrastructure.
C. break out of Covid-19 in India shows the lack of proper infrastructure and budget allocation.
D. there is a uniform distribution of funds and medical facilities throughout India.
E. None of these

44. How can people tackle the laxity and expensiveness of the healthcare sector?

A. people become reluctant towards medical facilities.
B. They tend to prefer other conventional methods of treatment and medicines.
C. They are now moving to government hospitals where free medicines and treatments are provided.
D. People are now opting for insurance as a safeguard for their health coverage.
E. None of these

45. What is the aim of the government for increasing the health care budget in Budget allocation?

A. the number of employees under the governmental healthcare coverage has increased.
B. to make free medical service available to all the people throughout India.
C. as India is committed to provide medical equipment to neighboring countries.
D. to robust the healthcare sector especially medical infrastructure.
E. None of these

46. Which of the following is/are the reason(s) for the precarious insurance schemes in India?

A. Only a few people are aware of the insurance and its benefits in the country.
B. Meagre spending on healthcare reduces the capacity to fight against a catastrophic situation.
C. Poor management of the records by several national surveys.
D. Both (A) and (C)
E. Both (B) and (C)

47. Which of the following statement(s) is/are incorrect as per the information given in the passage?

(*i*) there is a modest increase in the budget allocation of the healthcare sector from the previous financial year.
(*ii*) India follows the conventional method of investing in the healthcare sector.
(*iii*) The only allocated healthcare budget is the Union Ministry of Health and Family Welfare budget.

A. All (*i*), (*ii*) & (*iii*)
B. Only (*iii*)
C. Only (*iii*) & (*ii*)
D. Only (*i*)
E. Only (*i*) and (*iii*)

48. Which of the following words is most similar in meaning to "gradually" as given in the passage?

A. squander
B. bolster
C. array
D. overwhelm
E. moderately

49. Which of the following words is most similar in meaning to "incremental" as given in the passage?

A. confine
B. progressive
C. preventive
D. prodded
E. unswervingly

50. Which of the following words is most opposite in meaning to "persistent" as given in the passage?

A. grant
B. assassination
C. ambitious
D. intermittent
E. conclude

REASONING

Directions (Qs. No. 51 to 55): *Study the given information carefully and answer the questions that follow:*

(*i*) A, B, C, D, E, F and G are sitting on a wall and all of them are facing east.

(*ii*) C is on the immediate right of D.

(*iii*) B is at an extreme end and has E as his neighbour.

(*iv*) G is between E and F.

(*v*) D is sitting third from the south end.

51. Who is sitting to the right of E?

A. A B. C
C. D D. F
E. None of these

52. Which of the following pairs of people are sitting at the extreme ends?

A. AB B. AE
C. CB D. FB
E. Cannot be determined

53. Name the person who should change place with C such that he gets the third place from the north end.

A. E B. F
C. G D. D
E. None of these

54. Immediately between which of the following pairs of people is D sitting?

A. AC B. AF
C. CE D. CF
E. None of these

55. Which of the conditions (*i*) to (*v*) given above is not required to find out the place in which A is sitting?

A. (*i*) B. (*ii*)
C. (*iii*) D. All are required
E. None of these

Directions (Qs. No. 56 to 60): *Answer the given questions based on the following English alphabet:*

A B C D E F G H I J K L M N O P Q R S T U V W X Y Z

56. Which letter is fifth to the right of the eighteenth letter from your right?

A. C B. D
C. E D. M
E. N

57. If all the vowels are removed from the alphabet, which letter will be the seventh to the right of the fifth letter from the left?

A. L B. M
C. N D. P
E. None of these

58. If every alternate letter, starting with A, is removed from the alphabet, which letter among the remaining letters would be the third to the right of the fifth letter from the right?

A. X B. V
C. L D. J
E. None of these

59. If A and B are written as B and A, C and D as D and C, E and F as F and E and so on till the end of the alphabet, what will be the position of M from your right?

A. 11th
B. 12th
C. 13th
D. 14th
E. None of these

60. If the above alphabet is arranged in reverse order, which letter will be twelfth to the left of the sixteenth letter from your left?

A. D B. V
C. W D. X
E. None of these

Directions (Qs. No. 61 to 64): *In the following questions, the symbols @, #, $, %, * are used with the following meanings as illustrated below:*

'A @ B' means 'A is not greater than B';

'A # B' means 'A is greater than or equal to B';

'A $ B' means 'A is neither greater than nor less than B';

'A % B' means 'A is less than B';

'A * B' means 'A is neither less than nor equal to B'.

Now, in each of the following questions, assuming the given statements to be true, find which of the three conclusions I, II and III given below them is/are definitely true.

61. Statement: K @ L, L % N, E # N

Conclusions:

I. K % E II. E * L III. N * K

A. Only I and II are true
B. Only II and III are true
C. Only I and III are true
D. All are true
E. None of these

62. Statement: D $ T, T * P, M @ P

Conclusions:

I. D * M II. M % T III. D # P

A. Only I is true
B. Only I and II are true
C. All are true
D. Only I and III are true
E. None of these

63. Statement: T # R, R % L, L * K

Conclusions:

I. T % L II. K * R III. T # K

A. Only I is true
B. Only I and II are true
C. All are true
D. Only II and III are true
E. None of these

64. Statement: N % S, S # U, U * M

Conclusions:

I. M % S II. N % U III. N * M

A. Only I is true
B. Only II is true
C. All are true
D. Only I and II are true
E. None is true

Directions (Qs. No. 65 to 69): *Read the following information carefully and answer the questions given below:*

(*i*) Six flats on a floor in two rows facing North and South are allotted to P, Q, R, S, T and U.

(*ii*) Q gets a North facing flat and is not next of S.

(*iii*) S and U get diagonally opposite flats.

(*iv*) R, next to U, gets a South facing flat and T gets a North facing flat.

65. Which of the following combinations get South facing flats?

A. URP B. UPT
C. QTS D. Data inadequate
E. None of these

66. The flats of which of the other pairs than SU, is diagonally opposite to each other?

A. PT B. QP
C. QR D. TS
E. None of these

67. Whose flats is between Q and S?

A. T B. U
C. R D. P
E. Data inadequate

68. If the flat of T and P are interchanged, whose flat will be next to that of U?

A. Q B. T
C. P D. R
E. None of these

69. To arrive at the answer to the above questions, which of the following statements can be dispensed with?

A. None B. (*i*) only
C. (*ii*) only D. (*iii*) only
E. None of these

Directions (Qs. No. 70 and 71): *Read the following statements and answer the questions given below:*

A is the father of C. But C is not his son. E is the daughter of C. F is the spouse of A. B is the brother of C. D is the son of B. G is the spouse of B. H is the father of G.

70. Who is the son-in-law of H?

A. C
B. A
C. D
D. B
E. None of these

71. Who is the grand-daughter of A?

A. H
B. D
C. B
D. E
E. None of these

72. If it is possible to make a meaningful word with the fourth, the seventh, the eleventh and the thirteenth letters of the word CATEGORISATION, which of the following will be the first letter of that word? If no such word can be made, give 'X' as the answer. If more than one such words can be made, give 'M' as the answer.

A. O
B. R
C. T
D. X
E. M

Directions (Qs. No. 73 to 77): *These questions are based on the following information:*

From time to time, the Managing Director of a Company appoints Planning Committees, each consisting of exactly three members. Eligible for appointment are three executives from Finance– B, C, and D– and three executives from Operations– E, F and M.

Any given committee is subject to the following restrictions on appointments:

(*i*) At least one member must be from Finance, and at least one member must be from Operations.

(*ii*) If B is appointed, C cannot be appointed.

(*iii*) Neither D nor F can be appointed unless the other is also appointed.

(*iv*) If E is appointed, M must be appointed.

73. Which of the following is an acceptable committee?

A. E, F and M
B. D, E and F
C. D, F and M
D. B, D and M
E. None of these

74. If appointees from Operations are in majority in a committee, that committee must include:

A. M
B. F
C. E
D. C
E. None of these

75. If the restrictions on appointments apply also to a four-member committee appointed from the same group of executives, which of the following will be true?

A. If B is appointed, M must also be appointed.
B. If F is appointed, C must also be appointed.
C. If C is appointed, E must also be appointed.
D. None of the above will be true.
E. None of these

76. If B is appointed to the same committee as M, which of the following will be true of that committee?

A. E is not a committee member.
B. F is a committee member.
C. Appointees from Finance are in majority.
D. Appointees from Operations are in majority.
E. None of these

77. If appointees from Finance are in majority on a committee, that committee must include:

A. B
B. C
C. F
D. M
E. None of these

78. How many pairs of letters are there in the word MOTHERLY which are as many letters apart in the word as they are in the alphabet series?

A. 0
B. 1
C. 2
D. 3
E. More than 3

Directions (Qs. No. 79 and 80): *In each question below are given two statements followed by two conclusions numbered I and II. You have to take the two given statements to be true even if they seem to be at variance from commonly known facts and then decide which of the given conclusions logically follows from the two given statements, disregarding commonly known facts. Read both the statements and given answer:*

A. If only conclusion I follows.
B. If only conclusion II follows.
C. If either I or II follows.
D. If neither I nor II follows.
E. If both I and II follows.

79. Statements: I. All rivers are mountains.
II. Some rivers are deserts.
Conclusions: I. Some mountains are deserts.
II. Some deserts are not mountains.

80. Statements: I. All men are horses.
II. All horses are elephants.
Conclusions: I. All men are elephants.
II. All elephants are men.

81. In each of the following questions, some groups of letters are given, all of which, except one, share a common similarity while one is different. Choose the odd one out.

A. VRT B. RMP
C. YUW D. FBD
E. MIK

Directions (Qs. No. 82 to 86): *Read the following information to answer the questions:*

(*i*) A, B, C, D, E, F and G are sitting in a circle facing at the centre and playing cards.
(*ii*) E is neighbour of A and D.
(*iii*) G is not between F and C.
(*iv*) F is to the immediate right of A.

82. Which of the following does not have the pair of persons sitting adjacent to each other?

A. BA B. CB
C. DE D. GD
E. None of these

83. Which of the following pairs has the second person sitting immediately to the right of the first?

A. AB B. CB
C. EA D. DG
E. None of these

84. What is the position of F?

A. Third to the left of C
B. Second to the right of C
C. To the immediate left of A
D. To the immediate right of B
E. None of these

85. Who are the neighbours of B?

A. A and F B. C and D
C. F and C D. Data inadequare
E. None of these

86. Which of the following persons are sitting adjacent to each other from left to right in the order as shown?

A. BGC B. FBC
C. CDG D. EDG
E. None of these

Directions (Qs. No. 87 to 90): *Study the following arrangement carefully and answer the questions given below:*

R E 5 D A P S 3 T I Q 7 9 B # 2 K % U 1 M W 4 * J 8 N

87. Which of the following is exactly in the middle between 3 and 1 in the above arrangement?

A. B B. K
C. 9 D. #
E. None of these

88. How many such numbers are there in the above arrangement, each of which is immediately preceded by a consonant and not immediately followed by a consonant?

A. None B. One
C. Two D. Three
E. None of these

89. How many such vowels are there in the above arrangement, each of which is immediately followed by a number but not immediately preceded by a consonant?

A. None B. One
C. Two D. Three
E. Four

90. Which of the following is seventh to the left of the sixteenth from the left in the above arrangement?

A. A B. U
C. 4 D. T
E. None of these

Directions (Qs. No. 91 and 92): *In a certain code language.*

(*a*) '*mxy das zci*' means '*good little frock*';
(*b*) '*jmx cos zci*' means '*girl behaves good*';
(*c*) '*nvg drs cos*' means '*girl makes mischief*';
(*d*) '*das ajp cos*' means '*little girl fell*'.

91. Which word in that language stands for '*frock*'?

A. *zci* B. *das*
C. *nvg* D. *ajp*
E. None of these

92. Which of the given statements is superfluous and can be dispensed with while answering the above question?

A. (*a*) B. (*b*)
C. (*c*) D. (*d*)
E. None of these

Directions (Qs. No. 93 to 95): *In a certain code, 'il be pee' means 'roses are blue', 'sik hee' means 'red flowers' and 'pee mit hee' means 'flowers are vegetables'.*

93. How is '*red*' written in that code?

A. hee
B. sik
C. be
D. Cannot be determined
E. None of these

94. How is '*roses*' written in that code?

A. il
B. pee
C. be
D. Cannot be determined
E. None of these

95. How is '*vegetables are red flowers*' written in this code?

A. pee sik mit hee
B. sik pee hee be
C. il sik mit hee
D. Cannot be determined
E. None of these

96. How many such pairs of digits are there in the number 531268947 each of which has as many digits between them in the number as when they are arranged in descending order?

A. None B. One
C. Two D. Three
E. More than three

97. A meaningful word starting with A is made from the first, the second, the fourth, the fifth and the sixth letters of the word CONTRACT. Which of the following is the middle letter of the word?

A. C B. O
C. R D. T
E. None of these

Directions (Qs. No. 98 to 100): *Read the following information carefully and answer the questions given below it:*

Eight students A, B, C, D, E, F, G and H are planning to enjoy car racing. There are only two cars and following are the conditions:

(*i*) One car can accommodate maximum five and minimum four students.
(*ii*) A will sit in the same car in which D is sitting but H is not in the same car.
(*iii*) B and C can't sit in the same car in which D is sitting.

(*iv*) F will sit in the car of four people only along with A and E but certainly not with G.

98. If H and G are sitting in the same car, who are other two students sitting in the same car?

A. B and C B. C and D
C. B and D D. E and B
E. None of these

99. If E and A are sitting in the same car, which of the following statements are true?

A. Five students are sitting in the same car.
B. B is sitting in the same car.
C. F is not sitting in the same car.
D. G is not sitting in the same car.
E. None of these

100. Which of the following statements is superfluous for the above sitting arrangements?

A. only (*i*) B. only (*ii*)
C. only (*iii*) D. only (*iv*)
E. None of these

GENERAL AWARENESS

101. Which of the following is called a 'bankers' cheque?

A. DD B. IPO
C. FD D. RD
E. None of the above

102. Who is the only Prime Minister to have served as the Governor of RBI?

A. P.V. Narsimha Rao
B. Manmohan Singh
C. Lal Bahadur Shastri
D. Indira Gandhi
E. Chaudhari Charan Singh

103. Global Financial Development Report provides an update on the state of public and private credit reporting. The report is published by which of the following institutions?

A. Niti Aayog B. World Bank
C. IMF D. WHO
E. None of these

104. What do we call the banking oriented towards mass welfare and financial inclusion of the poor?

A. Mass banking B. Narrow banking
C. Social banking D. Hundi
E. None of the above

105. Which of the following operations are undertaken by Small Finance Banks?

A. Accepting Deposits
B. Disbursing small loans
C. Sell Insurance Products
D. To supply credit to small and marginal farmers
E. All of the above

106. Which among the following has entered into partnership with digital payments infrastructure provider (PPRO) to facilitate global e-commerce payments through UPI?

A. Razorpay
B. Bill Desk
C. NPCI International Payements
D. Paytm
E. None of these

107. How much money is the Central Government required to maintain as minimum cash balance with RBI on a daily basis?

A. ₹ 50 crore B. ₹ 10 crore
C. ₹ 1 crore D. ₹ 1000 crore
E. None of these

108. What distinguishes an Adjustable-Rate Mortgage (ARM) from a Fixed-Rate Mortgage?

A. The interest rate is constant throughout the loan term.
B. The initial interest rate is higher than fixed-rate loans.

C. The interest rate changes periodically based on a reference index.
D. The borrower is required to pay the principal amount initially.
E. None of these

109. How can blockchain technology improve Know Your Customer (KYC) processes in banking?

A. By eliminating the need for customer verification
B. By decentralizing customer data storage
C. By enabling banks to share verified customer data securely and efficiently
D. By reducing the number of KYC checks required for high-risk clients
E. None of these

110. Which of the following is a qualitative tool of monetary policy?

A. Repo Rate
B. Bank Rate
C. Selective Credit Control
D. Cash Reserve Ratio
E. Reverse-Rapo-Rate

111. The portion of total deposits of a commercial bank which it has to keep with itself in the form of liquid aspects is called _____.

A. Statutory Liquidity Ratio
B. Cash Reserve Ratio
C. Statutory Reserve Ratio
D. Cash Ratio
E. None of these

112. What is the purpose of the C-bot, an autonomous underwater vehicle, launched by the CSIR-NIO in Goa?

A. Space exploration
B. Monitoring coral reefs
C. Agricultural research
D. Air quality measurement
E. Soil and water research

113. Professor B.R. Kamboj, who was announced winner of 14th M.S. Swaminathan Award, is associated with which field?

A. Agronomy
B. Veterinary Science
C. Environmental Science
D. Plant Biotechnology
E. Medical Technology

114. Which sport's tournament is known as the "Hopman Cup"?

A. Tennis
B. Polo
C. Badminton
D. Baseball
E. Cricket

115. What is the main objective of India's Chandrayaan-4 mission, as announced by ISRO Chief S. Somanath?

A. To collect moon rocks and soil and bring them back to Earth for scientific analysis
B. To establish a research station on moon
C. To explore water on the moon
D. Develop the technologies required for designing
E. None of these

116. Which city's airport has won the prestigious 'Best Airport Staff in India & South Asia 2024' award by Skytrax?

A. Hyderabad
B. New Delhi
C. Bengaluru
D. Chandigarh
E. Mumbai

117. What is the theme of 'World Earth Day 2024'?

A. Invest in Our Planet
B. Planet vs Plastics
C. Climate action
D. Restore Our Earth
E. Indigenous Technologies for Viksit Bharat

118. Which Indian Olympic gold medalist carried the Olympic torch in the Paris 2024 relay?

A. Neeraj Chopra
B. Abhinav Bindra
C. Vijender Singh
D. Saina Nehwal
E. Gukesh

119. Karthikeyan Murali, who was seen in the news, is located in which sports?

A. Chess
B. Cricket
C. Squash
D. Badminton
E. Kabaddi

120. Which cricketer equalled record of Sachin Tendulkar at 49 ODI centuries?

A. Rohit Sharma
B. Virat Kohli
C. Ravindra Jadeja
D. KL Rahul
E. AB Devillier

121. Who won the men's single title at the 2024 Wimbledon Tennis Championships?

A. Roger Federer
B. Novak Djokovic
C. Carlos Alcaraz
D. Max Purcell
E. Jannik Sinner

122. Which country emerged as the winner of U-19 Asia Cup 2023?

A. India
B. UAE
C. Pakistan
D. Bangladesh
E. Sri Lanka

123. Which team has won the 'Indian Premier League 2024'?

A. Kolkata Knight Riders
B. Sunrisers Hyderabad
C. Mumbai Indians
D. Chennai Super Kings
E. None of these

124. Who among the following was the 23rd Jain Tirthankara?

A. Nemi Natha
B. Mahavira
C. Parshvanath
D. Malinath
E. Rishabhdeva

125. Montagu-Chelmsford Reforms which formed the base of Government of India Act 1919, introduced which of the following in India?

A. Self governance
B. Dyarchy
C. Indian Administrative Services
D. Indian Police Services
E. Supreme Court of India

126. 'Shanti Swarup Bhatnagar Awards' are presented to individuals associated with which profession?

A. Sports person
B. Scientist
C. Social Worker
D. Politician
E. Author

127. In which state is Kongthong located, which received the 'Best Tourism Village (Bronze) Award 2023'?

A. Assam
B. Meghalaya
C. Arunachal Pradesh
D. Manipur
E. None of these

128. With reference to the rivers in India, the "Upper Yamuna" refers to the Yamuna river from its origin at Yamunotri to:

A. Tajewala in Yamuna Nagar district
B. Dak Pathar near Dehradun
C. Okhla Barrage in Delhi
D. Paonta Sahib in Himachal Pradesh
E. None of these

129. Most of the peninsular rivers in India are seasonal in nature. Which among the following is the least seasonal among all the rivers of the peninsula?

A. Godavari
B. Krishna
C. Kaveri
D. Tungbhadra
E. Luni

130. When we touch leaves of "Touch me not plant", they close, these movements are called _____.

A. Seismonastic movements
B. Photonastic movements
C. Nyctinastic movements
D. Chemonastic movements
E. None of these

131. Which blood group individuals are universally known as recipients because they can receive blood from any group?

A. Group O
B. Group A
C. Group B
D. Group AB
E. None of these

132. The waste management technique that involves the use of micro-organisms to remove or neutralize pollutants from contaminated site is called _____.

A. Bio magnification
B. Bio sensor
C. Bioremediation
D. Bio concentration
E. None of these

133. What is the multibranched polysaccharide of glucose that serves as a form of energy storage in animals and fungi?

A. Glycogen B. Pectin
C. Cellulose D. Chitin
E. Fructose

134. The *Jatropha curcas*, source of inedible vegetable oil that is used to produce biofuel and which works as a carbon sink is native to which of the following regions of the world?

A. Europe B. Central Africa
C. Central America D. South America
E. East Asia

135. Neknampur Lake, which is the largest floating treatment wetland in the country, is situated in which of the following place?

A. Hyderabad B. New Delhi
C. Odisha D. Manipur
E. Mumbai

136. The Reserve Bank of India follows the principle of reciprocity and single mode of presence with respect to the ______.

A. Private Banks
B. Foreign Banks
C. Regional Rural Banks
D. Urban Cooperative Banks
E. Cooperative Bank

137. What is the primary objective of the PM-PRANAM scheme, recently in news?

A. To increase the use of chemical fertilisers
B. To reduce the use of chemical fertilisers by incentivizing states
C. To provide free chemical fertilisers to farmers
D. To promote chemical fertilisers over organic ones
E. None of these

138. Which state government has launched the Sahakar Kisan Kalyan Yojana to boost farm productivity and increase farmers' income?

A. Gujarat B. Uttar Pradesh
C. Haryana D. Rajasthan
E. Bihar

139. What is the name of the scheme approved by the Union Cabinet to promote natural farming in India?

A. National Agricultural Development Scheme
B. National Mission on Natural Farming
C. Green Revolution 2.0
D. Sustainable Agriculture Promotion Scheme
E. Pradhan Mantri Kisan Maan-Dhan Yojana

140. What does the term 'fetch' refer to in the context of the fetch-decode-execute cycle?

A. The CPU retrieves the next instruction from memory
B. The CPU decodes the instruction
C. The CPU executes the instruction
D. The CPU stores the result
E. None of these

141. Which of the following components is responsible for storing data temporarily during processing?

A. Hard drive
B. RAM (Random Access Memory)
C. CPU
D. ROM (Read-Only Memory)
E. ALU (Arithmetic Logic Unit)

142. In an 8-bit processor, the maximum decimal value that can be stored in a register is:

A. 128 B. 255
C. 512 D. 1024
E. 1048

143. What do we call a CPU that is designed specifically to handle the communications processing task with main purpose is to off-load communications processing task from the host computer so that the host computer can be dedicated for applications and data processing jobs?

A. Backend processor
B. Front-end processor
C. Node processor
D. File Server
E. Embedded processor

144. Who was associated with the first large-scale digital computer known as the Harvard Mark I or the IBM Automatic Sequence Controlled Calculator?

A. Clifford Berry B. Howard Aiken
C. Konrad Zuse D. John Atanasoff
E. Oxford Aiken

145. The copies of data or program files are always stored as a safety. Which of the following is the name given to these copies?

A. Backups B. Programs
C. Extras D. Stores
E. None of these

146. Which regulatory framework in India promotes ESG disclosure and transparency in listed companies?

A. Basel III
B. Business Responsibility and Sustainability Report (BRSR)
C. FEMA Guidelines
D. Companies Act, 2013
E. FERA Guidelines

147. Which tech giant has RBL Bank collaborated with to improve client experience and integrate improved data management and analytics tools in its Abacus 2.0 digital platform?

A. Infosys B. Google
C. IBM D. Accenture
E. Intel

148. Vilasini Natyam is the folk dance of which of the following Indian states?

A. Gujarat B. Odisha
C. Andhra Pradesh D. Karnataka
E. Madhya Pradesh

149. "Bad money (if not limited in quantity) drives good money out of circulation". Which law in economics says this?

A. Keynes' law B. Wagner's law
C. Gresham's law D. Grimm's law
E. None of these

150. Under which ministry is the Monopolies and Restrictive Trade Practices Commission?

A. Ministry of Finance
B. Ministry of Commerce
C. Ministry of Home Affairs
D. Ministry of Corporate Affairs
E. Ministry of External Affairs

EXPLANATORY ANSWERS

1. (C): CAB is the correct sequence hence the sentence will be "Despite being in the spotlight, a range of issues in the constituency remain unaddressed, such as the delay in shifting of the mofussil bus stand, lack of industrial development".

2. (B): BAC is the correct sequence hence the sentence will be "Peak summer season is yet to begin but several interior places are already in the grip of a heatwave".

3. (E): CBA is the correct sequence hence the sentence will be "The interns have decided to boycott work indefinitely until their demands were met".

4. (B): ACB is the correct sequence hence the sentence will be "BioNTech-Pfizer said their vaccine showed 100% **efficacy** against the coronavirus in 12 to 15-year-old, as they eye **approval** for **adolescents** to get the jabs before the next school year"

5. (D): The highlighted phrase is incorrect because of 'forming' which should be 'form' as 'to' follows 'V1'. The correct choice is option (D). All other options are grammatically in contextually incorrect.

6. (B): In the highlighted phrase 'were' is incorrect because noun is singular. The correct choice is option (B). All other options are grammatically and contextually incorrect.

7. (E): The highlighted phrase is correct hence no replacement required.

8. (B): The correct choice is option (B) with reference to the first paragraph which mentions, "Doing so is both morally right and in everyone's interest. Therefore, we need global multilateral action to increase the production of vaccines and accelerate the roll-out worldwide."

9. (D): The correct choice is option (D) with reference to the second paragraph which mentions, "The pandemic is still killing thousands of people every day and at the current pace, the whole world will not be vaccinated before 2023. Yet, a widely vaccinated world population is the only way to end the pandemic; otherwise, the multiplication of variants is likely to undermine the effectiveness of existing vaccines."

10. (B): Only (I) and (II) are correct with reference to the paragraph.

For statement (I), refer to the first and last paragraph in which it has been mentioned that how the international organizations such as EU and WHO have been making efforts to provide vaccine throughout the world

For (II), refer to the third paragraph which mentions, "Therefore, the EU welcomes the $50 billion plan proposed by the International Monetary Fund in order to be able to vaccinate 40% of the world population in 2021 and 60% by mid-2022."

11. (C): The correct choice is option (C) which can be inferred from the last paragraph which mentions, "To achieve this goal, we need closely coordinated multilateral action. We must resist the threat posed by linking the provision of vaccines to political goals and "vaccine nationalism". The EU has rejected both since the beginning of the pandemic."

12. (B): The correct choice is option (B), which can be inferred from second paragraph which mentions, "Vaccination is also a prerequisite for lifting the restrictions that are holding back our economies and freedoms."

13. (B): The correct choice is option (B). "Undermine" means to make something weaker and "cripple" is similar word which means to seriously damage or harm somebody/something dawdle means to go somewhere very slowly supervene means occur as an interruption or change to an existing situation. draconian means harsh and severe

14. (A): The correct choice is option (A). "Accelerate" means increase in rate, amount, or extent and "expedite" is synonym which means make (an action or process) happen sooner or be accomplished more quickly noxious means harmful, poisonous, or very unpleasant. fervent means having or displaying a passionate intensity. fitful means active or occurring spasmodically or intermittently; not regular or steady.

15. (D): The correct choice is option (D). "Substantially" means to a great or significant extent and "paltry" is synonym which means very small or meagre. flout means openly disregard offensive means causing someone to feel resentful, upset, or annoyed. flawed means having or characterized by a fundamental weakness or imperfection.

16. (B): Here "mechanical" is grammatically incorrect because we need the adverb 'mechanically' for the verb 'granting'.

17. (E): All given highlighted words are correct here therefore the correct choice is option (E).

18. (A): Except 'spectulation' all other words are correctly spelled here. The correct spelling is 'speculation' which means 'the forming of a theory'.

19. (C): Except 'pesimism' all other words are correctly spelled here. The correct spelling is 'pessimism' which means 'a tendency to see the worst aspect of things or believe that the worst will happen.'

20. (A): Except 'arrey' all other words are correctly spelled here. The correct spelling is 'array' which means 'an impressive display or range of a particular type of thing.'

21. **(B):** The correct rearrangement of the parts of the statement will be "BCAD" which will make a grammatically correct and contextually meaningful statement. Hence, option (B) is the most suitable answer choice. The correct statement thus formed will be: "We are united by our democratic values and our commitment to a free, open and inclusive Indo-Pacific."

22. **(D):** The correct rearrangement of the parts of statement will be "DBCA" which will make a grammatically correct and contextually meaningful statement. Hence, option (D) is the most suitable answer choice. The correct statement thus formed will be: "Under the constitutional mandate, it is the duty of the State to not interfere with the functioning of the State Election Commission."

23. **(B):** The correct rearrangement of the parts of statement will be "BCDA" which will make a grammatically correct and contextually meaningful statement. Hence, option (B) is the most suitable answer choice. The correct statement thus formed will be: "The Serum Institute of India has an agreement with Novavax to manufacture a substantial volume of the vaccine."

24. **(C):** The correct rearrangement of the parts of statement will be "CBDA" which will make a grammatically correct and contextually meaningful statement. Hence, option (C) is the most suitable answer choice. The correct statement thus formed will be: "For the first time, the constituency itself will vote for a chief ministerial candidate, whose stint at the helm will be under scrutiny."

25. **(A):** The correct rearrangement of the parts of the statement will be "ABCD" which will make a grammatically correct and contextually meaningful statement. Hence, option (A) is the most suitable answer choice. The correct statement thus formed will be: "The daughter of a village temple priest, who was murdered along with his son for exposing encroachments on a waterbody district, has decided to take the political plunge."

26. **(B):** The above passage talks about the other means and tactics used by politicians to win an election. Hence, the correct word will be 'numerous' which means 'many'. All other words are contextually and grammatically incorrect.

    Defection means conscious abandonment of allegiance or duty.

    Absurdity means extremely unreasonable.

    Standard means a level of quality or attainment.

    Preserve means to keep alive, intact, or free from decay.

27. **(E):** The above passage talks about the other means and tactics used by politicians to win an election. Hence. the correct word will be 'impression' which means 'an idea, a feeling or an opinion that you get about somebody/something'. All other words are contextually and grammatically incorrect.

    Treasury means a collection of very valuable objects, for example gold, silver, jewellery, etc.

    Insulate means to protect something with a material that prevents electricity, heat or sound from passing through.

    Combat means a fight, especially in war.

    Stability means the quality, state, or degree of being stable.

28. **(D):** The above passage talks about the other means and tactics used by politicians to win an election. Hence, the correct word will be 'portrayal' which means 'description and image'. All other words are contextually and grammatically incorrect.

    Contrary means completely different; opposite.

    Reluctant means not wanting to do something because you are not sure it is the right thing to do.

    Direct means without intervening factors or intermediaries.

    Disqualify means declare (someone) ineligible for an office, activity, or competition because of an offence or infringement.

29. **(E):** The above passage talks about the other means and tactics used by politicians to win an election. Hence, the correct word will be 'reflection' which means 'a thing that shows what somebody/something is like'. All other words are contextually and grammatically incorrect.

    Delegate means a person who has been chosen to speak or take decisions for a group of people, especially at a meeting.

    Constitute means to be one of the parts that form something.

Acceptance means the action of consenting to receive or undertake something offered.

Complex means consisting of many different and connected parts.

30. **(C):** The above passage talks about the other means and tactics used by politicians to win an election. Hence, the correct word will be 'influence' which means 'the power to affect, change or control somebody/something'. All other words are contextually and grammatically incorrect.

Accountable means required or expected to justify actions or decisions; responsible.

Draft means a piece of writing, etc.

Plunge means to jump, drop or fall suddenly and with force.

Betrayed means to give information about somebody/something to an enemy; to make a secret known.

31. **(B):** The above passage talks about the other means and tactics used by politicians to win an election. Hence, the correct word will be 'determination' which means 'the quality of having firmly decided to do something, even if it is very difficult'. All other words are contextually and grammatically incorrect.

Ostensible means seeming or stated to be real or true, but not necessarily real or true.

Fora means a place or meeting where people can exchange and discuss ideas.

Detrimental means harmful.

Executive means concerned with managing, making plans, decisions, etc.

32. **(A):** In the given statements, only statement (*i*) is error free. In statement (*ii*), 'correct' should be 'correctly' as we need adverb here. In statement (*iii*), 'enable' which means 'to make it possible for somebody/something to do something' should be 'unable' which means 'stop someone/something from doing a task'.

33. **(C):** In the given statements, only statement (*iii*) is error free. In statement (*i*), 'explains' should be 'explain' because 'to' is always followed by 'V1'. In statement (*ii*), 'included' should be 'include' because modal verbs always followed by "V1'.

34. **(C):** In the given statements, only statement (*iii*) is error free. In statement (*i*), 'then' should be replaced with 'than' and in statement (*ii*), 'excess' which means 'more of something than is necessary' should be 'access' which means 'the chance or right to use or have something'.

35. **(E):** All the given statements are error free. Hence, option (E) is the correct choice here.

36. **(B):** The error lies in part (B) of the sentence. Since 'advice' is an uncountable noun, the right usage of the word would be 'dolling out advice to entrepreneurs.'

Hence, the right choice for the answer is option (B).

37. **(E):** There is no error in the given sentence. It is grammatically and contextually correct.

38. **(B):** The error lies in part (B) of the sentence. Instead of 'build, the correct form of the verb to be used here is 'built' since we can infer from the sentence that it is of the past tense.

Hence, the right choice for the answer is option (B).

39. **(C):** The error lies in part (C) of the sentence. Here, 'are' will replace 'is' since 'many' is the antecedent and pronouns like few, many, several, both, all, some will always take Plural form.

Hence, the right choice for the answer is option (C).

40. **(D):** The error lies in part (D) of the sentence. Here, 'particularly' will replace 'particular' because an adverb modifies an adjective, verb or adjective clause.

Hence, the right choice for the answer is option (D).

41. **(E):** There is no error in the given sentence. It is grammatically and contextually correct.

42. **(B):** The error lies in part (B) of the sentence. 'At' will replace 'on' because 'at' (preposition) is used for pointing out specific time.

Hence, the right choice for the answer is option (B).

43. **(B):** Throughout the first paragraph, statement (b) can be inferred. Refer to the lines of the first paragraph which mentions, "This is important because enough evidence exists on weak fund-absorbing capacities particularly in the backward States — at times, such unused funds have been to the tune of over half of the State's public health expenditure"

44. (D): Refer to the third paragraph of the passage which mentions, "Large expenditure projections and time constraints involved in the input-based strengthening of public health care have inspired the shift to the insurance route for achieving universal health coverage" therefore the correct choice is option (D).

45. (D): Option (D) is correct choice with reference to the second paragraph which mentions, "While the allocations still leave a lot to be desired, these could make the first steps of a journey that steadily builds towards sustainable universal health coverage through incremental strengthening of grass-root-level institutions and processes."

46. (B): The correct choice is option (B) For correct answer refer to the last paragraph which mentions, "Given these circumstances, making do with such paltry spending year after year would mean that the scheme benefits are being spread out too narrowly or too thin, implying the inability to afford enough protection against catastrophic health expenses to the poor. Beyond low allocations, poor budget reliability merits attention. Another related issue is the persistent and large discrepancies between official coverage figures and survey figures (for e.g. the National Sample Surveys, or NSS, and National Family Health Survey) across Indian States, indicating that official public health insurance coverage fails to translate into actual coverage on the ground."

47. (B): The correct choice is option (B). Only statement (*iii*) is incorrect.

For statement (*i*), refer to the second paragraph which mentions, "The Union Ministry of Health and Family Welfare budget for 2021-22, viz. ₹ 73,932 crore, saw a 10.2% increase over the Budget estimate (BE) of 2020-21."

For statement (*ii*), refer to the first paragraph which mentions, "What made this possible was a three decade-long tradition of investing gradually but steadily in public health infrastructure and manpower."

For statement (*iii*) which is incorrect, refer to second paragraph which mentions, "The Union Ministry of Health and Family Welfare budget for 2021-22, viz. ₹ 73,932 crore, saw a 10.2% increase over the Budget estimate (BE) of 2020-21. Also, a corpus of ₹ 64,180 crore over six years has been set aside under the PM Atma Nirbhar Swasth Bharat Yojana, (PMANSBY), and ₹ 13,192 crore has been allocated as a Finance Commission grant."

48. (E): 'Gradually' means 'proceeding by steps or degrees' and 'moderately' is synonym of it.
squander means to waste time, money, etc.
bolster means to support or encourage somebody/something; to make something stronger.
array means a large collection of things, especially one that is impressive and is seen by other people.
overwhelm means to cause somebody to feel such a strong emotion that he/she does not know how to react.

49. (B): 'Incremental' means 'increase' and 'progressive' is synonym of it which means 'happening or developing steadily'.
confine means to stay within the limits of something.
preventive means intended to stop or prevent something from happening.
prodded means to push or press somebody/something with your finger or a pointed object.
unswervingly means not changing or becoming weaker; steady or constant.

50. (D): 'Persistent' means 'determined to continue doing something even though people say that you are wrong or that you cannot do it' and 'intermittent' is antonym which means 'stopping for a short time and then starting again several times'.
grant means to (officially) give somebody what he/she has asked for.
assassination means murder.
ambitious means having a strong desire to be successful, to have power, etc.
conclude means to form an opinion as the result of thought or study.

For Qs. No. 51 to 55:

C is to the right of D.

D is third from south. So, B will be at the extreme end from north because it should have E as its neighbour. G is between E and F. So, the sequence is:

B →
E →
G →
F → East
D →
C →
A →

51. **(E):** G is sitting to the right of E.

52. **(A):** A and B are sitting at the extreme ends.

53. **(C):** G should change place with C to make it third from north.

54. **(D):** D is sitting between C and F.

55. **(D):** All the statements are required to determine the correct sequence.

56. **(E):** Counting from the right end of the given alphabet-series, *i.e.*, from Z, the eighteenth letter is I. Counting from I towards the right, the fifth letter is N.

So, the answer is (E).

57. **(D):** Removing all the vowels, *i.e.*, A, E, I, O, U, we obtain the following letter-series:

B C D F G H J K L M N P Q R S T V W X Y Z

Counting from the left in the above series, *i.e.*, from B, the fifth letter is G.

Counting from G towards right, the seventh letter is P.

So, the answer is (D).

58. **(A):** Leaving out A, C, E, G, ..., W, Y, we obtain the following letter-series.

B D F H J L N P R T V X Z

Counting from the right in the above letter-series, the fifth letter is R. Counting from R, the third letter to the right is X. So, the answer is (A).

59. **(C):** The new letter-series obtained is:

B A D C F E H G J I L K N M P O R Q T S V U X W Z Y

Counting from Y in the above series, M is the 13th letter. So, the answer is (C).

60. **(C):** We obtain the following letter-series on reversing the order of the alphabets:

Z Y X W V U T S R Q P O N M L K J I H G F E D C B A

Counting from the left, *i.e.*, from Z in the above series, the sixteenth letter is K. Counting from K towards left, the twelfth letter is W. So, the answer is (C).

For Qs. No. 61 to 64:

Clearly, We have:

$A @ B \Rightarrow A \ngtr B \Rightarrow A \leq B$; $A \# B \Rightarrow A \geq B$;

$A \$ B \Rightarrow A \ngtr B$ and $A \nless B \Rightarrow A = B$; $A \% B \Rightarrow A < B$;

$A * B \Rightarrow A \nless B$ and $A \neq B \Rightarrow A > B$.

61. **(D):** Given statements; $K \leq L$, $L < N$, $E \geq N$

I. Relation between K and E:

$K \leq L$, $L < N$, $N \leq E \Rightarrow K \leq L < N \leq E$

$\Rightarrow K < E$ *i.e.*, K % E.

II. Relation between E and L:

$E \geq N$, $N > L \Rightarrow E \geq N > L$

$\Rightarrow E > L$ *i.e.*, E * L.

III. Relation between N and K:

$N > L$, $L \geq K \Rightarrow N > L \geq K$

$\Rightarrow N > K$ *i.e.*, N * K.

So, all I, II and III are true.

62. **(B):** Given statements; $D = T$, $T > P$, $M \leq P$

I. Relation between D and M:

$D = T$, $T > P$, $P \geq M \Rightarrow D = T > P \geq M$

$\Rightarrow D > M$ *i.e.*, D * M.

II. Relation between M and T:

$M \leq P$, $P < T \Rightarrow M \leq P < T$

$\Rightarrow M < T$ *i.e.*, M % T.

III. Relation between D and P:

$D = T$, $T > P \Rightarrow D = T > P$

$\Rightarrow D > P$ *i.e.*, D * P.

So, Only I and II are true.

63. **(E):** Given statements; $T \geq R$, $R < L$, $L > K$

I. Relation between T and L:

$T \geq R$, $R < L \Rightarrow T \geq R < L$

⇒ no definite conclusion.

II. Relation between K and R:

$K < L$, $L > R \Rightarrow K < L > R$

⇒ no definite conclusion.

III. Relation between T and K:
$T \geq R$, $R < L$, $L > K \Rightarrow T \geq R < L > K$
$\Rightarrow$ no definite conclusion.
So, none I, II and III is true.

64. (A): Given statements; $N < S$, $S \geq U$, $U > M$
I. Relation between M and S:
$M < U$, $U \leq S \Rightarrow M < U \leq S$
$\Rightarrow M < S$ *i.e.*, M % S.
II. Relation between N and U:
$N < S$, $S \geq U \Rightarrow N < S \geq U$
$\Rightarrow$ no definite conclusion.
III. Relation between N and M:
$N < S$, $S \geq U$, $U > M \Rightarrow N < S \geq U > M$
$\Rightarrow N < S > M \Rightarrow$ no definite conclusion.
So, only I is true.

For Qs. No. 65 to 69:

The positions of flats occupied are:

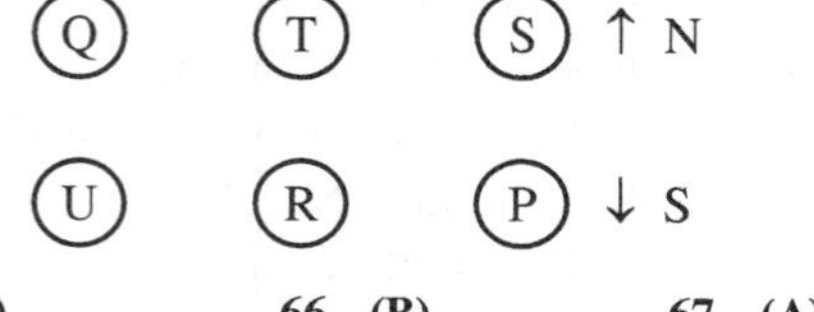

65. (A) **66. (B)** **67. (A)**

68. (D): The new positions will be:

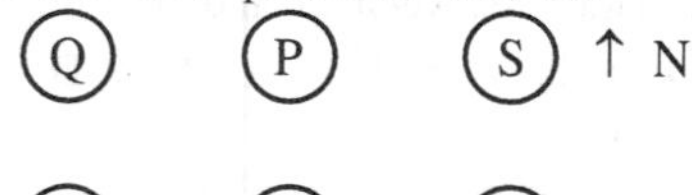

69. (A)

For Qs. No. 70 and 71:

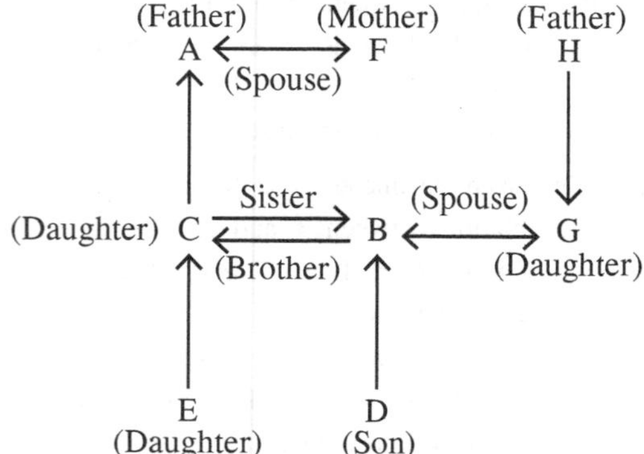

70. (D): 'H' is the father of 'G' and 'G' is the wife of 'B'. So, 'B' is the son-in-law of 'H'.

71. (D): 'E' is daugther of 'C'. 'C' is not a son of 'A' means 'C' is the daughter of 'A' and also mother of 'E'. So 'E' is the granddaughter of 'A'.

72. (E): The fourth, seventh, eleventh and thirteenth letters of the word CATEGORISATION are E, R, T and O respectively. The words formed are TORE and ROTE.

73. (C): (*a*) violates (*iii*) and so is not acceptable.
(*b*) violates (*iv*) and so is not acceptable.
(*d*) violates (*iii*) and so is not acceptable.

74. (A): Clearly, the committee has two executives from Operations and one executive from Finance. The two executives from Operations could be (E, F), (F, M) or (E, M). But, (E, F) violates (*iv*).

So, either (E, M) or (F, M) must be appointed. Thus, the committee must include M.

75. (A): If B is appointed, then C cannot be appointed. D and F have to be together. If E is appointed, then M also has to be appointed. So, B can form a four-member committee with D, F and M. Thus, (*a*) is true.

If F is appointed, then D is also appointed. Clearly, even if C is not appointed, F and D can form committee with (E and M) or (B and M). Thus, (*b*) is also false.

If C is appointed, then B cannot be appointed. Again, D and F have to be together and if E is appointed, M must also be appointed. So, C can form a four-member committee with D, F and M. So (*c*) is also false.

76. (D): Clearly, the committee has one more member apart from B and M. Now, if B is appointed, cannot be appointed. D and F have to be together. So, the third person appointed must be M. Thus, the committee has two executives from Operations.

77. (C): Clearly, the committee has two executives from Finance and one executive from Operations. Since B and C cannot go together, the two executives from Finance must be D and either B or C. If D is appointed, F must also be appointed. Thus, the committee must include F.

78. (C): MOTHERLY
NOPQ
: M and R have 'OTHE' in the word 'NOPQ' in the alphabet series.

MOTHERLY
UVWX
: T and Y have 'HERL' in the word and 'UVWX' in the alphabet series.

79. (E): When all rivers are mountains and some rivers are deserts, then some deserts cannot be mountains and also, some mountains need not be deserts. Therefore, both conclusion I and conclusion II are correct.

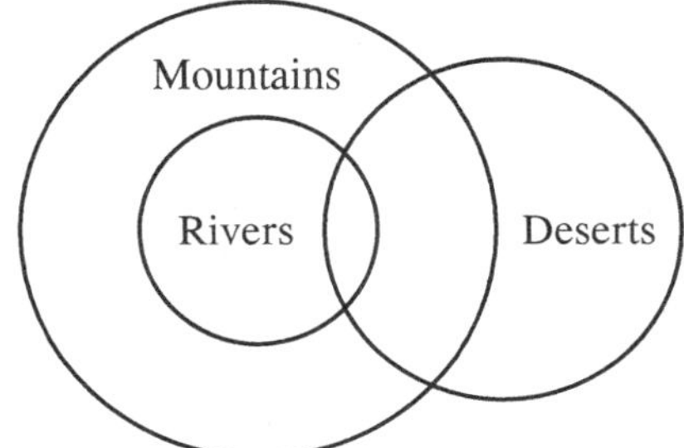

80. (A): When all men are horses and all horses are elephants then, naturally all men are elephants, but all elephants need not be men. Therefore, only conclusion I is correct.

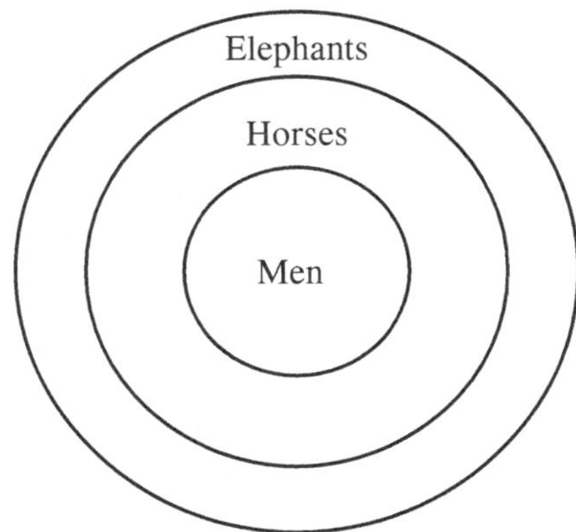

81. (B): In all other groups, the second, third and first letters are alternate letters of the alphabet in order.

For Qs. No. 82 and 86:

F is to the immediate right of A. E is neighbour of A and D, *i.e.*, E is between A and D.

G is not between F and C. So, B is between F and C.

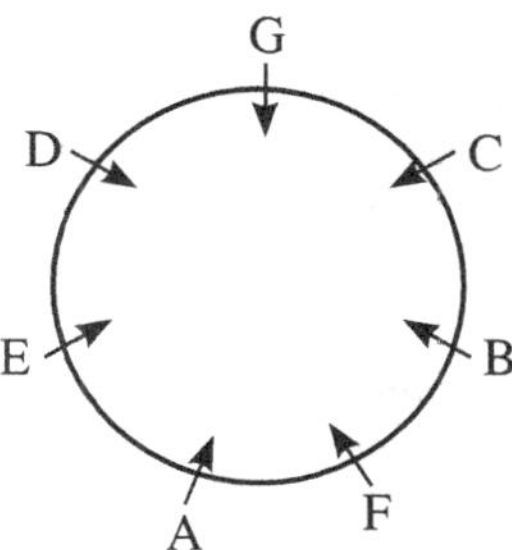

Thus, the arrangement is as shown in the adjoining figure.

82. (A): Each one of CB, DE and GD is a pair of persons sitting adjacent to each other, while BA is not.

83. (C): B is second to the right of A and to the immediate left of C, while G is to the immediate left of D. But A sits immediately to the right of E.

84. (E): F sits (*i*) second to the left of C; (*ii*) to the immediate right of A and (*iii*) to the immediate left of B.

85. (C): F and C are the neighbours of B.

86. (B): Clearly, the required group should contain three persons who are sitting in three consecutive positions in an anticlockwise order. Such a group is FBC.

87. (A): There are 11 elements between 3 and 1. So, the middle letter will be the sixth one, which of B.

88. (C): R E 5 D A P $ 3 T I Q 7 9 B # 2 K % U 1 M W 4 * J 8 N.

89. (B): R E 5 D A P $ 3 T I Q 7 9 B # 2 K % U 1 M W 4 * J 8 N

90. (D): The 16th element from the left is 2, and the element 7 steps to the left of 2 is T.

91. (E): In statements (*a*) and (*b*), the common code-word is '*zci*' and the common word is '*good*'. So, '*zci*' stands for '*good*'. In statements (*a*) and (*d*), the common code-word is '*das*' and the common word is '*little*'. So, '*das*' stands for '*little*'.

So, in (*a*), '*mxy*' stands for '*frock*'.

92. (C): Clearly, statement (C) is not required.

93. (B): In the second and third statements, the common code-word is '*hee*' and the common word is '*flowers*'. So, '*hee*' stands for '*flowers*'. Thus, in the second statement, '*sik*' stands for '*red*'.

94. (D): Since from the given information, we can only find the code for '*are*' in the first statement, it cannot be determined which of the remaining two codes stands for '*roses*'.

95. (A): Clearly, the required code will consists of the same codes as in the third statement with the code for '*red*' added to it.

96. (E): The given number is: 531268947.

Arranging the digits in descending order, we get: 987654321.

We have the following pairs of digits, satisfying the given conditions.

Digits in Given Number	Digits in Descending Order
5 3 1 2	5 4 3 2
3 1 2 6	6 5 4 3
1 2	2 1
1 2 6 8 9 4 7	7 6 5 4 3 2 1
2 6 8 9 4 7	7 6 5 4 3 2
8 9	9 8

Thus, we have 6 such pairs, namely (5, 2), (3, 6), (1, 2), (1, 7), (2, 7) and (8, 9).

Hence, the answer is (E).

97. (D): The first, second, fourth, fifth and sixth letters of the word CONTRACT are C, O, T, R, A respectively. The word formed is ACTOR, in which the middle letter is T.

For Qs. No. 98 and 100:

Consider two cars I and II.

A and D sit in the same car, say I.

H is not in the same car *i.e.*, H is in car II.

B and C are not in the same car in which D is sitting *i.e.*, B and C are in car II.

F sits along with A and E in the same car *i.e.*, car I.

G is in the other car *i.e.*, car II.

Thus, we have:

Car I → A, D, E, F

Car II → B, C, G, H

98. (A): B and C are sitting in the same car in which G and H are sitting.

99. (D): Clearly, G is not sitting in the car in which A and E are sitting.

100. (A): Clearly, statement (*i*) is not necessary.

101. (A): A banker's cheque or DD is a cheque issued by a bank, guaranteeing payment to the person whose name is written on it.

- It is prepaid: The person requesting it (the customer) gives the money to the bank first.
- The bank then writes the cheque from its own account (not the customer's).
- This makes it very safe and trustworthy for the person receiving it.

102. (B): Dr. Manmohan Singh is the only Indian Prime Minister who also served as the Governor of the RBI. His rare combination of deep economic knowledge and leadership helped shape modern India's economy. He is best known for:

- Being the 13th Prime Minister of India (2004–2014)
- Leading India's major economic reforms in 1991.
- Serving as Governor of the Reserve Bank of India (RBI) earlier in his career.

103. (B): The Global Financial Development Report (GFDR) is published by the World Bank and provides insights into the state of global financial systems. It focuses on topics like credit reporting, financial inclusion, and regulation. The report offers data and policy recommendations to help countries strengthen their financial sectors. It is aimed at supporting economic growth and poverty reduction through better financial infrastructure. Each edition focuses on a specific theme relevant to global financial development.

104. (C): Social banking is a banking approach aimed at promoting financial inclusion and welfare for the poor and underserved. It provides affordable banking services like loans, savings, and insurance to low-income groups. The goal is to help marginalized communities access formal financial systems and improve their livelihoods. Social banking supports inclusive economic growth by reducing barriers to credit and banking. It plays a key role in empowering disadvantaged sections of society.

105. (D): Small Finance Banks are specialized banks that primarily serve underserved and low-income segments by offering a range of financial services. They accept deposits from individuals and businesses, providing a safe place to save money. These banks also disburse small loans, including microloans and loans to small businesses and farmers, helping promote financial inclusion. Additionally, they sell insurance products and other financial services to meet the varied needs of their customers. Overall, Small Finance Banks play a crucial role in expanding access to banking and credit for those typically excluded from traditional banking.

106. (C): NPCI International Payments Ltd. (NIPL), a wholly-owned subsidiary of the National Payments Corporation of India (NPCI), has partnered with PPRO, a global digital payments infrastructure provider. This collaboration aims to enable seamless international e-commerce transactions using India's UPI (Unified Payments Interface). The partnership allows Indian consumers to pay global merchants using UPI, enhancing cross-border payment capabilities. It expands UPI's reach beyond India and supports its global adoption. PPRO will integrate UPI into its platform, connecting international merchants to Indian customers. This move supports the Indian government's vision of making UPI a global digital payment standard. The alliance also boosts convenience and accessibility for Indian users in global e-commerce markets.

107. (B): According to the Reserve Bank of India (RBI), the Central Government is required to maintain a minimum cash balance of ₹ 10 crore on a daily basis with the RBI. This arrangement ensures that the government has sufficient liquidity to meet its day-to-day expenditure needs. Additionally, on Fridays and at the end of March and July, the minimum balance requirement increases to ₹ 100 crore. If the government's balance falls below these stipulated minimum levels, it can avail of the RBI's Ways and Means Advances (WMA) facility to bridge the shortfall.

108. (C): An Adjustable-Rate Mortgage (ARM) has an interest rate that varies over time, usually linked to a benchmark or reference index like the LIBOR or Treasury rates. This means the rate—and therefore the monthly payments—can go up or down at specified intervals after an initial fixed period. In contrast, a Fixed-Rate Mortgage has an interest rate that stays the same throughout the loan term, providing predictable payments.

109. (C): Blockchain technology can improve KYC processes by allowing banks and financial institutions to share verified customer information securely and transparently through a decentralized ledger. This reduces duplication of efforts, speeds up customer onboarding, lowers costs, and enhances data privacy and security. Instead of each bank verifying the same customer repeatedly, blockchain enables trusted sharing of KYC data, making the process more efficient.

110. (C): Selective Credit Control is a qualitative tool of monetary policy used by the Reserve Bank of India to regulate the use of credit for specific purposes or sectors. It involves directing banks to restrict or encourage loans for certain industries or activities, helping control inflation or promote growth in targeted areas.

In contrast, tools like Repo Rate, Bank Rate, and Cash Reserve Ratio (CRR) are quantitative tools that influence the overall money supply and credit in the economy.

111. (A): Statutory Liquidity Ratio (SLR) is the portion of a commercial bank's total deposits that must be kept with itself in the form of liquid assets like cash, gold, or government-approved securities. It is mandated by the Reserve Bank of India (RBI) to ensure banks remain solvent and can meet withdrawal demands. SLR helps control credit growth and maintain financial discipline in the banking system. It is expressed as a percentage of Net Demand and Time Liabilities (NDTL). This reserve is different from CRR, which is kept with the RBI in cash form.

112. (B): The C-bot is an autonomous underwater vehicle developed by CSIR-NIO, Goa, designed to monitor coral reefs. It collects data on coral health and bleaching by navigating underwater and capturing images and environmental parameters. This helps scientists study the impact of climate change on coral ecosystems without needing human divers. Besides coral monitoring, C-bot can be used for underwater inspections and research. It supports marine conservation and advances oceanic scientific understanding.

113. (A): Professor B.R. Kamboj, Vice Chancellor of Chaudhary Charan Singh Haryana Agricultural University, received the 14th M.S. Swaminathan Award for his work in agronomy. His research has significantly improved farming practices and agricultural science. He has published around 300 research papers and articles. The award recognizes his contributions as a scientist and extension specialist. It was presented at an international conference focused on agricultural and health issues.

114. (A): The Hopman Cup is an international tennis tournament played in a mixed-team format, where each team consists of one male and one female player representing their country. It was named after Harry Hopman, a legendary Australian tennis player and coach. The tournament features singles and mixed doubles matches and is known for its unique and friendly competition style.

115. (A): ISRO Chief S. Somanath confirmed that the main objective of the Chandrayaan-4 mission is to soft-land on the Moon, collect lunar surface samples (rocks and soil), and then return them safely to Earth. This mission aims to demonstrate critical technologies like robotic drilling, ascent from the Moon, orbital docking, and safe re-entry—marking India's foray into lunar sample-return missions. The mission will help scientists better understand the Moon's geology and evolution and is a significant step forward in India's deep space exploration program.

116. (A): Hyderabad's Rajiv Gandhi International Airport won the 'Best Airport Staff in India & South Asia 2024' award from Skytrax. The award recognizes excellence in customer service, including staff behavior, efficiency, and helpfulness. It was based on global passenger feedback and surveys. This honor highlights the airport's commitment to world-class service standards. It strengthens Hyderabad's reputation as a top aviation hub in the region.

117. (B): The theme of World Earth Day 2024 was "Planet vs Plastics". It focused on raising awareness about the harmful impact of plastic pollution on the environment and human health. The campaign aimed to reduce global plastic production by 60% by 2040. It also called for a ban on single-use plastics and encouraged sustainable alternatives. The theme highlighted the urgent need to protect the planet from plastic waste.

118. (B): Abhinav Bindra, India's first individual Olympic gold medallist (Beijing 2008), carried the Olympic torch during the Paris 2024 torch relay in July 2024. He described the experience as an "honor beyond words", expressing his pride and humility at representing India. Bindra's selection celebrates his legacy and contributions to sports and the Olympic movement. His role in the relay reinforces India's growing presence in global athletics and the Olympic spirit.

119. (A): Karthikeyan Murali (born 5 January 1999 in Thanjavur, Tamil Nadu) is a celebrated Indian chess grandmaster, achieving his GM title in 2015. A prolific youth champion, he won the World U-12 (2011) and U-16 (2013) titles. He is a two-time Indian National Premier Champion, claiming the title in 2015 and 2016. In 2019, Karthikeyan finished runner-up at the highly competitive Gibraltar Masters and later made history in 2023 by becoming the third Indian to defeat Magnus Carlsen in a classical game at the Qatar Masters.

120. (B): Virat Kohli equalled Sachin Tendulkar's record of 49 ODI centuries, showcasing his consistency and excellence in limited-overs cricket. Both are regarded as two of the greatest batsmen in cricket history. Kohli achieved this milestone through remarkable performances over many years. His aggressive style and ability to chase targets have made him a standout player. This achievement highlights Kohli's place among cricket's all-time greats.

121. (C): Carlos Alcaraz won the 2024 Wimbledon men's singles title, defeating Novak Djokovic in straight sets: 6–2, 6–2, 7–6(4). This victory marked his second consecutive Wimbledon title and his fourth Grand Slam overall. Alcaraz became the youngest player in the Open Era to achieve the "Channel Slam" by winning both the French Open and Wimbledon in the same year. He is only the second man, after Roger Federer, to win his first four Grand Slam finals. The match lasted 2 hours and 27 minutes and was the first men's singles final at Wimbledon to end in straight sets since 2018.

122. **(D):** Bangladesh won the 2023 Under-19 Asia Cup by defeating the UAE by 195 runs in the final. They scored 282 runs, with Ashiqur Rahman Shibli making a century. The UAE was bowled out for just 87 runs. Bangladesh remained unbeaten throughout the tournament, winning all five matches. Ashiqur Rahman Shibli was named the Player of the Tournament for his outstanding performance.

123. **(A):** The Kolkata Knight Riders (KKR) won the 2024 Indian Premier League (IPL), defeating Sunrisers Hyderabad (SRH) by 8 wickets in the final held on May 26, 2024, at the M.A. Chidambaram Stadium in Chennai. Sunil Narine was awarded the Most Valuable Player of the tournament for his consistent all-round performances, scoring 488 runs and taking 17 wickets. This victory marked KKR's third IPL title, having previously won in 2012 and 2014.

124. **(C):** Parshvanath is the 23rd Jain Tirthankara, who lived before Mahavira, the 24th Tirthankara. He is known for reviving and teaching the principles of non-violence and truth. Parshvanath played a key role in shaping Jainism's ethical foundations. His teachings emphasized compassion towards all living beings. He is widely revered and considered one of the most important spiritual leaders in Jainism.

125. **(B):** The Montagu-Chelmsford Reforms of GOI act, 1919 introduced Dyarchy in Indian provinces, dividing governance into two parts. Transferred subjects were managed by Indian ministers accountable to the legislative councils. Reserved subjects remained under the control of the British governor and his officials. This system aimed to gradually involve Indians in administration while retaining British control. Dyarchy laid the foundation for further constitutional reforms in India.

126. **(B):** The Shanti Swarup Bhatnagar Award is given to scientists and researchers for outstanding contributions to science and technology in India. It is awarded annually by the Council of Scientific and Industrial Research (CSIR). The award covers fields like physics, chemistry, biology, engineering, mathematics, and more. It is considered one of the most prestigious science honors in the country. Only Indian citizens under the age of 45 are eligible for this award.

127. **(B):** Kongthong, a village located in the East Khasi Hills district of Meghalaya, India, was awarded the Best Tourism Village (Bronze) at the National Tourism Awards 2023. This recognition highlights Kongthong's unique cultural heritage, particularly its tradition of "Jingrwai Lawbei", where each resident is assigned a melodic tune instead of a conventional name. The village's picturesque landscapes and commitment to sustainable tourism practices also contributed to this honor. The award ceremony took place at Bharat Mandapam in New Delhi, with Meghalaya Chief Minister Conrad K. Sangma expressing pride in the achievement.

128. **(C):** The term "Upper Yamuna" refers to the stretch of the Yamuna River from its origin at Yamunotri in Uttarakhand up to the Okhla Barrage in Delhi. This portion of the river passes through Himachal Pradesh, Uttarakhand, Haryana, and Uttar Pradesh. It is crucial for water-sharing agreements among these states. The Upper Yamuna River Board (UYRB) manages this section for irrigation and water distribution. The Okhla Barrage marks the downstream end of the Upper Yamuna.

129. **(C):** Among the major rivers of Peninsular India, the Kaveri River is considered the most seasonal. It receives the majority of its flow from the monsoon rains, especially the southwest monsoon. During dry seasons, its water level drops significantly, affecting irrigation and water supply. Unlike rivers like the Godavari and Krishna, which have larger catchment areas, Kaveri has limited water availability year-round. Hence, it is more dependent on seasonal rainfall.

130. **(A):** The Touch-me-not plant (*Mimosa pudica*) responds to touch by rapidly closing its leaves. This movement is called a seismonastic movement, which is a type of nastic movement triggered by mechanical stimulation (like touch or shaking). It does not depend on the direction of the stimulus. The movement occurs due to changes in turgor pressure in the leaf cells. This response helps protect the plant from harm or grazing animals.

131. **(D):** Individuals with blood group AB are called universal recipients because they can receive blood from all other blood groups (A, B, AB, and O). This is due to the absence of anti-A and anti-B antibodies in their plasma. As a result, they do not attack any ABO blood type they receive. However, their donated blood cannot be given to people with other blood groups. This makes them ideal recipients but limited donors.

132. **(C):** Bioremediation is a waste management technique that uses microorganisms (like bacteria, fungi, or algae) to break down or neutralize pollutants in contaminated environments. It is commonly used to clean up oil spills, heavy metals, pesticides, and other hazardous substances. The microbes convert harmful substances into less toxic or non-toxic forms. This process is eco-friendly and cost-effective. It plays a key role in restoring polluted soils, water, and air.

133. **(A):** Glycogen is a highly branched polysaccharide made up of glucose units and serves as the primary energy storage molecule in animals and fungi. It is mainly stored in the liver and muscles of animals. When energy is needed, glycogen is broken down into glucose. Its branched structure allows for quick release of energy. In contrast, cellulose and chitin provide structural support, and pectin is found in plant cell walls.

134. **(C):** *Jatropha curcas* is a plant species known for producing inedible oil-rich seeds, which are used to make biofuels. It also acts as a carbon sink, helping to reduce greenhouse gases. The plant is native to Central America, although it is now widely cultivated in Africa, Asia, and India. Its hardy nature allows it to grow in arid and semi-arid conditions. Jatropha is valued for its role in sustainable energy and land rehabilitation.

135. **(A):** Neknampur Lake, recognized as the largest floating treatment wetland in India, is located in Manikonda, Hyderabad, Telangana. The innovative floating wetland—an artificial island planted with over 3,000 wetland plants—cleans the polluted lake using hydroponic techniques. This eco-friendly solution earned it national acclaim and recognition by NITI Aayog as a model for best restoration.

136. **(B):** The Reserve Bank of India (RBI) applies the principles of reciprocity and single mode of presence to foreign banks. Reciprocity means foreign banks can operate in India only if Indian banks get similar access in that foreign country. Single mode of presence means a foreign bank must choose either branch mode or subsidiary mode, not both. This ensures fair treatment and regulatory clarity. These rules help protect India's financial system while encouraging balanced international banking relations.

137. **(B):** The PM-PRANAM scheme stands for "PM Programme for Restoration, Awareness, Generation, Nourishment and Amelioration of Mother Earth". It is a government initiative in India aimed at promoting sustainable agriculture by reducing the use of chemical fertilisers. India has seen a rapid increase in the use of chemical fertilisers like urea, DAP (Di-ammonium Phosphate), MOP (Muriate of Potash), and NPK (Nitrogen-Phosphorus-Potassium). While these help increase crop yields, their excessive use harms soil health, pollutes water, and damages ecosystems. So, to protect the environment and promote sustainable farming, the government introduced this scheme.

138. **(D):** The Sahakar Kisan Kalyan Yojana was launched by the Rajasthan government to improve farm productivity and increase farmers' income. It offers interest subsidies on long-term cooperative loans provided through Primary Land Development Banks and Central Cooperative Banks. Farmers receive a 7% subsidy on agricultural loans and 5% on non-agricultural loans if they repay on time. This reduces the effective interest rate to 4% for agricultural and 3.5% for non-agricultural loans. The scheme is supported by a budget of ₹ 39.75 crore and covers projects like irrigation, solar energy systems, and beekeeping.

139. **(B):** The scheme approved by the Union Cabinet to promote natural farming in India is the National Mission on Natural Farming (NMNF). This initiative, launched as a standalone Centrally Sponsored Scheme, received approval in November 2024 to push chemical-free farming methods rooted in traditional knowledge, integrated livestock practices, and local agro-ecological principles.

140. **(A):** In the fetch-decode-execute cycle, the term 'fetch' means the CPU retrieves the next instruction from memory. This instruction is located using the Program Counter (PC), which keeps track of the current position in the program. Once fetched, the instruction is sent to the control unit for decoding. Fetching is the first step in the cycle that allows the CPU to know what to do next. It is essential for the CPU to begin processing any command or task.

141. (B): RAM (Random Access Memory) temporarily stores data and instructions that the CPU needs while running programs. It is fast and volatile, meaning it loses its data when the computer is turned off. This temporary storage helps the CPU quickly access information during processing. Unlike a hard drive, which stores data permanently, RAM is used only for active tasks. Therefore, RAM is essential for smooth and efficient computer operation.

142. (B): An 8-bit register can hold 8 binary digits (bits). Each bit can be either 0 or 1, giving $2^8 - 1 = 255$ possible combinations. Since counting starts from zero, the values range from 0 to 255. This means the highest decimal number an 8-bit register can store is 255. It defines the limit for data or instructions stored in such registers.

143. (B): A front-end processor is a special CPU designed to handle communication tasks like managing data transfer and protocols. It takes care of these tasks so the main computer can focus on running applications and processing data. By off-loading communication work, it improves overall system efficiency. It acts as a bridge between the host computer and communication networks. This helps in faster and more reliable data communication.

144. (B): Howard Aiken was the lead engineer behind the Harvard Mark I, one of the first large-scale digital computers. The machine, also called the IBM Automatic Sequence Controlled Calculator, was developed in the early 1940s. It was an electromechanical computer built in collaboration with IBM. Aiken's work laid the foundation for future computing machines. Other pioneers like Konrad Zuse and John Atanasoff worked on different early computers.

145. (A): Backups are copies of data or program files saved to prevent loss in case the original gets damaged or deleted. They act as a safety net, allowing recovery of important information. Regular backups protect against hardware failure, accidental deletion, or malware attacks. Without backups, data recovery becomes difficult or impossible. Therefore, backups are essential for data security and reliability.

146. (B): The Business Responsibility and Sustainability Report (BRSR) is a regulatory framework introduced by SEBI in India. It mandates the top 1000 listed companies to disclose their Environmental, Social and Governance (ESG) practices. BRSR promotes transparency and accountability in corporate sustainability efforts. It replaces the older Business Responsibility Report (BRR). The goal is to align Indian companies with global ESG standards and responsible business practices.

147. (B): RBL Bank has collaborated with Google to enhance its Abacus 2.0 digital platform. This partnership leverages Google Cloud's advanced data management and analytics tools. It aims to improve customer experience through better personalization and insights. The collaboration also helps the bank in digital onboarding and targeted product offerings. Overall, it supports smarter decision-making and scalable growth.

148. (C): Vilasini Natyam is a classical dance form that originated in Andhra Pradesh. It was traditionally performed by devadasis (temple dancers) in temples and royal courts. The dance includes ritualistic, expressive, and storytelling elements. It nearly disappeared after the decline of the devadasi system but has been revived in recent years. Today, it is recognized as an important part of India's classical dance heritage.

149. (C): Gresham's Law states that "bad money drives good money out of circulation" when both are accepted as legal tender. People tend to hoard valuable (good) money like gold or silver coins and spend less valuable (bad) money, such as debased coins or paper currency. Over time, the good money disappears from circulation. This happens especially when both types have the same face value but different real value. The law was named after Sir Thomas Gresham, who observed this in 16th-century England.

150. (B): Monopolies and Restrictive Trade Practices Commission (MRTPC) was set up under the Monopolies and Restrictive Trade Practices Act, 1969. The MRTPC is an organ of the Department of Company Affairs, Ministry of Corporate Affairs, Government of India. MRTPC is a quasi-judicial body.

YOUR SPACE

Previous Years' Paper

IBPS—SPECIALIST OFFICERS

Rajbhasha Adhikari and Law Officer, 2023*

Preliminary Exam

ENGLISH LANGUAGE

Directions (Qs. No. 1-10): *Read the following passage carefully and answer the questions given below it. Certain words have been highlighted for your attention.*

Most people spend (on average) half of their day tapping away at their hand-held devices. Either, surfing the net or checking notifications. Facebook ranks the highest in all social networking platforms, followed by Twitter, Instagram and so forth.

Social media is addictive—which is why so many people are 'hooked'. Often referred to as **Social networking addiction**, this phrase is often used to describe someone who spends too much time on Facebook, Twitter, Instagram and other channels. A blog post, Instagram post, tweet, or YouTube video can be produced easily by anyone and shared, which can then be viewed by millions for free. Psychologists and scientists have now taken the time to study social media in terms of why they believe it interferes with aspects of our daily life. There is no official medical term that identifies addiction and social networking. It cannot be deemed as a disease or disorder as the cases are not severe and the habit can easily be maintained or prevented. Furthermore, instead of spending long periods of time on social media, we dip into and out of these sites all day long. We check for updates from friends and family as well as news and information. However, the behaviour associated with the excessive use of these channels has become the subject of much public and sociological debate. We actively post, like, comment and share personal posts. Not only that, we tend to share and reshare expressions (of either negative or positive) **contagiously.** But, why?

Scientists believed some years ago that, dopamine was simply a pleasure chemical in the brain. Recent studies have shown that; dopamine actually produces the desire in people to 'want' by drawing out the need for us to - seek and search. Creating the ultimate drive to find what is that what we want.

Dopamine is spontaneous. It's stimulated by unpredictability and small bits of information as well as reward cues which are the same conditions that social media presents to all users. In addition, the pull of dopamine is so strong that recent studies have shown that tweeting, for example, can be harder to resist than cigarettes and alcohol!

Researchers at Chicago University studied the effects of social media. They concluded quite quickly that people presented higher levels of addiction to social media than the need to smoke or drink. Media cravings ranked higher.

And, let's not forget oxytocin, many call it the cuddle chemical because the brain releases pleasure chemicals that transpire usually when you kiss and hug- or tweet. It is also known as the hormone that builds the strong yet unique bond between mothers and their babies. Oxytocin is now regarded as the human stimulant of empathy, generosity, trust, and more. These are factors which many advertisers and marketers play on when promoting a brand or business over social media.

* **Based on Memory.**

Nevertheless, problems have arisen most commonly with school kids—whereby mobile phone devices have been **confiscated** because exam results have fallen severely due to lack of attention on homework or studies. Schools in many westernized countries have had to take drastic action - banning smartphones, iPad and most portable devices from school premises - as it is claimed to be a huge distraction. Whereas, other schools use it for educational purposes and as a rewards system for their pupils.

Research has also indicated unsurprisingly that Facebook is the most common activity that university students switch to, when studying. Worryingly, it has also found that those who most engage in this type of internet browsing tend to have lower levels of educational achievement.

Also, there have been many cases of students posting or sharing content that is unethical, which has caused parents and academic institutions to limit the use of these online networking channels.

1. Which is the most common activity that university students switch to when studying?
A. YouTube B. Facebook
C. Twitter D. WhatsApp
E. All of the above

2. Why is there no real medical term that identifies addiction and social networking?
A. Research is not yet done on the subject
B. It cannot be deemed as a disease or disorder as cases are not severe
C. The habit can easily be maintained or prevented
D. (A) and (B)
E. (B) and (C)

3. What stands true about Dopamine in the present scenario?
A. It creates the ultimate drive to find what is that what we want.
B. It's stimulated by unpredictability and small bits of information as well as reward cues.
C. Dopamine was simply a pleasure chemical in the brain
D. (A) and (B)
E. (B) and (C)

4. Why is Oxytocin regarded as the cuddle chemical?
A. The brain releases pleasure chemicals that transpire usually when you kiss and hug- or tweet.
B. It builds the strong yet unique bond between mothers and their babies.
C. It produces the desire in people to "want" by drawing out the need for us to - seek and search.
D. (A) and (B)
E. (B) and (C)

5. Which of the following words is the most similar in meaning to the word 'contagiously' as given in the passage?
A. Assail B. Ambivalent
C. Arboreal D. Malignant
E. Cogent

6. Which of the following words is the most opposite in meaning to the word 'confiscated' as given in the passage?
A. Cognizant B. Covet
C. Expiate D. Pithy
E. Relinquish

7. What were the conclusions taken out by the researchers at Chicago University on studying the effects of social media?
A. People presented higher levels of addiction to social media than the need to smoke or drink.
B. Levels of addiction of smoking and drinking were higher than that of media craving.
C. There was a higher rate of media cravings.
D. (A) and (B)
E. (A) and (C)

1. B	**2.** E	**3.** D	**4.** A	**5.** D	**6.** E	**7.** E

8. What actions are taken by schools for students regarding mobile phone devices as mentioned in the passage?
A. Punish students who bring mobile phones to schools.
B. Use it for educational purposes and as a rewards system for their pupils.
C. Banning smartphones, iPad and most portable devices from school premises
D. (A) and (B)
E. (B) and (C)

9. What does the phrase 'Social Networking Addiction' mean?
A. Stalking People Socially
B. Creating Fake profiles for fun
C. Finding your Friend Circle Online
D. Someone who spends too much time on social websites
E. Someone who is an introvert socially

10. Which of the below sentences summarizes the key idea of the passage?
A. The Psychology of Social Addiction
B. The Addiction in Students
C. The Science behind Addiction
D. Beliefs of Scientists for Social Life
E. None of the above

Directions (Qs. No. 11-15): *The following sentences form a paragraph. The sentences are—(a), (b), (c), (d), (e) and (f). Sentence (e) is fixed and its position cannot be changed. The rest of the sentences are not given in their proper order. Read the sentences and answer the following questions.*

(*a*) So a person that has integrity will act and behave as per set values and beliefs they hold dear.
(*b*) There is a famous saying which perfectly describes integrity.
(*c*) The word 'integrity' itself has a Latin origin.
(*d*) "Honesty is telling the truth to other people; integrity is telling the truth to myself."
(*e*) So it refers to the sense of completeness and togetherness one enjoys when they live their lives honestly and morally.
(*f*) It is derived from the word 'integer' and means to feel whole, i.e., a complete person.

11. Which sentence should be the sixth sentence in the paragraph?
A. (*f*) B. (*a*)
C. (*d*) D. (*c*)
E. (*b*)

12. Which sentence should be the fourth sentence in the paragraph?
A. (*f*) B. (*b*)
C. (*c*) D. (*d*)
E. (*a*)

13. Which sentence should be the third sentence in the paragraph?
A. (*a*) B. (*b*)
C. (*c*) D. (*d*)
E. (*f*)

14. Which sentence should be the second sentence in the paragraph?
A. (*b*) B. (*f*)
C. (*c*) D. (*a*)
E. (*d*)

15. Which sentence should be the first sentence in the paragraph?
A. (*a*) B. (*b*)
C. (*c*) D. (*d*)
E. (*f*)

Directions (Qs. No. 16-20): *In each of the questions given below, three words are given in bold. These three words may or may not be in their correct positions. The sentence is then followed by options with the correct combination of words that should replace each other in order to make the sentence grammatically and contextually correct. Find the correct combination of words that replace each other. If the sentence is correct as it is, select '(E)' as your option.*

8. E	**9.** D	**10.** A	**11.** B	**12.** A	**13.** C	**14.** E	**15.** B

16. **Approved** **(*a*)** on Saturday **said** **(*b*)** a third coronavirus vaccine for domestic use, Prime Minister Mikhail Mishustin **Russia** **(*c*)** on state TV.

A. (*a*) (*c*) (*b*) B. (*c*) (*a*) (*b*)
C. (*b*) (*a*) (*d*) D. (*a*) (*b*) (*c*)
E. None of the above

17. It is **mind** **(*a*)** that people should keep in **asserted** **(*b*)** the importance of adherence to COVID-19 appropriate **behaviour** **(*c*)**.

A. (*b*) (*a*) (*c*) B. (*c*) (*a*) (*b*)
C. (*a*) (*b*) (*c*) D. (*c*) (*b*) (*a*)
E. None of the above

18. The AstraZeneca company is going to **vaccine** **(*a*)** in Japan doses of the coronavirus **produce** **(*b*)** enough for 40 million **people** **(*c*)**, the executive director of the Japanese department of the firm said.

A. (*c*) (*a*) (*b*) B. (*a*) (*c*) (*b*)
C. (*a*) (*b*) (*c*) D. (*b*) (*a*) (*c*)
E. None of the above

19. The **received** **(*a*)** birthday party was the best **surprise** **(*b*)** Andrew could have **gift.** **(*c*)**

A. (*a*) (*b*) (*c*) B. (*b*) (*a*) (*c*)
C. (*b*) (*c*) (*a*) D. (*c*) (*a*) (*b*)
E. No rearrangement

20. The **blared** **(*a*)** parlour's owner **night** **(*b*)** really loud music all **tattoo** **(*c*)** long.

A. (*b*) (*c*) (*a*) B. (*a*) (*b*) (*c*)
C. (*c*) (*a*) (*b*) D. (*b*) (*a*) (*c*)
E. No rearrangement

Directions (Qs. No. 21-25): *Read the following sentence and determine whether there is an error in it. The error, if any, will be in one part of the sentence. If the sentence is error-free, then select 'No Error' as your answer.*

21. Psychiatrists feel that having a knowledge of (A) / the physical and mental changes that occurs in one's body (B) / and the reasons behind them (C) / have become essential for all teenagers. (D) / No error. (E)

22. As these books on science are (A) / published only in English, (B) / we seldom or ever (C) / find them in regional languages. (D) / No error. (E)

23. One evening of each week (A) / was set apart by him (B) / for the reception of whomsoever (C) / chose to visit him. (D) / No error (E)

24. Reports of researchers mysterious (A) / falling ill at the Wuhan Institute in late 2019, (B) / and other reports of a researcher (C) / who has reportedly gone missing. (D) / No Error (E)

25. Populist politics among the world has (A) / sought to privilege national sovereignty (B) / over universal values and commitments, (C) / slacking off efforts to tackle critical challenges that are transnational. (D) / No error (E)

Directions (Qs. No. 26-28): *Given below is a word, followed by three sentences that consist of that word. Identify the sentences(s) that best express(es) the meaning of the word.*

26. **Wind**

(*a*) That noise you can hear is the tape **winding** back.
(*b*) The blow to my stomach knocked the **wind** out of me.
(*c*) The sails flapped in the **wind**.

A. Only (*b*) B. (*a*) and (*c*)
C. (*b*) and (*c*) D. Only (c)
E. All of the above

27. **Fellow**

(*a*) He seemed like a decent **fellow**.
(*b*) He's a **fellow** of the Royal Institute of Chartered Surveyors.
(*c*) A member of staff was sacked for stealing from **fellow** employees.

A. Only (*a*) B. Only (*b*)
C. (*a*) and (*b*) D. (*a*) and (*c*)
E. All of the above

16. B	**17.** A	**18.** D	**19.** C	**20.** C	**21.** B	**22.** C	**23.** C
24. A	**25.** A	**26.** E	**27.** E				

28. Ascent

(*a*) She made her first successful **ascent** of Everest last year.
(*b*) She nodded her **ascent** to the proposal.
(*c*) His **ascent** to power was rapid and unexpected.

A. Only (*c*) B. Only (*a*)
C. (*a*) and (*c*) D. (*b*) and (*c*)
E. None of the above

Directions (Qs. No. 29 and 30): *A sentence/part of the sentence is emboldened. Five alternatives are given to the embolden part which will improve the sentence. Choose the correct alternative and choose the option corresponding to it. In case no improvement is needed, click the option corresponding to 'No improvement required'.*

29. He slapped the team into action and they headed for the town at a **more leisure pace**.

A. many leisurely
B. many leisured
C. more leisure paced
D. more leisurely pace
E. No improvement required

30. Although both the United States and China are formidable world powers, **India should side with the later.**

A. India should side along the later
B. India should side with the latter
C. India should side along the latter
D. India should be siding with the later
E. No improvement required

Directions (Qs. No. 31-36): *Each question below has one blank, which is indicating that something has been omitted. Find out which option can be used to fill up the blank in the sentence in the same sequence to make it meaningfully complete.*

31. Homemade gifts can be completely _______ to what the recipient likes.

A. Alters B. Firmed
C. Tailored D. Polite
E. Liability

32. After much thought, Ted __________ not to travel abroad this summer.

A. Resolved B. Concludes
C. Resolves D. Commence
E. Passed

33. Bryan is ________ in his belief that the earth is flat.

A. Tentative B. Hasten
C. Unlikely D. Provided
E. Confident

34. The noodle maker was __________ in making his noodles and would never let another person take over the task.

A. Careless B. Negligent
C. Cautious D. Exciting
E. Inattentive

35. If it weren't for the ________ circumstances, he would have certainly lost his job.

A. Sharp B. Intensify
C. Mitigating D. Increase
E. Aggravate

36. When asked about her father, she lost her outward enthusiasm and became rather ____.

A. Reserved B. Expansive
C. Talkative D. Extrovert
E. Outgoing

Directions (Qs. No. 37-40): *In each of the questions given below four words are given in bold. These four words may or may not be in their correct position. The sentence is then followed by options with the correct combination of words that should replace each other in order to make the sentence grammatically and contextually correct. Find the correct combination of the words that replace each other. If the sentence is correct as it then select option E as your choice.*

37. Some American officials **lead (A)** to hope that **resumed (B)** sanctions on Iran will **appear (C)** to a popular **uprising (D)**.

A. A-B B. A-C
C. B-D and A-C D. A-D
E. The sentence is correct

28. C **29.** D **30.** B **31.** C **32.** A **33.** E **34.** C **35.** C **36.** A **37.** B

38. **Tariffs (A)** has **imported (B)** higher **China (C)** on 603 items **imposed (D)** from the US.
A. Only A-B
B. Only B-C
C. Both A-B and B-D
D. Both A-C and B-D.
E. The sentence is correct.

39. NATO ally **world (A)** leads the **Turkiye (B)** in the **journalists (C)** of **number (D)** jailed.
A. A-B and C-D
B. Only B-C
C. A-C and B-D
D. A-D
E. The sentence is correct.

40. In 2016, **rising (A)** violence in **Pathankot (B)** by Islamic militants **culminated (C)** in attacks on Indian forces at Uri and **Kashmir (D).**
A. Both A-C and B-D
B. Both A-D and B-C
C. Only B-D
D. C-D
E. The sentence is correct.

Directions (Qs. No. 41-44): *Read each sentence to find out whether there is any grammatical or idiomatic error in it. The error, if any, will be in one part of the sentence. The number of that part is the answer. If there is 'No error', the answer is (E). (Ignore errors of punctuation, if any.)*

41. She held something (A)/ at her side which (B)/ was totally hiding (C)/ by the folds of her sari. (D)/ No error. (E)

42. The father forbade his son (A)/ to walk in the sun (B)/and play with (C)/ his friends on the road (D) / No error. (E)

43. The movement, which aims to (A)/ raise awareness about climate change, hopes (B)/ to bring people together to think about (C)/ what they can do for reduce harmful pollution. (D)/ No error (E)

44. I declined the invitation (A)/ not because I did not (B)/ want to go but (C)/ because I have no time. (D)/ No error (E)

Directions (Qs. No. 45-50): *In the following passage, some of the words have been left out, each of which is indicated by a number. Find the suitable word from the options given against each number and fill up the blanks with appropriate words to make the paragraph meaningfully complete.*

Stanford economist Nicholas Bloom is a true believer, and like many true believers, he lets his message __(45) __ his evidence. Based on a single study of a Chinese travel agency, he __(46) __ declares working from home a "future-looking technology" with "enormous potential." Not so fast. Bloom's study comes with serious limitations and is contradicted by a later Gallup report. However, while it is far too soon to draw broad __(47) __ from his findings, savvy business leaders can read between the lines and extract some valuable lessons for working __(48) __ with all employees.

Bloom __(49) __ on China's biggest travel agency, Ctrip, which wanted to expand while controlling office space costs. They __(50) __ a remote work trial, expecting that productivity would slip a little, but not enough to cancel out the savings. Instead, productivity shot up 13%, and attrition dropped 50%. When the work from home option was rolled out to the entire company and employees were given a choice, the productivity gains were 22%.

45. A. cut
B. outrun
C. exceeded
D. begin
E. choose

46. A. fast
B. enthusiastically
C. slowly
D. eager
E. appropriately

47. A. resulting
B. disappointments
C. conclusions
D. exercises
E. guarantees

48. A. optimally
B. extremely
C. competitively
D. abroad
E. everywhere

38. D **39.** A **40.** C **41.** C **42.** E **43.** D **44.** D **45.** B **46.** B **47.** C **48.** A

49. A. emphasising B. concentrates
C. learned D. matched
E. focused

50. A. establishes B. appointed
C. brought D. instituted
E. sold

REASONING

Directions (Qs. No. 51-55): *Study the following information carefully and answer the questions given below:*

Certain numbers of persons sit in a row face north direction. E sits 2nd to the right of F. Two persons sit between G and E. D sits immediate right of G. The numbers of persons sit to the left of D is same as to right of C. Four persons sit between D and H who does not sit near F. C sits 2nd to the left of H. B sits 2nd from the extreme end but not sit near E. No one sits left of F. A sits 2nd to the left of G.

51. Who sits 3rd to the right of D?
A. G B. E
C. A D. C
E. H

52. How many persons sit in the row?
A. 21 B. 17
C. 19 D. 18
E. 16

53. How many persons sit between C and A?
A. 1 B. 2
C. 3 D. 4
E. More than 4

54. Four of the following five are alike in a certain way and hence form a group. Which of the following does not belong to that group?
A. E B. G
C. A D. F
E. D

55. What is the position of E with respect to D?
A. 3rd to the right B. 4th to the left
C. Immediate right D. 2nd to the left
E. None of these

Directions (Qs. No. 56-60): *Study the following questions and answering the questions referring to the word sequence given below:*

ROW FIX FOG LAN COW

56. If first and second letter of each word is interchanged, then how many meaningful words will be formed?
A. Three B. Two
C. One D. Five
E. None of these

57. If each consonant is changed to its previous letter in the alphabetical series and each vowel is changed to its next letter in the alphabetical series, then how many words contain at least one vowel?
A. None B. One
C. Two D. Three
E. None of these

58. If words are arranged according to the dictionary order from left to right, which word is second from the right end?
A. FIX B. LAN
C. FOG D. COW
E. ROW

59. If all the letters in each word are arranged according to the alphabetical order from left to right, and then first and second letter are interchanged in each word then how many meaningful words will be formed?
A. Two B. One
C. None D. More than three
E. None of these

49. E **50.** D **51.** D **52.** E **53.** E **54.** D **55.** B **56.** E **57.** C **58.** B **59.** A

60. If last letter of each given word is changed to its next letter according to alphabetical series, then how many words contain more than one vowel?
A. One B. Two
C. Three D. More than three
E. None of these

Directions (Qs. No. 61-64): *In these questions, relationship between different elements is shown in the statements. These statements are followed by two conclusions. Give answer—*

61. Statements: $Q \geq S = D \geq C > F \leq G = T$

Conclusions: I. $D = F$ II. $S > F$
A. If only conclusion I is true
B. If only conclusion II is true
C. If either conclusion I or II is true
D. If neither conclusion I nor II is true
E. If both conclusion I and II are true

62. Statements: $W \leq Y > Z = X > P > J$

Conclusions: I. $J < Z$ II. $X < W$
A. If only conclusion I is true
B. If only conclusion II is true
C. If either conclusion I or II is true
D. If neither conclusion I nor II is true
E. If both conclusion I and II are true

63. Statements: $S > G \geq J \leq N < B > V = O$

Conclusions: I. $V \leq G$ II. $G < O$
A. If only conclusion I is true
B. If only conclusion II is true
C. If either conclusion I or II is true
D. If neither conclusion I nor II is true
E. If both conclusion I and II are true

64. Statements: $W \leq F < V = X \geq B \geq N$

Conclusions: I. $F > B$ II. $X \geq W$
A. If only conclusion I is true
B. If only conclusion II is true
C. If either conclusion I or II is true
D. If neither conclusion I nor II is true
E. If both conclusion I and II are true

Directions (Qs. No. 65-69): *Study the following information carefully and answer the questions given below:*

Six boxes i.e., B, Q, R, S, T and W are arranged one above the other but not necessarily in the same order. Three boxes are placed between box R and box S. Box Q is placed just above the box B. More than two boxes are placed below the box R. Box T is placed two places above the box Q.

65. Which box is placed just above box S?
A. Box R B. Box T
C. Box W D. None of these
E. Box B

66. How many boxes are placed between box W and box T?
A. One B. Two
C. Three D. Four
E. None

67. Which box is placed at the bottommost position?
A. Box S B. Box R
C. Box T D. Box W
E. Box B

68. How many boxes are placed below box Q?
A. Two B. Three
C. One D. Four
E. More than four

69. If all the boxes are arranged in alphabetical order from top to bottom then how many boxes remain unchanged?
A. One B. Two
C. Three D. Four
E. None

Directions (Qs. No. 70 and 71): *Study the following information carefully to answer the given questions:*

C is daughter-in-law of D who has only two children. A is grandmother of F who is niece of B. B is sister of E and child of D. G is grandchild of D who is married. No single parent lives in the family.

60. A **61.** B **62.** A **63.** D **64.** D **65.** C **66.** C **67.** A **68.** B **69.** E

70. How G is related to C?
A. Son
B. Daughter
C. Nephew
D. Niece
E. Either son or daughter

71. Four of the following five are alike in a certain way and thus form a group. Who among the following doesn't belong to the group?
A. A B. B
C. D D. F
E. C

72. If we form a four-letter meaningful word by using the second, third, fourth and eleventh letter from the left end of the word 'REPRODUCTION', then which of the following will be the fourth letter of the meaningful word thus formed. If more than one meaningful word is formed mark Z as your answer. If no meaningful word is formed, mark X as your answer?
A. R B. E
C. O D. X
E. Z

Directions (Qs. No. 73-77): *Study the following information carefully to answer the given questions:*

Seven persons are designated at seven different designations—Senior executive, Executive, SO, HR, Product head, ST and Admin in a company. The designations are given in decreasing order such as the Senior executive is the senior most designation and Admin is the junior most designation.

More than two persons are senior to R. Only two persons are designated between R and V. V is designated as senior to SO. Q is designated two persons senior to S but junior to R. As many persons designated between Q and S as between Q and U. P is senior to T.

73. How many persons are designated between V and Q?
A. Three B. Four
C. Five D. One
E. Two

74. Who among the following is designated as Executive?
A. R B. P
C. V D. Q
E. T

75. As many persons are senior to U as junior to _____.
A. R B. S
C. Q D. T
E. P

76. If V is related to U, in the similar way P is related to R then who among the following is related to S?
A. P B. T
C. U D. Q
E. V

77. Which among the following statements is/are true?
I. V is the senior most person among all
II. More than three persons are junior to R
III. Odd number of persons designated between P and T
A. Only III
B. Only II
C. Both I and II
D. All I, II and III
E. Both I and III

78. In the word 'REPLACED', how many pairs of the letters have the same number of letters between them (both forward and backward direction) in the word as in the alphabetical series?
A. Four B. Two
C. One D. Three
E. More than four

70. E **71.** C **72.** E **73.** A **74.** B **75.** C **76.** D **77.** E **78.** D

Directions (Qs. No. 79 & 80): *In the question below some statements are given followed by the conclusions. You have to take the given statements to be true even if they seem to be at variance with commonly known facts. Read all the conclusions and then decide which of the given conclusions logically follow from the given statements disregarding commonly known facts.*

79. **Statements** : Only a few fans are fridges. All fridges are cooler.

Conclusions : I. All fans are fridges.
II. No fans are fridges.

A. Either conclusion I or II follows
B. Only conclusion II follows
C. Only conclusion I follows
D. Both conclusions I and II follow
E. Neither conclusion I nor II follows

80. **Statements** : Only flavour is spices. Some taste is flavour.

Conclusions : I. No taste is spices.
II. All flavour can never be taste.

A. Neither conclusion I nor II follows
B. Either conclusion I or II follows
C. Only conclusion I follows
D. Both conclusions I and II follow
E. Only conclusion II follows

81. Find the odd one out?
A. BDI B. QSX
C. OLQ D. RTY
E. GIN

Directions (Qs. No. 82-86): *Study the following information carefully to answer the given questions:*

Eight persons sit around a square table such that four of them sit at the corners of the table and face towards the centre where the remaining four sit at the middle of the side and face away from the centre of the table.

D sits second to the right of H. One person sits between H and A. F sits adjacent to A and sits at the corner of the table. E sits second to the left of F but doesn't sit adjacent to A. G sits adjacent to both B and C who doesn't face F.

82. How many persons sit between G and E when counted from the right of G?
A. Five B. Three
C. Six D. Four
E. One

83. Four of the following five are alike in a certain way and thus form a group. Who among the following doesn't belong to the group?
A. B B. F
C. A D. C
E. E

84. Which among the following statement is true?
A. B doesn't face F
B. E sits two persons away from A
C. Three persons sit between C and F
D. G and D face the same direction
E. None is true

85. If all the persons sit in alphabetical order starts from A in clockwise direction, then the position of how many persons remains unchanged (excluding A)?
A. Two B. One
C. None D. Three
E. More than three

86. What is the position of A with respect to B?
A. Third to the left
B. Third to the right
C. Fifth to the left
D. Fourth to the right
E. Immediate left

79. E	**80.** D	**81.** C	**82.** D	**83.** C	**84.** D	**85.** B	**86.** A

Directions (Qs. No. 87-90): *Study the following alpha numeric symbol series carefully and answer the questions given below:*

9 M W @ Q 2 7 % J L & 2 T * U 9 6 # T Ω 1 Z 7 β L 6 3 μ Y 9

87. How many symbols are there in the above series which are immediately followed by a consonant and immediately preceded by a number?

A. None B. One
C. Two D. Three
E. Four

88. Which among the following element is 8th to the right of the number which is 4th from the left end in the above series?

A. T B. 6
C. U D. Ω
E. 9

89. If all the numbers are dropped from the above series, then which among the following will be the 18th element from the right end?

A. & B. @
C. W D. J
E. %

90. What is the sum of the numbers which are immediately followed by a symbol?

A. 23 B. 25
C. 22 D. 24
E. 32

Directions (Qs. No. 91-95): *Study the following information to answer the following questions.*

In a certain code,

"Ram goes to school" is written as "rx gw ts mh"

"He goes hospital" is written as "ez gw lp"

"He studies in school" is written as "ez yr ga mh"

"Ram works in hospital" is written as "rx kt ga lp"

91. What is code for word "school"?

A. rx B. mh
C. lp D. kt
E. Cannot be determined

92. What is code for word "goes hospital"?

A. kt lp B. rx gw
C. ez lp D. gw lp
E. yr mh

93. What is code for word "studies"?

A. gw B. ez
C. yr D. rx
E. Cannot be determined

94. What is code for word "works"?

A. kt B. qa
C. yr D. ez
E. Cannot be determined

95. What is code for word "Ram"?

A. gw B. mh
C. ts D. rx
E. Cannot be determined

96. How many such pairs of digits are there in the number '6315784' each of which has as many digits as between them in the number as are there in the general numerical order?

A. One B. Two
C. Three D. Four
E. Five

97. How many meaningful four-letter words (Not ending with F) can be made with the alphabets N, R, E and F each being used only once in each word?

A. One
B. Two
C. Three
D. More than three
E. None of these

87. E **88.** D **89.** C **90.** A **91.** B **92.** D **93.** C **94.** A **95.** D **96.** B **97.** A

Directions (Qs. No. 98-100): *Study the following information and answer the given questions.*

Eight candidates have exam on 5th and 20th of four months among March, May, June and July. H is one of the candidates. Two candidates have exam between A and B. C has exam on 20th May and immediate before A. E's exam is immediately after D's exam. F's exam is immediately after G's exam but not in same month. D has exam in the month, which has 30 days.

98. Who has exam on 5th July?
A. A B. B
C. C D. D
E. E

99. How many persons have exam after C?
A. Three
B. Four
C. One
D. Five
E. Two

100. Find odd one.
A. H B. None
C. G D. E
E. F

GENERAL AWARENESS

101. Which of these MFIs are NOT regulated by the RBI?
A. Small Finance Bank led MFIs
B. Non-profit MFIs
C. NBFC MFIs
D. More than one of the above
E. None of the above

102. Which of the following institutions do NOT come under the control of the RBI?
A. Co-operative banks
B. Co-operative societies
C. National housing banks
D. More than one of the above
E. None of the above

103. When was the National Stock Exchange of India (NSE) established?
A. 1988
B. 1990
C. 1992
D. 1994
E. None of the above

104. Which among the following is/are a segment of Reserve Money in Indian Economy?
1. RBI's net credit to the Government
2. Net forex reserve with the RBI
3. RBI's net credit to the commercial bank

A. 1 and 2
B. 2 and 3
C. 1 and 3
D. More than one of the above
E. None of the above

105. Which among the following are the functions of Money?
(*a*) Unit of value
(*b*) Standard for deferred payment
(*c*) Store of value
(*d*) Medium of exchange
A. (*a*), (*b*) and (*c*)
B. (*a*), (*c*) and (*d*)
C. (*a*), (*b*), (*c*) and (*d*)
D. More than one of the above
E. None of the above

106. Small Industries Development Bank of India (SIDBI) was established in which year?
A. 1990
B. 1988
C. 1992
D. 1994
E. None of these

98. E **99.** B **100.** C **101.** B **102.** B **103.** C **104.** D **105.** C **106.** A

107. Who is the only Prime Minister to have served as the Governor of RBI?
A. P.V. Narsimha Rao
B. Manmohan Singh
C. Lal Bahadur Shastri
D. Indira Gandhi
E. None of these

108. The headquarter of National Bank for Agriculture & Rural Development (NABARD) is in:
A. Delhi
B. Chandigarh
C. Kolkata
D. Mumbai
E. Lucknow

109. Which is the minimum amount which can be remitted through Real Time Gross Settlement (RTGS)?
A. ₹ 5,00,000
B. ₹ 2,00,000
C. ₹ 3,00,000
D. ₹ 1,00,000
E. None of the above

110. MCLR is the minimum lending rate below which a bank is not permitted to lend. What does 'M' Stand for?
A. Minimum
B. Marginal
C. Monetary
D. Money
E. Market

111. Which bank's licence was recently cancelled by the RBI due to inadequate capital and poor earning prospects?
A. Dhanlaxmi Bank
B. Purvanchal Co-operative Bank
C. Allahabad Bank
D. United Bank of India
E. State Bank of India

112. What is the purpose of the Reserve Bank of India (RBI) imposing an incremental Cash Reserve Ratio (CRR) on banks during periods of excess liquidity?
A. To increase the money supply in the economy
B. To help banks earn higher interest income
C. To absorb excess liquidity in the banking system
D. More than one of the above
E. None of the above

113. Which among the following is not a female reproductive part of plant?
A. Style
B. Stigma
C. Stamen
D. More than one of the above
E. None of the above

114. Who propounded the theory of Natural selection?
A. Mendel
B. Lamark
C. Darwin
D. More than one of the above
E. None of the above

115. A passenger in a moving bus is thrown forward when the bus suddenly stops. This is explained:
A. by Newton's first law
B. by Newton's second law
C. by Newton's third law
D. by the principle of conservation of momentum
E. None of the above

116. Which of the following instruments is 'not' a debt instrument?
A. Stocks
B. Debentures
C. Bonds
D. Mortgages
E. Promissory Note

107. B **108.** D **109.** B **110.** B **111.** B **112.** C **113.** C **114.** C **115.** A **116.** A

117. The working and activity of NBFCs are registered by the Reserve Bank of India within the framework of the ______.
A. Reserve Bank of India Act, 1934 (Chapter 10-12)
B. Banking Regulation Act, 1949
C. Companies Act, 1956
D. Banking Companies Act, 1970 (Chapter No. 4)
E. Corporate Act, 2001

118. The 'CGFMU' is a Credit Guarantee Fund established for guaranteeing loans sacrificed under the:
A. PMRY Scheme
B. PMMY Scheme
C. PMGSY Scheme
D. PMAY Scheme
E. PMUY Scheme

119. Payment solutions providers 'Oxigen Services' and 'PayU India' have been granted in-principle approval from Reserve Bank of India (RBI) to operate as _____ .
A. Payments Bank
B. Small Finance Bank
C. White Label ATM
D. Universal Bank
E. Bharat Bill Payments Operating Unit

120. According to RBI guidelines, a scheduled commercial bank can own stake in a payments bank to the extent permitted under Section 19(2) of the:
A. Public Financial Institutions Act, 1956
B. Banking Regulation Act, 1949
C. State Bank of India Act, 1955
D. Reserve Bank of India Act, 1934
E. Reserve Bank of India Act, 1953

121. 'LAF' is a monetary policy instrument which allows banks to borrow money through repurchase agreements. The alphabet 'L' in the abbreviation 'LAF' stands for ______ .
A. Leverage
B. Legitimate
C. Liquidity
D. Liability
E. Local

122. The Tarun Ramadorai panel setup by the Reserve Bank of India (RBI) has been tasked to look at the various facets of the _____ .
A. Household finance in India
B. Digital Banking initiatives
C. Demonetisation
D. Promotion of financial inclusion
E. Feasibility of Islamic banking in India

123. The statutory base for the Depositor Education and Awareness Fund (DEAF) constituted by the Reserve Bank of India is provided by _____ .
A. Section 21A of the Reserve Bank of India Act, 1935
B. Section 21A of the Banking Companies Act, 1976
C. Section 26A of the Reserve Bank of India Act, 1935
D. Section 26A of the Banking Regulation Act, 1949
E. Section 21A of the Banking Regulation Act, 1949

124. The India Aspiration Fund (IAF) is a fund of funds that would invest in venture capital funds for meeting the capital requirement of _____ .
A. Agriculture Sector
B. Housing Sector
C. Mid Corporates
D. MSME start-ups
E. Electronics Sector

125. 'Equity-linked Savings Scheme' (ELSS) is an open-ended diversified equity schemes offered by:
A. Stock exchanges
B. Commercial Banks
C. Primary Dealer
D. Mutual Funds
E. SEBI

117. A **118.** B **119.** E **120.** B **121.** C **122.** A **123.** D **124.** D **125.** D

126. The alphabet 'D' in the abbreviation 'NSDL' stands for:

A. Derivative B. Debt
C. Dematerialisation D. Depository
E. Demand

127. The 'IFSC Code' is an alphanumeric comprising of 11 characters that facilitates electronic fund transfer in the country. The alphabet 'I' in the abbreviation 'IFSC' stands for ....

A. Inter-bank
B. Indian
C. International
D. Intercontinental
E. Institutional

128. The Reserve Bank of India has authorized non-banks to operate 'White Label ATMs' under the provisions of ....

A. Reserve Bank of India Act, 1934
B. Negotiable Instruments Act, 1881
C. Negotiable Instruments (Amendment) Act, 2015
D. Banking Regulation Act, 1949
E. Payment & Settlement Systems Act, 2007

129. 'ONICRA is a leading ....

A. Credit and performance rating agency
B. Asset Reconstruction Company
C. White Label ATM Operator
D. Asset Management Company
E. None of those given as options

130. Which of the following is not a general credit control measure?

A. Bank rate
B. Variable reserve ratios
C. Open market operations
D. Regulation of margin requirements on advances against agricultural commodities
E. Other than those given as options

131. The term 'hyper-inflation' means ....

A. a situation with moderate rise in price level.
B. an inflationary situation where the external sources are the primary contributing factors.
C. a 'runway' or 'galloping' inflationary situation where the monetary unit becomes almost worthless.
D. a situation where the cost of living index is rising alarmingly.
E. Other than those given as options

132. 'Prathama Bank' is the first Regional Rural Bank (RRB) established in 1975 with its headquarters in Moradabad. It was sponsored by ______ .

A. Syndicate Bank
B. Allahabad Bank
C. Central Bank of India
D. Punjab National Bank
E. UCO Bank

133. The Nobel Prize in Chemistry 2023 was given for the development of ______.

A. Work on the structure of protein and insulin
B. Discovery and synthesis of quantum dots
C. Structure of atom
D. Radioactivity
E. None of the above

134. The National Unity Day was celebrated on 31st October in the remembrance of who among the following?

A. Indira Gandhi
B. Lal Bahadur Shastri
C. Sardar Vallabhbhai Patel
D. Chaudhari Charan Singh
E. Rajiv Gandhi

126. D **127.** B **128.** E **129.** A **130.** D **131.** C **132.** A **133.** B **134.** C

135. Kamlang tiger reserve is located in which state?
A. Manipur
B. Meghalaya
C. Arunachal Pradesh
D. Assam
E. Mizoram

136. Where is the headquarter of the International Atomic Energy Agency located?
A. Manila
B. Vienna
C. Paris
D. Washington DC
E. London

137. Pierre Agostini, Ferenc Krausz and Anne L'Huillier won the Nobel Prize in 2023 for which category?
A. Medicine
B. Chemistry
C. Physics
D. Economics
E. Peace

138. Who is the author of the book 'The Third Pillar-How Markets and the State leave the Community Behind'?
A. Raghuram Rajan
B. Anita Desai
C. Chetan Bhagat
D. Arundhati Roy
E. Ravinder Singh

139. Who among the following has been appointed as the first Lieutenant (Lt) Governor of Ladakh, the newly created Union Territories of India?
A. Dineshwar Sharma
B. Girish Chandra Murmu
C. Satya Pal Malik
D. P S Sreedharan Pillai
E. Radha Krishna Mathur

140. Helsinki is the capital of which country?
A. Norway
B. Sweden
C. Finland
D. Croatia
E. Belgium

141. Who won the men's singles title at the US Open 2023?
A. Roger Federer
B. Rafael Nadal
C. Novak Djokovic
D. John Millman
E. Daniil Medvedev

142. Kuchipudi is a folk dance of..............
A. Mizoram
B. Andhra Pradesh
C. Jammu & Kashmir
D. Maharashtra
E. Tamil Nadu

143. The headquarters of the International Solar Alliance (ISA) is headquartered in which city in India?
A. Chandigarh
B. Gurugram
C. Mysuru
D. Surat
E. None of the above

144. On August 6, 1945, the first nuclear bomb was dropped in which city?
A. Hiroshima
B. Tokyo
C. Nagasaki
D. Yakohama
E. Sendai

145. Which one of the following is the official mascot of Tokyo 2020 Olympic Games?
A. Soohorang
B. Vinicius de Moraes
C. The Hare, the Polar Bear and the Leopard
D. Miraitowa
E. Bandabi

135. C **136.** B **137.** C **138.** A **139.** E **140.** C **141.** C **142.** B **143.** B **144.** A **145.** D

146. Which Indian Shooter won gold in the women's 50 m rifle 3 position event at the Asian Games 2023 with a record score of 469.6 points?

A. Manu Bhaker
B. Mehuli Ghosh
C. Sift Kaur Samra
D. Rajeshwari Kumari
E. Esha Singh

147. .... is an internet-based computing solution where shared resources are provided.

A. Cloud Computing
B. Networking
C. LAN
D. None of the above
E. None of the above/More than one of the above

148. What is the shortcut key for a manual line break in MS-Word?

A. Ctrl + Enter
B. Alt + Enter
C. Shift + Enter
D. Space + Enter
E. None of the above

149. The k-Means algorithm is an .... algorithm.

A. Supervised Learning
B. Unsupervised Learning
C. Semi-supervised Learning
D. Reinforcement Learning
E. None of the above

150. LAN, WAN and MAN are computer networks covering different areas. Their first alphabets L, W and M respectively stand for:

A. Local, World and Middle
B. Long, Wireless and Metropolitan
C. Local, Wide and Metropolitan
D. Least, Wireless and Maximum
E. List, Word and Maximum

EXPLANATORY ANSWERS

1. (B): University students frequently switch to Facebook when studying. This is backed by research indicating Facebook is the primary distraction among university students. Additionally, it is the most common activity for them when studying, suggesting a significant impact on their focus and educational performance.

2. (E): There is no real medical term identifying addiction and social networking because cases are not severe enough to classify it as a disease or disorder, and the habit can be easily maintained or prevented. This highlights the fact that while social media use is widespread, its impact is generally manageable.

3. (D): In the present scenario, dopamine creates the ultimate drive to find what we want and is stimulated by unpredictability, small bits of information, and reward cues. These elements are prevalent in social media interactions, making dopamine a key factor in why social media is so engaging and potentially addictive.

5. (D): 'Contagiously' is most similar in meaning to 'malignant'. In the passage, it refers to the spread of emotions or behaviors among people through social media, similar to how a malignant disease spreads, emphasizing the viral nature of online interactions.

6. (E): 'Confiscated' is opposite in meaning to 'relinquish'. Confiscated means to take

146. C **147.** A **148.** C **149.** B **150.** C

away, often as a penalty, while relinquish means to voluntarily give up something. This contrast highlights the different approaches to managing possession and control over objects or behaviours.

7. **(E):** Researchers at Chicago University concluded that people presented higher levels of addiction to social media than the need to smoke or drink, and media cravings ranked higher. This indicates the strong pull of social media, surpassing even traditional addictive substances like cigarettes and alcohol.

8. **(E):** Schools have taken actions such as banning smartphones, iPads, and most portable devices from school premises due to their distracting nature. Some schools, however, use these devices for educational purposes and as a rewards system for students, showing a dual approach to technology in education.

9. **(D):** 'Social Networking Addiction' refers to someone who spends too much time on social websites. This is characterized by excessive use of platforms like Facebook, Twitter, and Instagram, often leading to a significant impact on daily life and productivity.

10. **(A):** The passage primarily discusses the psychology behind social addiction, explaining how chemicals like dopamine and oxytocin drive our engagement with social media. It highlights the addictive nature of social networking and its impact on behaviour, making it the central theme.

11. **(B):** The sentence (*a*) should be the sixth sentence in the paragraph because it logically concludes the discussion on integrity by explaining how a person with integrity acts and behaves based on their values and beliefs. This ties back to the concept of integrity described in the previous sentences, creating a coherent end to the paragraph.

12. **(A):** The sentence (*f*) should be the fourth sentence in the paragraph because it directly follows the fixed sentence (*e*), explaining the Latin origin of the word 'integrity' and its meaning of feeling whole or complete. This flows naturally from the explanation given in (*e*) about living life honestly and morally.

13. **(C):** The sentence (*c*) should be the third sentence in the paragraph because it introduces the origin of the word 'integrity,' which sets the stage for the subsequent explanation in (*f*) and aligns with the logical flow of the passage.

14. **(E):** The sentence (*d*) should be the second sentence in the paragraph because it logically follows the first sentence (*b*), which introduces a famous saying about integrity. The saying itself is quoted in sentence (*d*): "Honesty is telling the truth to other people; integrity is telling the truth to myself." This creates a clear connection between the introduction and the fixed sentence (*e*), explaining the meaning of integrity.

16. **(B):** The correct combination is (*c*), (*a*), (*b*): The sentence should read: "Russia on Saturday approved a third coronavirus vaccine for domestic use, Prime Minister Mikhail Mishustin said on state TV." Rearranging the words makes the sentence grammatically and contextually correct, indicating the approval of a vaccine by Russia.

17. **(A):** The correct combination is (*b*), (*a*), (*c*): The sentence should read: "It is asserted that people should keep in mind the importance of adherence to COVID-19 appropriate behaviour." This rearrangement corrects the sentence structure, ensuring it is grammatically and contextually accurate.

18. **(D):** The correct combination is (*b*), (*a*), (*c*): The sentence should read: "The AstraZeneca

company is going to produce in Japan doses of the coronavirus vaccine enough for 40 million people, the executive director of the Japanese department of the firm said." This rearrangement ensures the sentence is grammatically and contextually appropriate.

19. (C): The correct combination is (*b*), (*c*), (*a*): The sentence should read: "The surprise birthday party was the best gift Andrew could have received." This rearrangement corrects the sentence structure, making it grammatically and contextually correct.

20. (C): The correct combination is (*c*), (*a*), (*b*): The sentence should read: "The tattoo parlour's owner blared really loud music all night long." This rearrangement corrects the sentence structure, ensuring it is grammatically and contextually appropriate.

21. (B): The error is in part (B). The correct sentence should be "Psychiatrists feel that having a knowledge of the physical and mental changes that occur in one's body and the reasons behind them have become essential for all teenagers." The verb "occurs" should be "occur" to agree with the plural noun "changes."

22. (C): The error is in part (C). The correct sentence should be "As these books on science are published only in English, we seldom if ever find them in regional languages." The phrase "seldom or ever" should be "seldom if ever" to be grammatically correct.

23. (C): The error is in part (C). The correct sentence should be "One evening of each week was set apart by him for the reception of whosoever chose to visit him." The word "whomsoever" should be "whosoever" to be grammatically correct.

24. (A): The error is in part (A). The correct sentence should be "Reports of researchers mysteriously falling ill at the Wuhan Institute in late 2019, and other reports of a researcher who has reportedly gone missing." The adverb "mysteriously" should be used instead of the adjective "mysterious" to describe the manner in which the researchers are falling ill.

25. (A): The error is in part (A). The correct sentence should be "Populist politics around the world has sought to privilege national sovereignty over universal values and commitments, slacking off efforts to tackle critical challenges that are transnational." The phrase "among the world" should be "around the world" to be grammatically correct.

26. (E): All of the above. The word "wind" is used correctly in all three sentences, expressing different meanings of the word. (*a*) refers to the action of winding or coiling, (*b*) refers to the air knocked out of someone, and (*c*) refers to moving air.

27. (E): All of the above. The word "fellow" is used correctly in all three sentences. (*a*) describes a decent man, (*b*) refers to a member of a professional institute, and (*c*) refers to colleagues.

28. (C): (*a*) and (*c*). The word "ascent" means climbing or moving up in (*a*) and rising to a position of power in (*c*). Sentence (*b*) uses the incorrect spelling; the correct word should be "assent," which means agreement.

29. (D): "more leisurely pace." The correct phrase is "more leisurely pace," meaning a slower, more relaxed speed. This phrase correctly matches the context of the sentence, indicating the team's change in pace.

30. (B): "India should side with the latter." The correct word is "latter," which refers to the second of two mentioned entities, in this case, China. "Later" refers to time, so "latter" is the appropriate word to use in this context.

31. (C): The correct sentence is: “Homemade gifts can be completely tailored to what the recipient likes.” The word “tailored” means customized or adapted to fit specific needs or preferences, which makes the sentence meaningful.

32. (A): The correct sentence is: “After much thought, Ted resolved not to travel abroad this summer.” The word “resolved” means decided firmly, which fits the context of making a decision after much thought.

33. (E): The correct sentence is: “Bryan is confident in his belief that the earth is flat.” The word “confident” means sure or certain, which fits the context of a strong belief.

34. (C): The correct sentence is: “The noodle maker was cautious in making his noodles and would never let another person take over the task.” The word “cautious” means careful, which fits the context of someone who is very careful about their work.

35. (C): The correct sentence is: “If it weren’t for the mitigating circumstances, he would have certainly lost his job.” The word “mitigating” means making something less severe, which fits the context of circumstances that prevent a negative outcome.

36. (A): The correct sentence is: “When asked about her father, she lost her outward enthusiasm and became rather reserved.” The word “reserved” means quiet and restrained, which fits the context of someone losing enthusiasm and becoming more withdrawn.

37. (B): The correct combination is A-C. The sentence should read: “Some American officials appear to hope that resumed sanctions on Iran will lead to a popular uprising.” This rearrangement makes the sentence grammatically and contextually correct.

38. (D): The correct combination is: “Tariffs has imposed higher China on 603 items imported from the US.” However, considering the context, it makes more sense if rearranged to: “China has imposed higher tariffs on 603 items imported from the US.”

39. (A): The correct combination is: “NATO ally Turkiye leads the world in the number of journalists jailed.” This rearrangement makes the sentence grammatically and contextually correct, indicating Turkiye’s position in terms of jailed journalists.

40. (C): The correct combination is: “In 2016, rising violence in Kashmir by Islamic militants culminated in attacks on Indian forces at Pathankot and Uri.” This rearrangement makes the sentence grammatically and contextually correct.

41. (C): The correct sentence is: “She held something at her side which was totally hidden by the folds of her sari.” The error is in part (C). The phrase “was totally hiding” should be “was totally hidden” to correctly form the passive voice, indicating that the object was obscured by the sari.

42. (E): The sentence “The father forbade his son to walk in the sun and play with his friends on the road.” is grammatically correct. “Forbade” correctly uses the infinitive “to walk,” and the sentence structure is clear and logical.

43. (D): The correct sentence is: “The movement, which aims to raise awareness about climate change, hopes to bring people together to think about what they can do to reduce harmful pollution.” The phrase “to reduce” should replace “for reduce” to correctly form the infinitive verb.

44. (D): The correct sentence is: “I declined the invitation not because I did not want to go but because I had no time.” The phrase “have no time” should be “had no time” to maintain consistent past tense throughout the sentence.

45. (B): The correct word is "outrun." The sentence should read: "Stanford economist Nicholas Bloom is a true believer, and like many true believers, he lets his message outrun his evidence." "Outrun" suggests that his message goes beyond the available evidence.

46. (B): The correct word is "enthusiastically." The sentence should read: "Based on a single study of a Chinese travel agency, he enthusiastically declares working from home a 'future-looking technology' with 'enormous potential.'" "Enthusiastically" correctly conveys the strong, positive endorsement.

47. (C): The correct word is "conclusions." The sentence should read: "However, while it is far too soon to draw broad conclusions from his findings, savvy business leaders can read between the lines and extract some valuable lessons for working optimally with all employees." "Conclusions" appropriately fits the context of making inferences.

48. (A): The correct word is "optimally." The sentence should read: "Savvy business leaders can read between the lines and extract some valuable lessons for working optimally with all employees." "Optimally" means in the best or most effective way, fitting the context.

49. (E): The correct word is "focused." The sentence should read: "Bloom focused on China's biggest travel agency, Ctrip, which wanted to expand while controlling office space costs." "Focused" indicates the main subject of his study.

50. (D): The correct word is "instituted." The sentence should read: "They instituted a remote work trial, expecting that productivity would slip a little, but not enough to cancel out the savings." "Instituted" means to establish or introduce, fitting the context of starting a trial.

For Qs. No. 51-55: From given information

51. (D): C sits 3rd to the right of D.

52. (E): 16 persons are sitting in the row.

53. (E): (5 persons) more than 4 persons sit between C and A.

54. (D): Only F is on left end.

55. (B): The position of E with respect to D is 4th to the left.

56. (E): ⇒ ORW, IFX, OFG, ALN, OCW

⇒ No one meaningful word.

57. (C): ⇒ QPV, EJW, EPF, KBM, BPV

⇒ 2 words contain at least one vowel.

58. (B): ⇒ COW, FIX, FOG, LAN, ROW

⇒ LAN is second from the right end.

59. (A): ⇒ ORW, FIX, FGO, ALN, COW

⇒ ROW, IFX, GFO, LAN, OCW

2 meaningful words will be formed.

60. (A): ⇒ ROX, FIY, FOH, LAO, COX

⇒ Only one word (LAO) contain more than one vowel.

61. (B): From given statement:

$Q \geq S = D \geq C > F \leq G = T$

$\Rightarrow S > F$

Only conclusion II is true.

62. (A): Given, statement:

$W \leq Y > Z = X > P > J$

$\Rightarrow \quad Z > J$

$\Rightarrow \quad J < Z$

Only conclusion I is true.

For Qs. No. 65-69: From given information arrangement of boxes:

Boxes
T
R
Q
B
W
S

65. **(C)** **66.** **(C)** **67.** **(A)**

68. **(B)** **69.** **(E)**

For Qs. No. 70-71: From given information

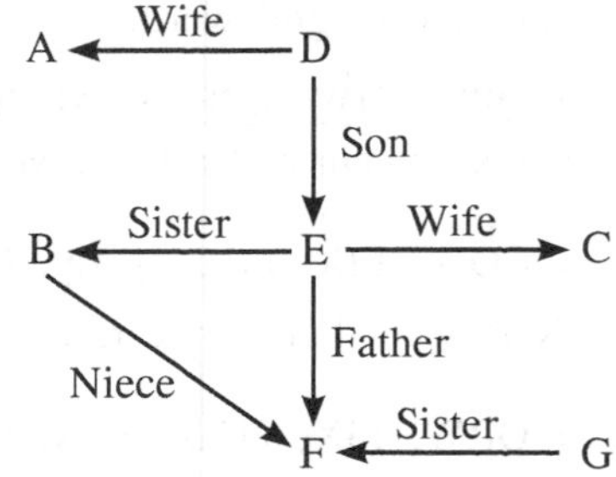

70. **(E):** G is either son or daughter.

71. **(C):** Except D, all are female member.

72. **(E):** E, P, R, O ⇒ REPO, ROPE
More than one meaningful word is formed.

For Qs. No. 73-77: From given information

Designations	**Persons**
Senior executive	V
Executive	P
SO	U
HR	R
Product head	Q
ST	T
Admin	S

73. **(A):** 3 persons are designated between V and Q.

74. **(B):** P is designated as executive.

75. **(C):** As many persons are Senior to U as Junior to Q.

76. **(D):** Given, V is related to U, P is related to R.
Similarly, Q is related S.

77. **(E):** Both I and III are true.

78. **(D):** 3 pairs of the letters (AD, DE, PR) have the same number of letters between them (both forward and backward direction) in the word as in the alphabetical series.

79. **(E):** From given statements:

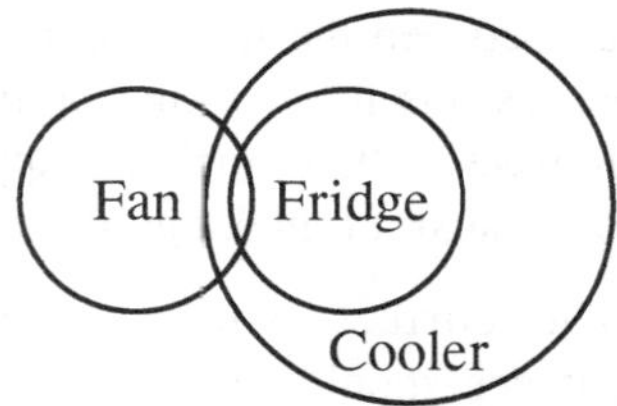

Conclusions:

I. All fans are fridge. (False)

II. No fans are fridge. (False)

Therefore, neither conclusion I nor II follows.

80. **(D):** From given statements:

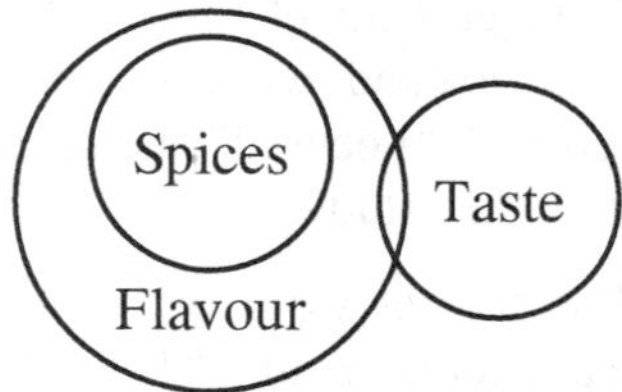

Conclusions:

I. No taste is spices. (True)

81. (C): (A) (B)

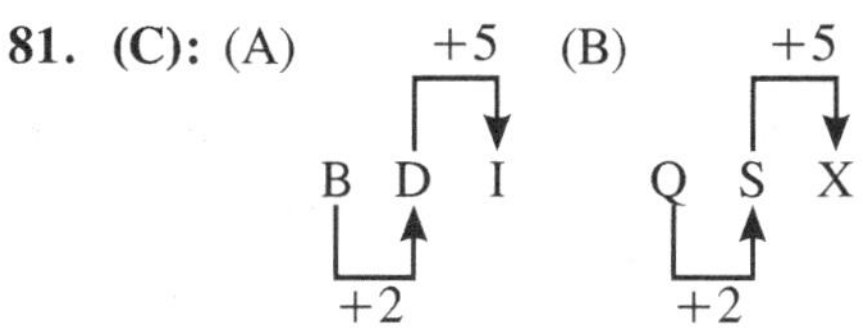

(C) (D)

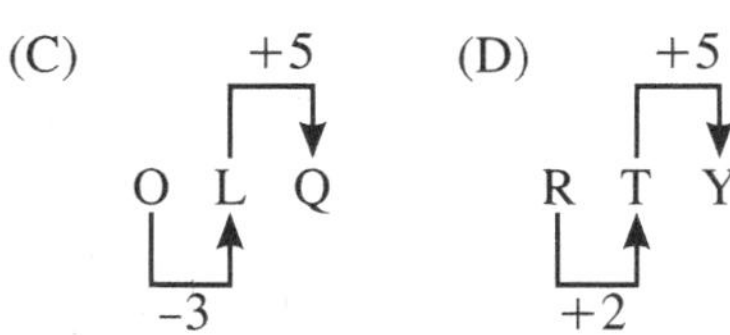

(E)

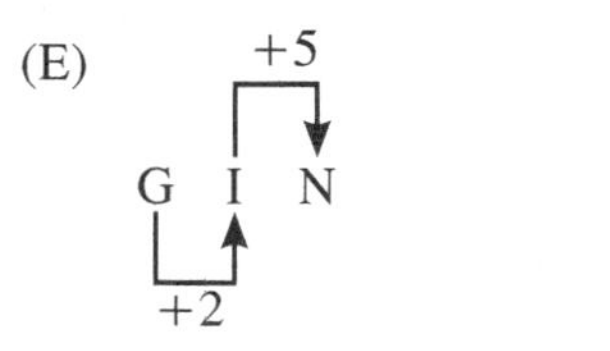

Option (C) is the odd one out.

For Qs. No. 82-86: From given information

8 persons sit around a square table:

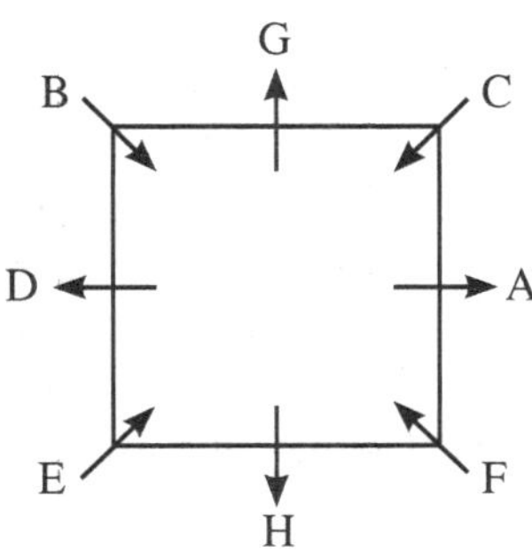

82. (D): 4 persons sit between G and E when counted from the right of G.

83. (C): A does not belong to the group, because face away from the centre.

84. (D): G and D face the same direction. (True)

85. (B): The position of one person remains unchanged. (Excluding (A)).

86. (A): The position of A is third to the left with respect to B.

87. (E): [7 % J, 6 # T, 7 β L, 3 μ Y].

88. (D): 4th number from left end = 2,

8th element to the right of 2 = Ω.

89. (C): Given all the numbers are dropped from given series.

So, 18th element from the right end = W.

90. (A): Sum = 7 + 6 + 7 + 3 = 23.

(91-95)

From given direction

In a certain code,

"Ram goes to school" = "rx gw ts mh" ...(*i*)

"He goes hospital" = "ez gw lp" ...(*ii*)

"He studies in school" = "ez yr ga mh" ...(*iii*)

"Ram works in hospital" = "rx kt ga lp" ...(*iv*)

91. (B): From (*i*) and (*iii*), we obtain,

"School" = mh

92. (D): From (*i*) and (*ii*)

"goes" = "gw"

From (*ii*) and (*iv*)

"hospital" = lp

∴ gw lp is code for word "goes hospital".

93. (C): From (*ii*) and (*iii*)

"He" = ez

From (*iii*) and (*iv*)

in = ga

From (*i*) and (*iii*)

"school" = mh

∴ "studies" = yr.

94. (A): From (*i*) and (*iv*)

Ram = rx and "works" = kt

95. (D): From (*i*) and (*iv*)

"Ram" = rx

96. (B): Given,

'6 3 1 5 7 8 4'

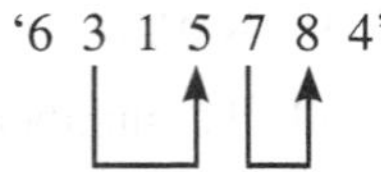

There are 2 such pair of digits (3&5, 7&8) in the given number, according to general numerical order.

97. (A): Meaningful four-letter word = FERN (a plant).

(98-100)

From given information,

March		May		June		July	
5th	20th	5th	20th	5th	20th	5th	20th
H	G	F	C	A	D	E	B

8 candidates have exam on 5th and 20th of four months among March, May, June and July.

98. (E): E has exam on 5th July.

99. (B): 4 persons have exam after C.

100. (C): (A) H — 5th March

(C) G — 20th March

(D) E — 5th July

(E) F — 5th May

As H, E & F have exam on 5th of every month & only G has on 20th of the month.

Hence, option (C) is the odd one.

101. (B): Non-profit MFIs are not regulated by the Reserve Bank of India (RBI). The RBI regulates financial institutions that engage in lending and deposit activities. Non-profit MFIs typically rely on grants and donations, and do not offer services like deposits that require RBI oversight.

102. (B): Co-operative societies do not come under the direct control of the RBI. The RBI regulates financial institutions that deal with monetary policy and financial stability. Co-operative societies are primarily governed by state laws and focus on community-based resources and benefits, not financial services regulated by the RBI.

103. (C): The National Stock Exchange of India (NSE) was established in 1992. It was set up to provide a modern, fully automated screen-based trading system with national reach. The NSE has played a crucial role in Indian financial markets, particularly in reforming the trading and settlement processes.

104. (D): More than one of the above. Reserve money, also known as high-powered money, includes several components such as RBI's net credit to the government, net forex reserves, and RBI's net credit to commercial banks. These elements contribute to the base level of money in the economy from which other forms of money are created.

105. (C): The functions of money include being a unit of value, a standard for deferred payment, a store of value, and a medium of exchange. Money enables consumers and businesses to measure the value of goods and services, save purchasing power for the future, and facilitate the exchange of goods and services.

106. (A): The Small Industries Development Bank of India (SIDBI) was established in 1990. SIDBI provides financial services to the small-scale industrial sector in India, helping small businesses and industries with loans, advances, and other financial services.

107. (B): Manmohan Singh is the only Prime Minister who has served as the Governor of the RBI. He held the position of RBI Governor during 1982 to 1985 before his political career, which later led to him becoming India's Prime Minister (2004-2014).

108. (D): The headquarters of the National Bank for Agriculture & Rural Development (NABARD) is located in Mumbai. NABARD is a key institution that provides finance and development assistance for agriculture and rural development in India.

109. (B): The minimum amount that can be remitted through Real Time Gross Settlement (RTGS) is ₹ 2,00,000. RTGS is used for large value transactions, and this minimum limit ensures the system is used for substantial transfers.

110. (B): 'M' in MCLR stands for Marginal. MCLR, or Marginal Cost of Funds based Lending Rate, is the minimum interest rate of a bank below which it cannot lend, except in some cases allowed by the RBI. It is designed to more accurately reflect the cost of funds for the bank.

111. (B): Purvanchal Co-operative Bank's license was recently cancelled by the RBI due to insufficient capital and poor earning prospects. This measure is often taken to protect depositors and ensure financial system stability when a bank's financial health deteriorates beyond viable correction measures.

112. (C): The purpose of the Reserve Bank of India imposing an incremental Cash Reserve Ratio (CRR) on banks during periods of excess liquidity is to absorb this excess liquidity. By requiring banks to hold a larger proportion of their deposits as reserves, the RBI can control excessive money flow, which could otherwise lead to inflation.

113. (C): The stamen is not a female reproductive part of a plant; it is actually the male reproductive part. The female parts of a plant are the stigma, style, and ovary, which together form the pistil.

114. (C): Charles Darwin propounded the theory of natural selection. This theory, central to evolutionary biology, describes the process whereby organisms better adapted to their environment tend to survive and produce more offspring.

115. (A): This scenario is best explained by Newton's first law of motion, which states that an object in motion will remain in motion unless acted upon by an external force. When the bus stops suddenly, the passenger's body continues to move forward due to inertia.

116. (A): Stocks are not considered debt instruments. Stocks represent equity ownership in a company, providing voting rights and dividends, unlike debt instruments like bonds and debentures which represent a loan made by an investor to a borrower.

117. (A): The activities of Non-Banking Financial Companies (NBFCs) are regulated by the Reserve Bank of India under the framework of the Reserve Bank of India Act, 1934, specifically chapters 10 to 12. These provisions outline the registration, operation, and regulation of NBFCs.

118. (B): The 'CGFMU' is a Credit Guarantee Fund established for guaranteeing loans given under the PMMY Scheme. This scheme aims to provide loans to micro-businesses and individual entrepreneurs to promote small business growth and employment.

119. (E): Oxigen Services and PayU India have been granted in-principle approval from the Reserve Bank of India to operate as Bharat Bill Payments Operating Units (BBPOUs). BBPOUs facilitate the payment of bills under an integrated and interoperable platform ensuring standardization across service providers.

120. (B): According to RBI guidelines, a scheduled commercial bank can own a stake in a payments bank up to the extent permitted under Section 19(2) of the Banking Regulation Act, 1949. This regulation ensures that the investments are managed within safe and permissible limits to avoid excessive risk concentration.

121. (C): 'LAF' stands for Liquidity Adjustment Facility. It is a tool used by the Reserve Bank of India to modulate the liquidity in the banking system. Banks can borrow money through repurchase agreements (repos) or park excess funds with the RBI in reverse repos.

122. (A): The Tarun Ramadorai panel set up by the RBI is focused on exploring the various facets of household finance in India. The aim is to enhance financial services penetration and promote better financial planning among Indian households.

123. (D): The statutory base for the Depositor Education and Awareness Fund (DEAF) constituted by the Reserve Bank of India is provided by Section 26A of the Banking Regulation Act, 1949. This section empowers the RBI to establish and manage the DEAF, which is used to enhance depositor education and fund claims against banks that fail.

124. (D): The India Aspiration Fund (IAF) is a fund of funds designed to invest in venture capital funds that meet the capital requirements of MSME start-ups. This initiative helps boost innovation and entrepreneurship in the Micro, Small and Medium Enterprises sector.

125. (D): Equity-linked Savings Scheme (ELSS) are open-ended diversified equity schemes offered by mutual funds. ELSS funds are popular for tax savings under Section 80C of the Income Tax Act, as they offer potential for higher returns through equity investments while saving on taxes.

126. (D): The 'D' in 'NSDL' stands for Depository. NSDL, or National Securities Depository Limited, provides services related to the handling of securities in dematerialized form in the Indian financial market, acting as a security depository.

127. (B): 'IFSC' stands for Indian Financial System Code. It is an alphanumeric code that facilitates electronic funds transfer within the country, used specifically to identify branches of banks participating in various online money transfer options like NEFT and RTGS.

128. (E): The Reserve Bank of India has authorized non-banks to operate White Label ATMs under the provisions of the Payment & Settlement Systems Act, 2007. This act provides the legal foundation for setting up and managing payment systems in India.

129. (A): ONICRA is a leading credit and performance rating agency. It provides rating services that assess the creditworthiness and operational performance of companies, helping investors and other stakeholders make informed decisions.

130. (D): Regulation of margin requirements on advances against agricultural commodities is not a general credit control measure. It is a specific control measure targeting a particular sector to manage the risk associated with lending against agricultural products. General measures include bank rate adjustments, open market operations, and variable reserve ratios.

131. (C): 'Hyper-inflation' describes an extreme inflationary situation where the price level increases so rapidly and excessively that the currency essentially becomes worthless. This scenario often leads to economic instability as the purchasing power of the currency collapses, forcing people to resort to barter systems or foreign currencies for transactions.

132. (A): Prathama Bank, the first Regional Rural Bank in India, was established in 1975 with its headquarters in Moradabad. It was sponsored by Syndicate Bank. This initiative was part of a national effort to provide banking services in rural areas to enhance financial inclusion.

133. (B): The Nobel Prize in Chemistry 2023 was awarded for the discovery and synthesis of quantum dots. Quantum dots are nanoscale semiconductor particles that have quantum mechanical properties, which can be used in various applications, including medical imaging and electronics.

134. (C): National Unity Day is celebrated on October 31st in memory of Sardar Vallabhbhai Patel, known as the Iron Man of India. This day commemorates his efforts in unifying the diverse states of the newly independent India into a single nation.

135. (C): Kamlang Tiger Reserve is located in Arunachal Pradesh. It is one of the key protected areas in the Northeast India region, providing habitat to a diverse array of wildlife, including tigers, under the Project Tiger initiative to conserve this endangered species.

136. (B): The headquarters of the International Atomic Energy Agency (IAEA) is located in Vienna, Austria. The IAEA is an international organization that promotes the peaceful use of nuclear energy and aims to prevent the use of nuclear energy for military purposes.

137. (C): In 2023, Pierre Agostini, Ferenc Krausz, and Anne L'Huillier were awarded the Nobel Prize in Physics. Their pioneering work has significantly contributed to the field of laser physics, advancing our understanding of light-matter interaction.

138. (A): Raghuram Rajan is the author of 'The Third Pillar - How Markets and the State Leave the Community Behind.' In this book, Rajan discusses the balance between markets, states, and communities in a global economy, emphasizing how the neglect of communities can lead to significant economic and social instability.

139. (E): Radha Krishna Mathur was appointed as the first Lieutenant Governor of Ladakh after its designation as a Union Territory in 2019. His appointment was part of the administrative reorganization following the bifurcation of Jammu and Kashmir into two separate Union Territories.

140. (C): Helsinki is the capital of Finland. It is the country's largest city and plays a significant role in Finland's political, educational, financial, cultural, and research activities, being a major global city in the Nordic region.

141. (C): Novak Djokovic won the men's singles title at the US Open 2023. His victory added another Grand Slam trophy to his collection, highlighting his enduring excellence and dominance in the sport of tennis.

142. (B): Kuchipudi is a classical dance form from Andhra Pradesh, not a folk dance. It originated in the village of Kuchipudi in the 17th century as a dance drama form, and it is known for its graceful movements and strong narrative character.

143. (B): The headquarters of the International Solar Alliance (ISA) is located in Gurugram, India.

ISA is an initiative jointly launched by India and France in 2015, aiming to promote solar energy among countries rich in sunlight.

144. (A): The first nuclear bomb during World War II was dropped on the city of Hiroshima on August 6, 1945. This historical event marked the first ever use of nuclear weapons and had devastating effects on the population and infrastructure of Hiroshima.

145. (D): Miraitowa is the official mascot of the Tokyo 2020 Olympic Games. The mascot represents modernity and tradition, with a name that combines the Japanese words for future and eternity, reflecting the enduring spirit of the Olympics.

146. (C): Sift Kaur Samra won the gold medal in the women's 50 m rifle 3 positions event at the Asian Games 2023. Her record score of 469.6 points set a new benchmark for excellence in this shooting discipline.

147. (A): Cloud Computing is an internet-based computing solution where shared resources, like servers, storage, and applications, are provided on demand to users over the internet. It enables organizations to use resources efficiently without the need for direct active management by users.

148. (C): The shortcut key for a manual line break in Microsoft Word is Shift + Enter. This key combination allows users to insert a line break into a document, which starts a new line without starting a new paragraph.

149. (B): The k-Means algorithm is a type of Unsupervised Learning algorithm used primarily for clustering. It involves partitioning n observations into k clusters in which each observation belongs to the cluster with the nearest mean, serving as a prototype of the cluster.

150. (C): LAN, WAN, and MAN stand for Local Area Network, Wide Area Network, and Metropolitan Area Network, respectively. These terms describe networks that cover different geographical areas, with LANs typically limited to a single building or site, WANs spanning broader geographical areas, and MANs usually encompassing a city.

Previous Paper (Solved)

IBPS—SPECIALIST OFFICERS

Law Officer and Rajbhasha Adhikari

Common Preliminary Exam, 2022*

ENGLISH LANGUAGE

Directions (Qs. No. 1-10): *Read the following passage carefully and answer the questions given below it. Certain words have been highlighted for your attention.*

Most people spend (on average) half of their day tapping away at their hand-held devices. Either, surfing the net or checking notifications. Facebook ranks the highest in all social networking platforms, followed by Twitter, Instagram and so forth.

Social media is addictive—which is why so many people are 'hooked'. Often referred to as **Social networking addiction**, this phrase is often used to describe someone who spends too much time on Facebook, Twitter, Instagram and other channels. A blog post, Instagram post, tweet, or YouTube video can be produced easily by anyone and shared, which can then be viewed by millions for free. Psychologists and scientists have now taken the time to study social media in terms of why they believe it interferes with aspects of our daily life. There is no official medical term that identifies addiction and social networking. It cannot be deemed as a disease or disorder as the cases are not severe and the habit can easily be maintained or prevented. Furthermore, instead of spending long periods of time on social media, we dip into and out of these sites all day long. We check for updates from friends and family as well as news and information. However, the behaviour associated with the excessive use of these channels has become the subject of much public and sociological debate. We actively post, like, comment and share personal posts. Not only that, we tend to share and reshare expressions (of either negative or positive) **contagiously**. But, why?

Scientists believed some years ago that, dopamine was simply a pleasure chemical in the brain. Recent studies have shown that; dopamine actually produces the desire in people to 'want' by drawing out the need for us to - seek and search. Creating the ultimate drive to find what is that what we want.

Dopamine is spontaneous. It's stimulated by unpredictability and small bits of information as well as reward cues which are the same conditions that social media presents to all users. In addition, the pull of dopamine is so strong that recent studies have shown that tweeting, for example, can be harder to resist than cigarettes and alcohol!

Researchers at Chicago University studied the effects of social media. They concluded quite quickly that people presented higher levels of addiction to social media than the need to smoke or drink. Media cravings ranked higher.

And, let's not forget oxytocin, many call it the cuddle chemical because the brain releases pleasure chemicals that transpire usually when you kiss and hug- or tweet. It is also known as the hormone that builds the strong yet unique bond between mothers and their babies. Oxytocin is now regarded as the

* Based on Memory.

human stimulant of empathy, generosity, trust, and more. These are factors which many advertisers and marketers play on when promoting a brand or business over social media.

Nevertheless, problems have arisen most commonly with school kids—whereby mobile phone devices have been **confiscated** because exam results have fallen severely due to lack of attention on homework or studies. Schools in many westernized countries have had to take drastic action - banning smartphones, iPad and most portable devices from school premises - as it is claimed to be a huge distraction. Whereas, other schools use it for educational purposes and as a rewards system for their pupils.

Research has also indicated unsurprisingly that Facebook is the most common activity that university students switch to, when studying. Worryingly, it has also found that those who most engage in this type of internet browsing tend to have lower levels of educational achievement.

Also, there have been many cases of students posting or sharing content that is unethical, which has caused parents and academic institutions to limit the use of these online networking channels.

1. Which is the most common activity that university students switch to when studying?
A. YouTube B. Facebook
C. Twitter D. WhatsApp
E. All of the above

2. Why is there no real medical term that identifies addiction and social networking?
A. Research is not yet done on the subject
B. It cannot be deemed as a disease or disorder as cases are not severe
C. The habit can easily be maintained or prevented
D. (A) and (B)
E. (B) and (C)

3. What stands true about Dopamine in the present scenario?
A. It creates the ultimate drive to find what is that what we want.
B. It's stimulated by unpredictability and small bits of information as well as reward cues.
C. Dopamine was simply a pleasure chemical in the brain
D. (A) and (B)
E. (B) and (C)

4. Why is Oxytocin regarded as the cuddle chemical?
A. The brain releases pleasure chemicals that transpire usually when you kiss and hug-or tweet.
B. It builds the strong yet unique bond between mothers and their babies.
C. It produces the desire in people to "want" by drawing out the need for us to - seek and search.
D. (A) and (B)
E. (B) and (C)

5. Which of the following words is the most similar in meaning to the word 'contagiously' as given in the passage?
A. Assail
B. Ambivalent
C. Arboreal
D. Malignant
E. Cogent

6. Which of the following words is the most opposite in meaning to the word 'confiscated' as given in the passage?
A. Cognizant B. Covet
C. Expiate D. Pithy
E. Relinquish

7. What were the conclusions taken out by the researchers at Chicago University on studying the effects of social media?
A. People presented higher levels of addiction to social media than the need to smoke or drink.
B. Levels of addiction of smoking and drinking were higher than that of media craving.
C. There was a higher rate of media cravings.
D. (A) and (B)
E. (A) and (C)

8. What actions are taken by schools for students regarding mobile phone devices as mentioned in the passage?
A. Punish students who bring mobile phones to schools.
B. Use it for educational purposes and as a rewards system for their pupils.
C. Banning smartphones, iPad and most portable devices from school premises
D. (A) and (B)
E. (B) and (C)

9. What does the phrase 'Social Networking Addiction' mean?
A. Stalking People Socially
B. Creating Fake profiles for fun
C. Finding your Friend Circle Online
D. Someone who spends too much time on social websites
E. Someone who is an introvert socially

10. Which of the below sentences summarizes the key idea of the passage?
A. The Psychology of Social Addiction
B. The Addiction in Students
C. The Science behind Addiction
D. Beliefs of Scientists for Social Life
E. None of the above

Directions (Qs. No. 11-15): *The following sentences form a paragraph. The sentences are—(a), (b), (c), (d), (e) and (f). Sentence (e) is fixed and its position cannot be changed. The rest of the sentences are not given in their proper order. Read the sentences and answer the following questions.*

(*a*) So a person that has integrity will act and behave as per set values and beliefs they hold dear.
(*b*) There is a famous saying which perfectly describes integrity.
(*c*) The word 'integrity' itself has a Latin origin.
(*d*) "Honesty is telling the truth to other people; integrity is telling the truth to myself."
(*e*) So it refers to the sense of completeness and togetherness one enjoys when they live their lives honestly and morally.
(*f*) It is derived from the word 'integer' and means to feel whole, i.e., a complete person.

11. Which sentence should be the sixth sentence in the paragraph?
A. (*f*) B. (*a*)
C. (*d*) D. (*c*)
E. (*b*)

12. Which sentence should be the fourth sentence in the paragraph?
A. (*f*) B. (*b*)
C. (*c*) D. (*d*)
E. (*a*)

13. Which sentence should be the third sentence in the paragraph?
A. (*a*) B. (*b*)
C. (*c*) D. (*d*)
E. (*f*)

14. Which sentence should be the second sentence in the paragraph?
A. (*b*) B. (*f*)
C. (*c*) D. (*a*)
E. (*d*)

15. Which sentence should be the first sentence in the paragraph?
A. (*a*) B. (*b*)
C. (*c*) D. (*d*)
E. (*f*)

Directions (Qs. No. 16-20): *In each of the questions given below, three words are given in bold. These three words may or may not be in their correct positions. The sentence is then followed by options with the correct combination of words that should replace each other in order to make the sentence grammatically and contextually correct. Find the correct combination of words that replace each other. If the sentence is correct as it is, select '(E)' as your option.*

16. Approved (*a*) on Saturday **said (*b*)** a third coronavirus vaccine for domestic use, Prime Minister Mikhail Mishustin **Russia (*c*)** on state TV.
A. (*a*)(*c*)(*b*) B. (*c*)(*a*)(*b*)
C. (*b*)(*a*)(*d*) D. (*a*)(*b*)(*c*)
E. None of the above

17. It is **mind** *(a)* that people should keep in **asserted** *(b)* the importance of adherence to COVID-19 appropriate **behaviour** *(c)*.

A. *(b)(a)(c)* B. *(c)(a)(b)*
C. *(a)(b)(c)* D. *(c)(b)(a)*
E. None of the above

18. The AstraZeneca company is going to **vaccine** *(a)* in Japan doses of the coronavirus **produce** *(b)* enough for 40 million **people** *(c)*, the executive director of the Japanese department of the firm said.

A. *(c)(a)(b)* B. *(a)(c)(b)*
C. *(a)(b)(c)* D. *(b)(a)(c)*
E. None of the above

19. The **received** *(a)* birthday party was the best **surprise** *(b)* Andrew could have **gift.** *(c)*

A. *(a)(b)(c)* B. *(b)(a)(c)*
C. *(b)(c)(a)* D. *(c)(a)(b)*
E. No rearrangement

20. The **blared** *(a)* parlour's owner **night** *(b)* really loud music all **tattoo** *(c)* long.

A. *(b)(c)(a)* B. *(a)(b)(c)*
C. *(c)(a)(b)* D. *(b)(a)(c)*
E. No rearrangement

Directions (Qs. No. 21-25): *Read the following sentence and determine whether there is an error in it. The error, if any, will be in one part of the sentence. If the sentence is error-free, then select 'No Error' as your answer.*

21. Psychiatrists feel that having a knowledge of (A) / the physical and mental changes that occurs in one's body (B) / and the reasons behind them (C) / have become essential for all teenagers. (D) / No error. (E)

22. As these books on science are (A) / published only in English, (B) / we seldom or ever (C) / find them in regional languages. (D) / No error. (E)

23. One evening of each week (A) / was set apart by him (B) / for the reception of whomsoever (C) / chose to visit him. (D) / No error (E)

24. Reports of researchers mysterious (A) / falling ill at the Wuhan Institute in late 2019, (B) / and other reports of a researcher (C) / who has reportedly gone missing. (D) / No Error (E)

25. Populist politics among the world has (A) / sought to privilege national sovereignty (B) / over universal values and commitments, (C) / slacking off efforts to tackle critical challenges that are transnational. (D) / No error (E)

Directions (Qs. No. 26-28): *Given below is a word, followed by three sentences that consist of that word. Identify the sentences(s) that best express(es) the meaning of the word.*

26. Wind

(a) That noise you can hear is the tape **winding** back.
(b) The blow to my stomach knocked the **wind** out of me.
(c) The sails flapped in the **wind**.

A. Only *(b)* B. *(a)* and *(c)*
C. *(b)* and *(c)* D. Only *(c)*
E. All of the above

27. Fellow

(a) He seemed like a decent **fellow**.
(b) He's a **fellow** of the Royal Institute of Chartered Surveyors.
(c) A member of staff was sacked for stealing from **fellow** employees.

A. Only *(a)* B. Only *(b)*
C. *(a)* and *(b)* D. *(a)* and *(c)*
E. All of the above

28. Ascent

(a) She made her first successful **ascent** of Everest last year.
(b) She nodded her **ascent** to the proposal.
(c) His **ascent** to power was rapid and unexpected.

A. Only *(c)* B. Only *(a)*
C. *(a)* and *(c)* D. *(b)* and *(c)*
E. None of the above

Directions (Qs. No. 29 & 30): *A sentence/part of the sentence is emboldened. Five alternatives are given to the embolden part which will improve the sentence. Choose the correct alternative and choose the option corresponding to it. In case no improvement is needed, click the option corresponding to 'No improvement required'.*

29. He slapped the team into action and they headed for the town at a **more leisure pace**.
A. many leisurely
B. many leisured
C. more leisure paced
D. more leisurely pace
E. No improvement required

30. Although both the United States and China are formidable world powers, **India should side with the later**.
A. India should side along the later
B. India should side with the latter
C. India should side along the latter
D. India should be siding with the later
E. No improvement required

Directions (Qs. No. 31-36): *Each question below has one blank, which is indicating that something has been omitted. Find out which option can be used to fill up the blank in the sentence in the same sequence to make it meaningfully complete.*

31. Homemade gifts can be completely __________ to what the recipient likes.
A. Alters B. Firmed
C. Tailored D. Polite
E. Liability

32. After much thought, Ted __________ not to travel abroad this summer.
A. Resolved B. Concludes
C. Resolves D. Commence
E. Passed

33. Bryan is ________ in his belief that the earth is flat.
A. Tentative B. Hasten
C. Unlikely D. Provided
E. Confident

34. The noodle maker was __________ in making his noodles and would never let another person take over the task.
A. Careless B. Negligent
C. Cautious D. Exciting
E. Inattentive

35. If it weren't for the ________ circumstances, he would have certainly lost his job.
A. Sharp B. Intensify
C. Mitigating D. Increase
E. Aggravate

36. When asked about her father, she lost her outward enthusiasm and became rather ________.
A. Reserved B. Expansive
C. Talkative D. Extrovert
E. Outgoing

Directions (Qs. No. 37-40): *In each of the questions given below four words are given in bold. These four words may or may not be in their correct position. The sentence is then followed by options with the correct combination of words that should replace each other in order to make the sentence grammatically and contextually correct. Find the correct combination of the words that replace each other. If the sentence is correct as it then select option E as your choice.*

37. Some American officials **lead** (A) to hope that **resumed** (B) sanctions on Iran will **appear** (C) to a popular **uprising** (D).
A. A-B B. A-C
C. B-D and A-C D. A-D
E. The sentence is correct

38. **Tariffs** (A) has **imported** (B) higher **China** (C) on 603 items **imposed** (D) from the US.
A. Only A-B
B. Only B-C
C. Both A-B and B-D
D. Both A-C and B-D.
E. The sentence is correct.

39. NATO ally **world** (A) leads the **Turkey** (B) in the **journalists** (C) of **number** (D) jailed.
A. A-B and C-D B. Only B-C
C. A-C and B-D D. A-D
E. The sentence is correct.

40. In 2016, **rising** (A) violence in **Pathankot** (B) by Islamic militants **culminated** (C) in attacks on Indian forces at Uri and **Kashmir** (D).
A. Both A-C and B-D
B. Both A-D and B-C
C. Only B-D
D. C-D
E. The sentence is correct.

Directions (Qs. No. 41-44): *Read each sentence to find out whether there is any grammatical or idiomatic error in it. The error, if any, will be in one part of the sentence. The number of that part is the answer. If there is 'No error', the answer is (E). (Ignore errors of punctuation, if any.)*

41. She held something (A)/ at her side which (B)/ was totally hiding (C)/ by the folds of her sari. (D)/ No error. (E)

42. The father forbade his son (A)/ to walk in the sun (B)/and play with (C)/ his friends on the road (D) / No error. (E)

43. The movement, which aims to (A)/ raise awareness about climate change, hopes (B)/ to bring people together to think about (C)/ what they can do for reduce harmful pollution. (D)/ No error (E)

44. I declined the invitation (A)/ not because I did not (B)/ want to go but (C)/ because I have no time.(D)/ No error (E)

Directions (Qs. No. 45-50): *In the following passage, some of the words have been left out, each of which is indicated by a number. Find the suitable word from the options given against each number and fill up the blanks with appropriate words to make the paragraph meaningfully complete.*

Stanford economist Nicholas Bloom is a true believer, and like many true believers, he lets his message __**(45)** __ his evidence. Based on a single study of a Chinese travel agency, he __**(46)** __ declares working from home a "future-looking technology" with "enormous potential." Not so fast. Bloom's study comes with serious limitations and is contradicted by a later Gallup report. However, while it is far too soon to draw broad __**(47)** __ from his findings, savvy business leaders can read between the lines and extract some valuable lessons for working __**(48)** __ with all employees.

Bloom __**(49)** __ on China's biggest travel agency, Ctrip, which wanted to expand while controlling office space costs. They __**(50)** __ a remote work trial, expecting that productivity would slip a little, but not enough to cancel out the savings. Instead, productivity shot up 13%, and attrition dropped 50%. When the work from home option was rolled out to the entire company and employees were given a choice, the productivity gains were 22%.

45. A. cut B. outrun C. exceeded D. begin E. choose

46. A. fast B. enthusiastically C. slowly D. eager E. appropriately

47. A. resulting B. disappointments C. conclusions D. exercises E. guarantees

48. A. optimally B. extremely C. competitively D. abroad E. everywhere

49. A. emphasising B. concentrates C. learned D. matched E. focused

50. A. establishes B. appointed C. brought D. instituted E. sold

REASONING

Directions (Qs. No. 51 and 52): *Study the following information carefully and answer the questions given below:*

R is married to U. U is the mother of L. L is the sister of D. U has only one daughter. D is married to J. K is the son of J. F is the mother of J.

51. How is D related to F?
A. Cannot be determined
B. Daughter
C. Daughter-in-law
D. Son-in-law
E. Son

52. How is R related to K?
A. Cannot be determined
B. Grandfather
C. Grandmother
D. Father
E. Uncle

Directions (Qs. No. 53-55): *Study the following information carefully and answer the questions given below:*

Each of the six buildings P, Q, R, S, T and U houses different number of offices. S has more offices than only T and R. Q has more number of offices than P but less than U. R does not house the least number of offices. The building which houses the least number of offices has 5 offices. The building which has second highest number of offices has 23 offices. S has 11 less number of offices than Q.

53. Which of the following buildings has the second least number of offices?
A. Q B. U
C. R D. P
E. T

54. The number of offices in P is an even number which is divisible by 2 as well as 3. How many offices does P have?
A. 20 B. 24
C. 16 D. 18
E. 12

55. Which of the following is the number of offices in the building R?
A. 25 B. 12
C. 13 D. 14
E. 11

Directions (Qs. No. 56-60): *Study the following information carefully and answer the questions given below:*

Seven persons, P, Q, R, S, T, U and V have a seminar but not necessarily in the same order, on seven different months (of the same year) namely Junuary, February. March, June, August, October and December. Each of them also likes a different fruit namely Banana, Grapes, Papaya, Orange, Mango, Litchi and Apple but not necessarily in the same order.

R has a seminar in a month which has less than 31 days. Only two persons have a seminar between R and S. The one who likes Banana has a seminar immediately before T. Only one person has a seminar before the one who likes Papaya. Q has a seminar immediately after the one who likes Papaya. Only three persons have a seminar between Q and the one who likes Mango. T likes neither Mango nor Papaya. P has a seminar immediately before T. V likes Apple. The one who likes Grapes has a seminar in the month, which has less than 31 days. The one who has a seminar in March does not like Orange.

56. Which of the following represents the month in which S has a seminar?
A. January
B. Cannot be determined
C. October
D. December
E. June

57. Which of the following represents the people who have a seminar in January and June respectively?
A. V, S B. U, S
C. Q, T D. U, R
E. V, R

58. How many persons have a seminar between the months in which V and R have a seminar?
A. None B. Three
C. Two D. One
E. More than three

59. As per the given arrangement, R is related to Banana and P is related to Orange following a certain pattern, with which of the following is U related to following the same pattern?
A. Mango B. Litchi
C. Apple D. Papaya
E. Grapes

60. Which of the following fruits, does U like?
A. Papaya B. Mango
C. Banana D. Grapes
E. Orange

Directions (Qs. No. 61-65): *Study the following information carefully and answer the questions given below:*

Ten persons are sitting in two parallel rows containing five persons each, in such a way that there is equal distance between adjacent persons. In row—1. J, K, L, M and N are seated (not necessarily in the same order) and all of them are facing south. In row—2. V, W, X, Y and Z are seated (not necessarily in the same order) and all of them are facing north. Therefore in the given seating arrangement each member seated in row faces another member of the other row.

Z sits third to the right of W. V sits second to the left of Z. The person facing V sits to the immediate right of K. Only one person sits between K and M. J is not an immediate neighbour of K. Only two persons sit between J and L. Neither K nor J faces Y.

61. Who amongst the following is facing N?
A. Y B. V
C. X D. W
E. Z

62. Which of the following statements is true regarding M?
A. M faces one of the immediate neighbours of X
B. K is one of the immediate neighbours of M
C. None of the given statements is true
D. L sits to the immediate right of M
E. Only one person sits between M and N

63. Who amongst the following is facing X?
A. K B. L
C. M D. J
E. N

64. What is the position of Z with respect to Y?
A. Third to the right
B. Second to the right
C. Immediate left
D. Immediate right
E. Second to the left

65. Four of the following five are alike in a certain way based on the given arrangement and hence form a group. Which of them does not belong to that group?
A. M B. J
C. Y D. W
E. N

Directions (Qs. No. 66-70): *In each of the question given below two/three statements followed by two Conclusions numbered I and II have been given. You have to take the two/three given statements to be true even if they seem to be at variance from commonly known facts and then decide which of the given Conclusions logically follows from the given statements disregarding commonly known facts.*

Give answer—
A. if only Conclusion II follows
B. if only Conclusion I follows
C. if both the Conclusion I and Conclusion II follow
D. if either Conclusion I or Conclusion II follows
E. if neither Conclusion I nor Conclusion II follows

66. Statements : All races are sprints.
Some races are contests.
Conclusion : I. Some contests are sprints.
II. All contest are sprints.

67. Statements : No bank is a locker.
All banks are stores.
No store is panel.
Conclusion : I. No store is a locker.
II. No panel is a bank.

68-69. Statements: Some strikes are hits.
No strike is a raid.
All attacks are raids.

68. Conclusion : I. Some hits are definitely not raids.
II. All hits being strikes is a possibility.

69. Conclusion : I. No attack is a strike.
II. All attacks being hits is a possibility.

70. Statements : Some equations are formulae.
All equations are terms.
All terms are symbols.
Conclusion : I. All equations are symbols.
II. No symbol is a formula.

Directions (Qs. No. 71-75): *Study the following information carefully and answer the questions given below:*

In a certain code language,

'festival for woman only' is written as 'pa ge bo xu'

'provide peace to women' is written as 'wr dl nj ge'

'women like to celebrate' is written as 'ge ct fx wr'

'celebrate peace in festival' is written as 'dl bo sv ct'

(All codes are two letter codes only)

71. What may be the possible code for 'provide idea' in the given code language?

A. fx hy B. xu bo
C. hy nj D. nj xu
E. wr fx

72. What is the code for 'celebrate' in the given code language?

A. ct B. wr
C. sv D. dl
E. fx

73. In the given code language what does the code 'pa' stand for?

A. peace
B. either 'for' or 'only'
C. either 'women' or 'to'
D. celebrate
E. festival

74. What is the code for 'women' in the given code language?

A. bo
B. xu
C. ct
D. Other than those given as options
E. ge

75. If 'peace to mind' is coded as 'zg wr dl' in the given code language, then what is the code for 'mind in festival'?

A. zg bo dl B. dl zg sv
C. zg nj wr D. bo sv zg
E. sv wr bo

Directions (Qs. No. 76-80): *In each of the following questions relationship between different elements is shown in the statements. The statements are followed by two Conclusions numbered I and II. Study the Conclusions based on the given statements and select the appropriate answer.*

Give answer—

A. if only Conclusion II is true
B. if only Conclusion I is true
C. if both the Conclusion I and Conclusion II are true
D. if either Conclusion I or Conclusion II is true
E. if neither Conclusion I nor Conclusion II is true

(76-77): Statements : $S \le L \le I = P \ge E > R; L > Q$

76. Conclusions : I. $P \ge S$ II. $I > R$

77. Conclusions : I. $L < R$ II. $E \ge Q$

(78-79): Statements : $G > R \ge E = A \le T \le S;$ $D \le A \le J$

78. Conclusions : I. $T \ge D$ II. $R > S$

79. Conclusions : I. $J > E$ II. $J = E$

80. Statements : $A \ge B > C \le D \le E < F$
Conclusions : I. $A \ge E$ II. $C < F$

Directions (Qs. No. 81-85): *Study the following information carefully and answer the questions given below:*

Ten person — J, K, L, M, N, O, P, Q, R and S — are sitting around a circular table facing the centre with equal distances between each other (but not necessarily in the same order). Each one of them is also related to M in some way or the other.

Only two persons sit between Q and L. M sits second to the left of Q. Only three persons sit between L and M's sister. M's son sits second to the right of M's sister.

Only one person sits between M's son and S. J sits to the immediate right of R. R is neither the son nor the mother of M.

S is an immediate neighbour of M's mother. Only three persons sit between M's mother and M's brother. M's daughter sits second to the left of M's brother.

M's father is not an immediate neighbour of M. M's wife sites third to the right of K. L is to the right of Q. Only four persons sits between M and M's father.

81. Who sits second to the right of R?
A. M's brother
B. M
C. R
D. N
E. M's daughter

82. How many persons sit between K and L, when counted from the left of K?
A. Six
B. One
C. None
D. Two
E. Four

83. Which of the following statements is true with respect to the given information?
A. R sits second to the right of M's wife.
B. K is an immediate neighbour of R.
C. M sits second to the left of L.
D. All the given options are true.
E. S is the daughter of L.

84. How is K related to R?
A. Son-in-law
B. Uncle
C. Brother
D. Niece
E. Daughter

85. Who amongst the following is the wife of M?
A. J
B. L
C. O
D. Q
E. N

Directions (Qs. No. 86 to 90): *Read the following information carefully and answer the questions given below.*

L, M, N, O, P, Q and R are seven employees who are working in the same company. They attend meeting in different department viz; Administrative, Security, Finance and HR department on different days from Monday to Sunday but not necessarily in the same order. One employee attends only one meeting and only one meeting is held on each day. There are two employees who attend meeting in administrative, security, HR department and only one employee attends meeting in Finance department.

L attends meeting on Thursday. There are two persons who attend meeting between L and the person who attends meeting in HR department. There are three persons who attend meeting between the persons who attend meeting in Administrative department and the one who attends meeting in Finance department. The one who attends meeting in administrative department attends before the one who attends in finance department. The one who attends meeting in finance department does not attend on Saturday. The number of persons who attend meeting between L and the one who attend meeting in finance department is same as the number of persons who attend meeting between O and the one who attends meeting in security department. The one who attends meeting in security department attend before O. O does not attend meeting in HR department. Q attends meeting on the day immediately before the day on which L attends meeting. O does not attend meeting on the day just after the day on which L attends meeting. The number of persons who attend meeting between L and P is same as the number of persons who attend meeting between L and R. P attends meeting in one of the day before the day on which R attends meeting. N attends meeting in administrative department. R does not attend meeting in security department.

86. Who among the following person attend meeting on Friday?
A. O
B. M
C. P
D. N
E. R

87. Which of the following combinations of "Person – Day" is true with respect to the given arrangement?
A. R – Friday
B. M – Saturday
C. Q – Thursday
D. P – Friday
E. P – Tuesday

88. L attends meeting in which of the following department?
A. Security
B. HR
C. Administrative
D. Finance
E. Either (A) or (B)

89. In this arrangement, Q is related to Monday, L is related to Security then N is related to?
A. Thursday

B. Wednesday
C. None of the given options is true
D. HR
E. Sunday

90. How many persons attend meeting between P and O?
A. 3 B. 4
C. 2 D. 1
E. None of these

Directions (Qs. No. 91 to 95): *Study the following information and answer the given questions:*

A, B, C, D, E, F, G & H are eight friends and sitting around a circular table but not necessarily in same order. Some of them are facing inside and some of them are facing outside. A sits third to right of H. There is two people sits between H and B. C sits second to left of B. There is three people sits between B and E. D is second to left of F, who is not immediate neighbour of A. Immediate neighbours of H faces same direction as H. F sits third to left of A, who faces centre. The immediate neighbours of A face opposite to the direction of A.

91. Who is sitting third to right of F?
A. C B. B
C. A D. E
E. D

92. Who is facing inside?
A. AD B. AGH
C. AB D. ADC
E. None of these

93. Who sits opposite to H?
A. A B. D
C. F D. E
E. G

94. How many people are sitting between C and B, when counted from left of C?
A. Two B. Three
C. One D. Four
E. Five

95. Who is sitting exactly between D and C when counted from right of D?
A. HE B. CE
C. FH D. BF
E. DF

Directions (Qs. No. 96 and 97): *Read the following information carefully to answer the given questions.*

A certain number of persons are seated in a row. The Row is arranged in a vertical manner and all are facing to north direction. Ranjan sits fourth from the left end of the row. There are two persons sit between Ranjan and Seema. Puja sits immediate right of Seema. There are as many persons sit between Puja and Seema as sit between Dinesh and Pooja. Dinesh does not sit to the left of Ranjan.

96. What is the position of Puja with respect to Ranjan?
A. Immediate right B. Third to the left
C. None of these D. Second to the left
E. Fourth to the right

97. How many persons sit in a row?
A. 4 B. 6
C. 0 D. 11
E. 9

Directions (Qs. No. 98 to 100): *Read the following information carefully to answer the given questions.*

There are six persons S, T, U, V, W and X, who got different marks in the examination. S got more marks than only U and X. T got less marks than W, who did not get the highest marks in the examination. The Second highest person got 92 marks.

98. How many persons got more marks than U?
A. Four
B. Two
C. Five
D. Can't be determined
E. One

99. If S got 69 marks and U got 68 marks, then which of the following statement is true?
A. X got the lower marks.
B. U got the fifth highest marks.
C. Five persons got more marks than X
D. All are true
E. X got 66 marks is a possibility

100. V got which of the following possible score?
A. 85 B. 66
C. 92 D. 89
E. 94

GENERAL AWARENESS

101. An account for which a bank acts as an uninterested third party is termed as?

A. Savings Account
B. Current Account
C. Reserve Account
D. Escrow Account
E. Fixed Account

102. A signed undertaking from one party containing a promise to pay a stated sum to a specified person or a company is known as _________

A. Power of Attorney
B. Promissory Note
C. Purchasing Power Parity
D. Plastic Notes
E. None of the given options is true

103. Which of the following is defined as the difference between current assets and current liabilities?

A. Venture Capital
B. Working Capital
C. Equitable Mortgage
D. Loss Assets
E. Profit and Loss Account

104. Who has won women's single title in US open 2019 and has become youngest and first ever from Canada to win this title?

A. Bianca Andreescu
B. Svetlana Kuznetsova
C. EliseMertens
D. Belinda Bencic
E. None of these

105. Which film won the "Golden Lion for Best Film" in the 76th edition of the annual Venice International Film Festival Awards for 2019?

A. Lion King
B. Avengers : Endgame
C. Joker
D. J'accuse
E. None of these

106. Abhishek Nayar is associated to which sports?

A. Football
B. Cricket
C. Volleyball
D. Wrestling
E. None of these

107. _________ is the rate at which commercial bank needs to maintain in the form of cash, or gold or government approved securities (Bonds) before providing credit to its customers.

A. Reverse Repo Rate
B. Repo Rate
C. CRR Rate
D. SLR Rate
E. Bank Rate

108. Which organization has released the draft guidelines to modify the loan system for delivery of bank credit, making the rules stricter to regulate larger borrowers enjoying working capital facility from the banking system?

A. RBI
B. SEBI
C. NABARD
D. SBI
E. Finance Ministry

109. CAG of India is an authority, established by Article 148 of the Constitution of India. CAG Stands for _______.

A. Comptroller and Auditor General of India
B. Constant and Author General of India
C. Constant Auditor General of India
D. Central Auditor General of India
E. None of the given options is true

110. Under which act National Housing Bank was set up as an apex institute of housing finance in the country?

A. National Housing Bank Act, 1986
B. National Housing Bank Act, 1987
C. National Housing Bank Act, 1988
D. National Housing Bank Act, 1989
E. None of these

111. Scheduled commercial bank can take equity stake in a payments bank to the extent permitted under Section 19 (2) of the:
A. Indian Societies Registration Act, 1860
B. Banking Regulation Act, 1949
C. Reserve Bank of India Act, 1934
D. Companies Act, 1956
E. Securities and Exchange Board of India Act, 1992

112. Senior Citizen Saving Scheme (SCSS) is exclusively meant for people over the age of 60 years. They shall come into force on:
A. August 2004 B. August 2002
C. August 2010 D. August 2008
E. August 2006

113. Bihu dance is famous in which state?
A. Odisha B. Assam
C. West Bengal D. Manipur
E. None of these

114. Name the First Indian bank to open branch outside India in London in 1946.
A. Union Bank of India
B. State Bank of India
C. Central Bank of India
D. Bank of India
E. None of these

115. Periyar National Park is located in which state?
A. Kerala B. Tamil Nadu
C. Andhra Pradesh D. Telangana
E. None of these

116. Name the player who beat Carolina Marin in Denmark Badminton Open 2020 to lift women's single title.
A. Sayaka Hirota
B. Yuki Fukushima
C. Misaki Matsutomo
D. Akane Yamaguchi
E. Nozomi Okuhara

117. Which country has won the Visvesvaraya award of the ISA Solar Awards 2020 from the Asia Pacific region?
A. Japan B. India
C. Singapore D. Australia
E. China

118. What is theme of World Osteoporosis Day 2020?
A. Love Your Bones - protect your future
B. THAT'S OSTEOPOROSIS
C. Strong Women Make Stronger Women
D. Serve up Bone Strength
E. Real Men Build Their Strength from Within

119. With which of the following is SARFAESI Act 2002 related _______ .
A. Recovery of bad loans
B. Regulation of foreign exchange
C. Fixation of interest rates
D. Fixation of base rate
E. None of these

120. The payments bank will be registered as a public limited company under the Companies Act, 2013, and licensed under Section _______ of the Banking Regulation Act, 1949.
A. Section 21 B. Section 22
C. Section 11 D. Section 16
E. None of these

121. According to Insurance (Amendment) Bill, 2021; Foreign Direct Investment (FDI) limit increased from 49 to _______ %.
A. 51% B. 74%
C. 81% D. 69%
E. None of these

122. Life Insurance Corporation of India (LIC) is the _______ strongest brand and _______ most valuable insurance brand globally as per the 'Insurance 100 2021' report by London-based consultancy firm Brand Finance.
A. 2nd, 7th B. 1st, 10th
C. 3rd, 10th D. 1st, 4th
E. None of these

123. Which of the following is the first life insurance company in India?
A. Life Insurance Corporation of India
B. United India Life Insurance Company
C. Bombay Mutual Life Assurance Society
D. National Insurance of India
E. None of these

124. When was the first time RBI issued Currency Notes?
A. January 1939 B. February 1949
C. April 1936 D. January 1938
E. January 1947

125. Who has been received the Indian Council for Cultural Relations (ICCR) Distinguished Indologist award for 2021?
A. Alice Boner
B. Prasanna Kumar
C. Maurice Bloomfield
D. Jeffrey Armstrong
E. Heinrich Freiherr Von Stietencron

126. Teachers' Day or Shikshak Divas marks the birthday of the country's first Vice President (1952-1962) __________ .
A. V.V. Giri
B. Zakir Hussain
C. Dr Sarvapalli Radhakrishnan
D. Gopal Swarup Pathak
E. Mohanmmad Hidayatullah

127. NaBFID, the new bank which is proposed to be set up, is to finance which sector?
A. Agriculture B. Infrastructure
C. MSMEs D. Fishery
E. None of these

128. What is India's rank in the 2020 Democracy Index?
A. 53 B. 57
C. 61 D. 67
E. None of these

129. "FutureSkills Prime" is a Digital Skill Development initiative of NASSCOM in association with which ministry?
A. Ministry of Education
B. Ministry of Skill Development
C. Ministry of Electronics and IT
D. Ministry of Home Affairs
E. None of these

130. World Anti-Doping Agency (WADA) restored the accreditation of National Dope Testing Laboratory (NDTL). Where is the headquarters of World Anti-Doping Agency (WADA)?
A. Montreal, Canada
B. Lausanne, Switzerland
C. Washington, D.C., United States
D. Kuala Lumpur, Malaysia
E. Munich, Germany

131. Recently, which of the following bank has announced the launch of 'Green Fixed Deposits'?
A. IndusInd Bank B. Axis Bank
C. ICICI Bank D. HDFC Bank
E. SBI Bank

132. Section 142 of the Social Security Code, 2020 is associated with which document?
A. PAN Card
B. MGNREGA Identity Card
C. Aadhar Card
D. NFSA Beneficiary Card

133. The General Insurance (Amendment) Act, 2021 removes the provision which required the Central Government to have atleast _____ ownership in four subsidiaries of General Insurance Company, namely, National Insurance, New India Assurance, Oriental Insurance, United India Insurance.
A. 75% B. 49%
C. 51% D. 80%
E. 74%

134. What are White Label ATMs (WLAs)?
A. ATMs set up, owned and operated by non-banks are called WLAs
B. ATMs set up, owned and operated by foreign financial institution in India are called WLAs
C. ATMs set up, owned and operated by RBI are called WLAs
D. Both (A) and (C)
E. None of these

135. ________ is a legal declaration of a person who is unable to pay off debts.
A. Bankruptcy
B. Credit Crunch
C. Amortisation
D. Bancassurance
E. None of these

136. Which of the following is NOT an instrument of RBI's monetary policy?
A. CRR
B. MSP
C. Repo Rate
D. LAF
E. SLR

137. 'Human Rights Day' is observed on _______.
A. 10 December
B. 9 December
C. 10 November
D. 10 October
E. None of these

138. In March, 2019 the merger of Bank of Baroda, Vijaya Bank and _______ has beed proposed.
A. Dena Bank
B. Bank of India
C. Canara Bank
D. Punjab National Bank
E. None of these

139. In banking sector GNPA refers to?
A. Gross Non-performing Advances
B. Gross National Performing Assets
C. Gross National Productive Assets
D. Gratuitous Non-performing Advances
E. None of these

140. On what does the dollar-rupee exchange rate in India depend?
A. Demand-supply equilibrium
B. Monetary Policy of RBI
C. Government control
D. The stock market fluctuations
E. None of these

141. Please provide the full form for CGTMSE, a scheme meant for Micro and Small Enterprises:
A. Credit Guarantee Trust for Micro and Small Enterprises,
B. Credit Guarantee Fund Trust for Micro and Small Enterprises
C. Credit Guarantee Fund towards Micro and Small Enterprises
D. Collateral Guarantee Trust for Micro and Small Enterprises
E. None of these

142. Consider the following statements about a classical dance form
(*a*) Tribhanga is a special feature of this dance.
(*b*) The torso movement is very important and is a unique feature of this dance.
(*c*) Many of today's Gurus of this style belong to the Gotipua tradition.

Identify the classical dance form using the above clues.
A. Kuchipudi B. Odissi
C. Sattriya D. Kathakali
E. None of these

143. Which of the following organization has decided to formulate Digital Payment Index?
A. NITI Aayog
B. Reserve Bank of India
C. Ministry of Finance
D. SEBI
E. None of these

144. If the Balance of Payment of a country is adverse, then which institution will help that country?
A. World Bank
B. World Trade Organization
C. International Monetary Fund
D. Asian Development Bank
E. None of these

145. Who translated the book 'The Story of My Experiments with Truth' written by M.K. Gandhi from Gujarati to English?
A. Mahadev Desai
B. J. B. Kripalani
C. Mohanlal Pandya
D. Vinoba Bhave
E. None of these

146. The world's first Yoga University outside India — 'Vivekananda Yoga University' was launched on 23rd June 2020 in which city?
A. New York
B. London
C. Berlin
D. Los Angeles
E. None of these

147. Which of the following indigenous sports has not been included in Khelo India Youth Games 2021?
A. Kalaripayattu
B. Gatka
C. Thang-Ta
D. Vallamkali
E. None of these

148. Which author and natural historian has been confered with Indira Gandhi Peace Prize 2019?
A. Ela Bhatt
B. David Attenborough
C. Wangari Maathai
D. Sadoko Ogata
E. None of these

149. In contrast to what was previously recognized by Nepal, the height of Mt. Everest has now been found to be higher by how many centimetres?
A. 85 cm
B. 84 cm
C. 86 cm
D. 88 cm
E. None of these

150. State Financial Corporations mainly give assistance to develop which of the following?
A. Small and medium scale industries
B. Agricultural farms
C. Cotton industry
D. Large scale industries
E. None of these

ANSWERS

1. (B)	2. (E)	3. (D)
4. (A)	5. (D)	6. (E)
7. (E)	8. (E)	9. (D)
10. (A)	11. (B)	12. (A)
13. (C)	14. (E)	15. (B)
16. (B)	17. (A)	18. (D)
19. (C)	20. (C)	21. (B)
22. (C)	23. (C)	24. (A)
25. (A)	26. (E)	27. (E)
28. (C)	29. (D)	30. (B)
31. (C)	32. (A)	33. (E)
34. (C)	35. (C)	36. (A)
37. (B)	38. (D)	39. (A)
40. (C)	41. (C)	42. (E)
43. (D)	44. (D)	45. (B)
46. (B)	47. (C)	48. (A)
49. (E)	50. (D)	

For Qs. No. 51-52.

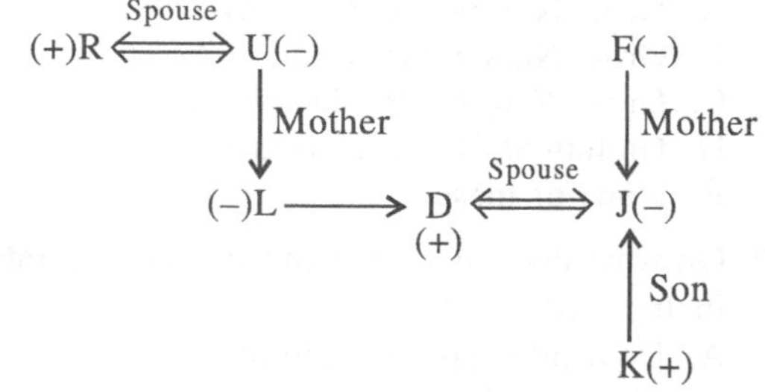

51. (D) 52. (B)

For Qs. No. 53-55.

Arrangement of six building (houses) according to decreasing number of offices.

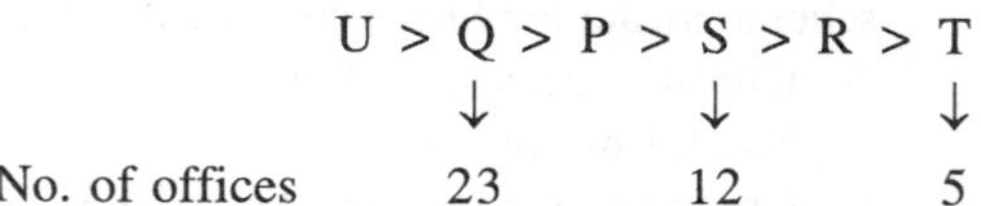

53. **(C):** R has second least no. of offices.

54. **(D):** Even number between 12 and 23 which is divisible by 2 and 3 is 18.

55. **(E):** Number of offices in building R should be less than 12 but greater than 5.

For Qs. No. 56-60.

Based on question, we have:

Months	Fruit	Person
January	Apple	V
February	Papaya	U
March	Litchi	Q
June	Grapes	R
August	Banana	P
October	Orange	T
December	Mango	S

56. (D) **57. (E)** **58. (C)**

59. (B) **60. (A)**

For Qs. No. 61-65.

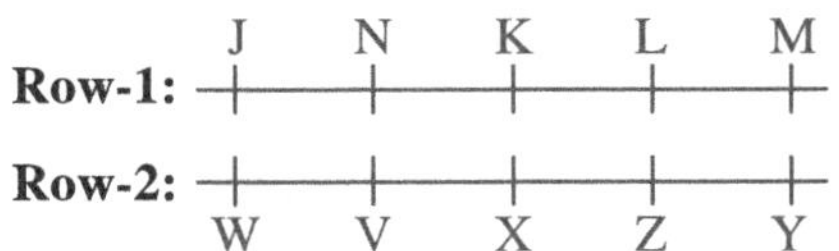

61. (B) **62. (D)** **63. (A)**

64. (C) **65. (E)**

66. (B):

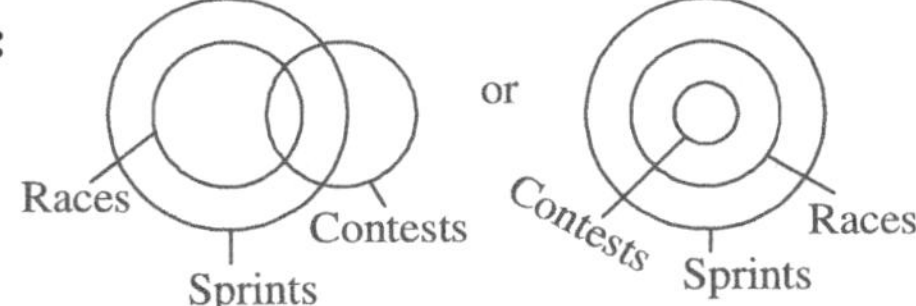

67. (A):

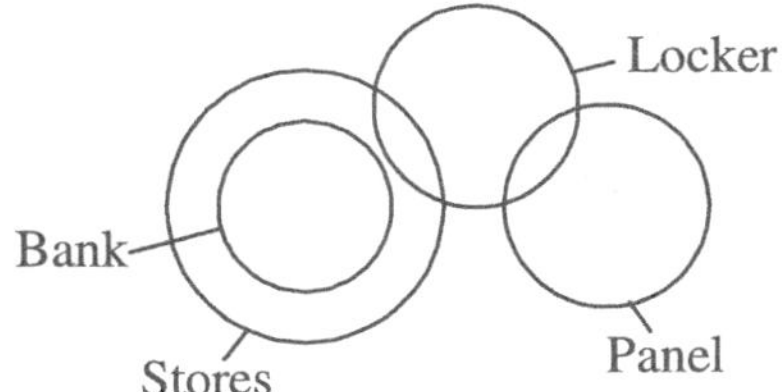

68. (C):

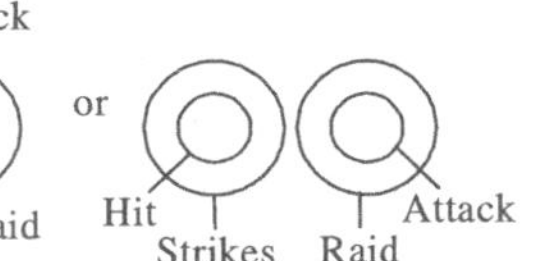

69. (C):

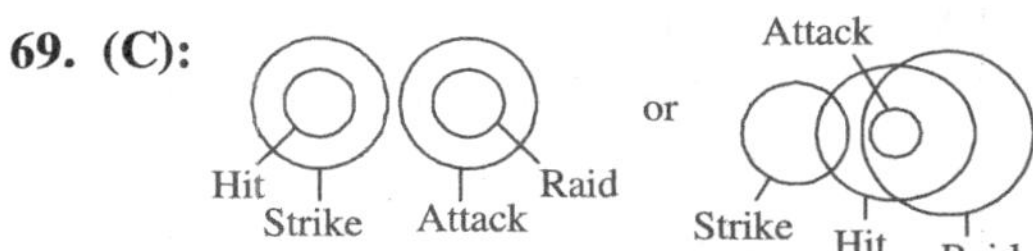

70. (B):

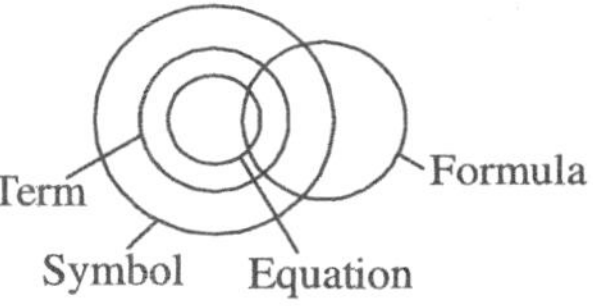

For Qs. No. 71-75.

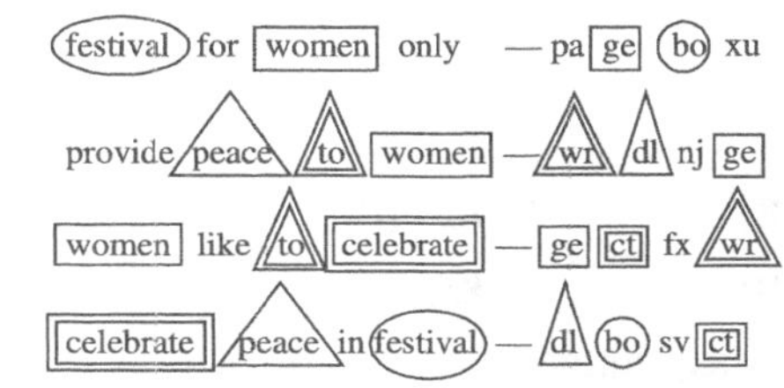

71. (C): 'hy' code is not used in this question so, 'hy' is the code for the word 'idea'.

72. (A) **73. (B)** **74. (E)**

75. (D)

76. (C): I. $P = I \geq L \geq S$

$\Rightarrow P \geq S$ (True).

II. $I = P \geq E > R$

$\Rightarrow I > R$ (True).

77. (E): I. $L \leq I = P \geq E > R$

$\Rightarrow$ No relation between L and R.

$\therefore L < R$ (False)

II. $Q < L \leq I = P \geq E$

$\Rightarrow$ No relation between Q and E.

$\therefore E \geq Q$ (False)

78. (B): $E = A \leq T$ and $D \leq A$

$\Rightarrow D \leq E = A \leq T$

$\Rightarrow D \leq T$ (True);

$R \geq E = A \leq T \leq S$

$\Rightarrow$ No relation between R and S

$\therefore R > S$ (False)

79. (D): I & II: $E = A \leq J$

$\Rightarrow$ either $J > E$ or $J = E$ (True).

80. (A): I. $A \geq B > C \leq D \leq E$

$\Rightarrow$ No relation between A and E.

$\therefore A \geq E$ (False)

II. $C \leq D \leq E < F \Rightarrow F > C$ (True).

For Qs. No. 81-85.

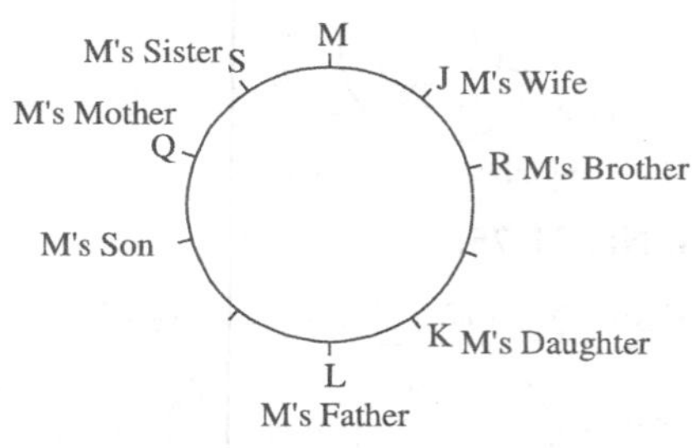

81. (B) **82. (C)** **83. (E)**

84. (D) **85. (A)**

For Qs. No. 86-90.

Day	Employees	Department
Monday	M	HR
Tuesday	P	Security
Wednesday	Q	Administrative
Thursday	L	Security
Friday	N	Administrative
Saturday	R	HR
Sunday	O	Finance

86. (D) **87. (E)** **88. (A)**

89. (B) **90. (B)**

For Qs. No. 91-95.

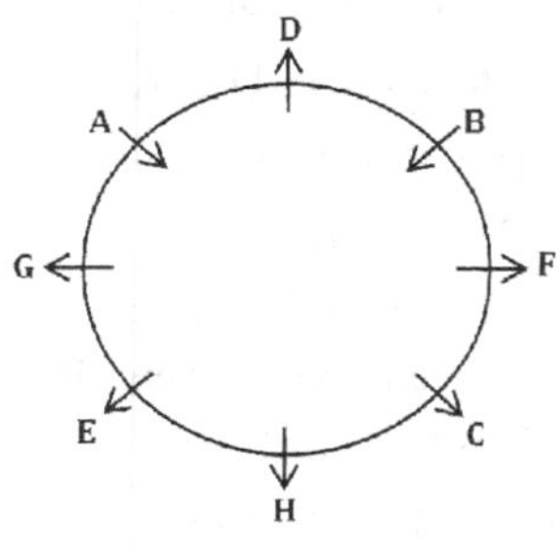

91. (D) **92. (C)** **93. (B)**

94. (C) **95. (D)**

For Qs. No. 96-97.

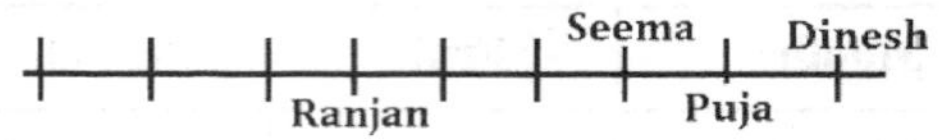

96. (E) **97. (E)**

98. (D): $V > W > T > S > U/X > X/U$

92

99. (D): $V > W > T > S > U > X$

92 69 68

100. (C): $V > W > T > S > U/X > X/U$

92

101. (D): An escrow account is a temporary pass through account held by a third party during the process of a transaction between two parties. Definition: An escrow account is a temporary pass through account held by a third party during the process of a transaction between two parties.

102. (B): A promissory note is a legal instrument in which one party (the maker or issuer) promises in writing to pay a determinate sum of money to the other (the payee).

103. (B): The capital of a business (working capital) which is used in its day-to-day trading operations, calculated as the current assets minus the current liabilities.

104. (A): Bianca Andreescu, a 19-year-old rising star from Canada, defeated Williams 6-3, 7-5 to win the 2019 U.S. Open women's singles tournament, becoming the first teenager to capture a major since Maria Sharapova won in 2006.

105. (C): Joaquin Phoenix's "Joker" was awarded the Golden Lion for Best Film at the 76th Annual Venice Film Festival.

106. (B)

107. (D): Section 24 and Section 56 of the Banking Regulation Act 1949 mandates all commercial banks in India to maintain SLR. It becomes pertinent to know in detail about the components of the SLR. These are assets one can easily convert into cash - like gold, treasury bills, govt-approved securities, government bonds and cash reserves.

108. (A): The Reserve Bank of India (RBI) released the draft guidelines to modify the loan system for delivery of bank credit, making the rules stricter to regulate larger borrowers enjoying working capital facility from the banking system. The draft specifies a minimum level of loan component in fund based working capital finance and a mandatory Credit Conversion Factor (CCF) for the undrawn portion of cash credit availed of by large borrowers.

109. (A): The Comptroller and Auditor General (CAG) of India is an authority, established by Article 148 of the Constitution of India, which audits all receipts and expenditure of the Government of India and the state governments, including those of bodies and authorities substantially financed by the government.

110. (B): National Housing Bank (NHB), a Government of India owned entity, was set up on 9 July 1988 under the National Housing Bank Act, 1987. NHB is an apex financial institution for housing.

111. (B): A promoter/promoter group can have a joint venture with an existing scheduled commercial bank to set up a payments bank. However, scheduled commercial bank can take equity stake in a payments bank to the extent permitted under Section 19 (2) of the Banking Regulation Act, 1949.

112. (A): Senior Citizen Saving Scheme (SCSS) is exclusively meant for people over the age of 60 years. They shall come into force on 02nd day of August in 2004.

113. (B): Bihu dance is a group dance in which males and females dance together. The Bihu dance is an indigenous folk from the Indian state of Assam. The dance is performed to traditional Bihu music.

114. (D): Bank of India was founded in 1906 in Mumbai. It became the first Indian bank to open a branch outside India in London in 1946 and the first to open a branch in continental Europe at Paris in 1974.

115. (A): Periyar National Park is located in Kerala, also known as 'God's own country'.

116. (E): Former World Champion Nozomi Okuhara clinched the women's singles in Denmark Open title after beating three-time world champion Spain's Carolina Marin. The Japanese Badminton star clinched the title while World Champion P V Sindhu opted not to participate in the event. Anders Antonsen of Denmark clinched the men's title.

117. (A)

118. (B): The World Osteoporosis Day (WOD) is observed globally on 20 October. The day is celebrated to raise global awareness of the prevention, diagnosis and treatment of osteoporosis and metabolic bone disease. WOD is organized by the International Osteoporosis Foundation (IOF), by the launch of a year-long campaign with a specific theme. WOD aims to make osteoporosis and fracture prevention a global health priority by reaching out to health-care professionals, the media, policymakers, patients, and the public at large.

In 2020 the Global WOD Campaign theme is “THAT'S OSTEOPOROSIS”, highlighting emotionally impactful visuals and stories of real people living with osteoporosis in all regions of the world.

119. (A)

120. (B): The bank must use the term “payments bank” in its name to differentiate it from other types of bank. The banks will be licensed as payments banks under Section 22 of the Banking Regulation Act, 1949, and will be registered as public limited company under the Companies Act, 2013.

121. (B) **122. (C)** **123. (C)**

124. (D): The 5 Rupee note was the first paper currency issued by RBI in January 1938. The Rs 5 note had the portrait of George VI. Then within the same year, currency notes of ₹ 10, ₹ 100, ₹ 1,000 and ₹ 10,000 were issued.

125. (D) **126. (C)** **127. (B)**

128. (A)

129. (C): NASSCOM, Union Ministry of Electronics and IT (MeITY) and the IT Industry have come together to launch "FurtureSkills Prime", which is a Digital re-skilling/up-skilling platform. It is an aggregator learning platform, which offers technologies such as AI, IoT, Data Analytics, cloud computing whose curriculum are globally accepted.

130. (A) **131. (A)**

132. (C): The Ministry of Labour & Employment, has notified Section 142 of the Social Security Code, 2020, which covers the applicability of Aadhar. It has been mandated to seek the 12-digit unique identification number from people like employees and unorganised sector workers who seek registration, avail services or receive payment under various schemes under the Social Security Code 2020.

133. (C) **134. (A)** **135. (A)**

136. (B): MSP is a form of government intervention to insure the farmers against a steep decline in the prices of their goods and to help them prevent losses. The government of India sets the MSP twice a year for 24 commodities. This is done by the government to protect the farmers against a fall in prices in a year of bumper production. When the market price falls below the declared MSP, the government would purchase the entire quantity from the farmers at MSP.

137. (A): Human Rights Day is observed by the international community every year on 10 December. It commemorates the day in 1948 the United Nations General Assembly adopted the Universal Declaration of Human Rights. The formal inception of Human Rights Day dates from 1950, after the Assembly passed resolution 423 (V) inviting all States and interested organizations to adopt 10 December of each year as Human Rights Day.

138. (A)

139. (A): GNPA stands for Gross Non-performing Assets. GNPA is an absolute amount. It tells you the total value of gross non-performing assets for the bank in a particular quarter or financial year as the case may be.

140. (A)

141. (B): The Board of Trustees of Credit Guarantee Fund Trust for Micro and Small Enterprises (CGTMSE), had framed a Scheme for the purpose of providing guarantees in respect of credit facilities extended by Lending Institutions to the borrowers in Micro and Small Enterprises (MSEs).

- The Scheme shall be known as the Credit Guarantee Fund Scheme for Micro and Small Enterprises (CGS-I) [earlier known as Credit Guarantee Fund Scheme for Small Industries (CGFSI)]. Subsequent to the enactment of MSMED Act-2006, the Trust was renamed as Credit Guarantee Fund Trust for Micro and Small Enterprises and scheme as Credit Guarantee Fund Scheme for Micro and Small Enterprises.
- The Scheme had come into force from August 1, 2000 and had covered eligible credit facilities extended by the lending institutions to eligible borrowers effective from June 1, 2000.
- The scheme was modified from time to time for ease of operations, enhancement of credit flow to MSE sector and to meet the requirements of the MSEs as well as Lending Institutions.

142. (B) **143. (B)** **144. (C)**

145. (A) **146. (D)** **147. (D)**

148. (B) **149. (C)** **150. (A)**

Previous Paper (Solved)

IBPS—SPECIALIST OFFICERS

Law Officer and Rajbhasha Adhikari

Common Preliminary Exam-2018*

General Awareness

1. The committee on Banking Regulations and Supervisory Practices which released the agreed frame work on international convergence of capital measures and capital standards in July 1988 is popularly known as _______.
A. Vaz Committee
B. Cooks Committee
C. Basel Committee
D. Rao Committee
E. None of the given options is true

2. Which is the first Indian Private Sector Bank set up a branch in China?
A. ICICI Bank
B. Syndicate Bank
C. Axis Bank
D. HDFC Bank
E. State Bank of India

3. In the term STRIPS, the first "S" denotes:
A. Single
B. Small
C. Special
D. Savings
E. Separate

4. What is the full form of IFRS?
A. International Financial Reporting Standards
B. Indian Financial Rating Standards
C. International Financial Rating Standards
D. Indian Functional Reporting Standards
E. None of the given options is true

5. Short-term assets, representing amounts due to a vendor or suppliers of goods or services that were sold on credit terms is known as _____.
A. Account Receivable
B. Fixed Asset
C. Deposit Asset
D. Current Liabilities
E. None of the given options is true

6. CAG of India is an authority, established by Article 148 of the Constitution of India. CAG Stands for _______.
A. Comptroller and Auditor General of India
B. Constant and Author General of India
C. Constant Auditor General of India
D. Central Auditor General of India
E. None of the given options is true

7. The Reserve Bank of India (RBI) permitted the Foreign Portfolio Investors (FPI) to buy fully or partly defaulted bonds under sections 10(4) and 11(1) of which Act?
A. The Foreigners Act, 1946
B. Foreign Exchange Management Act, 1999
C. Foreign (Contribution) Regulation Act, 2010
D. Undisclosed Foreign Income and Assets (Imposition of Tax) Act, 2015
E. None of these

8. Which State published the first draft of the National Register of Citizens (NRC)?
A. Arunachal
B. Assam
C. Meghalaya
D. Tripura
E. Mizoram

9. Which one of the following countries, applied Value Added Tax (VAT) for the first time on 1st January, 2018?
A. UAE
B. Qatar
C. Oman
D. Kuwait
E. None of these

* *Based on Memory.*

10. Who wins the Australian Open Women's Single title in 2018?
A. Angelique Kerber
B. Simona Halep
C. Caroline Wozniacki
D. Garbiñe Muguruza
E. None of these

11. What do we celebrate on 10th December every year?
A. Human Rights Day
B. Earth Day
C. World Thyroid Day
D. Anti-Tobacco Day
E. Legal Service Day

12. Buenos Aires is the Capital of which country?
A. Japan B. Angola
C. Argentina D. Azerbaijan
E. Bolivia

13. In March 2019, merger of Bank of Baroda, Vijaya Bank and Dena Bank has been proposed Winner of Santosh Trophy 2018:
A. Bihar B. Kerala
C. Assam D. Gujarat
E. Tamil Nadu

14. "Bharat Ratna Atal Bihari Vajpayee Ekana" Stadium is located at:
A. Bhopal B. Jaipur
C. Hyderabad D. Ahmedabad
E. Lucknow

15. Winner of Ramon Magsaysay Award 2018 from India:
A. Sonam Wangchuk B. Azizbek Ashurov
C. Adam Harper D. Naaz Joshi
E. Wangchuk Sherpa

16. Konkan joint military exercise 2018 was held between India and:
A. USA B. Japan
C. Russia D. United Kingdom
E. China

17. Dharma Guardian 2018 joint military exercise was held between India and Japan Height of "Statue of Unity" situated in Gujarat:
A. 160 metres B. 180 metres
C. 182 metres D. 190 metres
E. 187 metres

18. Indo-Russian Strategic Economic Dialogue 2018 was held in:
A. Russia B. China
C. Japan D. India
E. None of these

19. As per the RBI Guidelines for a damaged or torn ₹ 2000 note, minimum area required for a full refund:
A. 85 square cm B. 80 square cm
C. 93 square cm D. 99 square cm
E. 88 square cm

20. A Book written by Krishna Trilok:
A. Notes of a Dream
B. Edge of Time
C. Getting India Back on Track
D. I Do What I Do
E. None of these

21. First multi-modal terminal on Ganga river has been opened at:
A. Lucknow B. Varanasi
C. Bhopal D. Haridwar
E. Uttarkashi

22. 80th Policy Commission Meeting of World Customs Organisation was held in:
A. Hyderabad B. Lucknow
C. Amaravati D. Mumbai
E. Bhubaneswar

23. India's first interactive credit card with buttons launched by:
A. IndusInd Bank B. Yes Bank
C. ICICI Bank D. HDFC Bank
E. SBI Bank

24. ASEAN Summit 2018 held in:
A. Dubai B. Singapore
C. Beijing D. Bangkok
E. Doha

25. Headquarters of NSDL Payment Bank:
A. New Delhi B. Hyderabad
C. Mumbai D. Ahmedabad
E. Bhopal

26. Paul Romer & William Nordhaus have been awarded Nobel prize 2018 in which discipline?
A. Economic B. Medicine
C. Chemistry D. Physics
E. Peace

27. Singphan Wildlife Sanctuary has been declared as Singphan Elephant Reserve. In which state it is situated?
A. Assam
B. Manipur
C. Arunachal Pradesh
D. Nagaland
E. Meghalaya

28. Smriti Mandhana is associated with which sport?
A. Football B. Volleyball
C. Tennis D. Kabaddi
E. Cricket

29. Which Indian city will participate in UN Global Sustainable Cities 2025?
A. Noida & Greater Noida
B. Gurugram
C. Faridabad
D. Lucknow
E. Hyderabad

30. Author of "India ahead 2025 and beyond":
A. Anita Desai B. Amitav Ghosh
C. Bimal Jalan D. C.S. Pandit
E. Amrita Pritam

31. According to India Skills Report 2019, state with the highest Employability Rate:
A. Andhra Pradesh B. Gujarat
C. Odisha D. Assam
E. Jharkhand

32. With Reference to RBI, what does R stands for in PCR?
A. Regulation B. Registry
C. Regular D. Rate
E. Regional

33. Which of the following is the largest gulf in the world?
A. Gulf of Aden B. Gulf of Guinea
C. Persian Gulf D. Gulf of Mexico
E. Gulf of Alaska

34. Who abolished the use of Persian as court language and ordered the use of vernacular language?
A. William Bentinck B. Cornwallis
C. Warren Hastings D. John Shore
E. Lord Ripon

35. According to Swachh Survekshan 2017, which city is declared as Cleanest City in India?
A. Vishakhapatnam B. Bhopal
C. Idukki D. Indore
E. Ranchi

36. The statement "Tamsoma Jyotirgamya" was originally mentioned in:
A. Upanishad B. Mahakavya
C. Purana D. Shaddarshan
E. None of these

37. The Rashtriya Madhyamik Shiksha Abhiyan (RMSA) Scheme was launched in the year:
A. 2007 B. 2008
C. 2009 D. 2010
E. 2011

38. Who among the following attended all the three Round Table Conferences?
A. Madan Mohan Malviya
B. Annie Besant
C. Mahatma Gandhi
D. B.R. Ambedkar
E. None of these

39. Tulsidas was a contemporary of:
A. Babar B. Akbar
C. Jahangir D. Shahjahan
E. Humayun

40. Which of the following rights was described by Dr. B.R. Ambedkar as The Heart and Soul of the Constitution?
A. Right of Freedom of Religion
B. Right to Property
C. Right to Equality
D. Right to Constitutional Remedies
E. None of these

41. Which unit of valuation is known as 'Paper Gold'?
A. Petrodollar B. SDR
C. Eurodollar D. GDR
E. None of these

42. Who is the founder of World Economic Forum?
A. Klaus Schwab
B. John Kenneth Galbraith
C. Robert Zoellick
D. Paul Krugman
E. None of these

43. Where did the practice of 'Shadow Cabinet' originate?
A. USA B. Great Britain
C. Italy D. France
E. Japan

44. Gresham's law in Economics relates to:
A. Supply and demand
B. Circulation of currency
C. Consumption of supply
D. Distribution of goods and services
E. None of these

45. The capital of Pallavas was:
A. Arcot B. Kanchi
C. Malkhed D. Banaras
E. None of these

46. Lunar Eclipse is caused when:
A. The sun and the moon and the earth are in a line
B. The earth comes between the sun and the moon
C. The sun and the earth are on either side of the moon
D. The sun comes between the earth and the moon
E. None of these

47. The planets shine because:
A. they emit light
B. they are illuminated by nearby stars
C. they reflect light reaching them from the sun
D. they reflect light reaching them from the earth
E. None of these

48. Vitamin E deficiency causes:
A. Haemophilia B. Sterlity
C. Falling of hair D. Weakness
E. All of these

49. Which one of the following blood groups is universal recipient?
A. AB B. A
C. O D. B
E. All of these

50. The father of Embryology is:
A. S.C. Maheshwari
B. B.M. Johri
C. P. Maheshwari
D. K.G. Mukerji
E. None of these

Reasoning

Directions (Qs. No. 51-55): *Read the following information carefully to answer the following questions.*

Twelve friends P, Q, R, S, T, U, A, B, C, D, E and F are sitting in a straight line facing north but not necessarily in the same order. F sits third to the right of S. B sits fourth to the right of P, who is not the immediate neighbour of U. C and D are not immediate neighbours of F, who sits second to the right of E. There are two persons between U and A. There are two persons between D and Q. S is not an immediate neighbour of A. E sits at the fifth position from the right end. F is sixth to the right of T. C is not an immediate neighbour of D and Q.

51. Who among the following sit at the extreme ends of the line?
A. B, C B. P, D
C. T, C D. R, F
E. None of these

52. Who among the following sits third to the right of the fourth to the left of Q?
A. R B. C
C. A D. E
E. None of these

53. How many persons are there between C and the one who sits on the immediate left of S?
A. Two B. Three
C. Four D. One
E. None of these

54. Who among the following are immediate neighbours of R?
A. F and D B. E and T
C. A and C D. F and Q
E. None of these

55. Which of the following statements is/are true?
A. There are three friends between F and R
B. T and B are immediate neighbours
C. C sits at one of the ends of the line
D. P is on the immediate left of D
E. None of these

Directions (Qs. No. 56-60): *Study the following information carefully and answer the given questions:*

Twelve persons are sitting in two parallel rows containing six persons each, in such a way that there is an equal distance between adjacent persons. In row-1, J, K, L, M, N and O are seated (but not necessarily in the same order) and all of them are facing south. In row-2, C, D, E, F, G and H are seated (but not necessarily in the same order) and all of them are facing north. Therefore, in the given seating arrangement each person seated in a row faces another person of the other row.

M sits third to the left of J. The person facing M sits second to the left of H. Two persons are sitting between H and E. L and K are immediate neighbours. L and K do not sit at any of the extreme ends of the line. Only one person sits between N and L. The person facing K is an immediate neighbour of C. G is not an immediate neighbour of E. D does not face M.

56. Who amongst the following sits seconds to the right of the person who faces F?
A. L B. K
C. N D. J
E. Cannot be determined

57. Which of the following statements regarding N is true?
A. N sits second to the left of L
B. M sits to immediate left of N
C. H faces N
D. K is an immediate neighbour of N
E. The person who faces N is an immediate neighbour of D

58. Who amongst the following faces E?
A. M B. K
C. L D. J
E. Cannot be determined

59. Who amongst the following sits exactly between H and F?
A. G B. C
C. D D. E
E. Cannot be determined

60. Four of the following live are alike in a certain way based on the given seating arrangement and thus form a group. Which is the one that does not belong to the group?
A. O B. C
C. H D. L
E. J

Directions (Qs. No. 61-65): *Study the information given below and answer the questions based on it.*

Some persons were born in the same year but in different months *i.e.* from January to December. Only two persons were born before A. R is the youngest person. The number of person born before Q is same as after R. Two months gap between R and C. P is the 2nd eldest person. S was born in May. M is elder to C but younger to S. K was born in a month which was having 31 days. The number of persons born before A is same as after C. The number of month gap between Q and S is same as M and R. P was not born in March and C was not born in July. R was not born in December. The number of month gap between A and M is same as M and K.

61. Who among the following was born in October?
A. No one B. R
C. K D. S
E. M

62. What is the total number of person?
A. 6 B. 7
C. 8 D. 9
E. 5

63. Who among the following is the eldest?
A. Q B. A
C. C D. R
E. K

64. Which of the following is TRUE?
A. Q was born in February
B. Only one person was born after R

C. M was born in March
D. A was born in a month which was having 30 days
E. C was born in October

65. Who among the following is the youngest?
A. Q B. A
C. C D. R
E. K

Directions (Qs. No. 66-70): *Study the information given below and answer the questions based on it.*

A, B, C, D, E, F, G and H are eight students of a school. They study in standards VI, VII, and VIII with not more than three in any standard. Each of them has a favourite subject from Physics, Geography, English, Marathi, Mathematics, Chemistry, Biology and Economics but not necessarily in the same order.

D likes Chemistry and studies in standard VIII with only H. B does not study in standard VII. E and A study in the same standard but not with B. C and F study in the same standard. Those who study in standard VI do not like Mathematics or Biology. F likes Physics. The one who studies in standard VIII likes English. C does not like Geography. A's favourite subject is Marathi and G does not like Biology.

66. Which of the following groups of students studied in VII standard?
A. DHA B. EAG
C. BCF D. ABC
E. Cannot be determined

67. Which of the following combinations of student-standard-subject is correct?
A. D-VIII-Biology B. A-VI-Marathi
C. G-VII-Math D. F-VIII-Economics
E. None of these

68. What is C's favourite subject?
A. Chemistry B. English
C. Biology D. Economics
E. Geography

69. In which standard does C study?
A. VI B. VII
C. VIII D. Either VI or VIII
E. None of these

70. Which subject does H like?
A. Marathi B. Physics
C. English D. Geography
E. None of these

Directions (Qs. No. 71-75): *Study the information given below and answer the questions based on it.*

Nine boys Vikash, Kamal, Sunil, Saurabh, Rohit, Sanjay, Amit, Anit and Sushil stays in a nine floor building and all of them stays on different floors. Each of them likes different girls namely—Sanjana, Surabhi, Amita, Anita, Komal, Suhana, Kumkum, Saroj and Susheela. Each boys belongs to different cities *i.e.* Patna, Lucknow, Chennai, Varanasi, Mirzapur, Allahabad, Mathura, Noida and Agra but necessarily in the same order. The topmost floor is numbered 9, the floor below it is numbered 8 and so on, and the ground floor is numbered 1.

The one who likes Surabhi stays on an even numbered floor. Sanjay does not belong to Allahabad. The one who belongs to Lucknow stays on the topmost floor. The one who likes Sanjana stays immediately below the one who likes Amita. Sanjay likes Anita and does not stay on the ground floor. Vikash belongs to Chennai and stays on an even numbered floor and he likes Sanjana. Saurabh stays on the second floor and belongs to Mirzapur. There are three boys between the one who likes Suhana and the one who likes Komal. The one who likes Suhana stays below the boy who likes Komal. The one who belongs to Allahabad stays on the third floor. The one who likes Saroj does not stay on sixth floor. There is one floor between the floors in which the one who likes Susheela and the one who likes Kumkum stay. Kamal stays on an even numbered floor below the floor on which Vikash stays. There are two floors between the floors on which the boys who are from Mathura and Chennai. The boy who likes Komal is from Mathura. Sushil belongs to Patna. The one who belongs to Noida stays on the fourth floor. Kamal does not belong to Varanasi and does not like Anita and Komal. There are three floors between the floors on which Sushil and Amit stay. Sunil stays on a floor immediately above the Anit's floor. The one who likes Kumkum stays immediately above Sushil. There is one floor between the floors on which Sanjay and Amit stay.

71. Which among the following boys likes Anita?
A. Sanjay B. Amit
C. Anit D. Rohit
E. Vikash

72. Who among the following stays between the floor of Sunil and Saurabh?
A. Anit B. Amit
C. Kamal D. Vikash
E. Rohit

73. Which of the following combinations is true?
A. Sanjay – Suhana – Varanasi
B. Amit – Amita – Allahabad
C. Rohit – Saroj – Varanasi
D. Sunil – Susheela – Noida
E. Kamal – Surabhi – Chennai

74. If 'Sanjay' is related to 'Mathura', 'Vikash' is related to 'Agra', in the same way 'Kamal' is related to?
A. Allahabad B. Patna
C. Chennai D. Noida
E. Varanasi

75. How many boys stay between the one who likes Amita and the one who likes Kumkum?
A. Five B. Two
C. One D. Six
E. Four

Directions (Qs. No. 76-80): *In these questions, a relationship between different elements is shown in the statements. The statements are followed by two conclusions.*

76. Statements : $A \geq P = S > T, V < B = T > X$
Conclusions : I. $A > X$ II. $P < B$
A. only conclusion I is true
B. only conclusion II is true
C. either conclusion I or II is true
D. neither conclusion I nor II is true
E. both conclusions I and II are true

77. Statements : $S > U > V, Y < U < Z, Z < X > W$
Conclusions : I. $S < Z$ II. $X > Y$
A. only conclusion I is true
B. only conclusion II is true
C. either conclusion I or II is true
D. neither conclusion I nor II is true
E. both conclusions I and II are true

78. Statements : $P < X < Y < Q, S > Y < T, P = V > R$
Conclusions : I. $V < S$ II. $T > R$
A. only conclusion I is true
B. only conclusion II is true
C. either conclusion I or II is true
D. neither conclusion I nor II is true
E. both conclusions I and II are true

79. Statements : $A \geq B > C, D \geq E = F \geq G, H \geq I = E$
Conclusions : I. $H < C$ II. $H > D$
A. only conclusion I is true
B. only conclusion II is true
C. either conclusion I or II is true
D. neither conclusion I nor II is true
E. both conclusions I and II are true

80. Statements : $A \geq B > C, D \geq E \geq F > B, P \geq Q > E = S$
Conclusions : I. $P < B$ II. $S > A$
A. only conclusion I is true
B. only conclusion II is true
C. either conclusion I or II is true
D. neither conclusion I nor II is true
E. both conclusions I and II are true

Directions (Qs. No. 81-85): *In each of the questions below are given four statements followed by four conclusions numbered I, II, III and IV. You have to take the given statements to be true even if they seem to be at variance from commonly known facts. Read all the conclusions and then decide which of the given conclusions logically follows from the given statements disregarding commonly known facts.*

81. Statements : All lotus are beautiful.
All beautiful are Rose.
No Rose are stinky.
All sky are Rose.

Conclusions: I. All stinky are beautiful is a possibility.
II. Some stinky are lotus.
III. Some Rose are Stinky is a possibility.
IV. All beautiful can never be Sky.

A. None follows
B. Only I and IV follow

C. Only II follows
D. Only II and III follow
E. None of these

82. Statements : Some planes are waters.
Some waters are doors.
All doors are guitars.
No guitar is a flat.

Conclusion : I. At least some guitars are Planes.
II. All doors are flat is a possibility.
III. Some planes are both waters and doors.
IV. At least some flat is a door.

A. Only IV follows
B. Only either II or III follow
C. Only III follows
D. Only I follows
E. None follows

83. Statements : Some red are blue.
Some blue are grey.
All grey are white.
No white is black.

Conclusion : I. No black is grey.
II. Some blue are white.
III. Some black are red.
IV. No black is red.

A. Only I and II follow
B. Only either III or IV follows
C. Only I and either III or IV follow
D. Only I, II and either III or IV follow
E. None of these

84. Statements : All red are white.
Some white are pink.
Some pink are yellow.
No yellow is blue.

Conclusion : I. No blue is pink.
II. Some pink are red.
III. Some blue are red.
IV. Some blue are pink.

A. None follows
B. Only either I or IV follows
C. Only I follows
D. Only III & IV follow
E. All follow

85. Statements : All green are pink.
Some pink are black.
Some black are blue.
All blue are white.

Conclusions: I. Some black are white.
II. Some blue are pink.
III. Some pink are green.
IV. No green is white.

A. None follows
B. Only I and III follows
C. Only III follows
D. Only either I or II follows
E. None of these

Directions (Qs. No. 86-90): *In each question below is given a statement followed by two courses of action numbered I and II. You have to assume everything in the statement to be true and on the basis of the information given in the statement. Decide which of the suggested courses of action logically follow(s) for pursuing. Give answer:*

86. Statement : The government of India has launched a new scheme known as "Digital India" to help promote Digital Banking.

Course of action:
I. Traditional Banks should embrace the new scheme as it relates to the modern trend of digitalized banking.
II. Traditional Banks should do nothing as a bunch of money transaction apps cannot replace the traditional banking system, and hail it as a useless scheme.

A. If only course of action I follows
B. If only course of action II follows
C. If both I and II follow
D. If neither I nor II follows
E. If either I or II follows

87. Statement : A student was caught cheating in a class-test.

Course of action:
I. The teacher should report him to the principal.
II. Teacher should accept his test answer sheet and leave him with a final warning.

A. Only course of action I follows
B. Only course of action II follows

C. Both I and II follow
D. Neither I nor II follows
E. Either I or II follows

88. Statement : IT companies have stated that a large number of Engineers employed in their firms are not suitable for employment as they lack basic programming skills.

Course of action:

I. They should fire all unskilled and unproductive employees.
II. They should not fire the employees.

A. Only course of action I follows
B. Only course of action II follows
C. Both I and II follow
D. Neither I nor II follows
E. Either I or II follows

89. Statement : State police of Bihar came under the cloud with recent news that 9 lakh liters of liquor has been missing from the police station after the declaration of Bihar a dry state. The police department claimed that the whole of the liquor had been drunk by rats.

Course of Actions:

I. A thorough investigation should be ordered and those who are liable if any then they must have to be punished.
II. Suspension of those police officers who claim that rats drunk the liquor.

A. If only course of action I follow
B. If only course of action II follows
C. If both the course of action follows
D. If neither course of action fallows
E. Data inadequate

90. Statement : There has been an allegation on some of army officers that they had been involved in illegal arms trade with a few arms smuggler.

Course of Actions:

I. An investigation should be ordered by the Indian government to reveal the actual culprits.
II. They should be punished with court marshal.

A. Only course of action I follows
B. Only course of action II follows
C. Both I and II follow
D. Neither I nor II follows
E. Either I or II follows

Directions (Qs. No. 91-95): *The question below, there is a statement followed by two conclusions/ assumptions numbered I and II. You have to assume everything in the statement to be true. Then consider the two conclusion/assumption together and decide which of them follows/implicit beyond a reasonable doubt from the information given in the statement.*

91. Statement : High pressure boilers are hazardous pieces of equipment, which are strictly regulated with special laws.

Conclusions:

I. If not regulated, high pressure boilers will be easily available in the market
II. High pressure boilers are rare.

A. Only conclusion I follows
B. Only conclusion II follows
C. Both conclusion I and II follows
D. Neither conclusion I nor II follows
E. Either conclusion I or II follows

92. Statement : The principal announced that students who score more than 95% will get special prize and medal. Kevin scored 96% but was found to have cheated in some of the exams.

Conclusions:

I. Kevin is going to get special prize and medal.
II. Kevin might not get any prize.

A. Only conclusion I follows
B. Only conclusion II follows
C. Both conclusion I and II follows
D. Neither conclusion I nor II follows
E. Either conclusion I or II follows.

93. Statement : Using calculator for simpler calculations adversely affects mathematical abilities of children.

Assumptions:

I. Using calculator for complex calculations may not affect mathematical abilities adversely.

II. Complex calculations cannot be done manually without the help of a calculator.

A. Only I is implicit
B. Only II is implicit
C. Either I or II is implicit
D. Neither I or II is implicit
E. Both I and II are implicit

94. Statement : An advertisement by Easy Air, a private airliner reads: 'Travel to Meerut by our airlines and get a chance to win an all-expenses-paid holiday to Bangkok'.

Assumptions:

I. Easy Air flights are available for Bangkok.
II. The city of Meerut has an airport.

A. Only I is implicit
B. Only II is implicit
C. Either I or II is implicit
D. Neither I or II is implicit
E. Both I and II are implicit

95. Statement : Ms. Suu Kyi, a recipient of the Nobel Peace Prize, has found it pragmatic not to challenge the official rhetoric in Myanmar, which suggests the military's actions were aimed at tackling "terror" in Rakhine.

Conclusions:

I. Ms. Suu Kyi does not want to upset the fragile balance of power.
II. Ms. Suu Kyi's action shows lack of empathy for the Rohingya in a country.

A. only conclusion I follows
B. only conclusion II follows
C. both conclusion I and II follow
D. neither conclusion I nor II follows
E. either conclusion I or II follows

Directions (Qs. No. 96-100): *Each of the question below consists of a question and three statements numbered I, II and III given below it. You have to decide whether the data provided in three statement are sufficient to answer the question.*

96. How many daughters does W have?

I. B and D are the sister of M.
II. M's father T is the husband of W.
III. Out of the three children which T has, only one is a boy.

A. I and III are sufficient to answer the question
B. All I, II and III are required to answer the question
C. I and II are sufficient to answer the question
D. Question cannot be answered even with all I, II and III
E. II and III are sufficient to answer the question

97. Among A, B, C, D, E, F and G, is B greater than F?

I. A is either greater or equal to B which is lesser than C which is equal to D which is greater than E which is either greater or equal to F which is equal to G.
II. A is lesser or equal to B which is equal to C which is greater to D which is greater to E which is lesser to F which is lesser to G.
III. A is greater to B which is greater to C which is equal to D which is greater or equal to E which is greater to F which is lesser to G.

A. I and II
B. II and III
C. III
D. Any Two
E. All of the above

98. In which direction is M with respect to N?

I. M is to the south of G, which is to the west of H. G is to the east of T.
II. N is between G and H.
III. N is to the north-west of T.

A. Only I and II
B. Only I
C. Only II and III
D. Only I and III
E. Only I and either II or III

99. Are writers not words?

I. Some writers are covers. No cover is a page.
II. All writers are books. Some books are covers.
III. No book is a word. Some words are pens.

A. Only I
B. Only II and III
C. Only I and III
D. I, II and III together are not sufficient
E. Only I and II

100. Who among Nitesh, Mahi, Rita, Priya, Neha and Rahul, each having different heights, is the tallest?

I. Mahi is taller than Nitesh but shorter than Neha.
II. Only two of them are shorter than Rita.
III. Priya is taller than only Rahul.

A. Only I and III
B. Only I and II
C. Only II and III
D. All I, II and III together
E. None of these

English Language

Directions (Qs. No. 101-105): *Read the following passage carefully and answer the questions that follow. Certain words/phrases are printed in bold to help you locate them while answering some of the questions.*

The Cabinet decision to allow spectrum trading will give a huge **impetus** to the on-going efforts for making broadband available in even the remotest parts of the country under the Digital India campaign. There are many compelling reasons why the time is ripe for the introduction of spectrum trading. One of the objectives of the new National Telecom Policy is to achieve a base of 600 million broadband users, with a minimum access speed of 2 Mbps by 2020. The Centre wants to create digital infrastructure to provide utility services like banking, education and healthcare to every Indian citizen. These ambitious targets can be achieved only if every operator in the country has access to adequate spectrum. The more spectrums an operator holds, the more data traffic it can carry over its network. Despite several rounds of auctions in the last two years, the quantum of airwaves with Indian telecom companies is less than that of their global counterparts. Mobile companies in the US and Japan, for instance, are able to offer high speed video services because they have 30-40 MHz of spectrum. In contrast, a 3G operator in India has only 5 MHz. Spectrum trading will allow the operators to get access to a larger pool of air waves, in turn ensuring that spectrum does not lie fallow. The option to trade spectrum also introduces an element of liquidity to its value. Interest in future auctions will increase because operators can bid with the knowledge that they can get returns by further leasing the airwaves. For smaller operators who are looking for an exit, trading gives them the opportunity to monetize their key asset without going through complex merger or acquisition deals.

However, the guidelines approved by the Cabinet have some concern areas which, if not addressed, could make it difficult for operators to trade spectrum. For example, the spectrum seller will have to pay 11 to 13 per cent of the proceeds to the government in the form of licence fee and spectrum usage charge. This could be a major **deterrent** if the operator is debt-laden or in an exit mode. The other big concern is the rule asking operators who bought spectrum in the 800 MHz band in the 2013 auctions, to first pay the price arrived at in the 2015 auction if they want to enter into a trading deal. Though the prices arrived at in the 2013 auctions were significantly lower than in 2015, both were market-driven processes. Thus the Centre's view that it did not receive the full price then is misplaced.

The benefits of sharing resources can be seen in the telecom tower business where operators were able to drive down costs and improve efficiencies by sharing space on towers. Similar sharing is now happening in the optical fibre cable infrastructure. Spectrum trading will benefit consumers, since at least those operators with adequate spectrum will be able to offer better quality of service. That said, quality improvement across the board will be achieved only when more spectrum is made available.

101. According to the given passage, which among the following is TRUE?
- A. Mobile companies in the US and Japan are able to offer high speed video services.
- B. Mobile companies in US and Japan have 30-40 MHz of spectrum.
- C. A 3G operator in India has only 5 MHz Spectrum trading.
- D. All are true
- E. Only A and B are true.

102. According to the passage, how will Spectrum trading benefit the consumers in India?
- A. Quality of services will improve.
- B. Broad spectrum will be made available.
- C. The cost of telecom companies will rise.
- D. All the above
- E. Only A and B

103. Which of the following concerns in the guidelines approved by the Cabinet needs to be addressed by the Government?
- A. The spectrum seller will have to pay license fee and spectrum usage charge to the government.
- B. The cost was higher for the bidders in the auction of 2013.
- C. The rule asking operators who bought spectrum in the 2013 auctions, to first pay the price arrived at in the 2015 auction if they want to enter into a trading deal.
- D. All of the above
- E. Only A and C

104. Which of the following is the MOST SIMILAR in meaning to "impetus"?
- A. Momentum
- B. Block
- C. Check
- D. Hindrance
- E. Incentive

105. Which of the following is the MOST OPPOSITE in meaning to "deterrent"?
- A. Disincentive
- B. Encouragement
- C. Damper
- D. Curb
- E. Restraint

Directions (Qs. No. 106-115): *Read the following passage carefully and answer the questions that follow. Certain words are printed in bold to help you locate them while answering some of these.*

With half the fiscal year nearly complete, it is not surprising that the government is beginning to **fret** over the slow progress of the disinvestment programme. Of the budgeted ₹ 69,500 crore from PSU stake sales, only ₹ 12,700 crore has been raised so far. Reports that the Centre wants the EPFO to park part of the money that it has been allowed to invest in equity market in the CPSE ETF, highlights this desperation. Almost half the stocks in this ETF are companies that have been hard hit by the crash in commodity prices. This is not an asset the EPFO should be investing in now. The Centre, staring at yet another failure to meet its divestment target, appears ready to use any means to inch towards the target set for this year.

The urgency stems from the tight fiscal condition that the country is currently in. The fiscal deficit for the April to June period has already covered 69.3 per cent of the current year's target. This is despite a 36 per cent increase in indirect tax collection in the first five months of the current fiscal, thanks to the steep hike in excise duty on petrol and diesel, and the higher rate of service tax. A slowdown in income tax collection, along with a wide shortfall in the money raised through selling stakes in public sector companies, can make it a challenge for the Centre to meet this fiscal year's targeted deficit of 3.9 per cent of GDP. The increase in pension pay-outs for defence personnel is expected to add pressure on this goal. Inability to raise sufficient revenue can result in the government cutting back on investments, **pegging** back growth.

But the Centre has only itself to blame for this **predicament.** That the divestment department has gone about its task in a very **lackadaisical** manner in recent times is borne out by the fact that the gap between proceeds from stake sales and the budgeted target has been between 20 and 65 per cent since 2011-12. Given the decision to almost double its target for this fiscal, the Centre could have shown more **alacrity** in front-loading the sales this fiscal year, when the equity market was buoyant. The success of the REC's offer for sale in April highlights investor willingness to subscribe when the outlook for stocks is rosy. The divestment department needs to employ professionals to advise it on the timing of the sales better. Anyone who was tuned in to the stock market would have known that the second half of the year was expected to be rocky for stocks, given the impending monetary policy normalisation by the Fed. The offer for sale mechanism being employed for these stake sales also needs a rethink. With a retail discount of 5 per cent and the almost immediate availability of allotted shares, many investors have taken to short-term speculation through these offers.

106. What is the author of the above passage trying to suggest through it?
A. The tardiness in PSU stake sales will pressure the fiscal deficit.
B. The offer for sale mechanism for stake sales of companies must be remodelled.
C. The disinvestment programme is not furthering with a desired pace.
D. Only A and C
E. All of the above

107. Why the author believes that it is a challenge for the Centre to meet this fiscal year's targeted deficit of 3.9 per cent of GDP?
A. The fiscal deficit for the April to June period has already covered 69.3 per cent of the current year's target.
B. Slowdown in income tax collection.
C. Wide shortfall in the money collected through selling stakes in public sector companies.
D. All of the above
E. None of the above

108. Which among the following statements is **TRUE** according to the passage given above?
A. ₹ 12,500 crore has been raised so far through PSU stake sales.
B. In the first five months of the current fiscal there has been a 36 per cent increase in indirect tax collection.
C. The difference in proceeds from stake sales and the budgeted target is around 20 and 55 per cent since 2011-12.
D. Only A and C
E. Only B and C

109. What could be the results of the Centre's inability to raise sufficient revenues?
A. Government might cut back its investments.
B. The growth of the country could be pegged back.
C. Steep hike in excise duty on petrol and diesel may take place.
D. Only A and B
E. All A, B and C

110. Which among the following is **NOT TRUE** according to the passage given above?
A. A person who knows about stock market would have known that the second half of the year would be unhealthy for stock sales.
B. Many investors have bought the shares of the disinvestment portfolio just because of the 5% retail discount and immediate availability of stocks.
C. The targeted deficit of fiscal year 2011-12 is 3.9% of the GDP.
D. Only B and C
E. All are correct

111. Which among the following express the opposite meaning of the word "Fret" as given in the passage?
A. Affront B. Calm
C. Anguish D. Brood
E. Chafe

112. Which among the following express the opposite meaning of the word "Pegging" as given in the passage?
A. Clinch B. Fasten
C. Remove D. Tighten
E. Pin

113. Which among the following express the similar meaning of the word "Predicament" as given in the passage?
A. Fix B. Fortune
C. Solution D. Quandary
E. Ease

114. Which among the following express the SIMILAR meaning of the word "Lackadaisical" as given in the passage?
A. Abstracted B. Careful
C. Active D. Hard-working
E. Caring

115. Which among the following express the similar meaning of the word "Alacrity" as given in the passage?

A. Avidity B. Cessation
C. Idleness D. Repose
E. Inaction

Directions (Qs. No. 116-121): *In the following passage there are blanks each of which has been numbered. These numbers are printed below the passage and against each, five words/phrases are suggested, one of which fits the blank appropriately.*

Citing intensifying regulatory uncertainty, Wells Fargo is ___**116**___ roughly 200 agreements with builders, brokers and other real estate firms that the bank uses to bolster its mortgage business. One of the nation's largest mortgage lenders, Wells Fargo ___**117**___ that it was ending all mortgage marketing services and desk rental agreements with builders and real estate brokers. These arrangements are widespread throughout the highly competitive mortgage industry, where lenders scrap to find ___**118**___ borrowers. Such arrangements involve, for example, Wells renting desk space from a home builder in an effort to more easily sell mortgages to the home buyers passing through the sales office. "The decision was made as a result of increasing ___**119**___ surrounding regulatory oversight of these types of arrangements," the bank said in a statement. A bank spokesman said the move was not related to a specific regulatory problem or investigation. Rather, he said, the bank was responding to broader regulatory scrutiny of such arrangements, which are ___**120**___ by the Real Estate Settlement Procedures Act. The federal law is meant to ___**121**___ mortgage lenders, real estate brokers, builders and any other party involved in the home buying process from handing out or receiving kickbacks in exchange for referrals.

116. Find out the appropriate word in each case.

A. serving B. giving
C. signed D. having
E. proclaiming

117. Find out the appropriate word in each case.

A. noticed B. say
C. announced D. given
E. established

118. Find out the appropriate word in each case.

A. good B. eligible
C. sustainable D. amiable
E. passable

119. Find out the appropriate word in each case.

A. confusion B. burden
C. pressures D. uncertainty
E. curiosity

120. Find out the appropriate word in each case.

A. held B. told
C. acclaimed D. given
E. governed

121. Find out the appropriate word in each case.

A. provide B. prevent
C. allow D. accept
E. pause

Directions (Qs. No. 122-127): *In the given question, select the sentence which should follow the given statement in a grammatically and conceptually appropriate manner.*

122. Even though the school premises had a lot of space _____________.

A. there were plenty of play areas for the children
B. there was no playground for the children
C. yet it remain underutilized
D. there was no shortage of classrooms
E. none of the above

123. Political power is just as permanent as today's newspaper. Ten years down the line, _______ the most powerful man in any state today.

A. Political power shall have shifted weight into the hands of
B. New political parties shall have emerged
C. Few shall know, or care about
D. A new party may have absorbed into its ranks
E. None of these

124. Evolving in the mid-eighteenth century, from the pleasure houses of Japan where courtesans who would entertain the samurai, ________.

A. would discuss the state matters secretly.
B. would hold plays which would entertain the crowd.
C. the first geisha was actually men.

D. the first geisha were actually men, who entertained the guests with drums and music.
E. the first geisha will be actually men, who entertained the guests with drums and music and were all warriors.

125. The media's relationship with democracy has allowed people ______.
A. As well as the conviction that media should be democratic itself and media ownership concentration is not democratic
B. The right to participate in media and share the information they found and want to contribute to the people through the media.
C. To be seen as a theater in modern societies in which political participation is enacted through a medium of talk and a realm of social life which public opinion can be formed
D. To communicate with one another through digital media and share the information they want to
E. None of the above

126. The influences in our lives—family, school, church, work environment, friends _______
A. all have made their silent unconscious impact on us and help shape our frame of reference, our paradigms, our maps.
B. try to change outward attitudes and behaviours which does very little good in the long run
C. shows how powerfully our paradigms affect the way we interact with other people.
D. begin to realize that others see them differently from their own apparently equally clear and objective point of view
E. None of the above

127. To enjoy good health, to bring true happiness to one's family, to bring peace to all, one must first discipline _______.
A. to clear a good place for man's dwelling
B. and control one's own mind
C. to create a hindrance in the music that is in nature
D. to know the vast world outside
E. None of the above

Directions (Qs. No. 128-132): *Select the phrase/connector from the given three options which can be used to form a single sentence from the two sentences given below, implying the same meaning as expressed in the statement sentences. Pick out the option which when used to start a sentence combines both the above sentences in one.*

128. Flagging off partnerships in a host of economic and development projects through a Memorandum of Understanding has been done. The two Prime Ministers have set the stage for long-term collaboration in spheres ranging from energy and infrastructure to special economic zones.
I. Since
II. While
III. The reason behind the
A. Only I
B. Only II
C. Only III
D. All of the above
E. None of these

129. New Delhi's anxiety over Chinese presence might be justified. It should avoid using the China lens to view Sri Lanka, respecting the country's autonomy to engage with any willing partner.
I. While
II. Awhile
III. Among
A. Only I
B. Only II
C. Only III
D. Both I and III
E. None of these

130. The Modi government's fiscal deficit bumped to 3.5% of GDP in 2017-18, a slippage from the figure targeted in the budget. 3% of the GDP was envisaged in the fiscal consolidation unveiled earlier.
I. In the first place
II. Although
III. As a result
A. Only I
B. Only III
C. Only II
D. Both II and III
E. All of these

131. The partition was enforced by the ruling government. People started rushing towards their side of the town before the riots began.
I. Nevertheless
II. As soon as
III. In place of
A. Only I
B. Only III

C. Only I and III D. Only II and III
E. None of these

132. The U.S. Administration announced its intent to withdraw from the Paris Agreement on climate change against a backdrop of rising carbon emissions, extreme weather events that devastated homes; and one of the top three hottest years on record. The momentum continued as other countries held firm in their determination to honour national and international commitments under Paris, in the face of the U.S. announcement.

I. Additionally
II. By comparison
III. Yet

A. Only I B. Only II
C. Both I and III D. Only III
E. All of these

Directions (Qs. No. 133-137): *In the given question, there are five sentences numbered 1,2,3,4 and 5. Read the sentences and find out which of the combinations is correct and mark the respective option.*

133. 1. Goa has so much for the fun-loving tourists.
2. Goa is always ready to welcome its guests.
3. No place can beat Goa in India.
4. Thus tourists receive a very warm treatment in Goa.
5. Whenever we think of a beach holiday,

A. 12453 B. 15324
C. 15432 D. 12543
E. 12345

134. 1. Safdar, Ajay and I dashed out of the classroom as the bell rang.
2. He was our leader.
3. It was the lunch break and we had a whole hour to play.
4. Safdar was the tallest, also the strongest amongst us.
5. Ajay and I followed him meekly like lambs.

A. 14523 B. 15423
C. 12345 D. 13524
E. 13425

135. 1. When you infuse creativity into your writing, you try to
2. You can paint it with your words thus selection of words is important
3. Stoke the emotions of your readers by narrating a story
4. In this way you can make a story that they can relate to easily
5. Thus creative writing classes are getting popular these days

A. 13425 B. 13245
C. 14523 D. 13254
E. 12543

136. 1. Online bingo or Internet bingo sites are virtual in nature.
2. It includes online blackjack, slots, roulette and poker.
3. The odds are undoubtedly better online.
4. These sites allow users to place bets on bingo games.
5. There are several benefits of playing online.

A. 14253 B. 12345
C. 12435 D. 14325
E. 15432

137. 1. Hospitals require one centralized software
2. Since all the functions and working of the hospital will depend on it
3. System which smartly manages a lot of functions
4. It should be able to manage a huge crowd and Should not crash easily
5. The entire hospital can then be easily managed by one software solution

A. 12345 B. 13245
C. 12354 D. 13425
E. 14325

Directions (Qs. No. 138-142): *In the following question, a part of the sentence is printed in bold. Below the sentence alternatives to the bold part are given at (A), (B), (C) and (D) which may help improve the sentence. Choose the correct alternative. In case the given sentence is correct, your answer is (E) i.e. No correction required.*

138. Many subsequent attempts at human **self-definition has faced similar problems** in relation to exceptionality.

A. self-defining has faced similar problems
B. self-definition have faced similar problems
C. self-definition has faced similar problem
D. self-definition has faced similarity problems
E. No correction required

139. They wanted to show how desire interacts with the material world, and to **examine how it were entwined with politics.**

A. examination how it were entwined with politics
B. examine how it were entwine with politically
C. examine how it was entwined with politics
D. examine why it were entwined at politics
E. No correction required

140. That all meaningful experience **requires tapping in to a divine realm** will trigger a severe frown in any non-believer.

A. required tapping in to a divine realm
B. requires tapping into a divine realm
C. requires tapping in to at divine realm
D. required tapped in to a divine realms
E. No correction required

141. Although China has recognized India's sovereignty over Sikkim and had initiated the trade at Nathu La pass, the Doklam fiasco **could mean trouble at all** ends.

A. could mean trouble by all
B. could mean trouble for all
C. could meant trouble at all
D. can mean trouble by all
E. No correction required

142. For centuries, caste dictated almost every aspect of Hindu religious and social life, **with every group occupying** a specific place in this complex hierarchy.

A. by every group occupying
B. with each group occupying
C. by each group occupying
D. through every group occupying
E. No correction required

Directions (Qs. No. 143-147): *Rearrange the following six sentences (a), (b), (c), (d), (e) and (f) in the proper sequence to form a meaningful paragraph: then answer the questions given below them.*

(*a*) Having a bank account for the purpose of savings and remittances has always been the central objective behind banking.

(*b*) Keeping in mind the goal of financial inclusion and extending finance to small businesses and low-income households, under-serviced by traditional commercial banks.

(*c*) The Reserve Bank of India's decision to allow 10 players to set up small finance banks out of the 72 applicants may seem conservative.

(*d*) The need for institutions with greater penetration and wide distribution models has, to some extent, been met with the issue of payments banks licences.

(*e*) With more than half the population in India still unable to access such basic services,

(*f*) But by permitting eight microfinance institutions (MFIs) to set up small banks, the RBI has chosen wisely.

143. Which of the following will be the **Fourth** sentence?

A. (*a*) B. (*b*)
C. (*f*) D. (*d*)
E. (*c*)

144. Which of the following will be the **First** sentence?

A. (*a*) B. (*f*)
C. (*c*) D. (*d*)
E. (*e*)

145. Which of the following will be the **Last** sentence?

A. (*f*) B. (*d*)
C. (*c*) D. (*e*)
E. (*a*)

146. Which of the following will be the **Third** sentence?

A. (*a*) B. (*b*)
C. (*c*) D. (*d*)
E. (*e*)

147. Which of the following will be the **Fifth** sentence?

A. (*a*) B. (*f*)
C. (*c*) D. (*d*)
E. (*e*)

Directions (Qs. No. 148-150): *In each question below, a sentence is broken into four parts which are marked as (A), (B), (C) and (D). One of them may be grammatically or structurally wrong in the context of the sentence. The letter of that word is the answer. If there is no wrong word or group of words, your answer will be (E), i.e., 'No error'. (Ignore the errors of punctuation, if any).*

148. (A) There is just not enough/(B) timing in my job to sit around/(C) talking about how we feel/(D) about each other./(E) No error.

149. (A) Reasonable ambition, if supported/(B) at persistent efforts,/(C) is likely to yield/(D) the desired results./(E) No error.

150. (A) Even after worked in the office/(B) for as many as fifteen years,/(C) he still does not understand/(D) the basic objectives of the work./(E) No error.

ANSWERS

1	2	3	4	5	6	7	8	9	10
C	C	E	A	A	A	B	B	A	C
11	**12**	**13**	**14**	**15**	**16**	**17**	**18**	**19**	**20**
A	C	B	E	A	D	C	A	E	A
21	**22**	**23**	**24**	**25**	**26**	**27**	**28**	**29**	**30**
B	D	A	B	C	A	D	E	A	C
31	**32**	**33**	**34**	**35**	**36**	**37**	**38**	**39**	**40**
A	B	D	A	D	A	C	D	B	D
41	**42**	**43**	**44**	**45**	**46**	**47**	**48**	**49**	**50**
B	A	B	B	B	B	C	B	A	C
51	**52**	**53**	**54**	**55**	**56**	**57**	**58**	**59**	**60**
B	D	B	A	B	B	A	C	A	D
61	**62**	**63**	**64**	**65**	**66**	**67**	**68**	**69**	**70**
C	C	A	D	D	B	C	D	A	C
71	**72**	**73**	**74**	**75**	**76**	**77**	**78**	**79**	**80**
A	A	D	D	D	A	B	E	D	D
81	**82**	**83**	**84**	**85**	**86**	**87**	**88**	**89**	**90**
A	E	D	B	B	A	B	B	A	A
91	**92**	**93**	**94**	**95**	**96**	**97**	**98**	**99**	**100**
D	B	D	E	C	E	C	E	B	B
101	**102**	**103**	**104**	**105**	**106**	**107**	**108**	**109**	**110**
D	E	E	A	B	E	D	B	D	E
111	**112**	**113**	**114**	**115**	**116**	**117**	**118**	**119**	**120**
B	C	D	A	A	A	C	B	D	E
121	**122**	**123**	**124**	**125**	**126**	**127**	**128**	**129**	**130**
B	B	C	D	B	A	B	C	A	C
131	**132**	**133**	**134**	**135**	**136**	**137**	**138**	**139**	**140**
A	D	B	E	B	A	D	B	C	B
141	**142**	**143**	**144**	**145**	**146**	**147**	**148**	**149**	**150**
A	B	A	C	B	B	E	B	B	A

EXPLANATORY ANSWERS

For Qs. 51-55:

- F sits third to the right of S.
- F is sixth to the right of T.
- C and D are not immediate neighbours of F, who sits second to the right of E.
- E sits at the fifth position from the right end.
- B sits fourth to the right of P, who is not the immediate neighbour of U.
- There are two persons between U and A.
- There are two persons between D and Q.
- S is not an immediate neighbour of A.
- C is not an immediate neighbour of D and Q.

From the above statement, we conclude:

Facing North:

P	C	A	T	B	U	S	E	Q	F	R	D

For Qs. 56-60:

In row-1, J, K, L, M, N and O are seated and all of them are facing south. In row-2, C, D, E, F, G and H are seated and all of them are facing north

- M sits third to the left of J.
- The person facing M sits second to the left of H.
- Two persons are sitting between H and E.
- G is not an immediate neighbour of E.
- D does not face M.
- L and K are immediate neighbours.
- L and K do not sit at any of the extreme ends of the line.
- Only one person sits between N and L.
- The person facing K is an immediate neighbour of C.

According to above statement, we conclude:

J	K	L	M	N	O	Row 1 (Facing South)
C	D	E	F	G	H	Row 2 (Facing North)

For Qs. 61-65:

Month	Person
January (31)	Q
February (28/29)	P
March (31)	-
April (30)	A
May (31)	S
June (30)	-
July (31)	M
August (31)	C
September (30)	-
October (31)	K
November (30)	R
December (31)	-

For Qs. 66-70:

Students	Subjects	Standard
D	Chemistry	VIII
H	English	VIII
E	Biology	VII
A	Marathi	VII
G	Math	VII
C	Economics	VI
F	Physics	VI
B	Geography	VI

For Qs. 71-75:

Floor	Boy	Girl	City
9	Rohit	Amita	Lucknow
8	Vikash	Sanjana	Chennai
7	Sanjay	Anita	Varanasi
6	Kamal	Surabhi	Agra
5	Amit	Komal	Mathura
4	Sunil	Susheela	Noida
3	Anit	Saroj	Allahabad
2	Saurabh	Kumkum	Mirzapur
1	Sushil	Suhana	Patna

76. I. A > X → True (as A ≥ P = S > T > X)
II. P < B → False
Hence, only conclusion I follows.

77. I. S < Z → False (as S > U < Z)
II. X > Y → True (as Y < U < Z < X)
Hence, only conclusion II follows.

78. I. V < S → True (as V = P < X < Y < S)
II. T > R → True (as T > Y > X > P = V > R)
Hence, both conclusions follow.

79. I. H < C → False (as there is no relation between H and C)
II. H > D → False (as H ≥ I = E ≤ D)
Hence, no conclusion follows.

80. I. P < B → False (as P ≥ Q > E ≥ F > B)
II. S > A → False (as P ≥ Q > E = S ≥ F > B ≤ A)
Hence, no conclusion follows.

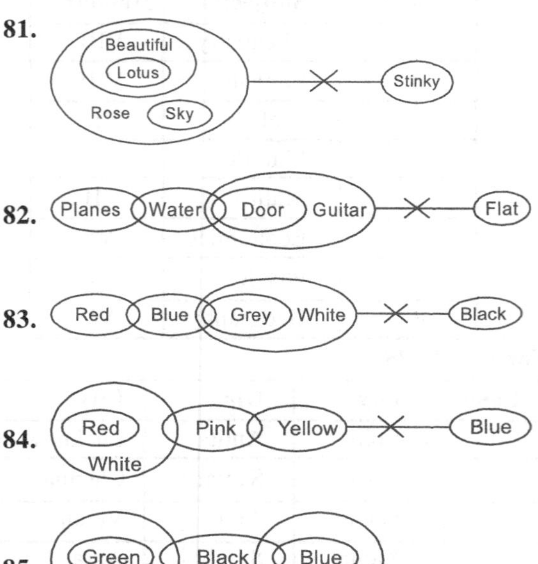

97. From I, A ≥ B < C = D > E ≥ F = G
We can't compare B and F.
From II, A ≤ B = C > D > E < F < G
We can't compare B and F.
From III, A > B > C = D ≥ E > F < G
Clearly B is greater to F.
So, Only III is sufficient. Hence, option C.

98. From I, T → G ← H, G → M

From II, N is between G and H.
From III, N ↖ T

From I and II,

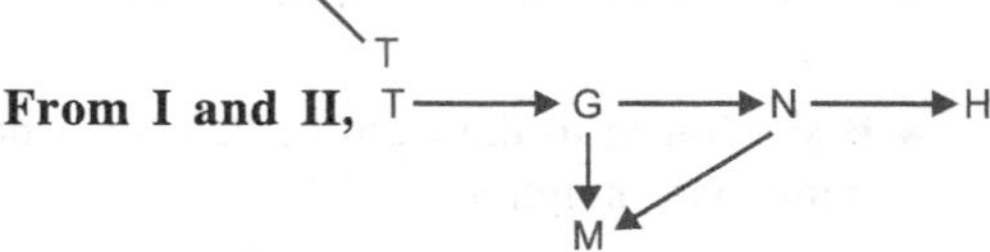

Hence, M is to the south-west of N.
From I and III,

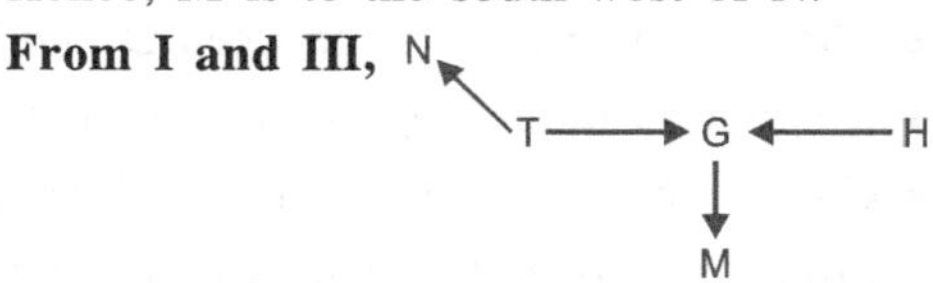

Thus, M is to the south-east of N.
So answer can be found by using I and either II or III.

99. From I, writer – cover – page

In this only 'writer' is given nothing information about 'word'.

From II,

In this only 'writer' is given nothing information about 'word'.

From III,

No information about 'writer'

From II and III,

If we combine both II and III we can get that 'no writer is word'.
So, both II and III will be answer.

100. From I. Neha > Mahi > Nitesh
From II. – > – > – > Rita > – > –
Now combining all the statements, we have
Neha > Mahi > Nitesh > Rita > – > –
Thus, Neha is the tallest.

Previous Paper (Solved)

IBPS—SPECIALIST OFFICERS

Law Officer and Rajbhasha Adhikari

Online Preliminary Recruitment Exam-2017*

Reasoning

1. Twenty per cent of all energy consumed in the country is consumed by home appliances. If appliances that are twice as energy-efficient as those currently available are manufactured, this figure will eventually be reduced to about ten per cent.

The argument above requires which of the following assumptions?

A. Home-appliance usage would not increase along with the energy efficiency of the appliances.
B. It would not be expensive to manufacture home appliances that are energy-efficient.
C. Home-appliance manufacturers now have the technology to produce appliances that are twice as energy-efficient as those currently available.
D. The cost of energy to the consumer would rise with increases in the energy efficiency of home appliances.
E. None of these

Directions (Qs. No. 2-6): *Study the following information carefully and answer the questions which follow—*

In a certain code language, some statements are coded as follows:

'give solution for problem' is coded as '*N8 #R3 %M7 @E4'

'pure fruit sell plants' is coded as '@T5 %E4 *L4 #S6'

'pet sensed ghostly farm' is coded as '#M4 *D6 @Y7 %T3'

'spa guards picked flake' is coded as '%D6 @S6 #E5 *A3'.

2. Which of the following will be the code for 'fruit picked teach game'?

A. @T5 %D5 #H4 *E4
B. @T5 %D6 @H5 *E4
C. @T5 #H4 *E4 %D6
D. @T5 #H5 *E4 %D6
E. @T5 #H4 *E4 %D6

3. What will be the code for 'ghostly'?

A. #Y6 B. @Y7
C. %D7 D. *E4
E. %D6

4. Which of the following will be the code for 'pure water spa tune'?

A. *A3 %E4 @R5 *E4
B. @R5 *E3 %A4 #E4
C. %A4 #E4 @R4 *E4
D. %E4 @R4 #E4 *A3
E. *A3 %E4 @R5 #E4

5. If 'solution farm grain seem' is coded as '*N8 %M4 @N5 #M4', then what is code for 'plants means grain seem'?

A. #S6 *S5 %M4 #N5
B. %A4 #E4 @R4 *E4
C. @N5 #S6 *S5 %M4
D. *S5 %M4 #N5 @S6
E. None of these

6. What will be the code for 'problem good'?

A. #Y6 #D4 B. %M7 @D4
C. @M7 %D4 D. %S7 @D4
E. @D4 %D6

* ***Based on Memory.***

Directions (Qs. No. 7-11): *Read the given information carefully and answer the given questions.*

Twelve friends are sitting in two parallel rows containing six people each in such a way that there is equal distance between adjacent persons. In row 1 A, B, C, D, E and F are seated and all of them are facing north and in row 2 P, Q, R, S, T and U, are seated and are facing south, but not necessarily in the same order.

There are four person, sits to the right of R. R's daughter is immediate neighbour of the one, who faces R. There is one person's sit between R's son and R's daughter. Q is married to F. R's son-in-law sits third to the left of the one, who faces the person, who is immediate left of A's brother. Two persons sit between S and T. R's brother sits second to the right of R's sister. S does not sit one of the extreme ends. A is brother-in-law of B. A's father sits second to the right of A's brother. E is married to S. only one person sits between A's brother and R's mother. R's son-in-law does not sit one of the extreme ends. A's sister-in-law faces S. A's sister-in-law sits third to the left of R's daughter. P faces E, who sits one of the extreme left end. B sits third to the right of E. Q sits immediate right of the person, who faces R's wife. R's mother sits third to the left of the one, who faces the one, who sits immediate right of R's son-in-law. R's brother-in-law sits fourth to the left of R's wife. C sits diagonally opposite to the one, who is immediate right of U. A is son-in-law of D.

7. Who sits immediate left of the one, who is sister-in-law of A?
A. B
B. C's brother
C. Q's brother
D. E's brother-in-law
E. Q

8. Who is grandmother of B?
A. T
B. D's mother-in-law
C. Person sits one of the extreme left end.
D. E's mother-in-law
E. All are true

9. Who sits second to the left of the one, who faces the person, who sits second to the left of P?
A. R's brother B. Q
C. None is true D. A
E. S's husband

10. Who is the niece of P?
A. B B. T's son
C. Q's wife D. Q's sister-in-law
E. Q

11. If P related to A's sister-in-law in the same way as Q related to R's daughter. Which of the following is U related to, following the same pattern?
A. R's brother B. C's brother
C. F D. A
E. None of these

Directions (Qs. No. 12-13): *Each question consists of some conclusion followed by five statements. Consider the given conclusion to be true even if they seem to be at variance with commonly known facts. Read the conclusions and then decide from which statement, the conclusion can be possible.*

12. Conclusion : No toxic is injection.
Some injections are glucose.

Statement :
A. All toxics are tablet.
No tablet is glucose.
Some glucose are medicine.
All medicines are injections.
B. Some toxics are tablet.
All tablets are injection.
Some injection are glucose.
All glucose are medicine.
C. All tablet are toxic.
No injection is toxic.
Some glucose are injections.
All glucose are medicines.
D. Some injections are toxics
All injections are tablet.
Some toxics are glucose.
All glucose are medicine.
E. Some medicines are toxics.
Some toxics are injections.
Some injections are tablets.
All tablets are glucose.

13. Conclusion : Some clocks are watches.
Some wheels are buses.

Statement:

A. All watches are clocks.
Some clocks are tyres.
Some tyres are wheels.
Some wheels are buses.

B. Some watches are wheels.
All wheels are tyre.
Some tyres are buses.
All buses are clocks.

C. Some buses are tyre.
Some tyres are clocks.
All clocks are watch.
Some watch are wheels.

D. All tyres are buses.
Some buses are wheels.
Some wheels are clocks.
No clocks is watch.

E. Some buses are watchs.
Some watches are tyre.
Some tyres are clocks.
Some clocks are wheels.

14. Statement : By asking five prominent hospitals in the national capital to deposit nearly ₹ 600 crore to compensate for their failure to treat poor patients, the Delhi government has drawn attention to the social obligation of healthcare providers in the corporate sector as well as the need for timely enforcement of applicable regulations. According to the Delhi government, trusts and registered societies to which public land was allotted to establish hospitals were required to earmark a percentage of their medical facilities and services for indigent patients.

Assumptions:

I. This strengthens the case for private hospitals to dedicate a part of their services to those who cannot afford treatment.

II. Social responsibility of hospitals must be monitored and central government should ensure compliance by the corporate hospitals.

III. There is a great need for the government to monitor and enforce "health services" so that the poor who cannot afford modern health facilities that are extremely costly - are able to be benefitted.

A. All are implicit
B. Only III is implicit
C. Only I and III are implicit
D. Only I and II are implicit
E. None is implicit

15. The ancient Nubians inhabited an area in which typhus occurs, yet surprisingly few of their skeletons show the usual evidence of this disease. The skeletons do show deposits of tetracycline, an antibiotic produced by a bacterium common in Nubian soil. This bacterium can flourish on the dried grain used for making two staples of Nubian diet, beer and bread. Thus, tetracycline in their food probably explains the low incidence of typhus among ancient Nubians.

Which of the following is an assumption that can be drawn from the passage?

I. Infectious diseases other than typhus to which the ancient Nubians were exposed are unaffected by tetracycline.

II. Tetracycline is not rendered ineffective as an antibiotic by exposure to the process involved in making bread and beer.

III. Typhus cannot be transmitted by ingesting bread or beer contaminated with the infectious agents of this disease.

IV. Bread and beer were the only items in the diet of the ancients Nubians which could have contained tetracycline.

V. Typhus is generally fatal.

A. Only II follows
B. Only III and V follow
C. Only III follows
D. Only II, III, IV and V follow
E. None of these

16. It is not often that professional footballers retire from internationals at the peak of their game. When the 29-year-old Lionel Messi, widely reckoned to be the most skilled footballer today, announced after the 2016 Copa America Final against Chile that he would not wear the Argentinian shirt again, he took everyone by surprise. It is not clear if he has made the retirement call in the heat of the moment. It came after Messi failed, yet again, to win a major title with the Argentinian team; he also missed a crucial penalty in the shootout against Chile after efficient but goal-less play in regulation and extra time. In fact, Messi's overall international record with Argentina has been good, if not spectacular. With him, the team has reached the finals of four important tournaments: the World Cup in 2014 and the Copa America in 2007, 2015 and 2016.

According to the given question, you have to decide which statement(s) is/are strong on the basis of the given passage:

After defeating in Copa America Final, should Messi continue his international career for two years more?

I. Yes, because it is the only way he can prove himself to the world as a challenging person.
II. No, it is his personal decision to play no more for Argentina and as a player he gave a lot of contribution to his nation. So we should respect his decision.
III. No, because Messi's record as a player of Barcelona is quite better than as a player of Argentina. So he should focus on one side rather than playing for both of them.

A. Only II and III are strong
B. Only I and III are strong
C. Only II is strong
D. Only III is strong
E. None is strong

Directions (Qs. No. 17-21): *Read the given information carefully and answer the given questions.*

Ten people G, H, I, J, K, L, W, X, Y and Z live in a building with four floors. Each floor has 3 flats - flat 1, flat 2 and flat 3 in the same order from left to right. Ground floor is numbered floor 1 and topmost floor is floor 4. Each flat is built in such a way that Flat 1 of floor 2 is just above Flat 1 of floor 1 and so on. The two flats in which no one lives are on even numbered floor and in even numbered flat. G does not live on even numbered floor and even numbered flat. W lives in the flat just above H. The flat between K and X is vacant and K lives in one of the flats above X. L lives in an odd numbered flat which is in the left of X. Z and Y live on the same floor and no one else is living with them on that floor. G lives on a floor and flat just above W's floor and flat. I lives on one of the floors on which one flat is vacant. Z and I both live in the flat which is numbered 1.

17. Who is living just above X?
A. K
B. G
C. J
D. Z
E. No one

18. Which of the following statements is true about G?
A. G lives on an even numbered flat
B. K is the immediate neighbour of G
C. G lives on a floor on which one flat is vacant
D. G and W live on the same floor
E. None is true

19. Which of the following lives on the ground floor?
A. G
B. I
C. L
D. W
E. Both A and C

20. Which of the following does not belong to a certain group?
A. J
B. L
C. W
D. H
E. Y

21. Who is living in flat 1 on floor 4?
A. Z
B. Y
C. W
D. G
E. No one

Directions (Qs. No. 22-24): *Each question consists of four statements followed by five conclusions. Consider the given statements to be true even if they seem to be at variance with commonly known facts. Read all the conclusions and then decide which of the given conclusions does not logically follow from the given statements using all statements together and mark that conclusion as your answer.*

22. Statements : All chairs are tables.
Some tables are books.
All books are pens.
No pen is a copy.

Conclusions:

A. Some tables are not copies.
B. All tables being pen is a possibility.
C. At least some copies are pens.
D. All books are not copies.
E. Some pens are books.

23. Statements : Some pencils are kites.
Some kites are desks.
All desks are cups.
All cups are tea.

Conclusions:

A. All tea are cups is a possibility.
B. Some cups are definitely pencils
C. Some tea are desks.
D. Some cups are kites.
E. Some pencils can be desks

24. Statements : Some boards are papers.
All clips are papers.
Some papers are lanes.
All lanes are roads.

Conclusions:

A. Some roads can be boards
B. Some lanes are papers
C. Some boards are clips
D. All roads are clips
E. Some roads are papers

Directions (Qs. No. 25-29): *Read the given information carefully and answer the given questions.*

J, K, L, M, S, T, U and V are eight employees of an organization. They will attend a meeting in the four months (March, June, October and November). The meeting is held in each month on 13th and 22nd date. Only two meetings are held in a month. No person can attend the meeting after L. M attends the meeting in the month which has less than 31 days. S and U attend meeting after M on 22nd of different months, while J and K attend before M and K attend after J in the same month. V does not attend the meeting in the month in which either S attends or L attends.

25. How many people attend the meeting between S and L?

A. 1 B. 2
C. 3 D. 4
E. None of these

26. Four of the following follow a same pattern. Find the one which does not follow.

A. J – March B. S – 13
C. U – October D. U – 22
E. T – November

27. Who attends the meeting in November?

A. T, L B. M, T
C. S, T D. S, U
E. None of these

28. Who attends the meeting immediately after M?

A. U B. S
C. V D. T
E. L

29. S attends the meeting in the month of:

A. June B. October
C. November D. March
E. None of these

30. Targeted Delivery of Government subsidies and benefits to ensure that they reach the poor and the deserving. What would be the cause of the above government budget?

A. Some portion is still untouched from new subsidies and other scheme.
B. Some urban sector can get subsidy scheme profit.
C. DBT ensures related information about the poor people for subsidies.
D. The transparency and clearance will be increased.
E. None of these

Directions (Qs. No. 31-35) : *Read the following information to answer the questions given below it:*

(*i*) In a family of six persons, there are people from three generations. Each person has separate profession and also they like different colours. There are two couples in the family.

(*ii*) Rohan is a CA and his wife is neither a doctor nor likes green colour.

(*iii*) The engineer likes red colour and his wife is a teacher.

(*iv*) Mohini is mother-in-law of Sunita and she likes orange colour.

(*v*) Vinod is grandfather of Tanmay, and Tanmay, who is a principal, likes black colour.

(*vi*) Nanu is grand-daughter of Mohini and she likes blue colour. Nanu's mother likes white colour.

31. Who is an engineer?
A. Nanu
B. Mohini
C. Sunita
D. Cannot be determined
E. None of these

32. What is the profession of Sunita?
A. Engineer
B. Doctor
C. Teacher
D. Cannot be determined
E. None of these

33. Which of the following is the correct pair of two couples?
A. Mohini-Vinod and Rohan-Sunita
B. Vinod-Mohini and Rohan-Nanu
C. Rohan-Sunita and Tanmay-Nanu
D. Cannot be determined
E. None of these

34. How many ladies are there in the family?
A. Two
B. Three
C. Four
D. Cannot be determined
E. None of these

35. Which colour is liked by CA?
A. Green
B. White
C. Either White or Green
D. Cannot be determined
E. None of these

Directions (Qs. No. 36-40) : *Read the following information carefully and answer the questions given below it:*

(*i*) Six flats on a floor in two rows facing North and South are allotted to P, Q, R, S, T and U.

(*ii*) Q gets a North facing flat and is not next to S.

(*iii*) S and U get diagonally opposite flats.

(*iv*) R, next to U, gets a South facing flat and T gets a North facing flat.

36. Which of the following combinations gets South facing flats?
A. QTS B. UPT
C. URP D. Data inadequate
E. None of these

37. Whose flat is between Q and S?
A. T B. U
C. R D. P
E. Data inadequate

38. If the flats of T and P are interchanged, whose flat will be next to that of U?
A. P B. Q
C. R D. T
E. None of these

39. The flats of which of the other pairs than SU, is diagonally opposite to each other?
A. QP B. QR
C. PT D. TS
E. None of these

40. To arrive at the answers to the above questions, which of the following statements can be dispensed with?
A. None B. (*i*) only
C. (*ii*) only D. (*iii*) only
E. None of these

Directions (Qs. 41-45): *Each of the following questions below consists of a question and two statements numbered I and II given below it. You have to decide whether the data provided in the statements are sufficient to answer the questions. Read both the statements and give answer.*

A. If the data in statement I alone are sufficient to answer the question, while the data in statement II alone are not sufficient to answer the question.

B. If the data in statement II alone are sufficient to answer the question, while the data in statement I alone are not sufficient to answer the question.

C. If the data in statement I alone or in statement II alone are sufficient to answer the question.
D. If the data in both the statements I and II are not sufficient to answer the question.
E. If the data in both the statements I and II together are necessary to answer the question.

41. How many members belong to Gymkhana club?
I. There are 50 members who belong to Dine club.
II. This year 120 new members have taken membership in Gymkhana Club.

42. What was Champa's income in 2001?
I. Her total income for last three years was ₹ 10000.
II. She earned 25% more in 2000 than she earned in 1999.

43. Is the number divisible by 8?
I. The number is divisible by 4.
II. The last three digits of the number are zeros.

44. Among five colleagues A, B, C, D, E who is the highest salary earner?
I. B's salary is less than the sum of the salaries of A and C but more than the sum of salaries of E and D.
II. A's salary is more than that of C who ranks second in the descending order of their salaries.

45. What are the dimensions of a certain rectangle?
I. The diagonal of the rectangle is 7.
II. The perimeter of the rectangle is 22.

Directions (Qs. 46-50): *Study the following information and answer the given questions.*

A word arrangement machine, when given an input line of words, rearranges them following a particular rule in each step. The following is an illustration of input and the steps of rearrangement.

Input : Go for to Though By easy To Access at
Step I : Access Go for to Though By easy To at
Step II : Access at Go for to Though By easy To
Step III : Access at By Go for to Though easy To
Step IV : Access at By easy Go for to Though To
Step V : Access at By easy for Go to Though To
Step VI : Access at By easy for Go Though to To
Step VII : Access at By easy for Go Though To to
(and Step VII is the last step for this input)

As per the rules followed in the above steps, find out in the given questions the appropriate step for the given input.

46. **Input :** story For around on was He at
Which of the following will be Step IV for the given input?
A. around at For He on was story
B. around at For He on story was
C. around at For He story on was
D. around at He For story on was
E. None of these

47. **Input :** every and peer to an for
Which of the following steps would be 'an and every for peer to'?
A. II
B. III
C. IV
D. V
E. None of these

48. **Input :** Together over series on feast the so
Which of the following steps will be the last but one?
A. II
B. III
C. IV
D. V
E. None of these

49. **Input :** Over Go For through at one
Which step number will be the last step of the above input?
A. III
B. V
C. VI
D. VII
E. None of these

50. The Step II of an input is as follows:
and Do pet to on that
Which of the following would definitely be the input?
A. Do on pet to and that
B. Do pet to and that on
C. Do and pet to on that
D. Cannot be determined
E. None of these

General Knowledge

51. Which Bank's headquarter is located in Chennai?
A. Indian Bank
B. SBI
C. Dena Bank
D. Oriental Bank of Commerce
E. None of the above

52. The capital of Mozambique is:
A. Jakarta B. Maputo
C. Teheran D. Baghdad
E. None of the above

53. Social Media Banking Application launched by SBI, is:
A. SBI Google B. SBI Phoning
C. SBI Mingle D. SBI Twitter
E. None of the above

54. Fino paytech is:
A. Payment Gateway
B. Financial Outdoor
C. Financial Orbit
D. Fixed Payment Target
E. None of the above

55. What is the maximum amount in BSBDA account?
A. 5 Lakhs B. 8 Lakhs
C. 3 Lakhs D. 1 Lakh
E. None of the above

56. Rani Jhansi Marine National Park is located in:
A. Andaman and Nicobar Islands
B. Kerala
C. Tamil Nadu
D. Manipur
E. None of the above

57. NATO summit 2016 was held in:
A. Paris B. London
C. Warsaw D. New York
E. None of the above

58. Who is the MD of Bandhan Bank?
A. Shashi Prabha
B. Raghav Mazumdar
C. Subrato Sen
D. Chandra Shekhar Ghosh
E. None of the above

59. The meeting of World Economic Forum 2016 was held in:
A. Warsaw B. Davos
C. Paris D. Baghdad
E. None of the above

60. Madhavrao Scindia cricket ground is located in:
A. Surat B. Rajkot
C. Nasik D. Ahmedabad
E. None of the above

61. Maximum loan amount in Mudra Scheme is:
A. 5 Lakhs B. 8 Lakhs
C. 10 Lakhs D. 7 Lakhs
E. None of the above

62. World Bank classify India as:
A. Lower Income Economy
B. Lower Middle Income Economy
C. Middle Income Economy
D. High Income Economy
E. None of the above

63. Lakhwar Dam-Dehradun is located in river:
A. Ganga B. Ghaghra
C. Yamuna D. Bhadra
E. None of these

64. Krishi Kalyan Cess was introduced on:
A. 1st June, 2016
B. 5 April, 2016
C. 3 December, 2016
D. 10 August, 2016
E. None of the above

65. Capital Local Area Bank Headquarters is located in:
A. Jodhpur B. Jalandhar
C. Mohali D. Ludhiana
E. None of the above

66. Kavinder Singh and Satish Kumar is related to which game?
A. Wrestling B. Boxing
C. Archery D. Shooting
E. None of these

67. As per report of Stockholm International Peace Research Institute (SIPRI) India's military expenditure in 2016 grew by:
A. 8.1% B. 8.7%
C. 8.5% D. 8.8%
E. None of these

68. What is the meaning of "C" in PCA?
A. Personal access code
B. Prompt corrected action
C. Prompt Corrective Action
D. Prompt code action
E. None of these

69. India Licensing Expo (ILE), India's first and most influential brand licensing show will take place on August 20-21 in:
A. Mumbai B. New Delhi
C. Kolkata D. Manipur
E. None of these

70. Who is highest wicket-taker in women's ODIs?
A. Jhulan Goswami
B. Ekta Bisht
C. Rajeshwari Gayakwad
D. Neetu David
E. None of these

71. The Insolvency and Bankruptcy Board of India (IBBI) has constituted a Technical Committee in accordance with Regulation 14 of the IBBI (Information Utilities) Regulations, 2017. The Technical Committee (Committee) will be headed by:
A. Justin Shrikrishna
B. Dr R. B. Barman
C. Vibhushan Kastirirangan
D. Manhendra Nath Pande
E. None of these

72. India's growth for 2018-19 as projected by IMF?
A. 7.7% B. 7.8%
C. 7.9% D. 8%
E. None of these

73. National Financial Switch (NFS) is run by:
A. RBI B. NIC
C. NPCI D. IDRBT
E. None of these

74. Who was elected as head of FIFA's governance committee at the world football governing body's 67th Congress in Bahrain's capital city of Manama?
A. Mukul Mudgal B. Rajiv Kumar
C. Dipak Mishra D. Gianni Infuntinu
E. None of these

75. Foreign direct investment (FDI) in India grew 18 per cent during 2016 to touch ________ data released by the Department of Industrial Policy and Promotion (DIPP).
A. $ 46 B. $ 36
C. $ 50 D. $ 56
E. None of these

76. Fiscal deficit target for 2017-18 pegged at __________ of GDP?
A. 4.8% B. 3.2%
C. 3.5% D. 4.0%
E. None of these

77. The government has decided to make tax evasion of over _________ under the proposed Goods and Services Tax (GST) the regime as a non-bailable offence.
A. ₹ 5 crore B. ₹ 4 crore
C. ₹ 8 crore D. ₹ 10 crore
E. None of these

78. What is the meaning of "S" in MSF?
A. Market Standing Facility
B. Moderate Standing Facility
C. Medium Standing Facility
D. Marginal Standing Facility
E. None of these

79. What is the meaning of "P" in APBS?
A. Aadhaar Payment Bridge System
B. Aadhaar paid Bridge System
C. Aadhaar Payment Bridge Source
D. Aadhaar Payment Bridge Secure
E. None of these

80. The target of digital transactions through UPI, USSD, Aadhar, IMPS for 2017-18?
A. 3,000 crore digital transactions
B. 2,500 crore digital transactions
C. 3,500 crore digital transactions
D. 4,000 crore digital transactions
E. None of these

81. Cheque written by drawer and dated at some point in past is called?
A. Ante-dated cheque B. Post dated cheque
C. open cheque D. State cheque
E. None of these

82. As per RBI norms on small banks, initial promoter stake for first 5 years should not be less than?
A. 30% B. 45%
C. 50% D. 40%
E. None of these

83. Which of the following full form of UPI?
A. Unique Payments Interface
B. Unified Payments Interface
C. Unified Power Income
D. Unique Power Income
E. None of these

84. The base year for calculating key economic growth from 2004-05 changed to?
A. 2011-12 B. 2013-14
C. 2014-15 D. 2015-16
E. None of these

85. One Question was, increase in repo rate signifies?
A. Is the rate at which the RBI lends to state government
B. Is the rate at which the International aid agencies lends to RBI
C. Is the rate at which the RBI lends to Bank
D. Is the rate at which the Bank lends to RBI
E. None of these

86. Finland has become the first country in Europe to pay its unemployed citizens a basic monthly income, amounting to:
A. 600 euros B. 570 euros
C. 590 euros D. 560 euros
E. None of these

87. Total number of ATMs of SBI after the merger?
A. 70,000 ATMs B. 65,000 ATMs
C. 59,000 ATMs D. 58,000 ATMs
E. None of these

88. The government of India (GOI) has approved 681 crores as seed capital for building a venture for electronic devices with total corpus?
A. ₹ 6,831 crore B. ₹ 5832 crore
C. ₹ 6,859 crore D. ₹ 7832 crore
E. None of these

89. How much amount has allocated by the government to MGNREGA in this year's (2017-18) Budget?
A. ₹ 48,000 crore B. ₹ 35000 crore
C. ₹ 50,000 crore D. ₹ 60,000 crore
E. None of these

90. Risk of collapse of entire financial system on entire market is called:
A. Systemic risk B. Capital risk
C. Systematic Risk D. Marginal Risk
E. None of these

91. Payments bank not permitted to?
A. can offer loans
B. can offer advances
C. can't offer advances
D. cannot offer loans
E. None of these

92. The NBFCs are allowed to accept/renew public deposits for a minimum period of 12 months and the maximum period of _____ months.
A. 60 months B. 70 months
C. 55 months D. 65 months
E. None of these

93. Government of India has changed CII base year from 1981 to:
A. 2001 B. 2002
C. 2004 D. 2008
E. None of these

94. Metric which defines operating liquidity available to business is known as?
A. Paid up capital B. Net Capital
C. Working capital D. Authorised capital
E. None of these

95. An estimated USD _________ in black money entered India during 2005-2014, US-based think tank Global Financial Integrity (GFI).
A. 770 billion B. 780 billion
C. 790 billion D. 800 billion
E. None of these

96. Name the person, who will head a task force to assess the extent of employment creation at different points of time, based on "credible data."

A. Amitabh Kamant B. C. Rangarajan
C. Ajay Tyagi D. Arvind Panagriya
E. None of these

97. Institute for Development & Research in Banking Technology (IDRBT) is located in?
A. Hyderabad B. Mumbai
C. New Delhi D. Kolkata
E. None of these

98. Class of derivative whose value is at least partly derived from one or more underlying stock exchange securities? (Trade, Commodity, Credit, Interest Rate, Equity)
A. Trade B. Equity Derivative
C. Credit D. Derivative
E. None of these

99. The framework of Joint Lenders' Forum (JLF) by RBI is to strengthen the system for revitalising the...............?
A. stressed assets in the economy
B. Restrustring assets
C. Destressed assets
D. Investment fluctuation assets
E. None of these

100. Amendment to Section _______ of Negotiable Instruments Acts to include the electronic image of a truncated cheque and a cheque in electronic form.
A. 6 B. 4
C. 5 D. 7
E. None of these

English Language

Directions (Qs. 101-105): *In each question given below, a sentence is broken into four parts which are marked as A, B, C and D. One of them may be grammatically or structurally wrong in the context of the sentence. The letter of that word is the answer. If there is no wrong word or group of words, your answer will be E, i.e., 'No error'. (Ignore the errors of punctuation, if any).*

101. (A) Due to certain inevitable circumstances/(B) the scheduled programme had to be/(C) postponed indefinite/(D) but the members could not be informed./(E) No error.

102. (A) Scarcely had/(B) he gone/(C) when a policeman/(D) knocked at the door./(E) No error.

103. (A) Do not trouble/(B) yourself about writing to me/(C) unless you are quite/(D) in the humour for it./(E) No error.

104. (A) In a very harsh tone,/(B) he shouted at his servants/(C) and told them that/(D) he does not need their services./(E) No error.

105. (A) Our system of assigning/(B) different jobs to different people/(C) should be based on/(D) their strengths and weaknesses./(E) No error.

Directions (Qs. 106-123): *Read the following passages carefully and answer the questions given below each of them. All answers should be given in the context of the given passage. Certain words/phrases are printed in bold to help you locate them while answering some of the questions.*

PASSAGE-1

Today, with a Nobel Prize to its credit. Grameen is one of the largest microfinance organisations in the world. It started out lending small sums to poor entrepreneurs in Bangladesh to help them grow from a subsistence living to a livelihood. The great discovery its founders made was that even with few assets, these entrepreneurs repaid on time. Grameen and microfinance have since become financial staples of the developing world. Grameen's approach, unlike other microfinancers, uses the group-lending model. Costs are kept down by having borrowers vet one another, tying together their financial fates and eliminating expensive loan officers entirely. The ultimate promise of Grameen is to use business lending as a way for people to lift themselves out of poverty.

Recently Grameen has taken on a different challenge—by setting up operations in the United States. Money may be tight in the waning recession, but it is still a nation of 1,00,000 bank branches. Globally, the working microfinance equation consists of borrowing funds cheaply and keeping loan defaults and overhead expenses sufficiently low. Microlenders, including Grameen, do this by charging **colossal** interest rates—as high as 60% or 70%—which is necessary to compensate for the risk and attract bank funding. But loans at rates, much above the standard 15% would most likely be attacked as usurious in America.

So, the question is whether there is a role for a Third World lender in the world's largest economy? Grameen America, believes that in a few years it will be successful and turn a profit, thanks to 9 million United States households untouched by mainstream banks and 21 million using the likes of payday loans and pawn shops for financing. But enticing the unbanked won't be easy. After all, profit has long **eluded** United States microfinanciers and if it is not lucrative; it is not microlending—but charity. When Grameen first went to the United States, in the late 1980s, it tripped up. Under Grameen's tutelage, banks started micro loans to entrepreneurs with a shocking 30% loss. But Grameen America says that this time results will be different because Grameen employees themselves will be making the loans, not training an American bank to do it. More often than not, the borrowers. Grameen finds in the United States already have jobs (as factory workers for example) or side businesses—selling toys, cleaning houses etc. The loans from Grameen, by and large, provide a steadier source of funding, but they don't create businesses out of nothing. But money isn't everything. More importantly for many entrepreneurs, group members are tremendous sources of support to one another. So even if studies are yet to determine if Grameen is a clear-cut pathway out of poverty, it still achieves something useful.

106. What has adversely affected the success of microfinance institutions in the United States?

A. The focus of these institutions is on making a profit at any cost instead of being charitable to the needy

B. American banks engaged in microlending were the most severely hit during the recession

C. Widespread perception among bankers that these institutions are better suited to developing countries

D. Their failure to attract those outside the formal banking system as customers

E. Americans are too proud to accept aid from third world countries

107. Why has Grameen made a second attempt to launch in the United States?

A. The willingness of U.S. banks to provide the necessary staff and funds to facilitate the spread of microfinance

B. The rates of interest on loans in the U.S. are exorbitant making it easier to recover capital

C. The realisation that a large percentage of the American population not reached by mainstream banks can be tapped

D. Recognition of the fact that disbursing credit developing countries during the recession is too risky

E. None of the above

108. Which of the following can be inferred from the passage?

A. Microfinance has been successful only in Asian countries

B. Microfinance makes individual borrowers dependent rather than independent

C. America has the largest number of banks in the world

D. There is scope for microfinance institutions to profitable in developed countries

E. There are no informal sources of credit in developed countries

109. According to the author, what has enhanced the likelihood of success for Grameen America at present?

A. Its success in Bangladesh and other developing countries

B. Absence of other microfinance institutions for competition

C. The fact that America is currently in the midst recession

D. It provides loans at nominal rates of interest i.e. below 15 per cent

E. None of the above

110. Which of the following can be said about Grameen?
1. Its success in developing countries will ensure success in developed countries
2. It ensures that the poor in developing countries enjoy a subsistence standard of living
3. It has demonstrated that the poor are far more likely to repay loans than the affluent

A. None B. Only 1
C. Only 1 and 3 D. Only 2
E. Only 3

111. What is the central theme of the passage?
A. The contention that Grameen is doomed to fall in developed countries
B. A comprehensive evaluation of the current status of the American economy
C. A discussion about the prospects of Grameen and micro finance in the U.S.
D. The role of banks in facilitating micro-lending efforts in developed nations
E. Microfinance efforts are useful in developing countries but are futile in developed ones

112. Why was Grameen America's initial U.S. initiative a flop?
1. Lack of proper training to Grameen America personnel
2. Grameen's refusal to adapt their system to meet the needs of the American poor
3. It ended up giving loans at half their customary rates of interest

A. None B. Only 1
C. Only 1 and 3 D. Only 2
E. Only 3

113. Which of the following is a benefit of the Grameen system of microfinance?
A. If a single member is unable to repay a loan other group members will repay it
B. Dispensing with the expense of technology networks to monitor advances
C. It utilises the vast bank network already existing in a country
D. Group members can sanction loans and verify if borrowers have sufficient collateral
E. Backing that borrowers receive from other group members

114. Which of the following is **most similar** in meaning to the word **'eluded'** as used in the passage?
A. Avoided B. Duped
C. Abandoned D. Intangible
E. Betrayed

115. Which of the following is **most opposite** in meaning to the word **'colossal'** as used in the passage?
A. Short B. Lavish
C. Minority D. Frugal
E. Insignificant

PASSAGE-2

We should recognise the indebtedness of the country to its farm families who toil to safeguard national food security. Loan waiver is the price we have to pay for the neglect of rural India over the past several decades. There has been a gradual decline in investment in key sectors related to agriculture such as infrastructure, marketing, post harvest technology etc. The four crore farmers whose debt is to be **relieved** will be eligible for institutional credit for their cultivation expenses during Kharif 2008. The challenge is to prevent them from getting into the debt trap again. For this purpose the Central and various State governments should set up an Indebted Farmers' Support Consortium, comprising scientists, panchayat raj officials and others relevant to assisting farmers to improve the profitability and productivity of their farms in an environmentally sustainable manner. The smaller the farm, the greater is the need for marketable surplus to reduce indebtedness.

The Indebted Farmers' Support Consortium should aim to get all the four crore farmers all the benefits of the government schemes such as the Rashtriya Krishi Vikas Yojana, Irrigation Benefit Programme and others. If this is done, every farm family released from the debt trap should be able to produce at least an additional half tonne per hectare of foodgrains. This should help increase food production by about 20 million tonnes by 2008-10. At a time when global and national food stocks are dwindling and prices are rising, this will be a timely gain for our national food security. We need to ensure that the outcome of the debt waiver is enhanced farmers' income and production. The prevailing **gap** between potential and actual yields in the crops of rainfed areas such as pulses and oilseeds is over 200 per cent even with the necessary technologies on the shelf. We are now importing without duty large quantities of pulses and oilseeds. If helped, farmers can produce these at a lower cost.

Opportunities for **assured** and remunerative marketing are essential if loan waiver is not to become a recurring event leading to the destruction of the credit system. This is why the Minimum Support Price is necessary for all, not just for a few crops which is the case at present. This is the single most effective step to make loan waivers history. There is another urgent step which needs to be taken. The loan waiver does not cover those who borrow from moneylenders. It will not be possible for the government to scrutinise the veracity of such private deals but steps can be taken such as giving them Smart Cards which will entitle them to essential inputs like seeds and fertilizers. The gram sabha can be entrusted with the task of identifying these farmers so that there is transparency in the process and elimination of the chances for falsification and corruption. Fear of occasional misuse should not come in the way of enabling millions of poor farmers who have borrowed from informal sources if we are to achieve the goal of four per cent growth in agriculture.

116. What is the likely impact of ensuring farmers' benefit from government schemes?
1. They can use the credit from these schemes to repay moneylenders
2. The government can control the price rise
3. Increased agricultural production

A. Both 1 and 2 B. All 1, 2 and 3
C. Only 3 D. Both 2 and 3
E. None of the above

117. Why does the author feel that rural India has been overlooked in the past?
1. Institutional credit was only made available for Kharif crops
2. Drop in investment in central areas related to agriculture
3. Records of those eligible for loan waivers have not been maintained over time

A. Only 2 B. Both 1 and 2
C. Only 3 D. All 1, 2 and 3
E. None of the above

118. How can small farmers avoid debt?
A. They need to acquire additional land holdings
B. They need to take advantage of both government schemes as well as credit from moneylenders
C. They have to ensure a sufficient amount of their farm produce is sold
D. The Government should provide periodic loan waivers
E. None of the above

119. What is the objective of the Indebted Farmers' Support Consortium?
A. It is a support group for the families of indebted farmers
B. It has to devise new government schemes for farmers
C. It has to track farmers eligible for government schemes
D. It has to evaluate government schemes and weed out the inefficient ones
E. None of the above

120. What does the author mean by the phrase "indebtedness of the country to its farm families"?
A. If farmers are in debt, it impacts the entire country
B. Citizens should be grateful to farmers and their families for the hardships borne by them to cultivate crops
C. India's food production has fallen causing it to be in debt since it has to import food
D. The number of farmers' descendants taking up agriculture has fallen
E. None of the above

121. What is the author's opinion of recurring loan waivers?
A. They are beneficial to farmers
B. They are detrimental to the system of lending
C. They will reduce the need for a Minimum Support Price for agricultural products
D. Farmers will no longer be in debt to moneylenders
E. None of the above

122. Which of the following is **true** in the context of the passage?

A. The Minimum Support Price for agricultural products is yet to be implemented

B. Loan waiver is a permanent solution to indebtedness of farmers

C. Current agricultural growth is below four per cent

D. India's food production has increased in 2008

E. Moneylenders benefit from loan waivers

123. Why does the loan waiver not cover credit taken from moneylenders?

1. It is difficult to verify these contracts between farmers and moneylenders
2. It will increase the deficit in the budget
3. There is a risk that the funds may be misappropriated

A. Both 1 and 3 B. All 1, 2 and 3

C. Only 2 D. Both 1 and 2

E. None of the above

Directions (Qs. 124 and 125): *Choose the word which is **most similar** in meaning to the word printed in bold as used in the passage.*

124. Assured

A. insured B. definite

C. doubted D. confident

E. reliance

125. Relieved

A. exempted B. backed

C. supported D. calmed

E. substituted

Directions (Qs. 126-130): *Rearrange the sentences marked with numbers to form a meaningful paragraph and select the option with correct order.*

126.
1. Many so-called indicators for stocks and indexes take on complex hues, such as taking on moving averages of moving averages and so on.
2. A moving-average-based indicator will always be a little late, and you should naturally be suspicious of any 'formula' that can predict the next move, based purely on moving averages of price.
3. The moving average is simply a "smoothing" function — it gets rid of periodic volatility to tell you the recent trend.
4. At best, they can tell you a trend, and if the hypothesis is that the trend will sustain, and that bears out historically in enough instances, you might have a hope with it.
5. But smoothing has its disadvantages; it reacts slowly to sudden changes, so it will only tell you that the trend has changed after the trend has changed, sometimes too late to actually take action.

A. 1 2 3 4 5 B. 4 2 3 1 5

C. 1 3 5 2 4 D. 2 5 3 1 4

E. 3 2 1 5 4

127.
1. From Sweden to the UK to Greece to even the US in the early part of the century, housing prices have fallen.
2. But wasn't that just correlation?
3. Housing bubbles have been known to go bust in the past, and in different countries.
4. "The real estate market has never gone down in any meaningful way" —this statement was often quoted by real estate agents and brokers in the US, and it might have even been statistically valid, with over 50 years of data supporting it.
5. While the argument is moot today (US House Prices are still falling, after more than three years of a downward trend) it remains alive in pockets of the world.

A. 3 4 1 2 5 B. 3 4 2 1 5

C. 4 2 3 1 5 D. 2 5 4 1 3

E. 1 2 3 4 5

128.
1. For pure vegetarians India is a heaven.
2. India can boast for its innumerable varieties of tasty and nutritious vegetarian dishes.
3. These are also prepared using different methods of cooking like baking, boiling, frying etc.
4. Vegetables are an integral part of our food and we consume them in a number of ways.
5. Indians like their vegetable curries real hot 'n' spicy and so add a number of spices to make them really exotic.

A. 2 3 1 4 5 B. 1 5 3 4 2

C. 3 5 2 4 1 D. 4 1 2 5 3

E. 5 1 2 3 4

129. 1. Over the last few decades green tea has undergone many scientific and medical studies to determine the extent of its long health benefits.
2. In China there is a proverb – "Better to be deprived of food for three days, than tea of one" – and they were using the tea as a cure for headache, depression and many other ailments.
3. But it's true that Chinese people were well aware about green tea from ancient time.
4. We came to know about this green tea very late.
5. If I had said that tea is a healthy drink some years before the introduction of green tea, I might have been ridiculed.

A. 5 4 3 2 1 B. 3 4 2 1 5
C. 5 2 4 1 3 D. 4 5 3 1 2
E. 1 2 3 4 5

130. 1. In simpler terms, it is the Indian version of the Razzies.
2. The 3rd Golden Kela Awards will be hosted by Cyrus Broacha this year.
3. It was created in order to ridicule the bad performances and as a revenge for wasting our precious time and money on such idiotic films.
4. The Golden Kela Awards is held each year where awards are given for the year's worst in Bollywood.
5. It was created by Random magazine, India's longest running humor magazine in the year 2009.

A. 4 1 5 3 2 B. 2 1 3 4 5
C. 1 3 5 4 2 D. 3 5 1 4 2
E. 5 1 2 3 4

Directions (Qs. 131-135): *In each of the following sentences, some part of the sentence or the entire sentence is italicised. Beneath each sentences you will find four different ways of phrasing the italicised part. Choose the best alternative among the four in the context of standard written English. If none of the four options seems right to you, select option 'E' as your answer.*

131. In a move towards full account convertibility, the foreign exchange dealers are expecting the Reserve Bank *of keeping its hands away from any sort of intervention directly or indirectly in the foreign exchange market.*

A. .... of keeping its hands away from any sort of intervention directly or indirectly in the foreign exchange market.
B. .... to remain away of all sorts of intervention directly or indirectly of the foreign exchange market.
C. .... to keep its hands away from direct or indirect sort of intervention in the market of foreign exchange.
D. .... to keep its hands off any sort of intervention in the foreign exchange market either directly or indirectly.
E. None of the above

132. The prime lending rates of banks have been out of sync with other rates of interest for the last two years. *Though the banks are willing to provide lower rates to good clients, they do not extend the same privilege to other borrowers.*

A. Though the banks are willing to provide lower rates to good clients, they do not extend the same privilege to other borrowers.
B. Though the banks are willing to offer lower rates to good clients, they did not extend the same courtesy to other borrowers.
C. The banks do not provide the same courtesy to the other borrowers which they are ready to offer to good clients.
D. The lower rates which the banks are willingly giving to its good clients are not being offered to the other borrowers.
E. None of the above

133. The one percent cut in interest rates *did not expand credit and left a lot of liquidity with banks which per force found its way to the bond market.*

A. .... did not expand credit and left a lot of liquidity with banks which per force found its way to the bond market.
B. .... has not expanded credit and has left a massive liquidity for banks which under pressure found its route to the bond market.

C. .... caused a lot of liquidity instead of expanding credit thereby forcing banks to find its way to the bond market.
D. .... resulted not in expanding credit but in massive liquidity for banks which per force found its way in the bond market.
E. None of the above

134. We must see that our thoughts, our actions are inspired by a deep love of humanity, and that our conduct and our worship *is freed wherever it necessitates of the bondage of custom and to conform as far as possible to the surer standard of our conscience.*
A. .... is freed wherever it necessitates of the bondage of custom and to conform as far as possible to the surer standard of our conscience.
B. .... is freed wherever it necessitates of the bondage of custom and to conform as far as possible to the surer standard of our conscience as far as possible.
C. .... are freed where necessary from the bondage of custom and made to conform as far as possible to the surer standard of our conscience.
D. .... are freed from the bondage of custom as far as possible when necessary and made to conform with the surer standard of our conscience.
E. None of the above

135. *Of course the teachings and the methods and the subjects taught in these days must be made to suit our new exigencies and environments,* but the spirits animating the teachings must be the same as that which led the first settlers to cross the Vindhya Range, and establish their colonies in the south.
A. Of course the teachings and the methods and the subjects taught in these days must be made to suit our new exigencies and environment, but ....
B. There is no doubt that the teachings, methods and subjects taught, all should be in accordance to our new exigencies and environment, but ....
C. It can be said without any doubt that all sorts of teachings, methods and subjects of present must conform to our latest exigencies and present environment,
D. No doubt, our new exigencies and environment demand such teachings, methods and subjects that conform to it, but ....
E. None of the above

Directions (Qs. 136-140): *In each of the following sentences, there are two blank spaces. Below each sentence there are five pairs of words denoted by number A, B, C, D and E. Find out which word/ pair of words can be filled up in the blanks in the sentence in the same sequence to make the sentence meaningfully complete.*

136. The demand to ..... the ancient monument of the town was long ..... with the state administration.
A. excavate, extinct
B. maintain, maintained
C. dispose, clear
D. preserve, pending
E. demolish, considered

137. Four of the ..... were hanged against whom, the judge had ..... the verdict.
A. criminals, passed
B. thieves, entered
C. accomplices, declared
D. murderers, declared
E. murderers, entered

138. Students have ..... using wrong procedures in the examinations because they are aware that these could be ..... .
A. started, false
B. stopped, detected
C. detected, stopped
D. tried, detected
E. detected, proved

139. Some animals can live comfortably both ..... water and ..... land.
A. into, at
B. on, in
C. inside, over
D. in, on
E. over, on

140. Although the ceremony was ..... scheduled for three days, yet it was ..... later to one day.
A. originally, curtailed
B. formerly, declared
C. timely, decide
D. decided, curtailed
E. therefore, curtailed

Directions (Qs. 141-150) : *In the following passage there are blanks, each of which has been numbered. These numbers are printed below the passage and against each, five words are suggested, one of which fits the blank appropriately. Find out the appropriate word that fits the blank.*

In these days of economic liberalisation, globalisation, etc., materialistic values have assumed **...(141)...** importance. Money physical comforts and luxuries are the most sought after aspects. There has been **...(142)...** competition. Such competition **...(143)...** undue stress. The stress leads to **...(144)...** of health of the people. Indian culture has **...(145)...** its striking uniqueness, as against the Western culture, in the fact that there is a **...(146)...** place for spiritualism in our value system in all walks of life. The spirituality is a very **...(147)...** force which helps us in maintaining our physical and mental health. It gives us **...(148)...** to cope with the stress. Westerners have now **...(149)...** the importance of spirituality and therefore, they have started **...(150)...** us in the matter of spirituality.

141. A. usual B. little C. tangible D. least E. greater

142. A. critical B. unhealthy C. unequalled D. no E. absolute

143. A. releases B. deserves C. generates D. demonstrates E. suppresses

144. A. neglect B. illness C. generation D. deterioration E. encroachment

145. A. maintained B. illustrated C. marginalised D. bestowed E. forsaken

146. A. vast B. brief C. formal D. clean E. distinct

147. A. dormant B. dedicated C. vital D. common E. dynamic

148. A. strength B. tips C. clearance D. sermons E. ideals

149. A. informed B. narrated C. intensified D. realised E. invented

150. A. encouraging B. imitating C. blaming D. preaching E. assuming

ANSWERS

1	2	3	4	5	6	7	8	9	10
A	D	B	E	C	B	C	E	E	D
11	**12**	**13**	**14**	**15**	**16**	**17**	**18**	**19**	**20**
B	C	A	C	A	C	E	B	C	B
21	**22**	**23**	**24**	**25**	**26**	**27**	**28**	**29**	**30**
A	C	B	D	C	B	A	B	A	A
31	**32**	**33**	**34**	**35**	**36**	**37**	**38**	**39**	**40**
E	D	A	B	A	C	A	C	A	A
41	**42**	**43**	**44**	**45**	**46**	**47**	**48**	**49**	**50**
D	D	B	B	E	C	B	D	E	E
51	**52**	**53**	**54**	**55**	**56**	**57**	**58**	**59**	**60**
A	B	C	A	D	A	C	D	B	B
61	**62**	**63**	**64**	**65**	**66**	**67**	**68**	**69**	**70**
C	B	C	A	B	B	C	C	A	A
71	**72**	**73**	**74**	**75**	**76**	**77**	**78**	**79**	**80**
B	A	C	A	A	B	A	D	A	B

81	82	83	84	85	86	87	88	89	90
A	D	B	A	C	D	C	A	A	A
91	**92**	**93**	**94**	**95**	**96**	**97**	**98**	**99**	**100**
D	A	A	C	A	D	A	B	A	A
101	**102**	**103**	**104**	**105**	**106**	**107**	**108**	**109**	**110**
C	E	D	D	D	A	C	D	E	E
111	**112**	**113**	**114**	**115**	**116**	**117**	**118**	**119**	**120**
C	A	E	A	D	B	A	E	A	B
121	**122**	**123**	**124**	**125**	**126**	**127**	**128**	**129**	**130**
B	C	A	B	A	C	C	D	A	A
131	**132**	**133**	**134**	**135**	**136**	**137**	**138**	**139**	**140**
D	B	A	C	A	D	A	B	D	A
141	**142**	**143**	**144**	**145**	**146**	**147**	**148**	**149**	**150**
E	B	C	D	A	E	C	A	D	B

EXPLANATORY ANSWERS

1. This argument is based on the assumption that if the appliances become more efficient, then more homes would not be tempted to increase their utility/consumption in the household.

For Qs. No. 7-11.

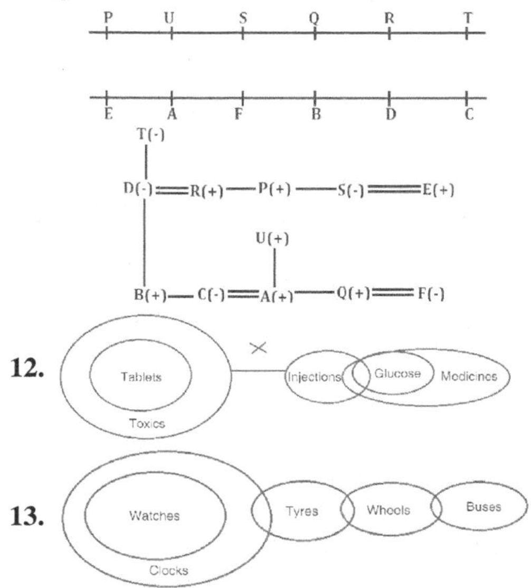

For Qs. No. 17-21.

Floor	Flat 1	Flat 2	Flat 3
Floor 4	Z	-	Y
Floor 3	J	K	G
Floor 2	I	–	W
Floor 1	L	X	H

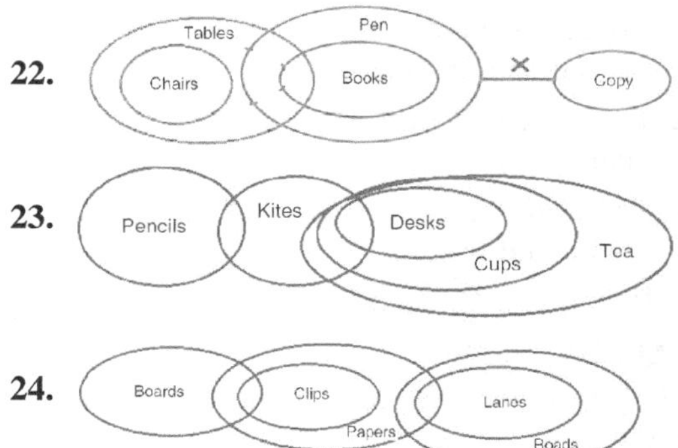

For Qs. No. 25-29.

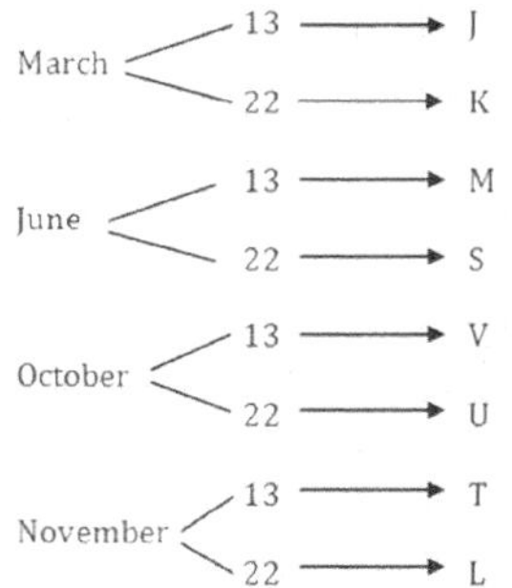

30. Govt. promulgate about subsidies and benefits to give benefit to untouched portion of our Population.

For Qs. No. 31-35.

Mohini is mother-in-law of Sunita and grandmother of Nanu. Vinod is grandfather of

Tanmay. So, Nanu and Tanmay represent third generation.

Mohini and Vinod form a couple and represent first generation.

Clearly, Rohan and Sunita form the other couple and represent second generation.

Rohan is a CA. Since engineer is married, so Vinod is an engineer and likes red colour.

Mohini is a teacher and likes orange colour.

Nanu likes blue colour.

Tanmay is a Principal and likes black colour.

Sunita, Nanu's mother, likes white colour.

Clearly, Rohan likes green colour.

31. Vinod is an engineer.

32. The only clue that Sunita, Rohan's wife, is not a doctor, cannot lead to her correct profession. So, the data is inadequate.

33. The two couples are Mohini-Vinod and Rohan-Sunita.

34. There are three ladies in the family—Mohini, Sunita and Nanu.

35. Rohan is a CA and likes green colour.

For Qs. No. 36-40.

Q gets a North-facing flat and is not next to S means.

Q		S

S and U get diagonally opposite flats means

U		
Q		S

R, next to U, gets a South facing flat and T gets a north facing flat means.

U	R	P
Q	T	S

So, the arrangement is:

South facing flats	U	R	P
North facing flats	Q	T	S

36. The South facing flats are U, R, P.

37. T's flat is between Q and S.

38. The flat next to U's flat is that of R, which remains unchanged if the flats of T and P are interchanged.

39. The diagonally opposite pairs are SU and QP.

40. Clearly, all the statements are necessary to answer the given questions.

41. Statement I is not sufficient as member of Gymkhana Club is not related to Dine Club. Statement II says about new member but does not provide information about previous member. Hence, both the statements I and II are not sufficient to answer the question. ∴ Option (D) is correct.

42. Both the statements I and II are not sufficient to answer the question. ∴ Option (D) is correct.

43. Statement I is not sufficient because 12 is divisible by 4 but not by 8. Statement II is sufficient to answer the question because for any number if the last three digits are zeros, the number is divisible by 8.

∴ Option (B) is correct.

44. From Statement I : $A + C > B > E + D$ ...(*i*)

From Statement II : $A > C$ ...(*ii*)

As the statement II states that C is 2nd in order and $A > C \Rightarrow A$ is 1st.

∴ Only statement II is sufficient to answer the question. ∴ Option (B) is correct.

45.

From Statement I

$$\therefore \quad x^2 + y^2 = 49 \quad ...(i)$$

From Statement II

$$2(x + y) = 22$$

$$\therefore \quad x + y = 11 \quad ...(ii)$$

Solving Equations (*i*) and (*ii*), we can get the value of x and y, *i.e.*, dimension of rectangle. Hence, both the statements together are necessary to answer the question.

∴ Option (E) is correct.

ENGLISH LANGUAGE

CHAPTER 1

Comprehension Passages

Comprehension is a very important part of General English paper. The questions on comprehension lay particular stress on understanding a given passage. You are required to read a passage and answer a few questions based on it. Various comprehension questions are set solely with the objectives named below:

1. To test your ability to detect the central idea or the focal point in the given passage.
2. To test your ability to understand and interpret the given passage.
3. To judge your capability to pick out the various arguments put forward by the writer for or against something.
4. To test your accuracy and richness of vocabulary.
5. To test your academic ability to understand the implied and the clearly and fully expressed ideas of the writer of the passage.
6. To test, occasionally, your power of appreciating critically the views contained in the given passage.

While answering comprehension questions, you must comply with the following important points:

1. First, read the whole passage attentively, carefully and quickly.
2. Read it for the second time, slowly but steadily.
3. Work out the probable meaning of new words, from the context in which they have been used.
4. Underline and look for transitional words and phrases as an aid to comprehension.
5. The process of elimination should be used while selecting the correct answer.
6. Recheck your answers before marking in the answersheet.

Directions: *Read the following passages carefully and answer the questions given below them. All answers should be given in the context of the given passage. Certain words/phrases are printed in* ***Bold*** *to help you to locate them while answering some of the questions.*

PASSAGE-1

After the "Liberalization," "Globalization" and the consequent change in the new international economic order as well as new information technology order, a new catch-phrase is being coined: 'A New Health Order.' Talking about setting it up is the theme of the WHO-sponsored international conference on primary health and medical care, currently being held at Milan in Italy. While much has been said and written on establishing "new order," little has actually been done. Will the conference at Milan too swear by the "new health order" go home and then forget about it, while the present medical and healthcare set-up in poor countries further **entrenches** itself? This does not have to be the fate of the radical resolutions that will undoubtedly be passed at Milan. Unlike creating a new world economic or information order, establishing a new heatlh set-up is essentially a matter for individual countries to accomplish. No conflict of international interests is involved. But this-advantage is, at least until it begins to take concrete shape, only theoretical. The million-dollar question is whether individual third-world governments are able and willing to **muster** the will, the resources, the administrative and other infrastructure to carry out what it is entirely within their power to attain and implement.

The dimensions of the problem are known and the solutions broadly agreed on. The present medical and healthcare system is urban-based, closely geared to drugs, hospitals and expensively trained apathetic doctors. The bulk of the population in poor countries, who live in rural areas, are left untouched by all this and must rely on traditional healers. The answer is to turn out medical/health personnel sufficiently, but not expensively, trained to handle routine complaints and to get villagers to pay adequate attention to cleanliness, hygienic sanitation, garbage disposal and other elementary but **crucial** matters. More complicated ailments can be referred to properly equipped centres in district towns, cities and metropolises. Traditional healers, whom villagers trust, can be among these intermediate personnel. Some third-world countries, including India, have **launched** or are preparing elaborate schemes of this nature. But the experience is not quite happy. There is **resistance** from the medical establishment which sees them as little more than licensed quackery but is not prepared either to offer **condensed** medical courses such as the former licentiate course available in this country and unwisely scrapped. There is the question of how much importance to give to indigenous system of medicine. And there is the difficult matter of striking the right balance between preventive healthcare and curative medical attention. These are complex issues and the Milan conference would perhaps be more fruitful if it were to discuss such specific subjects.

1. It can be inferred from the contents of the passage that the author's approach is
   A. sarcastic B. constructive
   C. indifferent D. fault-finding
   E. hostile

2. The contents of the passage indicate that the author is opposed to
   A. traditional healers
   B. licentiate practitioners
   C. allopathic system of medicines
   D. hospitals
   E. None of these

3. The author thinks that the solution to the problem of medical/healthcare lies in
   A. opening hospitals is rural areas
   B. conducting inexpensive medical courses
   C. improving the economic condition of the masses
   D. expediting the setting up of a new health order
   E. making cheap drugs available

4. The author is doubtful whether
   A. an individual country can set up a new health order
   B. the Milan Conference would pass radical resolutions
   C. underdeveloped countries have the capacity to organize their resources
   D. traditional healers could be trained as intermediate health personnel
   E. the problem has been understood at all

5. To make the conference really useful, the author suggests
   A. resolving the international conflicts involved
   B. that it should address itself to specific issues
   C. it should give importance to indigenous system of medicine
   D. that it should not pass radical resolutions
   E. None of these

6. The medical establishment seems to be reluctant to trust the
   A. allopathic medical practitioners
   B. traditional healers
   C. urban-based medical practitioners
   D. expensively trained allopathic doctors
   E. None of these

7. What does the author suggest for the cure of the cases involving complications?
   A. Treating such cases at well equipped hospitals in district places
   B. Training such victims in preliminary hygiene
   C. Training semi-skilled doctors to treat such cases
   D. Issuing licenses to semi-skilled doctors to treat such cases
   E. None of these

Directions (Qs. 8 to 10): *Choose the word which is most nearly the SAME in meaning as the word printed in BOLD as used in the passage.*

8. MUSTER
A. enlist B. summon
C. manifest D. extend
E. enrich

9. ENTRENCH
A. being deteriorating
B. surround completely
C. establish firmly
D. enclose carefully
E. finish radically

10. LAUNCHED
A. participated B. accomplished
C. elevated D. planned
E. started

Directions (Qs. 11 to 13): *Choose the word which is most nearly OPPOSITE in meaning of the word printed in BOLD as used in the passage.*

11. CONDENSED
A. concentrated B. envigoured
C. expanded D. lengthened
E. inexplicable

12. RESISTANCE
A. opposition B. agreement
C. repulsion D. acceptance
E. compliance

13. CRUCIAL
A. trivial B. critical
C. significant D. marvellous
E. conspicuous

PASSAGE-2

Management is a set of processes that can keep a complicated system of people and technology running smoothly. The most important aspects of management include planning, budgeting, organising, staffing, controlling, and problem solving. Leadership is a set of processes that creates organisations in the first place or adapts them to significantly changing circumstances. Leadership defines what the future should look like, aligns people with that vision, and inspires them to make it happen despite the obstacles. This distinction is absolutely crucial for our purposes here: Successful transformation is 70 to 90 per cent leadership and only 10 to 30 per cent management. Yet for historical reasons, many organisations today don't have much leadership. And almost everyone thinks about the problem here as one of managing change. For most of this century, as we created thousands and thousands of large organisations for the first time in human history, we did not have enough good managers to keep all those bureaucracies functioning. So many companies and universities developed management programmes, and hundreds and thousands of people were encouraged to learn management on the job. And they did. But, people were taught little about leadership. To some degree, management was the main item on the twentieth-century agenda because that's what was needed. For every entrepreneur or business builder who was a leader, we needed hundreds of managers to run their ever-growing enterprises.

Unfortunately for us today, this emphasis on management has often been institutionalised in corporate cultures that discourage employees from learning how to lead. Ironically, past success is usually the key ingredient in producing this outcome. The syndrome, as I have observed it on many occasions, goes like this: success creates some degree of marked dominance, which in turn produces much growth. After a while keeping the ever-larger organisation under control becomes the primary challenge. So attention turns inwards, and managerial competencies are **nurtured**. With a strong emphasis on management but not leadership, bureaucracy and an inward focus take over. But with continued success, the result mostly of market dominance, the problem often goes unaddressed and unhealthy arrogance begins to evolve. All of these characteristics then make any transformation effort much more difficult.

Arrogant managers can overvalue their current performance and competitive position, listen poorly, and learn slowly. Inwardly focussed employees can smother those who want to respond to shifting conditions. And the lack of leadership leaves no force inside these organisations to break out of the morass.

1. Why, according to the author, a distinction between management and leadership is crucial?

A. Leader are reactive whereas managers are proactive
B. Organisations are facing problems of not getting good managers
C. Organisations are pursuing the strategy of status-quo
D. In today's context organisations need leaders much than managers in transforming them
E. None of these

2. Why did companies and universities develop programmes to prepare managers in such a large number?
A. Companies and Universities wanted to generate funds through these programmes
B. The large number of organisations were created and they needed managers in good number
C. Organisations did not want to spend their scarce resoruces in training managers
D. Organisations wanted to create communication network through trained managers
E. None of these

3. Which of the following statements is NOT TRUE in the context of the passage?
A. Bureaucratic culture smothers those who want to respond to changing conditions
B. Leadership produces change and has the potential to establish direction
C. Pressure on managers comes mostly from within
D. Leadership centre on carrying out important functions such as planning and problem solving
E. Managers believe that they are the best and that their idiosyncratic traditions are superior

4. Which of the following is NOT the characterstic of bureaucratic culture?
A. Managers listen poorly and learn slowly
B. Managerial competencies are nurtured
C. Employees clearly see the forces that present threats and opportunities
D. Prevalence of unhealthy arrogance
E. Managers tend to stifle initiative and innovation

5. Which of the following is SIMILAR in meaning of the word 'SMOTHER' as used in the passage?
A. suppress
B. encourage
C. instigate
D. criticise
E. attack

6. How has the author defined management?
A. It is the process of adapting organisations to changing circumstances
B. It is the system of aligning people with the direction it has taken
C. It refers to creating a vision to help direct the change effort
D. Creating better performance through customer orientation
E. None of these

7. Management education was emphasised in the management programmes because
A. establishing direction was the main focus of organisations
B. motivating employees was thought to be done by managers
C. strategies for producing change was the main focus of organisations
D. organisations wanted to create powerful guiding coalition
E. management was the main item of agenda in organisations

8. What is the historical reason for many organisations not having leadership?
A. A view that leaders are born, they are not made
B. Leaders lack managerial skills and organisations need managers
C. Leaders are weak in carrying out traditional functions of management
D. Leaders allow too much complacency in organisations
E. None of these

9. In the passage, management is equated with
A. Organisation
B. Leadership
C. Organisation vision
D. Bureaucracy
E. Managerial training

10. Why does the attention of large organisations turn inward?

A. Their managers become arrogant
B. They have to keep themselves under control
C. Their success creates market dominance
D. They want to project their predictability
E. None of these

11. Which of the following is SIMILAR in meaning of the word 'NURTURED' as used in the passage?

A. created　　B. developed
C. thwarted　　D. surfaced
E. halted

12. What, according to the author, is leadership?

A. Process which keeps system of people and technology running smoothly
B. Planning the future and budgeting resources of the organisation
C. Inspiring people to realise the vision
D. Carrying out the crucial functions of management
E. None of these

13. Which of the following characteristics help organisations in their transformation efforts?

A. Emphasis on leadership but not management
B. A strong and dogmatic culture
C. Bureaucratic and inward looking approach
D. Failing to acknowledge the value of customers and shareholders
E. None of these

14. Why were people taught little about leadership in management programmes?

A. Teachers were busy in understanding the phenomenon of leadership
B. Enough study material was not available to facilitate teaching of leadership
C. Focus of these programmes was on developing managers
D. Leadership was considered only a political phenomenon
E. None of these

15. Which of the following statement is/are DEFINITELY TRUE in the context of the passage?

(1) Bureaucracy fosters strong and arrogant culture
(2) Leadership competences are nurtured in large size organisation
(3) Successful transformation in organisations is 70 to 90 per cent leadership

A. Only (1) and (2)　　B. Only (1) and (3)
C. Only (2) and (3)　　D. Only (2)
E. Only (3)

PASSAGE-3

The happy man is the man who lived objectively, who has free affections and wide interest, who secures his happiness through these interests and affections and through the fact that they, in turn, make him an object of interest and affection to many others. To be the recipient of affection is a potent cause of happiness, but the man who demands affection is not the man upon whom it is **bestowed.** The man who receives affection is, speaking broadly, the man who gives it. But it is useless to attempt to give it as a calculation, in the way in which one might lend money at interest, for a calculated affection is not genuine and is not felt to be so by the recipient.

What then can a man do who is unhappy because he is encased in self? So long as he continues to think about the cause of his unhappiness, he continues to be self-centred and therefore does nto get outside, the vicious circle if he is to get outside it, it must be by genuine interests, not by simulated interest accepted merely as a medicine. Although this difficulty is real, there is nevertheless much that he can do if he has rightly diagnosed his trouble. If, for example, his trouble is due to a sense of sin, conscious or unconscious he can first persuade his conscious mind that he has no reason to feel sinful, and then proceed, to plant this rational conviction in his unconscious mind, concerning himself meanwhile with some more or less neutral activity. If he succeeds in **dispelling** the sense of sin, it is possible that genuine objective interests will arise spontaneously. If his trouble is self-pity, he can deal with it in the same manner after first persuading himself that there is nothing extraordinarily unfortunate in his circumstances.

If fear is his trouble, let him practice exercises designed to give courage. Courage has been recognised from time immemorial as an important virtue, and a great part of the training of boys and young men has been devoted to producing a type of character capable of fearlessness in battle. But moral courage and intellectual courage have been much less studied, they also, however, have their technique, admit to yourself every day at least one painful truth, your will find this quite useful. Teach yourself to feel that life still be worth living even if you were not, as of course you are immeasurably superior to all your friends in virtue and in intelligence. Exercises of this sort prolonged through several years will at last enable you to admit facts without **flinching** and will, in so doing, free you from the empire of fear over a very large field.

1. If a man is suffering from a sense of sin...
   A. he should invite opinion of others
   B. he should admit his sin at once
   C. he should consciously realize that he has no reason to feel sinful
   D. he should develop a fearless character
   E. he should develop an internal locus of control

2. What happens to a man who demands affection?
   A. His feelings are reciprocated by others
   B. He tends to take a calculated risk
   C. He becomes a victim of a viscious circles
   D. He takes affection for granted from others
   E. None of these

3. What should a man do who is suffering from the feeling of self-pity?
   A. He should control his passions and emotions
   B. He should persuade himself that everything is alright in his circumstances
   C. He should seek affection from others
   D. He should develop a feeling of fearlessness
   E. He should consult an expert to diagnose his trouble

4. Which of the following, according to the passage, has not been studied much?
   A. Feeling of guilt and self-pity
   B. The state of mind of a unhappy man
   C. How to get absorbed in other interests
   D. Moral and intellectual courage
   E. None of these

5. Which of the following words is SIMILAR in meaning of the word 'BESTOWED' as used in the passage?
   A. conferred   B. accommodated
   C. thrusted   D. withdrawn
   E. directed

6. Which of the following virtues, according to the passage has been recognised for long as an important virtue?
   A. Patriotism
   B. Sacrifice
   C. Courage
   D. Self-consciousness
   E. None of these

7. Which of the following statements in NOT TRUE in the context of the passage?
   A. Happy man has wide interests
   B. Courage has been recognised as an important virtue
   C. Unhappy man is encased in self
   D. A man who suffers from the sense of sin must tell himself that he has no reason to be sinful
   E. Issue of intellectual courage has been extensively studied

8. Who according to the passage, is the happy man?
   A. Who is encased in self
   B. Who has free affection and wide interests
   C. Who is free from wordly passions
   D. Who has extremely centred passions
   E. None of these

9. According to the passage, calculated affection...
   A. appears to be false and fabricated
   B. makes other person to love you
   C. turns into permanent affection over a period of time
   D. leads to self-pity
   E. gives a feeling of courage

10. What happens when you think about cause of your unhappiness?
   A. You try to introspect and look critically at yourself
   B. You realize that the life can be lived in different ways
   C. You try to practise exercise designed to give courage
   D. You remain a self-centred person
   E. None of these

11. What according to the passage is the real cause of happiness?
   A. Material rewards and incentives received
   B. Critical analysis of the happy state of mind
   C. Affection received from others
   D. Calculated risks taken
   E. None of these

12. Which of the following words is OPPOSITE in meaning of the word 'DISPELLING' as used in the passage?
   A. giving B. accumulating
   C. projecting D. scattering
   E. receiving

13. How to get out of the viscious circle mentioned in the passage?
   A. By practicing skills of concentration
   B. By inculcating the habit of self-absorption
   C. Being true of others and ones internal circumstances
   D. Admitting to oneself that others could be right
   E. None of these

14. Which of the following words is SIMILAR in meaning to the word 'FILINCHING' as used in the passage?
   A. wincing B. convincing
   C. explaining D. providing
   E. debating

15. Which of the following statements is TRUE in the context of the passage?
   A. All passions stem from unhappiness
   B. The happy man lives subjectively
   C. Any virtue has a dark side also
   D. One feels happy if one receives affection
   E. Any affection is always genuine

PASSAGE-4

Globalization, liberalization and free market are some of the most significant modern trends in economy. **Most economists** in our country seem **captivated** by the spell of the free market. Consequently, nothing seems good or normal that does not accord with the requirements for the free marekt. A price that is determined by the seller or, for that matter, established by anyone other than the aggregate of consumers seems **pernicious.** Accordingly, it requires a major act of will to think of price-fixing as both normal and having a valuable economic function. In fact, price-fixing is normal in all industrialized societies because the industrial system itself provides, as an effortless consequence of its own development, the price-fixing that it requires. Modern industrial planning requires and rewards great size. Hence a comparatively small number of large firms will be competing for the same group of consumers. That each large firm will act with consideration of its own needs and thus avoid selling its products for more than its competitors charge is commonly recognised by **advocates** of free-market economic theories. But each large firm will also act with full consideration of the needs that it has in common with the other large firms competing for the same customers. Each large firm will thus avoid significant price-cutting, because price-cutting will be prejudicial to the common interest in a **stable** demand for products. Most economists do not see price-fixing when it occurs because they expect it to be brought about by a number of **explicit** agreements among large firms, it is not.

Moreover, those economists who argue that allowing the free-market to operate without interference is the most efficient method of establishing prices have not considered the economics of non-socialist countries. Most of these economics employ intentional price-fixing, usually in an **overt** fashion. Formal price-fixing by cartel and informal price-fixing by agreements covering the members of an industry are common place. Were there something peculiarly efficient about the free market and inefficient about price-fixing, the countries that have avoided the first and used the second would have suffered drastically in their economic development. There is no indication that they have.

Socialist industry also works within a framework of controlled prices. In the early 1970's the Soviet Union began to give firms and industries some flexibility in adjusting prices that a informal evolution has accorded the capitalist system. Economists in the USA have hailed the change as a return to the free-market. But the then Soviet firms were not in favour of the prices established by a free-market over which they exercised little influence; rather. Soviet firms acquired some power to fix prices.

1. The author's primary objective of writing the passage seems to:
   A. belie the popular belief that the free-market helps enhance development of industrial societies
   B. advocate that price-fixing is unavoidable and it is beneficial to the economy of any industrialized society
   C. explain the methodology of fixing price to stabilize free-market
   D. prove that price-fixing and free-market are compatible and mutually beneficial to industrialized society
   E. create awareness among the general public regarding combating price-fixing by large firms

2. Which of the following statements (1), (2) and/or (3) is/are TRUE in the context of the information given in the passage?
   The information in the passage is helpful to:
   1. know some of the ways in which prices can be fixed
   2. identify the products for which price-fixing can be more beneficial
   3. differentiate between the economics of various countries

   A. Only (1) B. Only (2)
   C. Only (3) D. Only (1) and (2)
   E. None of these

3. Considering the literal meaning and connotations of the words used in the passage, the author's attitude towards "Most economists" can best be described as:
   A. derogatory and antagonistic
   B. impartial and unbiased
   C. spiteful and envious
   D. critical and condescending
   E. indifferent

4. The author feels that price fixed by seller seems pernicious because:
   A. people do not have faith in large firms
   B. people do not want the Government to fix prices
   C. most economists believe that consumers should determine prices
   D. most economists believe that no group should determine prices
   E. people do not want to decide prices

5. Which of the following statements is DEFINITELY TRUE in the context of the passge? Price fixing is:
   A. a profitable result of economic development
   B. an inevitable result of the industrial system
   C. the joint result of a number of carefully organized decisions
   D. a phenomenon uncommon to industrialized societies
   E. a result of joint venture of the Government and industry

6. According to the passage, price-fixing in non-socialistic countries is generally:
   A. intentional and widespread
   B. illegitimate, but beneficial
   C. conservative and inflexible
   D. legitimate and innovative
   E. conservative and scarce

7. What was the result of the then Soviet Union's change in economic policy in the 1970's?
   A. They showed greater profits
   B. They had less control over the free-market
   C. They were able to adjust to techno-advancement
   D. They acquired some authority to fix prices
   E. They became more responsive to free-market

8. The author's primary concern seems to:
   A. summarise conflicting view points

B. make people aware of recent discoveries
C. criticise a point of view
D. predict the probable results of a practice
E. prepare a research proposal

9. Which of the following statements about the Socialist industry is/are false?
1. It works under certain price restrictions.
2. It has no authority to determine prices
3. It hails the strategy of price fixing, as a major deviation

A. Only (1) is false
B. Only (2) is false
C. Only (3) is false
D. (1) and (2) are false
E. (2) and (3) are false

PASSAGE-5

Amnesty International's charge that 'tens of thousands' of political prisoners, including prisoners of conscience, are **languishing** in Indian jails and that prisoners are routinely tortured in this country has to be seen in a much wider contest than the organisation's annual report cares to do. In its overall appraisal of 151 countries, Amnesty has accused 112 of torturing prisoners, 63 of harbouring prisoners of conscience, 61 of resorting to political killings and 53 of detaining people without a trial. Of these apparently **overlapping** categories, India seems to have been excluded from the list of the 61 which undertake political killings. The report has, however, pointed out that **scores** of people in India die for torture in police and military custody and that many also simply disappear. Clearly, only a thin line separates the 61 charged with political murder from the rest. Before coming to such conclusions, however, it may also be necessary to classify the various countries according to their political systems. Torture by the security forces and killings at the behest of the government make no difference to the victims whether they are in a democratic country or a totalitarian one. It is also nobody's case that a democratic country is less **culpable** than a dictatorship in the vent of human rights violations. But the point perhaps still needs to be made that torture or 'disappearances' represent a failure of the system in a democracy in contrast to being an integral part of state policy in a country ruled by an autocrat who is answerable to no one.

India may be guilty of keeping 'tens of thousands' behind bars and of the other human rights abuses mentioned by Amnesty, but it still remains a qualitatively different place from a totalitarian country. It is in this respect that Amnesty has been less than fair. It has chosen to ignore the distinctions between the good, the bad and the ugly. The openness of Indian soceity will be evident to anyone who spends half an hour in one of its chaotic market-places or visits the law courts or watches a political rally or reads a newspaper or **strikes up** a conversation with any person on the roads. There is no sense of fear in India, as in a dictatorship. There is also scope for securing relief from the heavy-handed behaviour of the authorities, even if the human rights commission has not yet lived up to expectations. Unless such points are recognised, Amnesty's assessment will seem to be a dry recital of statistics which may **pillory** India simply because of its larger population. Mercifully, Amnesty nowadays at least notes that the terrorists also indulge in human rights violations and that India has to cope with several insurgencies **fomented** by a country where the military does not always seem to be under the control of the elected government. True, there is much that is wrong in India's prison system and with the way the terrorist challenge in sometimes meet, but the stress should be on activating the self-correcting mechanism within a democracy and not merely on painting a grim, even biased, picture.

1. The author suggests classification of various countries on one additional dimension. Which of the following is that dimension?

A. Economic progress
B. Industrial progress
C. Political systems
D. Human rights
E. None of these

2. According to the passage, through which media or forum Amnesty International has hurled the charges?

A. Its International Meet
B. Its Annual Report

C. Seminar on Human Rights
D. Its Regional Meet
E. None of these

3. The author of the passage
A. agrees with the report
B. disagrees with the report
C. disagrees that conditions of prisons in India is bad
D. supports the totalitarian approach
E. disagrees with report on terrorists

4. The Amnesty International report is based on the information of how many countries?
A. 112 B. 63
C. 131 D. 115
E. None of these

5. In the report, India has been excluded from which of the following categories of violating human rights?
A. Political killings
B. Torturing prisoners
C. Detaining without trial
D. Harbouring prisoners of conscience
E. None of these

6. According to the passage, what does political murder in a democratic country signify?
A. Policy of the country
B. Need for autocratic rule
C. Openness of society
D. Failure of system
E. Heavy-handed behaviour of the authorities

7. Which of the following seems to be the main purpose of writing this passage?
A. To highlight the role of Amnesty International
B. To further the cause of human rights
C. To highlight the sufferings of prisoners
D. To condemn political killings
E. None of these

8. Which of the following is NOT TRUE in the context of the passage?
A. There is overlapping of cases in the categories of human rights abuses
B. India was one of the countries appraised by Amnesty International
C. India is guilty of some human rights abuses
D. Amnesty International appraised all the democratic countries
E. The report notes that the terrorists also violate human rights

9. Which of the following is the meaning of the phrase STRIKE UP as used in the passage?
A. discussion B. hit sharply
C. protest D. initiate
E. undertake

10. According to the author, among the good, the bad and the ugly, what at worst is the situation in India?
A. Good B. Bad
C. Ugly D. Good or Ugly
E. Bad of Ugly

11. Which of the following is TRUE, according to the passage?
A. The Human Rights Commission has done commendable service
B. There is a need to check political killings in India
C. There is a need to improve India's prison system
D. India is not at all guilty of human rights violations
E. None of these

12. Which of the following human rights violation is most prevalent among the countries?
A. Torturing prisoners
B. Detaining without trial
C. Killing with political motive
D. Harbouring prisoners of conscience
E. None of these

PASSAGE-6

We have inherited the tradition of secrecy about the budget from Britain where also the system has been strongly attacked by eminent economists and political scientists including Peter Jay. Sir Richard Clarke, who was the originating genius of nearly every **important** development in the British budgeting techniques during the last two decades, has spoken out about the abuse of budget secrecy: "The problems of long-term tax policy should surely be **debated** openly with the facts on the table. In my opinion, all governments should have just the same **duty** to publish their expenditure policy. Indeed, this obligation to publish taxation policy is really essential for the control of public expenditure in order to get realistic taxation implications." Realising that democracy **flourishes** best on the principles of open government, more and more democracies are having an open public debate on budget proposals before introducing the appropriate Bill in the legislature. In the United States the budget is conveyed in a message by the President to the Congress, which comes well in advance of the date when the Bill is introduced in the Congress. In Finland the Parliament and the people are already discussing in June the tentative budget proposals which are to be introduced in the Finnish Parliament in September. Every budget contains a cartload of figures in black and white— but the dark figures represent the **myriad** lights and shades of India's life, the contrasting tones of poverty and wealth and of bread so dear and flesh and blood so cheap, the deep tints of adventure and enterprise and man's ageless struggle for a brighter morning. The Union budget should not be an annual **scourge** but a part of presentation of annual accounts of a partnership between the Government and the people. The partnership would work much better when the nonsensical secrecy is replaced by openness and public consultations, resulting in fair laws and the people's acceptance of their moral duty to pay.

1. The author seems to be in favour of
- A. maintaining secrecy of budget
- B. judicious blend of secrecy and openness
- C. transparency in budget proposals
- D. replacement of public constitution by secrecy
- E. None of these

2. The author thinks that openness in budget is essential as it leads to
- A. prevention of tax implications
- B. people's reluctance to accept their moral duties
- C. exaggerated revelation of the strengths and weaknesses of economy
- D. making our country on par with Finland
- E. None of these

3. How do the British economists and political scientists react to budget secrecy? They are
- A. in favour of having a mix of secrecy and openness
- B. indifferent to the budgeting techniques and taxation policies
- C. very critical about maintenance of budget secrecy
- D. advocates of not disclosing in advance the budget contents
- E. None of these

4. The secrecy of the budget is maintained by all of the following countries EXCEPT
- (1) Finland
- (2) India
- (3) Unites States
- A. only (1)
- B. only (2)
- C. only (3)
- D. (1) and (3)
- E. (2) and (3)

5. Sir Richard Clarke seems to deserve the credit for
- A. transformation in the British budgetary techniques
- B. maintenance of secrecy of the British budget
- C. detection of abuse of transparency in budget
- D. bringing down the tax load on British people
- E. None of these

6. From the contents of the passage, it can be inferred that the author is
- A. authoritarian in his approach
- B. a democratic person
- C. unaware of India's recent economic developments
- D. a conservative person
- E. None of these

7. For making the budget realistic, the Government should
- A. refrain from making public the proposed provisions before finalisation
- B. discuss it secretly within themselves
- C. encourage the public to send in their suggestions
- D. consult the public, defend their own plans and accept public suggestions
- E. None of these

8. Which of the following statements is DEFINITELY TRUE in the context of the passage?

A. The British Government has been religiously maintaining budget secrecy
B. Budget secrecy is likely to lead to corrupt practices
C. Consulting unjustifiable taxes with public helps make them accept those taxes
D. There should be no control on public expenditure in democratic condition
E. None of these

9. Which of the following statement(s) is/are DEFINITELY FALSE in the context of the passage?

(1) Transparency helps unscrupulous elements to resort to corrupt practices
(2) Open approach of Government is a sign of healthy democracy
(3) People's acceptance of their moral duties can best be achieved through openness and public consultations

A. only (1) B. only (2)
C. only (3) D. (1) and (2)
E. (2) and (3)

Directions (Qs. 10 to 12): *Choose the word which is most nearly the SAME in meaning to the word printed in capital letters as used in the passage.*

10. MYRIAD
A. adequate B. functional
C. incompatible D. abundant
E. excellent

11. SCOURGE
A. ritual B. presentation
C. whip D. compromise
E. remedy

12. DUTY
A. obligation B. imposition
C. tax-liability D. function
E. job

Direciont (Qs. 13 to 15): *Choose the word which is most OPPOSITE in meaning to the word printed in capital letters as used in the passage.*

13. IMPORTANT
A. major B. uncountable
C. significant D. unscheduled
E. trivial

14. DEBATED
A. questioned severely
B. opposed strongly
C. accepted unconditionally
D. discussed frankly
E. implemented forcibly

15. FLOURISHES
A. disappears B. degenerates
C. vanishes D. blooms
E. opens

PASSAGE-7

An independent, able and upright judiciary is the hallmark of a free democratic country. Therefore, the process of judicial appointments is of vital importance. At present, on account of the Supreme Court's last advisory opinion, the role of the executive and its interference in the appointment of judges is minimal, which, **in the light of our previous experience,** is most welcome. However, there is a strong demand for a National Judicial Commission on the ground of wider participation in the appointment process and for greater transparency. The composition, the role and the procedures of the proposed National Judicial Commission, must be clearly spelt out, **lest it** be a case of **jumping from the frying pan into the fire**.

Recently, there has been a lively debate in England on the subject. A judicial commission has been proposed but there are not many takers for that proposal. In the paper issued this month by the Lord Chancellor's Department on judicial appointments, the Lord Chancellor has said, "I want every vacancy on the Bench to be filled by "the best person available. Appointments must and will be made on merit— irrespective of ethnic origin, gender, marital status, political affiliation, sexual orientation, religion or disability. These are not mere words. They are firm principles. I will not tolerate any form of discrimination."

At present, there are hardly any persons from the ethnic minorities manning the higher judiciary and so far not a single woman has made it to the House of Lords. The most significant part of Lord Chancellor's paper is the requirement that "allegations of professional misconduct made in the course of consultations about a candidate for judicial office must be specific and subject to disclosure to the candidate." This should go a long way in ensuring that principles of natural justice and fair play are not **jettisoned** in the appointment process, which is not an uncommon phenomenon.

1. Which of the following could be in the author's mind when he says *'in the light of our previous experience'*?
   A. Not having enough judges from backward communities
   B. Interference of the executive in the appointment of judges
   C. Professional misconduct of judges
   D. Delays occurred in the judicial appointment
   E. None of these

2. According to the passage, there has been a demand for a National Judicial Commission to
   A. clear the backing of court cases
   B. make judiciary see eye to eye with executive
   C. wipe out corruption at the highest places
   D. make the appointment process of judges more broad based and clear
   E. None of these

3. What, according to the passage should go a long way in judicial appointments?
   A. Decision that all sections of the society are represented
   B. Candidates' qualifications and seniority are considered
   C. Candidate must know the charge of professional misconduct levelled against him
   D. There should be strong reason for discrimination
   E. None of these

4. The role and procedure of the National Commission must be spelt out clearly
   A. because executive wing will depend on it heavily
   B. because judges will take judicial decisions on the basis of it
   C. as it will be represented by the cross section of the society
   D. as it will bring a qualitative change in the interpretation of law
   E. None of these

5. Which of the following words is SIMILAR in meaning as the word 'JETTISON' as used in the passage?
   A. Sacrifice B. Accept
   C. Modify D. Destroy
   E. None of these

6. Which of the following group of words is SIMILAR in meaning as the word 'LEST' as used in the passage?
   A. In spite of B. For fear that
   C. For want of D. In order to
   E. With regard to

7. What does the expression "jumping from the frying pan into the fire" mean?
   A. Seeing one dream after the other
   B. Making plan after plan
   C. Crossing one hurdle after the other
   D. Jumping from one high place to another
   E. None of these

8. What, according to the author, is the typical characteristic of an independent democratic country?
   A. Objective process of judicial appointments
   B. Supreme Court's advisory opinion on legal matters
   C. Responsible, free and fair judiciary
   D. Lively and frank debate in the society on the role of judiciary
   E. None of these

9. What has been the subject of lively debate in England?
   A. Role of judiciary in free and democratic nations
   B. Appointment of judicial commisison
   C. Seniority as the basis of appointment of judges
   D. Appointment of judicial posts
   E. None of these

10. Which, according to the passage, is not an uncommon phenomenon?

A. An independent and upright judiciary
B. Delays taking place in legal pronouncements
C. Justice being denied to poor people
D. Partiality and subjectivity in judicial appointments
E. None of these

11. Which one of the following forms part of what the Lord Chancellor has said?
A. Appointments to judicial posts must take into consideration the aspirations of the weaker sections of the society
B. Vacancies in the judiciary must not remain unfilled
C. Merit should be the sole criterion for judicial appointments
D. Selective discrimination may be preached and also practised
E. None of these

12. Which of the following, according to the author, is the most welcome thing?
A. The negligible role played by the executive in the appointment of judges
B. Coordinating role played by the executive in the appointment of judges
C. The appointment of judges from the ethnic minority classes
D. Appointment of judges purely on the basis of merit
E. None of these

PASSAGE-8

Economists, ethicists, and business sages **persuade** us that honesty is the best policy, but their evidence is weak. We hoped to find data that would support their theories and thus, perhaps encourage higher standards of business behaviour. To our surprise, our pet theories failed to **stand up.** Treachery, we found, can pay. There is no compelling economic reason to tell the truth or keep one's word—punishment for the treacherous in the real world is neither swift nor sure.

Honesty is, in fact, primarily a moral choice. Business people do tell themselves that, in the long run, they will do well by doing good. But there is little/factual or logical basis for this conviction. Without values, without a basic preference for right over wrong, trust based on such self-delusion would crumble in the face of temptation. Most of us choose virtue because we want to believe in ourselves and have others respect and belief in us.

And for this, we should be happy. We can be proud of a system in which people are honest because they want to be, not because they have to be. Materially, too, trust based on morality provides great advantages. It allows us to join in great and exciting enterprises that we could never undertake if we relied on economic incentives alone.

Economists tell us that trust is enforced in the market place through retaliation of reputation. If you violate a trust your victim is apt to seek revenge and others are likely to stop doing business with you, at least under favourable terms. A man or woman with a reputation for fair dealing will prosper. Therefore, profit maximizers are honest. This sounds plausible enough until you look for concrete examples. Cases that apparently demonstrate the awful consequences of trust turns out to be few and weak, while evidence that treachery can pay seems **compelling.**

1. What do economists and ethicists, according to the passage, want us to believe?
A. Businessmen should be honest at all times
B. Businessmen cannot be honest at all times
C. Businessmen turn dishonest at times
D. Businessmen are honest only at times
E. None of these

2. What did the author find out about the theory that honesty is the best policy?
A. It is correct on many occasions
B. It is correct for all businessmen
C. It is a useless theory
D. It is a theory which seems to be correct only occasionally
E. None of these

3. Why are businessmen, according to the author of the passage, honest in their dealings?
A. Businessmen are all God-fearing
B. Businessmen are by nature honest as a choice

C. Businessmen are by nature honest
D. All businessmen are caught if they are dishonest
E. None of these

4. Which of the following, according to the author of the passage, is the reason for being honest in business?
A. It gives no immediate benefits
B. It gives long-term benefits
C. It makes a person self-seeking
D. It brings disrespect of others
E. It does not make others respect you

5. Why does the author say that one can be proud of the present situation?
A. People are self-respecting
B. People are respect seekers
C. People are unselfish
D. People are honest without compulsion
E. None of these

6. What is the material advantage which the author sees in being honest?
A. It permits one to undertake activities which may not be economically attractive
B. It permits one to be honest for the sake of honesty alone
C. It permits one to make a lot of profit in various areas
D. It permits one to form various trusts to make profits
E. None of these

7. Why do businessmen, according to economists, remain honest?
A. Dishonest businessmen can make more money
B. Dishonest businessmen make money in the long run
C. Dishonest businessmen cannot stay in business for long
D. Dishonest businessmen are flogged in the market place
E. Dishonest businessmen are always prosecuted

8. Which of the following word(s) is most nearly the SAME in meaning as the word 'PERSUADE' as it has been used in the passage?
A. Give assurance B. Give opinion
C. Try to convince D. Cheat
E. Motivate

9. Which of the following is FALSE according to the passage?
A. Economists believe that all businessmen are dishonest
B. Generally people are honest to earn self-respect
C. Virtuous behaviour earns the self-respect of others
D. People are generally honest because it pays in the long run
E. All dishonest men are not caught

10. Which of the following word(s) is most nearly the SAME in meaning as the phrase 'STAND UP' as it has been used in the passage?
A. Get up B. Get established
C. Hold up D. Failed
E. Supported

11. Which of the following best describes what the author is trying to point out through the last sentence, of the passage, "Cases that ......compelling?"
A. The consequences of dishonesty
B. Theories do not seem to be true
C. Economists predict correctly
D. The contradictions in the real world
E. All theories are nonsense

12. Which of the following word is most nearly the SAME in meaning as the word 'COMPELLING' as it has been used in the passage?
A. Coercive B. Forceful
C. Binding D. Mandatory
E. True

PASSAGE-9

Economic growth involves both benefits and costs. The desirablity of increasing production has frequently been challenged in recent years and some have even maintained that economic growth is merely a quantitative enlargement that has no human meaning or value. However, economic growth is an increase in the capacity to produce goods and services that people want. Since the product of economic growth can be measured by its value to someone, it is important to ask whose standard of valuation counts.

In the United States, the value of a product is what purchasers pay for it. This is determined by the purchasers' preferences combined with conditions of supply, which in turn reflect various other factors, such as natural and technological circumstances at any given time and the preferences of those who supply capital and labour. The value by which we measure a product synthesizes all these factors Gross National Product (GNP) is the market value of the nation's total output of goods and services.

Gross National Product is not a perfect measure of all the activities involved in economic output. It does not account for deterioration or improvements in the environment, even when they are incidental results of the production process. On the other hand, it does not take into account many benefits provided as side effects of the economic process; it does not include 'productive but unpaid work' (such as that done by a housewife); and it does not reckon with such other factors as the burdensomeness of work, the length of the work, week and so forth.

Nonetheles, the GNP concept makes an important contribution to our understanding of how the economy is working. While it is not a complete measure of economic productivity and even less so of "welfare" the level and rate of increase of the GNP are clearly and positively associated with what most people throughout the world see as an improvement in the quality of life.

Although there has been much soul searching about the role of increasing material affluence in the good life, it seems quite certain that most Americans prefer a rapidly growing GNP and its consequences. This does not mean that growth of the GNP is an absolute requirement that must be furthered at all costs, and beyond a certain point they are not worth paying. Moreover people wants thing that are not measured in the GNP. Still, while human values and conditions of the life change and might conceivably make the social cost of a rising GNP seem too high, it is likely that we would still be concerned about the growth of our nation's GNP.

In any case, since there is little evidence of decline in the value assigned to economic output as a whole, the factors that influence our capacity to produce remain of great importance. In the long run, the same factors result in a growing GNP and in other social benefits. They are size and competence of population, state of knowledge, amount of capital and the effectiveness with which these are combined and utilized.

1. Those who decide the value of a product are
A. the GNP B. economic theorist
C. its advertisers D. its patent holders
E. its purchasers

2. The rhetorical purpose of the third paragraph of the passage is to
I. anticipate objection to what the GNP fails to take into account
II. cite examples of "products" the GNP ought to include
III. develop the definition of paragraph two with specific details
A. I only B. II only
C. III only D. I and II only
E. I, II and III

3. The main purpose of the passage is to
A. define the limitation of using GNP to measure the nation's well-being
B. contrast the American and the European GNPs
C. argue for the value of increased economic output
D. explain the disadvantages of measuring the quality of life using a scale of material affluence
E. define Gross National Product

4. A critic of the limitations of the measurement of the GNP might cite its failure to consider all the following except
A. the steady increase in American worker's leisure then
B. cooperative baby-sitting projects among parents with young children

C. the widespread existence of chemicals in American rivers
D. the value of the time a salaried stock broker spends on research
E. the valuation of family household management

5. We might assume that the author favours the continuing growth of the GNP because
A. although he mentions that the GNP has its costs, he doesn't examine those costs
B. it does not include such factors as the burdensomeness of work
C. he wishes to represent a minority opinion
D. he does not believe in perfect measure of economic growth
E. he believes that human values and the conditions of life are subject to change

6. We can infer from the passage the factor that does not influence the growth of the GNP is
A. the condition of the population
B. a dependence on spiritual values
C. the capital available in the country
D. knowledge related to production of goods and services
E. the efficiency of the production process

7. As it is used in the fourth paragraph of the passage, the word "welfare" can be best defined as
A. a measure of economic productivity
B. the quality of life of the public as a whole
C. government-supported payments to the indigent
D. public payments for unpaid production work such as child care
E. state-supported income supplements

PASSAGE-10

The political system always dominates the entire social scene; and hence those who wield political power are generally able to control all the different social sub-systems and manipulate them to their own advantage. The social groups in power, therefore, have always manipulated the education systems, especially when these happen to depend upon the State for their very existence, to strengthen and perceptuate their own privileged position. But herein lies a contradiction. For the very realization of their selfish ends, the social groups in power are compelled to extend the benefits of these educational systems to the under-privileged groups also. The inevitable task is generally performed with three precautions abundantly taken care of:

(1) the privileged groups continue to be the principal beneficiaries of the educational system, dominate the higher stages of education or the hard core of prestigious and quality institutions or the most useful of course, so as to safeguard their dominant position of leadership in all walks of life;

(2) the system is so operated that under-privileged groups can utilize it only marginally in real terms and the bulk of them become either drop-outs or push-outs and get reconciled to their own interior status in society; and

(3) the few from the weaker sections that survive and succeed in spite of all the handicaps are generally co-opted within the system to prevent dissatisfaction. But education is essentially a liberating force so that, as time passes some under-privileged groups do manage to become aware of the reality, the number of the educated persons soon becomes too large to be fully co-opted, and many able individuals among them strive to organize the liberate the weak and the under-privileged. The resultant awareness of the people, combined with suitable organization necessary, leads to adjustment in the social structure and to an increase in vertical mobility so that new groups begin to share power. Eventually, other social changes also follow and the traditional, inegalitarian, and hierachical social structure tends to be replaced by another which is more modern, less hierarchical and more egalitarian. The educational system, therefore, is never politically neutral, and it always performs three functions simultaneously viz., it helps the privileged to dominate, domesticates the under-privileged to their own status in society, and also tends to liberate the oppressed. Which of these functions shall dominate and to what

extent, depends mostly on one crucial factor, viz., the quality and quantity of the political education which the system provides or upon its 'political content',

The developments in Indian society, polity and education during the past 175 years should be viewed against the background of this broad philosophy. From very ancient times, the Indian society has always been elitist and power, wealth and education were mostly confined to the upper castes of the society. What is important to note is that the system has an infinite capacity to adjust or to absorb and, for that very reason, it is extremely resistant to any **radical** transformation. The social system continued to exist almost unchanged till the British administrators began to lay the foundation of the modern system of education.

1. According to the passage, the Indian society has always been:
   A. insensitive to the needs of elite groups
   B. less hierachical
   C. politically neutral
   D. conscious about the sufferings of the under-privileged
   E. None of these

2. In the context of the passage, which of the following statements is true regarding those who control political power?
   A. They try to establish a just social order
   B. They try to control all the different social sub-systems
   C. They facilitate the upward mobility of the under-privileged classes
   D. They manipulate the economic system for the benefits of the under-privileged
   E. None of these

3. According to the passage, the social groups in power have manipulated the educational system because:
   A. they wanted to preserve their special status
   B. they wanted to give maximum benefits to the under-privileged
   C. they wanted to introduce social changes through the educational system
   D. they wanted to make it politically neutral
   E. None of these

4. According to the passage, the Indian social system is resistant to the major changes because:
   A. it is basically elitist
   B. power, wealth and education are mostly confined to the upper classes
   C. it is extremely traditional and conservative
   D. it can absorb social changes without changing its basic framework
   E. None of these

5. According to the passage, why do the majority of under-privileged groups become drop-outs?
   A. They constantly suffer from the feeling of inferiority
   B. They do not possess the required intellectual potential to survive in the educational system
   C. The system is so manipulated that they cannot utilize it meaningfully
   D. The privileged groups continue to be the major beneficiaries of the system
   E. None of these

6. Which of the following statements is not true in the context of the passage?
   A. Educational system tends to enlighten the minds of the under-privileged
   B. Credit for bringing modern system of education goes to Britishers
   C. The privileged groups try to deprive the 'have nots' of the real benefits of education
   D. The privileged class depends upon the Government for their survival
   E. The educational system is never politically biased

7. Which of the following is most opposite in meaning of the word 'RADICAL' as used in the passage?
   A. superficial   B. slow
   C. narrow   D. simple
   E. extreme

8. According to the passage, social groups in power extend the benefits of education to the under-privileged groups because:
   A. they have realized that the growth of a nation depends upon the spread of education

B. they want to achieve their selfish objectives
C. they want to create an egalitarian society
D. they want to abdicate their dominant position of leadership in all walks of life
E. None of these

9. According to the passage, sharing of power by new groups is an outcome of:
A. the total replacement of the traditional social structure by a modern one
B. a politically neutral educational system
C. a liberal democratic approach of the privileged class
D. increase in the vertical mobility of the under-privileged groups
E. None of these

10. According to the passage, how education works for ameliorating the lot of the under-privileged classes?
A. It helps the under-privileged people to dominate others
B. It helps them to achieve higher goals in life
C. Some educated persons from this class organise and liberate the weak people
D. It encourages them to demosticate the privileged people
E. None of these

PASSAGE-11

Educational planning should aim at **meeting** the educational needs of the entire population of all age groups. While the traditional structure of education as a three layer hierarchy from the primary stage to the university represents the core, we should not overlook the periphery which is equally important under modern conditions workers need to rewind, or renew their enthusiasm, or strike out in a new direction, or improve their skills as much as any university professor. The retired and the aged have their needs as well. Educational planning, in their words, should take care of the needs of everyone.

Our structures of education have been built up on the assumption that there is a terminal point to education. This basic defect has become all the more harmful today. A UNESCO report entitled "Learning to Be" prepared by Edgar Faure and others in 1973 asserts that the education of children must prepare the future adult for various forms of self-learning. A viable educational system of the future should consist of modules with different kinds of functions serving a diversity of constitutent. And performance, not the period of study, should be the basis for credentials. The writing is already on the wall.

In view of the fact that the significance of a commitment of lifelong learning and lifetime education is being discussed only in recent years even in educationally advanced countries, the possibility of the idea becoming an **integral** part of educational thinking seems to be **a far cry**. For, to move in that direction means such more than some simple rearrangement of the **present** organisation of education. But a good beginning can be made by developing open university programmes for older learners of different categories and introducing extension services in the conventional colleges and schools. Also these institutions should learn to coorporate with the numerous community organisations such as libraries, museums, municipal recreational programmes, health services, etc.

1. According to the passage, the present education structures assume which of the following:
A. Education is a one time process.
B. All people can be educated as per their needs.
C. Discussions on lifelong learning should continue for some more time
D. Present educational planning is very much practical
E. Simple rearrangement of the present educational system is a must

2. According to the author, educational planning should attempt to:
A. decide a terminal point to education
B. train the people at the core
C. fulfil the educational needs of everyone
D. encourage conventional schools and colleges
E. overlook the people on the periphery

3. According to the author, what should be the basis for awarding credentials?
A. Duration of the course
B. Diversity of the topics covered
C. Participation in community activities
D. Real grasp of matter or skill
E. Competence of the course-teachers

4. In the context of the passage, what is the meaning of the sentence "The writing is already on the wall"?
A. The signs of change are already visible
B. Everything is uncertain nowadays
C. It is a mysterious process
D. Changes have already taken place
E. You cannot change the future

5. According to the author, the concept of "lifetime education" is:
A. not practical
B. not desirable
C. in vogue in advanced countries
D. still in formative stages
E. as old as traditional education

6. Which of the following is not true in the context of the passage?
A. 'Learning to Be' defends that there is a terminal point to education
B. Needs of aged and retired should also be considered
C. Lifelong learning is a recent concept
D. Schools and colleges should open extension services
E. 'Workers' knowledge and skills also need to be updated constantly

7. Which of the following best describes the purpose of the author?
A. To criticise the present educational system
B. To strengthen the present educational practices
C. To present a satirical style
D. To present a pragmatic point of view
E. To support non-conventional educational organisations

8. What is the main thrust of the author?
A. One should never cease to learn
B. Traditional systems should be strengthened
C. There is no substitute for the extant system of education
D. Formal education is more important than non-formal
E. It is impossible to meet the needs of everyone

9. Integrating the concepts of lifelong learning with the educational structure:
A. simple rearrangement of present educational organisations
B. longer durations for all formal courses
C. more weightage for actual performance than real understanding
D. closing dawn conventional schools and colleges
E. None of these

10. What should be the major characteristic of the future educational system?
A. Different modules with same function
B. Same module for different groups
C. No modules but compulsory standard programme for all
D. Rearrangement of various course contents
E. None of these

11. According to the author, what measures should open university adopt to meet modern conditions?
A. Open more colleges on traditional lines
B. Primary education should be under the control of the open universities
C. Develop various programmes for adult learners
D. De-recognition of various community organisations
E. Cater to the needs of those who represent 'Core'

12. Which of the following is most opposite in meaning of the phrase 'A FAR CRY' as used in the passage?
A. Next to impossible
B. Making loud noise
C. Very funny
D. A reality
E. A theoretical suggestion

13. Which of the following is most nearly the same in meaning as the word 'PRESENT' as used in the passage?
A. gift B. existing
C. given D. new
E. outward

14. Which of the following is most opposite in meaning of the word 'INTEGRAL' as used in the passage?
A. minor B. major
C. essential D. independent
E. unwilling

15. Which of the following is most nearly the same in meaning as the word 'MEETING' as used in the passage?
A. satisfying B. contacting
C. representing D. looking
E. approaching

PASSAGE-12

The past decade has upset many preconceptions about development and this, more than anything else, makes it difficult to be **overly** definite about what the next decade has in store. But there are a few things that one can assert with some confidence. First, education, health and productive employment are crucial both for growth and for equity. We have tended to assume that all of these are the consequences of rapid economic growth and that only growth can generate the resources required for these purposes. But, increasingly, it appears that these are better seen as causes rather than as consequences of development. Virtually, every case of successful development involves a prior improvement in literacy, technical skills, health status and access to productive work.

Second, technological competence is the most important endowment and it explains a far larger proportion of growth in output and trade than more conventional factors like natural resources or capital accumulation. The competence required is not just in research. In fact technological dynamism in the factory and the farm is more important than the presence of a **large** research establishment.

Third, the environmental imperative can no longer be ignored. Today, as an international issue, it is second only to disarmament. Nationally, the developmental consequences of environmental neglect are increasingly obvious.

In the Indian context there are at least two further factors which **reinforce** the above propositions. The first is population growth. Given the pace of expansion of the population and the workforce, human resource development acquires an added urgency. Population growth is also one, but not necessarily the most important factor, which underlines environmental stress in rural and urban areas. The second factor is that as a large country we cannot **carve** out an independent position in the global system without building up a substantial capacity for self-reliant growth. The acquisition of technical competence is crucial for this **purpose**.

Until now we have tended to **treat** human resource development, technology issues and environment as subsidiary to the main task of planning. The thrust has been on: quantitative expansion of infrastructure and production with a focus on production targets like tonnes of steel, kWh of electricity, etcetera; capacity targets like road length, rail kilometerage; and coverage targets like number of schools and students, number of villages electrified, etcetera, —**Catching up** with known technologies—fuller use of natural resources—maximum mobilisation of financial resources.

1. According to the passage, we have so far placed more emphasis on which of the following?
A. Maximum utilisation of available finances
B. Following known technologies
C. Increased number of basic facilities and meeting number targets
D. Optimum use of available natural resources
E. All of these

2. According to the author which of the following factors support and strengthen his point of view?
(1) Necessity for carrying out growth on the basis of our own strength
(2) Increased emphasis on production and coverage targets.

A. Only (1) and not (2)
B. Only (2) and not (1)
C. Either (1) or (2)
D. Both (1) and (2)
E. Not mentioned in the passage

3. Which of the following statements is NOT TRUE in the context of the passage?
A. We will have bright future by only catching up with known technologies
B. Optimum self-reliance is the need of the day
C. We have to now emphasise aspects of human resource development
D. Technological competence has to be given due priority over more conventional factors
E. We cannot afford to ignore the importance of environment

4. According to the author, which of the following cannot be viewed as cause of development?
A. Improvement in literacy
B. Betterment in health services
C. Increase in underemployment
D. Speedy economic growth
E. Enhancement in technical skills

5. What seems to be the purpose of the author in writing this passage?
A. To show how the policy makers have failed
B. Review of the past with a view to evolve positive directions for future
C. A review of world affairs with special emphasis on developed countries
D. To prove how his predictions have turned out to be correct
E. To appreciate the steps taken by our Government in the past and doubts about future

6. According to the authors at the national level, with passage of time, the effects of which of the following are being felt?
A. Progressive degradation of technological competence in urban areas
B. Emphasis on slow rate of disarmament as compared to other nations
C. Expansion of workforce of high quality
D. Lack of attention and action for protecting environmental wealth
E. Reduction in growth rate of population

7. According to the author, which of the following is a less important factor resulting in environmental stress in rural and urban areas?
A. Continued environmental neglect
B. Rapid economic growth
C. Rate of growth of population
D. Availability of productive employment
E. Increase in capital accumulation

8. What seems to be the approach of the author regarding present status of research?
(1) He desires that more research establishments should come up
(2) Application of new technologies in factories and field is more vital than setting up of research laboratories
A. Only (1)
B. Only (2)
C. Neither (1) nor (2)
D. Both (1) and (2)
E. Not mentioned in the passage

Directions (Qs. 9 to 12): *Choose the word which is most nearly the SAME in meaning as the word or group of words given in capital letters as used in the passage.*

9. CARVE
A. cover B. decide
C. drive D. acquire
E. forget

10. LARGE
A. long B. free
C. uncontrolled D. diverse
E. bis

11. CATCHING UP
A. drawing level with B. coming down
C. leading from D. lifting up
E. throwing up

12. PURPOSE
A. use B. outcome
C. effect D. reason
E. ability

Directions (Qs. 13 to 15): *Choose the word which is most OPPOSITE in meaning of the word given in capital letters as used in the passage.*

13. OVERLY
A. inwardly B. casually
C. certainly D. minutely
E. insignificantly

14. TREAT
A. consider B. dislike
C. misbehave D disregard
E. unwind

15. REINFORCE
A. strengthen B. weaken
C. remove D. delink
E. simplify

PASSAGE-13

One could, in theory, conceive of a country "specialising" entirely in agriculture and obtaining all its industrial requirements from abroad. But it could never become a high income country simply because technologically developed agriculture could never absorb more than a fraction of the working population on the available land. Though in all undeveloped countries the greater part of the working population is "occupied" in agriculture, most of this represents disguised unemployment; a rural community maintains all its membes and expects everyone to share in the work. Much of the greater part of this labour could be withdrawn from agriculture if alternative employment opportunities were available without any **adverse** effect, and pobably with a beneficial effect, on total agricultural output. For the relief of the pressure of labour on the land is itself a most potent factor in **inducing** improvements in technology which raise yields per acre, as well as the yield per man. These improvements normally require an increase in the capital employed on the land; but the savings necessary for the increase in capital are themselves a by-product of reduced population pressure. The reduction in the agricultural population, and the increased use of capital in agriculture are thus different aspects of the same process. As there are fewer mouths to feed, the "agricultural surplus" rises (the excess of agricultural production over the self-consumption of the farming population). The rise in the "surplus" enables the farmers to plough back a higher proportion of their output—in the form of better tools, improved seeds, fertilisers, etc., and such improvements tend to both "labour saving" and "land saving"; they **diminish** the labour requirements at the same time as they increase the yield of the land.

1. What, according to the passage, will be the achievement of inducing improvement in technology?
A. Higher specialisation in agriculture
B. Better employment opportunities
C. Beneficial effects on quality of life of people
D. Relieving the pressure of employment
E. None of these

2. According to the passage, it is theoretically possible to think of country .....
A. advanced both in agriculture and industry
B. specialised in industry, but not in agriculture
C. backward both in agriculture and industry
D. specialised in agriculture but not in industry
E. borrowing all its requirements from abroad

3. What could be done, according to the passage, to induce improvement in agricultural technology?
A. Import of better agricultural technology
B. Providing better weather forecasts
C. To relieve pressure of labour on land
D. Providing irrigation facilities
E. None of these

4. According to the passage, in underdeveloped countries .....
A. agriculture is in a primitive stage
B. per acre yield is very high
C. land is available in plenty
D. alternative employment opportunities will have adverse effect on the lives of people
E. significant proportion of working population works in agriculture

5. Which of the following statements is TRUE in the context of the passage
 A. Underdeveloped countries are rapidly growing industrially
 B. Technologically developed agriculture solves all the problems of unemployment
 C. Relief of the pressure of labour on land raises yields per acre
 D. Yield per acre and yield per man are unrelated
 E. Surplus in agriculture is spent for domestic purposes

6. Why, according to the passage, a country specialised in agriculture only cannot become a high income country?
 A. It simply cannot borrow all its industrial requirements from abroad
 B. It can absorb only a fraction of its working population
 C. Agriculture needs huge investments and infrastructural facilities
 D. Technological advancements in agriculture has limitations
 E. None of these

7. Which of the following staements is NOT TRUE in the context of the passage?
 A. Theoretically there could be a country specialised entirely in agriculture
 B. Capital is required to increase the per acre yield of the land
 C. Agriculture surplus will rise if there are fewer mouths to feed
 D. Technologically developed agriculture will absorb most of the working population on the available land
 E. A rural community maintains all its members and expects everyone to share in the work.

8. Which of the following is most nearly the SAME in meaning as the word 'DIMINISH' as used in the passage?
 A. reduce B. shorten
 C. prohibit D. increase
 E. worsen

9. Which of the following is most OPPOSITE in meaning of the word 'ADVERSE' as used in the passage?
 A. negative B. facilitating
 C. supplementary D. derogative
 E. decorative

10. Which of the following is most nearly the SAME in meaning as the word 'INDUCING' as used in the passage?
 A. causing B. augmenting
 C. reducing D. developing
 E. increasing

PASSAGE-14

Peace and order are necessary, not just in our own country but also at the international level, if we are to secure national progress and development. The different countries in the world are coming closer today due to faster means of transport and communication. Economically, they have become increasingly interdependent. If peace is disturbed in one part of the world, it has adverse effects in other parts of the world as well. Nuclear weapons have already threatened the world with nuclear war. If the conflicts between different nations are not settled in time, they might **culminate** in a nuclear war destroying the whole world. It is therefore in our own interest that the world is free of conflicts. If at all there are any, they must be settled promptly and peace should be restored. That is why we have declared the establishment of international peace and understanding as an objective of our foreign policy.

We need the help and co-operation of other countries for our scientific, industrial and economic development, especially in those fields where we have yet to achieve self-sufficiency. We obtain the latest machinery, technology and financial aid from the developed countries. On our part we, too, offer help to the underdeveloped countries. We are keen on maintaining friendly relations with other countries. Such friendly relations **foster** international understanding.

We have always exerted ourselves to see that the disputes arising between the different nations are settled through peaceful negotiations. We play an active role in the United Nations, the South Asian Association for Regional Co-operation, the Commonwealth of Nations and other such international organisations. We make it a point to participate in the international conferences on issues like energy crisis, environmental imbalance, nuclear arms race, etc. We always offer a helping hand to other nations affected by natural calamities such as famines, earthquakes, floods and so on. We strive to maintain peaceful and friendly relations with our neighbouring countries. Why do we do all this? We sincerely believe that the conflits in today's world should be minimised, making way for better cooperation among the nations. If this is achieved, human resources will no longer be wasted in things like war or aggression. There will be no destruction of wealth. We believe that, in a peaceful world, there will be greater scope for the economic and cultural development of countries.

1. Which of the following statements is NOT TRUE in the context of the passage?
   A. International conflicts must be settled promptly
   B. We try to maintain friendly relations with our neighbours
   C. We participate in many international conferences
   D. Friendly relations with other countries foster international understanding
   E. Each country can be considered isolated and insulated from the effects of other countries

2. Which of the following words is largely SIMILAR in meaning of the word 'CULMINATE' as used in the passage?
   A. Reach the highest point
   B. Stretch to the maximum
   C. Absolute standards
   D. Total destruction
   E. Coming of age

3. According to the passage, maintaining friendly relations with other countries facilitate
   A. developing international understanding
   B. exchange of scientists and technologists
   C. strategic planning in defence matters
   D. import and export of several vital commodities
   E. none of the above

4. If the conflicts between nations do not cease
   A. international bodies will have to take up these issues
   B. international understanding will not be fostered
   C. nuclear war will destroy the whole world
   D. the means of transport and communication will be disrupted
   E. none of these

5. Which of the following is obtained by us from the developed countries, according to the passage?
   A. Fertilisers B. Foodgrains
   C. Leather Products D. Technology
   E. Crude Oil

6. Which of the following according to the passage, is facilitating the process of different countries coming together?
   A. Emerging world order
   B. Asian Association for Regional Cooperation
   C. Our participation in international conferences
   D. Need for self-sufficiency
   E. Faster means of transport and communication

7. Minimising the conflicts and making way for better co-operation among the nations will result in
   A. useful and purposive utilisation of human resources
   B. better utilisation of means of transport and communication
   C. culmination of nuclear war destroying the world
   D. keenness on maintaining friendly relations with other countries
   E. preservation of our national unity and integrity

8. The question "Why do we do all this" is asked in the passage in which of the following contexts?

A. We always offer a helping hand to other nations in improving their technology
B. We endeavour to maintain peaceful and friendly relations with our neighbours
C. We obtain the latest machinery, technology and financial aid from the developed countries
D. We have shaped our foreign policy in a balanced and purposeful manner
E. None of these

9. Does any of the following sentences contain any idea expressed in the passage?
A. We have to make conscious efforts to preserve our national unity
B. Our country is huge in size and population where many languages are spoken
C. We have adopted the objective of democracy in the interest of overall development of our country
D. Citizens must be well-informed about public issues in order to participate meaningfully in public life
E. None of these statements contain any idea expressed in the passage

10. Which of the following words is most OPPOSITE in meaning of the word 'FOSTER' as used in the passage?
A. advocate B. hinder
C. obviate D. facilitate
E. jettison

PASSAGE-15

There is no field of human endeavour that has been so misunderstood as health. While health, which **connotes** well-being and the absence of illness, has a low profile, it is illness representing the failure of health, which virtually monopolizes attention because of the fear of pain, disability and death. Even Sushruta has warned that this provides the medical practitioner power over the patient which could be misused.

Till recently, patients had implicit faith in their physician whom they loved and respected, not only for his knowledge but also in the total belief that practitioners of this noble profession, guided by ethics, always placed the patient's interest above all other considerations. This rich interpersonal relationship between the physician, patient and family has, barring a few exceptions, prevailed till the recent past, for caring was considered as important as curing. Our indigenous systems of medicine like ayurveda and yoga have been more **concerned** with the promotion of the health of both the body and mind and with maintaining a harmonious relationship not just with fellow beings but with nature itself, of which man is an integral part. Healthy practices like cleanliness, proper diet, exercise and meditation are part of our culture which sustain people even in the prevailing conditions of poverty in rural India and in the unhygienic urban slums.

These systems consider disease as an **aberration** resulting from disturbance of the equilibrium of health, which must be corrected by gentle restoration of this balance through proper diet, medicines and the establishment of mental peace. They also teach the graceful acceptance of old age with its infirmities resulting from the normal **degenerative** process as well as of death which is **inevitable**.

This is in marked contrast to the western concept of life as a constant struggle against disease, aging and death which must be fought and conquered with the knowledge and technology **derived** from their science: a science which, with its narrow dissective and quantifying approach, has provided us the understanding of the microbial causes of communicable diseases and provided highly effective technology for their prevention, treatment and control. This can rightly be claimed as the greatest contribution of western medicine and justifiably termed as 'high' technology. And yet the contribution of this science in the field of non-communicable diseases is remarkably poor despite the far greater inputs in research and treatment for the problems of aging like cancer, heart diseases, paralytic strokes and arthritis which are the major problems of affluent societies today.

1. What caution proponents of indigenous systems have sounded against medical practitioners?
A. Their undue concern for the health of the person

B. Their emphasis on research on non-communicable diseases
C. Their emphasis on curing illness rather than preventive health measures
D. Their emphasis on restoring health for afluent members of the society
E. None of these

2. Which of the following has been described as the most outstanding benefit of modern medicine?
(1) The real course and ways of control of communicable diseases
(2) Evolution of the concept of harmony between man and nature
(3) Special techniques for fighting aging.
A. Only (2) and (3) B. Only (1) and (2)
C. Only (1) D. Only (2)
E. Only (3)

3. In India traditionally the doctors were being guided mainly by which of the following?
A. High technology
B. Good knowledge
C. Professional ethics
D. Power over patient
E. Western concept of life

4. Why does the author describe the contributions of science as remarkably poor?
A. It concentrates more on health than on illness
B. It suggests remedies for the poor people
C. It demands more inputs in terms of research and technology
D. The cost of treatment is low
E. None of these

5. Which of the following can be inferred about the position of the author in writing the passage?
(1) Ardent supporter of western system in present context
(2) Supremacy of ancient Indian system in today's world
(3) Critical and objective assessment of the present situation
A. Only (1) B. Only (2)
C. Only (3) D. Neither (2) nor (3)
E. None of these

6. Why was the field of health not been understood properly?
A. Difficulty in understanding distinction between health and illness
B. Confusion between views of indigenous and western system
C. Highly advanced technology being used by the professionals
D. Not given in the passage
E. None of these

7. Why, according to the author, people in India have survived inspite of poverty?
A. Their natural resistance to communicable diseases is very high
B. They have easy access to western technology
C. Their will to conquer diseases
D. Their harmonious relationship with the physician
E. None of these

8. Which of the following pairs are mentioned as 'contrast' in the passage?
A. Western concept of life and science
B. Technology and science
C. Western physician and western educated Indian physician
D. Indian and western concept of life
E. Knowledge and technology

9. The author seems to suggest that
A. we should give importance to improve the health rather than curing of illness
B. we should move towards becoming an affluent society
C. ayurveda is superior to yoga
D. good interpersonal relatoinship between the doctor and patient is necessary but not sufficient
E. ayurvedic medicine can be improved by following western approches and methods of sciences

Directions (Qs. 10 to 12): *Choose the word which is most OPPOSITE in meaning of the word printed in capital letters as used in the passage.*

10. CONCERNED
A. diluted B. liberated
C. indifferent D. divested
E. relaxed

11. DEGENERATIVE
A. recuperative
B. revolving
C. productive
D. innovative
E. integrative

12. INEVITABLE
A. undesirable
B. unsuitable
C. detestable
D. avoidable
E. available

Directions (Qs. 13 to 15): *Choose the word which is most nearly the SAME in meaning as the word printed in capital letters as used in the passage.*

13. ABERRATION
A. observation
B. alternative
C. deviation
D. outcome
E. stimulate

14. CONNOTES
A. helps
B. cures
C. follows
D. confirms
E. implies

15. DERIVED
A. constructed
B. sprung
C. directed
D. processed
E. continued

ANSWERS

PASSAGE-1

1	2	3	4	5	6	7	8	9	10
B	E	B	C	B	B	A	A	C	E
11	**12**	**13**							
D	D	A							

PASSAGE-2

1	2	3	4	5	6	7	8	9	10
D	D	D	B	A	C	E	B	C	A
11	**12**	**13**	**14**	**15**					
B	C	A	D	C					

PASSAGE-3

1	2	3	4	5	6	7	8	9	10
C	A	B	D	A	C	E	B	A	D
11	**12**	**13**	**14**	**15**					
C	E	C	A	D					

PASSAGE-4

1	2	3	4	5	6	7	8	9
B	A	B	C	B	A	E	A	C

PASSAGE-5

1	2	3	4	5	6	7	8	9	10
D	B	B	E	A	D	C	D	D	D
11	**12**								
C	A								

PASSAGE-6

1	2	3	4	5	6	7	8	9	10
B	E	C	D	A	B	D	E	A	D
11	**12**	**13**	**14**	**15**					
C	D	E	D	B					

PASSAGE-7

1	2	3	4	5	6	7	8	9	10
B	D	A	C	A	B	C	A	D	C
11	**12**								
B	D								

PASSAGE-8

1	2	3	4	5	6	7	8	9	10
A	D	B	B	D	A	C	C	A	B
11	**12**								
B	B								

PASSAGE-9

1	2	3	4	5	6	7
E	A	A	A	E	B	D

PASSAGE-10

1	2	3	4	5	6	7	8	9	10
E	B	A	D	C	E	A	B	D	C

PASSAGE-11

1	2	3	4	5	6	7	8	9	10
A	C	D	E	A	A	D	A	E	E
11	**12**	**13**	**14**	**15**					
C	D	B	D	A					

PASSAGE-12

1	2	3	4	5	6	7	8	9	10
C	A	A	C	A	D	C	B	D	E
11	**12**	**13**	**14**	**15**					
A	B	B	D	B					

PASSAGE-13

1	2	3	4	5	6	7	8	9	10
E	D	C	E	C	B	D	A	B	B

PASSAGE-14

1	2	3	4	5	6	7	8	9	10
E	A	A	C	D	E	A	B	E	B

PASSAGE-15

1	2	3	4	5	6	7	8	9	10
C	C	C	E	B	A	E	D	A	C
11	**12**	**13**	**14**	**15**					
A	D	C	E	B					

CHAPTER 2

Cloze Test

A cloze test is a procedure in which you are asked to supply words which have been removed from a passage. It is meant to test your ability to comprehend text. Try and practise it to master it in this chapter.

Directions: *In the following passages there are some blanks, each of which has been numbered. These numbers are also printed below the passages and against each five words are suggested, one of which fits the blank appropriately. Find out the appropriate words in each case.*

PASSAGE-1

The world economy is in recession — the deepest and the most widespread ... **1** ... the 1930s. There are ... **2** ... of ... **3** ... in the industrial countries, but most serious economic ... **4** ... anticipate that rates of growth and levels of economic activity will remain low.

In all that has been written about world ... **5** ..., the ... **6** ... have been overwhelmingly and narrowly economic. Few have ... **7** ... the human consequences in more than a superficial manner. Not a single international study has ... **8** ... the recession's ... **9** ... on the most vulnerable half of the world's population—the children.

The need for ... **10** ... clearly the ... **11** ... between world economic conditions and child welfare has thus become even more urgent in the last few years. The worldscale of current child distress also makes it artificial to restrict the analysis of causes to the ... **12** ... level.

1. A. in B. for C. by D. before E. since

2. A. risks B. glimmers C. studies D. tips E. histories

3. A. development B. downfall C. recovery D. slackness E. impact

4. A. analysts B. journalists C. surveys D. findings E. students

5. A. development B. economy C. wars D. recession E. conflicts

6. A. emphasis B. aims C. glimpses D. suppositions E. preoccupations

7. A. delved B. taught C. propagated D. investigated E. manifested

8. A. understood B. analysed C. highlighted D. prepared E. planned

9. A. analysis B. undercurrents C. impact D. overtures E. study

10. A. chalking out B. curbing C. bringing out D. implementing E. propagating

11. A. linkages B. fallouts C. dependence D. contrasts E. similarities

12. A. international B. political C. low D. national E. highest

PASSAGE-2

Conventional medical wisdom does not advise taking ... **1** ... vitamins as pills and capsules. On the contrary there was a strong lobby which ... **2** ... the supplementary intake of vitamins. This used to leave the ... **3** ... person confused. However, modern research is ... **4** ... a surprise. More and more scientists are beginning to ... **5** ... that ... **6** ... medical views on vitamins has been ... **7** ... . Evidence shows that ... **8** ... extra vitamins plays a role in assuring vitality and ... **9** ... health than was ... **10** ... thought.

1. A. some B. extra
C. insoluble D. strong
E. all

2. A. facilitate B. criticised
C. communicate D. projected
E. advocated

3. A. medical B. stick
C. scientific D. average
E. educated

4. A. trying B. manufacturing
C. practising D. holding
E. inventing

5. A. trust B. consider
C. refute D. forget
E. suspect

6. A. indigent B. all
C. traditional D. modern
E. allopathic

7. A. practical B. limited
C. feasible D. correct
E. confusing

8. A. marketing B. manufacturing
C. swallowing D. taking
E. buying

9. A. pleasurable B. manly
C. optimal D. stronger
E. useful

10. A. previously B. occasionally
C. seriously D. even
E. now

PASSAGE-3

Fundamentally, all human ... **1** ... possess combinations of fixed inherited traits. All men possess the ... **2** ... highly developed nervous system, back-bones, erect posture, hair, etc. Therefore, ... **3** ... among men arise only ... **4** ... changes of this ... **5** ... pattern. Racial ... **6** ... represent one of the finest distinctions and are based on certain ... **7** ... differences. Two races may be ... **8** ... in hair colour, in eye colour but ... **9** ... in stature while two others may be ... **10** ... in stature but differ in the colour of eyes and hair.

1. A. animal B. beings
C. mind D. society
E. thinking

2. A. large B. different
C. same D. natural
E. biological

3. A. sameness B. naturalness
C. growth D. substance
E. variations

4. A. no B. large
C. fundamental D. minor
E. artificial

5. A. fluctuating B. mad
C. picturesque D. basic
E. maddening

6. A. differences B. clashes
C. hatred D. tolerance
E. sameness

7. A. clearcut B. minor
C. unnoticeable D. massive
E. neat

8. A. alike B. different
C. mismatched D. beautiful
E. untouched

9. A. matched B. same
C. different D. close
E. tall

10. A. tall B. short
C. uncouth D. ugly
E. same

PASSAGE-4

Nowadays, under the ... **1** ... system of education, however good it may be, when a young man comes out of the University, there seems to be this ... **2** ... in him that the higher the standard of living rises, the less should a man work. Thus, mathematically higher the standard of living, according to this misconceived notion, the less the ... **3** .... Ultimately, what should be the highest standard of living then? ... **4** ... work! This leads to an unhealthy ... **5** ... among the workers. A typist who types over twenty letters a day asks his ... **6** ... how many letters he had typed that day. The latter ... **7** ... "fifteen". The former thinks, "Tomorrow I should type only fifteen or even ... **8** .... This tendency is quite ... **9** ..., and may ultimately lead to ... **10** .... Even one's family life may be affected adversely due to such tendency.

1. A. developed B. extinct C. outdated D. proposed E. modern
2. A. anxiety B. misconception C. realisation D. worry E. apprehension
3. A. salary B. comfort C. work D. energy E. time
4. A. Minimum B. Maximum C. Less D. No E. Ample
5. A. competition B. dispute C. delay D. jealousy E. ambition
6. A. employee B. subordinate C. boss D. client E. colleague
7. A. suggests B. remembers C. replies D. types E. all
8. A. less B. all C. more D. few E. some
9. A. discouraging B. heartening C. healthy D. unfortunate E. unnatural
10. A. evil B. retardation C. progress D. denial E. complexity

PASSAGE-5

The North-East India is Asia in miniature, a place ... **1** ... the brown and yellow races ... **2** ... and mingle. There are at least 262 ... **3** ... ethnic groups and the region is home to more than 150 million people, if one includes Bangladesh. Take ... **4** ... example the state of Manipur, which ... **5** ... Burma, with a population fo 1.8 million people. It is home to about 30 separate linguistic and ethnic groups including the Taraos, ... **6** ... number less than 400 individuals ... **7** ... the ages and the mountains, the people of this winding trail ... **8** ... an anthropological and sociological ... **9** ... to South East Asia, where the roots of many ... **10** ... lie.

1. A. when B. although C. where D. to E. if
2. A. meet B. desert C. form D. find E. went
3. A. identical B. closed C. corresponding D. homogeneous E. separate
4. A. from B. for C. again D. besides E. to
5. A. holds B. stretches C. rules D. borders E. side
6. A. who B. though C. amidst D. hence E. which
7. A. Bringing B. Demanding C. Beginning D. Allowing E. Stradling
8. A. construct B. form C. broke D. settled E. found
9. A. problem B. anathema C. bridge D. window E. series
10. A. opportunities B. sadly C. since D. still E. diseases

PASSAGE-6

Each species has its special place or habitat. An ... **1** ... bird-watcher can look at ... **2** ... forest, meadow, lake, swamp or field and ... **3** ... almost exactly what birds he ... **4** ... find there. ... **5** ... birds are found all over the world; others ... **6** ... themselves to certain areas. Still ... **7** ... migrate from one country to another in ... **8** ... in search of warmth and ... **9** ... and then return in spring, ... **10** ... the season is more favourable.

1. A. expert B. experienced C. advanced D. active E. old
2. A. the B. some C. a D. certain E. any
3. A. predict B. suggest C. prophesy D. calculate E. count
4. A. should B. must C. might D. will E. need
5. A. More B. Some C. Most D. All E. These
6. A. keep B. entrust C. confine D. involve E. adjust
7. A. some B. others C. few D. all E. fewer
8. A. winter B. summer C. spring D. autumn E. rains
9. A. seeds B. crops C. fruit D. food E. nests
10. A. while B. until C. after D. when E. then

PASSAGE-7

Four cases of burglary have been ... **1** ... with the arrest of one ... **2** ... criminal. The police have ... **3** ... gold and silver jewellery from him. The police increased their public contacts with the residents of the area after following a spate of burglaries. They held corner meetings to ... **4** ... the residents on steps to ... **5** ... prevention. They were ... **6** ... to inform their neighbours if they had to ... **7** ... their houses unattended. Consequently, some ... **8** ... of the locality observed one ... **9** ... leaving an empty house. He was ... **10** ... and a cases was registered.

1. A. connected B. adjusted C. solved D. deferred E. dealt
2. A. notorious B. more C. thief D. imprisoned E. extremely
3. A. withdrawn B. amassed C. sold D. recovered E. stolen
4. A. harass B. arrest C. probe D. threaten E. educate
5. A. loss B. crime C. its D. burglar E. their
6. A. required B. forbidden C. instructed D. entrusted E. forced
7. A. paint B. sell C. protect D. leave E. build
8. A. criminals B. neighbours C. burglars D. pedestrains E. residents
9. A. stranger B. resident C. neighbour D. entrant E. alien
10. A. misled B. apprehended C. neglected D. boycotted E. informed

PASSAGE-8

... **1** ... can be injected ... **2** ... human blood for ... **3** ... diptheria, pneumonia and severe wounds ... **4** ... surgical operations, penicillin is given to ... **5** ... to ... **6** ... the bacterial infections from spereading. After this ... **7** ... several other antibiotics ... **8** ... discovered. Today, these antibiotics are ... **9** ... the lives of lakhs of ... **10** ... all over the world.

1. A. Antibiotics B. Penicillin C. Streptomycin D. Teramycin E. Medicine

2. A. within B. through
C. on D. into
E. over

3. A. treating B. operating
C. discovering D. spreading
E. monitoring

4. A. In B. Over
C. While D. After
E. During

5. A. children B. injured
C. patients D. doctors
E. nurses

6. A. study B. prevent
C. dismiss D. spread
E. remove

7. A. treatment B. patient
C. cause D. discovery
E. operation

8. A. were B. may be
C. have D. are
E. would be

9. A. multiplying B. providing
C. saving D. infecting
E. growing

10. A. children B. species
C. women D. medicos
E. people

PASSAGE-9

... 1 ... change is the ... 2 ... of the day, a proper orientation to ... 3 ... with the change becomes a natural necessity ... 4 ... asured organisational stability. In this ... 5 ... of organisational change and survival, the author brings in the concept of 'praxis', ... 6 ... it as the dynamo of change and uses it for ... 7 ... a conceptual and methodological ... 8 ... for the identification of training needs. Training, ... 9 ... perceived as only one of the many elements in the organisational reflection process, is believed to stand ... 10 ... as the means for relevant learning.

1. A. Few B. Many
C. No D. If
E. Why

2. A. order B. scope
C. large D. direction
E. result

3. A. assist B. renew
C. become D. try
E. cope

4. A. in B. for
C. from D. which
E. but

5. A. end B. decision
C. context D. scope
E. focus

6. A. describes B. throws
C. rejects D. leaves
E. derives

7. A. neglecting B. developing
C. calculating D. experiencing
E. diluting

8. A. routine B. idea
C. book D. follow up
E. framework

9. A. be B. may
C. though D. gets
E. as

10. A. in B. against
C. through D. out
E. with

PASSAGE-10

Each year, middle class Indian children ... 1 ... hundreds of crores of rupees in pocket money and ... 2 ... a heavy burden on parental ... 3 ... . Like adults, these kids have ... 4 ... connected with budgeting and saving money. Unfortunately, basic money ... 5 ... is ... 6 ... taught in schools. At home, very few parents ... 7 ... money matters with their children. Kids who ... 8 ... about money ... 9 ... have been found to be way ahead of their peers. Indeed, learning to ... 10 ... with money properly fosters discipline, good work habits and self-respect.

1. A. spend B. steal
C. save D. give
E. invest

2. A. move B. take
C. risk D. put
E. lift

3. A. promises B. payments
C. demands D. attitudes
E. incomes

4. A. expenses B. experience
C. problems D. guidance
E. necessities
5. A. availability B. inflation
C. economics D. problem
E. management
6. A. carefully B. rarely
C. generally D. always
E. thoroughly
7. A. discuss B. understand
C. teach D. reveal
E. advise
8. A. quarrel B. ask
C. learn D. waste
E. spend
9. A. slowly B. early
C. timely D. lately
E. regularly
10. A. decide B. earn
C. control D. deal
E. pay

PASSAGE-11

Architecture is a unique ... **1** ... of art and science that has ... **2** ... out of man's primary need for shelter. It is concerned with the design and ... **3** ... of buildings in their sociological, technological and environmental context. This field is not only ... **4** ... but also provide the ... **5** ... of designing and building pleasing and ... **6** ... refined structures to serve various needs. ... **7** ... the fairly large number of practising architects, the countrywide ... **8** ... in building activity offers scope for more. And though the initial earnings in the field are relatively ... **9** ... what you make thereafter will depend entirely on your ... **10** ... .

1. A. procedure B. process
C. portion D. blend
E. subject
2. A. drifted B. fizzled
C. contrived D. earned
E. arisen
3. A. painting B. construction
C. decoration D. repairing
E. appearance
4. A. fatiguing B. strenuous
C. encouraging D. vast
E. rewarding
5. A. satisfaction B. facility
C. infrastructure D. amenities
E. decorum
6. A. practically B. ideologically
C. aesthetically D. principally
E. readily
7. A. Considering B. Having
C. Assuming D. Regarding
E. Despite
8. A. variation B. slack
C. lethargy D. spurt
E. deterioration
9. A. escalating B. modest
C. unpredictable D. negligible
E. exorbitant
10. A. ambition B. appearance
C. expectation D. experience
E. need

PASSAGE-12

Without science there is no future for any society. Even with science, ... **1** ... it is controlled by some spiritual impulses, there is also no future. One great thing about science is that it does not accept anything on mere ... **2** ... . Everything has to be ... **3** ... beyond any doubt. All acceptance comes after experiement which has no room for any ... **4** ... . This is the reason ... **5** ... development of science and technology has revolutionised human life all over the world. There are very few spheres of human activity which have not experienced the ... **6** ... of such development. However, despite its manifold ... **7** ... science has not been ... **8** ... to solve any of man's moral or spiritual problems. Society is still ... **9** ... in the dark to find out what its future will be. The need, therefore, is to make science ... **10** ... for the ultimate truth.

1. A. unless B. without
C. if D. before
E. because
2. A. principles B. conjecture
C. experiment D. research
E. experience
3. A. accepted B. demonstrated
C. proved D. performed
E. understood

4. A. precision B. exactness
C. confirmation D. speculation
E. apprehension

5. A. for B. how
C. that D. about
E. why

6. A. impact B. futility
C. causes D. problems
E. nature

7. A. limitations B. benefits
C. shortcomings D. researches
E. inventions

8. A. employed B. developed
C. able D. entrusted
E. taught

9. A. engulfed B. lost
C. enlightening D. investigating
E. groping

10. A. useful B. worthy
C. ready D. search
E. fit

PASSAGE-13

Studies of cognitive development have shown that the child's ... **1** ... to use generalised ... **2** ... develops more slowly in history than in any other schools subjects. This ... **3** ... development of reasoning in historical ... **4** ... makes it necessary for the historian to ... **5** ... upon events that may be included in the text. In many cases, the historian may need to ... **6** ... with special effort a generalised understanding of key-concepts to be used in a... **7** ... . This ... **8** ... may well mean that school history can not cover as many events as it does at present. Also, school histories may have to provide for topic work or theme-based ... **9** ... rather than merely observe ... **10** ... conformity.

1. A. power B. intellect
C. preparedness D. ability
E. alertness

2. A. tasks B. concepts
C. procedures D. theories
E. principles

3. A. typical B. matured
C. slower D. accelerated
E. rapid

4. A. chronology B. arena
C. perspective D. conformity
E. contexts

5. A. deliver B. build
C. focus D. dwell
E. plan

6. A. tackle B. grapple
C. provide D. deliver
E. trade

7. A. text B. forum
C. debate D. reference
E. discussion

8. A. necessity B. requirement
C. understanding D. rationale
E. fact

9. A. projects B. description
C. work-outs D. analysis
E. presentation

10. A. internal B. metaphorical
C. eternal D. chronological
E. time-bound

PASSAGE-14

Faced with an ... **1** ... number and variety of products on the market, managers are finding it more difficult to ... **2** ... demand and plan production and order ... **3** ... . As a result ... **4** ... forecasts are increasing and, along with them, the costs of those errors. Many managers today, ... **5** ... speed is the ... **6** ... , have turned to one or another popular production scheduling system. But these tools tackle only part of the problem. ... **7** ... really needed is a way to ... **8** ... forecasts and simultaneously redesign planning processes to ... **9** ... the impact of ... **10** ... forecasts.

1. A. exact B. equal
C. optimum D. eccentric
E. unprecedented

2. A. meet B. predict
C. ignore D. accept
E. register

3. A. immediately B. quickly
C. accordingly D. positively
E. spontaneously

4. A. inaccurate B. buoyant
C. frequent D. inadequate
E. exorbitant

5. A. consider B. neglecting
C. visualising D. believing
E. notwithstanding

6. A. problem B. answer
C. source D. outcome
E. lacuna

7. A. What's B. That's
C. One D. Managers
E. Companies

8. A. ignore B. obtain
C. vitiate D. negate
E. improve

9. A. rationalise B. substantiate
C. minimise D. counter
E. tolerate

10. A. dangerous B. absolute
C. unpredicted D. erroneous
E. popular

PASSAGE-15

In view of the ... **1** ... demand for personnel with commerce background, in the post-liberalisation period, courses in commerce have ... **2** ... the attention of students and parents. There is growing ... **2** ... for these courses not only in schools but also in colleges. But the ... **4** ... of commerce education in schools leaves ... **5** ... to be desired. Its popularity, importance and quality, to a large extent, depends much on the teaching methodology being ... **6** ... in schools. Of course, the ... **7** ... review and ... **8** ... of syllabic also ... **9** ... . But this aspect is ... **10** ... taken care of suitably, by the concerned organisations.

1. A. exaggerated B. unreasonable
C. tremendous D. increasing
E. diminishing

2. A. distorted B. ameliorated
C. attracted D. weighed
E. encouraged

3. A. demand B. contempt
C. dissatisfaction D. commotion
E. urgency

4. A. awareness B. intricacy
C. status D. necessity
E. quality

5. A. scope B. much
C. short D. everything
E. nothing

6. A. abandoned B. practised
C. contemplated D. assimilated
E. taught

7. A. unscrupulous B. partial
C. expert D. general
E. periodical

8. A. discussions B. perusal
C. reduction D. updating
E. formulation

9. A. matters B. flourishes
C. desires D. encompasses
E. needs

10. A. duly B. seldom
C. being D. often
E. never

ANSWERS

PASSAGE-1

1	2	3	4	5	6	7	8	9	10
E	A	D	A	B	B	A	B	C	C
11	**12**								
D	D								

PASSAGE-2

1	2	3	4	5	6	7	8	9	10
B	E	B	D	A	D	D	D	C	A

PASSAGE-3

1	2	3	4	5	6	7	8	9	10
B	C	E	C	D	D	C	A	C	E

PASSAGE-4

1	2	3	4	5	6	7	8	9	10
E	B	C	D	E	C	C	A	A	B

PASSAGE-5

1	2	3	4	5	6	7	8	9	10
C	A	D	B	D	A	D	B	B	E

PASSAGE-6

1	2	3	4	5	6	7	8	9	10
A	C	D	B	B	C	A	A	D	D

PASSAGE-7

1	2	3	4	5	6	7	8	9	10
C	A	D	E	B	A	D	E	A	B

PASSAGE-8

1	2	3	4	5	6	7	8	9	10
B	D	A	D	C	B	D	A	C	E

PASSAGE-9

1	2	3	4	5	6	7	8	9	10
D	A	E	B	C	A	B	E	C	D

PASSAGE-10

1	2	3	4	5	6	7	8	9	10
A	D	E	C	E	B	A	C	C	D

PASSAGE-11

1	2	3	4	5	6	7	8	9	10
D	E	B	D	C	C	E	D	B	D

PASSAGE-12

1	2	3	4	5	6	7	8	9	10
A	B	C	D	E	A	B	C	E	E

PASSAGE-13

1	2	3	4	5	6	7	8	9	10
D	B	C	E	C	C	A	A	D	D

PASSAGE-14

1	2	3	4	5	6	7	8	9	10
E	B	C	A	D	B	A	E	C	E

PASSAGE-15

1	2	3	4	5	6	7	8	9	10
D	C	A	E	B	B	E	D	A	A

CHAPTER 3

Synonyms

English is the most popular language in the world. It comprises thousands of words. No one can remember all the words and their meanings but everyone must try to read and learn maximum number of words and their meanings. One must keep and use a dictionary religiously.

TYPE-I

Directions: *In the following questions choose the words which best expresses the meaning of the given words.*

1. INDICT
A. Condemn B. Reprimand
C. Accuse D. Allege
E. Trap

2. SCINTILLATING
A. Smouldering B. Gilittering
C. Touching D. Warming
E. Glowing

3. REFECTORY
A. Restaurant B. Parlour
C. Living Room D. Dining Room
E. Factory

4. DISTINCTION
A. Diffusion B. Disagreement
C. Difference D. Degree
E. Honour

5. IMPROVEMENT
A. Advancement B. Betterment
C. Promotion D. Preference
E. Enhance

6. ADVERSITY
A. Failure B. Helplessness
C. Misfortune D. Crisis
E. Negativity

7. TURN UP
A. Land up B. Show up
C. Crop up D. Come up
E. Rotate

8. DEIFY
A. Flatter B. Challenge
C. Worship D. Face
E. Obstruct

9. ERROR
A. Misadventure B. Misgiving
C. Ambiguity D. Blunder
E. Flaw

10. SHALLOW
A. Artificial B. Superficial
C. Foolish D. Worthless
E. Deep

11. MASSACRE
A. Murder B. Stab
C. Assassinate D. Slaughter
E. Shoot

12. COMBAT
A. Conflict B. Quarrel
C. Feud D. Fight
E. Jostle

13. VORACIOUS
A. Wild B. Hungry
C. Angry D. Quick
E. Beautiful

14. IMPROMPTU
A. Offhand B. Unimportant
C. Unreal D. Effective
E. Punctual

15. RABBLE
A. Mob B. Noise
C. Roar D. Rubbish
E. Erase

16. TEPID
A. Hot B. Warm
C. Cold D. Boiling
E. Sticky

17. MAYHEM
A. Jubilation B. Havoc
C. Excitement D. Defeat
E. Movement

18. TIMID
A. Fast B. Slow
C. Medium D. Shy
E. Rapid

19. CANTANKEROUS
A. Quarrelsome B. Rash
C. Disrepectful D. Noisy
E. Obese

20. PRECARIOUS
A. Cautious B. Critical
C. Perilous D. Brittle
E. Sharp

21. TACITURNITY
A. Dumbness B. Changeableness
C. Hesitation D. Reserveness
E. Preserve

22. INEBRIATED
A. Dreamy B. Stupefied
C. Unsteady D. Drunken
E. Broken

23. HARBINGER
A. Massenger B. Steward
C. Forerunner D. Pilot
E. Performer

24. INTIMIDATE
A. To hint B. Frighten
C. Bluff D. Harass
E. Inform

25. IRONIC
A. Inflexible
B. Bitter
C. Good-natured
D. Disguisedly sarcastic
E. Hard

26. STRINGENT
A. Tense B. Stringy
C. Strict D. Causing to shrink
E. Liberal

27. ECSTATIC
A. Animated B. Bewildered
C. Enraptured D. Illful
E. Gloomy

28. COMMENSURATE
A. Measurable B. Proportionate
C. Beginning D. Appropriate
E. Finish

29. DESTITUTION
A. Humility B. Moderation
C. Poverty D. Beggary
E. Orphanage

30. ASCEND
A. Leap B. Grow
C. Deviate D. Mount
E. Invite

31. UNCOUTH
A. Ungraceful B. Rough
C. Slovenly D. Dirty
E. Gracious

32. LYNCH
A. Hang B. Madden
C. Kill D. Shoot
E. Start

33. LAUD
A. Lord B. Eulogy
C. Praise D. Extolled
E. Clap

34. CORRESPONDENCE
A. Agreements B. Contracts
C. Documents D. Letters
E. News

35. VENUE
A. Place B. Agenda
C. Time D. Duration
E. Ceremony

36. STERILE
A. Barren B. Arid
C. Childless D. Dry
E. Fertile

37. SYNOPSIS
A. Index B. Mixture
C. Summary D. Puzzle
E. End

38. GERMANE
A. Responsible B. Logical
C. Possible D. Relevant
E. Foreigner

39. PONDER
A. Think B. Evaluate
C. Anticipate D. Increase
E. Sprinkle

40. CANNY
A. Obstinate B. Handsome
C. Clever D. Stout
E. Container

41. ABUNDANT
A. Ripe B. Cheap
C. Plenty D. Absent
E. Closed

42. CONSEQUENCES
A. Results B. Conclusions
C. Difficulties D. Applications
E. Series

43. SHIVER
A. Shake B. Rock
C. Tremble D. Move
E. Cry

44. DILIGENT
A. Progressive B. Brilliant
C. Inventive D. Hard-working
E. Masculine

45. DISTANT
A. Far B. Removed
C. Reserved D. Separate
E. Unreachable

46. FORAY
A. Excursion B. Contest
C. Ranger D. Intuition
E. Light

47. FRUGALITY
A. Foolishness B. Extremity
C. Enthusiasm D. Economy
E. Weakness

48. GARNISH
A. Paint B. Garner
C. Adorn D. Abuse
E. Attract

49. VIGOUR
A. Strength B. Boldness
C. Warmth D. Enthusiasm
E. Vitality

50. CANDID
A. Apparent B. Explicit
C. Frank D. Bright
E. Sweet

51. BRIEF
A. Limited B. Small
C. Little D. Short
E. Compress

52. GARRULITY
A. Credulity B. Senility
C. Loquaciousness D. Speciousness
E. Misery

53. FURORE
A. Excitement B. Worry
C. Flux D. Anteroom
E. Noise

54. NEUTRAL
A. Unbiased B. Non-aligned
C. Undecided D. Indifferent
E. Unmoved

55. LAMENT
A. Regret B. Comment
C. Condone D. Console
E. Sadden

56. MASTERLY
A. Crafty B. Skilful
C. Meaningful D. Cruel
E. Rightfully

57. MOROSE
A. Annoyed B. Gloomy
C. Moody D. Displeased
E. Happy

58. BARE
A. Uncovered B. Tolerate
C. Clear D. Neat
E. Least

59. FEEBLE
A. Weak B. Vain
C. Arrogant D. Sick
E. Sleek

60. PRESTIGE
A. Influence B. Quality
C. Name D. Wealth
E. Strength

61. WARRIOR
A. Soldier B. Sailor
C. Pirate D. Spy
E. Juggler

62. ENTIRE
A. Part B. Quarter
C. Whole D. Half
E. Tiring

63. RESCUE
A. Command B. Help
C. Defence D. Safety
E. Problem

64. INFREQUENT
A. Never B. Usual
C. Rare D. Sometimes
E. Often

65. WRETCHED
A. Poor B. Foolish
C. Insane D. Strained
E. Broken

66. DIVERSION
A. Amusement B. Distortion
C. Deviation D. Bylane
E. Subway

67. AWAKENED
A. Enlightened B. Realised
C. Shook D. Waken
E. Walking

68. HESITATED
A. Stopped B. Paused
C. Slowed D. Postponed
E. Obstructed

69. PIOUS
A. Pure B. Pretentious
C. Clean D. Devout
E. Thirsty

70. TORTURE
A. Torment B. Chastisement
C. Harassment D. Terror
E. Beat

71. ATTEMPT
A. Serve B. Explore
C. Try D. Explain
E. Chance

72. RESTRAINT
A. Hindrance B. Repression
C. Obstacle D. Restriction
E. Tolerance

73. CHASTE
A. Honest B. Dignified
C. Virtuous D. Noble
E. Truthful

74. INSOMNIA
A. Lethargy B. Sleeplessness
C. Drunkenness D. Unconsciousness
E. Blindness

75. TRANSIENT
A. Transparent B. Fleeting
C. Feeble D. Fanciful
E. Flowing

76. MANDACIOUS
A. Full of confidence B. False
C. Encouraging D. Provocative
E. Thinkable

77. VORACIOUS
A. Truthful B. Gluttonous
C. Funny D. Venturous
E. Fearful

78. CONNOISSEUR
A. Ignorant B. Lover of art
C. Interpreter D. Delinquent
E. Officer

79. REPERCUSSION
A. Clever reply B. Recollection
C. Remuneration D. Reaction
E. Discussion

80. REPEAL
A. Sanction B. Perpetuate
C. Pass D. Cancel
E. Appeal

81. INFAMY
A. Dishonour B. Glory
C. Integrity D. Reputation
E. Beauty

82. FAKE
A. Original B. Imitation
C. Trustworthy D. Loyal
E. Lie

83. DEBACLE
A. Collapse B. Decline
C. Defeat D. Disgrace
E. Mistake

84. ADMONISH
A. Punish B. Curse
C. Dismiss D. Reprimand
E. Admit

85. EMBEZZLE
A. Misappropriate B. Balance
C. Remunerate D. Clear
E. Mix

86. CORPULENT
A. Lean B. Gaunt
C. Emaciated D. Obese
E. Corrupt

87. AUGUST
A. Common B. Ridiculous
C. Dignified D. Petty
E. Month

88. STRINGENT
A. Dry B. Strained
C. Rigorous D. Shrill
E. Thready

89. INSOLVENT
A. Poor B. Bankrupt
C. Penniless D. Broke
E. Unsoluble

90. EXTRICATE
A. Pull B. Free
C. Tie D. Complicate
E. Expel

91. INEXPLICABLE
A. Confusing
B. Unaccountable
C. Chaotic
D. Unconnected
E. Undesired

92. GRATIFY
A. Appreciate B. Frank
C. Indulge D. Pacify
E. Regard

93. ALERT
A. Energetic B. Observant
C. Intelligent D. Watchful
E. Smart

94. UNTIE
A. Unfold B. Unchain
C. Undo D. Unhinge
E. Free

95. OBJECT
A. Challenge B. Disapprove
C. Deny D. Disobey
E. Refuse

96. BROWSE
A. Heal B. Deceive
C. Examine D. Strike
E. Vision

97. SALACITY
A. Bliss B. Depression
C. Indecency D. Recession
E. Urban

98. ZANY
A. Clown B. Pet
C. Thief D. Magician
E. Virtuous

99. WARY
A. Sad B. Vigilant
C. Distorted D. Tired
E. Different

100. RECKLESS
A. Courageous B. Rash
C. Bold D. Daring
E. Disorganised

TYPE-II

Directions: *In each of the sentences given below a word is printed in* **bold**. *Below it five choices are given. Pick up the one which is most nearly the SAME in meaning as the word printed in* **bold** *and can replace it without altering the meaning of the sentence.*

101. When youngesters do not have good role-models to **emulate** they start searching for them amongst Sportsmen of Filmstars.
A. imitate B. modify
C. molify D. inhabit
E. target

102. The **aberration** in the India Economy can be attributed to short-sightedness of its political masters.
A. procrastination B. privilege
C. deviation D. steadfastness
E. corruption

103. The claims of students look hollow when they **attribute** their poor performance to difficulty of examination.
A. infer B. impute
C. inhere D. inundate
E. claim

104. As soon as he finished his speech, there was **spontaneous** applause from the audience.
A. well-timed B. willing
C. instinctive D. instantaneous
E. momentary

105. The soldier proved his **mettle** in the battlefield.
A. persistence
B. stamina and strength
C. courage and endurance
D. heroism
E. constituent

106. He listened of my request with **indifference**.
A. disinterest B. concern
C. displeasure D. caution
E. seperation

107. The accident occurred due to his **lapse**.
A. trick B. interval
C. error D. ignorance
E. speed

108. Being a member of this Club, he has certain **rights**.
A. status B. truth
C. virtues D. privileges
E. favours

109. He is **averse** to the idea of holding elections now.
A. convinced B. angry
C. agreeable D. opposed
E. known

110. Silence is **mandatory** for meditation to be effective.
A. compulsory B. necessary
C. required D. needed
E. optional

111. The underworld still makes solid profit out of **illicit** liquor.
A. indigenous B. illegitimate
C. illegal D. country
E. duplicate

112. When I look back over the wartime years I cannot help feeling that time is an inadequate and even **capricious** measure of their duration at one moment they seem so long, at another so short.
A. misleading B. whimsical
C. erratic D. unpredictable
E. effective

113. The tablet **alleviated** the pain, and the patient was soon feeling much better.
A. mitigated B. moderated
C. removed D. lightened
E. eliminated

114. The leader nodded his **approbation.**
A. understanding B. approval
C. admiration D. appreciation
E. enquiry

115. We should always try to maintain and promote communal **amity**.
A. bondage B. contention
C. friendship D. understanding
E. peace

116. Many species of animals have become **extinct** during the last hundred years.
A. aggressive B. non-existent

C. scattered D. feeble
E. rare

117. True religion does not require one to **proselytise** through guile or force.
A. translate B. hypnotise
C. attack D. convert
E. fight

118. That the plan is both inhuman and **preposterous** needs no further proof.
A. heartless B. impractical
C. absurd D. abnormal
E. destructive

119. She **baffled** all our attempts to find her.
A. defeated B. thwarted
C. foiled D. circumvented
E. knew

120. Instead of putting up a united front against of common enemy, the medieval states frittered away their energy in **internecine** warfare.
A. mutually destructive
B. baneful
C. pernicious
D. detrimental
E. communal

121. The bullet wound proved to be **fatal** and the soldier died immediately.
A. grievous B. dangerous
C. serious D. deadly
E. accurate

122. Whatever opinion he gives is **sane**.
A. rational B. obscure
C. wild D. arrogant
E. clear

123. He **corroborated** the statement of his brother.
A. confirmed B. disproved
C. condemned D. seconded
E. refuted

124. Whatever the **verdict** of history may be, Chaplin will occupy a unique place in its pages.
A. judgement B. voice
C. outcome D. prediction
E. chapter

125. The attitude of the Western countries towards the Third World countries is rather **callous** to say the least.
A. passive B. unkind
C. cursed D. unfeeling
E. unfair

126. The story is too fantastic to be **credible**.
A. believable B. false
C. readable D. praiseworthy
E. payable

127. Catching snakes can be **hazardous** for people untrained in the art.
A. tricky B. harmful
C. difficult D. dangerous
E. deadly

128. After the **dismal** performance of the team in the series concluded yesterday, the captain offered his resignation to the president of the club.
A. poor B. sorrowful
C. minimum D. short
E. failing

129. The small boy was able to give a **graphic** description of the thief.
A. picture B. drawing
C. vivid D. broad
E. designer

130. The prisoner has been **languishing** in the jail for the last many years.
A. convicted B. suffering
C. attempting D. avoiding
E. learning

131. Some of the Asian countries have been **enmeshed** in an inescapable debt trap.
A. entagled B. hit
C. struck D. ensured
E. caged

132. In spite of their efforts, the team of scientists could not make much **headway** to solve the problem.
A. progress B. thinking
C. efforts D. start
E. attempt

133. On scrutiny the police officer found out that the documents provided by the landlord were totally **fabricated**.
A. forged B. historical
C. prepared D. genuine
E. designed

134. The soldier displayed **exceptional** courage and saved the Major from the enemy's hand.
A. avoidable B. unusual
C. strange D. abnormal
E. optimal

135. He found a **lucrative** assignment.
A. good B. profitable
C. excellent D. significant
E. creative

136. The novel was so interesting that I was **oblivious** of my surroundings.
A. precarious B. unmindful
C. aware D. watchful
E. cut

137. The great dancer impressed the appreciative crowd by his **nimble** movements.
A. unrhythmic B. lively
C. quickening D. clear
E. agile

138. The president of the party **deprecated** the move of the Government to introduce electoral reforms in a haste.
A. welcomed B. denied
C. protested D. humiliated
E. announced

139. It took him a long time to **come round** after the operation.
A. recover B. walk
C. move D. eat
E. rotate

140. Few teachers have been spared the problem of an **obstreperous** pupil in the class.
A. sullen B. unruly
C. lazy D. awkward
E. stupid

141. His visit to foreign countries brought about a **sea-change** in his outlook and his attitude to people.
A. complete change
B. partial change
C. favourable change
D. unfavourable change
E. visual

142. Swift is known in the world of letters for his **misogynism**.
A. hate for mankind
B. hate for womankind
C. love for the reasonable
D. love for womankind
E. love for unisex

143. He was warned at the **outset** of his career.
A. end B. beginning
C. middle D. entrance
E. peak

144. The time I spent in the library was a most **rewarding** one.
A. profitable B. paying
C. serviceable D. precious
E. prizing

145. That young is quite **sanguine** about the result of his competitive examination.
A. depressed B. pessimistic
C. anxious D. optimistic
E. sure

146. The courage shown by the soldiers at this moment of crisis is **exemplary**.
A. suitable B. clear
C. elementary D. admirable
E. exceptional

147. The notice said that the meeting would begin **precisely** at 9.30 a.m.
A. approximately B. exactly
C. accurately D. concisely
E. aptly

148. The inspector was a **vigilant** young man.
A. intelligent B. ambitious
C. watchful D. smart
E. agile

149. A **rupture** in the relationship of the two brothers is quite apparent.
A. break B. damage
C. breach D. gap
E. blast

150. "I have learnt a great deal working in factories, and for a time I've been a weaver. Here are my **testimonials,** Mr. Davis."
A. witnesses B. testaments
C. tokens D. credentials
E. reports

ANSWERS

1	**2**	**3**	**4**	**5**	**6**	**7**	**8**	**9**	**10**
C	B	D	C	B	C	B	C	D	B
11	**12**	**13**	**14**	**15**	**16**	**17**	**18**	**19**	**20**
D	D	B	A	A	B	B	D	A	B
21	**22**	**23**	**24**	**25**	**26**	**27**	**28**	**29**	**30**
D	D	C	B	D	C	C	B	C	D
31	**32**	**33**	**34**	**35**	**36**	**37**	**38**	**39**	**40**
A	C	C	D	A	A	C	D	A	C
41	**42**	**43**	**44**	**45**	**46**	**47**	**48**	**49**	**50**
C	A	C	D	A	A	D	C	A	C
51	**52**	**53**	**54**	**55**	**56**	**57**	**58**	**59**	**60**
D	C	A	A	A	B	B	A	A	C
61	**62**	**63**	**64**	**65**	**66**	**67**	**68**	**69**	**70**
A	C	B	D	A	C	D	B	A	A
71	**72**	**73**	**74**	**75**	**76**	**77**	**78**	**79**	**80**
C	D	C	B	B	B	B	B	D	D
81	**82**	**83**	**84**	**85**	**86**	**87**	**88**	**89**	**90**
A	B	A	D	A	D	C	C	B	B
91	**92**	**93**	**94**	**95**	**96**	**97**	**98**	**99**	**100**
B	D	D	C	B	C	C	A	B	B
101	**102**	**103**	**104**	**105**	**106**	**107**	**108**	**109**	**110**
A	C	B	C	C	A	C	D	D	A
111	**112**	**113**	**114**	**115**	**116**	**117**	**118**	**119**	**120**
C	B	A	B	C	B	D	C	C	A
121	**122**	**123**	**124**	**125**	**126**	**127**	**128**	**129**	**130**
D	A	A	A	D	A	D	A	C	B
131	**132**	**133**	**134**	**135**	**136**	**137**	**138**	**139**	**140**
A	A	A	B	B	B	C	C	A	B
141	**142**	**143**	**144**	**145**	**146**	**147**	**148**	**149**	**150**
A	B	B	A	D	D	B	C	A	D

CHAPTER 4

Antonyms

In English, while learning the meanings of words, learning their opposite words is also equally important for a good learner. One must learn as many as one can, to score well.

TYPE-I

Directions: *In the following questions choose the word which is the exact OPPOSITE of the given words.*

1. DEAR
A. Priceless B. Free
C. Worthless D. Cheap
E. Expensive

2. FLAGITIOUS
A. Innocent B. Vapid
C. Ignorant D. Frivolous
E. Stupid

3. LIABILITY
A. Property B. Assets
C. Debt D. Treasure
E. Responsibilty

4. VIRTUOUS
A. Wicked B. Corrupt
C. Vicious D. Scandalous
E. Dishonest

5. ENCOURAGE
A. Dampen B. Disapprove
C. Discourage D. Warn
E. Land

6. MORTAL
A. Divine B. Immortal
C. Spiritual D. Eternal
E. Strong

7. LEND
A. Borrow B. Cheat
C. Pawn D. Hire
E. Ask

8. COMIC
A. Emotional B. Tragic
C. Fearful D. Painful
E. Adult

9. ADDITION
A. Division B. Enumeration
C. Subtraction D. Multiplication
E. Minus

10. MINOR
A. Big B. Major
C. Tall D. Heavy
E. Adult

11. REPEL
A. Attend B. Concentrate
C. Continue D. Attract
E. Expel

12. ARTIFICIAL
A. Red B. Natural
C. Truthful D. Solid
E. Superficial

13. CAPACIOUS
A. Limited B. Caring
C. Foolish D. Changeable
E. Spacious

14. PROVOCATION
A. Vocation B. Pacification
C. Peace D. Destruction
E. Convocation

15. METICULOUS
A. Mutual B. Shaggy
C. Meretricious D. Slovenly
E. Ridiculous

16. ABLE
A. Disable B. Inable
C. Unable D. Misable
E. Probable

17. COMFORT
A. Uncomfort B. Miscomfort
C. Discomfort D. Uneasy
E. Luxury

18. GAIN
A. Loose B. Fall
C. Lost D. Lose
E. Again

19. SYNTHETIC
A. Affable B. Natural
C. Plastic D. Cosmetic
E. Pathetic

20. ACQUITTED
A. Freed B. Burdened
C. Convicted D. Entrusted
E. Predicted

21. STRINGENT
A. General B. Vehement
C. Lenient D. Magnanimous
E. Astringent

22. FLIMSY
A. Frail B. Filthy
C. Firm D. Flippant
E. Fat

23. BUSY
A. Occupied B. Engrossed
C. Relaxed D. Engaged
E. Free

24. ADAPTABLE
A. Adoptable B. Flexible
C. Yielding D. Rigid
E. Solid

25. LOVE
A. Villainy B. Hatred
C. Compulsion D. Force
E. Fight

26. BALANCE
A. Disbalance B. Misbalance
C. Debalance D. Imbalance
E. Unbalance

27. RELINQUISH
A. Abdicate B. Renounce
C. Possess D. Deny
E. Occupy

28. MOUNTAIN
A. Plain B. Plateau
C. Precipice D. Valley
E. Ocean

29. FICKLE
A. Courageous B. Sincere
C. Steadfast D. Humble
E. Strong

30. PERENNIAL
A. Frequent B. Regular
C. Lasting D. Rare
E. Often

31. RARELY
A. Hardly B. Definitely
C. Frequently D. Periodically
E. Barely

32. STARTLED
A. Amused B. Relaxed
C. Endless D. Astonished
E. Finished

33. ADHERENT
A. Detractor B. Enemy
C. Alien D. Rival
E. Follower

34. QUIESCENT
A. Indifferent B. Troublesome
C. Weak D. Unconcerned
E. Silent

35. CONDENSE
A. Expand B. Distribute
C. Interpret D. Lengthen
E. Lighten

36. BENIGN
A. Malevolent B. Soft
C. Friendly D. Unwise
E. Kind

37. OBSCURE
A. Implicit B. Obnoxious
C. Explicit D. Pedantic
E. Incurable

38. HYPOCRITICAL
A. Gentle B. Sincere
C. Amiable D. Dependable
E. Critical

39. EVASIVE
A. Free B. Honest
C. Liberal D. Frank
E. Invasive

40. INDUSTRIOUS
A. Indifferent B. Indolent
C. Casual D. Passive
E. Serving

41. EXTRICATE
A. Manifest B. Palpable
C. Release D. Entangle
E. Intricate

42. LUCID
A. Glory B. Noisy
C. Obscure D. Distinct
E. Clear

43. INSIPID
A. Tasty B. Stupid
C. Discreet D. Feast
E. Flavoured

44. OBEYING
A. Ordering B. Following
C. Refusing D. Contradicting
E. Insulting

45. VICTORIOUS
A. Defeated B. Annexed
C. Destroyed D. Vanquished
E. Triumphant

46. COMMISSIONED
A. Started B. Closed
C. Finished D. Terminated
E. Salaried

47. VANITY
A. Pride B. Humility
C. Conceit D. Ostentious
E. Grace

48. ZENITH
A. Acme B. Top
C. Nadir D. Pinnacle
E. Core

49. TANGIBLE
A. Ethereal B. Concrete
C. Actual D. Solid
E. Delicious

50. REPRESS
A. Inhibit B. Liberate
C. Curb D. Quell
E. Suppress

51. EPILOGUE
A. Dialogue B. Prelude
C. Post script D. Epigram
E. Monologue

52. FRAUDULENT
A. Candid B. Direct
C. Forthright D. Genuine
E. Real

53. LOQUACIOUS
A. Reticent B. Talkative
C. Garrulous D. Verbose
E. Verbatim

54. NIGGARDLY
A. Frugal B. Thrifty
C. Stingy D. Generous
E. Mean

55. PERTINENT
A. Irrational B. Irregular
C. Insistent D. Irrelevant
E. Inconsistent

56. FAINT-HEARTED
A. Warm-hearted B. Full-blooded
C. Hot-blooded D. Stout-hearted
E. Kind-hearted

57. VIOLENT
A. Humble B. Harmless
C. Gentle D. Tame
E. Pet

58. STATIONARY
A. Active B. Mobile
C. Rapid D. Busy
E. Unfixed

59. HONORARY
A. Dishonourable B. Reputed
C. Paid D. Official
E. Obligatory

60. COMMON
A. Rare B. Small
C. Petty D. Poor
E. General

61. FRUGAL
A. Copious B. Extravagant
C. Generous D. Ostentatious
E. Thrifty

62. MALICIOUS
A. Kind B. Boastful
C. Generous D. Indifferent
E. Harmful

63. FAMILIAR
A. Unpleasant B. Dangerous
C. Friendly D. Strange
E. Known

64. PRELIMINARY
A. Final B. First
C. Secondary D. Initial
E. Main

65. DOUBTFUL
A. Famous B. Certain
C. Fixed D. Important
E. Vague

66. REMISS
A. Forgetful B. Watchful
C. Dutiful D. Harmful
E. Break

67. INDISCREET
A. Reliable B. Honest
C. Prudent D. Stupid
E. Credible

68. FRESH
A. Faulty B. Sluggish
C. Disgraceful D. Stale
E. Old

69. ANNOY
A. Praise B. Rejoice
C. Please D. Reward
E. Happy

70. TRANSPARENT
A. Semi-transparent B. Muddy
C. Opaque D. Dark
E. Clear

71. REVEALED
A. Denied B. Concealed
C. Ignored D. Overlooked
E. Appealed

72. EXTRAVAGANCE
A. Luxury B. Poverty
C. Economy D. Cheapness
E. Vengeance

73. CROWDED
A. Busy B. Congested
C. Quiet D. Deserted
E. Empty

74. SHRINK
A. Contract B. Spoil
C. Expand D. Stretch
E. Droop

75. ENMITY
A. Important B. Unnecessary
C. Friendship D. Likeness
E. Infamy

76. EXODUS
A. Influx B. Home-coming
C. Return D. Restoration
E. Entry

77. CULPABLE
A. Defendable B. Blameless
C. Careless D. Irresponsible
E. Bailable

78. SUBSERVIENT
A. Aggressive B. Straightforward
C. Dignified D. Supercilious
E. Submissive

79. AWARE
A. Uncertain B. Ignorant
C. Sure D. Doubtful
E. Beware

80. GRACEFUL
A. Rough B. Expert
C. Miserable D. Awkward
E. Beautiful

81. AUTONOMY
A. Slavery
B. Subordination
C. Dependence
D. Submissiveness
E. Democracy

82. NADIR
A. Modernity
B. Zenith
C. Liberty
D. Progress
E. Horizon

83. CONCEDE
A. Object
B. Refuse
C. Grant
D. Accede
E. Exceed

84. SUPPRESS
A. Encourage
B. Grow
C. Praise
D. Permit
E. Swell

85. FAMOUS
A. Disgraced
B. Notorious
C. Evil
D. Popular
E. Ugly

86. EXPAND
A. Contract
B. Condense
C. Congest
D. Conclude
E. Compact

87. ARROGANT
A. Polite
B. Cowardly
C. Meek
D. Gentlemanly
E. Vibrant

88. ENORMOUS
A. Soft
B. Average
C. Tiny
D. Weak
E. Gigantic

89. URBANE
A. Illiterate
B. Backward
C. Discourteous
D. Orthodox
E. Villager

90. HOSTILITY
A. Courtesy
B. Hospitality
C. Relationship
D. Friendliness
E. Casualty

91. BELITTLE
A. Praise
B. Flatter
C. Exaggerate
D. Adore
E. Decry

92. HAPLESS
A. Cheerful
B. Consistent
C. Fortunate
D. Shapely
E. Hopeful

93. HAPHAZARD
A. Fortuitous
B. Indifferent
C. Deliberate
D. Accidental
E. Random

94. GREGARIOUS
A. Antisocial
B. Glorious
C. Horrendous
D. Similar
E. Affable

95. VALUABLE
A. Invaluable
B. Worthless
C. Inferior
D. Lowly
E. Worthy

96. ABSOLUTE
A. Deficient
B. Faulty
C. Limited
D. Scarce
E. Whole

97. CONFESS
A. Deny
B. Refuse
C. Contest
D. Contend
E. Profess

98. GULLIBLE
A. Incredulous
B. Fickle
C. Easy
D. Stylish
E. Credulous

99. HIRSUTE
A. Scaly
B. Bald
C. Erudite
D. Quiet
E. Hairy

100. HINDRANCE
A. Aid
B. Persuasion
C. Cooperation
D. Agreement
E. Encumbrance

TYPE-II

Directions: *Each sentence below consists of a word or a phrase which is* ***bold****. It is followed by five words or phrases. Select the word or phrase which is closest to the OPPOSITE in meaning of the* ***bold*** *word or phrase.*

101. The atmosphere in that desolate place looked **ominous**.
A. pleasant B. encouraging
C. auspicious D. favourable
E. propitious

102. He spoke against corruption with **zeal**.
A. indifference B. calmness
C. despair D. passiveness
E. stoicism

103. The story told by the teacher **amused** children in the class.
A. frightened B. jolted
C. astonished D. saddened
E. anguished

104. In a literary work **obscurity** can be a virtue.
A. clarity B. precision
C. definiteness D. specificity
E. mystery

105. The managing director remarked that the secretary was an **asset** to the company.
A. loss B. liability
C. drag D. handicap
E. expense

106. He is extremely **intelligent** but proud.
A. dull B. weak
C. ignorant D. simple
E. apt

107. A **friendly** dog met us at the farmgate.
A. helpful B. understanding
C. quiet D. hostile
E. convivial

108. In ancient India, scholars had no interest in political power or **material** growth.
A. internal B. spiritual
C. psychic D. celestial
E. external

109. His short but pointed speech was **applauded** by all sections of the audience.
A. disapproved B. misunderstood
C. praised D. welcomed
E. lauded

110. Like poverty, **affluence** can sometimes create its own problems.
A. indigence B. opulence
C. sorrow D. exuberance
E. abundance

111. Adversity teaches man to be humble and self-reliant.
A. sincerity B. animosity
C. curiosity D. prosperity
E. success

112. History **abounds** in instances of courage.
A. shines B. lacks
C. suffices D. fails
E. bounds

113. He **abandoned** his family.
A. supported B. encouraged
C. pleased D. saved
E. renounced

114. The young leader was **reluctant** to shoulder the responsibilities of the ministerial office.
A. wanting B. willing
C. anxious D. eager
E. grudging

115. Unsettled conditions in the land led to the **exodus** of hundreds of its citizens.
A. invasion B. entry
C. immigration D. expulsion
E. massacre

116. In the interest of one's own reputation one should avoid **ostentation** while entertaining friends.
A. miserliness B. simplicity
C. purity D. innocence
E. flamboyance

117. Everything about him, especially his talkative nature, proclaims his **effeminacy**.
A. aggressiveness B. attractiveness
C. meaniness D. boorishness
E. verbosity

118. The habit of **squandering** money should not be encouraged.
A. discarding B. boarding
C. collecting D. saving
E. laundering

119. There was something strange and **morbid** about the whole house.

A. healthy B. cheerful
C. insipid D. appealing
E. unpleasant

120. Many people suffer setbacks in their career because of their inherent **levity**.
A. seriousness B. solemnity
C. religiosity D. gravity
E. laxity

121. This new magazine is known for its **comprehensive** coverage of news.
A. casual B. inadequate
C. indifferent D. superficial
E. compressive

122. His critics found in his **overt** statements some hidden designs.
A. converse B. pervert
C. covert D. contrived
E. subvert

123. Given these constraint, we had no alternative but to suggest **an improvised** solution.
A. a complete B. a pre-planned
C. a permanent D. a proscribed
E. an impromptu

124. Because of the economy drive, they very unwillingly surrendered some **superfluous** posts.
A. important B. relevant
C. significant D. essential
E. redundant

125. I **abhor** the ideas he sometimes expresses.
A. admire B. respect
C. applaud D. appreciate
E. abominate

126. You can hardly find any trace of **humility** in the man.
A. pride B. insolence
C. arrogance D. conceit
E. humbleness

127. The result of the tournament gave them a sense of **elation**.
A. despondency B. misery
C. disappointment D. despair
E. exultant

128. It was done in a **haphazard** manner.
A. planned B. excellent
C. extraordinary D. designed
E. random

129. The officer asked the clerk to **expedite** the matter.
A. postpone B. defer
C. adjourn D. delay
E. explain

130. The atmosphere in the institute he had newly joined was **congenial** to research.
A. disagreeable for
B. inconvenient for
C. unpleasant for
D. unsuitable for
E. compliant

131. He is the most **prudent** person I have ever come across.
A. shortsighted B. reckless
C. inconsiderate D. injudicious
E. sagacious

132. The members thought that the task was **feasible**.
A. impractical B. impossible
C. difficult D. impracticable
E. viable

133. I was surprised at his **stiff** attitude.
A. courteous B. flexible
C. soft D. lively
E. strange

134. The General Manager is quite **tactful** and handles the workers union very effectively.
A. disciplined B. naive
C. strict D. loose
E. discreet

135. His **vindictive** nature often came up for comment among his friends.
A. forgetful B. forgiving
C. obedient D. timid
E. rancorous

136. I thought about her a lot during the **following** months.
A. succeeding B. proceeding
C. preceding D. receding
E. coming

137. He was asked to **accelerate** the pace of work.
A. supervise B. slacken
C. control D. check
E. speed up

138. What he tells me **confirms** my ideas.
A. strengthens B. opposes
C. contradicts D. verifies
E. acquiesces

139. The error in the newspaper article is **accidental**.
A. intentional B. conventional
C. usual D. permissible
E. incidental

140. According to a great philosopher **magnanimity** in a man implies many other qualities.
A. enmity B. meanness
C. jealousy D. poverty
E. munificence

141. The minister gave a public speech on the controversial subject to **precipitate** the matter.
A. aggravate B. create
C. defer D. push
E. yield

142. The commission took two years to go through the **massive** collection of files and documents before preparing its report.
A. meagre B. heavy
C. light D. short
E. gaunt

143. Satish's point of view was correct but his behaviour with his father was quite **impertinent**.
A. healthy B. respectful
C. inadequate D. smooth
E. germane

144. The chairman **initiated** the proceedings with a brief speech.
A. confused B. closed
C. started D. complicated
E. committed

145. The club meets on the last Thursday of every month in a **dilapidated** palace.
A. neglected B. regenerated
C. renovated D. furnished
E. ruined

146. The inhabitants of the island were **barbarians**.
A. civilised B. cruel
C. uncivilised D. bad
E. gigantic

147. They had an **insipid** conversation.
A. lively B. argumentative
C. loud D. curious
E. vapid

148. The chairman **rebuked** the accounts officer for not supervising the work of his subordinates.
A. received B. awarded
C. invited D. praised
E. upbraided

149. The actor is well known both for his **humility** and courage.
A. pride B. determination
C. honesty D. gentleness
E. humanity

150. **Feasibility** of the project is under study.
A. unsuitability
B. cheapness
C. impropriety
D. impracticability
E. viability

ANSWERS

1	**2**	**3**	**4**	**5**	**6**	**7**	**8**	**9**	**10**
D	A	B	C	C	B	A	B	C	B
11	**12**	**13**	**14**	**15**	**16**	**17**	**18**	**19**	**20**
D	B	A	B	D	C	C	D	B	C
21	**22**	**23**	**24**	**25**	**26**	**27**	**28**	**29**	**30**
C	C	C	D	B	D	C	D	C	D

31	32	33	34	35	36	37	38	39	40
D	B	B	A	C	A	C	B	B	B
41	**42**	**43**	**44**	**45**	**46**	**47**	**48**	**49**	**50**
D	C	A	A	A	D	B	C	A	B
51	**52**	**53**	**54**	**55**	**56**	**57**	**58**	**59**	**60**
B	D	A	D	D	D	C	B	C	A
61	**62**	**63**	**64**	**65**	**66**	**67**	**68**	**69**	**70**
B	C	D	A	B	C	C	D	C	C
71	**72**	**73**	**74**	**75**	**76**	**77**	**78**	**79**	**80**
B	C	D	D	C	A	A	C	B	D
81	**82**	**83**	**84**	**85**	**86**	**87**	**88**	**89**	**90**
C	B	B	B	B	B	A	C	C	D
91	**92**	**93**	**94**	**95**	**96**	**97**	**98**	**99**	**100**
C	C	C	A	B	C	A	A	B	A
101	**102**	**103**	**104**	**105**	**106**	**107**	**108**	**109**	**110**
C	A	D	A	B	A	D	B	A	A
111	**112**	**113**	**114**	**115**	**116**	**117**	**118**	**119**	**120**
D	B	A	B	C	A	C	D	B	D
121	**122**	**123**	**124**	**125**	**126**	**127**	**128**	**129**	**130**
D	C	B	B	A	C	D	A	D	A
131	**132**	**133**	**134**	**135**	**136**	**137**	**138**	**139**	**140**
B	A	B	B	B	C	B	C	A	B
141	**142**	**143**	**144**	**145**	**146**	**147**	**148**	**149**	**150**
C	A	B	B	C	A	A	D	A	D

Spotting Errors

The most common errors in English are of grammar and usage of words and phrases. By regular practice, the errors can be minimised. Try and practise it in this chapter to master it.

Directions: *In each question below, a sentence is broken into four parts which are marked as (A), (B), (C) and (D). One of them may be grammatically or structurally wrong in the context of the sentence. The letter of that word is the answer. If there is no wrong word or group of words, your answer will be (E), i.e., 'No error'. (Ignore the errors of punctuation, if any).*

1. (A) There is just not enough/(B) timing in my job to sit around/(C) talking about how we feel/(D) about each other./(E) No error.
2. (A) Reasonable ambition, if supported/(B) at persistent efforts,/(C) is likely to yield/(D) the desired results./(E) No error.
3. (A) Even after worked in the office/(B) for as many as fifteen years,/(C) he still does not understand/(D) the basic objectives of the work./(E) No error.
4. (A) Why some people don't get/(B) what they deserve/(C) and why others get what they don't deserve/(D) is a matter decided by luck./(E) No error.
5. (A) the five-member committee were/(B) of the view that the present service conditions/(C) of the employees of this company/(D) are quite good./(E) No error.
6. (A) If you would have/(B) gone to his house/(C) before 10 a.m., you would have/(D) got his autograph./(E) No error.
7. (A) His speech was/(B) judged by many/(C) as one of the most important speech/(D) given in the function./(E) No error.
8. (A) I am contacting you/(B) sometime in next week/(C) to explain to you/(D) my problem in detail./(E) No error.
9. (A) Whatever he was/(B) today is only because/(C) of his mother who/(D) was a renowned scientist./(E) No error.
10. (A) The Head of the Department along with his colleagues/(B) are coming to attend/(C) the conference which is/(D) scheduled this afternoon./(E) No error.
11. (A) One of the most effective/(B) solutions is that/(C) she should work on Sunday/(D) and complete the assignment./(E) No error.
12. (A) He had to/(B) seek legal help in/(C) order for settling/(D) the dispute./(E) No error.
13. (A) Since I had been gone/(B) through the book/(C) long back, I could/(D) not remember the contents./(E) No error.
14. (A) We have to take/(B)him to the hospital yesterday/(C) because he was/(D) suffering from fever./(E) No error.
15. (A) The interviewer asked the actress/(B) how could she/(C) manage to attain fame/(D) in a short period./(E) No error.
16. (A) The Head of the Department/(B) advised all the staff/(C) to not to/(D) indulge in gossip./(E) No error.
17. (A) I shall be able/(B) to complete the work in/(C) stipulated time provide/(D) you do not disturb me./(E) No error.

18. (A) Having learn my lessons/(B) I was very careful/(C) in dealing with him/(D) in front of his room-mate./(E) No error.

19. (A) In spite of his/(B) being a Quiz Master/(C) show was/(D) a big flop./(E) No error.

20. (A) No sooner the/(B) clock strike six than/(C) all the employees/(D) rushed out of office./(E) No error.

21. (A) Naren could not/(B) decide as to which/(C) course he should do/(D) after obtaining his Degree./(E) No error.

22. (A) One of the objective/(B) of the meeting which/(C) was held today was to/(D) elect new office-bearers./(E) No error.

23. (A) Ketaki would have/(B) surely got the job/(C) if she would have/(D) attended the interview./(E) No error.

24. (A) When the national/(B) anthem was being/(C) sung, everyone were/(D) standing in silence./(E) No error.

25. (A) Rosy herself wash/(B) all the clothes and/(C) never gives them/(D) to the laundry./(E) No error.

26. (A) But for your/(B) kind help this/(C) task could not/(D) have been completed./(E) No error.

27. (A) Since it was a memory test/(B) the students were instructed/(C) to learn the/(D) passage with heart./(E) No error.

28. (A) So longer as/(B) you are honest/(C) and forthright I will/(D) support you in this task./(E) No error.

29. (A) The customer scarcely had/(B) enough money to pay/(C) to the cashier/(D) at the cash counter./(E) No error.

30. (A) Neither the earthquake/(B) nor the subsequent fire/(C) was able to dampen/(D) the spirit of the residents./(E) No error.

31. (A) Not one of the children/(B) has ever sang/(C) on any occasion/(D) in public before./(E) No error.

32. (A) If the by-stander had not been/(B) familiar with first-aid techniques,/(C) the driver which had met/(D) with the accident would have died./(E) No error.

33. (A) Even after requesting/(B) him, he did not/(C) tell us that how/(D) he solved the problem/(E) No error.

34. (A) We never thought/(B) that Mahesh is/(C) oldest than the other/(D) players in the team./(E) No error.

35. (A) No sooner did he/(B) got up from bed/(C) than he was sent/(D) to the dairy./(E) No error.

36. (A) By arresting the local criminals/(B) and encouraging good people/(C) we can end/(D) hostilities of that area./(E) No error.

37. (A) The apparently obvious solutions/(B) to most of his problems/(C) were overlook by/(D) many of his friends./(E) No error.

38. (A) In spite of the difficulties/(B) on the way,/(C) they enjoyed their/(D) trip to Gangothri./(E) No error.

39. (A) We decided not tell to/(B) the patient about/(C) the disease he was/(D) suffering from./(E) No error.

40. (A) The principals of equal justice/(B) for all is one of/(C) the cornerstones of our/(D) democratic way of life./(E) No error.

41. (A) The Trust has succeeded/(B) admirably in raising/(C) money for/(D) its future programmes./(E) No error.

42. (A) Honesty, integrity and being intelligent/(B) are the qualities which/(C) we look for when/(D) we interview applicants./(E) No error.

43. (A) In order to save petrol,/(B) motorists must have to/(C) be very cautious/(D) while driving along the highways./(E) No error.

44. (A) The committee is thankful to Shri Desai/(B) for preparing not only the main report/(C) but also for preparing/(D) the agenda notes and minutes./(E) No error.

45. (A) All of you will agree with me/(B) that no problem faced by our society/(C) is as grave and intractable/(D) as this problem is/(E) No error.

46. (A) I would have lost/(B) my luggage and other belongings/(C) if I would have left the compartment/(D) and gone out to fetch drinking water./(E) No error.

47. (A) Ramesh did not like/(B) leaving his old parents alone in the house/(C) but he had no alternative/(D) as he has to go out to work./(E) No error.

48. (A) I was being astonished/(B) when I heard that/(C) he had left the country/(D) without informing anyone of us./(E) No error.

49. (A) According to one survey/(B) only those forests which were/(C) not under village management/(D) succumbed from fires recently./(E) No error.

50. (A) We can not handle/(B) this complicated case today/(C) unless full details are not given/(D) to us by now./(E) No error.

51. (A) We will pack not only/(B) the material properly/(C) but will also deliver it/(D) to your valued customers./(E) No error.

52. (A) While Mahendra was away/(B) on a long official tour/(C) his office receive an important letter/(D) which was marked 'Urgent'./(E) No error.

53. (A) We now look forward for/(B) some great achievements/(C) which to some extent/(D) can restore the country's prestige once again./(E) No error.

54. (A) Mahatma Gandhi did not solve/(B) all the problems of the future/(C) but he did solve/(D) problems of his own age./(E) No error.

55. (A) No country can long endure/(B) if its foundations/(C) were not laid deep/(D) in the material prosperity./(E) No error.

56. (A) Though he suffered of fever,/(B) he attended office/(C) and completed all the pending/(D) work by sitting late./(E) No error.

57. (A) As always have been said,/(B) parents should not/(C) impose their desires/(D) on their wards./(E) No error.

58. (A) Being a very fast worker,/(B) he is always liking/(C) by all his colleagues./(D) and superiors too./(E) No error.

59. (A) We fail to understand/(B) why do most educated people/(C) lose their temper even/(D) without any apparent reason./(E) No error.

60. (A) You may not always/(B) get whatever you deserve/(C) but that does not belittle/(D) the importance for your work./(E) No error.

61. (A) On resuming his duty,/(B) he asked his Superiors/(C) that whether he would be/(D) permitted to leave early./(E) No error.

62. (A) We don't deny/(B) your right to know/(C) whatever happened while/(D) you were not in the office./(E) No error.

63. (A) Jayesh loved his Guru immensely/(B) and gave him fullest loyalty,/(C) yet he had his own/(D) independent way of thinking./(E) No error.

64. (A) We have done everything/(B) that could be done/(C) to avert the storm/(D) which is now coming on./(E) No error.

65. (A) Our school is making/(B) every possible effort/(C) to provide best facilities/(D) and personal attention for each child./(E) No error.

66. (A) They have been/(B) struggling with the management/(C) from the past five years/(D) but their demands are not considered./(E) No error.

67. (A) When I stood up spontaneously/(B) and questioned the speaker;/(C) someone commented that/(D) it was a boldly step./(E) No error.

68. (A) Their only demand/(B) for additional wages were/(C) considered sympathetically/(D) by the progressive management./(E) No error.

69. (A) He has been undergoing/(B) the special training course/(C) which each of the employees/(D) is required to./(E) No error.

70. (A) You must had/(B) a kind and gentle heart/(C) if you want/(D) to be a successful doctor./(E) No error.

71. (A) If you cannot/(B) sympathy with the poor,/(C) how will you be/(D) able to do social work?/(E) No error.

72. (A) He loosened his temper/(B) whenever he knows/(C) things do not take place/(D) as per his planning./(E) No error.

73. (A) They wanted money/(B) to purchase certain things/(C) for themselves and/(D) for donated to their colleagues./(E) No error.

74. (A) As the ticket was/(B) firm affixed/(C) on the envelope, he/(D) could not remove it./(E) No error.

75. (A) I asked him/(B) whom he thought/(C) would be able to/(D) get the first prize./(E) No error.

76. (A) He was too/(B) irritated to/(C) concentrate on his work/(D) for a long time./(E) No error.

77. (A) Both the brothers are/(B) so good-natured that/(C) they look at their/(D) old and aged parents very well./(E) No error.

78. (A) The observers felt that/(B) the stronger team had to face/(C) defeat because the players/(D) didn't play wholehearted./(E) No error.

79. (A) Every animal in the zoo/(B) is fed regularly/(C) and attended to/(D) very promptly./(E) No error.

80. (A) How you eat/(B) is as important/(C) as what/(D) you eat./(E) No error.

81. (A) All his relatives/(B) expect his daughter/(C) have gone on/(D) a month's vacation tour./(E) No error.

82. (A) All renew licences/(B) may be collected from/(C) the cashier's counter after/(D) paying the fees./(E) No error.

83. (A) We are happy/(B) to know that/(C) the project completed/(D) strictly as per the schedule./(E) No error.

84. (A) They would not/(B) have able to plan/(C) the details of the job,/(D) if you had no cooperated./(E) No error.

85. (A) Very few employees./(B) in our company are/(C) so dedicated as/(D) Mahesh will./(E) No error.

86. (A) Rajesh won the case as/(B) he argued very forcefully and/(C) in such the intelligent way/(D) that the judge changed his opinion./(E) No error.

87. (A) The basket of apples/(B) sent by the gardener/(C) contained a number of/(D) green mangoes also./(E) No error.

88. (A) In the absence of/(B) clear instructions/(C) one cannot be expected/(D) to be functioned effectively./(E) No error.

89. (A) They could have/(B) helped him/(C) had they approached by him./(D) for help well in advance./(E) No error.

90. (A) He has in/(B) his possession a/(C) price collection of very old coins./(D) and some ancient paintings./(E) No error.

91. (A) Everyone is/(B) impress by/(C) his zeal/(D) and enthusiasm./(E) No error.

92. (A) The patient recover/(B) so fast that/(C) the expert doctors/(D) also were surprised/(E) No error.

93. (A) His father told me/(B) that though his son had/(C) worked very hard,/(D) but he had failed to make any mark in the examination./(E) No error.

94. (A) We must go/(B) and congratulate him for/(C) his brilliant/(D) performance./(E) No error.

95. (A) He deserted the path of honour/(B) in order to/(C) satisfy his ambition/(D) and then went down his doom very quickly./(E) No error.

96. (A) At last the rain ceased/(B) and the sky was/(C) cleared by clouds/(D) and lightening./(E) No error.

97. (A) Mr. Raman said that/(B) he had a difference/(C) with/(D) the chairman at his statement./(E) No error.

98. (A) The future is/(B) yet to come/(C) but you have a/(D) right to shape it./(E) No error.

99. (A) We have keep/(B) our promise and/(C) you can expect/(D) a lot from us in future./(E) No error.

100. (A) Mohan has collected/(B) all the necessary documents/(C) and have written a good paper/(D) for this conference./(E) No error.

101. (A) Mohan has collected/(B) assembled on the ground/(C) and are waiting for/(D) the Principal to come./(E) No error.

102. (A) The book is making/(B) waves and the sale/(C) is quite brisk in/(D) all major cities./(E) No error.

103. (A) Well, I spend six or seven years/(B) after high school/(C) trying to find a job for me/(D) but could not succeed in it./(E) No error.

104. (A) I do not recall/(B) exactly what he said to me/(C) but when I was quit/(D) he said something to me./(E) No error.

105. (A) We wanted to purchase/(B) something but all the three stores/(C) in that area/(D) were closed on that day./(E) No error.

106. (A) I have had to work/(B) at the fountain for almost/(C) ten hours before it could/(D) start functioning well./(E) No error.

107. (A) No sooner had the jeep/(B) arrives the station/(C) than a young police officer/(D) jumped out of it./(E) No error.

108. (A) No girl/(B) in her troupe is/(C) so sprightly as/(D) your daughter./(E) No error.

109. (A) It seems evidently/(B) to me that/(C) the visits they made to the island/(D) were not very frequent./(E) No error.

110. (A) He was very disappointed/(B) when he found/(C) that someone else/(D) had secured higher marks./(E) No error.

111. (A) Scarcely had/(B) he gone a few steps/(C) that he was told/(D) that his mother was no more./(E) No error.

112. (A) After toiling very hard/(B) over a long period/(C) he found/(D) he had hardly made no profit at all./(E) No error.

113. (A) Day in and day out/(B) he keep telling/(C) his friends that/(D) he wants to go abroad./(E) No error.

114. (A) Whatever work/(B) that which you undertake/(C) put your best/(D) efforts in it./(E) No error.

115. (A) If the teacher/(B) is good the students/(C) will respond/(D) positively to them./(E) No error.

116. (A) I will put on/(B) a note in this regard/(C) for your considera-tion/(D) and necessary decision./(E) No error.

117. (A) The mission provides/(B) able service to all/(C) the needy people in this area/(D) during last few years./(E) No error.

118. (A) I am pleased to sanction/(B) one special increment/(C) to all the employees/(D) with this month./(E) No error.

119. (A) Each cigarette/(B) a person smoke/(C) does some harm and eventually/(D) it may cause a serious disease./(E) No error.

120. (A) This is one of/(B) the most interesting book/(C) I have/(D) ever read./(E) No error.

121. (A) In my opinion/(B) the balance sheet exhibits/(C) a true and fair/(D) view of the state of affairs of the bank./(E) No error.

122. (A) He neglects/(B) attending lectures/(C) regularly/(D) though college was only a few yards away from his house./(E) No error.

123. (A) We have helped them not only/(B) with money but also/(C) with new machinery/(D) and raw material./(E) No error.

124. (A) Of all the men/(B) known to me none is/(C) less inclined than he is/(D) to think ill to others./(E) No error.

125. (A) The new facts he/(B) has discovered and the new/(C) arguments he has advanced/(D) has not changed my opinion/(E) No error.

126. (A) The teacher promised/(B) that he will explain it/(C) if they come/(D) before school the following day./(E) No error.

127. (A) Hindi and Marathi are/(B) different forms of the Sanskrit/(C) which were once spoken/(D) in almost every part of India./(E) No error.

128. (A) The student/(B) answered to/(C) the question/(D) asked by the Inspector./(E) No error.

129. (A) We/(B) have been living/(C) in this house/(D) since two years./(E) No error.

130. (A) Looking forward/(B) to/(C) meet you/(D) here./(E) No error.

131. (A) He/(B) has seen/(C) the picture/(D) yesterday./(E) No error.

132. (A) Ten kilometres/(B) are/(C) a/(D) long distance./(E) No error.

133. (A) What/(B) you will think/(C) if school boys/(D) make fun of you?/(E) No error.

134. (A) I cannot/(B) make from/(C) what you are saying/(D) about him./(E) No error.

135. (A) He is/(B) a mason/(C) who/(D) built my house./(E) No error.

136. (A) Pass on/(B) the salt/(C) please,/(D) do you?/(E) No error.

137. (A) Looking forward/(B) to seeing/(C) you/(D) soon./(E) No error.

138. (A) The institute/(B) imparts training/(C) in/(D) the French./(E) No error.

139. (A) Your machine would not have/(B) given you so much trouble/(C) if you had/(D) maintained it proper./(E) No error.

140. (A) He ought/(B) not have/(C) done such a/(D) filthy thing./(E) No error.

141. (A) Generally, people have not receptive/(B) and fail to notice the/(C) irrelevant answers they/(D) get for straight questions./(E) No error.

142. (A) He could succeed/(B) in catching the ball/ (C) before it reaches/(D) the boundary line./(E) No error.

143. (A) Even at the planning stage/(B) Rajesh was quite sure./(C) that the scheme was/(D) binding to fail/(E) No error.

144. (A) The environment in which/(B) companies operating/(C) today is/(D) undergoing Frenetic changes./(E) No error.

145. (A) The minister's speech/(B) has been reported/(C) to the newspaper/(D) today./(E) No error.

146. (A) No sooner/(B) we reached there/(C) than it started raining/(D) heavily./(E) No error.

147. (A) The man/(B) is/(C) a/(D) social animal./(E) No error.

148. (A) Twenty-five kilometres/(B) from Bhubaneswar to Cuttack/(C) are/(D) a long distance./(E) No error.

149. (A) What is needed today is/(B) a new breed of managers/(C) with a new set of concepts/(D) and a flexible way about thinking./(E) No error.

150. (A) Motivating employees with/(B) traditional authority and financial/(C) incentives have become/(D) increasingly difficult./(E) No error.

151. (A) Several issues raising/(B) in the meeting could/(C) be amicably resolved/(D) due to his tactful handling./(E) No error.

152. (A) The health workers are/(B) being tried their best/(C) to popularise/(D) preventive measures./ (E) No error.

153. (A) Of the two/(B) sisters/(C) Meena is/(D) the elder./(E) No error.

154. (A) Bible/(B) can be/(C) regarded as/(D) a great/ (E) No error.

155. (A) Such/(B) rules do not/(C) apply to/(D) you and I/(E) No error.

156. (A) While luminaries of the dance world/(B) have a derth of opportunities to display their art,/(C) upcoming dancers suffer from/(D) an unfortunate lack of exposure./(E) No error.

157. (A) The job is much worse than I expected./(B) If I would have realised/(C) how awful it was going to be/(D) I would not have accepted it./ (E) No error.

158. (A) Kamlesh asked the dealer/(B) what was the price/(C) of that bicycle and whether/(D) it is really made in Germany?/(E) No error.

159. (A) I am trying to finish/(B) this letter for the last one hour./(C) I wish you would/(D) go away or stop disturbing me./(E) No error.

160. (A) He served/(B) the country with/(C) heart and soul/(D) but got nothing in return./(E) No error.

161. (A) I have/(B) the firm/(C) belief in the basic goodness of/(D) all men./(E) No error.

162. (A) We play/(B) tennis together/(C) every morning/(D) since last June./(E) No error.

163. (A) According to me/(B) the Indians in general is/(C) not a vigilant/(D) and security conscious people./(E) No error.

164. (A) A lot of money/(B) is wasted in/(C) the duplication of work/(D) in any organisation./ (E) No error.

165. (A) I see you/(B) in Kanpur/(C) during my next visit./(D) in the month of May./(E) No error.

166. (A) The last year proved/(B) quite bad/(C) as major industries/(D) witness lot of problems./ (E) No error.

167. (A) I offered him part-time work/(B) but he turned it over/(C) saying that he would/(D) rather wait for a full-time job./(E) No error.

168. (A) The foremost criterion of selection we adopted/(B) were the number of years of training/(C) a dancer had received/(D) under a particular guru./(E) No error.

169. (A) He fixed a metal ladder/(B) for the wall below his window/(C) so as to be able to/(D) escape if there was a fire./(E) No error.

170. (A) Scarcely had I/(B) finished washing the car/(C) than the master came/(D) and asked me to clean the floor of the house./(E) No error.

171. (A) I personally feel that/(B) cleanliness in the city/(C) is one proof of the/(D) efficiently civic administration./(E) No error.

172. (A) When I/(B) last see him/(C) he was/(D) in Calcutta./(E) No error.

173. (A) During last days/(B) I was continuously trying/(C) to contact you/(D) but you were not available./(E) No error.

174. (A) The historian/(B) has been working/(C) on the project/(D) from last 12 years./(E) No error.

175. (A) A detailed inquiry/(B) in the incident/(C) has been initiated/(D) by the Central Government./(E) No error.

176. (A) The soap brought in the/(B) market recently is not/(C) very fragrant and/(D) is too expensive./(E) No error.

177. (A) Somewhere along the/(B) line I lost/(C) track of what Ashish/(D) says about heart ailments/(D) No error.

178. (A) Even though it was/(B) raining bad I/(C) went out to/(D) get some medicines./(E) No error.

179. (A) Developmental activities of/(B) the government come/(C) to a standstill due/(D) to paucity of funds./(E) No error.

180. (A) Foolishly Rajani opened/(B) the cooker when/(C) it was full steam/(D) and burnt her hands./(E) No error.

181. (A) From a tiny roon in/(B) the slums, they have/(C) managed to move to a good/(D) house in a better locality./(E) No error.

182. (A) Even if the doctor/(B) put in his best efforts, he/(C) could not succeed in/(D) saving the patient./(E) No error.

183. (A) Yesterday, a visitor to/(B) the park was attacked/(C) by a tiger and/(D) had to hospitalise./(E) No error.

184. (A) Rajdeep always introduces/(B) himself by his/(C) first name and never mentions/(D) his family name./(E) No error.

185. (A) Ketan had a lot/(B) of work to complete yesterday/(C) and wishes/(D) that he had my help./(E) No error.

186. (A) Sarang is the only/(B) person who can/(C) complete this work/(D) within stipulated deadline./(E) No error.

187. (A) Unintentionally I let/(B) out the secret/(C) by talking about/(D) it loudly in the library./(E) No error.

188. (A) Schools in that area which/(B) had English as a/(C) medium of instruction/(D) as the majority there spoke English./(E) No error.

189. (A) The recent study has/(B) indicated that there is/(C) perceptible change in/(D) the attitudes of the people./(E) No error.

190. (A) Had I come/(B) to know about/(C) his difficulties/(D) would have certainly helped./(E) No error.

191. (A) Ever since the government/(B) announced its new policy,/(C) the private institutions had/(D) run into heavy weather./(E) No error.

192. (A) The majority of the/(B) computer professionals recommends/(C) that effective measures/(D) should be taken against software piracy./(E) No error.

193. (A) Mangesh cannot be able/(B) to finish this work/(C) unless he takes the/(D) help of his colleagues./(E) No error.

194. (A) We were shocking/(B) to hear the news/(C) of the untimely death/(D) of the leader./(E) No error.

195. (A) As it was Ramesh's/(B) first interview he dressed him/(C) in his most/(D) formal suit./(E) No error.

196. (A) A high level meeting/(B) of officials is reporting/(C) to have discussed/(D) the issue in great detail./(E) No error.

197. (A) While going/(B) through the report/(C) yesterday I find/(D) several factual mistakes./(E) No error.

198. (A) On his attitude/(B) it seems that what he wants/(C) is that the decision-making power/(D) should rest with him./(E) No error.

199. (A) No sooner did/(B) the chairman begin speaking/(C) some participants started/(D) shouting slogans./(E) No error.

200. (A) I was standing/(B) at the bus stop/(C) waiting for him/(D) since eight o'clock./(E) No error.

ANSWERS

1	**2**	**3**	**4**	**5**	**6**	**7**	**8**	**9**	**10**
B	B	A	A	A	A	C	B	A	B
11	**12**	**13**	**14**	**15**	**16**	**17**	**18**	**19**	**20**
E	C	A	A	B	C	C	A	C	A
21	**22**	**23**	**24**	**25**	**26**	**27**	**28**	**29**	**30**
E	A	C	C	A	E	D	A	A	C
31	**32**	**33**	**34**	**35**	**36**	**37**	**38**	**39**	**40**
B	C	C	C	B	C	C	E	A	A
41	**42**	**43**	**44**	**45**	**46**	**47**	**48**	**49**	**50**
E	A	B	C	B	C	D	A	D	C
51	**52**	**53**	**54**	**55**	**56**	**57**	**58**	**59**	**60**
A	C	A	B	C	A	A	B	B	D
61	**62**	**63**	**64**	**65**	**66**	**67**	**68**	**69**	**70**
C	E	D	A	D	C	D	B	D	A
71	**72**	**73**	**74**	**75**	**76**	**77**	**78**	**79**	**80**
B	A	D	B	B	E	C	D	C	E
81	**82**	**83**	**84**	**85**	**86**	**87**	**88**	**89**	**90**
C	A	C	B	D	C	E	D	C	C
91	**92**	**93**	**94**	**95**	**96**	**97**	**98**	**99**	**100**
B	A	D	B	D	C	D	A	A	C
101	**102**	**103**	**104**	**105**	**106**	**107**	**108**	**109**	**110**
E	C	A	B	C	A	B	C	A	E
111	**112**	**113**	**114**	**115**	**116**	**117**	**118**	**119**	**120**
C	D	B	B	D	A	A	D	B	B
121	**122**	**123**	**124**	**125**	**126**	**127**	**128**	**129**	**130**
E	D	E	D	D	B	C	B	D	C
131	**132**	**133**	**134**	**135**	**136**	**137**	**138**	**139**	**140**
B	B	B	B	B	D	B	D	D	B
141	**142**	**143**	**144**	**145**	**146**	**147**	**148**	**149**	**150**
A	C	D	B	C	B	A	C	D	C
151	**152**	**153**	**154**	**155**	**156**	**157**	**158**	**159**	**160**
A	B	D	A	D	B	B	B	A	B
161	**162**	**163**	**164**	**165**	**166**	**167**	**168**	**169**	**170**
B	A	B	B	A	D	B	B	B	C
171	**172**	**173**	**174**	**175**	**176**	**177**	**178**	**179**	**180**
D	B	A	D	B	A	D	B	B	C
181	**182**	**183**	**184**	**185**	**186**	**187**	**188**	**189**	**190**
C	A	D	D	C	D	E	A	C	D
191	**192**	**193**	**194**	**195**	**196**	**197**	**198**	**199**	**200**
C	A	A	A	B	B	C	A	C	A

CHAPTER 6

Sentence Improvement

A sentence will convey its true meaning and make the right impact if it is written in a grammatically correct way. One must learn the general rules of grammar and practise well to improve one's English regularly.

Directions: *Which of the phrases given below each sentence should replace the phrase printed in* **bold** *type to make the sentence grammatically correct? If the sentence is correct as it is, mark 'E' as the answer.*

1. The research study is an eye-opener and **attempts to acquaint** us with the problems of the poor nations.
   A. attempted to acquaint
   B. attempts at acquainting
   C. attempt to acquaint
   D. attempting to acquaint
   E. No correction required
2. The man who has committed such a serious crime must **get the mostly severe** punishment.
   A. be getting the mostly severely
   B. get the most severe
   C. have got the most severely
   D. have been getting the severemost
   E. No correction required
3. Acquisition of certain specific skills **can be facilitated from** general awareness, education and exposure to novel situations.
   A. can be facilitated by
   B. may facilitate through
   C. can be felicitated with
   D. may be felicitated with
   E. No correction required
4. He confidently asked the crowd if they thought he was right and the crowd shouted **that they did.**
   A. that he did
   B. that they had
   C. that he is
   D. that he didn't
   E. No correction required
5. If he has to spend five hours in the queue, it **was really a wastage.**
   A. is a really wastage
   B. is real a wastage
   C. has really a wastage
   D. is really a wastage
   E. No correction required
6. Why **did you not threw** the bag away?
   A. did you not throw
   B. had you not threw
   C. did you not thrown
   D. you did not thrown
   E. No correction required
7. They **are not beware of** all the facts
   A. are not aware for
   B. are not aware of
   C. are not to be aware
   D. must not to be aware for
   E. No correction required
8. **If I would have** realised the nature of the job earlier, I would not have accepted it.
   A. If I have had
   B. In case I would have
   C. Had I been
   D. Had I
   E. No correction required
9. The moment they saw me, they **were delight**
   A. had delighted

B. were delighted
C. are delighted
D. have been delighted
E. No correction required

10. The small child does whatever his father **was done.**
A. has done B. did
C. does D. had done
E. No correction required

11. It was unanimously resolved that the parties **should unitedly undertook** launching of popular programmes.
A. should be united undertook
B. should be unitedly undertaken
C. should be unitedly undertake
D. should unitedly undertake
E. No correction required

12. One of my drawbacks is that **I do not have to** tolerance of ambiguity.
A. do not have B. cannot have to
C. am not D. did not have to
E. No correction required

13. They **should have calmly thought of** the advantages that would accrue to them.
A. should have been calm in thinking about
B. should be calmly thought of
C. shall have to calmly thought of
D. should have calmly think of
E. No correction required

14. Their earnings are such that they find it difficult **to make both ends to meet**.
A. to making both ends meet
B. to make both ends for meeting
C. to make both ends meet
D. for making both ends to meet
E. No correction required

15. They **were all shocked at** his failure in the competition.
A. were shocked at all
B. had all shocked at
C. had all shocked by
D. had been all shocked on
E. No correction required

16. He is too impatient **for tolerating** any delay.
A. to tolerate B. to tolerating
C. at tolerating D. with tolerating
E. No correction required

17. Why **should the candidates be** afraid of English Language is not clear.
A. the candidates should be
B. do the candidates be
C. should be the candidates
D. are the candidates
E. No correction required

18. Ramesh is **as tall if not,** taller than Mahesh.
A. not as tall but B. not so tall but as
C. as tall as, if not D. as if not
E. No correction required

19. The easiest **of the thing to do** is to ask the address to the postman.
A. of the things to do
B. among the things did
C. of the thing to be done
D. of all the things done
E. No correction required

20. The player was asked **that why he had not** attended the prayer.
A. why had he not
B. that why had he not
C. why he was not
D. is hesitated to listen to
E. No correction required

21. He **hesitated to listen to** what his brother was saying.
A. listened to hesitate
B. hesitated listen to
C. hesitates to listening
D. is hesitated to listen to
E. No correction required

22. Hardly **does the sun rise** when the stars disappeared.
A. have the sun rose B. had the sun risen
C. did the sun rose D. the sun rose
E. No correction required

23. The police has **so far succeeded in recovering** only a part of the stolen property.
A. thus far succeeded for recovery
B. so far succeed in the recovery of
C. as far as succeeded in recovery of
D. so far succeed to recover
E. No correction required

24. **What happens to** all those travellers on the ship was not known?
A. What happened of
B. That is what happens to
C. What is that happens to
D. What happened to
E. No correction required

25. Because of his ill health, the doctor has advised him **not to refrain** from smoking.
A. to not refrain from
B. to resort to
C. to refrain from
D. to be refrained from
E. No correction required

26. The courts **are actively to safeguard** the interests and the rights of the poor.
A. are actively to safeguarding
B. have been actively safeguarding
C. have to active in safeguarding
D. are actively in safeguarding
E. No correction required

27. He is a singer of repute, but his **yesterday's performance was** quite disappointing.
A. performances for yesterday were
B. yesterday performance was
C. yesterday performances were
D. performances about yesterday were
E. No correction required

28. **Despite of their** differences on matters of principles, they all agree on the demand of hike in salary?
A. Despite their B. Despite of the
C. Despite for their D. Despite off their
E. No correction required

29. The orator **had been left** the auditorium before the audience stood up.
A. had been leaving B. was left
C. left D. would leave
E. No correction required

30. This is one of the most important **inventions of this century**.
A. invention of this century
B. invention of these centuries
C. inventions of centuries
D. inventions of the centuries
E. No correction required

31. Can you tell me **why did you not speak** the truth?
A. why did not you speak
B. that why did you not speak
C. why you did not speak
D. why did you not spoke
E. No correction required

32. The chemist **hadn't hardly any of those kind** of medicines.
A. had hardly any of those kinds
B. had hardly not any of those kind
C. had scarcely any of those kind
D. had hardly any of those kind
E. No correction required

33. She cooks, washes dishes, does her homework and **then relaxing.**
A. relaxing then B. then is relaxing
C. relaxing is then D. then relaxes
E. No correction required

34. Anyone interested in the use of computers can learn much if **you have access** to a personal computer.
A. they have access
B. access can be available
C. he or she has access
D. one of them have access
E. No correction required

35. **By such time** you finish that chapter, I will write a letter.
A. The time when B. By the time
C. By that time D. The time
E. No correction required

36. **Had I realised** how close I was to the edge of the valley, I would not have carried the bags there.
A. Had I been realised
B. If I would have realised
C. When I realised
D. Had I had realised
E. No correction required

37. Later he became unpopular because he tried **to lord it on** his followers.
A. to lord it for B. to lord over
C. to lord it over D. to lord it over on
E. No correction required

38. **The long or short of it** is that I do not want to deal with that new firm.
A. The long and short of it
B. The long and short for it
C. The long or short for it
D. The short and long of it
E. No correction required

39. The people generally try to **curry favour** with the corrupt but influential person.
A. cook favour B. seek favour
C. extract favour D. display favour
E. No correction required

40. My hair **stood off ends** when I saw the horrible sight.
A. stood at ends B. stood on ends
C. stood to ends D. stands on ends
E. No correction required

41. "Friends and comrades, the light has gone **away from** our lives and there is darkness everywhere."
A. off B. out of
C. out from D. out off
E. No correction required

42. We **can not always convey** ourselves in simple sentences.
A. cannot always convey
B. can not always express
C. cannot always express
D. can not always communicate
E. No correction required

43. **Shapes** of gods and goddesses are worshipped by people.
A. Images B. Reflections
C. Clay shapes D. Clay toys.
E. No correction required

44. The crops are dying; **it must not had** rained.
A. must had not
B. must not be
C. must not have
D. must not have been
E. No correction required

45. It is always better to make people realise the importance of discipline than to **impose them on it.**
A. impose it with them
B. impose them with it
C. imposing them on it
D. impose it on them
E. No correction required

46. The performance of our players was rather **worst than I had expected.**
A. bad as I had expected
B. worse than I had expected
C. worse than expectation
D. worst than was expected
E. No correction required

47. For some days the new professor lectured **above the heads of** his pupils.
A. over the head of
B. over the heads of
C. on the heads of
D. through the heads of
E. No correction required

48. For many centuries in Indian history there was no city so famous **like** the city of Ujjain.
A. as B. such as
C. likewise D. so like
E. No correction required

49. Making friends is more rewarding than **to make enemies**.
A. to be unsociable B. to be sociable
C. being unsociable D. making enemies
E. No correction required

50. **You need not come unless you want to.**
A. You don't need to come unless you want to
B. You come only when you want to
C. You come unless you don't want to
D. You needn't come until you don't want to
E. No correction required

51. The drama had many scenes which were so humorous that it was **hardly possible to keep** a straight face.
A. hardly possible for keeping
B. hardly impossible keeping
C. hardly impossible to keep
D. hardly possible keeping
E. No correction required

52. The moment the manager came to know of the fradulent action of his assistant, he **order immediately dismissed him**.

A. immediately ordered his dismissed
B. ordered his immediate dismissal
C. immediately order dismissal of his
D. ordered for immediately dismissal him
E. No correction required

53. We met him immediately after the session in which he **had been given** a nice speech.
A. would be giving
B. has been given
C. will have given
D. had given
E. No correction required

54. The world has seen **small** real attempt at population and resource planning.
A. few B. little
C. less D. a few
E. No correction required

55. One of the most significant **phenomenons** of our time has been the development of the cinema.
A. phenomenon B. phenomena
C. phenomna D. phenomns
E. No correction required

56. **It was until many years** later that Gandhi became a rebel against authority.
A. It was not until many years
B. It was till many years
C. It was not many years
D. Until it was many years
E. No correction required

57. There are not many men who are so famous that they are frequently referred to by their **short names** only.
A. initials B. signatures
C. pictures D. middle names
E. No correction required

58. Though we **have kept in mind to try and maintain** most facilities, we would like to request you to kindly bear with us any inconvenience that may be caused.
A. must keep in mind to try and maintain
B. have kept in mind trying and maintain
C. would keep in mind to try and maintain
D. should have kept in mind to try and to maintain
E. No correction required

59. The tea-estate administration is **in such mess there** is no leader to set the things right.
A. in such a mess here
B. in a such mess that here
C. in such a mess that there
D. with such a mess that there
E. No correction required

60. My doctor knew that I would eventually recover and do the kind of work **I would be doing** before.
A. would have been doing
B. would have done
C. had been done
D. had been doing
E. No correction required

61. If you are thinking about investigation overseas, **isn't it makes** sense to find an experience guide?
A. it is not making
B. doesn't it make
C. does it make
D. is it making
E. No correction required

62. The **crime has growth rapidly** in Russia since the disintegration of the communist system.
A. rapid crime has grown
B. crime has grown rapid
C. crimes grow rapidly
D. crimes have been rapidly grown
E. No correction required

63. Technology **must use to feed** the forces of change.
A. must be used to feed
B. must have been using to feed
C. must use having fed
D. must be using to feed
E. No correction required

64. In addition **to enhanced their reputations** through strategic use of philanthropy, companies are sponsoring social initiatives to open new markets.
A. of enhancing their reputations
B. to having enhance their reputation
C. to enhancing their reputation
D. to have their reputation enhancing
E. No correction required

65. They failed **in their attempt to repair** the demolished portion of the building.
A. for their attempt to repair
B. in their attempting to repair
C. with their attempt to repair
D. in their attempt for repairs
E. No correction required

66. We don't know **how did the thief made** an escape.
A. how the thief did make
B. how the thief does make
C. how the thief made
D. how was the thief made
E. No correction required

67. They have a scheme of rewarding **the best of the performers** every year.
A. a best performer
B. the best among the performer
C. a best among performers
D. the best of the performer
E. No correction required

68. No sooner **do the bells ring** than the curtain rose.
A. did the bell ring
B. did the bells ring
C. had the bell rang
D. had the bell rung
E. No correction required

69. Most of the Indian workers are **as healthy as, if not healthier** than, the British workers.
A. as if healthy as and not healthier
B. healthier but not as healthy
C. as healthy, if not healthier
D. so healthy, if not healthier
E. No correction required

70. He admired the speed with which he completed the work and **appreciating the method adopted** by him.
A. appreciate the method being adopted
B. appreciated the method adopted
C. appreciate the method of adoption
D. appreciated the adopting method
E. No correction required

71. The population of Tokyo is **greater than that of any other** town in the world.
A. greatest among any other
B. greater than all other
C. greater than those of any other
D. greater than any other
E. No correction required

72. They examined both the samples very carefully but failed to detect **any difference** in them.
A. some difference in
B. some difference between
C. any difference between
D. any difference among
E. No correction required

73. Tax evaders **should heavily fined** as they do it intentionally.
A. should be heavy fined
B. should have heavily fined
C. shall have heavy fine
D. should be heavily fined
E. No correction required

74. He never **has and ever will take** such strong measures.
A. had taken nor will ever take
B. had taken and will ever take
C. has and never will take
D. had and ever will take
E. No correction required

75. The intruder stood quietly **for few moments**.
A. for few time
B. for the few moments
C. for moments
D. for a few moments
E. No correction required

76. He **should not had** done it.
A. had not
B. should had not
C. should not have
D. should have
E. No correction required

77. The meeting was **attended to by all** the invitees.
A. all attended to by
B. attended by all
C. fully attended to by
D. like attending to all
E. No correction required

78. I have got some tea, but I do not have **a** sugar.
A. some
B. got
C. more
D. any
E. No correction required

79. I need not offer any explanation regarding this incident—my behaviour **is speaking itself**.

A. will speak to itself
B. speaks for itself
C. has been speaking
D. speaks about itself
E. No correction required

80. Anand has the guts **to rise from** the occasion and come out successfully.

A. in rising from B. to raise with
C. to rise against D. to rise to
E. No correction required

81. Maria unnecessarily **picked up** a quarrel with Rani and left the party hurriedly.

A. has picked up B. picked on
C. picked D. picking up
E. No correction required

82. The train will leave at 8.30 p.m., we **have been** ready by 7.30 p.m. so that we can reach the station in time.

A. were B. must be
C. are D. should have
E. No correction required

83. He dislikes the word dislike, **isn't he**?

A. didn't he B. doesn't he
C. hasn't he D. does he
E. No correction required

84. The prosecution failed **in** establish in every case today.

A. to B. on
C. as D. upon
E. No correction required

85. We were still standing in the queue when the **film was beginning**.

A. film began
B. film had begun
C. beginning of the film was over
D. film begins
E. No correction required

86. I **earnestly believe that** you will visit our relatives during your forthcoming trip to Mumbai.

A. had hardly believe that
B. sincerely would believe
C. certainly believing that
D. could not believe
E. No correction required

87. We must **take it granted** that Madhu will not come for today's function.

A. take it for granted
B. taking it granted
C. took it as granted
D. have it granted
E. No correction required

88. He has received no other message than an urgent telegram **asking** him to **rush his village** immediately.

A. asked him to rush his village
B. asking him to have rush his village
C. asking him to rush to his village
D. asking him rushing at his village
E. No correction required

89. They continued to work in the field **despite of the heavy rains**.

A. even though there is heavy rain
B. although heavily rains
C. in spite the heavy rains
D. even though it rained heavily
E. No correction required

90. **Had you been told** me about your problem, I would have helped you.

A. If you would have told
B. Had you have told
C. had you told
D. If you have told
E. No correction required

91. They felt humiliated because they realised that they **had cheated**.

A. have been cheated
B. had been cheated
C. had been cheating
D. were to be cheated
E. No correction required

92. He found the gold coin **as he cleans** the floor.

A. as he had cleaned
B. while he cleans
C. which he is cleaning
D. while cleaning
E. No correction required

93. Because of his mastery in this field, his suggestions **are wide accepted**.

A. are widely accepted
B. are wide acceptance

C. have widely accepted
D. have been wide accepted
E. No correction required

94. The man to **who I sold** my house was a cheat.
A. to whom I sell
B. to who I sell
C. who was sold to
D. to whom I sold
E. No correction required

95. **If I was you,** I would not have joined the party.
A. If I am you B. If I be you
C. As you D. Were I you
E. No correction required

96. You will be late if you **do not leave** now.
A. did not leave
B. left
C. will not leave
D. do not happen to leave
E. No correction required

97. All the allegations **levelled against** him were found to be baseless.
A. level against B. level with
C. levelling with D. levelled for
E. No correction required

98. What **does agonise me most** is not this criticism, but the trivial reason behind it.
A. most agonising me
B. agonises me most
C. agonising me most
D. I most agonised
E. No correction required

99. The accused now flatly denies **have admitted** his guilt in his first statement.
A. having admitted
B. had admitted
C. have been admitting
D. has admitting
E. No correction required

100. We demonstrated to them how we **were prepared** the artistic patterns.
A. are prepared
B. have prepared
C. are preparing
D. had prepared
E. No correction required

ANSWERS

1	2	3	4	5	6	7	8	9	10
B	B	A	E	D	A	B	D	B	C
11	**12**	**13**	**14**	**15**	**16**	**17**	**18**	**19**	**20**
D	A	E	C	E	A	A	C	A	D
21	**22**	**23**	**24**	**25**	**26**	**27**	**28**	**29**	**30**
E	B	E	D	C	B	E	A	C	E
31	**32**	**33**	**34**	**35**	**36**	**37**	**38**	**39**	**40**
C	A	D	C	B	E	C	A	E	B
41	**42**	**43**	**44**	**45**	**46**	**47**	**48**	**49**	**50**
B	C	A	C	D	B	B	A	D	A
51	**52**	**53**	**54**	**55**	**56**	**57**	**58**	**59**	**60**
E	B	D	B	B	A	A	E	C	D
61	**62**	**63**	**64**	**65**	**66**	**67**	**68**	**69**	**70**
B	B	A	C	E	C	E	B	E	B
71	**72**	**73**	**74**	**75**	**76**	**77**	**78**	**79**	**80**
E	C	D	A	D	C	B	D	B	D
81	**82**	**83**	**84**	**85**	**86**	**87**	**88**	**89**	**90**
C	B	B	A	B	E	A	C	D	C
91	**92**	**93**	**94**	**95**	**96**	**97**	**98**	**99**	**100**
B	D	A	D	D	E	E	B	A	D

CHAPTER 7

Reordering Words

Different words form a sentence and convey their true meaning only when they are arranged in a proper order. One must try and practise it regularly.

Directions: *In the following questions, some parts of the sentence have been jumbled up. You are required to rearrange these parts which are labelled P, Q, R and S to produce the correct sentence. Choose the option with proper sequence.*

1. We are doing
P : to the people
Q : to give relief
R : all we can
S : but more funds are needed
The correct sequence should be
A. P Q R S B. R Q P S
C. Q P R S D. S P Q R
E. P R Q S

2. The man
P : when he was
Q : in the office last evening
R : could not finish
S : all his work
The correct sequence should be
A. P Q R S B. Q R S P
C. R Q P S D. R S P Q
E. P R Q S

3. The people decided
P : they were going
Q : how much
R : to spend
S : on the construction of the school building
The correct sequence should be
A. Q P R S B. P Q R S
C. P R Q S D. S Q P R
E. Q R P S

4. The man said that
P : those workers
Q : would be given a raise
R : who did not go on
S : strike last month
The correct sequence should be
A. P Q R S B. P R S Q
C. Q P R S D. R S P Q
E. P R Q S

5. I think
P : the members
Q : are basically in agreement
R : of the group
S : on the following points.
The correct sequence should be
A. R Q P S B. S Q R P
C. P R Q S D. P Q S R
E. Q R P S

6. While it was true that
P : I had
Q : to invest in industry
R : some lands and houses
S : I did not have ready cash
The correct sequence should be
A. P Q R S B. P R S Q
C. S Q P R D. Q P R S
E. Q P S R

7. P : But your help
Q : to finish this work
R : it would not have been possible
S : in time

The correct sequence should be
A. P R Q S B. S P Q R
C. R P Q S D. P Q R S
E. Q P R S

8. The boy
P : in the competition
Q : who was wearing spectacles
R : won many prizes
S : held in our college
The correct sequence should be
A. P Q R S B. R P S Q
C. Q R P S D. Q P S R
E. S P Q R

9. About 200 years ago,
P : in the south of India
Q : an old king
R : ruled over a kingdom
S : called Rajavarman
The correct sequence should be
A. Q S R P B. P Q R S
C. Q P S R D. Q S P R
E. Q P R S

10. P : his land
Q : a wooden plough
R : the Indian peasant still uses
S : to cultivate
The correct sequence should be
A. R Q P S B. Q P S R
C. S R Q P D. R Q S P
E. Q P R S

11. He was a man,
P : even if he had to starve
Q : who would not beg
R : borrow or steal
S : from anyone
The correct sequence should be
A. P Q R S B. P R Q S
C. Q R S P D. Q P R S
E. P S R Q

12. P : in the progress of
Q : universities play a crucial role
R : our civilization
S : in the present age
The correct sequence should be
A. S Q P R B. Q R S P
C. Q R P S D. S Q R P
E. P Q R S

13. P : far out into the sea
Q : for the next two weeks there were further explosions
R : which hurled
S : ashes and debris
The correct sequence should be
A. Q R P S B. R S P Q
C. Q R S P D. S R P Q
E. P Q R S

14. William Shakespeare,
P : in his lifetime
Q : the great English dramatist
R : wrote thirty-five plays
S : and several poems
The correct sequence should be
A. P Q R S B. R S P Q
C. Q S R P D. Q R S P
E. P R Q S

15. Whenever I am,
P : with an old friend of mine
Q : in New Delhi
R : to have dinner
S : I always try
The correct sequence should be
A. S Q P R B. Q S R P
C. R P S Q D. P R Q S
E. P Q R S

16. P : I don't know
Q : must have thought
R : what people sitting next to me
S : but I came away
The correct sequence should be
A. R S Q P B. R Q S P
C. P Q R S D. P R Q S
E. P S R Q

17. P : in estimating the size of the earth
Q : but they were hampered by the lack of instruments of precision
R : ancient astronomers
S : used methods which were theoretically valid

Which one of the following is the correct sequence?

A. R P Q S B. P R Q S
C. R S Q P D. R P S Q
E. P Q R S

18. P : It is a pity that
Q : by offering a handsome dowry
R : a number of parents think that
S : they will be able to ensure the happiness of their daughters

Which one of the following is the correct sequence?

A. S Q R P B. P R S Q
C. P S R Q D. P R Q S
E. P Q R S

19. The common man
P : in nurturing
Q : a more active role
R : communal harmony
S : should play

Which one of the following is the correct sequence?

A. P R S Q B. S Q P R
C. S Q R P D. P R Q S
E. P Q R S

20. The doctor
P : able to find out
Q : what has caused
R : the food poisoning
S : has not been

Which one of the following is the correct sequence?

A. S P R Q B. P R Q S
C. P R S Q D. S P Q R
E. P Q R S

21. P : was suspended
Q : the officer being corrupt
R : before his dismissal
S : from service

Which one of the following is the correct sequence?

A. Q P S R B. Q P R S
C. R S Q P D. R S PQ
E. P Q R S

22. With an unsteady hand
P : on my desk
Q : from his pocket
R : he took an envelope
S : and threw it

Which one of the following is the correct sequence?

A. Q R P S B. Q R S P
C. R Q P S D. R Q S P
E. P Q R S

23. P : she gave her old coat
Q : to a beggar
R : the one with the brown fur on it
S : shivering with cold

Which one of the following is the correct sequence?

A. S Q R P B. S P R Q
C. P R Q S D. P S Q R
E. P Q R S

24. It is a privilege
P : to pay tax
Q : of every citizen
R : as well as the duty
S : as well as the duty who is well-placed

Which one of the following is the correct sequence?

A. R P S Q B. S P R Q
C. R Q S P D. S Q R P
E. P Q R S

25. It is not good
P : of the wicked persons
Q : to overthrow
R : to accept the help
S : the righteous persons

Which one of the following is the correct sequence?

A. R S Q P B. Q S R P
C. R P Q S D. Q P R S
E. P Q R S

26. Life is judged
P : and not by
Q : of work done
R : the longevity of years
S : by the quality

Which one of the following is the correct sequence?

A. Q S P R B. S Q R P
C. Q S R P D. S Q P R
E. P Q R S

27. P : When he learns that
Q : you have passed the examination
R : in the first division
S : your father will be delighted
Which one of the following is the correct sequence?
A. Q P S R B. S P Q R
C. Q R S P D. S R Q P
E. P Q R S

28. P : The journalist
Q : saw
R : countless number of the dead
S : driving across the field of battle
Which one of the following is the correct sequence?
A. P Q S R B. P Q R S
C. P S Q R D. S R Q P
E. R P Q S

29. P : Jane planned
Q : some stamps
R : to buy
S : this afternoon
Which one of the following is the correct sequence?
A. P R Q S B. P S Q R
C. Q R P S D. Q S P R
E. R P Q S

30. Her mother
P : when she was
Q : hardly four years old
R : began to teach Neha
S : English
Which one of the following is the correct sequence?
A. R S Q P B. S R P Q
C. R S P Q D. S R Q P
E. R P Q S

31. P : Bill had
Q : a friend
R : an appointment
S : to meet
Which one of the following is the correct sequence?
A. P S R Q B. P R S Q
C. Q S R P D. Q R S P
E. R P Q S

32. For fear
P : that may or may not affect them perhaps at first
Q : of upsetting young people
R : only healthy people over 80 should be sequenced
S : about their genetic propensities
Which one of the following is the correct sequence?
A. S Q P R B. Q S R P
C. S Q R P D. Q S P R
E. P Q R S

33. While traditional
P : under made-up Americans aliases pretending familiarity with a culture and climate
Q : India sleeps a dynamic young cohort of highly skilled articulate professionals
R : they've never actually experienced earning salaries that were undreamt of by their elders
S : work through the night in the call centres functioning on US time
Which one of the following is the correct sequence?
A. P R Q S B. Q S P R
C. P S Q R D. Q R P S
E. P Q R S

34. IITs are
P : of great self-confidence and competitive advantage for India today
Q : in science and technology which has become a source
R : as they epitomize his creation of an infrastructure for excellence
S : perhaps Jawaharlal Nehru's most consequential legacy

Which one of the following is the correct sequence?

A. Q P S R B. S R Q P
C. Q R S P D. S P Q R
E. P Q R S

35. As India

P : from nearly 250 years of the British rule in India
Q : first major struggle for independence from the British rule
R : celebrates the Diamond Jubilee of its independence
S : it also observes simultaneously the 150th Anniversary of the Great Indian Mutiny

Which one of the following is the correct sequence?

A. R S P Q B. Q P S R
C. R P S Q D. Q S P R
E. P Q R S

36. There have been

P : a day after high intensity violence left at least 50 persons
Q : sporadic clashes between
R : dead in the northern city of Tripoli
S : the Lebanese army and militants

Which one of the following is the correct sequence?

A. Q S R P B. S Q R P
C. Q S P R D. S Q P R
E. P Q R S

37. Although

P : of non-owner managers came to be widely appreciated
Q : political freedom from the British masters
R : came to us in 1947 it was not until
S : well into the following decade that the role

Which one of the following is the correct sequence?

A. S P Q R B. Q R S P
C. S R Q P D. Q P S R
E. P Q R S

38. Conditions

P : for marketing in the U.S. and Canada
Q : Mexico as a manufacturing base
R : that Indian companies aspiring to tap
S : would have to fulfil include the complex rules of origin

Which one of the following is the correct sequence?

A. R Q P S B. S P Q R
C. R P Q S D. S Q P R
E. P Q R S

39. Aside

P : of the same three-storey building in the military academy
Q : from eating in the same dining hall
R : half to the north of the entrance half to the south
S : the 206 troops live side by side on the ground floor

Which one of the following is the correct sequence?

A. R P S Q B. Q S P R
C. R S P Q D. Q P S R
E. P Q R S

40. Russia's test firing

P : to US steps that have sparked an arms race
Q : of an intercontinental ballistic missile on
R : and undermined world security
S : Tuesday was in response

Which one of the following is the correct sequence?

A. S Q P R B. Q S R P
B. S Q R P D. Q S P R
E. P Q R S

41. Marks, cities, civilization —

P : on the verge of globalization; poised to
Q : the slow ascent to where he is today, poised
R : it is in this order that primitive man made
S : achieve universal prosperity and abundance

Which one of the following is the correct sequence?

A. R Q P S B. P S R Q
B. R S P Q D. P Q R S
E. S R P Q

42. I bow my head

P : for their sense of the beautiful in

Q : nature and for their foresight in investing beautiful

R : manifestations of nature with a religious significance

S : in reverence to our ancestors

Which one of the following is the correct sequence?

A. Q R S P
B. S P Q R
B. Q P S R
D. S R Q P
E. P Q R S

43. With all the crime and sleaze

P : I am not sure how many parents will be able to

Q : how many will have the courage to satisfy the child's uncomfortable queries

R : that dominates the front page of the newspapers today

S : read out the headlines to their children and if they do so

Which one of the following is the correct sequence?

A. R P S Q
B. S Q R P
C. R Q S P
D. P R S Q
E. P Q R S

44. The way

P : processes that govern their actions

Q : nutrients become integral parts

R : depends on the physiological and biochemical

S : of the body and contribute to its functions

Which one of the following is the correct sequence?

A. Q R S P
B. P S R Q
C. Q S R P
D. S P R Q
E. P Q R S

45. Thus,

P : international surveys would hence forth record

Q : if dirt-poor people in the developing world

R : their wealth of happiness alongside their material poverty

S : display a general sense of well-being

Which one of the following is the correct sequence?

A. S Q R P
B. Q S P R
C. S Q P R
D. Q S R P
E. P Q R S

46. It's

P : someone who's grieving but

Q : natural to feel uncomfortable

R : that prevent you from being there

S : or awkward when you have to help

Which one of the following is the correct sequence?

A. Q P S R
B. R S P Q
C. Q S P R
D. R P S Q
E. P Q R S

47. Developing countries

P : along the equator, which

Q : could become leaders in energy production

R : are expected to face the brunt of global warming

S : with a solar energy breakthrough

Which one of the following is the correct sequence?

A. Q S P R
B. P R Q S
C. Q R P S
D. P S Q R
E. S R P Q

48. A diversified

P : use as a heating or power generation fuel by converting gas into

Q : adding a new dimension to the traditional use of gas

R : of natural gas is emerging

S : amongst other products, high quality diesel transportation fuel virtually free of sulphur

Which one of the following is the correct sequence?

A. R P Q S
B. S Q P R
C. R Q P S
D. S P Q R
E. P Q R S

49. As things stand

P : but a majority still does not have access to English

Q : linguistic edge they are equipped with

R : after globally because of the

S : Indian professionals are much sought

Which one of the following is the correct sequence?

A. R S P Q B. S R Q P
C. R S Q P D. S R P Q
E. P Q R S

50. While advocates

P : of its provisions with the
Q : there is some misguided concern about a possible clash of some
R : of social reform have generally hailed the new legislation
S : religious and customary practices in vogue in the country

Which one of the following is the correct sequence?

A. R Q P S B. Q R S P
C. R Q S P D. Q R P S
E. P Q R S

51. Public Interest Litigations

P : as they are subjected to massive misuse
Q : but today they contribute to the backlog
R : were instituted as a means to help ordinary people side-step judicial delays to secure justice
S : also called postcard petitions

Which one of the following is the correct sequence?

A. R S Q P B. S R P Q
C. R S P Q D. S R Q P
E. P Q R S

52. Among

P : the soldier's mindset from fighting
Q : the doctrine's other directives is the need to reorient
R : namely terrorists hiding among civilians
S : the enemy to fighting his own people

Which one of the following is the correct sequence?

A. P Q R S B. Q P S R
C. P Q S R D. Q PRS
E. S R P Q

53. Indeed

P : on how to nurture young talent at the grassroots level
Q : as the powerhouse of women's hockey
R : is an instructive lesson for Indian hockey bosses
S : the non-descript town's emergence

Which one of the following is the correct sequence?

A. Q S R P B. S Q P R
C. S Q R P D. Q S P R
E. P Q R S

54. With pressure

P : to submit a report on the retreat of glaciers in Uttarakhand and also its impact
Q : mounting from every corner
R : a committee comprising scientists, geologists and technical experts
S : the state government has finally constituted

Which one of the following is the correct sequence?

A. Q S P R B. S Q R P
C. Q S R P D. S Q P R
E. P Q R S

55. This could

P : while out on sea-right from an engine break down to a human problem
Q : they shoulder great responsibility and have to take care of any eventuality
R : because while seafarers do look forward to some fun on the decks
S : not be further from the truth

Which one of the following is the correct sequence?

A. P R Q S B. S Q R P
C. P Q R S D. S R Q P
E. R S P Q

56. The producer must

P : give enough information so that the consumer
Q : will understand how the product differs from the competition
R : about the product but to buy it, the producer must
S : inform the consumer of his product and if he wants the consumer to not only know

Which one of the following is the correct sequence?

A. P R S Q B. S Q P R
C. P Q S R D. S R P Q
E. R S P Q

57. The bigoted

P : reality that additional hands also mean additional mouths to feed, cloths and house

Q : in order to augment their incomes, plead for more children, ignoring the resultant

R : not only to the national interests but also to those families which

S : belief—the more, the marrier—has done immense harm

Which one of the following is the correct sequence?

A. S Q R P B. P R Q S
C. S R Q P D. P Q R S
E. R S P Q

58. Critics

P : cover up the essentially inequalitarian

Q : and unjust nature of a Third World State

R : has been basically a sugar-coated concept that tries to

S : also point out that development administration

Which one of the following is the correct sequence?

A. P Q S R B. S R P Q
C. P R S Q D. S Q P R
E. Q P R S

59. For

P : are determined by nature and which by nurture

Q : about two decades now

R : aspects of cognition and behaviour in the human brain

S : scientists have been trying to figure out which

Which one of the following is the correct sequence?

A. S Q R P B. Q S P R
C. S Q P R D. Q S R P
E. P Q R S

60. A school of psychology argues that

P : is one of the manifestations of impulse control disorder, a condition in which

Q : an act harmful to oneself or others

R : motorcycling—like gambling or sky-diving—

S : an individual cannot resist the impulse or temptation to perform

Which one of the following is the correct sequence?

A. R P S Q B. Q S P R
C. R S P Q D. Q P S R
E. P Q R S

61. With six of its neighbours

P : there is a renewed warning for India

Q : and safeguard its own strategic interests

R : ranking high on a global roster of failed states

S : to reassess its policy towards them

Which one of the following is the correct sequence?

A. P R S Q B. R P Q S
C. P R Q S D. R P S Q
E. P Q R S

62. Faced with the

P : traditional culture in the pre-independence India

Q : challenge of the intrusion of colonial culture and ideology

R : developed during the nineteenth century

S : an attempt to reinvigorate traditional institutions and to realise the potential of

Which one of the following is the correct sequence?

A. P R Q S B. Q S P R
C. P S Q R D. Q R P S
E. S R P Q

63. Looking back,

P : two wars I had been through

Q : life in the Army had all along been truly joyous

R : and the innumerable postings and below par accommodation at many stations

S : despite the vicissitudes and hardships of the

Which one of the following is the correct sequence?

A. S R P Q B. Q P R S
C. S P R Q D. Q R P S
E. P Q R S

64. Polluted

P : on aqua life while

Q : Kerala rivers threatens the indigenous varieties

R : rivers are wreaking havoc

S : the introduction of exotic fish in the

Which one of the following is the correct sequence?

A. R P S Q B. Q S P R
C. R S P Q D. Q P S R
E. P Q R S

65. Typically,

P : despite the overwhelming evidence of the negative role

Q : or for the destruction of natural habitats,

R : played by commercial logging and mining interest

S : it is local communities who are blamed for deforestation

Which one of the following is the correct sequence?

A. P R S Q B. S Q P R
C. P Q S R D. S R P Q
E. R Q P S

66. If the idyllic

P : and rehabilitation work being carried out across several nations,

Q : only a cursory mention in the massive restoration

R : island of Car Nicobar has found

S : part of the reason could be inaccessibility of these islands

Which one of the following is the correct sequence?

A. R Q P S B. S P Q R
C. R P Q S D. S Q P R
E. P Q R S

67. The real founder

P : and Humayun's son Akbar, the greatest ruler

Q : of the Mughal Empire was Babur's grandson

R : Ashoka a millennium and half earlier

S : to sit on an Indian throne after

Which one of the following is the correct sequence?

A. S P Q R B. Q R S P
C. S R Q P D. Q P S R
E. P Q R S

68. In the neighbourhood

P : of the equator there is little need of clothes of fire,

Q : stretched out on the bare ground beneath the shade of a tree

R : and no danger to health, to pass the livelong day

S : and it is possible with perfect comfort

Which one of the following is the correct sequence?

A. P R S Q B. Q S R P
C. P S R Q D. Q R S P
E. P Q R S

69. Hospitality

P : to commendation on this account

Q : is a virtue for which the natives of the east

R : and the people of Egypt are well entitled

S : in general are highly and deservedly admired;

Which one of the following is the correct sequence?

A. Q S R P B. P R S Q
C. Q R S P D. P S R Q
E. P Q R S

70. It is possible

P : between Finland and Sweden, which was an international accord

Q : to find a solution to the Kashmir issue

R : settling a territorial dispute on the basis of *status quo*

S : on the lines of the agreement on the Aland Islands

Which one of the following is the correct sequence?

A. Q R P S B. P S Q R
C. Q S P R D. P R Q S
E. S R P Q

71. Once an

P : Shanghai has metamorphosed into

Q : in China's economic development strategy

R : a major international city which is a key element

S : obscure fishing town,
Which one of the following is the correct sequence?
A. R P S Q B. S Q R P
C. R Q S P D. S P R Q
E. Q P R S

72. When factors
P : to the growth of biotechnology come together,
Q : it heralds the arrival of a new venture
R : and a government that is dedicated
S : like rich biodiversity, a conducive climate, a network of established research institutes, educated and skilled manpower.
Which one of the following is the correct sequence?
A. Q P R S B. S R P Q
C. Q R P S D. S P R Q
E. P Q R S

73. Brazil's Guaranis
P : from being Internet savvy
Q : are an ancient tribe who live in the country's remote jungles,
R : excluded them
S : but that has not.
The proper sequence should be:
A. P S R Q B. Q R S P
C. P R S Q D. Q S R P
E. P Q R S

74. A game host
P : that could be used at the airport duty-free shops
Q : and the winner walked away with
R : shot out ten witty questions
S : vouchers worth 200 Singapore dollars.
The proper sequence should be:
A. P S Q R B. R Q S P
C. P Q S R D. R S Q P
E. P Q R S

75. And while
P : without adequate international support
Q : the US military has been forced into remaining in Iraq
R : the overthrow of Saddam Hussein may have been quick,
S : longer than anticipated.
The proper sequence should be:
A. R S Q P B. P Q S R
C. R Q S P D. P S Q R
E. P Q R S

ANSWERS

1	2	3	4	5	6	7	8	9	10
B	D	A	B	C	C	A	C	A	D
11	**12**	**13**	**14**	**15**	**16**	**17**	**18**	**19**	**20**
C	A	C	D	B	D	C	B	B	D
21	**22**	**23**	**24**	**25**	**26**	**27**	**28**	**29**	**30**
B	D	C	C	B	D	B	C	A	B
31	**32**	**33**	**34**	**35**	**36**	**37**	**38**	**39**	**40**
B	D	B	B	C	C	C	A	B	D
41	**42**	**43**	**44**	**45**	**46**	**47**	**48**	**49**	**50**
A	B	A	C	B	C	B	A	B	A
51	**52**	**53**	**54**	**55**	**56**	**57**	**58**	**59**	**60**
D	B	C	C	D	D	C	B	D	A
61	**62**	**63**	**64**	**65**	**66**	**67**	**68**	**69**	**70**
D	B	C	A	B	A	D	C	A	C
71	**72**	**73**	**74**	**75**					
D	B	D	B	C					

CHAPTER 8

Reordering Sentences

A paragraph is formed from sentences, it will convey its true meaning and purpose only when the sentences are arranged in a proper manner. One must try and practise it regularly.

Directions (Qs. 1 to 50): *Each of these question sets has a group of sentences marked with numbers. Rearrange them in proper sequence to form a meaningful paragraph; then answer the questions given below each set.*

SET-1

1. After examining him, the doctor smiled at him mischievously and took out a syringe.
2. Thinking that he was really sick, his father summoned the family doctor.
3. That day, Mintu wanted to take a day off from school.
4. Immediately, Mintu jumped up from his bed and swore that he was fine.
5. Therefore; he pretended to be sick and remained in bed.

1. Which sentence should come **fourth** in the pargaraph?

A. 1 B. 2
C. 3 D. 4
E. 5

2. Which sentence should come **last** in the paragraph?

A. 1 B. 2
C. 3 D. 4
E. 5

3. Which sentence should come **first** in the paragraph?

A. 1 B. 2
C. 3 D. 4
E. 5

4. Which sentence should come **third** in the paragraph?

A. 1 B. 2
C. 3 D. 4
E. 5

5. Which sentence should come **second** in the paragraph?

A. 1 B. 2
C. 3 D. 4
E. 5

SET-2

1. In his literacy work he spoke of that province of human life which mere intellect does not speak.
2. He has also given innocent joy to many children by his stories like 'Kabuliwalah'.
3. Thsese songs are sung not only in Bengal but all over the country.
4. Rabindranath's great works sprang from intensity of vision and feelings.
5. He sang of beauty and heroism, nobility and charm.

6. Which sentence should come **third** in the sequence?

A. 1 B. 2
C. 3 D. 4
E. 5

7. Which sentence should come **fourth** in the sequence?

A. 1 B. 2
C. 3 D. 4
E. 5

8. Which sentence should come **second** in the sequence?

A. 1 B. 2
C. 3 D. 4
E. 5

9. Which sentence should come **first** in the sequence?
A. 1 B. 2
C. 3 D. 4
E. 5

10. Which sentence should come **fifth** in the sequence?
A. 1 B. 2
C. 3 D. 4
E. 5

SET-3

1. I reached office at 11 o'clock after sending the money.
2. Some money had to be sent to my parents.
3. After that, I spent almost an hour at the Post Office.
4. Therefore, I went to the bank to withdraw some money.
5. However, I had no money with me.

11. Which statement should come **first** in the paragraph?
A. 1 B. 2
C. 3 D. 4
E. 5

12. Which statement should come **second** in the paragraph?
A. 1 B. 2
C. 3 D. 4
E. 5

13. Which statement should come **third** in the paragraph?
A. 1 B. 2
C. 3 D. 4
E. 5

14. Which statement should come **fourth** in the paragraph?
A. 1 B. 2
C. 3 D. 4
E. 5

15. Which statement should come **fifth** in the paragraph?
A. 1 B. 2
C. 3 D. 4
E. 5

SET-4

1. In fact, it prevents us from helping children to analyse conflict, to learn to cope with it and counter it.
2. Children have always known that there is conflict in the adult world.
3. However, the make-believe world that nineteenth century rationally imposed on childhood in Europe and which we impose in an institutionalised manner through our modern education system can hardly be described as related in this regard.
4. We may therefore conclude that conflict in an institutionalised manner is not a matter of faith in children's capacities, rather, it is a lack of faith in ourselves as adults.
5. Further, psychologists tell us and story tellers have always known that the child's desire to search for order and coherence gathers strength from the knowledge of conflict.

16. Which of the following should be the **last** sentence in the paragraph?
A. 1 B. 2
C. 3 D. 4
E. 5

17. Which of the following should be the **first** sentence in the paragraph?
A. 1 B. 2
C. 3 D. 4
E. 5

18. Which of the following should be the **fourth** sentence in the paragraph?
A. 1 B. 2
C. 3 D. 4
E. 5

19. Which of the following should be the **third** sentence in the paragraph?
A. 1 B. 2
C. 3 D. 4
E. 5

20. Which of the following should be the **second** sentence in the paragraph?
A. 1 B. 2
C. 3 D. 4
E. 5

SET-5

1. A case in point is the programme involving the Sardar Sarovar Dam which would displace about 2,00,000 people.
2. Critics decry the fact that a major development institution appears to absorb more capital than it distributes to borrowers.
3. For all its faults critics however, concede that the bank remains a relatively efficient instrument for distribution of development-aid money.
4. One of the key complaints focuses on this non-profit bank's recent "profitability".
5. Although the lives of millions of people around the globe have been improved by the bank's activities, it is now under fire.
6. The bank is also being blamed for large-scale involuntary resettlement to make way for dams and other constructions projects.

21. Which sentence should come **third** in the paragraph?

A. 2 B. 5
C. 1 D. 4
E. 6

22. Which sentence should come **fourth** in the paragraph?

A. 6 B. 3
C. 5 D. 2
E. 1

23. Which sentence should come **first** in the paragraph?

A. 4 B. 6
C. 3 D. 2
E. 5

24. Which sentence should come **second** in the paragraph?

A. 3 B. 1
C. 4 D. 6
E. 5

25. Which sentence should come **last** (*i.e.* **sixth**) in the paragraph?

A. 5 B. 4
C. 2 D. 1
E. 3

SET-6

1. Chandrakant was shocked when he realised that the leg had lost sensation.
2. When he tried to get up, he felt his left leg was very heavy.
3. He had to lie down hopelessly, till he saw a flashlight.
4. It was an odd night time and hence nobody heard his voice.
5. Due to sudden sprain Chandrakant fell down.
6. Nervous with this realisation, he called out for help.

26. Which of the following should be the **third** sentence?

A. 1 B. 2
C. 3 D. 4
E. 5

27. Which of the following should be the **sixth (last)** sentence?

A. 6 B. 5
C. 4 D. 3
E. 2

28. Which of the following should be the **first** sentence?

A. 1 B. 2
C. 3 D. 4
E. 5

29. Which of the following should be the **second** sentence?

A. 1 B. 2
C. 3 D. 4
E. 5

30. Which of the following should be the **fourth** sentence?

A. 1 B. 2
C. 6 D. 4
E. 5

SET-7

1. The history of mankind is full of such fightings between communities, nation and people.
2. From the primitive weapons of warfare, man has advanced to the modern nuclear weapons.

3. Ever since the dawn of civilisation man has been fighting with man.
4. A modern war is scientific in character, but the effect is the same wiping human existence out of this earth.
5. The only difference now seems to be in the efficiency of the instruments used for killing each other.

31. Which of the following should be the **fifth (last)** sentence?
A. 1 B. 2
C. 3 D. 4
E. 5

32. Which of the following should be the **fourth** sentence?
A. 1 B. 2
C. 3 D. 4
E. 5

33. Which of the following should be the **first** sentence?
A. 1 B. 2
C. 3 D. 4
E. 5

34. Which of the following should be the **second** sentence?
A. 1 B. 2
C. 3 D. 4
E. 5

35. Which of the following should be the **third** sentence?
A. 1 B. 2
C. 3 D. 4
E. 5

SET-8

1. Its current was very powerful and could take away big tree trunks.
2. There were some children, playing on the bank of the waterway.
3. In the forest of Madhubani, there is a big lake.
4. The excess water started flowing forcefully through the waterway.
5. Once there was a very heavy rain because of which the lake started overflowing.
6. A poor man noticed it and rushed to save them.

36. Which of the following should be the **first** sentence?
A. 6 B. 5
C. 4 D. 3
E. 2

37. Which of the following should be the **third** sentence?
A. 6 B. 5
C. 4 D. 3
E. 2

38. Which of the following should be the **sixth (last)** sentence?
A. 6 B. 5
C. 4 D. 3
E. 2

39. Which of the following should be the **fourth** sentence?
A. 5 B. 4
C. 3 D. 2
E. 1

40. Which of the following should be the **second** sentence?
A. 6 B. 5
C. 4 D. 3
E. 2

SET-9

1. The means and methods they employ to deal with public pressures are also different.
2. They will make no move unless the gallery is packed.
3. The poorest are over-hesitant, evasive and preoccupied with their relationships with others.
4. Enormous difference is generally observed in the ways in which various public officials respond to public pressures.
5. The best possess understanding of the forces that must be taken into account, determination not to be swerved from the path of public interest.
6. They confront all embarrasments with a stale general formula.

41. Which of the following should be the **third** sentence?

A. 1 B. 2
C. 3 D. 4
E. 5

42. Which of the following should be the **sixth (last)** sentence?

A. 2 B. 3
C. 4 D. 5
E. 6

43. Which of the following should be the **first** sentence?

A. 6 B. 5
C. 4 D. 3
E. 2

44. Which of the following should be the **second** sentence?

A. 1 B. 2
C. 3 D. 4
E. 5

45. Which of the following should be the **fourth** sentence?

A. 2 B. 3
C. 4 D. 5
E. 6

SET-10

1. A taxi was summoned and Venu was taken to Lifeline Hospital.
2. While hurrying home from school.
3. Since they did not succeed, they decided to take him to a hospital.
4. When Venu opened his eyes, he found himself surrounded by doctors and nurses.
5. Some people rushed towards him and tried to bring him to his senses.
6. He was thrown a couple of feet away and lost consciousness.

46. Which sentence should come **third** in the paragraph?

A. 6 B. 2
C. 5 D. 1
E. 4

47. Which sentence should come **fourth** in the paragraph?

A. 3 B. 5
C. 6 D. 2
E. 1

48. Which sentence should come **first** in the paragraph?

A. 4 B. 6
C. 2 D. 5
E. 3

49. Which sentence should come **last** (*i.e.*, **sixth**) in the paragraph?

A. 2 B. 3
C. 1 D. 4
E. 5

50. Which sentence should come **second** in the paragraph?

A. 5 B. 1
C. 4 D. 3
E. 6

Directions (Qs. 51 to 65): *In each question rearrange the given sentences in the proper sequence to form a meaningful paragraph; then mark the correct sequence as the answer.*

51. 1. Now under liberated economy they are learning to compete domestically and globally.
2. In India corporations until recently achieved success by avoiding competition, using protected and regulated domestic markets.
3. The trend is irreversible
4. Business leaders are preparing themselves to meet competitive challenges and to avoid being swept away.

A. 1 2 4 3 B. 2 4 3 1
C. 2 4 1 3 D. 3 4 2 1
E. 2 1 4 3

52. 1. Such a system will help identify and groom executives for positions of strategists.
2. Evaluation of performance is more often than not done for the purpose of reward or punishment for past performance.
3. They must become an integral part of the executive evaluation system.

4. Even where the evaluation system is for one's promotion to assume higher responsibilities, it rarely includes items that are a key for playing the role of strategists effectively; e.g. the skills for playing the role of change agent and creative problem solving.

A. 4 2 1 3 B. 4 3 2 1
C. 1 2 3 4 D. 2 4 3 1
E. 3 4 2 1

53. 1. However, different rulers and governments dealt with the different groups in a compartmentalised manner.
2. Various situational and political changes have taken place over the past three and half centuries.
3. This tendency resulted in deeply embedded fragmented South African society which became even more prominent in the period 1948 until the commencement of the new Constitution on May 10, 1994.
4. South Africa is a racially divided society since the first European settlers arrived in 1652.

A. 2 4 1 3 B. 4 2 1 3
C. 3 1 2 4 D. 1 3 4 2
E. 2 1 3 4

54. 1. Recovery was given inadequate attention and consequently some bank branches regularly incurred heavy losses and their parent bodies had to bale them out.
2. As a result, banks indulged in extensive lending to borrowers who had little or no potential to make repayments.
3. To fulfil the social objectives laid down by the masters of nationalisation, banks were asked to lend to indentified priority sectors.
4. 1992-93 results showed that the loss making branches of public sector banks increased from 10,000 to 13,000 and the quantum of losses showed at Rs. 3,369 crores.

A. 2 1 3 4 B. 4 1 2 3
C. 3 2 1 4 D. 2 3 1 4
E. 3 4 2 1

55. 1. Much of the argument that goes on around the alternative solution occurs because people hold different perceptions of the problem.
2. One of the reasons that Japanese Managers are perceived as making superior decisions compared to Western Managers is that they spend a great deal of effort and time determining that the problem is correctly defined.
3. Unfortunately, too often in the West, Managers assume that the initial definition of the situation is correct.
4. Up to half the time in meetings is spent in asking "Is this the real problem?"

A. 2 4 3 1 B. 2 3 4 1
C. 3 2 4 1 D. 1 3 4 2
E. 1 2 3 4

56. 1. Participation involves more than the formal sharing of decisions.
2. Through anticipation, individuals or organisations consider trends and make plans, shielding institutions from trauma of learning by shock.
3. Innovative learning involves both anticipation and participation.
4. It is an attitude characterised by cooperation, dialogue and empathy.

A. 2 3 1 4 B. 1 2 4 3
C. 4 1 3 2 D. 3 2 1 4
E. 1 3 2 4

57. 1. This feeling of an extensive group gives rise to a fellow feeling, a feeling of brotherhood among the citizens.
2. This feeling takes us beyond the bounds of family, caste, religion and region and helps us develop a broad perspective that we all of us together constitute an extensive group called the nation.
3. National integration is the feeling among all the citizens of a country that they are all a part of one nation.
4. We do not then limit our thinking to our own caste or religion but think about all our fellow citizens.

A. 3 4 1 2 B. 3 1 2 4
C. 3 4 2 1 D. 3 2 4 1
E. 3 2 1 4

58. 1. The facts speak for themselves so they need exposition only, not demonstration.
2. At the present moment, it is widely recognised that India holds the balance in the worldwise competition between rival ideologies.
3. It is not, of course, only in geographical sense that India is in a key position.
4. India's key position simply needs pointing out.

A. 4 1 3 2 B. 3 4 1 2
C. 2 3 4 1 D. 2 4 1 3
E. 4 1 2 3

59. 1. But categorisation schemes are not always helpful in determining what one can do with or about organisational culture.
2. Much of the literature on organisational culture is focused on categorising types of cultures.
3. It has taken the understanding of corporate culture far beyond what used to be called 'the informal organisation'.
4. This literature is both interesting and informative.

A. 2 4 1 3 B. 2 1 4 3
C. 2 3 4 1 D. 4 1 2 3
E. 4 2 1 3

60. 1. Finally the bureaucratic organisation took over from the pioneering enterprise.
2. The nineteenth century was the age of entrepreneur, the self-made man.
3. Thoughtful business administration took over from action-centred business entrepreneurship.
4. In the twentieth century the rational executive took command.

A. 4 2 1 3 B. 3 1 2 4
C. 2 4 3 1 D. 2 3 4 1
E. 4 2 1 3

61. 1. It also gives rise to a feeling of animosity among the different sections of society.
2. In a democratic system, frequent use of power is never desirable, it on the part of government or the people.
3. Therefore, citizens should never resort to violent ways and means in democracy, though they have the right to oppose the government.
4. It destroys the stability and security in public life.

A. 4 2 1 3 B. 2 4 1 3
C. 2 4 3 1 D. 4 1 3 2
E. 4 3 2 1

62. 1. The Puritans went much farther; during the commonwealth they actually abolished all the festivals, including even Christmas.
2. They lost many of their maypoles; but there were ugly scenes when the magistrate's man tramped into Church to pull down the Christmas holly.
3. Leisure began to diminish at about the time of the Reformation.
4. That was more than the people of England would endure.
5. The leaders of the Church approved the festivals decently kept, with many sports, and with dancing in the Churchyard after Evensong; but they drastically reduced the old calendar — and with every saint omitted, a holiday vanished as well.

A. 5 3 1 4 2 B. 1 5 3 2 4
C. 5 1 2 4 3 D. 3 5 1 4 2
E. 2 1 5 3 4

63. 1. He was so busy with them that he did not get time to eat.
2. Thousands of people came to him and asked different types of questions.
3. No one cared to see that he had his food or rest that night.
4. Swami Vivekanand once stayed in a small village.

A. 2 3 4 1 B. 3 2 1 4
C. 4 2 1 3 D. 4 2 3 1
E. 1 2 3 4

64. 1. Learn a kind of tenderness towards the vanity of others.
2. And indeed towards all their prejudices.
3. Who make a cult of sincerity.

4. Men accustomed to difficult negotiations.
5. Which is infinitely shocking to these.

A. 4 3 5 1 2   B. 3 4 5 2 1
C. 4 1 2 5 3   D. 3 4 2 5 1
E. 4 3 5 2 1

65. 1. It buys programmes and services from many sources, which are then put on the system's channels
2. The early cable supermarkets had only a dozen channels on which to display their goods, but new systems boast more than 100 channels.
3. A cable system is like a supermarket.
4. By the end of the 1980s cable television will offer as many as 200 different channels of entertainment and services.
5. For a monthly fee, individual subscribers order the programmes and services that suit them.
6. Extra fees are charge for some programmes (including movies) brought in by satellite.
7. The cable system deliver all local television programming, television programming from nearby cities, and programming from distant networks whose signals are sent by satellite.

A. 2 3 1 4 7 6 5
B. 3 1 5 7 6 2 4
C. 1 2 3 4 5 6 7
D. 6 2 7 1 3 4 5
E. 7 1 2 4 3 6 5

ANSWERS

1	2	3	4	5	6	7	8	9	10
A	D	C	B	E	B	E	A	D	C
11	**12**	**13**	**14**	**15**	**16**	**17**	**18**	**19**	**20**
B	E	D	C	A	D	B	C	A	E
21	**22**	**23**	**24**	**25**	**26**	**27**	**28**	**29**	**30**
B	A	D	C	E	A	D	E	B	C
31	**32**	**33**	**34**	**35**	**36**	**37**	**38**	**39**	**40**
E	D	C	A	B	D	C	A	D	B
41	**42**	**43**	**44**	**45**	**46**	**47**	**48**	**49**	**50**
C	E	C	A	D	C	A	C	D	E
51	**52**	**53**	**54**	**55**	**56**	**57**	**58**	**59**	**60**
E	D	B	C	A	D	E	C	A	D
61	**62**	**63**	**64**	**65**					
B	D	C	C	B					

CHAPTER 9

Sentence Completion

Sentence completion is such an exercise which starts with the primary education and continues in the highest level of examinations. One must practise it regularly to score well.

SINGLE WORD

Dircections: *Pick out the most effective word from the given words to fill in the blank to make the sentence meaningfully complete.*

1. Leadership defines what the future should look like and ...... people with that vision.
A. aligns B. develops
C. trains D. encourages
E. transforms

2. We upset ourselves by responding in an ...... manner to someone else's actions.
A. unabashed B. irrational
C. arduous D. arguable
E. invalid

3. All the people involved in that issue feel a great ...... to his suggestion.
A. contradiction B. adherence
C. indifference D. objection
E. repugnance

4. These elections will be remembered as much for its anti-incumbency mood as for its ...... mandate.
A. invincible B. rational
C. unprecedented D. deliberate
E. pervasive

5. How do you expect us to stay in such a ...... building even if it can be hired on a nominal rent?
A. scruffy B. disparate
C. fragmented D. robust
E. damaging

6. ...... efforts from all concerned are required to raise the social and economic conditions of our countrymen.
A. Perpetual B. Dynamic
C. Massive D. Exploring
E. Penetrative

7. Many companies see technology as a ...... for a whole host of business problems.
A. consideration B. preference
C. linking D. panacea
E. craving

8. Known as devout and serious person, she also has ...... sense of humour.
A. better B. plentiful
C. quick D. beautiful
E. good

9. The matter would have become serious if ...... action had not been taken.
A. hasty B. fast
C. timely D. unusual
E. deliberate

10. The ...... with which he is able to yield the paint brush is really remarkable.
A. ease B. practice
C. majesty D. sweep
E. energy

11. The speaker did not properly use the time as he went on ...... on one point alone.
A. devoting B. deliberating
C. diluting D. distributing
E. dilating

12. They decided to ...... down their original plans for the bigger house and make it smaller.
A. climb B. turn
C. scale D. play
E. change

13. Usha was badly ...... by the news which she got in the letter.
A. electrified B. petrified
C. deranged D. shaken
E. frozen

14. In spite of her other ......, Kasthuri still managed to find time for her hobbies.
A. occupations B. preoccupations
C. predilections D. business
E. promises

15. Success comes to those who are vigilant not to permit ...... from the chosen path.
A. distraction B. deviation
C. alienation D. diversion
E. obstruction

16. It is advisable to ...... on this issue rather than create unnecessary problem by taking a rigid stand.
A. lose B. promise
C. evade D. compromise
E. forfeit

17. After a short holiday Rajini came back totally ......
A. rejuvenated B. reborn
C. refurbished D. revamped
E. restored

18. The victim tried to tell us what had happened but his ...... were not audible.
A. assailants B. sounds
C. letters D. proofs
E. words

19. The ...... between the twins is so slight that it is very difficult to identify one from the other.
A. similarity B. distance
C. resemblance D. difference
E. rift

20. The members were ...... of the date of the meeting well in advance.
A. communicated B. conveyed
C. ignorant D. informed
E. known

21. A ...... of ships was kept ready to scour the sea in case of an emergency.
A. group B. pack
C. unit D. fleet
E. battalion

22. I had not expected to meet him; it was quite an ...... meeting.
A. organised B. intentional
C. undesirable D. auspicious
E. accidental

23. The window of our room ...... the rear.
A. overlooks B. opens
C. opposes D. adjoins
E. precedes

24. I could ...... see the sight since it was dark.
A. clearly B. barely
C. obviously D. aptly
E. abruptly

25. The top-ranking manager ...... his success in the profession to his managing director's guidance.
A. account B. agrees
C. attributes D. claims
E. refers

26. Does your pride keep you ...... making the decision you know you should?
A. away B. alert
C. from D. quiet
E. intact

27. Their ...... to scale the mountain peak was an absolute failure.
A. attempt B. desire
C. anxiety D. proposal
E. dedication

28. The writer, like a spider ...... a web; the creatures caught in the web have no substance, no reality.
A. spins B. catches
C. writes D. compiles
E. finds

29. In a ...... move the chief minister today dropped two ministers from the cabinet.

A. secret B. delicate
C. continuous D. consistent
E. surprise

30. In his address to the teachers, the vice-chancellor ...... certain measures being taken for improving the quality of college education.
A. declined B. directed
C. advised D. highlighted
E. demanded

31. Change in the legal system are inevitable for we are not working for a ...... society.
A. backward B. dynamic
C. stagnant D. modern
E. ruthless

32. Modern science began ...... the influence of Copernicus, Kepler, Galileo and Newton.
A. by B. under
C. from D. upon
E. with

33. A meeting of senior police officers was held to ...... the law and order situation of the town.
A. review B. curb
C. cover D. support
E. criticise

34. The problems that India's economic development faces are ......
A. myopic B. dubious
C. enormous D. strong
E. morbid

35. In our zeal for progress we should not ...... the executive with more powers.
A. avoid B. arm
C. give D. enhance
E. improve

36. At present, all over the world, moral standards, ... to have fallen.
A. look B. wish
C. started D. appear
E. intend

37. He was one of the ...... spirits behind the successful agitation of the citizens for keeping the city clean.
A. revolving B. moving
C. evolving D. amazing
E. rising

38. The employees were unhappy because their salary was not increased ......
A. marginally B. abruptly
C. substantially D. superflously
E. negligibly

39. ...... the being a handicapped person, he is very co-operative and self-reliant.
A. Because B. Although
C. Since D. Basically
E. Despite

40. The child broke ...... from his mother and ran towards the painting.
A. away B. after
C. down D. with
E. heavily

41. With his ...... income, he finds it difficult to live a comfortable life.
A. brief B. sufficient
C. meagre D. huge
E. adequate

42. He could ...... a lot of money in such a short time by using his intelligence and working hard.
A. spend B. spoil
C. exchange D. accumulate
E. pay

43. Though the brothers are twins, they look ......
A. alike B. handsome
C. indifferent D. identical
E. different

44. Unfavourable weather conditions can ..... illness.
A. cure B. detect
C. treat D. enhance
E. diagnose

45. No sooner did the bell ring, ... the actor started singing.
A. when B. than
C. after D. before
E. through

46. If I ...... realised it, I would not have acted on his advice.
A. was B. had
C. were D. have
E. being

47. Why don't you ...... your work in advance before commencing it.
A. start B. complete
C. finish D. plan
E. execute

48. Contemporary economic development differs ...... from the Industrial Revolution of the 19th century.
A. usually B. specially
C. literally D. markedly
E. naturally

49. Mounting unemployment is the most serious and ...... problem faced by India today.
A. profound B. intractable
C. unpopular D. dubious
E. unattainable

50. Unemployment is not only ...... throughout the emerging world, but is growing worse, especially in urban areas.
A. endemic B. peripheral
C. absorbing D. prolific
E. endangering

TWO WORDS

Directions: *In each of the following sentences, there are two blank spaces. Below each sentence there are five pairs of words denoted by number (A), (B), (C), (D) and (E). Find out which word/pair of words can be filled up in the blanks in the sentence in the same sequence to make the sentence meaningfully complete.*

51. The WHO has ..... the government for taking prompt ..... action.
A. lauded, preventive
B. criticise, obligatory
C. blamed, ineffective
D. appreciated, hectic
E. admired, unreasonable

52. Though the hospital is extremely rich, the conditions there are ....
A. equally, rich
B. apallingly, poor
C. admirably, comfortable
D. extremely, conducive
E. frequently, tolerable

53. Nine members have ..... about the decision, but the tenth one views it ..... .
A. solution, critically
B. consensus, similarly
C. disagreement, collectively
D. grievance, grudgingly
E. agreement, differently

54. Vision is usually ..... most effectively when many different ..... are used.
A. developed, manifestations
B. adapted, organisations
C. communicated, vehicles
D. exhibited, forms
E. described, thought

55. People who have been through difficult, painful and not very ..... change efforts often end up ..... both pessimistic and angry conclusions.
A. successful, drawing
B. meaningful, projecting
C. reliable, evolving
D. strong, following
E. challenging, lamenting

56. If misery is the effect of ill-fortune, it ought to be pitied; if of ..... to be .....
A. virtue, criticised
B. calamity, reverenced
C. virtue, protected
D. vice, reverenced
E. virtue, reverenced

57. It is the ..... of selfishness for men, who fully ..... in their own case the great advantages of good education, to deny these advantages to women.
A. parody, demand B. height, appreciate
C. height, assimilate D. degree, appreciate
E. level, advance

58. His death ..... many tributes than have been paid at the ..... of any other human being in history.
A. brought, passing
B. directed, helm
C. delivered, description
D. invited, living
E. acknowledged, perpetuation

59. All the performances of human art, at which we look with praise or wonder, are ..... of the restless ..... of perserverence.
A. manifestations, pronouncement
B. projections, component
C. instances, force

D. proofs, humanity
E. visions, future

60. The issues could be ..... amicably only because of his ..... handling of the situation.
A. dropped, haphazard
B. raised, careful
C. discussed, enthusiastic
D. suppressed, emphatic
E. resolved, tactful

61. The only way to ensure best output from your vehicle is to provide it a ..... and ..... maintenance.
A. nurturing, expensive
B. proper, timely
C. careful, costly
D. trouble-free, everlasting
E. resolved, tactful

62. ..... your colleagues for important decision making activities ensures their ..... cooperation.
A. Counselling, wholehearted
B. Helping, occasional
C. Guiding, meagre
D. Neglecting, enthusiastic
E. Dominating, unstinted

63. The recent ..... in oil-prices has given an unexpected additional ..... to the cost-spiral.
A. slump, drawback
B. cut, blow
C. rise, twist
D. development, cut
E. deterioration, impetus

64. People ..... to work hard if you ..... certain conditions on them.
A. decide, negotiate
B. try, thrust
C. plan, invoke
D. hesitate, impose
E. volunteer, place

65. Our latest battle plan ..... some projects ..... at saving the earth's biological diversity.
A. destroys, stirring
B. covers, aimed
C. finances, looking
D. encompasses, looked
E. excludes, arriving

66. Unless the authorities adopt the principle ..... the strategies cannot become ..... .
A. wholeheartedly, successful
B. fully, defunct
C. mechanically, obsolete
D. legitimately, noteworthy
E. forcefully, trivial

67. Trying to ..... a team without a good and simple ..... system is like trying to drive a car without a steering wheel.
A. form, working
B. lead, exploratory
C. organise, empowering
D. run, guidance
E. achieve, developmental

68. ..... members of a group often ..... influence the outcome of a consensus forecast.
A. Permanent, exert
B. Majority, rightly
C. Vocal, legitimately
D. Minority, inadvertently
E. Dominant, unduly

69. Transforming ..... bureaucracies into dynamic, customer-driven organisations is ..... under any circumstances.
A. ideal, essential
B. lazy, undesirable
C. inefficient, challenging
D. civilized, ineffective
E. customer, unsurmountable

70. He was initially ..... at the suggestion but was soon ..... it himself.
A. frowning, rejecting
B. thrilled, propagating
C. shocked, advocating
D. impressed, negating
E. suspicious, trusting

71. The Minister felt that the ..... made by the Committee was ..... even though similar schemes had worked earlier.
A. election, acceptable
B. choice, profitable
C. decision, gainful
D. recommendation, infeasible
E. acceptance, approved

72. Nabeesa was not ..... by the criticism and paid no ..... even when her best friend talked against her.
A. threatened, warning
B. troubled, mind
C. deterred, heed
D. bothered, attention
E. shaken, indication

73. The activities of the association have ..... from the ..... objectives set for it in the initial years.
A. emerged, total B. deviated, original
C. grown, simple D. details, grand
E. increased, perverse

74. The ..... imposed for non-payment was too ..... for it to bring in improvement in collection.
A. penalty, low B. fine, severe
C. punishment, harsh D. toll, simple
E. damage, cruel

75. Although his first few attempts were ....., ultimately he ..... .
A. fruitful, won
B. futile, succeeded
C. laborious, gave up
D. appreciable, retarded
E. thwarted, lost

Directions: *In each question, an incomplete statement (Stem) followed by four fillers is given. Pick out the best one which can complete the incomplete stem correctly and meaningfully.*

76. He is so lazy that he .....
A. cannot depend on others for getting his work done.
B. cannot delay the schedule of completing the work.
C. can seldom complete his work on time.
D. dislike to postpone the work that he undertakes to do.
E. None of these

77. He always stammers in public meetings, but his today's speech .....
A. was fairly audible to everyone present in the hall.
B. was not received satisfactorily.
C. could not be understood properly.
D. was free from that defect.
E. None of these

78. In order to raise the company's profit, the employees .....
A. demanded two additional increments.
B. decided to go on paid holidays.
C. requested the management to implement new welfare schemes.
D. offered to work overtime without any compensation.
E. None of these

79. Although, he is reputed for making very candid statements, ...
A. his today's speech was not fairly audible.
B. his promises had always been realistic.
C. his speech was very interesting.
D. his today's statements were very ambiguous.
E. None of these

80. I felt somewhat more relaxed .....
A. but tense as compared to earlier.
B. and tense as compared to earlier.
C. as there was already no tension at all.
D. and tension-free as compared to earlier.
E. None of these

81. With great efforts his son succeeded in convincing him not to donate his entire wealth to an orphanage .....
A. and lead the life of a wealthy merchant.
B. but to a home for the forsaken children.
C. and make an orphan of himself.
D. as the orphange needed a lot of donations.
E. None of these

82. Even though it is a very large house, ...
A. there is a lot of space available in it for children.
B. there is hardly any space available for children.
C. there is no dearth of space for children.
D. the servants take a long time to clean it.
E. None of these

83. Practically, very little work could be completed in the last week as it was .....
A. full of working days.
B. a very hectic week.
C. full of holidays.
D. a very busy week.
E. None of these

84. He tames animals because he .....
A. is fond of them.
B. hates them.
C. is afraid of them
D. wants to set them free
E. None of these

85. He has no money now .....
A. although he was very poor once.
B. as he has given up all his wealth.
C. because he was very rich once.
D. because he has received huge donation.
E. None of these

86. The employer appeared to be in such an affable mood that Rohit .....
A. decided to ask for a raise in his salary.
B. was scared to talk to him about his leave.
C. felt very guilty for his inadvertent slip.
D. promised him that he would not commit mistake again.
E. None of these

87. Since people cannot learn through legitimate channels all that they are anxious to learn .....
A. they resort to ways and means without any ethical or moral considerations.
B. they join academics in order to quench their thirst for learning.
C. they adopt formal ways and means to achieve what they want to.
D. these social service organisations provide them the required input of knowledge.
E. None of these

88. It was an extremely pleasant surprise for the hutment-dweller when the Government officials told him that .....
A. he had to vacate hutment which he had been unauthorisedly occupying
B. he had been gifted with a furnished apartment in a multi-storeyed building.
C. he would be arrested for wrongfully encroaching on the pavement outside his dwelling.
D. they would not accede to his request.
E. None of these

89. Despite his best efforts to conceal his anger .....
A. we could detect that he was very happy.
B. he failed to give us an impression of his agony.
C. he succeeded in camouflaging his emotions.
D. people came to know that he was annoyed.
E. None of these

90. His appearance is unsmiling but .....
A. his heart is full of compassion for others.
B. he looks very serious on most occasions.
C. people are afraid of him.
D. he is uncompromising on matters of task performance.
E. None of these

91. The weather outside was extremely pleasant and hence we decided to .....
A. utilise our time in watching the television.
B. refrain from going out for a morning walk.
C. enjoy a morning ride in the open.
D. employ this rare opportunity for writing letters.
E. None of these

92. The officer who had neglected to file his income tax returns had to .....
A. return the files.
B. pay a fine.
C. be rewarded.
D. play mischief.
E. None of these

93. In order to help the company attain its goal of enhancing profit, all the employees .....
A. urged the management to grant paid leave.
B. appealed the management to implement new welfare schemes.
C. voluntarily offered to work overtime with lucrative compensation.
D. voluntarily offered to render additional services in lieu of nothing.
E. None of these

94. His behaviour is so unpredictable that he .....
A. never depends upon others for getting his work done.
B. is seldom trusted by others.
C. always finds it difficult to keep his word.
D. always insists on getting the work completed on time.
E. None of these

95. Since it is already midnight, we .....
A. had better leaving
B. ought to have leave
C. should take our leave
D. might as well as leave
E. None of these

96. It is not easy to remain tranquil when those around you .....
A. behave in a socially acceptable manner.
B. exhibit pleasant mannerism.
C. are losing their heads.
D. agree to whatever you say.
E. None of these

97. Although initial investigations pointed towards him, ...
A. the preceding events corroborated his involvement in the crime.
B. the additional information confirmed his guilt.

C. the subsequent events established that he was guilty.
D. the subsequent events proved that he was innocent.
E. None of these

98. Because he believes in democratic principles, he always .....
A. decides all the matters himself.
B. listens to others' views and enforces his own.
C. shown respect to others' opinions if they match his own.
D. reconciles with the majority's views and gives us his own.
E. None of these

99. Owing to the acute power shortage, the people of our locality have decided to .....
A. dispense with other non-conventional energy sources.
B. resort to abundant use of electricity for illumination.
C. off-switch the electrical appliance while not in use.
D. resort to use of electricity only when it is inevitable.
E. None of these

100. She never visits any zoo because she is a strong opponent of the idea of .....
A. setting the animals free into the forest.
B. feeding the animals while others are watching.
C. watching the animals in their natural abode.
D. holding the animals in captivity for our joy.
E. None of these

ANSWERS

1	2	3	4	5	6	7	8	9	10
A	A	E	C	A	A	D	E	C	A
11	**12**	**13**	**14**	**15**	**16**	**17**	**18**	**19**	**20**
E	C	D	B	A	D	A	E	D	D
21	**22**	**23**	**24**	**25**	**26**	**27**	**28**	**29**	**30**
D	E	A	B	C	C	A	A	E	D
31	**32**	**33**	**34**	**35**	**36**	**37**	**38**	**39**	**40**
C	B	A	C	B	D	B	C	E	A
41	**42**	**43**	**44**	**45**	**46**	**47**	**48**	**49**	**50**
C	D	E	D	B	B	D	D	B	A
51	**52**	**53**	**54**	**55**	**56**	**57**	**58**	**59**	**60**
A	B	E	A	B	C	C	A	C	E
61	**62**	**63**	**64**	**65**	**66**	**67**	**68**	**69**	**70**
B	A	C	D	B	A	A	E	C	C
71	**72**	**73**	**74**	**75**	**76**	**77**	**78**	**79**	**80**
D	C	B	A	B	C	D	D	D	D
81	**82**	**83**	**84**	**85**	**86**	**87**	**88**	**89**	**90**
C	B	C	A	B	C	A	B	D	A
91	**92**	**93**	**94**	**95**	**96**	**97**	**98**	**99**	**100**
C	B	D	B	D	C	D	D	D	D

CHAPTER 10

Idioms, Phrases and Proverbs

Directions (Qs. 1 to 20): *Some proverbs/idioms are given below together with their meanings. Choose the correct meaning of the proverb/idiom. If there is no correct meaning given, E i.e. 'None of these' will be the answer.*

1. To beg the question
- A. To refer to
- B. To take for granted
- C. To raise objections
- D. To be discussed
- E. None of these

2. To drive home
- A. To find one's roots
- B. To return to place of rest
- C. Back to original position
- D. To emphasise
- E. None of these

3. To hit the right nail on the head
- A. To do the right thing
- B. To destroy one's reputation
- C. To announce one's fixed views
- D. To teach someone a lesson
- E. None of these

4. To pick holes
- A. To find some reason to quarrel
- B. To destory something
- C. To criticise someone
- D. To cut some part of an item
- E. None of these

5. To smell a rat
- A. To see signs of plague epidemic
- B. To get bad smell of a dead rat
- C. To suspect foul dealings
- D. To be in a bad mood
- E. None of these

6. A black sheep
- A. An unlucky person
- B. A negro
- C. An ugly person
- D. A partner who takes no share of the profits
- E. None of these

7. To catch a tarter
- A. To trap wanted criminal with great difficulty
- B. To catch a dangerous person
- C. To meet with disaster
- D. To deal with a person who is more than one's watch
- E. None of these

8. To be above board
- A. To have a good height
- B. To be honest in any business deal
- C. To have no debts
- D. To try to be beautiful
- E. None of these

9. To keep one's temper
- A. To become angry
- B. To be in good mood
- C. To preserve one's energy
- D. To be aloof from
- E. None of these

10. To have an axe to grind
- A. A private end to serve
- B. To fail to arouse interest
- C. To have no result
- D. To work for both sides
- E. None of these

11. To cry wolf
A. to listen eagerly
B. to give false alarm
C. to turn pale
D. to keep off starvation
E. None of these

12. A man of straw
A. a man of no substance
B. a very active person
C. a worthy fellow
D. an unreasonable person
E. None of these

13. To make clean breast of
A. to gain prominence
B. to praise oneself
C. to confess without reserve
D. to destroy before it blooms
E. None of these

14. To end in smoke
A. to make completely understand
B. to ruin oneself
C. to excite great applause
D. to overcome someone
E. None of these

15. To leave someone in the lurch
A. to come to compromise with someone
B. constant source of annoyance to someone
C. to put someone at ease
D. to desert someone in his difficulties
E. None of these

16. To play second fiddle
A. To be happy, cheerful and healthy
B. To reduce importance of one's senior
C. To support the role and view of another person
D. To do back seat driving
E. None of these

17. To set one's face against
A. To oppose with determination
B. To judge by appearance
C. To get out of difficulty
D. To look at one steadily
E. None of these

18. To put one's hand to the plough
A. To take up agricultural farming
B. To take a difficult task
C. To get entangled into unnecessary things
D. Take interest in technical work
E. None of these

19. To join issue with
A. To cooperate with others for a cause
B. To join any voluntary organisation for good purpose
C. To resolve dispute and restore peace
D. To enter into argument over any issue
E. None of these

20. To do oneself justice
A. To dispense justice on our own
B. To treat others with due respect
C. To defend one's point of view
D. To follow the path of truth and justice
E. None of these

Directions (Qs. 21 to 150) *In following questions four alternatives are given for the idiom/phrase italicised in the sentence. Choose the alternative which best expresses the meaning of the idiom/phrase.*

21. How long will the people *put up with* the increasing economic hardships?
A. welcome
B. take easily
C. remain satisfied with
D. tolerate
E. None of these

22. Do not trust a man who *blows his own trumpet.*
A. flatters
B. praises others
C. admonishes others
D. praises himself
E. None of these

23. The dacoit murdered the man *in cold blood.*
A. coldly
B. boldly
C. ruthlessly
D. deliberately
E. None of these

24. My car *broke down* on way to the railway station.
A. stopped
B. met with an accident
C. ran out of petrol
D. failed to work
E. None of these

25. The time is running out, you must *look sharp.*
A. be careful B. make haste
C. be punctual D. be sensible
E. None of these

26. He visits the doctor *off and on.*
A. everyday B. regularly
C. never at all D. occasionally
E. None of these

27. The old father *brought home the moral of unity by asking each of his sons to break the bundle of sticks.*
A. emphasised B. voiced
C. declared D. suggested
E. None of these

28. He believes in the policy of *making hay while the sun shines.*
A. giving bribes to get his work done
B. seeking advice from one and all
C. helping those who help him
D. making the best use of a favourable situation
E. None of these

29. There is no *hard and fast rule* regarding this subject.
A. rule that is difficult
B. rule that is fast-changing
C. rule that cannot be broken or modified
D. rule that can be broken or modified
E. None of these

30. The University will have *to shelve* its plans for expansion in view of the present situation.
A. cancel B. discuss
C. reconsider D. postpone
E. None of these

31. He is an interesting speaker but tends to *go off at a tangent.*
A. change the subject suddenly
B. forget things in between
C. go on at great length
D. become boisterous
E. None of these

32. He has built a big business empire by his *sharp practices.*
A. extreme hard work
B. keen business skills
C. dishonest dealings
D. sharp intelligence
E. None of these

33. Despite the trust bestowed on the minister he turned out to be *a snake in the grass* during the revolution.
A. a secret enemy
B. a treacherous person
C. an unforeseen danger
D. an unexpected misfortune
E. None of these

34. The secretary and the treasurer are *hand in glove* with each other.
A. very good frineds
B. constantly fighting
C. associates in some action
D. suspicious of each other
E. None of these

35. Govind has left his country *for good.*
A. for better opportunities
B. on an important mission
C. forever
D. to return soon
E. None of these

36. He *went back on* his promise to vote for me.
A. withdrew B. forgot
C. reinforced D. supported
E. None of these

37. I met him after a long time, but he gave me *the cold shoulder.*
A. scolded me B. insulted me
C. abused me D. ignored me
E. None of these

38. The teacher warned the student *once for all* that no mischief shall be tolerated in the class.
A. authoritatively B. finally
C. angrily D. coldly
E. None of these

39. Why must you look a *gift horse in the mouth?*
A. welcome a gift
B. find fault with a gift
C. be fastidious
D. examine a gift carefully
E. None of these

40. Companies producing goods *play to the gallery* to boost their sales.
A. advertise
B. cater to the public taste
C. attempt to appeal to popular taste
D. depend upon the public for approval
E. None of these

41. The new C.M. *stuck his neck out* today and promised 10 kgs. free wheat a month for all rural families.
A. took an oath
B. took a risk
C. extended help
D. caused embarrassment
E. None of these

42. It was he who *put a spoke in my wheel.*
A. tried to cause an accident
B. helped in the execution of the plan
C. thwarted the execution of the plan
D. destroyed the plan
E. None of these

43. I did not mind what he was saying, he was only *talking through his hat.*
A. talking nonsense
B. talking ignorantly
C. talking irresponsibly
D. talking insultingly
E. None of these

44. In the organised society of today no individual or nation can *plough a lonely furrow.*
A. remain unaffected
B. do without the help of others
C. survive in isolation
D. remain non-aligned
E. None of these

45. The question of abolition of private property is still *a most point.*
A. undecided B. uncertain
C. unknown D. not clear
E. None of these

46. She was in a *brown study* and did not notice my entrance.
A. dream B. sleep
C. fear D. reverie
E. None of these

47. In spite of the immense pressure exerted by the militants, the Government has decided not to *give in.*
A. accede B. yield
C. oblige D. conform
E. None of these

48. While the ladies continued their *small talk* in the drawing room, I felt bored.
A. whispering
B. backbiting
C. gossip
D. light conversation
E. None of these

49. The old man was *cut to the quick* when his rich son refused to recognise him.
A. surprised B. hurt intensely
C. annoyed D. irritated
E. None of these

50. The party stalwarts have advised the President *to take it lying down for* a while.
A. to be cautious
B. to be on the defensive
C. to take rest
D. to show no reaction
E. None of these

51. There was opposition to the new policy by the *rank and file* of the Government.
A. the official machinery
B. the ordinary members
C. the majority
D. the Cabinet members
E. None of these

52. My father *strained every nerve* to enable me to get settled in life.
A. worked very hard
B. spent a huge-amount
C. tried all tricks
D. bribed several persons
E. None of these

53. He sold his house *for a song.*
A. at a reasonable price
B. at a discount
C. very cheaply
D. at a premium
E. None of these

54. He went to his friend's house in the evening *as was his wont.*
A. as usual
B. as he wanted
C. as his want was
D. as he wanted that day
E. None of these

55. As a politician he is used to being *in the limelight* all the time.
A. giving speeches
B. the object of admiration
C. the centre of attraction
D. an object of public notice
E. None of these

56. I am afraid he is burning *the candle at both ends* and ruining his life.
A. wasting his money
B. becoming overgenerous
C. overtaxing his energies
D. losing his objectives
E. None of these

57. This matter has been *hanging fire* for the last many months and must therefore be decided one way or the other.
A. going on slowly B. hotly debated
C. stuck up D. ignored
E. None of these

58. His speech *went down well with* the majority of the audience.
A. found acceptance with
B. was attentively listened to by
C. was appreciated by
D. was applauded by
E. None of these

59. I cannot get along with a man who *plays fast and loose.*
A. behaves in an unreliable and insincere way
B. has a loose tongue
C. lives a life of ease and luxury
D. does not know how to behave himself
E. None of these

60. The project did not appear to *hold out* bright prospects.
A. highlight B. show
C. offer D. promise
E. None of these

61. When he tells stories about himself, he is inclined to *draw the long bow.*
A. understate B. get emotional
C. exaggerate D. get excited
E. None of these

62. The arrival of the mother-in-law in the family *proved* a *rift in the lute.*
A. caused unnecessary worries
B. brought about disharmony
C. caused a pleasant atmosphere
D. brought about a disciplined atmosphere
E. None of these

63. The old beggar *ran amuck* and began to throw stones at the passersby.
A. became desperate B. ran about wildly
C. became annoyed D. felt disgusted
E. None of these

64. He was undecided. He *let the grass grow under his feet.*
A. loitered around B. stayed out
C. sat unmoving D. moved away
E. None of these

65. There is *no love lost* between the two neighbours.
A. close friendship
B. cool indifference
C. intense dislike
D. a love-hate relationship
E. None of these

66. The *die is cast* and now let us hope for the best.
A. project is over
B. decision is made
C. death is inevitable
D. cloth has been dyed
E. None of these

67. The class could not *keep a straight face* on hearing the strange pronunciation of the new teacher.
A. remain silent B. remain serious
C. remain mute D. remain disturbed
E. None of these

68. The prince did not *take after* the king.
A. run after B. follow
C. precede D. resemble
E. None of these

69. His plan was so complicated that it *floored* his listeners.

A. entertained B. puzzled
C. annoyed D. encouraged
E. None of these

70. The P.M. has *pulled up* Orissa partymen.

A. elevated B. rewarded
C. punished D. reprimanded
E. None of these

71. Turban is *in vogue* in some communities.

A. in fashion B. out of use
C. vaguely used D. never used
E. None of these

72. Don't lose patience, things will improve *by and by.*

A. soon B. finally
C. gradually D. unexpectedly
E. None of these

73. When he heard that he had once again not been selected he *lost heart.*

A. became desperate
B. felt sad
C. became angry
D. became discouraged
E. None of these

74. I felt *like a fish out of water* among all those business tycoons.

A. troubled B. stupid
C. uncomfortable D. inferior
E. None of these

75. His friends *let* him *down.*

A. failed B. comforted
C. succeeded D. stood by
E. None of these

76. The curious neighbours were disappointed as the young couple's quarrel was just a *storm in a tea cup.*

A. violent quarrel
B. fuss about a trifle
C. brittle situation
D. quarrel about tea cups
E. None of these

77. I requested him to *put in a word for* me.

A. introduce B. assist
C. support D. recommend
E. None of these

78. The rebels held out for about a month.

A. waited B. retreated
C. bargained D. resisted
E. None of these

79. The popularity of the yesteryears' superstar is *on the wane.*

A. at its peak B. at rock-bottom
C. growing more D. growing less
E. None of these

80. He is *out and out* a reactionary.

A. no more B. thoroughly
C. in favour of D. deadly against
E. None of these

81. The authorities *took him to task* for his negligence.

A. gave him additional work
B. suspended his assignment
C. reprimanded him
D. forced him to resign
E. None of these

82. I am sure they will fight *tooth and nail* for their rights.

A. with all their might
B. without any other weapon
C. resorting to violence
D. very cowardly
E. None of these

83. The detective *left no stone unturned* to trace the culprit.

A. took no pains
B. did very irrelevant things
C. resorted to illegitimate practices
D. used all available means
E. None of these

84. He resigned the post *of his own accord.*

A. which he liked
B. according to his convenience
C. voluntarily and willingly
D. according to his judgement
E. None of these

85. He *did me a good turn* by recommending me for the post of Vice-Principal.

A. returned my kindness
B. did an act of kindness
C. improved my prospects
D. became suddenly good
E. None of these

86. Harassed by repeated acts of injustice, he decided to *put his foot down*.
A. not to yield
B. resign
C. to accept the proposal unconditionally
D. withdraw
E. None of these

87. *He was in high spirits* when I met him in the restaurant.
A. He was in a drunken state
B. He was very cheerful
C. He talked incoherently
D. He was deeply engrossed in thoughts
E. None of these

88. Vikram said that he has got a problem to *square up* with the manager.
A. Consider
B. Discuss
C. Settle
D. Work out
E. None of these

89. His friends advised him to be *fair and square* in his dealings.
A. Careful
B. Considerate
C. Polite
D. Upright
E. None of these

90. Don't *thrust your nose into* my affairs.
A. Advise me about
B. Be in opposition
C. Deal with
D. Meddle officiously in
E. None of these

91. I felt that it was a *tall order* to expect Monisha to go home alone at twelve in the night.
A. Difficult
B. Too much
C. Customary
D. Simple
E. None of these

92. Rohit has *bitten off more than he can chew.*
A. Is trying to do too much
B. Is very greedy
C. Is always hungry
D. Has little regard for others
E. None of these

93. Jaya had a *chequered career* since I first knew him as an office assistant in the insurance company.
A. Had a variety of jobs and experiences
B. A career which helped him make lot of money
C. A career where he signed a lot of cheques
D. Did odd jobs
E. None of these

94. In his youth, he was practically *rolling in money.*
A. Spending more than his income
B. Borrowing money liberally
C. Very rich
D. Wasting a lot of money
E. None of these

95. You have to be *a cool customer* and be patient if you want to get the best buys.
A. Be calm and not be excitable
B. Have a cool head
C. Be uncommunicative
D. Be choosy
E. None of these

96. He never liked the idea of keeping his wife *under his thumb* and so he let her do what she liked.
A. Pressed down
B. Unduly under control
C. Below his thumb
D. Under tyrannical conditions
E. None of these

97. Mohan always *keeps himself to himself*
A. Is too busy
B. Is selfish
C. Is unsociable
D. Does not take sides
E. None of these

98. He *struck several bad patches* before he made good.
A. Came across bad soil
B. Had a bad time
C. Went through many illnesses
D. Had many professional difficulties
E. None of these

99. Do not imagine that Dharmendra is really sorry that his wife died. Those are only *crocodile tears.*
A. Pretended sorrow
B. Tears a crocodile
C. A weeping crocodile
D. Mild regret
E. None of these

100. Having sold off his factory, he is now *a gentleman at large.*
A. Has no serious occupation
B. Is living comfortably
C. Is respected by everybody
D. Is held in high esteem
E. None of these

101. There has been *bad blood* between the two communities even before the shooting.
A. Impure blood B. Ill feeling
C. Bloody fights D. Quarrels
E. None of these

102. Since he knew what would happen, he should be left to *stew in his own juice.*
A. Make a stew
B. Boil
C. Suffer in his own juice
D. Suffer for his own act
E. None of these

103. The parliamentary inquiry into the Bofors deal did not *bring to light* any startling facts.
A. Prove B. Probe
C. Highlight D. Disclose
E. None of these

104. Sanjay is *very diffident about* passing the Civil Services Examination this year.
A. Dead sure of
B. Very hopeful of
C. Lacking self-confidence about
D. Reasonably certain of
E. None of these

105. It is no longer easy to *strike gold* in Shakespeare's research since much work has already been done on him.
A. Hit a golden spot
B. Come across gold
C. Come across the word "gold"
D. Uncover or find a valuable line of argument or information
E. None of these

106. You cannot *have your cake and eat it too.*
A. Enjoy for ever
B. Have it both ways
C. Run away from responsibility
D. Absolve yourself of guilt
E. None of these

107. Sobhraj could be easily arrested because the police were *tipped off* in a advance.
A. Toppled over
B. Bribed
C. Given advance information
D. Threatened
E. None of these

108. Women should be paid the same as men when they do the same job, for, surely *what is sauce for the goose is sauce for the gander.*
A. What is thought suitable pay for a man should also be for a woman
B. Goose and gander eat the same sauce
C. Both goose and gander should be equally treated
D. The principle of equal treatment should be implemented
E. None of these

109. He *passed himself off* as a noble man.
A. Was regarded as
B. Pretended to be
C. Was thought to be
D. Was looked upon
E. None of these

110. Madhuri might *scream blue murder,* but I feel Deepali should get the promotion since she is better qualified for the job.
A. Someone has been murdered with some blue liquid
B. Someone is being murdered and has become blue
C. Suffer from persecution complex
D. Make a great deal of noise and object vehemently
E. None of these

111. In spite of the efforts of all peace loving people, world peace is still a *fry cry.*
- A. an impracticable idea
- B. an abstract ideal
- C. out of reach
- D. a long way off
- E. None of these

112. I hope it will not *put you out* if I am late.
- A. harm you
- B. irritate you
- C. please you
- D. worry out
- E. None of these

113. Some people now wonder whether we just *pay lip-service* or genuinely subscribe to democracy.
- A. pay oral tribute
- B. attach no value
- C. remain indifferent
- D. show only outward respect
- E. None of these

114. Pt. Nehru was *born with a silver spoon in his mouth.*
- A. born in a middle class family
- B. born in a wealthy family
- C. born in a royal family
- D. born in a family of nationalists
- E. None of these

115. Dowry is *a burning question* of the day.
- A. a widely debated issue
- B. a dying issue
- C. a relevant problem
- D. an irrelevant issue
- E. None of these

116. The cricket match proved to be a *big draw.*
- A. a keen contest
- B. a huge attraction
- C. a lovely spectacle
- D. a game without any result
- E. None of these

117. It is *high time* that India did something about the population problem.
- A. already late
- B. appropriate time
- C. desired occasion
- D. auspicious moment
- E. None of these

118. The new economic policy is likely to *run into rough weather.*
- A. create problems
- B. encounter difficulties
- C. confuse matters
- D. make things difficult
- E. None of these

119. The speaker gave *a bird's eye view* of the political conditions in the country.
- A. a personal view
- B. a general view
- C. a biased view
- D. a detailed presentation
- E. None of these

120. The sight of the accident made *my flesh creep*
- A. draw my attention
- B. confused me
- C. frightened me
- D. worried me
- E. None of these

121. We should *give a wide berth* to bad characters.
- A. give publicity to
- B. publicly condemn
- C. keep away from
- D. not sympathise with
- E. None of these

122. The thief *took to his heels* when he saw a policeman on the beat.
- A. had some pain in his heels
- B. ran away from the scene
- C. confronted the policeman
- D. could not decide what to do
- E. None of these

123. In the armed forces, it is considered a great privilege to *die in harness.*
- A. die on a horseback
- B. die in the battefield
- C. die while still working
- D. die with honour
- E. None of these

124. Though he has a lot of money, yet all his plans are *built upon sand.*
- A. established on insecure foundations
- B. based on inexperience
- C. resting on cheap material

D. resting on immature ideas

E. None of these

125. In modern democratic societies *lynch law* seems to have become a common feature in almost all the spheres of life.

A. law of the mob

B. law of the underworld

C. law of the constitution

D. law of the parliament

E. None of these

126. I *ran out of* money on my European tour.

A. exhausted my stock of

B. did not have enough

C. lost

D. carried a lot of

E. None of these

127. He is leaving the country *for a good*

A. for better prospects

B. for a good cause

C. for ever

D. for others' good

E. None of these

128. He is always *picking holes in every* project.

A. creating problems in

B. finding fault with

C. suggesting improvement in

D. asking irrelevant questions on

E. None of these

129. If you give John all your money, you are likely to *burn your fingers*.

A. be unhappy B. be happy

C. suffer D. be ill

E. None of these

130. The clerk *wiped the nose* of his employer by submitting a false bill and was dismissed from his job.

A. Cleaned the nose

B. Cheated

C. Abused

D. Slapped

E. None of these

131. Sanjay was the real *power behind the throne* and all politicians were aware of this.

A. The person who had the real control and power

B. The acknowledged leader

C. The person who controlled the monarch

D. The person who advised the queen

E. None of these

132. It is time that professors came down from their *ivory towers* and studied the real needs of the students.

A. Detachment and seclusion

B. A tower made of ivory

C. Prison

D. Dream lands

E. None of these

133. The case was *held over* due to the great opposition to it.

A. stopped B. postponed

C. dropped D. cancelled

E. None of these

134. Discipline is *on the wane* in schools and colleges these days.

A. declining B. increasing

C. spreading D. spiralling

E. None of these

135. The robber *took to his heels* when the police arrived

A. opened fire B. hid himself

C. ran off D. surrendered

E. None of these

136. The autographed bat from the famous cricketer Sunil Gavaskar is *worth a jew's eye.*

A. Not a worthy possession

B. Unnecessary

C. A costly items

D. A possession of high value

E. None of these

137. We were in hurry. The road being zigzag we had to *cut off a corner* to reach in time.

A. To cut a portion of the road

B. To take a short cut

C. To go fast

D. To take an alternative route

E. None of these

138. Although both the partners are running the show for the last ten years but their business is now *on its last legs.*
A. About to fructify
B. About to perish
C. About to produce results
D. About to take off
E. None of these

139. I *have a bone to pick* with you in this matter.
A. Am in agreement
B. Am angry
C. Am indebted
D. Will join hands
E. None of these

140. Leaders should not only make speeches; they should also be prepared to *bell the cat.*
A. To take lead in danger
B. To tie bell to a cat's neck
C. To be alert of the enemy
D. To make noise
E. None of these

141. He is in the habit of *throwing dust in* his superiors' *eyes.*
A. To put sand into eyes
B. To make blind
C. To deceive
D. To show false things
E. None of these

142. This regular absenteeism is *a bad business* since on work is being completed.
A. Bad for business
B. Unbusinesslike
C. An unfortunate event
D. Creating ill-will
E. None of these

143. He is always *standing up for* the weak and oppressed.
A. Boosting the claims of
B. Championing the cause of
C. Seeking help of others for
D. Moving about with
E. None of these

144. The recent film "Secular India" has tried *to keep the pot* of Muslim Women's Bill *boiling.*
A. Earning enough to keep body and soul together
B. Keep a controversy alive
C. Boil the Bill
D. Boil something in a pot
E. None of these

145. Why do you wish *to tread on their toes?*
A. To give offence to them
B. To follow them grudgingly
C. To treat them indifferently
D. To be kicked by them
E. None of these

146. The account of the murder *made her flesh creep.*
A. Made her sad
B. Surprised her
C. Made her cry bitterly
D. Filled her with horror
E. None of these

147. Their business is now *on its last legs.*
A. About to fructify
B. About to perish
C. About to produce results
D. About to take off
E. None of these

148. Although he has failed in the written examination, he is using *backstairs influence* to get the job.
A. Political influence
B. Backing influence
C. Deserving and proper influence
D. Secret and unfair influence
E. None of these

149. He intends *setting up* as a lawyer in the adjoining district.
A. To establish himself
B. To migrate
C. To join
D. To settle
E. None of these

150. I cannot *conceive* of a time when I was without a refrigerator.
A. Imagine
B. Give birth
C. Understand
D. Depend
E. None of these

ANSWERS

1	2	3	4	5	6	7	8	9	10
B	D	A	C	C	E	B	B	B	A
11	**12**	**13**	**14**	**15**	**16**	**17**	**18**	**19**	**20**
B	A	C	E	D	C	A	B	B	E
21	**22**	**23**	**24**	**25**	**26**	**27**	**28**	**29**	**30**
D	D	C	A	B	D	A	D	C	D
31	**32**	**33**	**34**	**35**	**36**	**37**	**38**	**39**	**40**
A	C	A	A	C	A	D	B	B	C
41	**42**	**43**	**44**	**45**	**46**	**47**	**48**	**49**	**50**
B	C	A	B	A	B	B	D	B	D
51	**52**	**53**	**54**	**55**	**56**	**57**	**58**	**59**	**60**
B	A	C	A	C	C	A	C	A	C
61	**62**	**63**	**64**	**65**	**66**	**67**	**68**	**69**	**70**
C	B	B	A	C	B	B	D	B	D
71	**72**	**73**	**74**	**75**	**76**	**77**	**78**	**79**	**80**
A	C	D	C	A	B	D	D	D	B
81	**82**	**83**	**84**	**85**	**86**	**87**	**88**	**89**	**90**
C	A	D	C	B	A	B	C	D	D
91	**92**	**93**	**94**	**95**	**96**	**97**	**98**	**99**	**100**
B	A	A	C	A	B	C	D	A	A
101	**102**	**103**	**104**	**105**	**106**	**107**	**108**	**109**	**110**
B	D	D	C	D	B	C	A	B	D
111	**112**	**113**	**114**	**115**	**116**	**117**	**118**	**119**	**120**
D	B	D	B	A	B	A	B	B	C
121	**122**	**123**	**124**	**125**	**126**	**127**	**128**	**129**	**130**
C	B	C	D	A	A	C	B	C	B
131	**132**	**133**	**134**	**135**	**136**	**137**	**138**	**139**	**140**
A	A	B	A	C	D	B	B	B	A
141	**142**	**143**	**144**	**145**	**146**	**147**	**148**	**149**	**150**
C	C	B	B	A	D	B	D	A	A

REASONING

1 Series

LETTER SERIES

In letter series, the letters follow a definite order. The given series of letters can be in natural order or in reverse order or combination of both. The letters may be skipped or repeated or consecutive. The given series may be single or may comprise two different series merged at alternate positions. While attempting questions on letter series one should note the pattern of alphabet series.

Alphabets in natural series

A B C D E F G H I J K L M N O P Q R S T U V W X Y Z
1st 5th 10th 15th 20th 25th

are:

Alphabets in reverse series

Z Y X W V U T S R Q P O N M L K J I H G F E D C B A
1st 5th 10th 15th 20th 25th

Note: On reaching Z, the series restarts from A and on reaching A, it restarts from Z.

Example

1. A Z B Y C ?

A. D B. X
C. U D. E
E. W

Ans.: (B) There are two alternate series.

Series I : A B C (Consecutive letters in natural series)

Series II : Z Y X (Consecutive letters in reverse series)

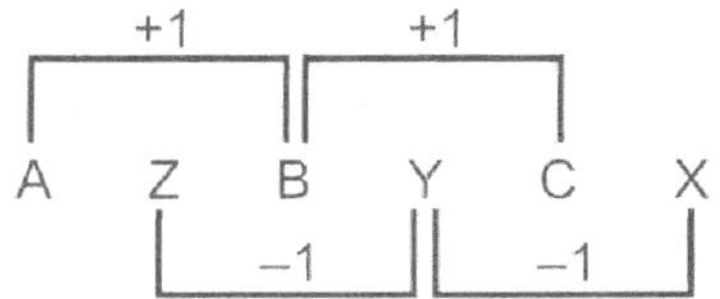

REPEAT SERIES

In this type of series small letters of the alphabet are used to make a set of letters which are repeated. The candidate has to find the set of letters which will fit the blanks left in the given series in such a manner that one section of the series is further repeated in the same manner.

Example

2. Which of the following groups of letters will complete the given series?

ba-b-aab-a-b

A. baab B. abba
C. abaa D. babb
E. aaab

Ans.: (B) The series is baab, baab, baab. Here the section 'baab' is repeated in the series. Solving steps : The candidate has to look for clues to solve such series pattern. 'aab' in the series indicates that 'b' in this series is preceded by two 'a' so, the first blank and the last blank will be filled by 'a'. Now the first set is formed, *i.e.*, 'baab' in the beginning. This set is repeated, so the second and third blanks will have 'b' filling them.

NUMBER SERIES

In this type of series, the set of given numbers in a series are related to one another in a particular pattern or manner. The relationship between the numbers may be (i) consecutive odd/even numbers; (ii) consecutive prime numbers; (iii) squares/cubes of some numbers with/without variation of addition or subtraction of some number; (iv) sum/product/ difference of preceding numbers; (v) addition/ subtraction/multiplication/division by some number; and (vi) many more combinations of the relationships given above.

Example

3. Complete the given series. 2, 14, 98, 686, ?
   A. 1976 B. 2548
   C. 980 D. 4802
   E. 890

Ans.: (D) The numbers are multiplied by 7 to obtain the next numbers.

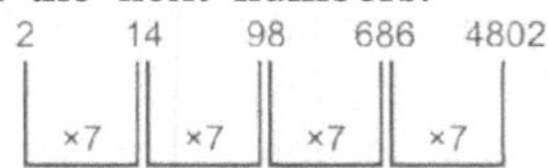

The given series may also comprise of two alternate series merged as one.

MIXED SERIES

Mixed series comprises of the combinations of letters and numbers. In this type of series, the letters and numbers may have a common sequence pattern or may have separate sequence patterns.

Example

4. What should come in the place of question mark in the following letter-number combination?

   F6, H8, J10, L12, ?

   A. N15 B. O14
   C. N14 D. O13
   E. N13

Ans.: (C) The letters are moved two steps forward and the number indicates the position of the letter in the alphabet series.

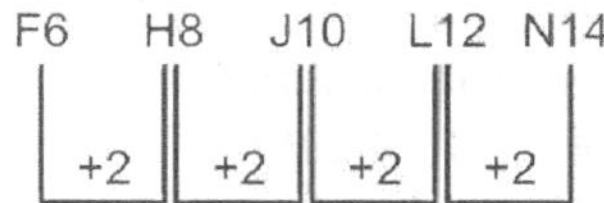

EXERCISE

Directions (Qs. No. 1 to 8): *In each of the following series determine the order of the letters. Then from the given options select the one which will complete the given series.*

1. GH, JL, NQ, SW, YD, ?
   A. EJ B. FJ
   C. EL D. FL
   E. EI
2. AI, BJ, CK, ?
   A. DL B. DM
   C. GH D. LM
   E. DE
3. b e d f ? h j ? l
   A. i m B. m i
   C. i n D. j m
   E. n i
4. ADVENTURE, DVENTURE, DVENTUR, ?, VENTU
   A. DVENT B. VENTURE
   C. VENTUR D. DVENTU
   E. None of these
5. PERPENDICULAR, ERPENDICULA, RPENDICUL, ?
   A. PENDICUL B. PENDIC
   C. ENDIC D. ENDICU
   E. None of these
6. ATTRIBUTION, TTRIBUTIO, RIBUTIO, IBUTI, ?
   A. IBU B. UT
   C. UTI D. BUT
   E. None of these
7. M, N, O, L, R, I, V, ?
   A. A B. E
   C. F D. H
   E. Z
8. A, CD, GHI, ?, UVWXY
   A. LMNO B. MNO
   C. MNOP D. NOPQ
   E. OPQR

Directions (Qs. No. 9 to 15): *Which letter(s) in each of the following series is wrong or is misfit in the series?*

9. Z A W B X C
   A. D B. C
   C. X D. W
   E. V

10. M L O N Q P T R
A. T B. O
C. Q D. L
E. U

11. D K R Y F L
A. L B. D
C. R D. Y
E. M

12. L N Q T W Z C F
A. C B. Q
C. L D. F
E. I

13. XW, DC, CB, NM, PQ, QP
A. NM B. CB
C. PQ D. XW
E. NO

14. B E I N S A I
A. A B. E
C. S D. I
E. O

15. Z T P K H F
A. Z B. P
C. T D. F
E. D

Directions (Qs. No. 16 to 20): *In each of the following letter series, some of the letters are missing which are given in that order as one of the alternatives below it. Choose the correct alternative.*

16. ba _ cb _ b _ bab _
A. acbb B. bacc
C. bcaa D. cabb
E. abcc

17. c _ bba _ cab _ ac _ ab _ ac
A. abebe B. acbcb
C. babec D. bcacb
E. babce

18. ab _ _ baa _ _ ab _
A. aaaaa B. aabaa
C. aabab D. baabb
E. abaaa

19. _ bc _ ca _ aba _ c _ ca
A. abcbb B. bbbec
C. bacba D. abbec
E. abcba

20. ab _ aa _ bbb _ aaa _ bbba
A. abba B. baab
C. aaab D. abab
E. baba

Directions (Qs. No. 21 to 25): *Choose the correct alternative that will continue the same pattern and replace the question mark in the given series.*

21. 3, 9, 27, 81, 243, ?
A. 486 B. 729
C. 972 D. 359
E. 739

22. 1, 6, 12, 19, 27 ?
A. 38 B. 35
C. 36 D. 54
E. 57

23. 125, 80, 45, 20, ?
A. 5 B. 8
C. 10 D. 12
E. 14

24. 120, 99, 80, 63, 48, ?
A. 35 B. 38
C. 39 D. 40
E. 42

25. 589654237, 89654237, 8965423, 965423, ?
A. 58965 B. 65423
C. 89654 D. 96542
E. 69452

Directions (Qs. No. 26–33): *In each series given below, what would come in place of the question-mark?*

26. 2B, 4C, 8E, 14H, ?
A. 20L B. 22L
C. 21I D. 16K
E. 19L

27. C(1)L, F(4)O, I(9)R, L(16)U, ?
A. P(27)W B. N(24)Y
C. M(23)X D. O(25)X
E. P(26)Y

28. 3F, 6G, 11I, 18L, ?
A. 27P B. 21O
C. 27Q D. 25N
E. 24P

29. W(1)A, X(4)Z, Y9Y, ?, A(25)W
A. X(11)Z B. Z(21)A
C. Z(16)X D. Z(14)X
E. Z(12)A

30. 81Y, 27S, 9N, 3J, ?
A. 0H B. IG
C. 0F D. IE
E. 1H

31. E5, K11, Q17, ?
A. X20 B. Y24
C. V22 D. W25
E. X23

32. D2, I3, N6, S18, ?
A. V72 B. W36
C. Y90 D. X108
E. U80

33. 3J, 6M, 12L, ?, 48N
A. 24O B. 8M
C. 26M D. 22O
E. 16N

Directions (Qs. No. 34 and 35) : *Which of the following does not fit in the letter number series given below?*

34. G4T, J10R, M20P, P43N, S90L
A. J10R B. S90L
C. M20P D. G4T
E. U30X

35. B0R, G3U, E3P, J7S, H9N
A. E3P B. J7S
C. H9N D. G3U
E. M4T

ANSWERS

1	2	3	4	5	6	7	8	9	10
D	A	A	C	E	C	B	C	D	A
11	**12**	**13**	**14**	**15**	**16**	**17**	**18**	**19**	**20**
A	C	C	C	B	B	B	B	A	B
21	**22**	**23**	**24**	**25**	**26**	**27**	**28**	**29**	**30**
B	C	A	A	D	B	D	A	C	B
31	**32**	**33**	**34**	**35**					
C	D	A	A	B					

EXPLANATORY ANSWERS

1. 1st letter:

G $\xrightarrow{+3}$ J $\xrightarrow{+4}$ N $\xrightarrow{+5}$ S $\xrightarrow{+6}$ Y $\xrightarrow{+7}$ (F)

2nd letter:

H $\xrightarrow{+4}$ L $\xrightarrow{+5}$ Q $\xrightarrow{+6}$ W $\xrightarrow{+7}$ D $\xrightarrow{+8}$ (L)

2. 1st letter: A $\xrightarrow{+1}$ B $\xrightarrow{+1}$ C $\xrightarrow{+1}$ (D)

2nd letter: I $\xrightarrow{+1}$ J $\xrightarrow{+1}$ K $\xrightarrow{+1}$ (L)

3. The series may be divided into groups as shown: b e d / f ? h / j ? l
Clearly in the first group, the second and third letters are respectively three and two steps ahead of the first letter. A similar pattern would follow in the second and third groups.

4. One letter from the beginning and one from the end of a term are removed, one by one, in alternate steps.

5. Each term of the series is obtained by removing two letters from the preceding term one from the beginning and one from the end. So, the missing term is PENDICU.

6. In the first step, one letter from the beginning and one from the end of a term are removed to give the next term. In the second step, two letters from the beginning of a term are removed. These two steps are repeated alternately.

7. The given sequence is a combination of two series: I. M, O, R, V and II. N, L, I, ?

The pattern in I is: M $\xrightarrow{+2}$ O $\xrightarrow{+3}$ R $\xrightarrow{+4}$ V

The pattern in II is: N $\xrightarrow{-2}$ L $\xrightarrow{-3}$ I $\xrightarrow{-4}$ (E)

8. Each term consists of consecutive letters in order. The number of letters in the terms goes on increasing by one at each step. Also, there is a gap of one letter between the last letter of the first term and the first letter of the second term; a gap of two letters between the last letter of the second term and the first letter of the third term; and so on. So, there should be a gap of three letters between the last letter of the third term and the first letter of the desired term.

9. There are two alternate series I. Z, Y, X and II. A, B, C

The pattern in I is : Z $\xrightarrow{-1}$ (Y) $\xrightarrow{-1}$ X

The pattern in II is : A $\xrightarrow{+1}$ B $\xrightarrow{+1}$ C

10. Two consecutive letters are written backwards.

ML ON OP SR
← ← ← ←

S should be in place of T.

11. The pattern in this series is moving the letters seven steps forward.

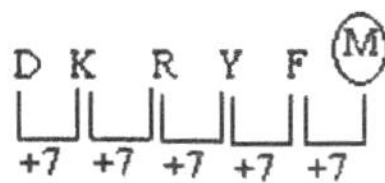

M should be in place of L.

12. The pattern in the series is +3

(K) N Q T W Z C F
+3 +3 +3 +3 +3 +3 +3

K should be in place of L.

13. The series is made with any two consecutive letters written backwards.

XW DC CB NM QP
← ← ← ← ←

Q should come before P in the series.

14. The difference between the letters is increased by one at each step.

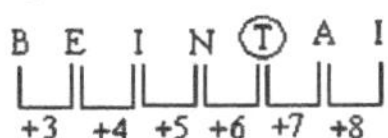

T should be in place of S.

15. The difference between the letters is decreased by one at each step.

Z T O K H F
-6 -5 -4 -3 -2

O should be in place of P.

16. The series is babc/babc/babc. Thus, the pattern 'babc' is repeated.

17. The series is cabbac/cabbac/cabbac. Thus, the pattern 'cabbac' is repeated.

18. The series is aba/aba/aba/aba. Thus, the pattern 'aba' is repeated.

19. The series is abc/bca/cab/abc/bca. Thus, the letters change places in a cyclic order.

20. The series is abb/aaabbb/aaaabbbb/a. Thus, the letters are repeated twice, then thrice, then four times and so on.

21. The numbers in the series are multiplied by 3 to get the next numbers.

22. The difference between the numbers in the series increases by 1, after beginning from 5,

i.e., 1 6 12 19 27 36
+5 +6 +7 +8 +9

23. The pattern is –45, –35, –25, ...
So, missing term = 20 – 15 = 5.

24. The pattern is –21, –19, –17, –15,.....
So, missing term = 48 – 13 = 35.

25. The digits are removed one-by-one from the beginning and the end in order alternately, so as to obtain the subsequent terms of the series.

26. The sequence of numbers is +2, +4, +6, +8 and sequence of letters is +1, +2, +3, +4.

27. The corresponding letters are moved 3 steps forward and the sequence of numbers is +3, +5, +7, +9.

28. The sequence of numbers is +3, +5, +7, +9 and the letters are moved 1, 2, 3, 4 steps forward.

29. The letters on the left are in reverse series, the letters on the right are in natural series, and the numbers are squares of numbers in natural order starting from 1.

30. The numbers are divided by 3 at each step and the letters are moved 6, 5, 4, 3 steps backward.

31. The series comprises of random letters and numbers indicate the position of the letter in alphabet series.

32. The letters are moved five steps forward and every third number is the product of two preceding numbers.

33. Every number is double the previous number and the sequence of letters is +3, –1 (3 steps forward, 1 step backward) which is repeated.

34. The letters on the left are moved 3 steps forward, the letters on the right are moved 2 steps backward and the sequence of numbers is $(4 \times 2) +1$, $(9 \times 2) +2$, $(20 \times 2) +3$, $(43 \times 2) +4$. So, J9R should be in place of J10R.

35. The sequence of letters on the left is +5, –2 (5 steps forward, 2 steps backward) which is repeated, the sequence of letters on the right is +3, –5 (3 steps forward, 5 steps backward) which is repeated, and the numbers are the sum of two preceeding numbers. So, J6S should be in place of J7S.

2 Coding-Decoding

Coding is a secretive language which is used to change the representation of the actual term/word/value. This coded language can be framed by

(*i*) moving the letters one or more steps forward or backward;
(*ii*) substituting numbers for letters and vice-versa;
(*iii*) writing the letters of the given word in reverse order in part or in whole; and
(*iv*) replacing the letters in their natural series by the same positioned letters in their reverse series.

Alphabet in natural series are :

A B C D E F G H I J K L M N O P Q R S T U V W X Y Z
1st 5th 10th 15th 20th 25th

Alphabet in reverse series are :

Z Y X W V U T S R Q P O N M L K J I H G F E D C B A
1st 5th 10th 15th 20th 25th

Note : On reaching Z, the series restarts from A and on reaching A, it restarts from Z

Example

1. If FACE is coded as GBDF, then BADE will be coded as :

A. CBEF B. CEBF
C. CFBE D. CBFE
E. CFB

Ans.: (A) The word is coded by moving the letters one step forward

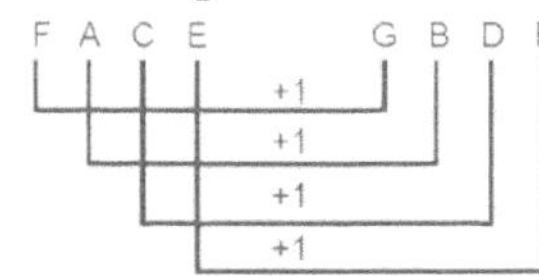

Similarly,

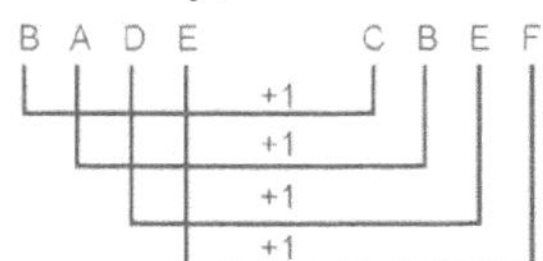

2. In a certain code 'ra mei ket' means 'he is rich'; 'rui pha jeu' means 'run for money'; and 'pha rui ket' means 'money for rich'. Which of the following is the code for 'rich'?

A. ra B. pha
C. ket D. jeu
E. for

Ans.: (C) The given information is :

Code	***Sentence***
1. ra mei ket	he is rich
2. rui pha jeu	run for money
3. pha rui ket	money for rich

After comparing codes and sentences 1 and 3, it is clear that word 'rich' is common and so is the code 'ket'.

3. If 'banana' is called 'jelly', 'jelly' is called 'green', 'green' is called 'apple'. 'apple' is called 'mango', what is the colour of leaf?

A. green B. mango
C. apple D. banana
E. jelly

Ans.: (C) Leaf is green in colour and according to the codes in the question 'green' is called 'apple'.

In another form of coding, the Digits and its coded Letters or vice versa are already given. One has to find out the answers to the given questions just by tallying the given codes.

EXERCISE

Directions (Qs. No. 1 to 8): *In the following questions select the right option which indicates the correct code for the word or letter given in the question.*

1. If PHILOSOPHY is coded as HPLISOPOYH, ornamental will be coded as :
A. ROANEMNTLA B. ONRAMNEALT
C. ROANEMTNLA D. ROANEMNATL
E. RAONMENATL

2. If OPFGBCST stands for NEAR, in the same manner IJVWHI will stand for :
A. HAG B. HUG
C. HUT D. KEG
E. GUH

3. If m is coded as g, g as o, a as *i* and *i* as y, then 'imagination' will be written as :
A. ygagynatyin B. ygioynityog
C. ygioynityon D. ygioyintyon
E. ygoiyintoyn

4. If OUT is coded as 152120, IN will be coded as :
A. 1015 B. 819
C. 1813 D. 914
E. 919

5. If BAD is coded as 7. HIS as 9, LOW will be coded as :
A. 50 B. 8
C. 23 D. 5
E. 25

6. In a certain code ABCD is written as 2468 and EFGH as 1357. How will CAGE be written in that code?
A. 6453 B. 6251
C. 6521 D. 6215
E. 6312

7. If HARD is coded as 1357 and SOFT as 2468, what will 21448 stand for?
A. SHAFT B. SHORT
C. SHOOT D. SHART
E. SHAAT

8. If FACE is coded as 6135, BIG as 297, HAD as 814 and BADGE as 21475, then what is the code for 'A'?
A. 3 B. 1
C. 2 D. 4
E. 5

Directions (Qs. No. 9 to 13): *In the following questions study the coded patterns and then select the right option from the given alternatives.*

9. In a certain language, A. 'FOR' stands for 'old is gold'; B. 'ROT' stands for 'gold is pure'; C. 'ROM' stands for 'gold is costly'. How will 'pure old gold is costly' be written?
A. TFROM B. FOTRM
C. FTORM D. TOMRF
E. OTFMR

10. In a certain code '643' means 'she is beautiful', '593' means 'he is handsome', and '567' means 'handsome meets beautiful'. What number will indicate the word 'meets'?
A. 5 B. 3
C. 7 D. 6
E. 4

11. In a certain code language, A. 'pic vic nic' stands for 'winter is cold'; B. 'to nic re' for 'summer is hot'; C. 're pic boo' for 'winter and summer' and D. 'vic tho pa' for nights are cold'. Which of the following word is the code for 'summer'?
A. nic B. boo
C. to D. re
E. vic

12. In a certain language 'mu mit es' means 'who is she' and 'elb mu es' means 'where is she'. What is the code for 'where' in this language?
A. es B. elb
C. mu D. mit
E. el

13. In a certain code language 'roi ja kyo twa' means ' Moody is writing letters', 'pok ju ja twa' means 'Woody is writing cards', 'trn kyo pos un' means 'they are writing letters', and 'koi rus pok' means 'gifts and cards'. What is the code word for 'Moody'?

A. ja
B. twa
C. roi
D. kyo
E. trn

Directions (Qs. No. 14 to 18): *Read the given coded information and choose the correct answer from the given options.*

14. If 'red' is called 'air', 'air' is called 'black', 'black' is called 'sky', 'sky' is called 'blue', 'blue' is called 'wind' and 'wind' is called 'white', where to birds fly?

A. air
B. sky
C. blue
D. wind
E. black

15. If 'green' is called 'pink', 'pink' is called 'blue', 'blue' is called 'purple', 'purple' is called 'white', 'white' is called 'orange' and 'orange' is called 'peach', what is the colour of snow?

A. peach
B. orange
C. purple
D. blue
E. white

16. If 'colour' is called 'blue', 'blue' is called 'light', 'light' is called 'showy', 'showy' is called 'dark' and 'dark' is called 'colour', what is the colour of ink?

A. blue
B. showy
C. dark
D. colour
E. light

17. If 'yellow', is called 'pale', 'pale' is called 'blue', 'blue' is called 'orange', 'orange' is called 'dull', 'dull' is called 'green' and 'green' is called 'yellow' , what is the colour of grass in a lawn?

A. pale
B. yellow
C. blue
D. green
E. orange

18. If 'black' is called 'pink', 'pink' is called 'blue', 'blue' is called 'brown', 'brown' is called 'orange', 'orange' is called 'violet', 'violet' is called 'red' and 'red' is called 'black', what is the colour of blood?

A. black
B. brown
C. pink
D. orange
E. red

Directions (Qs. No. 19 to 23): *The following questions are based on the code pattern given below:*

Letters :	T	R	A	H	U	X	C	I	B	L
Numbers :	3	0	1	7	4	9	6	8	2	5

Which of the given options has the correct coded form of the given letters?

19. RACIXT

A. 016823
B. 016873
C. 016843
D. 016893
E. 016863

20. BUHLAI

A. 247018
B. 247508
C. 247538
D. 247518
E. 247528

21. LBIHAR

A. 528471
B. 528710
C. 528947
D. 528103
E. 528301

22. UBAXTC

A. 421736
B. 421956
C. 421936
D. 421906
E. 421916

23. HULBRT

A. 745203
B. 723045
C. 752340
D. 732145
E. 732154

ANSWERS

1	2	3	4	5	6	7	8	9	10
C	B	C	D	D	B	B	B	A	C
11	**12**	**13**	**14**	**15**	**16**	**17**	**18**	**19**	**20**
D	B	C	C	B	E	B	A	D	D
21	**22**	**23**							
B	C	A							

EXPLANATORY ANSWERS

1. The places of two consecutive letters in the word are interchanged to form the coded word.

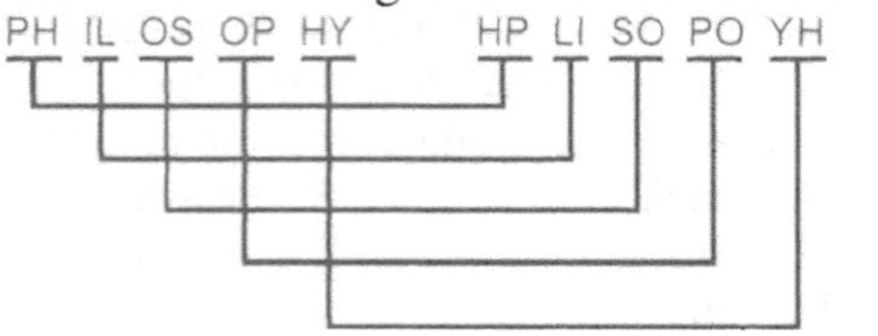

Similarly,

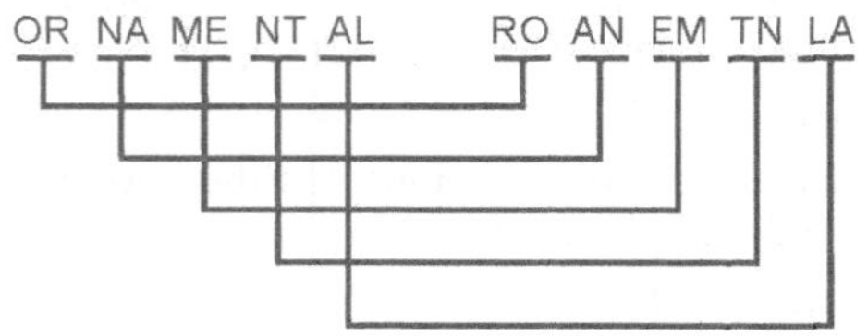

2. The manner of decoding is

↓ OP ↓ FG ↓ BC ↓ ST → codes
N E A R → given word

The letters preceeding two consecutive letters in the alphabetical series are picked to depict the words.

Similarly,

↓ IJ ↓ VW ↓ HI → given codes
H U G → answer word

3. Alphabet whose codes are given

m → g
g → o
a → i
i → y

All other alphabet will remain unchanged so, 'imagination' will be coded as :

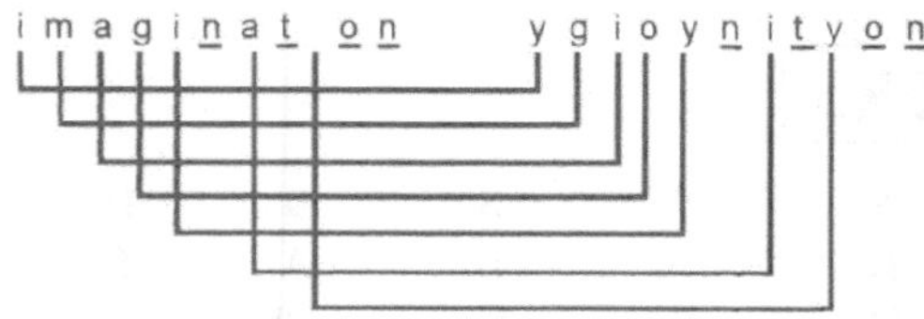

4. The coded number signifies the position of the alphabet in its natural alphabetical series (ABCD...)

O U T → OUT
15th 21st 20th→ 152120

Similarly,

I N → IN
9th 14th → 914

5. The coded number is the sum of number digits signifying the position of the alphabet in the natural order.

B A D
↓ ↓ ↓
2nd 1st 4th

i.e., 2 + 1 + 4 = 7

Similarly,

H I S
↓ ↓ ↓
8th 9th 19th

i.e., 8 + 9 + 19 = 36, further 3 + 6 = 9

Also,

L O W
↓ ↓ ↓
12th 15th 23rd

i.e., 12 + 15 + 23 = 50,

further, 5 + 0 = 5

6. The letters of the given groups are coded by numbers and the word CAGE is formed by letters from the given words. So, to find the answer, select the respective numbers.

A B C D E F G H → letters
2 4 6 8 1 3 5 7 → codes

So,

C A G E → letters
6 2 5 1 → answer codes

7. The numbers represent letters and to find the answer, select the respective letters.

1 3 5 7 2 4 6 8 → codes
H A R D S O F T → letters

So,

2 1 4 4 8 → codes
S H O O T → answer letters

8. The letter 'A' is present in three words and so is the number '1' in all the three words.

FACE	HAD	BADGE
6135	814	21475

9. ***Code*** ***Sentence***

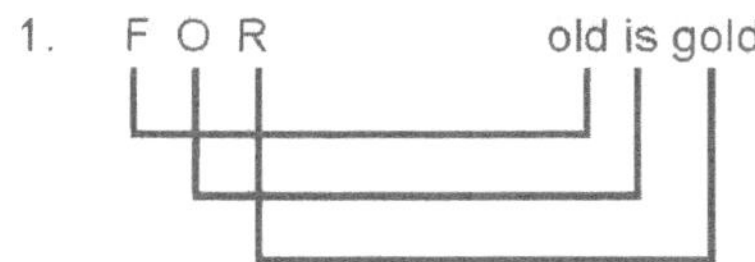

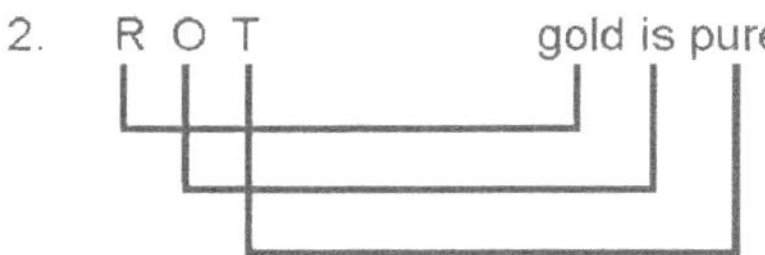

Therefore,

F stands for old
O stands for is
R stands for gold
T stands for pure
M stands for costly

So, 'pure old gold is costly' will be written as 'TFROM'.

10. ***Code*** ***Sentence***

	Code	Sentence
1.	643	she is beautiful
2.	593	he is handsome
3.	567	handsome meets beautiful

From 3rd code and its sentence, neither number '7' nor the word 'meets' is repeated.

11. ***Code*** ***Sentence***

	Code	Sentence
1.	pic vic nic	winter is cold
2.	to nic re	summer is hot
3.	re pic boo	winter and summer
4.	vic tho pa	nights are cold

The word 'summer' is common in 2nd and 3rd sentences and so is the code 're'

12. ***Code*** ***Sentence***

	Code	Sentence
1.	mu mite es	who is she
2.	**elb** mu es	**where** is she

The code words 'mu' and 'es' are repeated in Ist sentence. The only code left is 'elb' which means 'where'

13. ***Code Sentence***

	Code	Sentence
1.	**roi** *ja kyo twa*	**Moody** is *writing letters*
2.	pok ju *ja twa*	Woody is *writing* cards
3.	trn *kyo* pos un	they are writing *letters*
4.	koi rus pok	gifts and cards

'Moody' is in 1st sentence only. The code words 'ja' and 'twa' are repeated in 2nd sentence and 'kyo' in 3rd sentence. Only code 'roi' remains which stands for 'Moody'.

14. Birds fly in the 'sky' and 'sky' is called 'blue'.

15. Colour of snow is 'white' and 'white' is called 'orange'.

16. Colour of ink is 'blue' and 'blue' is called 'light'.

17. The colour of grass in a lawn is 'green' and 'green' is called 'yellow'.

18. Colour of blood is 'red' and 'red' is called 'black'.

❀ ❀ ❀

3 Symbol Substitution

Questions in these category are easy to attempt. Candidates must be quick in substituting symbols and calculations. The common pattern of questions asked are given below.

Example

1. If '+' stands for '×'; '×' stands for '÷'; '÷' stands for '–' and '–' stands for '+' then
   2 – 8 × 2 + 6 ÷ 7 = ?
   A. 32 B. 19
   C. 23 D. 9
   E. 15

Ans. After substituting the symbols in the given expression the new expression will be :
2 + 8 ÷ 2 × 6 – 7
The solving steps will be :
2 + 4 × 6 – 7
2 + 24 – 7
26 – 7 = 19

2. If ▲ stands for '+'
   ■ stands for '–'
   ● stands for '÷'
   ∗ stands for '×' then
   13 ▲ 5 ∗ 20 ● 10 ■ 9 = ?
   A. 26 B. 37
   C. 14 D. 55
   E. 20

Ans. After substituting the symbols the new expression will be :
13 + 5 × 20 ÷ 10 – 9
The solving steps will be :
13 + 5 × 2 – 9
13 + 10 – 9
23 – 9 = 14

EXERCISE

1. If × stand for addition, ÷ stands for subtraction, + stands for multiplication and – stands for division, then (20 × 6 ÷ 6 × 4) is equal to
   A. 5 B. 24
   C. 25 D. 80
   E. None of these
2. If "+" means "×"; "÷" means "–"; "×"means "÷" and "–" means "+", what will be the value of the following expression?
   4 + 11 ÷ 5 – 50 = ?
   A. 79 B. – 11
   C. 91 D. – 48.5
   E. None of these
3. If P = 6, J = 4, L = 8, M = 24, then which of the given values can replace the question mark (?) in the following?
   M × J ÷ L + J = ?
   A. 8 B. 36
   C. 52 D. 0
   E. 16
4. If A + B > C + D, B + E = 2 C and C + D > B + E, it necessarily follows that
   A. A > C B. A + B > 2D
   C. A + B > 2C D. A + B > 2E
   E. D + B < 2C
5. If A + D > C + E, C + D = 2B and B + E > C + D, it necessarily follows that
   A. A + D > B + E
   B. A + D > B + C
   C. A + B > 2D
   D. B + D > C + E
   E. A + D < B + C

6. What will be the correct mathematical signs that can be inserted in the following equation?
9 . . . 8 . . . 8 . . . 4 . . . 9 = 65
A. $- + \times \div$ B. $\div \times + -$
C. $\div + \times -$ D. $\times + \div -$
E. $+ \times \div -$

7. If "÷" means "+"; "–" means "÷"; "×"means "–" and "+" means "×", then
$32 \div 8 - 4 \times 12 + 4 = ?$
A. 40 B. 1/12
C. 16 D. 12
E. None of these

8. If "*x*" stands for "+"; "*y*" stands for "–"; "*z*"stands for "÷" and "*w*" stands for "×", then
$10w\ 2x\ 5y\ 5 = ?$
A. 15 B. 12
C. 20 D. 10
E. 25

9. If "–" stands for "×"; "×" stands for "+"; "+"stands for "÷" and "÷" stands for "–", then what will be the value of the following equation?
$8 - 4 + 16 \times 8 - 10 = ?$
A. 54 B. 82
C. 15 D. 10
E. 110

10. If Δ denotes =; + denotes >, – denotes <, □ denotes ≠, × denotes > and ÷ denotes < then a + b – c denotes
A. b Δ c □ a B. b □ a ÷ c
C. a ÷ b × c D. b – a + c
E. none of these

ANSWERS

1	2	3	4	5	6	7	8	9	10
B	E	E	C	B	D	E	C	B	D

EXPLANATORY ANSWERS

1. $20 + 6 - 6 + 4 = 24$

2. $4 \times 11 - 5 + 50$
$44 - 5 + 50 = 89$

3. $24 \times 4 \div 8 + 4$
$12 + 4 = 16$

4. $A + B > C + D > B + E$ or 2 C
$\therefore A + B > 2C$

5. 1. $A + D > C + E$
2. $B + E > C + D$ or 2 B
Since, the relation between 1 and 2 is not clear it is however certain that $A + D > B + C$ (combination with C is $< A + D$).

6. A. $9 - 8 + 8 \times 4 \div 9 = 65$
($8 \times 4 \div 9$ gives the result in fractions. So, there is no need for further calculation as the result 65 is a whole number.)

B. $9 \div 8 \times 8 + 4 - 9 = 65$
$9 + 4 - 9$ *ie* $4 = 65$

C. $9 \div 8 + 8 \times 4 - 9 = 65$
($9 \div 8$ gives the result in fraction)

D. $9 \times 8 + 8 \div 4 - 9 = 65$
$72 + 2 - 9$ *ie* $65 = 65$

E. $9 + 8 \times 8 \div 4 - 9$
$9 + 16 - 9$ *ie* $16 = 65$

7. $32 + 8 \div 4 - 12 \times 4$
$32 + 2 - 48 = - 14$

8. $10 \times 2 + 5 - 5$
$20 + 5 - 5 = 20$

9. $8 \times 4 \div 16 + 8 \times 10$
$2 + 80 = 82$

10. What is given is a > b < c
The equations are :
A. b = c ≠ a which is wrong
B. b ≠ a < c which is wrong
C. a < b > c which is wrong
D. b < a > c which is correct
Therefore, '*d*' is the answer.

❀ ❀ ❀

4 Blood Relation

Coded relationships problem involves interpreting a given relationship—string which is coded in a particular way and then matching it with the relationship mentioned in the questions. The process of decoding each and every relation and then interpreting from the given relationship—string the final relationship is a cumbersome process and doing it for all the choices makes it very time consuming. However systematic representation and some clever common sense observations may give a speedy solution.

BLOOD RELATIONSHIPS

While attempting questions on blood relations, one should be clear of all the relation patterns that can exist between any two individuals. Very well-known relations are:

Mother	Father	Son
Daughter	Brother	Sister
Niece	Nephew	Uncle
Aunt	Husband	Wife
Grandmother	Grandfather	Grandson
Granddaughter	Brother-in-law	Sister-in-law
Father-in-law	Mother-in-law	Son-in-law
Daughter-in-law	Cousin	

The patterns of some relationships which help in solving questions in these tests are :

Father's or Mother's Father – Grandfather (Paternal or Maternal)
Father's or Mother's Mother– Grandmother (Paternal or Maternal)
Father's or Mother's Son – Brother
Father's or Mother's Daughter – Sister
Father's Brother – Paternal Uncle
Father's Sister – Paternal Aunt
Mother's Brother – Maternal Uncle
Mother's Sister – Maternal Aunt
Uncle or Aunt's Son or Daughter – Cousin
Son's Wife – Daughter-in-law
Daughter's Husband – Son-in-law
Husband's or Wife's Brother – Brother-in-law
Husband's or Wife's Sister – Sister-in-law
Brother's Wife – Sister-in-law
Sister's Husband – Brother-in-law
Brother's Son – Nephew
Brother's Daughter – Niece

Example

1. R is the daughter of Q. M is the sister of B, who is the son of Q. How is M related to R?

A. Cousin
B. Niece
C. Sister
D. Aunt
E. None of these

Ans. C. B is the son of Q and R is the daughter of Q. This means M is sister of B and R.

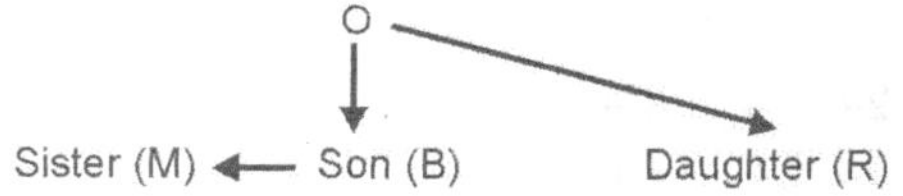

2. M is father of N. L is brother of M. P is mother of L. How is N related to P?

A. Grandson
B. Nephew
C. Granddaughter
D. Can't be determined
E. None of these

Ans. D. P is mother of L and M. N is child of M. Therefore, N is grandson or granddaughter of P.

Mother (P)
Father (M) → Brother (L)
(N)

EXERCISE

1. Introducing a boy, a girl said, "He is the son of the daughter of the father of my uncle." How is the boy related to the girl?
   A. Brother B. Nephew
   C. Uncle D. Son-in-law
   E. Father
2. Pointing to a photograph of a boy Suresh said, "He is the son of the only son of my mother." How is Suresh related to that boy?
   A. Brother B. Uncle
   C. Cousin D. Father
   E. Brother-in-law
3. If A + B means A is the brother of B; A – B means A is the sister of B and A × B means A is the father of B. Which of the following means that C is the son of M?
   A. M – N × C + F B. F – C + N × M
   C. N + M – F × C D. M × N – C + F
   E. M × N + C – F
4. If A is the brother of B; B is the sister of C; and C is the father of D, how D is related to A?
   A. Brother
   B. Sister
   C. Nephew
   D. Father
   E. Cannot be determined
5. If A + B means A is the mother of B; A – B means A is the brother of B; A % B means A is the father of B and A × B means A is the sister of B, which of the following shows that P is the maternal uncle of Q?
   A. Q – N + M × P B. P + S × N – Q
   C. P – M + N × Q D. Q – S % P
   E. Q × S + P
6. Pointing to a photograph Lata says, "He is the son of the only son of my grandfather." How is the man in the photograph related to Lata?
   A. Brother B. Uncle
   C. Cousin D. Father
   E. Data is inadequate
7. If D is the brother of B, how B is related to C? To answer this question which of the statements is/are necessary?
   1. The son of D is the grandson of C.
   2. B is the sister of D.
   A. Only 1
   B. Only 2
   C. Either 1 or 2
   D. 1 and 2 both are required
   E. Neither 1 nor 2
8. Pointing to a photograph. Balram said, "He is the son of the only daughter of the father of my brother." How Balram is related to the man in the photograph?
   A. Nephew B. Brother
   C. Father D. Maternal Uncle
   E. Brother-in-law
9. Pointing to a woman, Abhay said, "Her granddaughter is the only daughter of my brother." How is the woman related to Abhay?
   A. Sister B. Grandmother
   C. Mother-in-law D. Mother
   E. Sister-in-law
10. If A + B means A is the sister of B; A × B means A is the wife of B, A % B means A is the father of B and A – B means A is the brother of B. Which of the following means T is the daughter of P?
   A. P × Q % R + S – T
   B. P × Q % R – T + S
   C. P × Q % R + T – S
   D. P × Q % R + S + T
   E. P × Q % R – S – T
11. Deepak said to Naresh, "That boy playing with the football is the younger of the two brothers of the daughter of my father's wife." How is the boy playing football related to Deepak?
   A. Son B. Brother
   C. Cousin D. Brother-in-law
   E. Son-in-law

12. Reena who is the sister-in-law of Ashok, is the daughter-in-law of Kalyani. Dheeraj is the father of Suresh who is the only brother of Ashok. How Kalyani is related to Ashok?

A. Mother-in-law B. Aunt
C. Wife D. Mother
E. None of these

13. A and B are children of M. Who is the father of A? To answer this question which of the statements 1 and 2 is necessary?

1. C is the brother of A and the son of E.
2. F is the mother B.

A. Only 1 B. Only 2
C. Either 1 or 2 D. 1 and 2 both
E. Neither 1 nor 2

14. Anil said, "This girl is the wife of the grandson of my mother". How is Anil related to the girl?

A. Brother B. Grandfather
C. Husband D. Father-in-law
E. Father

15. Pointing towards a man, a woman said, "His mother is the only daughter of my mother." How is the woman related to the man?

A. Mother B. Grandmother
C. Sister D. Daughter
E. Wife

16. If P $ Q means P is the brother of Q; P # Q means P is the mother of Q; P * Q means P is the daughter of Q in A # B $ C * D, who is the father?

A. D B. B
C. C D. A
E. Data is inadequate

17. Introducing Shalu, Aamir says, "She is the wife of only nephew of only brother of my mother." How Shalu is related to Aamir?

A. Wife B. Sister
C. Sister-in-law D. Father
E. Data is inadequate

Directions (Qs. No. 18 and 19): *Read the following information to answer the questions:*

A + B means A is the father of B
A – B means A is the sister of B
A × B means A is the husband of B
A % B means A is the wife of B

18. Which of the following means 'T is the nephew of Q'?

A. Q × R – S + T
B. Q + R % S + T
C. Q – R % S + T
D. Q – R + S % T
E. None of these

19. Which of the following means S is granddaughter of R?

A. R + P % Q + S
B. K % R + P × Q – L + S
C. K % R + P % Q + S – L
D. K % R + P % Q + S + L
E. R % P + Q – S

20. If 'A + B' means 'A is brother of B', 'A – B' means 'A is sister of B', 'A × B' means 'A is wife of B' and 'A % B' means 'A is father of B', then which of the following indicates 'S is the son of P'?

A. P × Q % R + S – T
B. P × Q % S – R + T
C. P × Q % R – T + S
D. P × Q % R – S + T
E. P × Q – R % S + T

ANSWERS

1	2	3	4	5	6	7	8	9	10
A	D	D	E	C	A	D	D	D	B
11	**12**	**13**	**14**	**15**	**16**	**17**	**18**	**19**	**20**
B	E	B	D	A	A	A	E	C	D

EXPLANATORY ANSWERS

1. 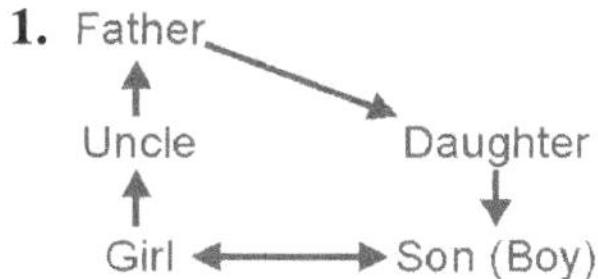

The father of the boy's uncle → the grandfather of the boy and daughter of the grandfather → sister of father.

2. 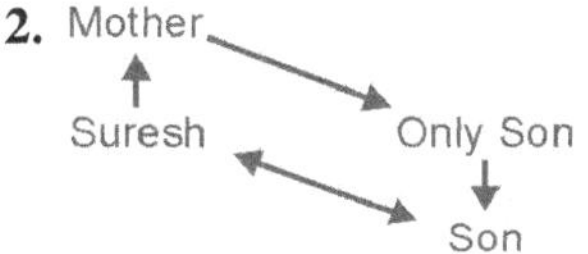

The boy in the photograph is the only son of the son of Suresh's mother *i.e.*, the son of Suresh. Hence, Suresh is the father of boy.

3. 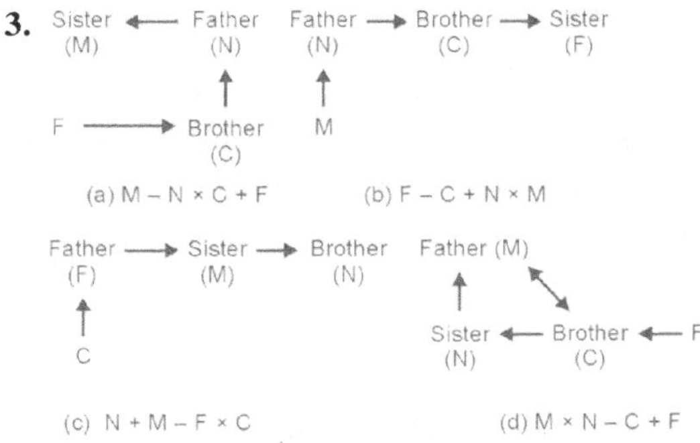

M × N → M is the father of N
N – C → N is the sister of C
and C + F → C is the brother of F.

Hence, M is the father of C or C is the son of M.

4. Father (C) ⟶ Sister (B) ⟶ Brother (A)
↑
D

If D is Male, the answer is Nephew.
If D is Female, the answer is Niece.
As the sex of D is not known, hence, the relation between D and A cannot be determined.

Note: Niece - A daughter of one's brother or sister, or of one's brother-in-law or sister-in-law.
Nephew - A son of one's brother or sister, or of one's brother-in-law or sister-in-law.

5. 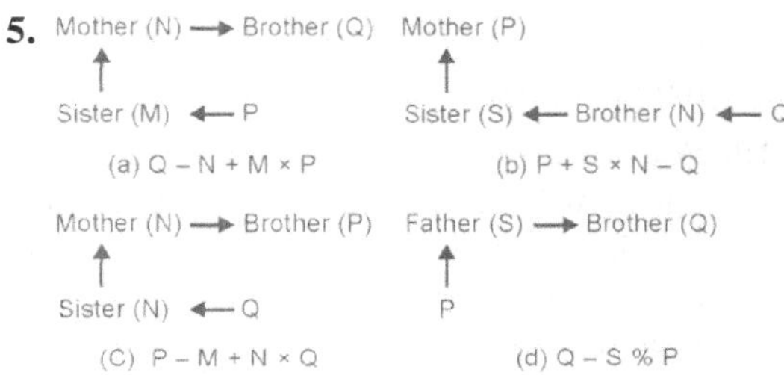

6. 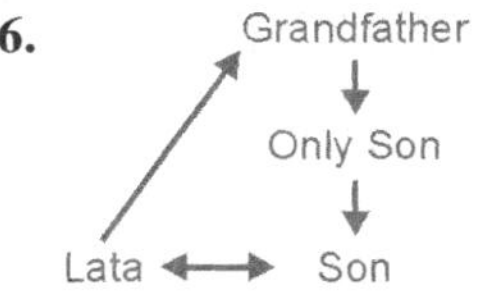

The man in the photograph is the son of the only son of Lata's grandfather *i.e.*, the man is the son of Lata's father. Hence, the man is the brother of Lata.

7. Father (C) Grandefather (C) ... St 1
(Sister ... St 2)B ⟶ Brother (D)
Son

Given: D is the brother of B.
From statement 1, we can detect that D is son of C (son of D is the grandson of C).
From statement 2, we can detect that B is 'Female' (sister of D).
Therefore, B is daughter of C.

8. 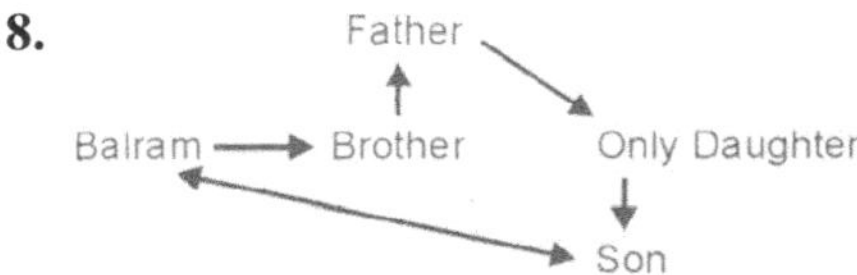

The man in the photograph is the son of the sister of Balram. Hence, Balram is the maternal uncle of the man in the photograph.

9. 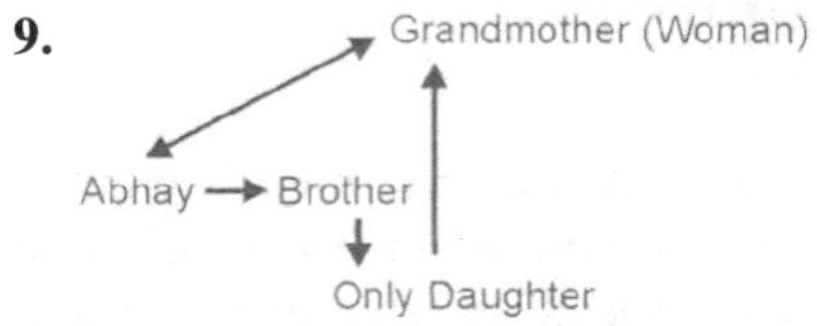

Daughter of Abhay's brother → niece of Abhay. Thus the granddaughter of the woman is Abhay's niece. Hence, the woman is the mother of Abhay.

10. We can note that sex of last person in each option will be unknown. Since T should be daughter of P so T will be definitely female in correct option. So options A and D are straightaway ruled out. Also in the correct option only '+' or '×' will follow T as T is definitely a female so option C is also ruled out.

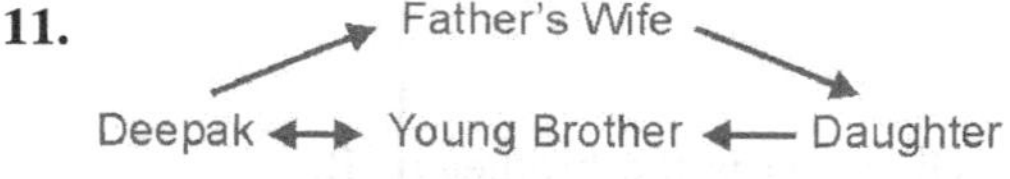

B. $P \times Q \% R - T + S$.

$P \times Q \rightarrow$ P is the wife of Q.

$Q \% R \rightarrow$ Q is the father of R.

$R - T \rightarrow$ R is the brother of T.

$T + S \rightarrow$ T is the sister of S.

Therefore, T is the daughter of P.

11. Father's Wife

Deepak ↔ Young Brother ← Daughter

Father's wife → mother.

Hence, the daughter of the mother means sister and sister's younger brother means brother. Therefore, the boy is the brother of Deepak.

12. 

Ashok is the only brother of Suresh and Reena is the sister-in-law of Ashok. Hence, Reena is the wife of Suresh. Kalyani is the mother-in-law of Reena. Kalyani is the mother of Ashok.

13. 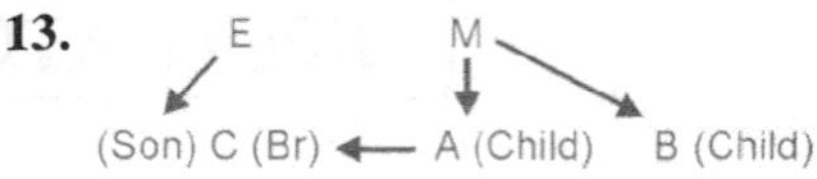

From main st. & st. 1

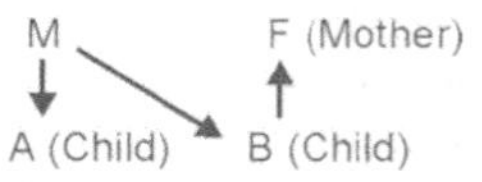

From main st. & st. 2

A and B are children of M. From 1, C is the brother B and son of E. Since, the sex of M and E are not known. Hence 1 is not sufficient to answer the question.

From 2. F is the mother of B. Hence, F is also the mother of A. Hence M is the father of A. Thus, 2 is sufficient to answer the question.

14. 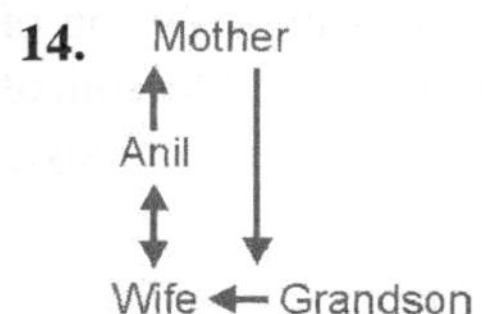

The girl is the wife of grandson of Anil's mother *i.e.*, the girl is the wife of son of Anil. Hence, Anil is the father-in-law of the girl.

15. 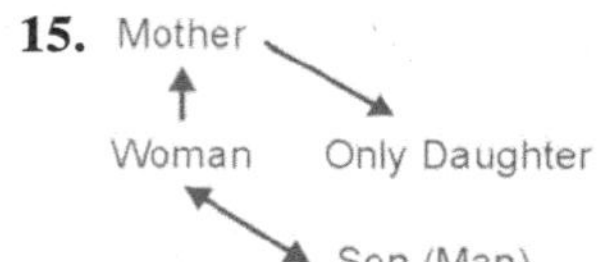

Only daughter of my mother → myself. Hence, the woman is the mother of the man.

16. 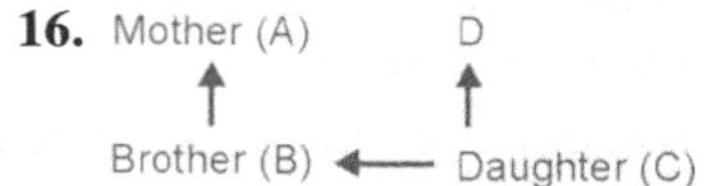

A is the mother of B, B is the brother of C and C is the daughter of D. Hence, D is the father.

17. 

Brother of mother means maternal uncle. Hence only nephew of Aamir's maternal uncle means Aamir himself. Therefore Shalu is the wife of Aamir.

18. Since 'T is the nephew of Q' so 'T' must be a male but sex of 'T' cannot be established in any of the option.

19. Choice A, B is not correct as sex of S is not known. D is ruled out because S is a male here. Representation for choice C is as follows:

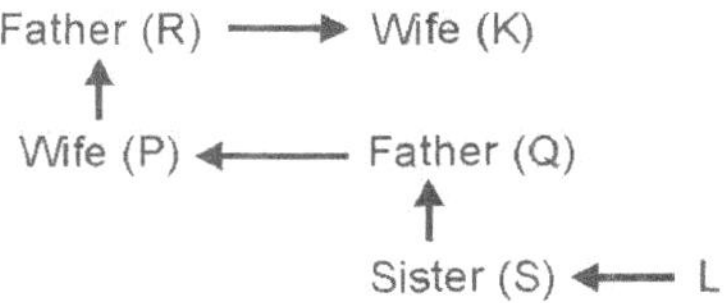

So, S is granddaughter of R is correct here.

20. As 'S' is female in option A and B, both are rejected directly. The sex of 'S' in option C is not known, hence it is also eliminated. Now, check option D.

Father (Q) ⟶ Wife (P)
↑
Sister (R) ⟵ Brother (S) ⟵ T

Clearly, S is son of P.

5 Direction Sense

In these type of tests, the directions in questions needs to be perceived, Such questions are based on the direction chart.

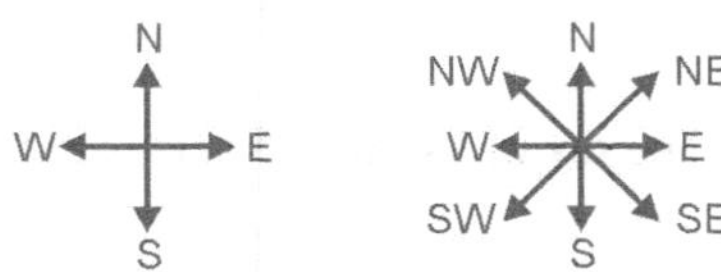

N = North, S = South, E = East, W = West

The sense of the different directions are guided by the left and righ turns or angular turns.

Example

1. Shobha was facing East. She walked 20 metres. Turning left she moved 15 metres and then turning right moved 25 metres. Finally, she turned right and moved 15 metres more. How far is she from her starting point?

A. 25 metres B. 35 metres
C. 50 metres D. 45 metres
E. 40 metres

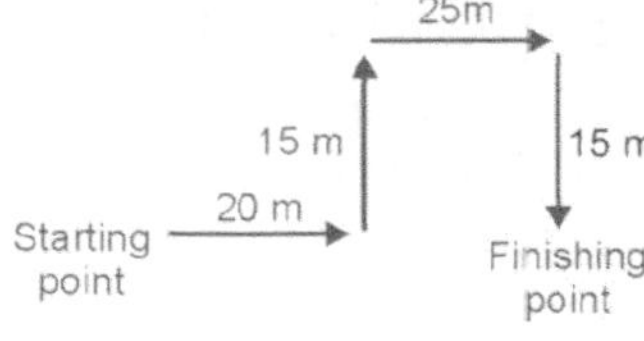

Ans.: Shobha turns left after walking 20 metres towards East. Now she walks 15 metres towards North. She turns right towards East again and walks 25 metres further. Finally turning right towards South, she walks 15 metres. The distance moved towards North and towards South is same, i.e., 15 metres. So, Shobha is 20 + 25 metres = 45 metres away from her starting point.

EXERCISE

1. One morning Urmilla and Vishal were talking to each other face to face at a crossing. If Vishal's shadow was exactly to the left of Urmilla, which direction was Urmilla facing?

A. East B. West
C. North D. South
E. North - East

2. If South-East becomes North, North-East becomes West and so on. What will West become?

A. North - East B. North - West
C. South - East D. South - West
E. North

3. Ravi put his timepiece on the table in such a way that at 6 P.M. hour hand points to North. In which direction the minute hand will point at 9.15 P.M. ?

A. South - East B. South
C. North D. West
E. North - East

4. Rakesh walked 20 m towards north. Then he turned right and walks 30 m. Then he turns right and walks 35 m. Then he turns left and walks 15 m. Finally he turns left and walks 15 m. In which direction and how many metres is he from the starting position?

A. 15 m West B. 30 m East
C. 30 m West D. 45 m East
E. 30 m North

5. Starting from the point X, John walked 15 m towards west. He turned left and walked 20 m. He then turned left and walked 15 m. After this he turned to his right and walked 12 m. How far and in which directions is now John from X?

A. 32 m, South B. 47 m, East
C. 42 m, North D. 27 m, South
E. 35 m North

6. Suman is 40 metres South – West of Ashok, Prakash is 40 metres South – East of Ashok. Prakash is in which direction of Suman?

A. South B. West
C. East D. North – East
E. North

7. Vijayan started walking towards South. After walking 15 metres he turned to the left and walked 15 metres. He again turned to his left and walked 15 metres. How far is he from his original position and in which direction?

A. 15 metres, North
B. 15 metres, East
C. 30 metres, South
D. 15 metres, West
E. 30 metres, North

Directions (Qs. No. 8 to 10): *Each of the following questions is based on the following information:*

1. P # Q means B is at 1 metre to the right of P.
2. P $ Q means B is at 1 metre to the North of P.
3. P * Q means B is at 1 metre to the left of P.
4. P @ Q means B is at 1 metre to the south of P.
5. In each question first person from the left is facing North.

8. According to X @ B * P, P is in which direction with respect to X?

A. North B. South
C. North - East D. South-West
E. East

9. According to M # N $ T, T is in which direction with respect to M?

A. North-West B. North-East
C. South-West D. South-East
E. North

10. According to P # R $ A * U, in which direction is U with respect to P?

A. East B. West
C. North D. South
E. North - East

Directions (Qs. No. 11 to 15): *P, Q, R and S are standing on four corners of a square piece of plot as shown in the given figure. They start moving, and the movements are explained in each of the questions. Read the question and select the right alternative.*

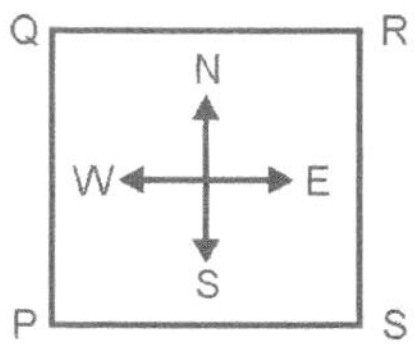

11. P, Q , R and S walk diagonally to opposite corners and from there Q and R walk one and a half sides anti-clockwise while P and S walk one side clockwise along the sides. Where is S now?

A. At the North – West corner
B. At the North -East
C. At the South – West corner
D. At the South-East
E. None of these

12. Q travelled straight to R, a distance of 10 m. He turned right and walked 7 m towards S, again he turned right and walked 8 m, and then finally turned right and walked 7m. How far is he from his original position?

A. 7 m B. 8 m
C. 2 m D. 3 m
E. 5 m

13. From the original position, S starts crossing the field diagonally. After walking half the distance he turns right; walks some distance and turns left. Which direction is S facing now?

A. South - East B. North - West
C. South - West D. North
E. South

14. P and S walk one and a half length of the side clockwise and anti-clockwise respectively. Which one of the following statements is true?

A. P is at midpoint between Q and R and S at the corner originally occupied by P

B. P and S are both at the midpoint between R and S

C. P and S are both at the midpoint between Q and R.

D. S is at midpoint between Q and R and P is at the midpoint between original side of R and S

E. P is the midpoint between R and S.

15. P, Q, R and S walk one and a half sides clockwise. Who is on the left of Q if he is facing West?

A. P B. R

C. S D. Q

E. None of these

ANSWERS

1	2	3	4	5	6	7	8	9	10
C	C	D	D	A	C	B	D	B	C
11	**12**	**13**	**14**	**15**					
B	C	B	C	B					

EXPLANATORY ANSWERS

1.

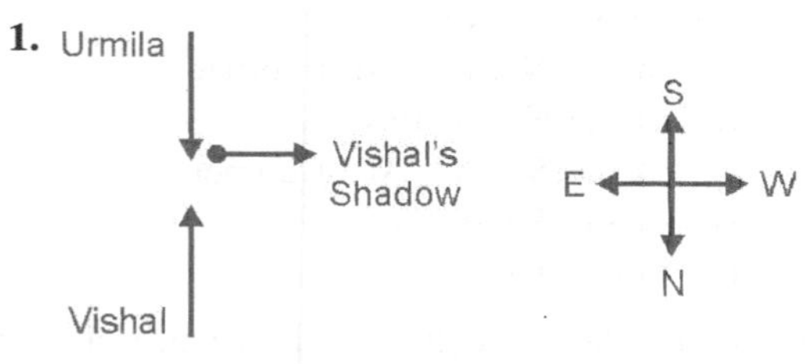

2.

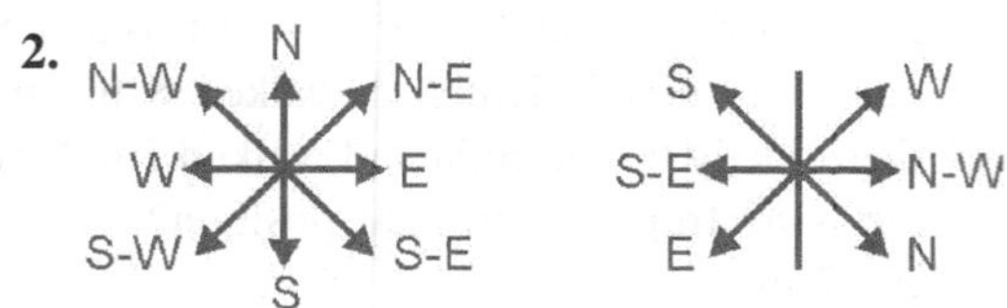

It is clear from the diagrams that new name of West will become South-East.

3.

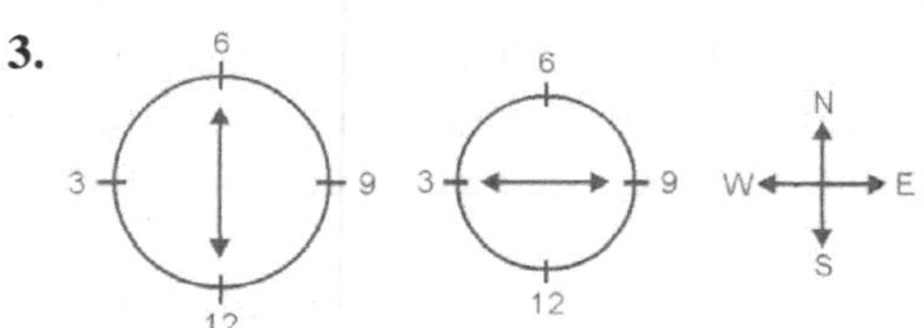

At 9.15 P.M., the minute hand will point towards west.

4.

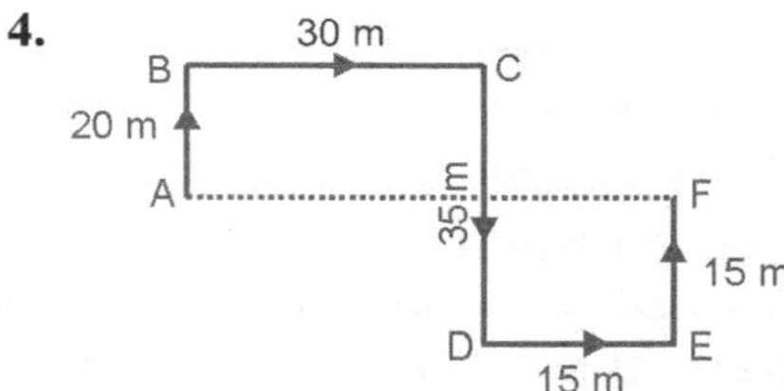

Required distance = AF = 30 + 15 = 45 m. From the above figure, F is in East direction from A. So the answer is '45 m East'.

5.

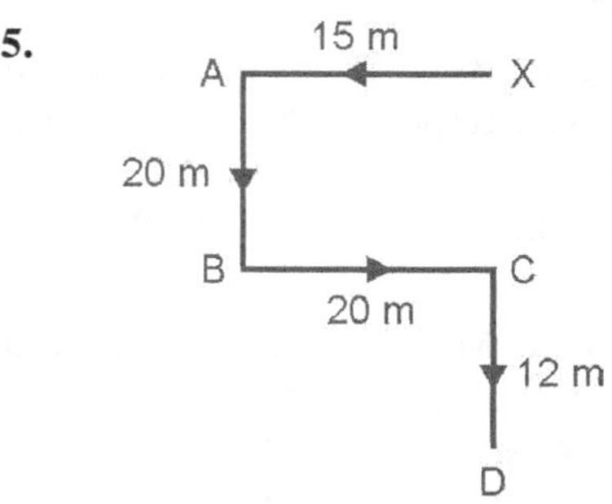

Required distance = 20 + 12 = 32 m South.

6.

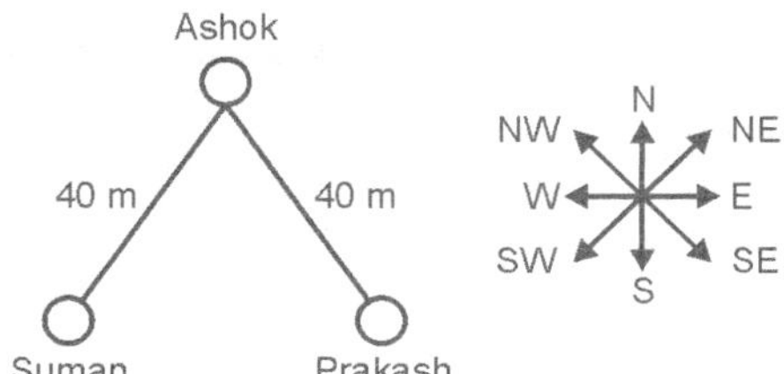

7. Starting point Finishing point

15 m 15 m

15 m

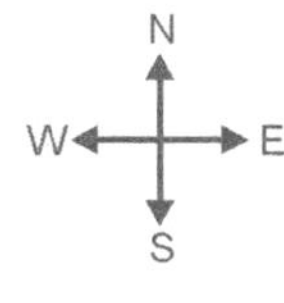

8. According to X @ B * Y

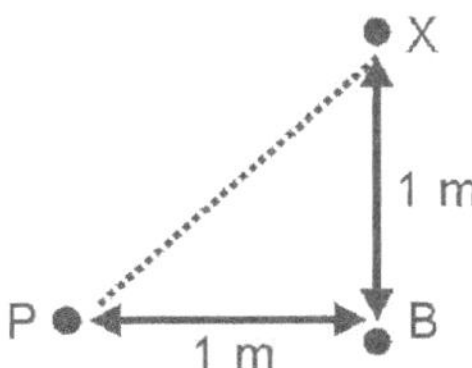

Hence, P is in South-West of X.

9. According to M # N $ T

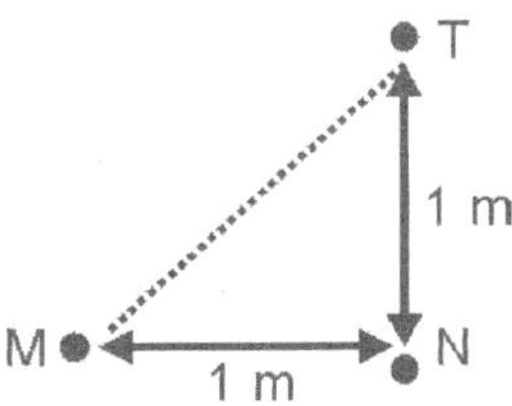

Hence, T is in the North-East of M.

10. According to P # R $ A * U

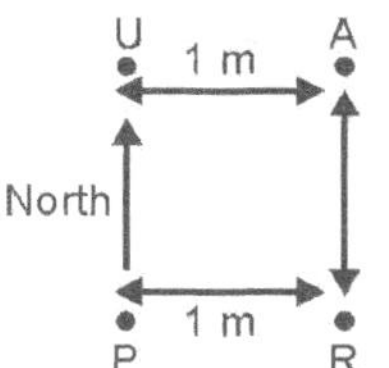

Hence, U is in North direction with respect to P.

11.

(1) (2) (3)

12. (10 m – 8 m = 2 m)

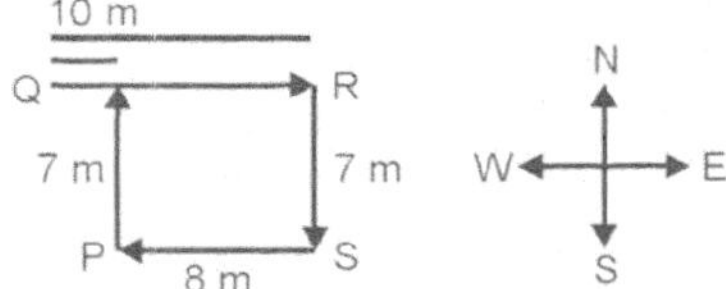

13.

14. The movements are :

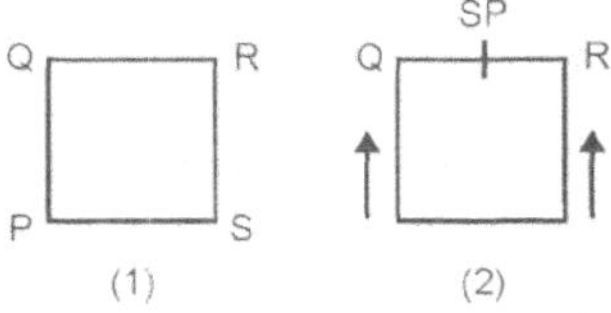

15.

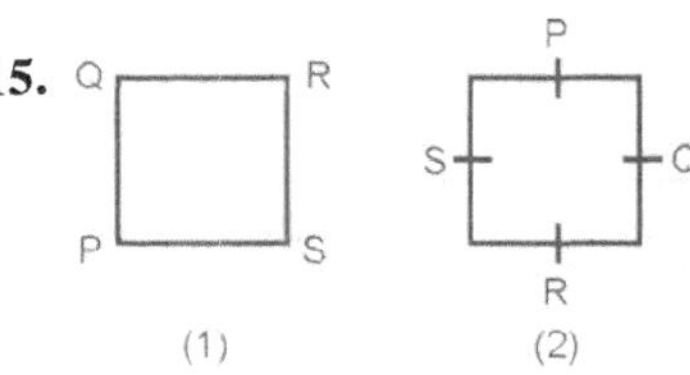

6 Statement Analysis

In these questions, a series of interlinked information or data is given. Quantitatively analysis of given information or data provides certain conclusions.

In Statement Analysis (Problem Solving) questions, all given information has to be interpreted and arranged step-by-step. One should be careful that no given data is left incorporated. A brief glimpse to all questions asked on given data is helpful in preparing the solution format.

Directions: *Read the following information carefully and answer the questions given below:*

In a family of six persons—A, B, C, D, E and F—there are three males and three females. There are two married couples and two persons are unmarried. Each one of them reads different newspapers, viz. Times of India, Indian Express, Hindustan Times, Financial Times, Navbharat Times and Business Standard. E, who reads Indian Express, is mother-in-law of A, who is wife of C. D is the father of F and he does not read Times of India or Business Standard. B reads Navbharat Times and is the sister of F, who reads Hindustan Times. C does not read Business Standard.

1. Who among the following reads the Times of India?
A. C B. D
C. A D. Data inadequate
E. None of these

2. How is F related to E?
A. Daughter B. Brother
C. Son D. Data inadequate
E. None of these

3. Which of the following is one of the married couples?
A. D-B B. D-E
C. B-F D. E-F
E. None of these

4. Which of the following newspapers is read by 'A'?
A. Times of India B. Navbharat Times
C. Financial Times D. Data inadequate
E. None of these

5. How many sons does E have?
A. Four B. Three
C. Two D. One
E. None of these

Following is the detail presentation of mental approach for solution of the given problem. In practice these questions are solved briefly.

E, who reads Indian Express, is mother-in-law of A, who is the wife of C

Person	Newspaper read	Sex	Information/Reasons
A		Fe	A-C Couple
B			
C		M	A is the wife of C
D			
E	I.E	Fe	mother-in-law of A
F			

D is the father of F and he does not read TOI or B.S

Person	Newspaper read	Sex	Information/Reasons
A		Fe	A-C Couple
B			
C		M	A is the wife of C
D	H.T or F.T or N.T	M	father of F, (TOI, B.S,I.E- not)
E	I.E	Fe	mother-in-law of A

As there are two married couples. This implies that D and E are couples. B reads N.T and is the sister of F, who reads H.T. C does not read B.S

Person	Newspaper read	Sex	Information/Reasons
A	B.S	Fe	A-C Couple
B	N.T	Fe	Sister of F
C	TOI	M	B.S -no
D	F.T	M	father of F
E	I.E	Fe	D-E, Couple
F	H.T	M	There are 3 males- 3 females

E is mother in law of A and A is wife of C implies C is Son of E. D is father of F and D-E are couples implies F is Son of E.

1. A **2.** C **3.** B **4.** E **5.** C

EXERCISE

Directions (Qs. No. 1 to 4): *Read the following information carefully and answer the questions given below:*

1. There are five types of cards viz. A, B, C, D and E. There are three cards of each type. These are to be inserted in envelopes of three colours—red, yellow and brown. There are five envelopes of each colour.
2. B, D and E type cards are to be inserted in red envelopes; A, B and C type cards are to be inserted in yellow envelopes; and C, D and E type cards are to be inserted in brown envelopes.
3. Two cards each of B and D type are inserted in red envelopes.

1. How many cards of E type are inserted in brown envelopes?

A. Nil B. One
C. Two D. Three
E. Data inadequate

2. Which of the following combinations of the type of cards and the number of cards is **definitely correct** in respect of yellow-coloured envelopes?

A. A-2, B-1, C-2 B. B-1, C-2, D-2
C. A-2, E-1, D-2 D. A-3, B-1, C-1
E. None of these

3. Which of the following combinations of types of cards and the number of cards and colour of envelope is **definitely correct**?

A. C-2, D-1, E-2, Brown
B. C-1, D-2, E-2, Brown
C. B-2, D-2, A-1, Red
D. A-2, B-2, C-1, Yellow
E. None of these

4. Which of the following combinations of colour of the envelope and the number of cards is **definitely correct** in respect of E type cards?

A. Red-2, Brown-1
B. Red-1, Yellow-2
C. Red-2, Yellow-1
D. Yellow-1, Brown-2
E. None of these

Directions (Qs. No. 5 to 7): *Read the following information carefully and answer the questions given below:*

Six persons A, B, C, D, E and F took up a job with a firm in a week from Monday to Saturday. Each of them joined for different posts on different days. The posts were of–Clerk, Officer, Technician, Manager, Supervisor, and Sales Executive, though not respectively. F joined as a Manager on the first day. B joined as a Supervisor but neither on Wednesday nor Friday. D joined as a Technician on Thursday. Officer joined the firm on Wednesday. E joined as a clerk on Tuesday. A joined as a Sales Executive.

5. Who joined the firm on Wednesday?
A. B B. C
C. B or C D. Data inadequate
E. None of these

6. Who was the last person to join the firm?
A. E B. F
C. A D. B
E. None of these

7. On which of the following days did the Sales Executive join?
A. Tuesday B. Thursday
C. Saturday D. Wednesday
E. None of these

Directions (Qs. No. 8 to 11): *Read the following information carefully and answer the questions given below:*

(*a*) An examination board has organised examination for ten s ubjects viz. A, B, C, D, E, F, G, H, I and J on six days of the week with a holiday on Sunday, not having more than two papers on any of the days.
(*b*) Exam begins on Wednesday with subject F.
(*c*) D is accompained by some other subject but not on Thursday. A and G are on the same day immediately after holiday.
(*d*) There is only one paper on last day and Saturday. B is immediately followed by H, which is immediately followed by I.
(*e*) C is on Saturday. H is not on the same day as J.

8. Examination for which of the following pairs of subjects is on Thursday?
A. HE B. DB
C. FD D. Data inadequate
E. None of these

9. Examination for which of the following subjects is on the next day of D?
A. B (2) C
C. I D. H
E. None of these

10. Examination for which of the following subjects is on the last day?
A. B B. E
C. J D. Data inadequate
E. None of these

11. Examination for subject F is on the same day as which of the following subjects?
A. E (2) D
C. I D. B
E. None of these

Directions (Qs. No. 12 to 16): *Study the following information to answer the given questions:*

P, Q, R, S, T, V, W and Z are travelling to three destinations Delhi, Chennai and Hyderabad in three different vehicles Honda City, Swift D'Zire and Ford Ikon. There are three females among them one in each car. There are atleast two persons in each car. R is not travelling with Q and W. T , a male, is travelling with only Z and they are not travelling to Chennai. P is travelling in Honda City to Hyderabad. S is sister of P and travels by Ford Ikon. V and R travel together. W does not travel to Chennai.

12. Who is travelling with W?
A. Only Q
B. Only P
C. Both P and Q
D. Cannot be determined
E. None of these

13. Members in which of the following combinations are travelling in Honda City?
A. PRS B. PQW
C. PWS D. Data inadequate
E. None of these

14. In which car are four members travelling?
A. None B. Honda City
C. Swift D'zire D. Ford Ikon
E. Honda City or Ford Ikon

15. Which of the following combinations represents the three female members?
A. QSZ
B. WSZ
C. PSZ
D. Cannot be determined
E. None of these

16. Members in which car are travelling To Chennai?
A. Honda City
B. Swift D'Zire
C. Ford Ikon
D. Either Swift D'Zire or Ford Ikon
E. None of the above

Directions (Qs. No. 17-23): *Each problem consists of three statements. Based on the first two statements, the third statement may be true, false, or uncertain.*

17. (i) Tanya is older than Easha.
(ii) Celina is older than Tanya.
(iii) Easha is older than Celina.
If the first two statements are true, the third statement is
A. True B. False
C. Uncertain D. Certain
E. None of these

18. (i) Blueberries cost more than strawberries.
(ii) Blueberries cost less than raspberries.
(iii) Raspberries cost more than both strawberries and blueberries.
If the first two statements are true, the third statement is
A. True B. False
C. Uncertain D. Certain
E. None of these

19. (i) Maria runs faster than Gail.
(ii) Lily runs faster than Maria.
(iii) Gail runs faster than Lily.
If the first two statements are true, the third statement is
A. True B. False
C. Uncertain D. Certain
E. None of these

20. (i) A fruit basket contains more apples than mangoes.
(ii) There are more mangoes in the basket than there are oranges.
(iii) The basket contains more apples than oranges.
If the first two statements are true, the third statement is
A. True B. False
C. Uncertain D. Certain
E. None of these

21. (i) Jullie is younger than Katrina.
(ii) Maya was born after Jullie.
(iii) Katrina is older than Maya.
If the first two statements are true, the third statement is
A. True B. False
C. Uncertain D. Certain
E. None of these

22. (i) The temperature on Monday was lower than on Tuesday.
(ii) The temperature on Wednesday was lower than on Tuesday.
(iii) The temperature on Monday was higher than on Wednesday.
If the first two statements are true, the third statement is
A. True B. False
C. Uncertain D. Certain
E. None of these

23. (i) All Lamels are Signots with buttons.
(ii) No blue Signots have buttons.
(iii) No Lamels are blue.
If the first two statements are true, the third statement is
A. True B. False
C. Uncertain D. Certain
E. None of these

ANSWERS

1	2	3	4	5	6	7	8	9	10
C	D	A	E	B	D	E	A	B	C
11	**12**	**13**	**14**	**15**	**16**	**17**	**18**	**19**	**20**
D	C	B	A	D	C	B	A	B	C
21	**22**	**23**							
A	C	A							

EXPLANATORY ANSWERS

Solution (1-4): From (2), Out of fifteen cards nine cards will be inserted as following:

Red envelope	Yellow envelope	Brown envelope
B	A	C
D	B	D
E	C	E

From (3) and using the above table, we get

Red envelope	Yellow envelope	Brown envelope
B(2)	A	C
D(2)	B(1)	D(1)
E(1)	C	E(2)

The digits in brackets shows the no. of cards. Now, From (1), it is clear that each colour of envelope contains five cards, so there are two cards of C-type in brown envelope. Hence the remaining one card of C-type is in yellow envelope. Hence all the three A-type are in yellow envelope.

4. Brown-2, Red-1.

Solution (5-7): Summarising the given information in tabular form, we get

Person	Posts	Days
F	Manager	Monday
B	Supervisor	*Saturday*
D	Technician	Thursday
C	Officer	Wednesday
E	Clerk	Tuesday
A	Sales Executive	*Friday*

The places of italized letter/words is the last left one and can be filled easily by fulfilling all other given conditions.

Solution (8-11):

Wed	Thu	Fri	Sat	Sun	Mon	Tue
F, B	H, E	I, D	C	Hol	A, G	J

12-16: T(m) Z(f) Swift D'Zire Delhi
QWP Honda City Hyderabad
V(m)R(m)S(f) Ford Ikon Chennai.

17. Because the first two statements are true, Easha is the youngest of the three, so the third statement must be false.

18. Because the first two statements are true, raspberries are the most expensive of the three.

19. We know from the first two statements that Lily runs fastest. Therefore, the third statement must be false.

20. There are fewer oranges than either apples or mangoes, so the statement is true. (another approach)

1. A fruit basket contains more apples than mangoes = App > Mang.
2. There are more mangoes in the basket than there are oranges = Mang > Org
   Now, Combine the above two results: App > Mang > Org.
3. The basket contains more apples than oranges (App > ... > Org) = Yes.

Therefore, the given 3rd statement is true.

21. Jullie is younger than Katrina and older than Maya, so Maya must be younger than Katrina.

22. We know from the first two statements that Tuesday had the highest temperature, but we cannot know whether Monday's temperature was higher than Tuesday's.

23. We know that there are Signots with buttons, or Lamels, and that there are blue Signots, which have no buttons. Therefore, Lamels do not have buttons and cannot be blue.

❀ ❀ ❀

7 Sitting Arrangement

Sitting arrangement around circle: Nowadays in some competitive exams problems based on sitting arrangement around circle is frequently asked. These questions appear very simple but are not a cakewalk and are often solved wrongly. Main confusing point is deciding between left hand side and right hand side of a person when all persons are sitting around a circle facing centre. Because the left hand side of a person in lower semicircle is right hand side of a person in upper semicircle. This confusion is not met when these problems are solved by numbered line method. In numbered line method all members are first placed on a numbered line numbered up to total number of persons starting from one. For extreme end members line is assumed to be continued with other extreme member as immediate neighbour. Right hand side or left hand side confusion is by passed in this method. Following solved problems will make the method very clear.

Example

Directions (Qs. No. 1 to 6): *Study the following information carefully and answer the questions given below:*

P, Q, R, S, T, V, W and Z are sitting around a circle facing at the centre. R is fourth to the left of P who is second to the right of S. V is fourth to the right of S. Q is fourth to the left of W who is not an immediate neighbour of P or S. Z is not an immediate neighbour of R.

1. Who is to the immediate right of V?
A. R B. W
C. Z D. Data inadequate
E. None of these

2. Who is to the immediate right of R?
A. T B. S
C. W D. Data inadequate
E. None of these

3. Who is second to the left of Z?
A. Q B. V
C. S D. W
E. None of these

4. In which of the following pairs is the first person sitting to the immediate right of the second person?
A. VW B. RT
C. WR D. QP
E. ZP

5. Which of the following pairs are the immediate neighbours of Z?
A. WQ B. VQ
C. WP D. VP
E. None of these

6. Who is third to the right of R?
A. P B. S
C. Q D. Data inadequate
E. None of these

Solution (1-6):

(a) R is fourth to the left of P who is second to the right of S.
(b) V is fourth to the right of S.
(c) Q is fourh to the left of W who is not an immediate neighbour of P or S.
(d) Z is not an immediate neighbour of R.

V .... (b)
R S P, ...(a)
1.....2.....3.....4.....5.....6.....7.....8
Z .... (d)
(c) .. Q W

R T S Q P Z V W
1.....2.....3.....4.....5.....6.....7.....8

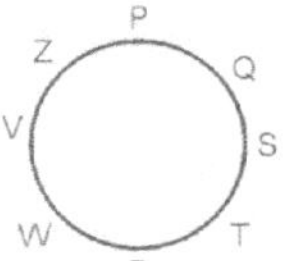

1. B **2.** A **3.** A **4.** E **5.** D **6.** C

EXERCISE

Directions (Qs. No. 1 to 5): *Study the following information carefully and answer the questions given below:*

M, P, J, B, R, T and F are sitting around a circle facing at the centre. B is third to the left of J who is second to the left of M. P is third to the left of B and second to the right of R. T is not an immediate neighbour of M.

1. Who is fourth to the right of M?

A. B B. T
C. J D. Data inadequate
E. None of these

2. Who is second to the left of T?

A. F B. M
C. P D. J
E. Data inadequate

3. In which of the following pairs the second person is sitting to the immediate right of the first person?

A. JR B. PJ
C. TR D. MP
E. None of these

4. What is F's position with respect to R?

A. Third to the left
B. Fourth to the right
C. Third to the right
D. Both A and B
E. None of these

5. Who is third to the right of B?

A. R B. J
C. M D. Data inadequate
E. None of these

Directions (Qs. No. 6 to 10): *Study the following information to answer the given questions:*

Representatives from eight different Banks viz. A, B, C, D, E, F, G and H are sitting around a circular table facing the centre but not necessarily in the same order. Each one of them is from a different Bank viz. UCO Bank, Oriental Bank of Commerce, Bank of Maharashtra, Canara Bank, Syndicate Bank, Punjab National Bank, Bank of India and Dena Bank. F sits second to right of the representative from Canara Bank. Representative from Bank of India is an immediate neighbour of the representative from Canara Bank. Two people sit between the representative of Bank of India and B. C and E are immediate neighbours of each other. Neither C nor E is an immediate neighbour of either B or the representative from Canara Bank. Representative from Bank of Maharashtra sits second to right of D. D is neither the representative of Canara Bank nor Bank of India. G and the representative from UCO Bank are immediate neighbours of each other. B is not the representative of UCO Bank. Only one person sits between C and the representative from Oriental Bank of Commerce. H sits third to left of the representative from Dena Bank. Representative from Punjab National Bank sits second to left of the representative from Syndicate Bank.

6. Who amongst the following sit exactly between B and the representative from Bank of India?

A. A and the representative from UCO Bank
B. F and G
C. H and the representative from Bank of Maharashtra
D. H and G
E. Representatives from Syndicate Bank and Oriental Bank of Commerce

7. Who amongst the following is the representative from Oriental Bank of Commerce?

A. A B. C
C. H D. G
E. D

8. Four of the following five are alike in a certain way based on the given arrangement and thus form a group. Which is the one that does not belong to that group?

A. H – UCO Bank
B. A – Canara Bank
C. D – Bank of Maharashtra
D. E – Syndicate Bank
E. F – Punjab National Bank

9. Who amongst the following sits second to left of B?
A. C
B. H
C. The representative from Canara Bank
D. The representative from Punjab National Bank
E. G

10. Which of the following is true with respect to the given sitting arrangement?
A. B is the representative from Bank of Maharashtra
B. C sits second to right of H
C. The representative from Dena Bank sits to the immediate left of the representative from UCO Bank
D. A sits second to right of the representative from Bank of India
E. The representatives from Bank of Maharashtra and Syndicate Bank are immediate neighbours of each other

Directions (Qs. No. 11 to 14): *Six friends P, Q, R, S, T and U are sitting around the hexagonal table each at one corner and are facing the centre of the hexagonal. P is second to the left of U. Q is neighbour of R and S. T is second to the left of S.*

11. Which one is sitting opposite to P?
A. R B. Q
C. T D. S
E. U

12. Who is the fourth person to the left of Q?
A. P B. U
C. R D. T
E. Data inadequate

13. Which of the following are the neighbours of P?
A. U and P
B. T and R
C. U and R
D. S and T
E. Data inadequate

14. Which one is sitting opposite to T?
A. R
B. Q
C. Cannot be determined
D. S
E. T

Direction (Qs. No. 15 and 16): *Five girls are sitting on a bench to be photographed. Seema is to the left of Rani and to the right of Bindu. Mary is to the right of Rani. Reeta is between Rani and Mary.*

15. Who is sitting immediate right to Reeta?
A. Bindu B. Rani
C. Mary D. Seema
E. Reeta

16. Who is in the middle of the photograph?
A. Seema B. Rani
C. Reeta D. Seema
E. Bindu

Directions (Qs. No. 17 to 20) : *In a class there are seven students (including boys and girls) A, B, C, D, E, F and G. They sit on three benches I, II and III. Such that at least two students on each bench and at least one girl on each bench. C who is a girl student, does not sit with A, E and D. F a boy student sits with only B. A boyfriend of D sits on the bench I with his best friends. G sits on the bench III. E is the brother of C.*

17. How many girls are there out of these 7 students?
A. 3 B. 3 or 4
C. 4 D. 2
E. Data inadequate

18. Which of the following is the group of girls?
A. BAC
B. BFC
C. BCD
D. CDF
E. BAD

19. Who sits with C?
A. B B. D
C. G D. E
E. C

20. On which bench there are three students?
A. Bench I
B. Bench II
C. Bench III
D. Bench I or II
E. Bench I or III

Directions (Qs. No. 21 to 25): *In an Exhibition seven cars of different companies—Tata, Ambassador, Fiat, Maruti, Mercedes, Bedford and Fargo are standing facing to east in the following order.*

I. Tata is next to right of Fargo.
II. Fargo is fourth to the right of Fiat.
III. Maruti car is between Ambassador and Bedford.
IV. Fiat which is third to the left of Ambassador, is at one end.

21. Which of the cars are on both the sides of Tata car?
A. Ambassador and Maruti
B. Maruti and Fiat
C. Fargo and Mercedes
D. Ambassador and Fargo
E. Maruti and Fargo

22. Which of the following statement is correct?
A. Maruti is next left of Ambassador.
B. Bedford is next left of Fiat.
C. Bedford is at one end.
D. Fiat is next second to the right of Maruti.
E. Maruti is next to Fiat

23. Which one of the following statements is correct?
A. Fargo car is in between Ambassador and Fiat.
B. Tata is next left to Mercedes car.
C. Fargo is next right of Tata.
D. Maruti is fourth right of Mercedes.
E. Maruti is next left to Tata.

24. Which of the following groups of cars is to the right of Ambassador?
A. Tata, Fargo and Maruti
B. Mercedes, Tata and Fargo
C. Maruti, Bedford and Fiat
D. Bedford, Tata and Fargo
E. Tata, Fiat and Fargo

25. Which one of the following is the correct position of Mercedes?
A. Next to the left of Tata
B. Next to the left of Bedford
C. Fourth to the right of Maruti
D. Fourth to the right of Maruti
E. Next to the right of Tata

ANSWERS

1	2	3	4	5	6	7	8	9	10
E	A	C	D	B	C	E	B	D	E
11	**12**	**13**	**14**	**15**	**16**	**17**	**18**	**19**	**20**
D	A	B	B	C	B	A	C	C	A
21	**22**	**23**	**24**	**25**					
C	A	B	B	D					

EXPLANATORY ANSWERS

1-5: (a) B is third to the left of J who is second to the left of M.

(b) P is third to the left of B and second to the right of R.

(c) T is not an immediate neighbour of M.

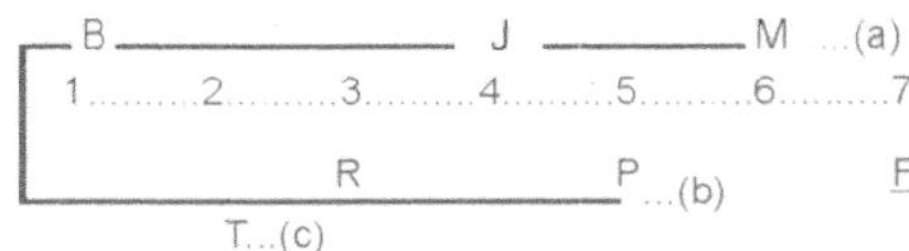

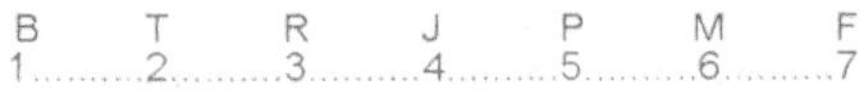

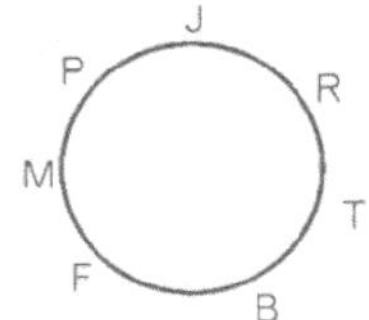

6-10:

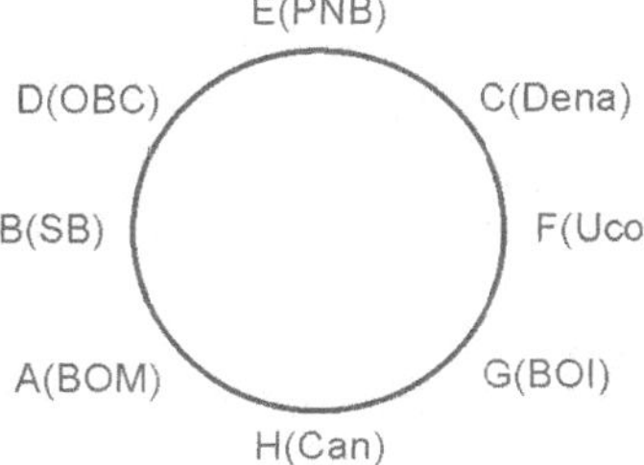

11-14:

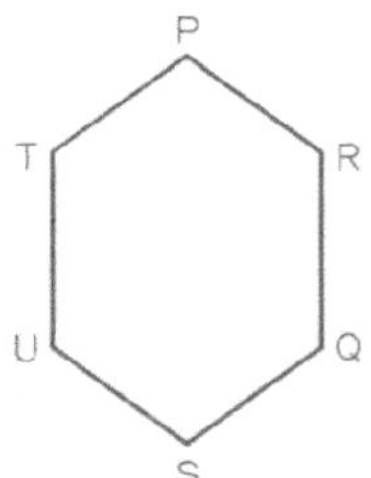

15-16:

● Bindu ● Seema ● Rani ● Reeta ● Mary

17-20:

Bench I	[A]	[E]	(D)
Bench II	[F]	(B)	
Bench III	[G]	(C)	

[ ] Boy

( ) Girl

21-25:

8 Data Sufficiency

In these questions, all one have to do is to analyse the given data and see if the answer to the problem can be given by all the data provided or by few of the data provided or cannot be answered with the data provided. Sometimes questions are qualitative in nature, wherein one has to apply his own value-judgement in order to reach a conclusion.

Example

Directions: *In the question below consists of a question and two or three statements given below it. You have to decide whether the data provided in the statements are sufficient to answer the question.*

1. Who is the North-East of R?

1. S is to the South-East of N, who is to the South-West of P, who is to the North of Q.
2. T is to the North-West of Q, who is to the South of P.
3. R, who is to the North of S, is midway between N and Q, N being to the West of R.

A. All 1, 2, 3 together are required
B. Only 1 and 3 together are sufficient
C. Only 2 and 3 together are sufficient
D. Either 1 and 3 together or 2 and 3 together are sufficient
E. None of these

Ans. D

EXERCISE

Directions (Qs. Nos. 1 to 30): *In each of the questions below consists of a question and two statements numbered I and II given below it. You have to decide whether the data provided in the statements are sufficient to answer the question. Read both the statements and* give answer:

A. If the data in statement I alone are sufficient to answer the question, while the data in statement II alone are not sufficient to answer the question.
B. If the data in statement II alone are sufficient to answer the question, while the data in statement I alone are not sufficient to answer the question.
C. If the data either in statement I alone or in statement II alone are sufficient to answer the question.
D. If the data given in both statements I and II together are not sufficient to answer the question and
E. If the data in both statements I and II together are necessary to answer the question.

1. The last Sunday of March, 2006 fell on which date?

Statements:

I. The first Sunday of that month fell on 5th.
II. The last day of that month was Friday.

2. In which year was Raju born?

Statements:

I. Raju at present is 25 years younger to his mother.
II. Raju's brother, who was born in 1964, is 35 years younger to his mother.

3. How many children does M have?

Statements:

I. H is the only daughter of X who is wife of M.
II. K and J are brothers of M.

4. How much was the total sale of the company?
Statements:
I. The company sold 8000 units of product A each costing ₹ 25.
II. This company has no other product line.

5. What will be the total weight of 10 rods, each of the same weight?
Statements:
I. One-fourth of the weight of each rod is 5 kg.
II. The total weight of three rods is 20 kilograms more than the total weight of two rods.

6. How is J related to Y?
Statements:
I. Y and Z are children of D who is wife of J.
II. R's sister J is married to Y's father.

7. How is T related to F?
Statements:
I. R's sister J has married T's brother L, who is the only son of his parents.
II. F is the only daughter of L and J.

8. What is the code for 'sky' in the code language?
Statements:
I. In the code language, 'sky is clear' is written as 'de ra fa'.
II. In the same code language, 'make it clear' is written as 'de ga jo'.

9. How is J related to P?
Statements:
I. M is brother of P and T is sister of P.
II. P's mother is married to J's husband who has one son and two daughters.

10. How many children are there between P and V in a row of children?
Statements:
I. P is fifteenth from the left in the row.
II. V is exactly in the middle and there are ten children towards his right.

11. B is the brother of A. How is A related to B?
Statements:
I. A is the sister of C.
II. E is the husband of A.

12. Who is to the immediate right of P among five persons P, Q, R, S and T facing North?
Statements:
I. R is third to the left of Q and P is second to the right of R.
II. Q is to the immediate left of T who is second to the right of P.

13. How is X related to Y?
Statements:
I. Y says, "I have only one brother".
II. X says, "I have only one sister".

14. How many children are there in the row of children facing North?
Statements:
I. Vibha who is fifth from the left end is eighth to the left of Ashish who is twelfth from the right end.
II. Rohit is fifth to the left of Nisha who is seventh from the right end and eighteenth from the left end.

15. How is Tannu related to the man in the photograph?
Statements:
I. Man in the photograph is the only son of Tannu's grandfather.
II. The man in the photograph has no brothers or sisters and his father is Tannu's grandfather.

16. On which day of the week was birthday of Salim?
Statements:
I. Salim celebrated his birthday the very next day on which Arun celebrated his birthday.
II. The sister of Salim was born on the third day of the week and two days after Salim was born.

17. How many doctors are practicing in this town?
Statements:
I. There is one doctor per seven hundred residents.
II. There are 16 wards with each ward having as many doctors as the number of wards.

18. How many pages of book C did Robert read on Sunday?
Statements:
I. The book has 300 pages out of which two-thirds were read by him before Sunday.
II. Robert read the last 40 pages of the book on the morning of Monday.

19. Among F, V, B, E and C, who is the third from the top when arranged in the descending order of their weights?
Statements:
I. B is heavier than F and C and is less heavier than V who is not the heaviest.
II. C is heavier than only F.

20. On a T.V. channel, four films A, B, C and D were screened, one on each day, on four consecutive days but not necessarily in that order. On which day was the film C screened?
Statements:
I. The first film was screened on 23rd, Tuesday and was followed by film D.
II. Film A was not screened on 25th and one serial was screened between films A and B.

21. Which word in the code language means 'flower'?
Statements:
I. 'de fu la pane' means 'rose flower is beautiful' and 'la quiz' means 'beautiful tree'.
II. 'de la chin' means 'red rose flower' and 'pa chin' means 'red tea'.

22. Who is C's partner in a game of cards involving four players A, B, C and D?
Statements:
I. D is sitting opposite to A.
II. B is sitting right of A and left of D.

23. How many students in a class play football?
Statements:
I. Only boys play football.
II. There are forty boys and thirty girls in the class.

24. Can Ramesh retire from office X in January 2020, with full pension benefits?
Statements:
I. Ramesh will complete 30 years of service in office X in April 2014 and desires to retire.
II. As per office X rules, an employee has to complete minimum 30 years of service and attain age of 60. Ramesh has 3 years to complete age of 60.

25. On which date in August was Kunal born?
Statements:
I. Kunal's mother remembers that Kunal was born before nineteenth but after fifteenth.
II. Kunal's brother remembers that Kunal was born before seventeenth but after twelfth.

26. Madan is elder than Kamal and Sharad is younger than Alok. Who among them is the youngest?
Statements:
I. Sharad is younger than Madan.
II. Alok is younger than Kamal.

27. What is the code for 'or' in the code language?
Statements:
I. 'nik sa te' means 'right or wrong', 'ro da nik' means 'he is right' and 'fe te ro' means 'that is wrong'.
II. 'pa nik la' means 'that right man', 'sa ne pa' means 'this or that' and 'ne ka re' means 'tell this there'.

28. What is Gagan's age?
Statements:
I. Gagan, Vimal and Kusum are all of the same age.
II. Total age of Vimal, Kusum and Anil is 32 years and Anil is as old as Vimal and Kusum together.

29. How much money do Vivek and Sunny have together?
Statements:
I. Sunny has 20 rupees less than what Tarun has.
II. Vivek has 30 rupees more than what Tarun has.

30. Who among P, Q, R, S and T is the lightest?
Statements:
I. R is heavier than Q and T but lighter than S.
II. S is not the heaviest.

ANSWERS

1	2	3	4	5	6	7	8	9	10
C	E	D	E	C	C	E	D	B	E
11	**12**	**13**	**14**	**15**	**16**	**17**	**18**	**19**	**20**
C	C	D	C	C	B	B	E	A	E
21	**22**	**23**	**24**	**25**	**26**	**27**	**28**	**29**	**30**
D	C	D	E	E	B	C	E	D	D

EXPLANATORY ANSWERS

1. From I, we conclude that 5th, 12th, 19th and 26th of March, 2006 were Sundays.
So, the last Sunday fell on 26th.
From II, we conclude that 31st March, 2006 was Friday. Thus, 26th March, 2006 was the last Sunday of the month.

2. From both I and II, we find that Raju is (35 – 25) = 10 years older than his brother, who was born in 1964. So, Raju was born in 1954.

3. From I, we conclude that H is the only daughter of M. But this does not indicate that M has no son. The information given in II is immaterial.

4. From I, total sale of product A = ₹ (8000 × 25) = ₹ 200000.

From II, we know that the company deals only in product A.

This implies that sale of product A is the total sale of the company, which is ₹ 200000.

5. From I, we conclude that weight of each rod = (4 × 5) kg = 20 kg.
So, total weight of 10 rods = (20 × 10) kg = 200 kg.

From II, we conclude that:
Weight of each rod = (weight of 3 rods) – (weight of 2 rods) = 20 kg.
So, total weight of 10 rods = (20 × 10) kg = 200 kg.

6. From I, we conclude that Y is the child of D who is wife of J i.e. J is Y's father.

From II, J is married to Y's father. This implies that J is Y's mother.

7. From I, we know that L is T's brother and J's husband. Since L is the only son of his parents, T is L's sister.

From II, we know that F is L's daughter. Thus, from I and II, we conclude that T is the sister of F's father i.e. T is F's aunt.

8. The only word common to I and II is 'clear' and as such, only the code for 'clear' can be ascertained from the given information.

9. From II, we know that P's mother is married to J's husband, which means that J is P's mother.

10. From II, V being in the middle, there are 10 children to his right as well as to his left. So, V is 11th from the left. From I, P is 15th from the left. Thus, from both I and II, we conclude that there are 3 children between P and V.

11. B is A's brother means A is either brother or sister of B. Now, each one of I and II individually indicates that A is a female, which means that A is B's sister.

12. From I, we have the order: R, –, P, Q.

From II, we have the order: P, Q, T. Clearly, each one of the above two orders indicates that Q is to the immediate right of P.

13. The statements in I and II do not provide any clue regarding relation between X and Y.

14. Since 8th to the left of 12th from the right is 20th from the right, so from I, we know that Vibha is 5th from left and 20th from right *i.e.* there are 4 children to the left and 19 to the right of Vibha.

So, there are (4 + 1 + 19) *i.e.* 24 children in the row.

From II, Nisha is 7th from right and 18th from left end of the row.

So, there are (6 + 1 + 17) = 24 children in the row.

15. From I, we conclude that the man is the only son of Tannu's grandfather *i.e.* he is Tannu's father or Tannu is the man's daughter.

From II, we conclude that the man's father is Tannu's grandfather. Since the man has no brothers or sisters, so he is Tannu's father or Tannu is the man's daughter.

16. I does not mention the day of the week on the birthday of either Arun or Salim. According to II, Salim's sister was born on Wednesday and Salim was born two days before Wednesday *i.e.* on Monday.

17. From I, total number of doctors in town = (1/700 × N), where N = total number of residents in town. But, the value of N is not known.

From II, total number of doctors in town
= (Number of wards in town) × (Number of doctors in each ward)
= 16 × 16 = 256.

18. From I and II, we find that Robert read (300 × 2/3) *i.e.* 200 pages before Sunday and the last 40 pages on Monday. This means that he read [300 – (200 + 40)] *i.e.* 60 pages on Sunday.

19. From I, we have: B > F, B > C, V > B. Thus, V is heavier than each one of B, F and C. But V is not the heaviest. So, E is the heaviest. Thus, we have the order:

E > V > B > T > C or E > V > B > C > F. Clearly, B is third from the top.

20. From I, we know that the films were screened on 23rd, 24th, 25th and 26th. Clearly, D was screened second *i.e.* on 24th, Wednesday.

From II, we know that one film was screened between A and B.

So, A and B were screened first and third, *i.e.* on 23rd and 25th. But, A was not screened on 25th.

So, A was screened on 23rd and B on 25th. Thus, C was screened on 26th, Friday.

21. From the given two statements in I, the code for the only common word 'beautiful' can be determined.

From the given two statements in II, the code for the only common word 'red' can be determined.

In I and II, the common words are 'rose and 'flower' and the common code words are 'de' and 'la'. So, the code for 'flower' is either 'de' or 'la'.

22. Clearly, each of the given statements shows that B is sitting opposite to C or B is the partner of C.

23. It is not mentioned whether all the boys or a proportion of them play football.

24. Clearly, the facts given in I and II contain two conditions to be fulfilled to get retirement and also indicate that Ramesh fulfils only one condition out of them.

25. From I, we conclude that Kunal was born on any one of the dates among 16th, 17th and 18th.

From II, we conclude that Kunal was born on any one of the dates among 13th, 14th, 15th and 16th.

Thus, from both I and II, we conclude that Kunal was born on 16th August.

26. As given, we have: M > K, A > S.

From II, K > A.

Thus, we have: M > K > A > S.

So, Sharad is the youngest. From I, M > S. Thus, we have: M > K > A > S or M > A > K > S or M > A > S > K.

27. I. In 'right or wrong' and 'he is right', the common word is 'right' and the common code word is 'nik'. So 'nik' means 'right'. In 'right or wrong' and 'that is wrong', the common word is 'wrong' and the common code word is 'te'. So, 'te' means 'wrong'. Thus, in 'right or wrong', 'sa' is the code for 'or'. II. In 'that right man' and 'this or that', the common word is 'that' and the common code word is 'pa'. So, 'pa' means 'that'. In 'this or that' and 'tell this there', the common word is 'this' and the common code word is 'ne'. So, 'ne' means 'this'. Thus, in 'this or that', 'sa' is the code for 'or'.

28. As given in I and II, we have: $G = V = K$, $V + K + A = 32$ and $A = V + K$.
Putting $V + K = A$ in $V + K + A = 32$, we have: $2A = 32$ or $A = 16$.
Thus, $V + K = 16$ and $V = K$. So, $V = K = 8$.
Thus, $G = 8$.

29. From I, we have: $S = T - 20$.

From II, we have: $V = T + 30$.

Thus, from both I and II, we have:

$V + S = (T + 30) + (T - 20) = (2T + 10)$.

So, to get the required amount, we need to know the amount that Tarun has.

30. From I, we have: $R > Q$, $R > T$, $S > R$ *i.e.* $S > R > Q > T$ or $S > R > T > Q$.
From II, S is not the heaviest. So, P is the heaviest.
Thus, we have: $P > S > R > Q > T$ or $P > S > R > T > Q$.
Hence, either T or Q is the lightest.

9 Coded Inequalities

To solve coded inequalities problem one's primarily task is to combine (visualise) two or more inequalities in to one combined notation.

Rule-Carry one directional lightest inequality to deduce conclusion from combined inequality Whenever inequalities are combined together in one combined notation writing common terms only once then conclusion will follow between any two terms if and only if all the inequalities between these two terms points in one same direction and conclusion will carry lightest ('<' is lighter than '≤' and '>'is lighter than '≥') inequality sign present between these two terms.

Basics of above rule

1. Two inequalities can be combined if and only if they have a common term.
2. Two inequalities can be combined (to give valid conclusion) if and only if the common term is greater than (or 'greater than or equal to') one and less than (or 'less than or equal to') the other.
3. The conclusion –inequality will have an '≥' sign (or a '≤' sign) if and only if both the signs in the combined inequality were '≥'(or '≤',as the case may be).

EXERCISE

Directions (Qs. No. 1 to 6): *In the following questions, the symbols @, ©, •, % and $ are used with the following meaning as illustrated below:*

'P © Q' means 'P is neither greater than nor smaller than Q'.

'P @ Q' means 'P is smaller than Q'.

'P $ Q' means 'P is greater than Q'.

'P • Q' means 'P is either smaller than or equal to Q'.

'P % Q' means 'P is either greater than or equal to Q'.

Now in each of the following questions assuming the given statements to be true, find which of the two conclusions I and II given below them is/are Definitely true?

Give answer :

A. if only conclusion I is true
B. if only conclusion II is true
C. if either conclusion I or II is true
D. if neither conclusion I nor II is true
E. if both conclusions I and II are true

1. Statements: J $ N, N % F, F • D
Conclusions: I. F @ J II. D % N

2. Statements: J % N, N © D, D @ K
Conclusions : I. D © J II. D @ J

3. Statements: R © M, M @ V, V $ F
Conclusions: I. F @ M II. V $ R

4. Statements: N @ K, K • F, F $ W
Conclusions: I. F % N II. W @ K

5. Statements: B •K, K $ R, R % E
Conclusions: I. E @ K II. E @ B

6. Statements: M• T, T @ R, R © K
Conclusions: I. K $ T II. R % M

Directions (Qs. Nos. 7 to 11): *In the following questions, the symbols @, ©, %, $ and β are used with the following meaning as illustrated below:*

'P © Q' means 'P is smaller than Q'.

'P @ Q' means 'P is either smaller than or equal to Q'.

'P % Q' means 'P is greater than Q'.

'P $ Q' means 'P is either greater than or equal to Q'.

'P β Q' means 'P is equal to Q'.

Now in each of the following questions

assuming the given statements to be true, find which of the two conclusions I and II given below them is/are Definitely true?

Give answer:

A. if only conclusion I is true
B. if only conclusion II is true
C. if either conclusion I or II is true
D. if neither conclusion I nor II is true
E. if both conclusions I and II are true

7. Statements: B © T, T β M, M % F
Conclusions: I. B © M   II. B © F

8. Statements: M β R, R % T, T $ K
Conclusions: I. K @ M   II. K © M

9. Statements: W © D, D @ H, H β N
Conclusions: I. N $ D   II. W © N

10. Statements: W @ D, D $ R, R © K
Conclusions: I. R β W   II. R % W

11. Statements : F $ J, J % V, V © N
Conclusions: I. N $ F   II. N % J

Directions (Qs. No. 12 to 16): *In the following questions, certain symbols have been used to indicate relationships between elements as follows:*

A % B means A is neither smaller than nor greater than B.
A $ B means A is greater than B.
A & B means A is either greater than or equal to B.
A @ B means A is smaller than B.
A # B means A is either smaller than or equal to B.

In each question, three statements showing relationships have been given, which are followed by two conclusions I and II. Assuming that the given statements are true, find out which conclusion(s) is/are definitely true.

Mark answer :

A. if only conclusion I is true
B. if only conclusion II is true
C. if either conclusion I or II is true
D. if neither conclusion I nor II is true
E. if both conclusions I and II are true

12. Statements: P & Q, Q $ R, Q % S
Conclusions: I. P @ S   II. R @ P

13. Statements: F & G, G % H, H $ K
Conclusions: I. H @ F   II. F % H

14. Statements: T # V, V $ X, X & Y
Conclusions: I. V $ Y   II. X # T

15. Statements: C % E, E # W, W @ Z
Conclusions: I. W & C   II. C @ Z

16. Statements : L # M, M @ N, N $ P
Conclusions: I. L # N   II. M & P

Directions (Qs. No. 17 to 22): *In the following questions, the symbols @, ©, %, $ and ? are used with the following meaning as illustrated below :*

'P © Q' means 'P is either smaller than or equal to Q.
'P Ω Q' means 'P is either greater than or equal to Q'.
'P % Q' means 'P is smaller than Q'.
'P $ Q' means 'P is greater than Q'.
'P @ Q' means 'P is equal to Q'

Now in each of the following questions assuming the given statements to be true, find which of the two conclusions I and II given below them is/are Definitely true?

Give answer:

A. if only conclusion I is true
B. if only conclusion II is true
C. if either conclusion I or II is true
D. if neither conclusion I nor II is true
E. if both conclusions I and II are true

17. Statements: M % T, T $ K, K © D
Conclusions: I. T $ D   II. D $ M

18. Statements: F @ B, B % N, N $ H
Conclusions: I. N $ F   II. H $ F

19. Statements: R Ω M, M @ K, K © J
Conclusions: I. J $ M   II. J @ M

20. Statements: B $ N, N Ω R, R @ K
Conclusions: I. K © N   II. B $ K

21. Statements: J © K, K $ N, N Ω D
Conclusions: I. J % N   II. D % K

22. Statements: R @ D, D © M, M $ T
Conclusions: I. T % D   II. M Ω R

Directions (Qs. No. 23 to 27): *In the following questions, the symbols $, •, %, Ω and @ are used with the following meaning as illustrated below :*

'P • Q' means ' P is neither greater than nor equal to Q'.
'P @ Q' means ' P is neither smaller than nor equal to Q,.
'P Ω Q' means ' P is not greater than Q'.
'P % Q' means 'P is not smaller than Q'.
'P $ Q' means 'P is neither greater than nor smaller than Q'.

Now in each of the following questions assuming the given statements to be true, find which of the two conclusions I and II given below them is/are Definitely true?

Give answer:

A. if only conclusion I is true
B. if only conclusion II is true
C. if either conclusion I or II is true
D. if neither conclusion I nor II is true
E. if both conclusions I and II are true

23. Statements: R % W, W @ F, F $ Z
Conclusions: I. F • R II. Z • W

24. Statements: B @ K, K % J, J • M
Conclusions: I. J • B II. M @ B

25. Statements: D $ T, T Ω H, H @ N
Conclusions: I. H $ D II. H @ D

26. Statements: H Ω N, N • K, K Ω D
Conclusions: I. D @ N II. H • K

27. Statements : W % E, E @ K, K $ J
Conclusions: I. J Ω E II. W % K

Directions (Qs. No. 28 to 30): *Read the information/ statement given in each question carefully and answer the questions.*

28. Which of the following expressions will be true if the expression' A > B ≥ C < D is definitely true?

A. A > D B. C ≤ A
C. D > B D. D ≥ A
E. None is true

29. Which of the following expressions will not be true if the expression ' F ≤ G = H < K' is definitely true?

A. K ≥ F B. H ≥ F
C. G < K D. F < K
E. None of these

30. In which of the following expressions will the expression 'P < Q' be definitely true?

A. P ≥ R > N = Q B. Q < R ≥ N > P
C. P < R ≤ Q > N D. P ≥ N ≥ M > Q
E. None is true

ANSWERS

1	2	3	4	5	6	7	8	9	10
A	C	B	D	A	A	A	B	E	D
11	**12**	**13**	**14**	**15**	**16**	**17**	**18**	**19**	**20**
D	B	C	A	E	D	D	A	C	E
21	**22**	**23**	**24**	**25**	**26**	**27**	**28**	**29**	**30**
D	B	E	A	C	E	D	E	A	C

EXPLANATORY ANSWERS

(1-6): © → = • → ≤ @ → < $ → > % → ≥

1. J $ N → J > N, N % F → N ≥ F,
F • D → F ≤ D
Therefore, J > N ≥ F ≤ D
Conclusions:
I. F @ J → F < J : True
II. D % N → D ≥ N: False

2. J % N → J ≥ N, N © D → N = D,
D @ K → D < K
Therefore, J ≥ N = D < K
Conclusions:
I. D © J → D = J : False
II. D @ J → D < J : False
Either I or II is true

3. R © M → R = M, M @ V → M < V,
V $ F → V > F
Therefore, R = M < V > F
Conclusions:
I. F @ M → F < M : False
II. V $ R → V > R : True

4. N @ K → N < K,
K • F → K ≤ F,
F $ W → F > W
Therefore, N < K ≤ F > W
Conclusions:
I. F % N → F ≥ N : False
II. W @ K → W < K : False

5. B • K → B ≤ K,
K $ R → K > R,
R % E → R ≥ E
Therefore, B ≤ K > R ≥ E
Conclusions:
I. E @ K → E < K : True
II. E @ B → E < B : False

6. M • T → M ≤ T,
T @ R → T < R,
R © K → R = K
Therefore, M ≤ T < R = K
Conclusions:
I. K $ T → K > T : True
II. R % M → R ≥ M : False

(7- 11): © → < @ → ≤ % → > $ → ≥ β → =

7. B © T → B < T,
T β M → T = M,
M % F → M > F
Therefore, B < T = M > F
Conclusions:
I. B © M → B < M : True
II. B © F → B < F : False

8. M β R → M = R,
R % T → R > T,
T $ K → T ≥ K
Therefore, M = R > T ≥ K
Conclusions:
I. K @ M → K ≤ M : False
II. K © M → K < M : True

9. W © D → W < D,
D @ H → D ≤ H,
H β N → H = N
Therefore, W< D ≤ H = N
Conclusions:
I. N $ D → N ≥ D : True
II. W © N → W < N : True

10. W @ D → W ≤ D,
D $ R → D ≥ R,
R © K → R < K
Therefore, W ≤ D ≥ R < K
Conclusions:
I. R β W → R = W : False
II. R % W → R > W : False

11. F $ J → F ≥ J,
J % V → J > V,
V © N → V < N
Therefore, F ≥ J > V< N
Conclusions:
I. N $ F → N ≥ F : False
II. N % J → N > J : False

(12- 16): A % B → A = B, A $ B → A > B, A & B → A ≥ B, A @ B → A < B, A # B → A ≤ B

12. P & Q → P ≥ Q,
Q $ R → Q > R,
Q % S → Q = S
Therefore, P ≥ Q = S > R
Conclusions:
I. P @ S → P < S : False
II. R @ P → R < P : True

13. F & G → F ≥ G,
G % H → G = H,
H $ K → H > K
Therefore, F ≥ G = H > K
Conclusions:
I. H @ F → H < F : False
II. F % H → F = H : False
H is either smaller than or equal to F.

14. T # V → T ≤ V,
V $ X → V > X,
X & Y → X ≥ Y
Therefore, T ≤ V > X ≥ Y
Conclusions:
I. V $ Y → V > Y : True
II. X # T → X ≤ T : False

15. C % E → C = E,
E # W → E ≤ W,
W @ Z → W < Z
Therefore, C = E ≤ W < Z
Conclusions:
I. W & C → W ≥ C : True
II. C @ Z → C < Z : True

16. L # M → L ≤ M, M @ N → M < N,
N $ P → N > P
Therefore, L ≤ M < N > P
Conclusions:
I. L # N → L ≤ N : False
II. M & P → M ≥ P : False

(17-22): @ → =, © → ≤, % → <, $ → >, Ω → ≥

17. M % T → M < T,
T $ K → T > K,
K © D → K ≤ D
Therefore, M < T > K ≤ D
Conclusions:
I. T $ D → T > D : False
II. D $ M → D > M : False

18. F @ B → F = B,
B % N → B < N,
N $ H → N > H
Therefore, F = B < N > H
Conclusions:
I. N $ F → N > F : True
II. H $ F → H > F : False

19. R Ω M → R ≥ M,
M @ K → M = K,
K © J → K ≤ J
Therefore, R ≥ M = K ≤ J
Conclusions:
I. J $ M → J > M : False
II. J @ M → J = M : False
J is either greater than M or equal to M.

20. B $ N → B > N,
N Ω R → N ≥ R,
R @ K → R = K
Therefore, B > N ≥ R = K
Conclusions:
I. K © N → K ≤ N : True
II. B $ K → B > K : True

21. J © K → J ≤ K,
K $ N → K > N,
N Ω D → N ≥ D
Therefore, J ≤ K > N ≥ D
Conclusions:
I. J % N → J < N : False
II. D % K → D < K: False

22. R @ D → R = D, D © M → D ≤ M,
M $ T → M > T
Therefore, R = D ≤ M > T
Conclusions:
I. T % D → T < D : False
II. M Ω R → M ≥ R : True

(23 – 27): • → <, @ → >, Ω → ≤, % → ≥, $ → =

23. Statements: R % W → R ≥ W,
W @ F → W > F,
F $ Z → F = Z
Therefore, R ≥ W > F = Z
Conclusions:
I. F • R → F < R : True
II. Z • W → Z < W: True

24. Statements: B @ K → B > K,
K % J → K ≥ J,
J • M → J < M
Therefore, B > K ≥ J < M
Conclusions:
I. J • B → J < B : True
II. M @ B → M > B : False

25. Statements: D $ T → D = T,
T Ω H → T ≤ H,
H @ N → H > N
Therefore, D = T ≤ H > N
Conclusions:
I. H $ D → H = D : False
II. H @ D → H > D: False
H is greater than or equal to D.
So either I or II is true

26. Statements: H Ω N → H ≤ N,
N • K → N < K,
K Ω D → K ≤ D
Therefore, H ≤ N < K ≤ D
Conclusions:
I. D @ N → D > N : True
II. H • K → H < K : True

27. Statements: W % E → W ≥ E,
E @ K → E > K,
K $ J → K = J
Therefore, W ≥ E > K = J
Conclusions:
I. J Ω E → J ≤ E : False
II. W % K → W ≥ K : False

28. A > B ≥ C < D None is true.

29. F ≤ G = H < K, we have K > F.
Therefore, K ≥ F is not true.

30. In P < R ≤ Q > N , P < Q is true.

❀ ❀ ❀

10 Input Interpretations

In input-output problems one is asked to imagine that there is some computer or a word-processing machine and it performs some operation on a given input. These operations are performed repeatedly as per a pre-fixed pattern and subsequently one has different output in different steps. One's primarily job is to deduce the rule followed by computer/ machine in arranging numbers and words. One should analyze final arranged step while deducing rule applied.

Example

Directions (Qs. No. 1 to 4): *Study the following information to answer the given questions:*
A word rearrangement machine when given an input line of words, rearranges them, following a particular rule, in each step. The following is an illustration of input and the steps of rearrangement.
Input: over you pat me crow easy to.
Steps: (I) pat over you crow easy to me
(II) crow pat over you to me easy
(III) over crow pat to me easy you
(IV) to over crow pat easy you me, and so on.

As per the rule followed in the above steps, find out the appropriate step for the given input in the following questions.

1. If step V of an input is 'put down col in as much sa', what would be the VIIIth step?
A. down in put much sa as col
B. in put down col much sa as
C. much in put down sa as col
D. col put down as much sa in
E. None of these

Ans. E. The steps followed are :
Step V : put down col in as much sa
Step VI : in put down col much sa as
Step VII : down in put much sa as col
Step VIII : much down in put as col sa

2. Input: but calm free are so not eat. Which of the following will be the IIIrd step for this input?
A. so free but calm eat are not
B. but calm are free not so eat
C. are but calm free not eat so
D. but so free eat are not calm
E. None of these

Ans. D. The step followed are :
Input : but calm free are so not eat
Step I : free but calm so not eat are
Step II : so free but calm eat are not
Step III : but so free eat are not calm

3. Input : rim bye eat klin fe to low. Which of the following steps would be 'fe low rim to bye klin eat'?
A. VIth B. Vth
C. IVth D. IIIrd
E. None of these

Ans. B. The step followed are :
Input : rim bye eat klin fe to low
Step I : eat rim bye fe to low klin
Step II : fe eat rim bye low klin to
Step III : rim fe eat low klin to bye
Step IV : low rim fe eat to bye klin
Step V : fe low rim to bye klin eat

4. If step II of an input is 'ge su he for game free but', what would be the step VI?
A. ge for but free he game su
B. for free ge game su he but
C. free ge for but game su he
D. he ge su but game free for
E. None of these

Ans. E. The step followed are :
Step II : ge su he for game free but
Step III : he ge su game free but for
Step IV : game he ge su but for free
Step V : ge game he but for free su
Step VI : but ge game he free su for

EXERCISE

Directions (Qs. No. 1 to 5): *Study the following information carefully and answer the questions given below:*

When an input line of words is given to a word arrangement machine, it rearranges them following a particular rule in each step.

Input: car some pour tie more tin bee goat
Step I : goat car some pour tie more tin bee
Step II : goat more car some pour tie tin bee
Step III : goat more pour car some tie tin bee
Step IV : goat more pour some car tie tin bee
Step V : goat more pour some bee car tie tin
and step V is the last output.

1. If the 3rd step of an input is:
bend take vide nut zeal pot car tin.
Which of the following will be the last step?
A. 6th B. 5th
C. 7th D. 4th
E. None of these

2. If the 2nd step of an input is:
coat some for die song kill bit son.
Which is certainly the input?
A. for come die song kill coat bit son
B. for die come song kill coat bit son
C. for die song come kill coat bit son
D. Can't be determined
E. None of these

3. Input : door site may for you mean now goal
Which of the following is the 3rd step of the above input?
A. door goal mean site for may now you
B. door goal mean site may for you now
C. door site goal mean may for you now
D. Can't be determined
E. None of these

4. Input: mute deal sit cut coat day long for
Which of the following will be the 4th step?
A. coat deal mute sit cut day long for
B. coat deal long mute sit cut day for
C. coat deal long mute cut sit day for
D. coat deal long mute cut day for sit
E. None of these

5. Input : ask not feel task opt sale dark den
Which of the following will be the last step?
A. 5th B. 6th
C. 4th D. 7th
E. None of these

Directions (Qs. No. 6 to 10): *Study the following information to answer the questions given below:*

A number arrangement machine when given an input of numbers, rearranges them following a particular rule in each step. The following is an illustration of input and steps of rearrangement.

Input:	48	245	182	26	99	542	378	297
Step I	542	48	245	182	26	99	378	297
Step II	542	26	48	245	182	99	378	297
Step III	542	26	378	48	245	182	99	297
Step IV	542	26	378	48	297	245	182	99
Step V	542	26	378	48	297	99	245	182

This is the final arrangement and step V is the last step for this input.

6. What will be the fourth step for an input whose second step is given below?
Step II: 765 42 183 289 542 65 110 350
A. 765 42 542 350 183 289 65 110
B. 765 42 542 65 110 183 289 350
C. 765 42 542 65 183 289 110 350
D. Cannot be determined
E. None of these

7. What should be the third step of the following input?
Input: 239 123 58 361 495 37
A. 495 37 361 123 239 58
B. 495 37 58 361 123 239
C. 495 37 58 123 361 239
D. 495 37 361 239 123 58
E. None of these

8. How many steps will be required to get the final output from the following input?
Input: 39 88 162 450 386 72 29
A. Two B. Three
C. Four D. Six
E. None of these

9. What should be the last step of the following input?
Input: 158 279 348 28 326 236
A. 348 28 326 158 279 236
B. 348 28 326 236 158 279
C. 348 28 236 158 279 326
D. 348 28 158 326 236 279
E. None of these

10. If the first step of an input is "785 198 32 426 373 96 49", then which of the following steps will be "785 32 426 49 198 373 96"?
A. Third B. Fourth
C. Fifth D. Second
E. None of these

Directions (Qs. No. 11 to 15): *A word-number arrangement machine, when given an input as a set of words and numbers, rearranges them following a particular rule and generates stepwise outputs till the rearrangement is complete following that rule.*

Followings is an illustration of input and steps of rearrangement till the last step.

Input: pour ask 57 dear 39 fight 17 28
Step I : ask pour 57 dear 39 fight 17 28
Step II : ask 57 pour dear 39 fight 17 28
Step III : ask 57 dear pour 39 fight 17 28
Step IV : ask 57 dear 39 pour fight 17 28
Step V : ask 57 dear 39 fight pour 17 28
Step VI : ask 57 dear 39 fight 28 pour 17
and Step VI is the last output.

As per the rule followed in the above steps find out the answer to each of the following questions:

11. If step II of an input is "cut 97 38 end for 29 46 down", which of the following will be the last step?
A. Fifth B. Fourth
C. Sixth 4 D. Seventh
E. None of these

12. If the 4th step of an input is "ago 85 elite 79 exile fat 26 41", which of the following will definitely be the 2nd step of the input?
A. ago 85 79 elite fat 41 26 exile
B. ago 85 exile elite 41 26 fat 79
C. ago 85 26 exile 41 elite 79 fat
D. Cannot be determined
E. None of these

13. If the 1st step of an input is "car 17 vas tiger 92 87 like 52", which of the following will be the 4th step?
A. car 92 like 87 tiger 52 17 vas
B. car 92 like 87 17 vas tiger 52
C. car 92 like 87 tiger 17 vas 52
D. car 92 like 17 vas tiger 87 52
E. None of these

14. Input: zeal for 49 31 high 22 track 12
Which of the following will be the 3rd step?
A. for 49 high 31 track 22 zeal 12
B. for 49 high 31 zeal 22 track 12
C. for 49 high zeal 31 22 track 12
D. for 49 high 31 track zeal 22 12
E. None of these

15. Input : 19 feat 34 28 dog bag take 43
Which of the following steps would be "bag 43 dog 19 feat 34 28 take"?
A. Second
B. Fourth
C. First
D. Cannot be determined
E. None of these

Directions (Qs. No. 16 to 20): *A word-number arrangement machine, when given an input as a set of words and numbers, rearranges them following a particular rule and generates stepwise outputs till the rearrangement is complete following that rule.*

Followings is an illustration of input and steps of rearrangement till the last step.

Input: sine 88 71 cos theta 14 56 gamma delta 26
Step I: cos sine 71 theta 14 56 gamma delta 26 88
Step II: delta cos sine theta 14 56 gamma 26 88 71
Step III: gamma delta cos sine theta 14 26 88 71 56
Step IV: sine gamma delta cos theta 14 88 71 56 26
Step V: theta sine gamma delta cos 88 71 56 26 14

And Step V is the last Step of the arrangement of the above input as the intended arrangement is obtained.

As per the rules followed in the above steps, find out in each of the following questions the appropriate steps for the given input, Input for the questions

Input : for 52 all 96 25 jam road 15 hut 73 bus stop 38 46

(all numbers are in two digits)

16. Which word/number would be at the 6th position from the left in Step V?
A. 25 B. stop
C. jam D. all
E. road

17. Which of the following would be the Step III?
A. hut for bus all 25 jam road 15 stop 38 96 73 52 46
B. for us all 25 jam road 15 hut 38 stop 96 46 73 52
C. hut for bus all jam road 15 stop 38 96 73 52 46 25
D. for bus all 25 jam road 15 hut stop 38 46 96 73 52
E. None of the above

18. Which word/number would be at the 8th position from the right in Step IV?
A. 15 B. road
C. hut D. jam
E. stop

19. Which of the following would be Step VII?
A. stop road jam hut for bus all 15 96 73 52 46 38 25
B. road jam hut for bus all stop 15 25 38 46 52 73 96
C. stop road jam hut for bus all 96 73 52 46 38 25 15
D. jam hut for bus all 25 road stop 15 96 73 52 46 38
E. There will be no such step as the arrangement gets established at Step VI

20. Which step number would be the following output?
bus all for 52 25 jam road 15 hut stop 38 46 96 73
A. There will be no such step
B. III C. II
D. V E. VI

Directions (Qs. No. 21 to 24.): *A word-number arrangement machine, when given an input as a set of words and numbers, rearranges them following a particular rule and generates stepwise outputs till the rearrangement is complete following that rule.*

Input : tall 48 13 rise alt 99 76 32 wise jar high 28 56 barn

Followings is an illustration of input and steps of rearrangement till the last step.

Input : tall 48 13 rise alt 99 76 32 wise jar high 28 56 barn

Step I: 13 tall 48 rise 99 76 32 wise jar high 28 56 barn alt

Step II: 28 13 tall 48 rise 99 76 32 wise jar high 56 alt barn

Step III: 32 28 13 tall 48 rise 99 76 wise jar 56 alt barn high

Step IV: 48 32 28 13 tall rise 99 76 wise 56 alt barn high jar

Step V: 56 48 32 28 13 tall 99 76 wise alt barn high jar rise

Step VI: 76 56 48 32 28 13 99 wise alt barn high jar rise tall

Step VII: 99 76 56 48 32 28 13 alt barn high jar rise tall wise

Step VII is the last step of the above input, as desired arrangement is obtained.

As per the rules followed in the above steps, find out in each of the following questions the appropriate steps for the given input.

Input: 84 why sit 14 32 not best ink feet 51 27 vain 68 92 (All the numbers are two digit numbers)

21. Which step number is the following output?
32 27 14 84 why sit not 51 vain 92 68 feet best ink
A. Step V B. Step VI
C. Step IV D. Step III
E. There is no such step

22. Which word/number would be at 5th position from the right in Step V?
A. 14 B. 92
C. feet D. best
E. why

23. How many elements (words or numbers) are there between 'feet' and '32' as they appear in the last step of the output?

A. One B. Three
C. Four D. Five
E. Seven

24. Which of the following represents the position of 'why' in the fourth step?
A. Eighth from the left
B. Fifth from the right
C. Sixth from the left
D. Fifth from the left
E. Seventh from the left

Directions (Qs. No. 25 to 30): *A word-number arrangement machine, when given an input as a set of words and numbers, rearranges them following a particular rule and generates stepwise outputs till the rearrangement is complete following that rule.*

Followings is an illustration of input and steps of rearrangement till the last step.

Input : rose girl 13 petal 16 go 35 ate 71 wild 22 87

Step I : go rose girl 13 petal 16 35 ate 71 wild 22 87

Step II : go 13 rose girl petal 16 35 ate 71 wild 22 87

Step III : go 13 ate rose girl petal 16 35 71 wild 22 87

Step IV : go 13 ate 16 rose girl petal 35 71 wild 22 87

Step V : go 13 ate 16 girl rose petal 35 71 wild 22 87

Step VI : go 13 ate 16 girl 22 rose petal 35 71 wild 87

Step VII: go 13 ate 16 girl 22 rose 35 petal 71 wild 87

Step VIII: go 13 ate 16 girl 22 rose 35 wild petal 71 87

Step IX : go 13 ate 16 girl 22 rose 35 wild 71 petal 87

and Step IX is the last step of the rearrangement.

25. Input: man 79 over 63 like 43 joy 15 never climbed 21 56
How many steps will be required to complete the arrangement?
A. Eight B. Nine
C. Ten D. Eleven
E. None of these

26. Step II of an input: to 13 world news 73 29 win 52.
How many more steps will be required to complete the arrangement?
A. Six B. Four
C. Five D. Two
E. None of these

27. Input : no 11 19 94 join for 81 style 37 matched.
Which of the following steps will be the last?
A. VI B. VII
C. VIII D. IX
E. None of these

28. Step III of an input is : we 12 you 19 meet 17 discuss 15 result 16.
Which of the following will be step II?
A. we 12 you 17 meet 19 discuss 15 result 16
B. we 12 17 you meet 19 discuss 15 result 16
C. we 12 you 15 17 meet 19 discuss result 16
D. Cannot be determined
E. None of these

29. Which of the following cannot be definitely Step V of an input?
A. be 13 did 27 eye 43 soon 34 39 wonder
B. be 13 did 27 eye 43 soon 39 34 wonder
C. be 13 did 27 soon 43 eye 39 wonder 34
D. Cannot be determined
E. None of these

30. If two given inputs gives identically same output, which of the following is definitely true?
A. Both require same number of steps for final arrangement.
B. Two inputs are identically same
C. Both contains same elements which may or may not be in same sequence
D. 2nd last step for both arrangements will be same
E. None of these

ANSWERS

1	2	3	4	5	6	7	8	9	10
B	D	E	C	A	C	D	E	A	B
11	**12**	**13**	**14**	**15**	**16**	**17**	**18**	**19**	**20**
A	D	B	C	E	A	D	B	C	A
21	**22**	**23**	**24**	**25**	**26**	**27**	**28**	**29**	**30**
E	D	B	C	C	B	A	D	C	C

EXPLANATORY ANSWERS

Solution (1 to 5): Following rule is followed here: Words are arranged according to their no. of letters. Words with largest no. of letters are arranged first. If two words have equal no. of letters then the word which comes first in English Dictionary is arranged first. In each step only one word is arranged and the rest shift one position rightwards. The process goes on until all the words are arranged.

1.

Step III: bend take vide nut zeal pot car tin
⑥ 4 ⑥ 5 ⑥

Step III : bend take vide nut zeal pot car tin
Step IV : bend take vide zeal nut pot car tin
Step V : bend take vide zeal car nut pot tin

2. Previous step can't be determined

3.

Input: door site may for you mean now goal
① ③ 3 2 1

Input : door site may for you mean now goal
Step I : door goal site may for you mean now
Step II : door goal mean site may for you now
Step III : door goal mean site for may you now

4.

Input: mute deal sit cut coat day long for
④ 2 4 1 3

Input: mute deal sit cut coat day long for
Step I: coat mute deal sit cut day long for
Step II: coat deal mute sit cut day long for
Step III: coat deal long mute sit cut day for
Step IV: coat deal long mute cut sit day for

5.

Input: ask not feel task opt sale dark den
⑤ ⑥ 2 4 ⑥ 3 4 5

Input : ask not feel task opt sale dark den
Step I : dark ask not feel task opt sale den
Step II : dark feel ask not task opt sale den
Step III : dark feel sale ask not task opt den
Step IV : dark feel sale task ask not opt den
Step V : dark feel sale task den ask not opt

Solution(6 to 10): On observing last step it is clear that there are two alternating series of numbers: one in descending order and the other in ascending order. When we reach step 1 through input, we find that the largest no. becomes the first and remaining numbers shift rightward. In the next step, the smallest no. becomes the second and the rest shift rightward. These two steps continue alternately until the two alternate series are formed.

6.

Step II: 765 42 183 289 542 65 110 350
3 4

Step II : 765 42 183 289 542 65 110 350
Step III : 765 42 542 183 289 65 110 350
Step IV : 765 42 542 65 183 289 110 350

7.

Input: 239 123 58 361 495 37
3 1 2

Input: 239 123 58 361 495 37
Step I : 495 239 123 58 361 37
Step II : 495 37 239 123 58 361
Step III : 495 37 361 239 123 58

8.

Input: 39 88 162 450 386 72 29
④ 4 1 3 5 2

Input: 39 88 162 450 386 72 29
Step I : 450 39 88 162 386 72 29

Step II : 450 29 39 88 162 386 72
Step III : 450 29 386 39 88 162 72
Step IV : 450 29 386 39 162 88 72
Step V : 450 29 386 39 162 72 88

9.

Input: 158 279 348 28 326 236
④ 4 1 2 3

Last step can be known directly.

10.

Step I : 785 198 32 426 373 96 49
1 2 3 4

Step I : 785 198 32 426 373 96 49
Step II : 785 32 198 426 373 96 49
Step III : 785 32 426 198 373 96 49
Step IV : 785 32 426 49 198 373 96

Solution (11 to 15): Following rule is followed here: Words are arranged in alphabetical order and nos. are arranged in decreasing order alternately. In output the word, which comes first in dictionary, comes to the first place and the rest shift one place rightwards. In the next step, the largest no. comes to the second place and the rest shift one place rightwards. These two steps occur alternately until the last step is obtained.

11.

Step II : <u>cut</u> <u>97</u> 38 end for 29 46 down
⑥ 5 ⑥ ⑥ 4 3

Step II : cut 97 38 end for 29 46 down
Step III : cut 97 down 38 end for 29 46
Step IV : cut 97 down 46 38 end for 29
Step V : cut 97 down 46 end 38 for 29

13.

Step I : <u>car</u> 17 vas tiger 92 87 like 52
2 4 3

Step I : car 17 vas tiger 92 87 like 52
Step II : car 92 17 vas tiger 87 like 52
Step III : car 92 like 17 vas tiger 87 52
Step IV : car 92 like 87 17 vas tiger 52

14.

Input: zeal for 49 31 high 22 track 12
1 2 3

Step I: for zeal 49 31 high 22 track 12
Step II: for 49 zeal 31 high 22 track 12
Step III: for 49 high zeal 31 22 track 12

15.

Input : 19 feat 34 28 dog bag take 43
3 1 2

Input : 19 feat 34 28 dog bag take 43
Step I : bag 19 feat 34 28 dog take 43
Step II : bag 43 19 feat 34 28 dog take
Step III : bag 43 dog 19 feat 34 28 take

Solution (16 to 20) : Here in Step I word which come first in dictionary takes first position from left and rest elements shifts one position rightwards and in the same step largest number takes first position from right and other elements shifts one step leftwards. In next step, same methodology is applied to only unarranged ones. Process continues until all words are arranged fzrom left to right in reverse dictionary order and numbers are arranged in increasing sequence from right to left.

Input: sine 88 71 cos theta 14 56 gamma delta 26
4 1B 2B 1 5 5B 3B 3 2 4B

Here, to get final arrangement sequence will be : 5 4 3 2 1 1B 2B 3B 4B 5B

(Note here first unnumbered from left or right will not be circled as no element could arrive at arranged position)

Input: for 52 all 96 25 jam road 15 hut73 bus stop 38 46
3 3B 1 1B 6B 5 6 7B 4 2B 2 7 5B 4B

Input : for 52 all 96 25 jam road 15 hut 73 bus stop 38 46
Step I : all for 52 25 jam road 15 hut 73 bus stop 38 46 96
Step II : bus all for 52 25 jam road 15 hut stop 38 46 96 73
Step III : for bus all 25 jam road 15 hut stop 38 46 96 73 52
Step IV : hut for bus all 25 jam road 15 stop 38 96 73 52 46
Step V : jam hut for bus all 25 road 15 stop 96 73 52 46 38
Step VI : road jam hut for bus all 15 stop 96 73 52 46 38 25
Step VII : stop road jam hut for bus all 96 73 52 46 38 25 15

Solution (21 to 24) : Here in Step I smallest number takes first position from left and rest elements shifts one position rightwards and in the same step word which comes first in dictionary takes first position from right and rest elements shifts one position leftwards. In next step, same methodology is applied to only unarranged ones. Process continues until all numbers are arranged in decreasing sequence from left to right and all words are arranged in reverse dictionary order from right to left.

Input: 84 why sit 14 32 not best ink feet 51 27vain 68 92
6 7B 5B 1 3 4B 1B 3B 2B 4 2 6B 5 7

Here, to get final arrangement sequence will be:

7 6 5 4 3 2 1 1B 2B 3B 4B 5B 6B 7B

(Note here first unnumbered from left or right will not be circled as no element could arrive at arranged position)

Input : 84 why sit 14 32 not best ink feet 51 27 vain 68 92
Step I : 14 84 why sit 32 not best ink feet 51 27 vain 68 92 best
Step II : 27 14 84 why sit 32 not ink 51 vain 68 92 best feet
Step III : 32 27 14 84 why sit not 51 vain 68 92 best feet ink
Step IV : 51 32 27 14 84 why sit vain 68 92 best feet ink not
Step V : 68 51 32 27 14 84 why vain 92 best feet ink not sit
Step VI : 84 68 51 32 27 14 why 92 best feet ink not sit vain
Step VII : 92 84 68 51 32 27 14 best feet ink not sit vain why

Solution (25 to 30) : Here numbers and words are arranged alternately. Numbers are arranged in increasing order while words are arranged in decreasing order of their dictionary placements. If a number or word is already arranged, then next member is arranged in the same step.

25.

Input :man 79 over63 like 43joy 15 never climbed21 56
③ 6 9 4 5 1 2 8 10 3 7

Input : man 79 over 63 like 43 joy 15 never climbed 21 56
Step I : joy man 79 over 63 like 43 15 never climbed 21 56
Step II : joy 15 man 79 over 63 like 43 never climbed 21 56
Step III : joy 15 man 21 79 over 63 like 43 never climbed 56
Step IV : joy 15 man 21 like 79 over 63 43 never climbed 56
Step V : joy 15 man 21 like 43 79 over 63 never climbed 56
Step VI : joy 15 man 21 like 43 over 79 63 never climbed 56
Step VII : joy 15 man 21 like 43 over 56 79 63 never climbed
Step VIII : joy 15 man 21 like 43 over 56 never 79 63 climbed
Step IX : joy 15 man 21 like 43 over 56 never 63 79 climbed
Step X : joy 15 man 21 like 43 over 56 never 63 climbed 79

26.

Step II: to 13 world news 73 29 win 52
⑦ 5 ⑦ 4 3 6

Step II: to 13 world news 73 29 win 52
Step III : to 13 win world news 73 29 52
Step IV : to 13 win 29 world news 73 52
Step V : to 13 win 29 news world 73 52
Step VI : to 13 win 29 news 52 world 73

This is the final arrangement.

27.

Input : no 11 19 94 join for 81 style 37matched
① ① ② ⑦ 2 1 5 4 3 6

Input : no 11 19 94 join for 81 style 37 matched
Step I : no 11 for 19 94 join 81 style 37 matched
Step II : no 11 for 19 join 94 81 style 37 matched
Step III : no 11 for 19 join 37 94 81 style matched
Step IV : no 11 for 19 join 37 style 94 81 matched
Step V : no 11 for 19 join 37 style 81 94 matched
Step VI : no 11 for 19 join 37 style 81 matched 94

This is the final arrangement.

28. Previous steps cannot be determined.

29. Step V of any input should have at least five elements arranged.

❀ ❀ ❀

11 Drawing Inference

In evaluating inferences problems a passage is followed by some inferences and the job is to decide whether a given inference follows or not in the context of the given passage. The most vital aspect of this question is intensity of probability of a particular inference. Some of the inferences can be easily and quickly judged because they are directly based on the facts given in the passage. But in some cases, an inference is indirect. Here the interference appears to be overlapping *i.e.* one may be confused between definitely true or probably true, probably true or data inadequate, data inadequate or probably false and probably false or data inadequate

The inference can

(1) directly follow from the passage

(2) be inferred from the passage

(3) be inferred with the help of some key words.

While evaluating inferences, first of all check whether it can be evaluated with the help of the passage directly. Check if the given inference is directly supported (or contradicted) by something in the passage. More or less direct inference is a restatement of something already stated in the passage.

EXERCISE

Directions (Qs. No. 1 to 20): *Below are given some passages followed by several possible inferences which can be drawn from the facts stated in the passage. You have to examine each inference separately in the context of the passage and decide upon its degree of truth or falsity.*

Mark answer

A. if the inference is definitely true, *i.e.* properly follows from the statement of facts given.

B. if the inference is probably true, though not 'definitely true' in the light of facts given.

C. if the data are inadequate, *i.e.* from the facts given you cannot say whether the inference is likely to be true or false.

D. if the inference is probably false, *i.e.* though not 'definitely false' in the light of the facts given.

E. if the inference is 'definitely false', *i.e.* it cannot possibly be drawn from the facts given or it contradicts the given facts.

PASSAGE 1

The immediate challenge is on the food front. Shortfalls in production have been allowed to affect supplies and hence prices. The government is planning to focus on investment in irrigation and strategy. It appears that the Green Revolution instruments to encourage farmers to invest are no longer effective. The Green Revolution strategy was based on the state taking out the risk of collapse in prices. Farmers were offered remunerative prices and a guaranteed procurement of their produce in case the open market could not absorb it. Farmers could then borrow from banks, acquire the Green Revolution Technology and produce as much as they could. The pressure on the food subsidy was manageable as long as there was a food shortage. Prices in the open market then tended to be above the procurement prices. But with the food surpluses the situation has changed. The situation was unsustainable not merely because of the magnitude of this subsidy. It was also inefficient. It meant farmers were being led to produce crops based just on the prices Government fixed and not in relation to any legal demand. In these circumstances, the Government was reluctant to keep increasing procurement prices at the pace that used to be the norm in earlier years.

1. The Government is planning to make crucial changes in the Green Revolution strategies.
2. The Government is no longer in a position to provide subsidy to farmers.
3. As the open market prices are lower, all the burden of procurement of crops is on the Government.
4. Demand is much higher than the quantity of crops produced by the farmers.
5. The farmers tend to produce the crops as per their convenience and not constant with the demand.

PASSAGE 2

Long term economic progress comes mainly from the invention and spread of improved technologies. The scientific revolution was made possible by the printing press, the industrial revolution by the steam engine and India's escape from famine by increased farm yields the so called 'Green Revolution'. Right now rich countries are changing the world's climate by emitting billions of tones of carbon dioxide each year from the use of coal, oil and natural gas. In future years, China and India will make massive contributions to increase carbon dioxide in the atmosphere. Yet no country rich or poor, is keen to cut its energy use, owing to concern that to do so would threaten jobs, incomes and economic growth. New technologies will provide a key part of the solution. Already, 'hybrid' automobiles, which combine gasoline and battery power, can roughly double fuel efficiency cutting carbon dioxide emission by half. Similarly, engineers have developed ways to capture the carbon dioxide that results from burning coal in power plants and store it safely underground. The new technology called "carbon capture and sequestration" can cut 80%, of the carbon dioxide emitted during the production of electricity.

6. It may not be practically possible to switch over to the new hybrid technologies from the present ones.
7. In the forthcoming years, India and China are going to be at the top of the list of world's developed countries.
8. The more developed is a country; less is the contribution to increase in air pollution.
9. The new technologies can control emission of carbon dioxide caused only during electricity generation.
10. The developing countries in the world are trying to evolve new technologies to reduce the emission of carbon dioxide.

PASSAGE 3

In the overall economy of India, agriculture is the largest sector of economic activity. It plays a crucial role in the country's economic development by providing food to its people and raw materials to industry. It accounts for the largest share to the national income. The share of the various agricultural commodities, animal husbandry and ancillary activities has been more than 40 per cent since independence. During the decade of the fifties, it actually contributed about half of the national output.

11. Agriculture is the mainstay of Indian economy.
12. The contribution of agricultural sector has decreased in recent years.
13. Agriculture is the only source of income in India.
14. The contribution of agriculture to Indian economy rose substantially after independence.
15. Agriculture contributes to national income more than all other activities put together.

PASSAGE 4

Gujarat has hardly 8.5 per cent of its total area under forest. Of this a considerable portion is covered by wild grass and marshes. Denuded of thick forests, fauna have disappeared from many places. Mandvi, for instance, had its share of panthers once. The state government has imposed a total ban on cutting of trees for five years from this year. The imminent destruction of over 40000 hectares of forest land by the Narmada project has led to nationwide strong protest.

16. People in Gujarat are quite conscious of the need of conservation of forests.

17. There is thick forest in 8.5 per cent of the total area of Gujarat.

18. Gujarat is the first state in India to impose a total ban on cutting of trees.

19. A dam on the Narmada river is planned.

20. Once there was thick forest in Mandvi.

ANSWERS

1	2	3	4	5	6	7	8	9	10
A	B	E	E	E	E	E	E	E	A
11	**12**	**13**	**14**	**15**	**16**	**17**	**18**	**19**	**20**
A	C	E	A	A	A	E	C	A	A

SOME SELECTED EXPLANATORY ANSWERS

6. A new technology is developed in view of its viability and acceptance. So, the inference is false.

7. A developed country does not emit huge quantity of carbon dioxide.

9. It is clear from the passage that the technologies are being developed to decrease the emission of carbon dioxide from automobiles as well as from the production of electricity.

Syllogism

Syllogism was introduced by Aristotle (a reasoning consisting two premises and a conclusion). Aristotle gives the following definition of syllogism in his fundamental treatise Organon.

"A syllogism is discourse, in which, certain things being stated, something other than what is stated follows of necessity from their being so". Things that have stated are known as premises and the one that follows from the premises is known as the conclusion of the syllogism.

A categorical syllogism is a type of argument with two premises and one conclusion. Each of these three propositions is one of four forms of categorical proposition.

Type	Form	Example
A	All S are P	All monkeys are mammals
E	No S is P	No monkeys are birds
I	Some S are P	Some philosophers are logicians
O	Some S are not P	Some logicians are not philosophers

These four type of proposition are called A, E, I and O type propositions, the variables S and P are place-holders for terms which represent out a class or category of thing, hence the name "categorical" proposition.

Example

Directions (Qs. 1 to 3): *Below are given three or four statements followed by three or four conclusions. You have to take the given statements to be true even if they appear to be at variance with commonly known facts, and then decide which of the conclusions logically follow(s) from the given statements. For each question, mark out an appropriate answer choice that you think is correct.*

1. Statements: **Solution:**

(*a*) All locks are keys (*a*) LL – K

(*b*) All keys are bats (*b*) KK – B

(*c*) Some clocks are bats (*c*) C – B

Conclusions:

1. Some bats are locks. 1. B – L
2. Some clocks are keys. 2. C – K ×
3. All keys are locks. 3. KK – LL ×

A. Only 1 and 2 follow
B. Only 2 and 3 follow
C. Only 1 follows
D. Only 2 follows
E. 1, 2 and 3 follow

<u>C. Only 1 follows</u>

2. Statements: **Solution:**

(*a*) Some cups are pots (*a*) C – P

(*b*) All pots are tubes (*b*) PP – T

(*c*) All cups are bottles (*c*) CC – B

Conclusions:

1. Some bottles are tubes. 1. B – T
2. Some pots are bottles 2. P – B
3. Some tubes are cups 3. T – C

A. Only 1 and 2 follow
B. Only 2 and 3 follow
C. Only 1 and 3 follow
D. 1, 2 and 3 follow
E. None follows

<u>D. 1, 2 and 3 follow</u>

3. Statements: **Solution:**

(*a*) All papers are books. PP – B

(*b*) All bags are books. BaBa – B

(*c*) Some purses are bags Pu – Ba

Conclusions:

1. Some papers are bags. P – Ba ×
2. Some books are papers. B – P
3. Some books are purses. B – Pu

A. Only 1 follow
B. Only 2 and 3 follow
C. Only 1 and 3 follow
D. Only 1 and 2 follow
E. 1, 2 and 3 follow

<u>D. Only 2 and 3 follow</u>

EXERCISE

Directions (Qs. Nos. 1 to 10): *In each question below are given two statements followed by two conclusions numbered I and II. You have to take the given two statements to be true even if they seem to be at variance from commonly known facts. Read the conclusion and then decide which of the given conclusions logically follows from the two given statements, disregarding commonly known facts.*

Give answer:

A. If only conclusion I follows
B. If only conclusion II follows
C. If either I or II follows
D. If neither I nor II follows and
E. If both I and II follow.

1. Statements: I. All tables are chalks.
II. All chalks are chairs.
Conclusions: I. All chairs are tables.
II. All tables are chairs.

2. Statements: I. Some radios are stones.
II. All stones are rods.

3. Statements: I. Some birds are flowers.
II. Some flowers are books.
Conclusions: I. Some birds are books.
II. No book is a flower.

4. Statements: I. Some cows are jackals.
II. No fox is a cow.
Conclusions: I. Some jackals are foxes.
II. Some jackals are not foxes.

5. Statements: I. Only cats are animals.
II. No dog is an animal.
Conclusions: I. Some cats are not dogs.
II. Some dogs are cats.

6. Statements : I. All shoes are carpets.
II. No carpet is a pullover.
Conclusions: I. No shoes are pullovers.
II. All carpets are shoes.

7. Statements: I. No window is a wall.
II. No wall is a door.
Conclusions: I. No window is a door.
II. No door is a window.

8. Statements: I. All players are tall.
II. Johan is tall.
Conclusions: I. Johan is a player.
II. Johan is not a player.

9. Statements: I. All dogs are wolves.
II. Some wolves are tigers.
Conclusions: I. Some dogs are tigers.
II. Tigers which are wolves are not dogs.

10. Statements: I. All cars fly.
II. Some cycles fly.
Conclusions: I. All cars are cycles.
II. Some cycles do not fly.

Directions (Qs. Nos. 11 to 20): *In each question below are given three statements followed by two conclusions numbered I and II. You have to take the given two statements to be true even if they seem to be at variance from commonly known facts. Read the conclusion and then decide which of the given conclusions logically follows from the two given statements, disregarding commonly known facts.*

Give answer:

A. If only conclusion I follows
B. If only conclusion II follows
C. If either I or II follows
D. If neither I nor II follows and
E. If both I and II follow.

11. Statements: I. Some spoons are pots.
II. All pots are cups.
III. Some cups are cards.
Conclusions: I. Some cards are spoons.
II. Some cups are spoons.

12. Statements: I. Some keys are locks.
II. Some locks are doors.
III. Some doors are windows.
Conclusions: I. Some windows are locks.
II. Some doors are keys.

13. Statements: I. Some boys are flowers.
II. All flowers are jungles.
III. All jungles are houses

Conclusions: I. Some houses are flowers.
II. Some houses are boys.

14. Statements: I. All bottles are tanks.
II. All tanks are drums.
III. All drums are pipes.

Conclusions: I. Some pipes are tanks.
II. Some drums are bottles.

15. Statements: I. All sticks are brushes.
II. No brush is a fruit.
III. Some fruits are trees.

Conclusions: I. Some trees are sticks.
II. No tree is stick.

16. Statements: I. Some shirts are pants.
II. All pants are clothes.
III. Some clothes are napkins.

Conclusions: I. Some napkins are shirts.
II. Some clothes are shirts.

17. Statements: I. All packets are tents.
II. All tents are houses.
III. Some boxes are houses.

Conclusions: I. Some houses are packets.
II. Some boxes are tents.

18. Statements: I. Some nuts are bolts.
II. Some bolts are hammers.
III. Some hammers are nails.

Conclusions: I. Some nails are bolts.
II. No nail is a bolt.

19. Statements: I. All windows are doors.
II. No door is mountain.
III. Some mountains are roads.

Conclusions: I. Some roads are windows.
II. Some roads are doors.

20. Statements: I. Some phones are bangles.
II. Some bangles are rings.
III. All rings are sticks.

Conclusions: I. Some rings are phones.
II. Some sticks are bangles.

Directions (Qs. Nos. 21 to 25): *In each question below are given four statements followed by four conclusions numbered I, II, III and IV. You have to take the given two statements to be true even if they seem to be at variance from commonly known facts. Read the conclusion and then decide which of the given conclusions logically follows from the two given statements, disregarding commonly known facts.*

21. Statements: I. All silver are metals.
II. All metals are steel.
III. Some steel are stones.
IV. All stones are stands.

Conclusions: I. Some stands are metals.
II. Some stones are silver.
III. Some stands are steel.
IV. Some stones are steel.

A. Only conclusions III and IV follow
B. Only conclusion I follows
C. Only conclusion II follows
D. Only conclusion III follows
E. None of these

22. Statements: I. All chairs are tables.
II. All tables are songs.
III. Some songs are rhythms.
IV. Some rhythms are pillows.

Conclusions: I. Some tables are chairs.
II. All tables are rhythms.
III. All chairs are songs.
IV. Some pillows are songs.

A. Only conclusions I and III follow
B. Only conclusions I and IV follow
C. Only conclusion I follows
D. Only conclusion III follows
E. None of these

23. Statements: I. Some mobiles are pens.
II. Some pens are covers.
III. Some covers are plates.
IV. All plates are papers.

Conclusions: I. All mobiles are covers.
II. Some pens are papers.
III. All plates are pens.
IV. Some papers are mobiles.

A. Only conclusion I follows
B. Only conclusion II follows
C. Only conclusions I and IV follow
D. Only conclusions II and IV follow
E. None follows

24. Statements: I. All shoes are tables.
II. Some tables are lanes.
III. All caps are lanes.
IV. Some lanes are row.

Conclusions: I. Some tables are rows.
II. Some tables are shoes.
III. Some rows are caps.
IV. Some lanes are shoes.

A. Only conclusions I and II follow
B. Only conclusion II follows
C. Only conclusion III follows
D. Only conclusion I either or conclusion IV follows
E. None of these

25. Statements: I. Some symbols are numbers.
II. Some numbers are letters.
III. All alphabets are symbols.
IV. All pianos are letters.

Conclusions: I. Some symbols are letters.
II. Some numbers are pianos.
III. No letter is symbol.
IV. Some symbols are alphabets.

A. Only conclusion I follows
B. Only conclusion II follows
C. Only conclusions III and IV follow
D. Only conclusion IV follows
E. Only either I or III and IV follow

ANSWERS

1	2	3	4	5	6	7	8	9	10
B	E	D	B	A	A	D	C	D	D
11	**12**	**13**	**14**	**15**	**16**	**17**	**18**	**19**	**20**
B	D	E	E	C	B	A	C	D	B
21	**22**	**23**	**24**	**25**					
A	A	E	B	E					

EXPLANATORY ANSWERS

1. [A + A = A, All tables are chairs]

2. [I + A = I, Some radios are rods. Also, some radios are stones *conversion* Some stones are radios.]

3. [I + I = no conclusion]

4. [Change order of the statements to align. Now, No fox is a cow + Some cows are jackals = E + I = O*, Some jackals are not foxes.]

5. [Change order first. Now, No dog is an animal + Only cats are animals *implies* No dog is an animal + All animals are cats = E + A = O*, Some cats are not dogs.]

6. [A + E = E]

7. [E + E = no conclusion]

8. [Align: Johan is tall + Some tall are players = A + I = no conclusion. But, Johan should either be a player or a non-player. Hence either of the two choices follows.

9. [A + I = no conclusion]

10. [After alignment, All cars fly + Some fly are cycles = no conclusion]

11. [Some spoons are *pots,+ All pots* are cups. I + A = I type of conclusion "Some spoons are cups". Conclusion II is converse of it.]

12. [All the three premises are I type. No conclusion follows from two I premises.]

13. Some boys are *flowers.* + *All flowers* are jungles. I + A = I type conclusion, "Some boys are jungles". Some boys are flowers + *All jungles* are houses.

I + A = I type conclusion, "Some boys are houses". Conclusion II is converse of it.

14. All bottles are tanks. + All tanks are drums. A + A = A – type of conclusion *i.e.* "all bottles are drums'. Conclusion II is converse of it. All tanks are drums + All drums are pipes A + A implies A-type of conclusion "All tanks are pipes". Conclusion I is converse of it.

15. All sticks are brushes + No brush is fruit. *i.e.* A + E = E type of conclusion. "No stick is fruit". No brush is fruit + Some fruits are trees. *i.e.* E + I = O*,"Some trees are not brushes". Conclusions I and II forms a complementary pair. Therefore, either I or II follows.

16. Some shirts are pants + All pants are clothes = Some shirts are clothes. Conclusion II is converse of it.

17. All packets are tents + All tents are houses = All packets are houses. Conclusion I is the converse of it.

18. All the three premises are particular affirmative. No conclusion can be reached from two particular premises (I type).

19. All windows are doors + No door is mountain = No window is mountain. No door is mountain + Some mountains are roads = Some roads are not doors.

20. Some bangles are rings + All rings are sticks = Some bangles are sticks. Conclusion II is converse of the third premise.

21. All silver are metals + All metals are steel = All silver are steel. Some steel are stones + All stones are stands = Some steel are stands conversion Conclusion III. Conclusion IV is converse of the third premise.

22. All chairs are tables + All tables are songs = All chairs are songs (Conclusion III) Conclusion I is converse of first premise.

23. Some covers are plates + All plates are papers = Some covers are papers.

24. All shoes are tables + Some tables are lanes = no conclusion.

Conclusion II is the converse of the first premise.

25. All alphabets are symbols + Some symbols are numbers = no conclusion.

Conclusion IV follows from the conversion of the third premise. Conclusion I and III form complementary pair.

❀ ❀ ❀

13 Cause & Effect

In these questions, the job is to determine whether a given event is the cause or the effect of some other event. Events do not just happen without any cause behind them. These causes are the conditions under which these events (or results or effects) happen. Cause is an event which leads to a said effect and this fact is either scientifically proven or logically expected. An immediate cause means a cause that immediately precedes the effect and a principal cause means a cause that immediately precedes the effect and a principal cause means a cause that was the most important reason behind the effect. Obviously cause must occur before the effect, we can merely look at the given two events first and by analyzing the time of occurrence, we can find which event can't be a cause.

Example

Directions (Qs. Nos. 1-4): *In each of the following questions, two statements numbered I and II are given. There may be cause and effect relationship between the two statements. These two statements may be the effect of the same cause or independent causes. These statements may be independent causes without having any relationship. Read both the statements in each question and mark your answer as*

A. If statement I is the cause and statement II is its effect;
B. If statement II is the cause and statement I is its effect;
C. If both the statements I and II are independent causes;
D. If both the statements I and II are effects of independent causes; and
E. If both the statements I and II are effects of some common cause.

1. Statements:
I. Police had resorted to lathi-charge to disperse the unruly mob from the civic headquarters.
II. The civic administration has recently hiked the property tax of the residential buildings by about 30 per cent.

Ans. D: Both the statements I and II are the effects of independent causes.

2. Statements:
I. The government has allowed private airline companies in India to operate to overseas destinations.
II. The national air carrier has increased its flights to overseas destinations.

Ans. A: Since the Government has allowed private airline companies in India to operate to overseas, so the national air carrier has increased its flights to overseas destinations.

3. Statements:
I. Many people visited the religious place during the week-end.
II. Few people visited the religious place during the week days.

Ans. E: Both the statements I and II are the effects of some common cause.

4. Statements:
I. The performance of Indian sports persons in the recently held Olympics could not reach the level of expectation the country had on them.
II. The performance of Indian sports person in the last Asian games was far better than any previous games.

Ans. E: Both the statements are effects of some common cause.

EXERCISE

Directions (Qs. Nos. 1 to 12): *In each of the following questions, two statements numbered I and II are given. There may be cause and effect relationship between the two statements. These two statements may be the effect of the same cause or independent causes. These statements may be independent causes without having any relationship. Read both the statements in each question and mark your answer as*

A. If statement I is the cause and statement II is its effect;
B. If statement II is the cause and statement I is its effect;
C. If both the statements I and II are independent causes;
D. If both the statements I and II are effects of independent causes; and
E. If both the statements I and II are effects of some common cause.

1. Statements:

I. The prices of petrol and diesel in the domestic market have remained unchanged for the past few months.

II. The crude oil prices in the international market have gone up substantially in the last few months.

2. Statements:

I. India has surpassed the value of tea exports this year over all the earlier years due to an increase in demand for quality tea in the European market.

II. There is an increase in demand of coffee in the domestic market during the last two years.

3. Statements:

I. The government has recently fixed the fees for professional courses offered by the unaided institutions which are much lower than the fees charged last year.

II. The parents of the aspiring students launched a severe agitation last year protesting against the high fees charged by the unaided institutions.

4. Statements:

I. The Reserve Bank of India has recently put restrictions on few small banks in the country.

II. The small banks in the private and co-operative sector in India are not in a position to withstand the competitions of the bigger in the public sector.

5. Statements:

I. All the schools in the area had to be kept closed for most part of the week.

II. Many parents have withdrawn their children from the local schools.

6. Statements:

I. There is unprecedented increase in the number of young unemployed in comparison to the previous year.

II. A large number of candidates submitted applications against an advertisement for the post of manager issued by a bank.

7. Statements:

I. The school authority has asked the X Std. students to attend special classes to be conducted on Sundays.

II. The parents of the X Std. students have withdrawn their wards from attending private tuitions conducted on Sundays.

8. Statements:

I. Majority of the students in the college expressed their opinion against the college authority's decision to break away from the university and become autonomous.

II. The university authorities have expressed their inability to provide grants to its constituent colleges.

9. Statements:

I. The police authority has recently caught a group of house breakers.

II. The citizens group in the locality have started night vigil in the area.

10. Statements:

I. The Government has imported large quantities of sugar as per trade agreement with other countries.

II. The prices of sugar in the domestic market have fallen sharply in the recent months.

11. Statements:

I. It is the aim of the city's civic authority to get the air pollution reduced by 20% in the next two months.

II. The number of asthma cases in the city is constantly increasing.

12. Statements:

I. The private medical colleges have increased the tuition fees in the current year by 200 per cent over the last year's fees to meet the expenses.

II. The Government medical colleges have not increased their fees in spite of price escalation.

ANSWERS

1	2	3	4	5	6	7	8	9	10
D	C	B	B	D	A	A	B	E	A
11	**12**								
B	C								

EXPLANATORY ANSWERS

1. The prices of petrol and diesel being stagnant in the domestic market and the increase in the same in the international market must be backed by independent causes.

2. The two statements discuss two separate statistical and generalised results.

3. The parents' protest against high fees being charged by the institutions led the government to interfere and fix the fees at a more affordable level.

4. The inability of the small banks to compete with the bigger ones shall not ensure security and good service to the customers, which is an essential concomitant that has to be looked into by the Reserve Bank. I seems to be a remedial step for the same.

5. Closing the schools for a week and the parents withdrawing their wards from the local schools are independent issues, which must have been triggered by different individual causes.

6. An increase in the number of unemployed youth is bound to draw in huge crowds for a single vacancy.

7. It seems quite evident that the parents have instructed their wards to abstain from private tuitions on Sundays and attend special classes organised by the school.

8. Clearly, the university's decision to refuse grant to the colleges must have triggered the college authority to become autonomous.

9. Both the statements are clearly backed by a common cause, which is clearly an increase in the number of thefts in the locality.

10. Since the Government has imported large quantities of sugar as per trade agreement with other countries, therefore, the prices of the sugar in the domestic market have fallen sharply in the recent months.

11. The increase in number of asthma cases must have alerted the authorities to take action to control air pollution that triggers the disease.

12. The increase in the fees of the private colleges and there being no increase in the same in Government colleges seem to be policy matters undertaken by the individual decisive boards at the two levels.

❀ ❀ ❀

14 Course of Action

In these questions, a situation is presented and some courses of action are suggested in the context of that situation. Job is to determine which of them should be followed. Such questions tests one's ability to judge a problem correctly, to determine the root cause of the problem and then to prescribe a suitable course of action.

Basically there are two broad types of patterns in such questions, it is a 'problem-solution' or 'fact-follow-up action' type.

To solve questions on 'course of action' first of all, determine whether it is a 'problem-solution' or 'fact-follow-up action' type.

Example

Directions (Qs. Nos. 1 and 2): *In each question given below a statement is followed by three courses of action denoted 1, 2 and 3. A course of action is a step or administrative decision to be taken for improvement, follow-up for further action in regard to the problem, policy etc. on the basis of the information given in the statement. You have to assume everything in the statement to be true, then decide which of the three given/suggested courses of action logically follows for pursuing and decide the answer.*

1. Statement: The chairman of the car company announced in the meeting that all trial of its first product of the new car model 'M' are over and company plans to launch its car in the market after six months.

Courses of action:

1. The network of dealers is to be finalised and all legal, financial and other matters in this connection will have to be finalised shortly.
2. The company will have to make plan for product other than car.
3. Material, managerial and other resources will have to be in fine tune to maintain production schedule.

A. 1 and 3 only B. Only 1
C. All the three D. Only 2
E. None of these

Ans. A: After trials, the best availability of material, managerial and other resources is necessary to maintain production schedule. Hence 3 follows. As stated 'model M is its first product', so it is necessary to finalise the network of dealers and all matters regarding the sale of the product. Hence 1 follows. 2 has no connection with the statement.

2. Statement: The Company 'X' has rejected first lot of valves supplied by company"Y' and has cancelled its entire huge order quoting use of inferior-quality material and poor crafts-manship.

Courses of action:

1. The Company 'Y' needs to investigate functioning of its purchase, production and quality control departments.
2. The Company 'Y' should inspect all the valves rejected by Company 'X'.
3. The Company 'Y' should inform Company 'X' that steps have been taken for improvement and renegotiate schedule of supply.

A. Only 1 and 2
B. Only 2
C. All 1, 2 and 3
D. 2 and either 1 or 3
E. None of these

Ans. 3: As stated 'rejection due to inferior-quality material and poor craftsmanship', since purchase deptt is responsible for purchasing the inferior quality material and for improper inspection. Hence investigation is compulsory for all the departments. Hence 1 follows. 2 follows because claim of company 'X' may not be true. 3 follows because relationships with a previous client should always be kept out.

EXERCISE

Directions (Qs. Nos. 1 to 15): *In each question below is given a statement followed by two courses of action numbered I and II. You have to assume everything in the statement to be true and on the basis of the information given in the statement, decide which of the suggested courses of action logically follow(s) for pursuing.*

A. If only I follows
B. If only II follows
C. If either I or II follows
D. If neither I nor II follows
E. If both I and II follow

1. Statement: Severe drought is reported to have set in several parts of the state.

Courses of Action:

I. Government should immediately make arrangement for providing financial assistance to those affected.
II. Food, water and fodder should immediately be sent to all these areas to save the people and cattle.

2. Statement: A large number of people in ward J of the city are diagnosed to be suffering from a fatal dengue type fever.

Courses of Action:

I. The city municipal authority should take immediate steps to carry out extensive fumigation in ward J.
II. The people in the area should be advised to take steps to avoid mosquito bites.

3. Statement: Since its launching in 2001, Kingfisher Airlines has so far accumulated losses amounting to ₹ 8000 crore.

Courses of Action:

I. Kingfisher Airlines should be directed to reduce wasteful expenditure and to increase passenger fare.
II. An amount of about ₹ 300 crore should be provided to Kingfisher Airlines to make the airliner economically viable.

4. Statement: Exporters in the town are alleging that commercial banks are violating a Reserve Bank of India directive to operate a post shipment export credit denominated in foreign currency at international rates from March this year.

Courses of Action:

I. The officers concerned in the commercial banks are to be suspended.
II. The RBI should be asked to stop giving such directives to commercial banks.

5. Statement: A large number of people suffer illness every year due to drinking polluted water during the rainy season.

Courses of Action:

I. The government should make adequate arrangements to provide safe drinking water to all its citizens.
II. The people should be educated about the dangers of drinking polluted water.

6. Statement: Most of those who study in premier government engineering colleges in India migrate to developed nations for better prospects in their professional pursuits.

Courses of Action:

I. All the students joining these colleges should be asked to sign a bond at the time of admission to the effect that they will remain in India at least for ten years after they complete education.

II. All those students who desire to settle in the developed nations should be asked to pay entire cost of their education which the government subsidies.

7. **Statement:** As stated in the last census report the female to male ratio is alarmingly low in most of the states.

Courses of Action:

I. The government should conduct another census to verify the results.

II. The government should immediately issue orders to all the departments to encourage people to improve the ratio.

8. **Statement:** The retired Professors of the S Institute should also be invited to deliberate on restructuring of the organization, as their contribution may be beneficial to the Institute.

Courses of Action:

I. Management may seek opinion of the employees before calling retired professors.

II. Management should involve experienced people for the systematic restructuring of the organization.

9. **Statement:** Three districts in State F have been experiencing severe drought for the last four years resulting into exodus of people from these districts.

Courses of Action:

I. The government should immediately start food for work programme in these districts to put a halt to the exodus.

II. The government should make sincere efforts to provide drinking/potable water to these districts.

10. **Statement:** The sale of a particular product has gone down considerably causing great concern to the company.

Courses of Action:

I. The company should make a proper study of rival products in the market.

II. The price of the product should be reduced and quality improved.

11. **Statement:** A recent study revals that children below five die in the cities of the developing countries mainly from diarrhoea and parasitic intestinal worms.

Courses of Action:

I. Governments of the developing countries should take adequate measures to improve the hygienic conditions in the cities.

II. Children below five years in the cities of the developing countries need to be kept under periodic medical check-up.

12. **Statement:** A recent survey shows that the teachers are still not familiarised with the need, importance and meaning of population education in the higher education system. They are not even clearly aware about their role and responsibilities in the population education programme.

Courses of Action:

I. Population education programme should be included in the college curriculum.

II. Orientation programme should be conducted for teachers on population education.

13. **Statement:** STAR TV is concerned about the quality of its programmes particularly in view of stiff competition it is facing from SAB and other satellite TV channels and is cont-emplating various measures to attract talent for its programmes.

Courses of Action:

I. In an effort to attract talent, the STAR TV should revise its fee structure for the artists.

II. The fee structure should not be revised until other electronic media also revise it.

14. **Statement:** The Asian Development Bank has approved a $285 million loan to finance a project to construct coal ports by Coal India Limited in Kerala.

Courses of Action:

I. India should use financial assistance from other international financial organisations to develop such ports in other places.

II. India should not seek such financial assistance from the international financial agencies.

15. Statement: The Rabi crops have been affected by the insects for consecutive three years in the district and the farmers on average harvested less than fifty percent of produce during these years.

Courses of Action:

I. The farmers should seek measures to control the attack of insects to protect their crops next year.

II. The Government should increase the support price of Rabi crops considerably to protect the economic interests of farmers.

ANSWERS

1	2	3	4	5	6	7	8	9	10
B	E	A	D	E	B	B	B	E	A
11	**12**	**13**	**14**	**15**					
E	B	A	A	E					

EXPLANATORY ANSWERS

1. In the break-out of a natural calamity, the basic duty of the government becomes to provide the basic amenities essential to save the lives of people and cattle. Providing financial assistance to all would put undue burden on the country's resources. So, only II follows.

2. Clearly, prevention from mosquitoes and elimination of mosquitoes are two ways to prevent dengue. So, both the courses follow.

3. Clearly, for better economic gain, losses should be reduced and income increased. So, only course I follows.

4. The statement mentions that the commercial banks violate a directive issued by the RBI. The remedy is only to make the banks implement the Act. So, none of the courses follows.

5. The situation demands creating awareness among people about the dangers of drinking polluted water so that they themselves refrain from the same, and at the same time taking steps to provide safe drinking water. So, both the courses follow.

6. Clearly, no student can be bound to live and work in the country against his wish. So, I does not follow. However, it is quite right to recover the extra benefits awarded to students if they do not serve their own country. So, II follows.

7. A census is always conducted with the utmost precision, leaving negligible chances of differences. So, I does not follow. Further, the ratio can be improved by creating awareness among the masses and abolishing female foeticide. Thus, only course II follows.

8. The statement stresses that the contribution of retired Professors shall be beneficial. This means that these people's experience regarding working of the organisation is helpful. So, only course II follows.

9. The exodus can be checked by providing the people conditions conducive to living. So, both the courses follow.

10. Clearly, a study of rival products in the market will help assess the cause for the lowering down of sales and then a suitable action can be taken. Thus, I follows. The second course may not be implementable.

11. Clearly, the two diseases mentioned are caused by unhygienic conditions. So, improving the hygienic conditions will check the spread of disease. Also, periodic medical check-up will help timely detection of the disease and hence a proper treatment. So, both I and II follow.

12. The statement stresses on teachers' lack of awareness and knowledge in population education and as such the best remedy would be to guide them in this field through orientation programmes. So, only course II follows.

13. Revised its fee structure for artists will attract talent and enchance quality of STAR TV programmes. It cannot wait till other media take action. So, only course I follows.

14. Clearly, such projects will provide employment and shall be an asset and a source of income to the country later on. So, course I shall follows. Course II will slowdown country's economic growth.

15. Clearly, the problem demands taking extra care and adequate precautions to protect crops from insects and extending help to farmers to prevent them from incurring huge losses. Thus, both the courses follow.

❀ ❀ ❀

15 Distinguishing Argument

Arguments are the fundamentals unit of logic. An argument contains two explict constituents: supporting premises and conclusion. Some supporting premises make strong arguments while some make weak arguments. The question statement is (usually) in the form of a suggested course of action. Followed by the statement are two arguments, one argument advocates the suggested course of action by stating out the positive features or positive results of that action and the other argues against the suggested course of action by stating out the negative features or harmful results of that action.

To determine forcefulness of argument it should be preliminary screened first to reject an argument on the basis of preliminary observations. An argument can be rejected if it is ambiguous or if it is 'half-hearted' or if it is too simple to be acceptable or if it is in the form of a question. If a argument is not rejected in preliminary screening then argument is subjected to three steps to ascertain its strength.

Thus, solution consists of four stages: 1. Preliminary screening 2. Check, whether the result really follows or not 3. Check, whether the result really desirable or not (or harmful, in case of negative arguments)? 4. Check, whether the argument and the suggested course of action are properly related or not?

If an argument passes all the four checks, it is a strong argument, otherwise it is weak.

Example

Directions (Qs. Nos. 1 and 2): *In making decisions about important questions, it is desirable to be able to distinguish between "strong" arguments and "weak" arguments insofar as they relate to the question. "Strong" arguments are those which are both important and directly related to the question. "Weak" arguments are those which are of minor importance and also may not be directly related to the question or may be related to a trivial aspect of the question.*

Instructions: Each statement below is followed by two arguments denoted by I and II. you have to decide which of the arguments is a "strong" argument and which is a "weak" argument.

Give answer:

A. if only argument I is "strong".
B. if only argument II is "strong".
C. if either I or II is "strong".
D. if neither I nor II is "strong".
E. if both I and II are "strong".

1. Statement: Should one close relative of a retiring government employee be given a job in government services in India?

Arguments:

I. Yes, where else relative get a job like this?
II. No, it will close doors of government service to competent and needy youth.

Ans. B: I is weak because that relative may not be suitable for the job. II is strong. As the seats will be filled by close relatives of retiring government employees, deserving and other needy youths won't get entry for government services.

2. Statement: Should purchase of gold by individuals be restricted in India to improve its foreign exchange position?

Arguments:

I. Yes, interference on customer's right and freedom is desirable.
II. No, business interest has to be guarded first.

Ans. D: I is weak because such interference is not desirable in a democracy. II is weak because it gives priority to business interest on foreign exchange position, which is undesirable.

EXERCISE

Directions (Qs. 1 to 10): *Each question given below consists of a statement, followed by two arguments numbered I and II. You have to decide which of the arguments is a 'strong' argument and which is a 'weak' argument.*

Give answer:

A. if only argument I is "strong".
B. if only argument II is "strong".
C. if either I or II is "strong".
D. if neither I nor II is "strong".
E. if both I and II are "strong".

1. Statement: Should there be a restriction on the migration of people from one state to another state in India?

Arguments:

I. No. Any Indian citizen has a basic right to stay at any place of his/her choice and hence they cannot be stopped.

II. Yes. This is the way to effect an equitable distribution of resources across the states in India.

2. Statement: Should there be a complete ban on use of all types of chemical pesticides in India?

Arguments:

I. No. The pests will destroy all the crops and the farmers will have nothing to harvest.

II. Yes. The chemical pesticides used in agriculture pollute the water underground and this has become a serious health hazard.

3. Statement: Should officers accepting bribe be punished?

Arguments:

I. No. Certain circumstances may have compelled them to take bribe.

II. Yes. They should do the job they are entrusted with, honestly.

4. Statement: Should cutting of trees be banned altogether?

Arguments:

I. Yes. It is very much necessary to do so to restore ecological balance.

II. No. A total ban would harm timber based industries.

5. Statement: Should all refugees, who make unauthorized entry into a country, be forced to go back to their homeland?

Arguments:

I. Yes. They make their colonies and occupy a lot of land.

II. No. They leave their homes because of hunger or some terror and on human grounds, should not be forced to go back.

6. Statement: Should all the practising doctors be brought under Government control so that they get salary from the Government and treat patients free of cost?

Arguments:

I. No. How can any country do such an undemocratic thing?

II. Yes. Despite many problems, it will certainly help minimize, if not eradicate, unethical medical practices.

7. Statement: Should there be a ban on product advertising?

Arguments:

I. No. It is an age of advertising. Unless your advertisement is better than your other competitors, the product will not be sold.

II. Yes. The money spent on advertising is very huge and it inflates the cost of the product.

8. Statement: Are nuclear families better than joint families?

Arguments:

I. No. Joint families ensure security and also reduce the burden of work.

II. Yes. Nuclear families ensure greater freedom.

9. Statement: Should there be compulsory medical examination of both the man and the woman before they marry each other?

Arguments:

I. No. This is an intrusion to the privacy of an individual and hence cannot be tolerated.

II. Yes. This will substantially reduce the risk of giving birth to children with serious ailments.

10. Statement: Should government stop spending huge amounts of money on international sports?

Arguments:

I. Yes. This money can be utilized for upliftment of the poor.

II. No. Sports persons will be frustrated and will not get international exposure.

ANSWERS

1	2	3	4	5	6	7	8	9	10
A	E	B	E	B	B	E	E	B	B

EXPLANATORY ANSWERS

1. Clearly, argument I holds strong, while argument II is vague.

2. Obviously, pesticides are meant to prevent the crops from harmful pests. But at the same time, they get washed away with water and contaminate the groundwater. Thus, both the arguments hold strong.

3. Obviously, officers are paid duly for the jobs they do. So, they must do it honestly. Thus, argument II alone holds.

4. Definitely, trees play a vital role in maintaining ecological balance and so must be preserved. So, argument I holds. Also, trees form the basic source of timber and a complete ban on cutting of trees would harm timber based industries. So, only a controlled cutting of trees should be allowed and the loss replenished by planting more trees. So, argument II is also valid.

5. Obviously, refugees are people forced out of their homeland by some misery and need shelter desperately. So, argument II holds. Argument I against the statement is vague.

6. A doctor treating a patient individually can mislead the patient into wrong and unnecessary treatment for his personal gain. So, argument II holds strong. Also, a policy benefiting common people cannot be termed 'undemocratic'. So, I is vague.

7. Obviously, it is the advertisement which makes the customer aware of the qualities of the product and leads him to buy it. So, argument I is valid. But at the same time, advertising nowadays has become a costly affair and the expenses on it add to the price of the product. So, argument II also holds strong.

8. Obviously, with so many people around in a joint family, there is more security. Also, work is shared. So, argument I holds. In nuclear families, there are lesser number of people and so lesser responsibilities and more freedom. Thus, II also holds.

9. Definitely, such a step would help to prevent the growth of diseases like AIDS. So, only argument II is strong.

10. Obviously, spending money on sports should not be avoided merely because it can be spent on socio-economic problems. So, argument I does not hold. Also, if the expenses on sports are curtailed, the sports persons would face lack of facilities and training and our country will lag behind in the international sports competitions. So, II holds.

❀ ❀ ❀

16 Drawing Conclusions

In this reasoning pattern, a statement is given followed by two conclusions. The statement is to be taken as the fact. Then based on it one has to decide which of the conclusion(s) definitely follows or does not follow from the given statement.

Example

In the questions below the answer is given as:

A. If only conclusion I follows
B. If only conclusion II follows
C. If either I or II follows
D. If neither I nor II follows and
E. If both I and II follow.

1. **Statement:** It is said that teachers should not go on strike. Why should they not? Strike is an inherent right.

   Conclusions:

   I. Teachers cannot get justice unless they go on strike.
   II. Every teacher should go on strike.

Ans. A: Only conclusion I follows from the given statements, *i.e.*, as an inherent right the teachers can get justice in appropriate cases if they go on strike. Conclusion II does not follow.

2. **Statement:** The government of country 'X' has recently announced several concessions and offered attractive package tours for foreign visitors.

   Conclusions:

   I. Now, more numbers of foreign tourists will visit the country.
   II. The government of country 'X' seems to be serious in attracting foreign tourists.

Ans. E: Concessions and attractive package tours will encourage tourists and country 'X' has taken the step only because it seems to be serious about foreign visitors. So both conclusion I and conclusion II follow from the given statement.

EXERCISE

Directions (Qs. Nos. 1 to 10): *In each question below is given a statement followed by two conclusions numbered I and II. You have to assume everything in the statement to be true, then consider the two conclusions together and decide which of them logically follows beyond a reasonable doubt from the information given in the statement*

Give answer:

A. If only conclusion I follows
B. If only conclusion II follows
C. If either I or II follows
D. If neither I nor II follows and
E. If both I and II follow.

1. **Statement:** In a one day cricket match, the total runs made by a team were 200. Out of these 160 runs were made by spinners.

   Conclusions:

   I. 80% of the team consists of spinners.
   II. The opening batsmen were spinners.

2. **Statement:** The old order changed yielding place to new.

   Conclusions:

   I. Change is the law of nature.
   II. Discard old ideas because they are old.

3. **Statement:** Government has spoiled many top ranking financial institutions by appointing bureaucrats as Directors of these institutions.

Conclusions:

I. Government should appoint Directors of the financial institutes taking into consideration the expertise of the person in the area of finance.

II. The Director of the financial institute should have expertise commensurate with the financial work carried out by the institute.

4. **Statement:** Population increase coupled with depleting resources is going to be the scenario of many developing countries in days to come.

Conclusions:

I. The population of developing countries will not continue to increase in future.

II. It will be very difficult for the governments of developing countries to provide its people decent quality of life.

5. **Statement:** Prime age school-going children in urban India have now become avid as well as more regular viewers of television, even in households without a TV. As a result, there has been an alarming decline in the extent of readership of newspapers.

Conclusions:

I. Method of increasing the readership of newspapers should be devised.

II. A team of experts should be sent to other countries to study the impact of TV. On the readership of newspapers.

6. **Statement:** The Government run company had asked its employees to declare their income and assets but it has been strongly resisted by employees union and no employee is going to declare his income.

Conclusions:

I. The employees of this company do not seem to have any additional undisclosed income besides their salary.

II. The employees union wants all senior officers to declare their income first.

7. **Statement:** The distance of 900 km by road between Bombay and Jafra will be reduced to 280 km by sea. This will lead to a saving of ₹ 7.92 crores per annum on fuel.

Conclusions:

I. Transportation by sea is cheaper than that by road.

II. Fuel must be saved to the greatest extent.

8. **Statement:** The manager humiliated Sachin in the presence of his colleagues.

Conclusion:

I. The manager did not like Sachin.

II. Sachin was not popular with his colleagues.

9. **Statements:** Nation X faced growing international opposition for its decision to explode eight nuclear weapons at its test site.

Conclusions:

I. The citizens of the nation favoured the decision.

II. Some powerful countries do not want other nations to become as powerful as they are.

10. **Statement:** National Aluminium Company has moved India from a position of shortage to self-sufficiency in the metal.

Conclusions:

I. Previously, India had to import aluminium.

II. With this speed, it can soon become a foreign exchange earner.

ANSWERS

1	2	3	4	5	6	7	8	9	10
D	A	E	B	D	D	B	D	D	E

EXPLANATORY ANSWERS

1. According to the statement, 80% of the total runs were made by spinners. So, I does not follow. Nothing about the opening batsmen is mentioned in the statement. So, II also does not follow.
2. Clearly, I directly follows from the given statement. Also, it is mentioned that old ideas are replaced by new ones, as thinking changes with the progressing time. So, II does not follow.
3. According to the statement, Government has spoiled financial institutions by appointing bureaucrats as Directors. This means that only those persons should be appointed as Directors who are experts in finance and are acquainted with the financial work of the institute. So, both I and II follow.
4. The fact given in I is quite contrary to the given statement. So, I does not follow. II mentions the direct implications of the state discussed in the statement. Thus, II follows.
5. The statement concentrates on the increasing viewership of TV. and does not stress either on increasing the readership of newspapers or making studies regarding the same. So, neither I nor II follows.
6. Nothing about the details of the employees' income or the cause of their refusal to declare their income and assets, can be deduced from the given statement. So, neither I nor II follows.
7. According to the statement, sea transport is cheaper than road transport in the case of route from Bombay to Jafra, not in all the cases. So, conclusion I does not follow. The statement stresses on the saving of fuel. So, conclusion II follows.
8. The manager might have humiliated Sachin not because of his dislike but on account of certain negligence or mistake on his part. So, I does not follow. Also, nothing about Sachin's rapport with his colleagues can be deduced from the statement. So, II also does not follow.
9. Neither the citizens response to the decision nor the reason for opposition by other nations can be deduced from the statement. So, neither I nor II follows.
10. According to the statement, National Aluminium Company has moved India from a position of shortage in the past to self-sufficiency in the present. This means that previously, India had to import aluminium. So, I follows. Also, it can be deduced that if production increases at the same rate, India can export it in future. So, II also follows.

17 Statement Assumptions

The mental recognition of cause-and-effect relationship is called reasoning. It may be the prediction of an event from an observed cause or the inference of a cause from an observed event. Logical reasoning is a process of passing from the known to the unknown. It is the process of deriving a logical inference from a hypothesis through reasoning.

Argumentation is fundamental to all logic. In logic, we advocate a certain point of view with the help of some evidences and certain assumptions. The whole thing is known as "argumentation". An argument contains two explict constituents: supporting premises and conclusion. There is also an implict (hidden) constituent called assumption. Conclusion is arrived at with the help of one or more than one statement, which may be called premise or proposition. In an argument, the number of premises can be more than one and it is not necessary that every argument have an assumption *i.e.* if an argument is complete in itself and does not have the hidden links, it will not have any assumptions. An assumption is something which is assumed, supposed and taken for granted.

Example

Directions: *In each question below is given a statement followed by two assumptions numbered 1 and 2. An assumption is something supposed or taken for granted. You have to consider the statement and the following assumptions and to decide which of the assumptions is implict in the statement.*

Give answer

A. if only assumption 1 is implict.
B. if only assumption 2 is implict.
C. if either 1 or 2 is implict.
D. if neither 1 nor 2 is implict.
E. if both 1 and 2 are implict.

1. Statement: The 'X' group of employees' association have opposed Voluntary Retirement Scheme to the employees of some organisations.

Assumptions:

1. Only those employees who are not efficient may opt for the scheme.
2. The response of the employees may be lukewarm towards the scheme and it may not the benefit the organisation to the desired level.

Ans. A: The employees association is generally concerned with the welfare of employees and not with benefit of the organisation, hence 2 is not implict. 1 is not related with the statement.

Alter: If assumptions 1 and 2 are considered wrong then too main statement is valid one so none of them follows.

2. Statement: In view of the statement on the ongoing strike of work by the employees, the government has agreed to work out an effective social security programme.

Assumptions:

1. The striking employees may not be satisfied with the announcement and continue the agitation.
2. The striking employees may withdraw their agitation with immediate effect and start working.

Ans. B: Assuming 2 only, the government has agreed to work out an effective social security programme.

Alter: If 1 is considered correct than the main statement is absurd so 1 does not follow. Main statement is meaningful only when 2 is considered correct, so 2 follows.

EXERCISE

Directions (Qs. Nos. 1-10): *In each question below is given a statement followed by two assumptions numbered I and II. You have to consider the statement and the following assumptions and decide which of the assumptions is implicit in the statement.*

Give answer

A. if only assumption I is implict.
B. if only assumption II is implict.
C. if either I or II is implict.
D. if neither I nor II is implict.
E. if both I and II are implict.

1. **Statement:** Many historians have done more harm than good by distorting truth.
Assumptions:
I. People believe what is reported by the historians.
II. Historians are seldom expected to depict the truth.

2. **Statement:** "As there is a great demand, every person seeking tickets of the programme will be given only five tickets."
Assumptions:
I. The organizers are not keen on selling the tickets.
II. No one is interested in getting more than five tickets.

3. **Statement:** "Computer education should start at schools itself."
Assumptions:
I. Learning computers is easy.
II. Computer educated is hardly unemployed.

4. **Statement:** "The programme will start at 6 p.m. but you can come there up to 7 p.m. or so and still there is no problem."
Assumptions:
I. The programme will continue even after 7 p.m.
II. The programme may not even start by that time.

5. **Statement:** The organization should promote employees on the basis of merit alone and not on the basis of length of service or seniority.
Assumptions:
I. Length of service or seniority do not alone reflect merit of an employee.
II. It is possible to determine and measure merit of an employee.

6. **Statement:** The higher echelons of any organization are expected to be models of observational learning and should not be considered as merely sources of reward and punishments.
Assumptions:
I. Employees are likely to be sensitive enough to learn by observing the behaviour of their bosses.
II. Normally bosses are considered as sources of reward and punishment.

7. **Statement:** "If you want to give any advertisement, give it in the newspaper X." — A tells B.
Assumptions:
I. B wants to publicise his products.
II. Newspaper X has a wide circulation.

8. **Statement:** Kundan left for Delhi on Tuesday by train to attend a function to be held on Friday at his uncle's house in Delhi.
Assumptions:
I. Kundan may reach Delhi on Wednesday.
II. Kundan may reach Delhi before Friday.

9. **Statement:** "Get rid of your past for future, get our new generation fridge at a discount in exchange of old".—An advertisement.
Assumptions:
I. The sales of the new fridge may increase in the coming months.
II. People prefer to exchange future with past.

10. **Statement:** "Ensure a good night's sleeps for your family with safe and effective X mosquito coil."—An advertisement.
Assumptions:
I. X mosquito coil is better than any other mosquito coil.
II. A good night's sleep is desirable.

ANSWERS

1	2	3	4	5	6	7	8	9	10
A	D	A	A	E	E	B	B	E	B

EXPLANATORY ANSWERS

1. The view that historians have done harm by distorting truth means that people believe what is reported by the historians. So, I is implicit. II does not follow from the statement and so is not implicit.

2. Clearly, the organizers are adopting this policy not to reduce the sale but to cope up with great demand so that maximum can get the ticket. So, I is not implicit. Also, due to great demand, the maximum number of tickets one person can get has been reduced to five. So, II is also not implicit.

3. Computer education can be started at the school level only if it is easy. So, I is implicit. Statement does not talk about the link between jobs and computer education. So, II is not implicit.

4. The statement tells that there is no problem if one comes up to 7 p.m. also. This means that the programme will continue even after 7 p.m. So, I is implicit. Also, it is clearly mentioned that the programme will start at 6 p.m. So, II is not implicit.

5. The statement advocates to award promotion to a person who has been displaying remarkable talent and performing extraordinarily for the organization rather than the one who has been working steadily for the organization since long. Thus, length of service does not alone prove a man worthy. His talent and his performance are the criteria to be considered. So, both I and II are implicit.

6. The statement advises people not to consider their bosses as mere 'instruments' to control and assess their acts, but as 'models' to imitate in their working. So, both I and II are implicit.

7. The statement speaks for any advertisement and it may not be restricted to promotion of products only. So I is not implicit. It is advised that advertisements be given in newspaper X. This means that X will help advertise better *i.e.*, it has wider circulation. So, II is implicit.

8. Clearly, it cannot be deduced as to which day Kundan would reach Delhi. But Kundan has left for Delhi to attend a function to be held on Friday. So, he must have planned his journey to reach Delhi before Friday. Thus, only II is implicit.

9. Obviously, the scheme is aimed to encourage those owning an old fridge to go for a new one at a reasonable price without the hassles of disposing off the old one. So, I is implicit. An advertisement highlights that which appeals to masses and which customers desire for. So, II is also implicit.

10. The statement mentions the good qualities of X coil but this does not necessitate it is the best. So, I is not implicit. Besides, an advertisement highlights the feature which is desirable by customers and can lure them. So, II is implicit.

❀ ❀ ❀

18 Cubes and Dice

The questions related to problems on cubes and dice are aimed to check the imaginative power of the candidate. The candidate must have the ability to visualise quickly in three-dimensional object for what is asked of it. To attempt such questions some basic facts should be kept in mind and the visualisation ability should be combined with fast and accurate calculations.

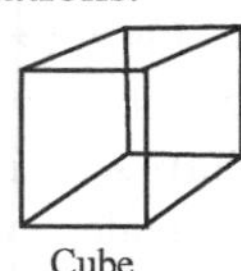

Cube

- Cube has six faces/sides and eight corners.
- Problems are based on the same or different coloured faces.
- Dice has six faces/sides.
- Problems are based only on the value occurring on the six faces.
- Problems are based on cutting the squares into specified number of smaller equal parts.

Dice

Diagrammatically, the explanation of a cube which is painted green on all sides can be understood easily taking one side of the cube.

a	b	a
b	c	b
a	b	a

This cube is divided into 3 × 3 × 3 = 27 equal small cubes.

There are four corner pieces 'a', so 4 × 2, *i.e.*, 8 pieces will be painted on 3 sides.

There are four middle pieces 'b', so 4 × 3, *i.e.*, 12 pieces will be painted on 2 sides

There is one middle piece 'c', so 1 × 6, *i.e.*, 6 pieces will be painted only on 1 side.

There will be one piece right in the centre of this cube, *i.e.*, piece will not have paint at all.

So, this cube has 8 + 12 + 6 + 1, *i.e.*, 27 smaller cubes.

EXERCISE

1. Two positions of a dice are shown below. When there are two circles at the bottom, the number of circles at the top will be :

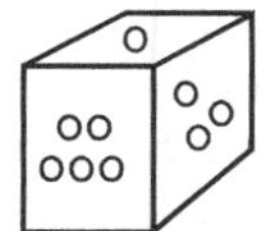

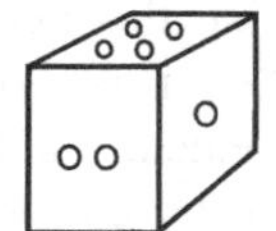

A. 5
B. 2
C. 3
D. 6
E. None of these

2. Two positions of a dice are shown below. When 4 is at the bottom, what number will be on the top?

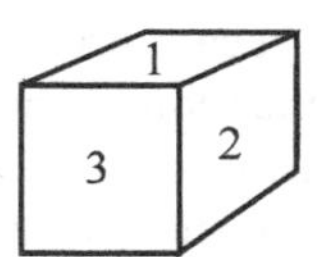

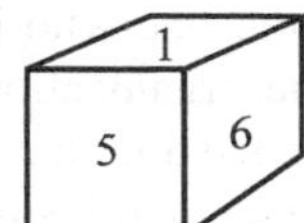

A. 1
B. 2
C. 5
D. 6
E. None of these

3. A cube is painted red on two adjacent faces and on one opposite face, yellow on two adjacent faces and green on the remaining face. It is then cut into 64 equal cubes. How many cubes have only one red and one green face?

A. 4 B. 8
C. 12 D. 16
E. None of these

4. A cube, on whose sides letters have been written, is shown below in different positions as can be seen from different directions. Find the missing letter?

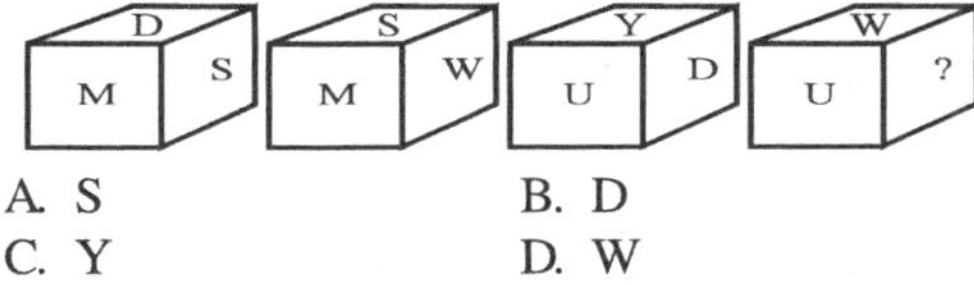

A. S B. D
C. Y D. W
E. None of these

5. In a dice a, b, c and d, are written on the adjacent faces, in a clockwise order and e and f at the top and bottom. When c is at the top, what will be at the bottom?

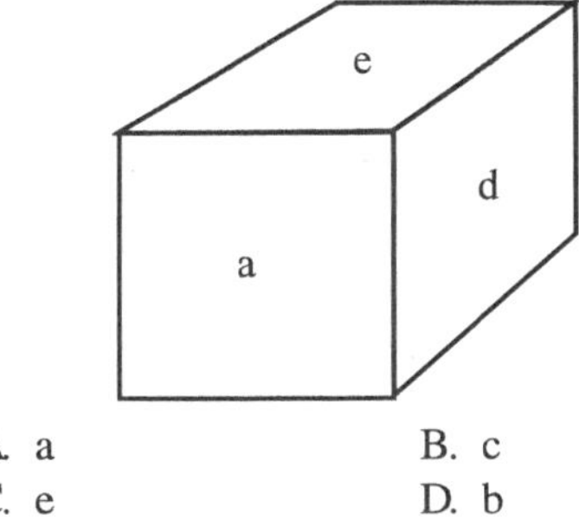

A. a B. c
C. e D. b
E. None of these

6. The number of cubes arranged one over the other in this figure will be :

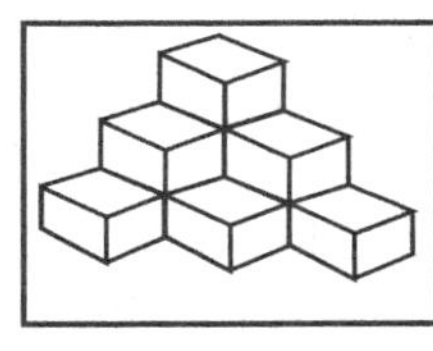

A. 8 B. 6
C. 5 D. 10
E. None of these

7. Two positions of a dice are shown below. When 2 is at the bottom, which number will be at the top?

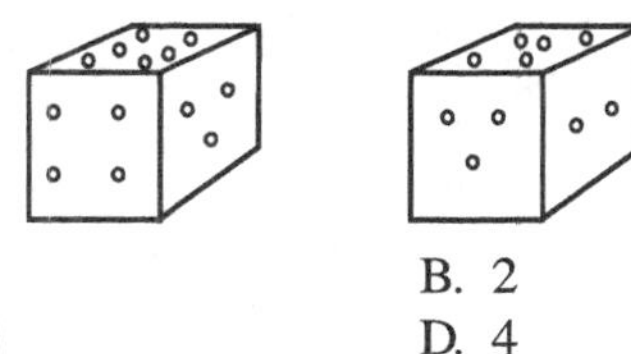

A. 1 B. 2
C. 3 D. 4
E. None of these

8. The sides of a cube are painted in different colours. Black side is opposite to red. White side is between black and red. Green side is adjacent to grey and blue side is adjacent to green. What colour will be on the side opposite to the white side of the cube?

A. Blue B. Green
C. Grey D. Data is insufficient
E. None of these

9. A cube is painted black on two adjacent faces and on one opposite face, red on two opposite faces and green on the remaining face. If it is cut into 64 equal cubes, then how many cubes will have only one black coloured face?

A. 32 B. 16
C. 12 D. 8
E. None of these

10. Six sides of a cube are coloured in the following manner

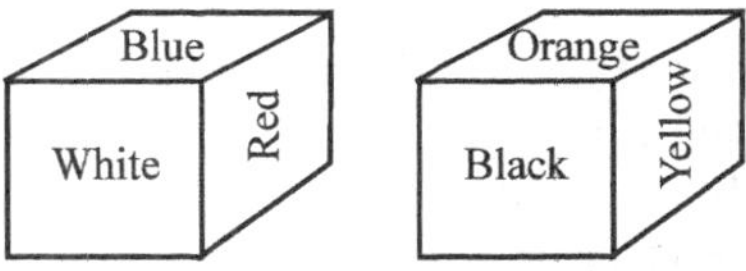

If blue and orange are opposite and red is on the top, which colour will be at the bottom?

A. Orange B. Purple
C. Black D. Yellow
E. None of these

11. A toy cube is painted orange on all sides. It is cut into 64 smaller cubes of equal size. How many smaller cubes are not painted at all?

A. 4 B. 8
C. 16 D. 20
E. None of these

Directions (Qs. 12-13) : *A die is thrown 4 times and its four different positions are given below :*

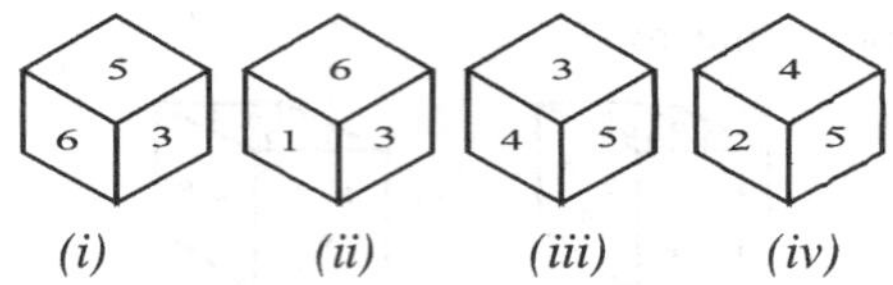

12. Find the number on the face opposite the face showing 3.

A. 2 B. 1
C. 5 D. 4
E. None of these

13. Find the number on the face opposite the face showing 6.

A. 5 B. 3
C. 4 D. 1
E. None of these

Directions (Qs. 14 to 16): *Study the information given below :*

The six faces of a cube are coloured black, brown, green, red, white and blue.

(*i*) Red is opposite of black
(*ii*) Green is between red and black
(*iii*) Blue is adjacent to white
(*iv*) Brown is adjacent to blue
(*v*) Red is at the bottom

14. Which colour is opposite of brown?

A. White B. Red
C. Green D. Blue
E. None of these

15. Which of the following can be deduced from (*i*) and (*v*)?

A. Black is on the top
B. Blue is on the top
C. Brown is on the top
D. Brown is opposite of black
E. None of these

16. The four adjacent colours are :

A. black, blue, brown, red
B. black, blue, brown, white
C. black, blue, red, white
D. black, blue, red, white
E. None of these

Directions (Qs. 17 to 19): *In each question below a dice has been marked with some letters or numerals and placed in three different positions. Answer the questions that follow :*

17. Which letter is opposite to Q?

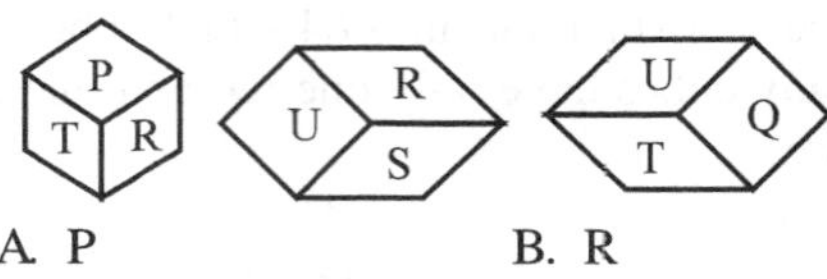

A. P B. R
C. S D. T
E. None of these

18. Which letter/numeral is opposite to 3?

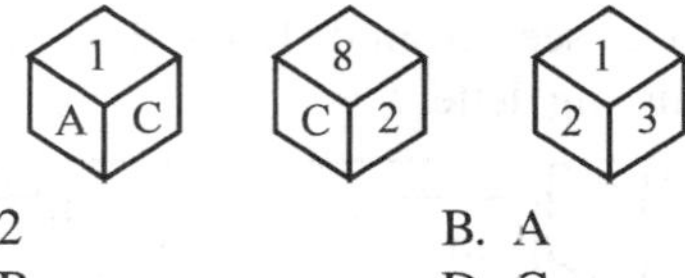

A. 2 B. A
C. B D. C
E. None of these

19. If one of the 3 visible faces of the cube is hidden, which letter is opposite to O?

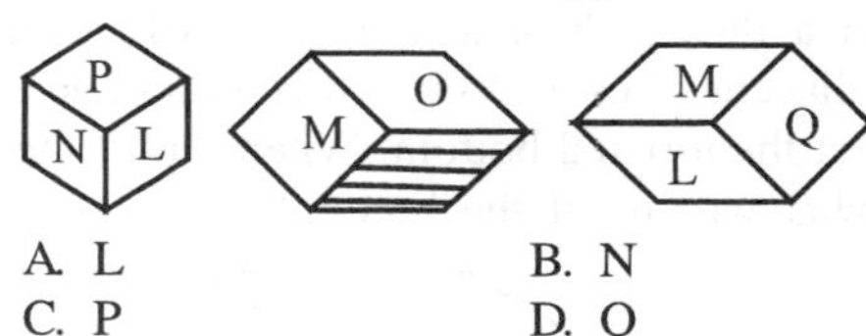

A. L B. N
C. P D. Q
E. None of these

Directions (Qs. 20 to 22): *Given below are the three positions of the same dice. Answer the questions that follow :*

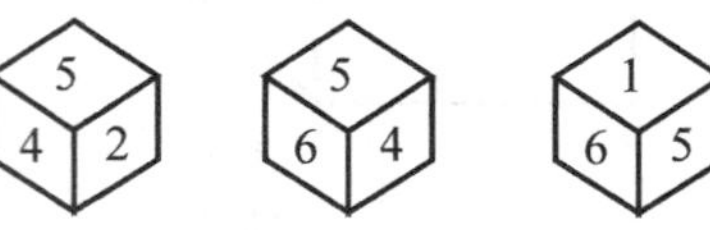

20. What is the number on the face opposite of face 2?

A. 1
B. 6
C. 5
D. Cannot be determined
E. None of these

21. In the third position of the dice which number lies on the face on the bottom?

A. 2 B. 3
C. 4 D. 5
E. None of these

22. When value 5 is on the face on the top, which value lies on the face on the bottom?

A. 3 B. 4
C. 1 D. 2
E. None of these

Directions (Qs. 23 to 25): *A solid cube with each side 3 cm has been painted red, blue and green on pairs of opposite faces. It is then cut into small cubes with each side 1 cm. Answer the questions that follow :*

23. How many cubes have one face painted red and one face painted green?

A. 12 B. 8
C. 6 D. 14
E. None of these

24. How many cubes have only one face painted?

A. 6 B. 4
C. 12 D. 9
E. None of these

25. How many cubes are painted blue on one face and either red or green on another face?

A. 4 B. 6
C. 8 D. 12
E. None of these

Directions (Qs. 26 to 29): *The questions are based on the following statement :*

A cube is painted red on two adjacent faces, yellow on two opposite faces and green on the remaining faces. It is cut into 64 smaller cubes of equal size.

26. How many cubes are painted on two faces only and that too with the same colour?

A. 0 B. 4
C. 8 D. 16
E. None of these

27. How many cubes have three faces painted?

A. 4 B. 8
C. 16 D. 32
E. None of these

28. How many cubes are painted on one face only and are yellow?

A. 32 B. 16
C. 8 D. 4
E. None of these

29. How many cubes are painted on all faces?

A. 0 B. 4
C. 8 D. 64
E. None of these

ANSWERS

1	2	3	4	5	6	7	8	9	10
A	A	B	C	A	D	D	B	C	D
11	**12**	**13**	**14**	**15**	**16**	**17**	**18**	**19**	**20**
B	A	C	A	A	D	B	D	A	B
21	**22**	**23**	**24**	**25**	**26**	**27**	**28**	**29**	
C	A	A	A	C	B	B	C	A	

SOME SELECTED EXPLANATORY ANSWERS

1. After observing the views of the same dice, the faces that can be clearly understood to be the opposites are :
2 – 5, 4 – 3 and 1 – 6.

3. 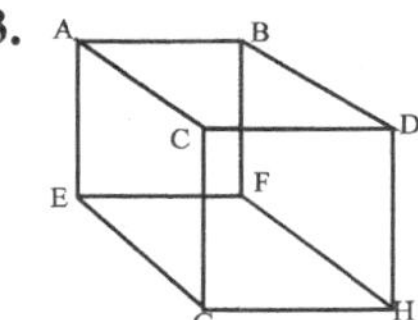

The red sides are EGAC, ABCD and BDFH.
The yellow sides are ABEF and EFGH
The green side is CDGH.

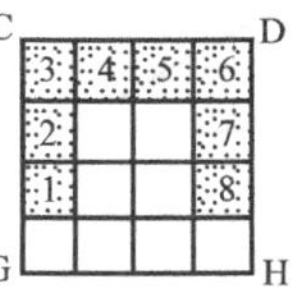

Sides GC, CD and DH are adjacent to red sides and side GH is adjacent to yellow side.

So, only 8 cubes will have one side red and one green.

4. The letters on the top and bottom sides are W and D respectively and the letters on the sides are U, Y, M and S clockwise.

5. The two positions of dice will be :

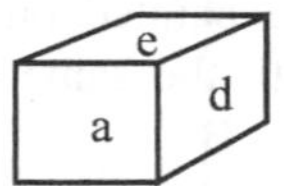

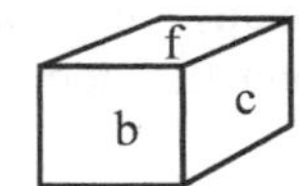

and the opposite sides will be a – c, b – d.

6. 

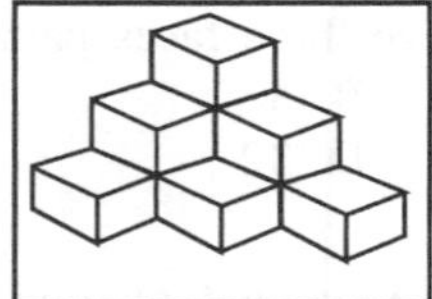

There are three columns containing 1 cube each. There are two columns containing 2 cubes each. There is one column containing 3 cubes. So, the total number of cubes is : $(3 \times 1) + (2 \times 2) + (1 \times 3)$, *i.e.*, $3 + 4 + 3 = 10$.

9. 

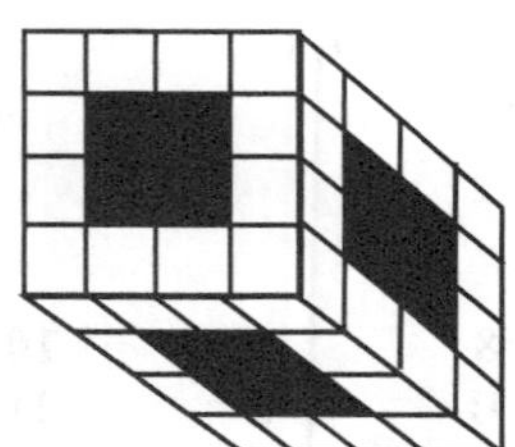

Three faces of the cube are painted black and the rest are in different colours. If this cube is cut into 64 equal cubes, then only the 4 cubes in centre of one face will come out with only one black coloured face. So, the total number of one black coloured face small cubes will be $4 \times 3 = 12$.

10. 

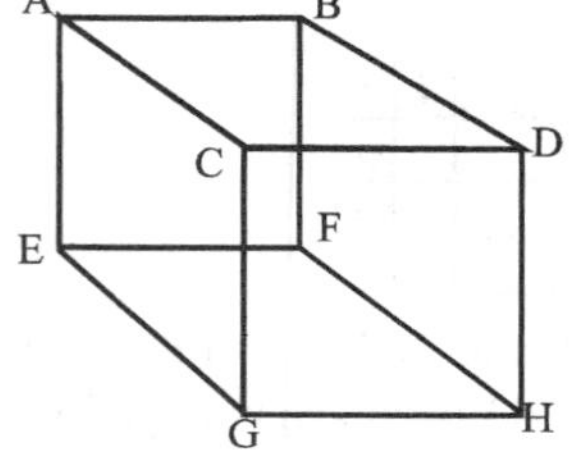

If side ABCD is red; then ABEF will be white; and ACEG will be blue. If side BDFH is orange (opposite to blue); then CDGH will be black; and EFGH will be yellow (opposite to red and at the bottom).

11. The smaller 64 pieces will be cut in the manner that :

1. 8 pieces will be painted on 3 sides,
2. 24 pieces on 2 sides.
3. 24 pieces on 1 side, and
4. 8 will not have paint at all.

Diagrammatically, the explanation taking one side of the cube will be :

a	b	b	a
b	c	c	b
b	c	c	b
a	b	b	a

1. 'a' are the corner pieces $[4 \times 2 = 8]$
2. 'b' are the centre pieces of the cornered sides $[8 \times 3 = 24]$
3. 'c' are the centre pieces $[4 \times 6 = 24]$
4. Remaining interior pieces
$= 64 - (8 + 24 + 24)$
$= 64 - 56 = 8$.

12. From figures (*i*), (*ii*) and (*iii*) it is clear that the faces adjacent to 3 have numbers 6, 5, 1 and 4. So, the number on face opposite of face 3 will be 2.

13. From figures (*i*), (*iii*) and (*iv*) it is clear that the faces adjacent to 5 have numbers 6, 3, 4 and 2. So, the number on face opposite of face 5 is 1. In earlier question the face opposite 3 was 2. Now the opposite faces are 3 – 2, 5 – 1 and 4 – 6.

14. A, 15. A, 16. D :

According to the given information the two positions of the cube will be :

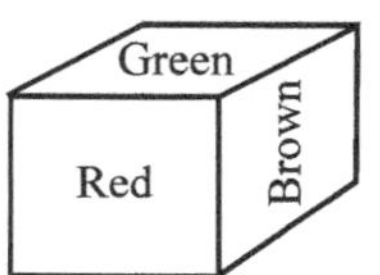

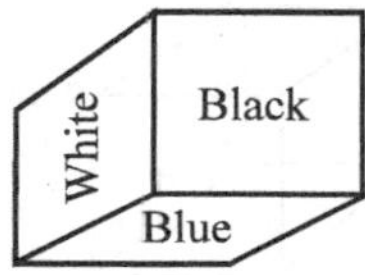

The whole cube will be :

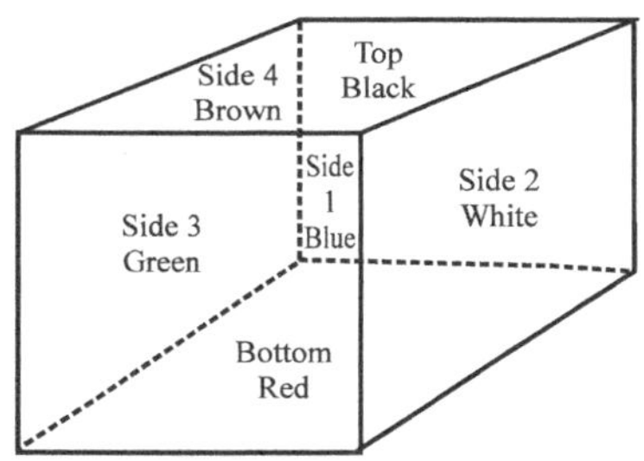

The colours on opposite faces will be : Red—Black, Green—Blue and Brown—White.

20. B, 21. C, 22. A,

The following observations can be made from the three positions of the same dice.

(*i*) Letters adjacent to 5 are 4, 2, 6 and 1. So, 3 is opposite 5.

(*ii*) Letters adjacent to 6 are 5, 4, 1 and necessarily 4. So, 2 is opposite 6.

(*iii*) When opposite numbers are 3–5 and 2–6 then 1 and 4 must be opposites.

23. A, 24. A, 25. C :

The whole cube is :

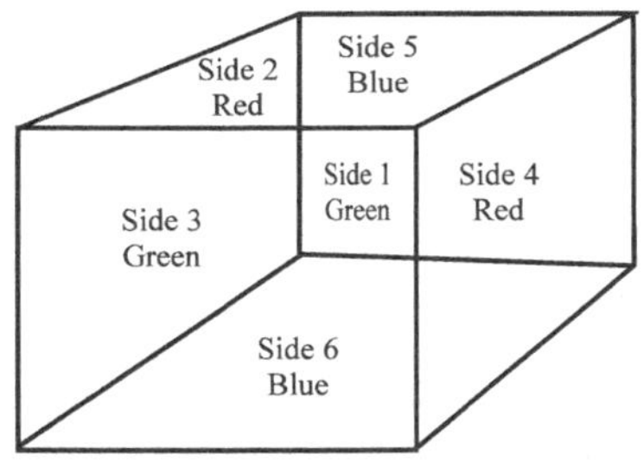

The divided cube is :

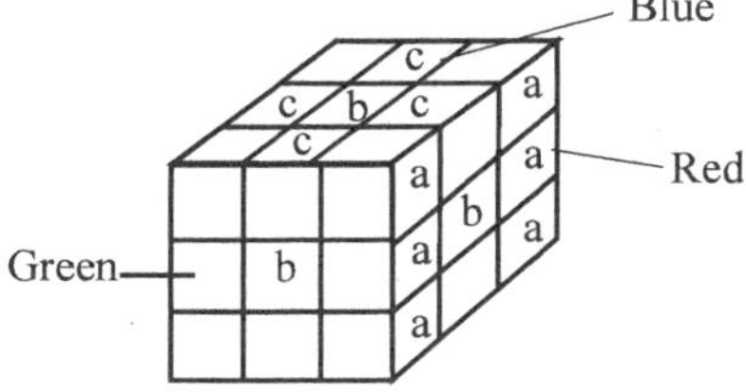

'a'— 12 cubes (6 each on opposite sides) have one face painted red and the other painted green.

'b'— 6 cubes (1 on each side) have only one face painted).

'c'— 8 cubes (4 each on opposite side) have one face painted blue and either red or green on the other.

26. B, 27. B, 28. C, 29. A :

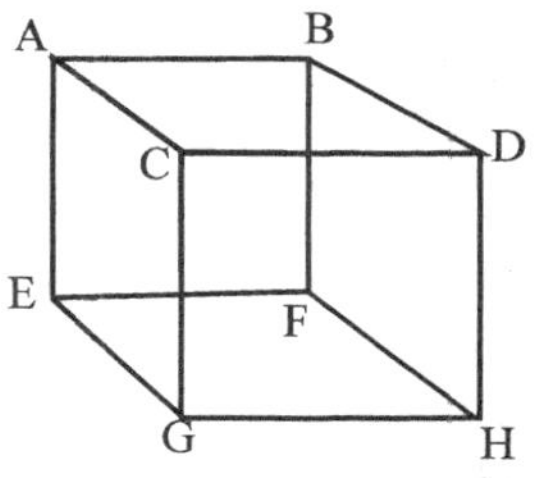

Red faces are ABCD and ABEF

Yellow faces are ACEG and BDFH

Green faces are EFGH and CDGH.

Note that Red and Green colours are on two adjacent faces. So, 2 corner cubical pieces of Red and 2 of Green (*i.e.,* total 4 cubes) will be painted on two faces only and that too with the same colour.

All the corners pieces of the cube will have three faces painted, *i.e.*, 8 cubes.

Yellow sides are on the opposites. Diagrammatically, the explanation taking one side will be :

a	b	b	a
b	c	c	b
b	c	c	b
a	b	b	a

'c' are the centered pieces and are painted on one face only in yellow. So, 4 × 2 (sides) *i.e.,* 8 cubes will have one side painted and in yellow.

Also, note that when a painted cube is cut into smaller cubes like this, not all pieces are coloured. The maximum number of sides painted in a small cube will be 3. No cube will be painted on all faces.

19 Figure Series

In this form of non-verbal series, which are the most common, four or five consecutive problem figures form a definite sequence and one is required to select the one figure from the given set of Answer Figures that will continue the same sequence.

One has to try different set of moves, changes, replacements, rotations, repetitions and a lot more variations to arrive at the logical pattern making the series. Practising alone will sharpen one's skill of solving such sequences.

Example

1. Problem Figures

Answer Figures

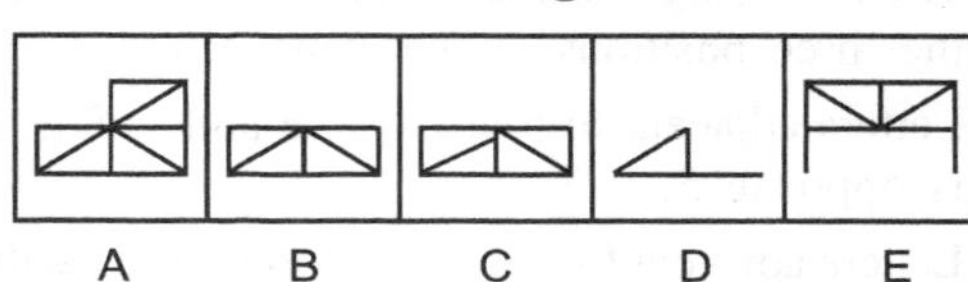

A B C D E

Answer E : Problem Figures consist of a rectangle divided into sections. At each step one of the lines is removed. First from the right, then left and then the centre. To continue this pattern, a right diagonal line is removed. In the answer figure a left diagonal line should be removed. Answer Figure 'E' continues the series.

EXERCISE

Directions : *Each of the following questions consist of problem figures followed by answer figures. Select a figure from amongst the answer figures which will continue the same series or pattern as established by the problem figures.*

1. Problem Figures

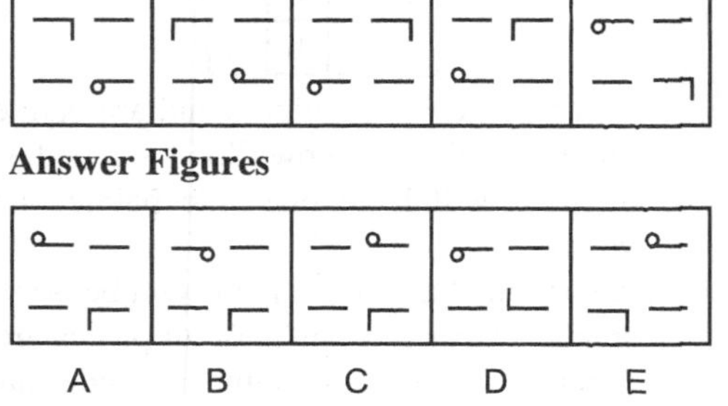

2. Problem Figures

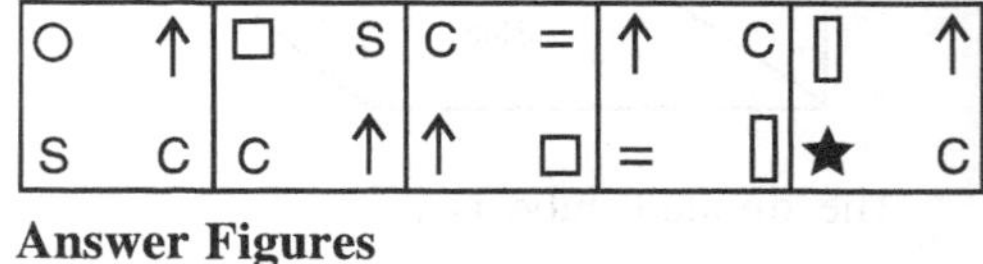

Answer Figures

A B C D E

3. Problem Figures

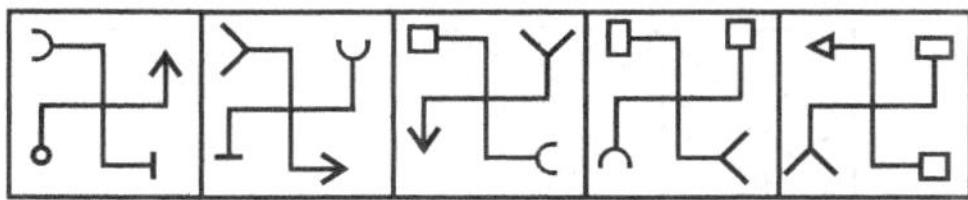

Answer Figures

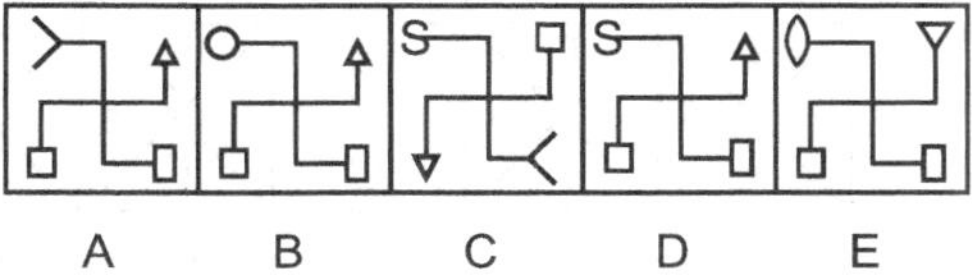

4. Problem Figures

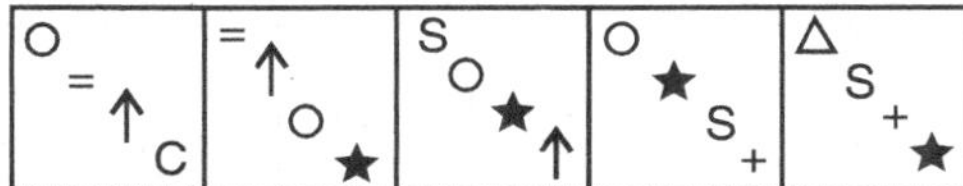

Answer Figures

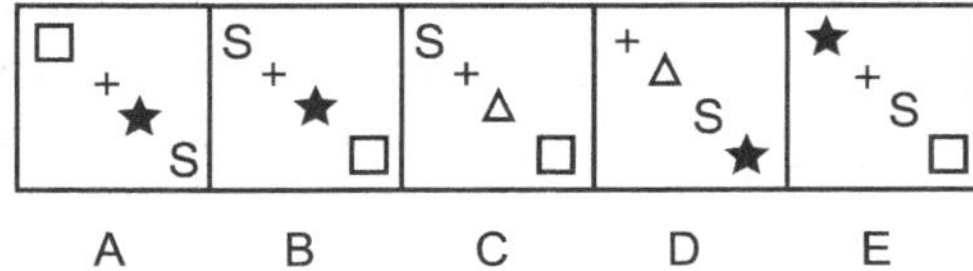

5. Problem Figures

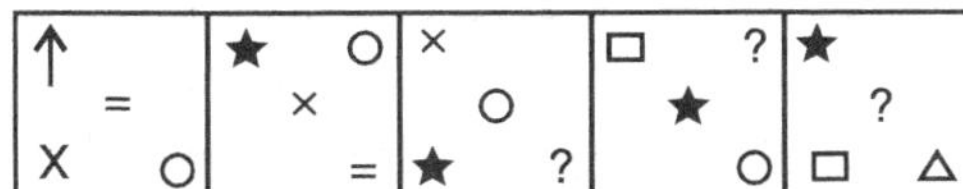

Answer Figures

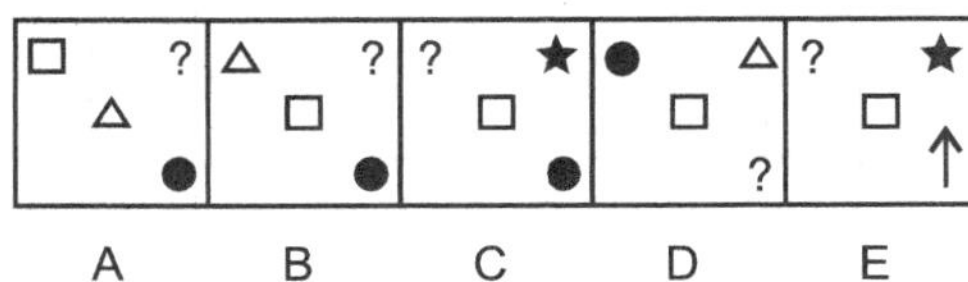

6. Problem Figures

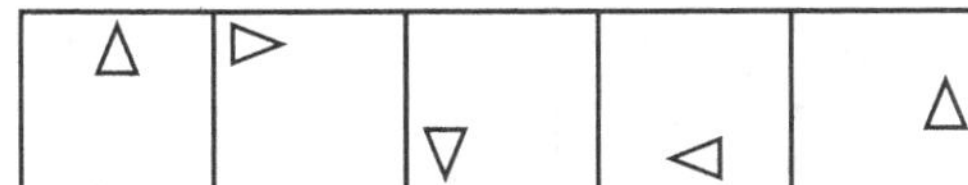

Answer Figures

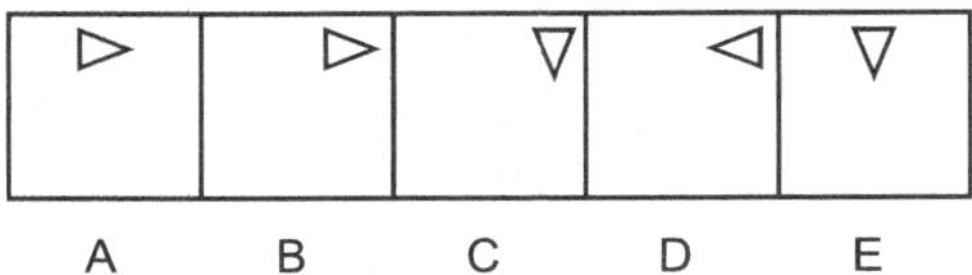

7. Problem Figures

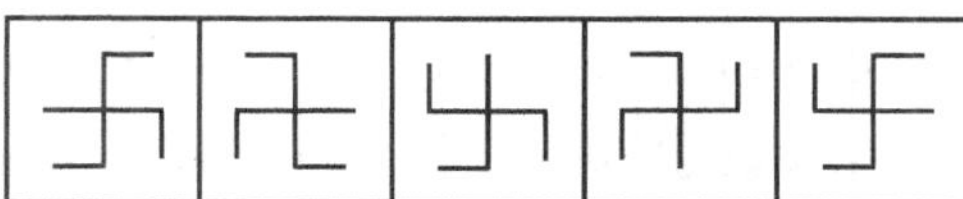

Answer Figures

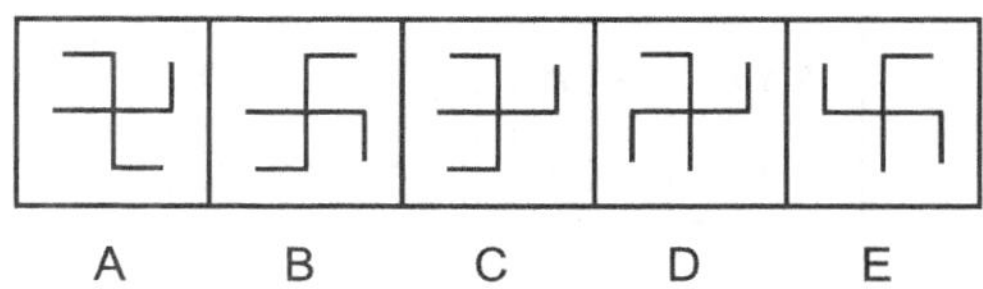

8. Problem Figures

Answer Figures

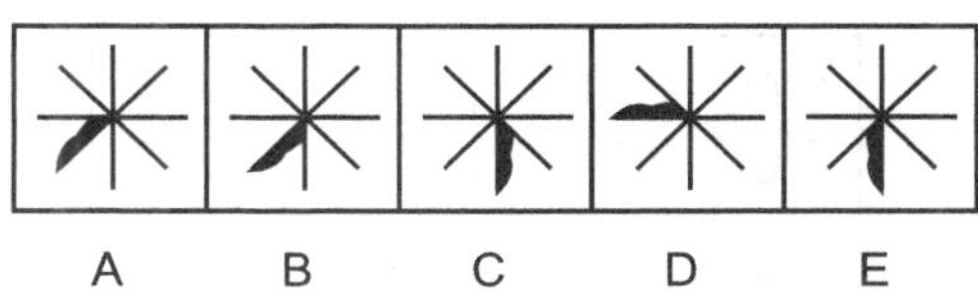

9. Problem Figures

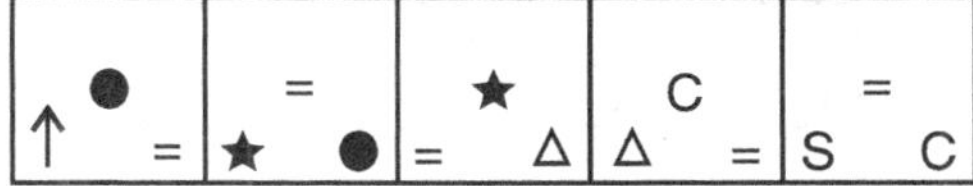

Answer Figures

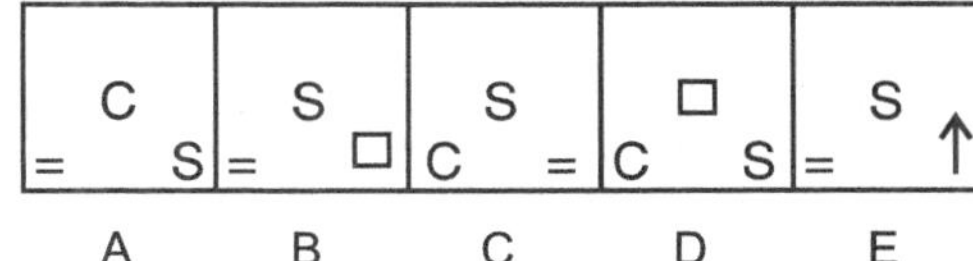

10. Problem Figures

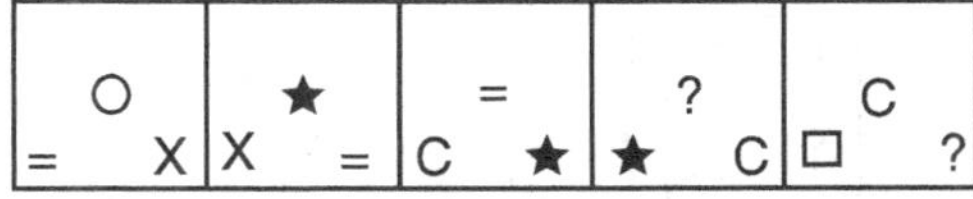

Answer Figures

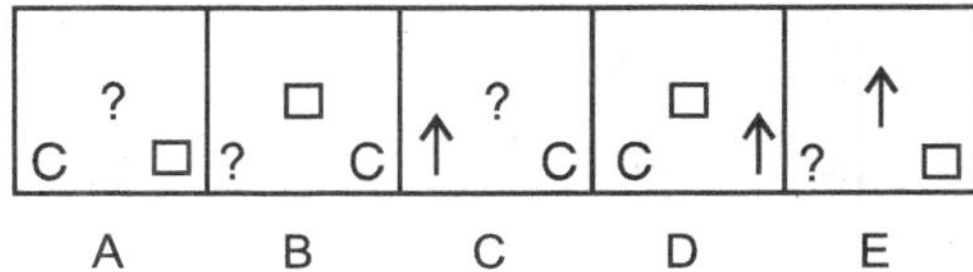

11. Problem Figures

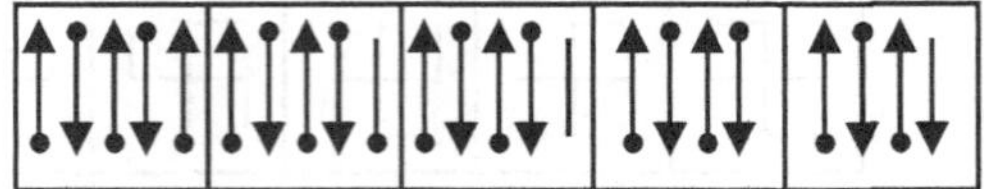

Answer Figures

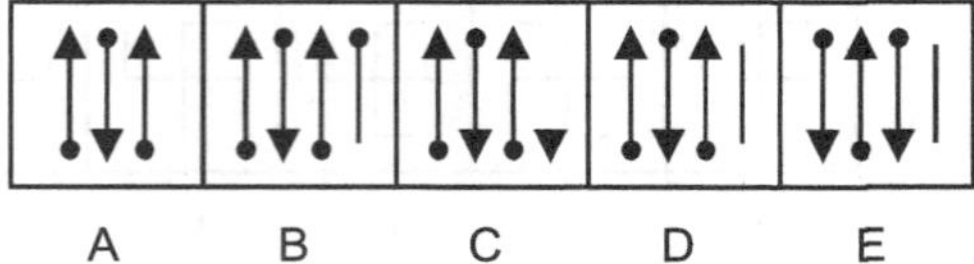

12. Problem Figures

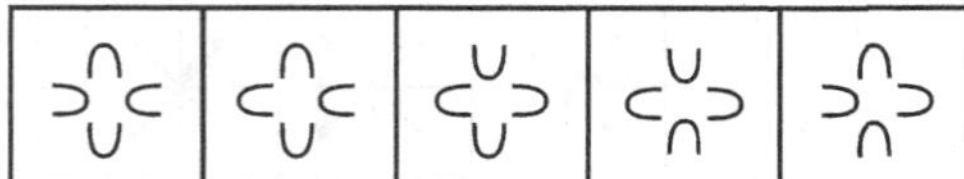

Answer Figures

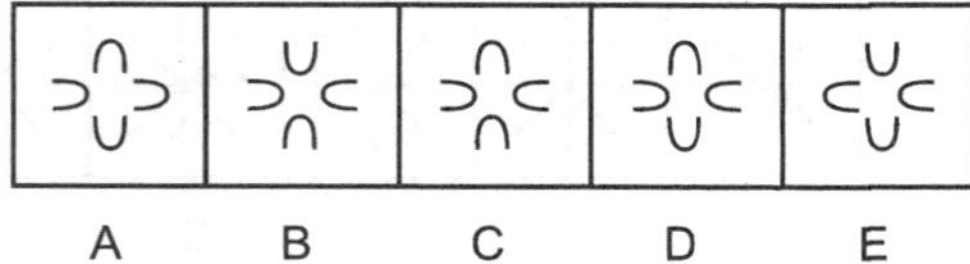

13. Problem Figures

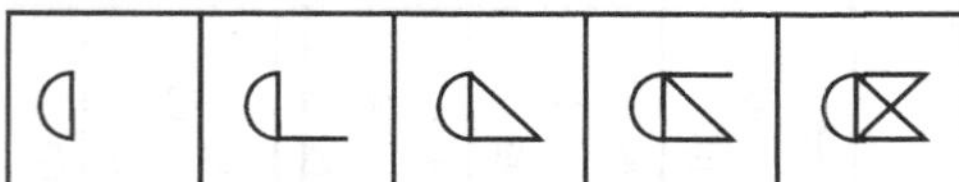

Answer Figures

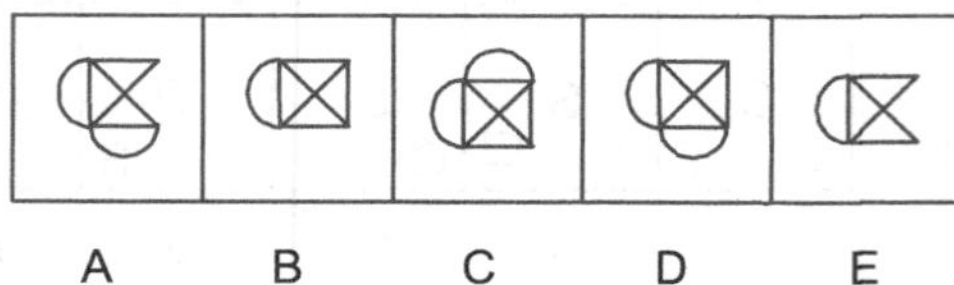

14. Problem Figures

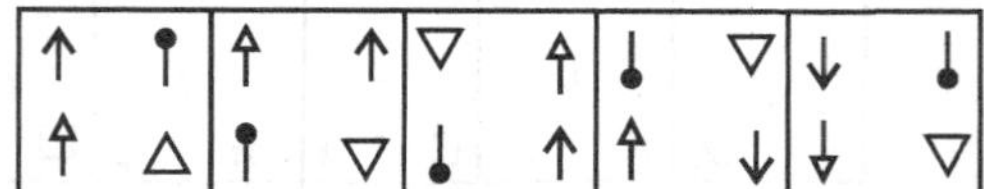

Answer Figures

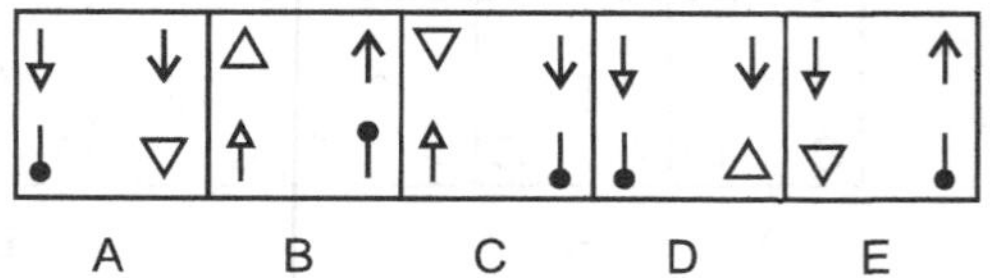

15. Problem Figures

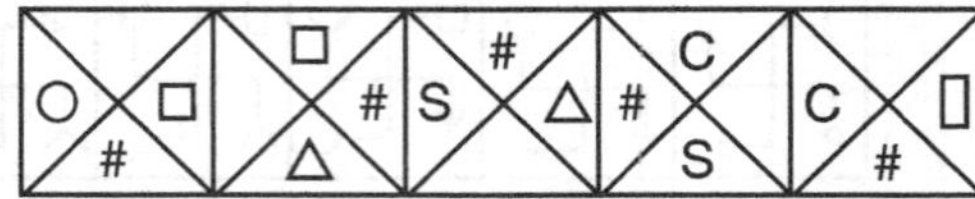

Answer Figures

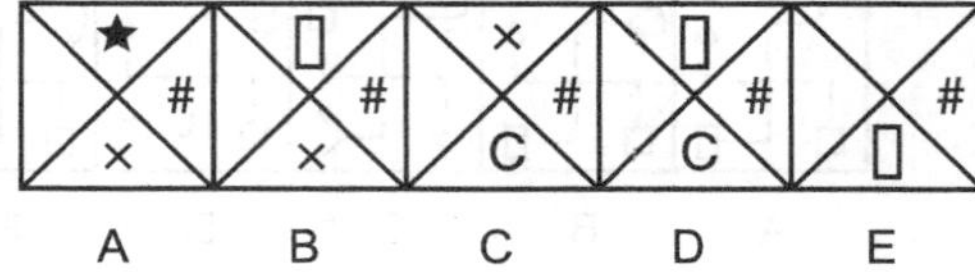

16. Problem Figures

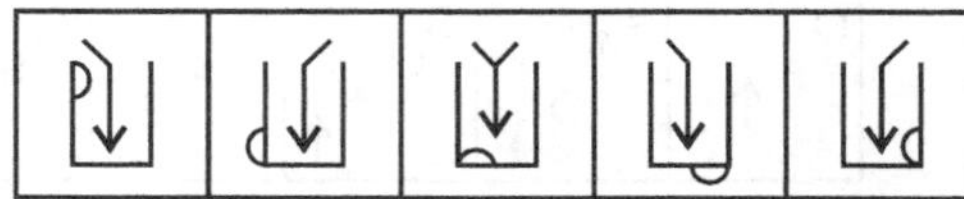

Answer Figures

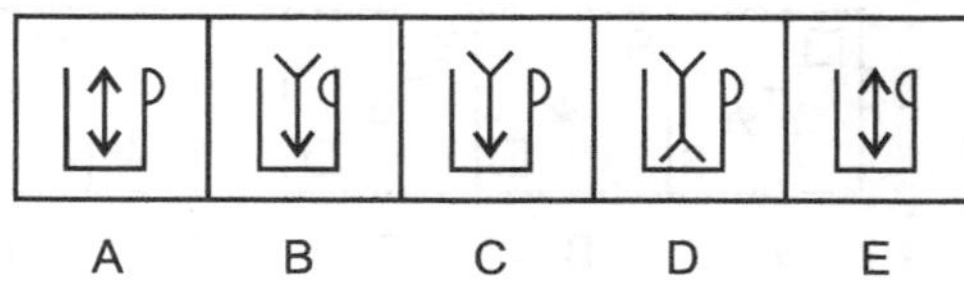

17. Problem Figures

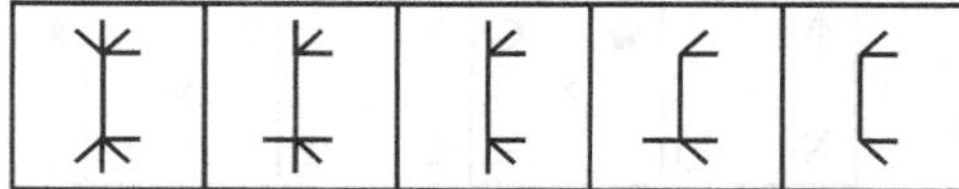

Answer Figures

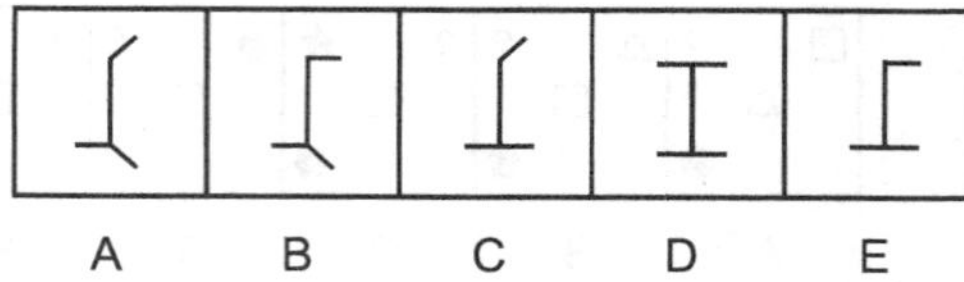

18. Problem Figures

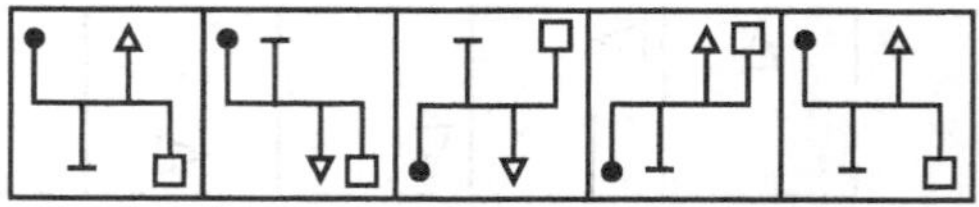

Answer Figures

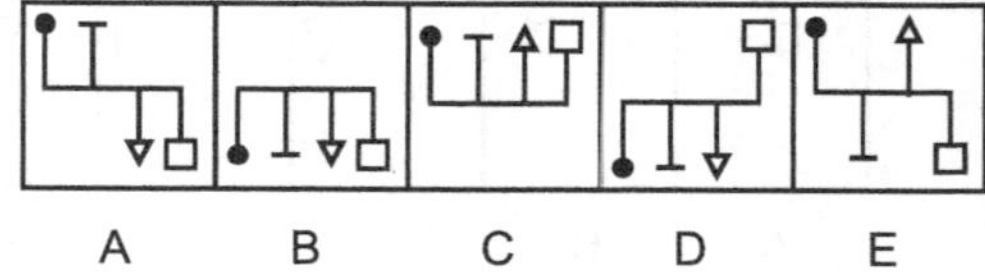

19. Problem Figures

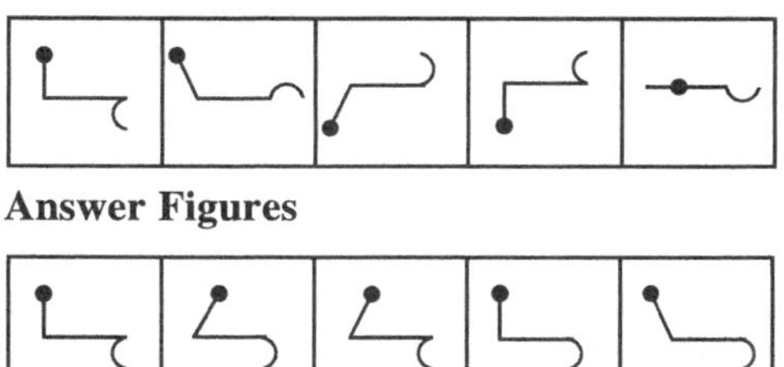

Answer Figures

A B C D E

20. Problem Figures

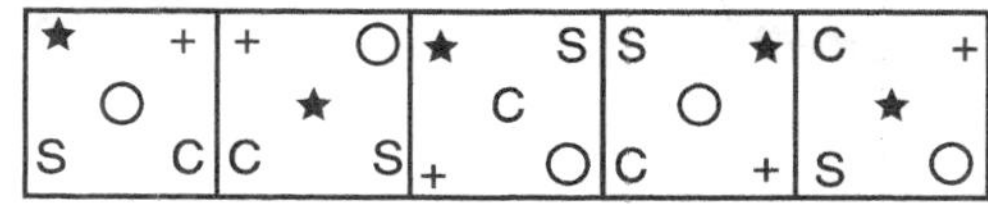

Answer Figures

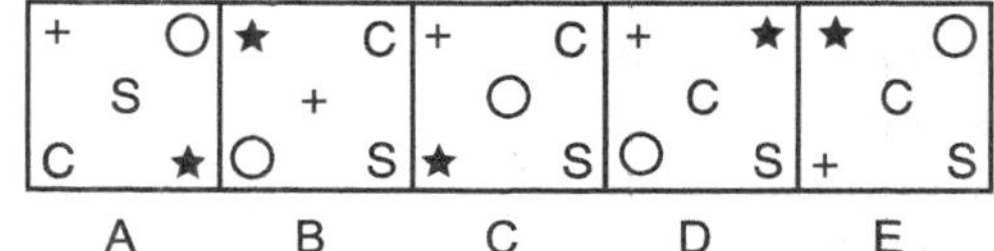

A B C D E

ANSWERS

1	2	3	4	5	6	7	8	9	10
A	B	D	C	D	B	A	E	B	E
11	**12**	**13**	**14**	**15**	**16**	**17**	**18**	**19**	**20**
D	C	A	D	B	C	E	A	B	D

SOME SELECTED EXPLANATORY ANSWERS

1. In alternate figures the four elements are moved clockwise.

3. The shape is turned 90° clockwise and the element attached to its top left side is replaced by an entirely new element.

6. The triangle is moved half and one steps anticlockwise alternately and turned 90° anticlockwise at each step.

7. In alternate figures the design is turned 90° clockwise.

8. The number of spikes the shade is moved anticlockwise, is increased by one at each step and the placement of the shade is same in alternate figures.

11. Starting from the extreme right element, at a time one part is removed in a set order. Answer Figure D continues the series.

12. Clockwise, starting from the left first one '*u*' shape and then two '*u*' shapes are turned by 180°. Option C fits the series.

13. Without lifting the pen one part is added to the figure at each step.

16. In alternate figures the semicircle is moved one step clockwise. The three stages of the arrow are repeated from the fourth figure.

18. First the two middle elements are turned to the other side of the horizontal line, then the two corner elements are turned. Also note, this series is repeated from the fifth figure.

20. Starting from the two bottom elements, anticlockwise, their places are interchanged, while the places of other three elements are changed one step anticlockwise.

20 Analogies or Relationships

Analogy is a process of reasoning between two parallel cases. It relates to agreement or correspon-dence in certain respects between two things. It is a process whereby the underlying relationship that exists between two figures, designs or patterns is determined. Under the process, one has to discover the features common to the two figures or designs. This common feature is a model or base. The question seeks solution on the basis of this model or base.

EXERCISE

Directions : *The second figure in the first unit of the Problem Figures bears a certain relationship to the first figure. Similarly, one of the figures in the Answer Figures bears the same relationship to the first figure in the second unit of the Problem Figures. Locate the figure which would fit the question mark.*

1. Problem Figures

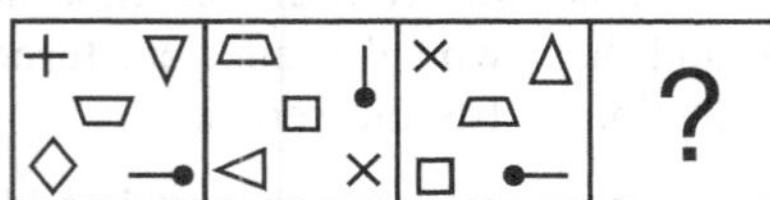

Answer Figures

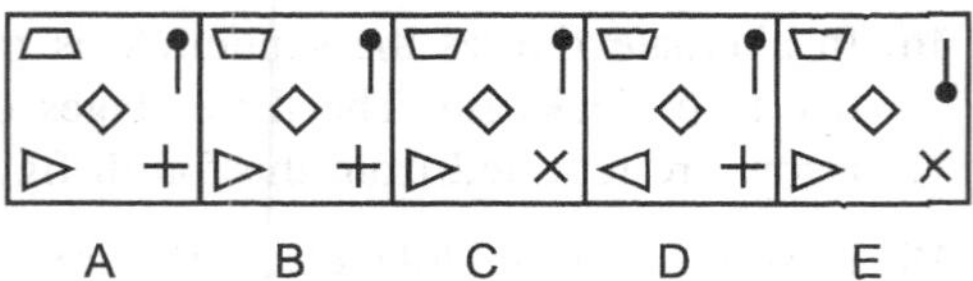

2. Problem Figures

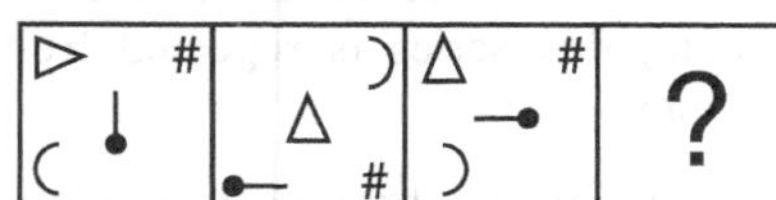

Answer Figures

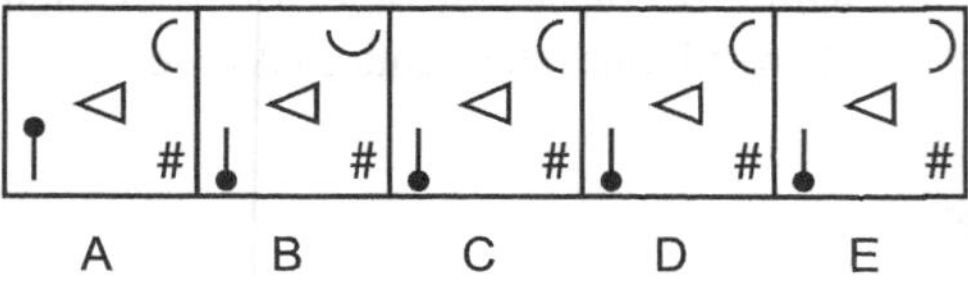

3. Problem Figures

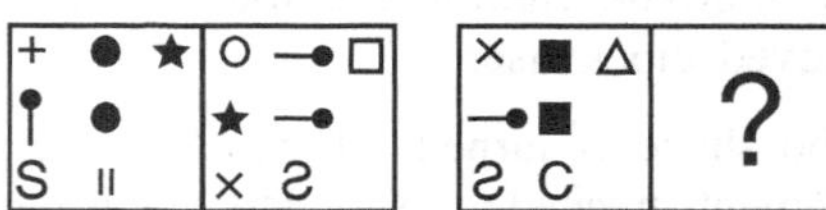

Answer Figures

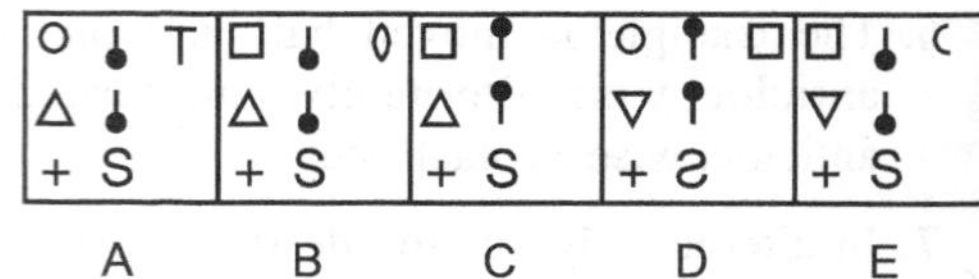

4. Problem Figures

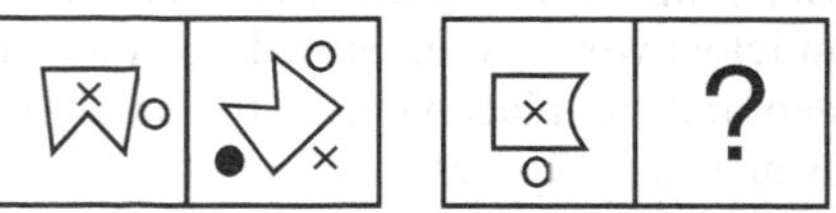

Answer Figures

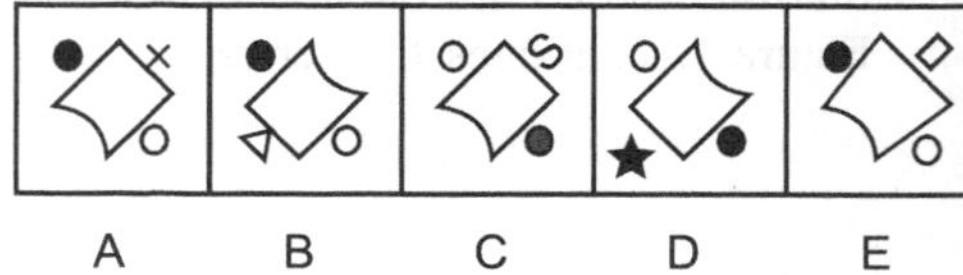

5. Problem Figures

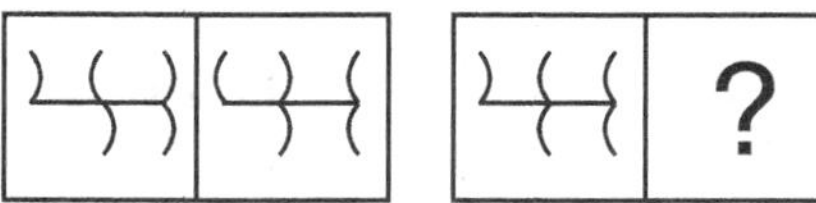

Answer Figures

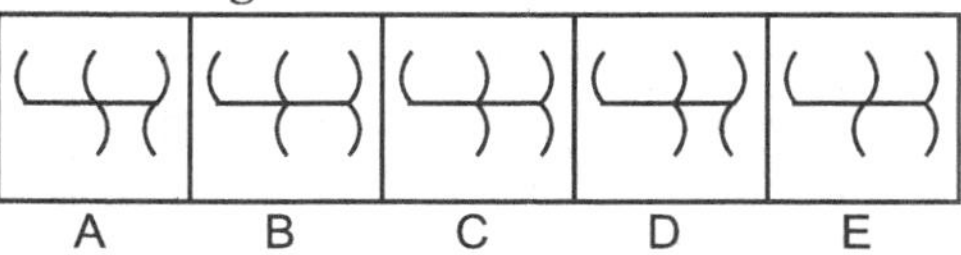

6. Problem Figures

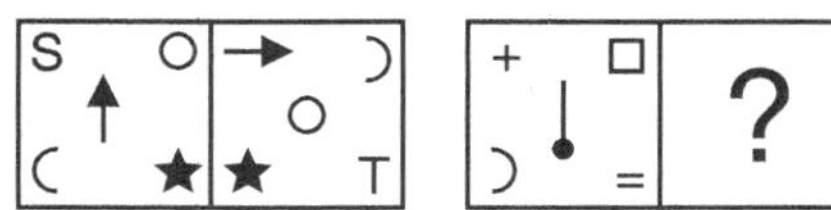

Answer Figures

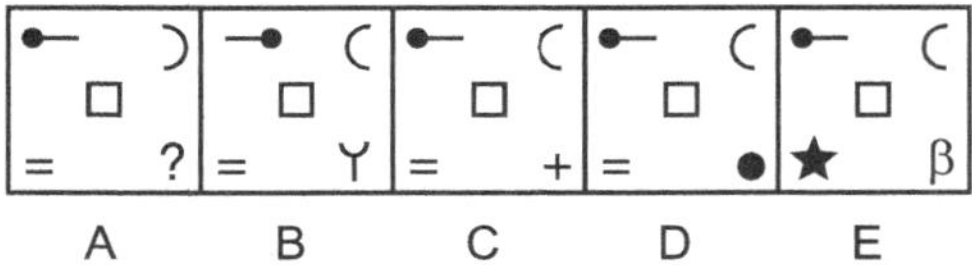

7. Problem Figures

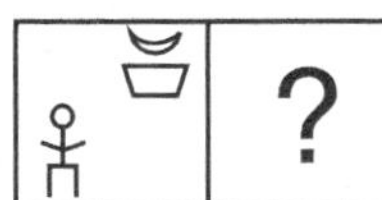

Answer Figures

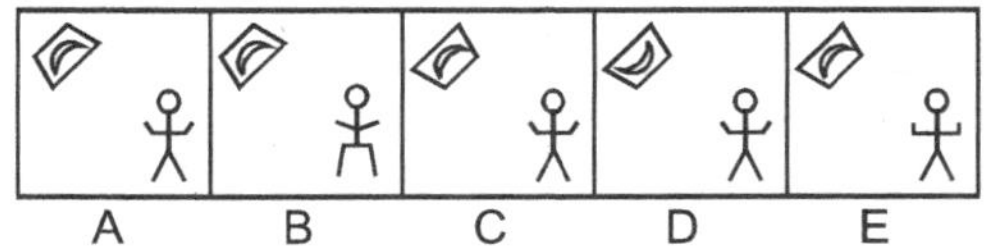

8. Problem Figures

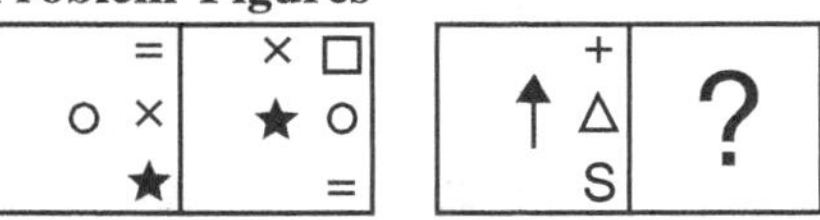

Answer Figures

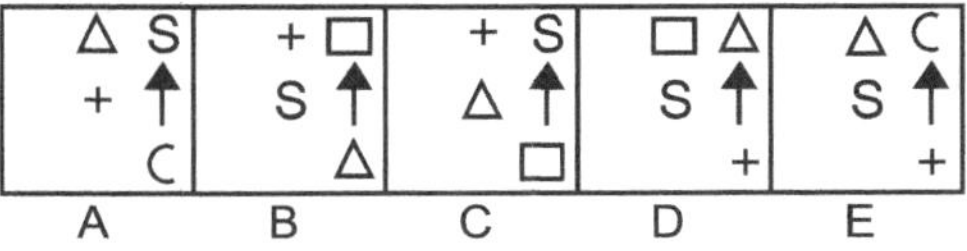

9. Problem Figures

Answer Figures

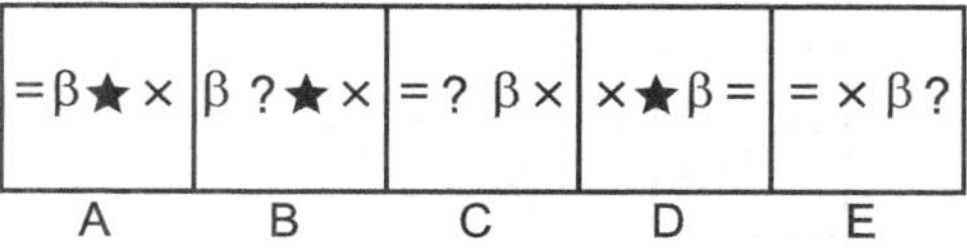

10. Problem Figures

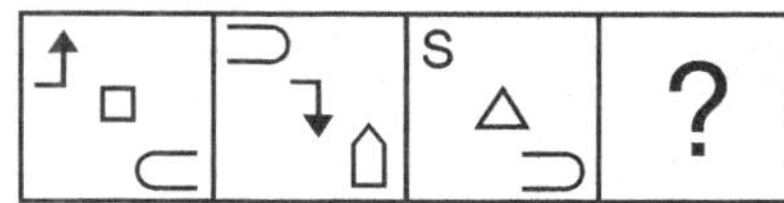

Answer Figures

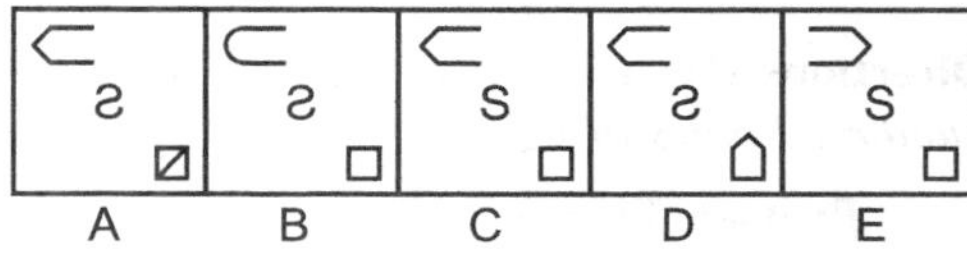

11. Problem Figures

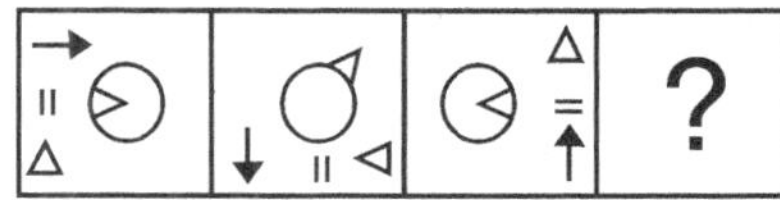

Answer Figures

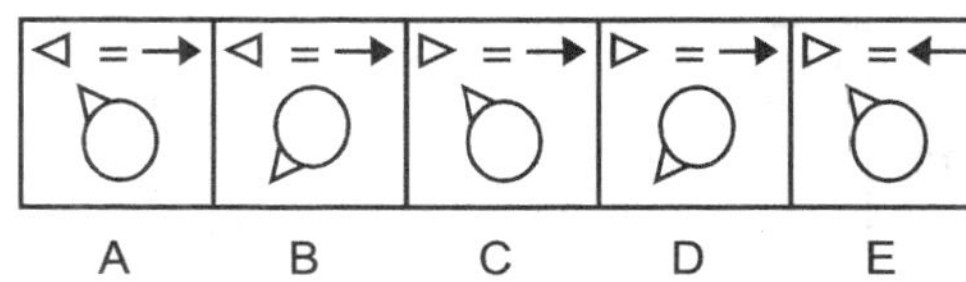

12. Problem Figures

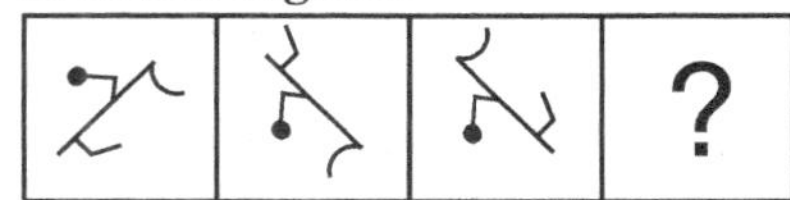

Answer Figures

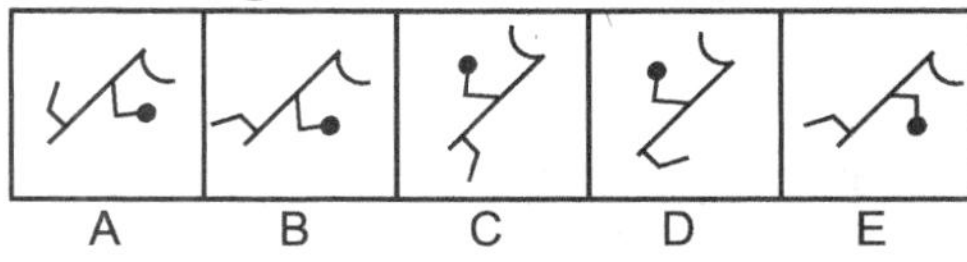

13. Problem Figures

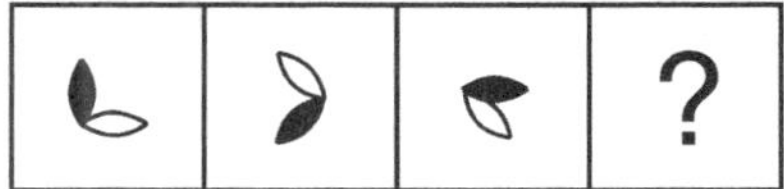

Answer Figures

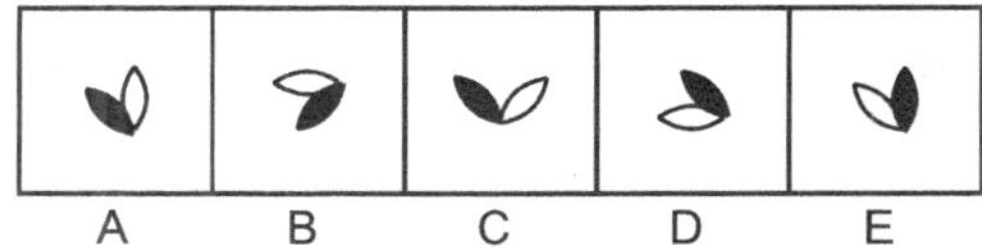

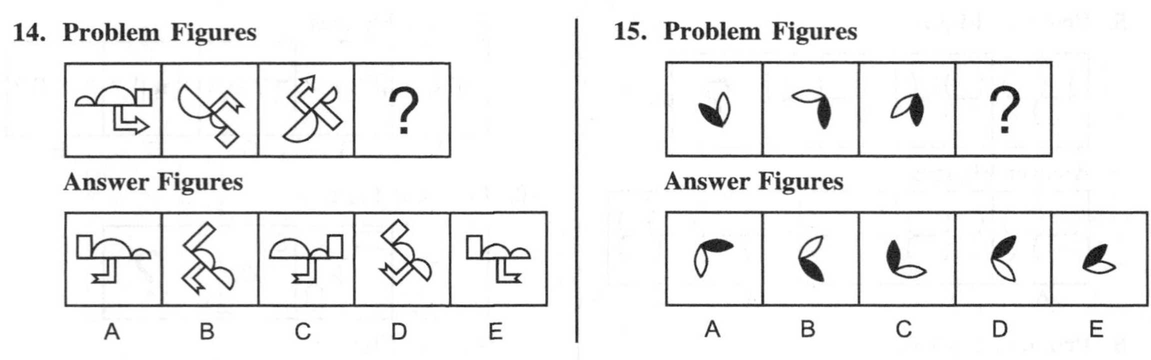

Directions (Q. 16–20): *In each of the following questions, a related pair of figures is followed by five numbered pairs of figures. Select the pair that has a relationship* ***similar*** *to that in the unnumbered pair.*

Problem Figure **Answer Figures**

16. I II | A B C D E

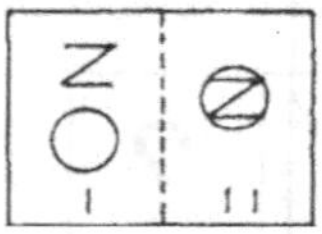

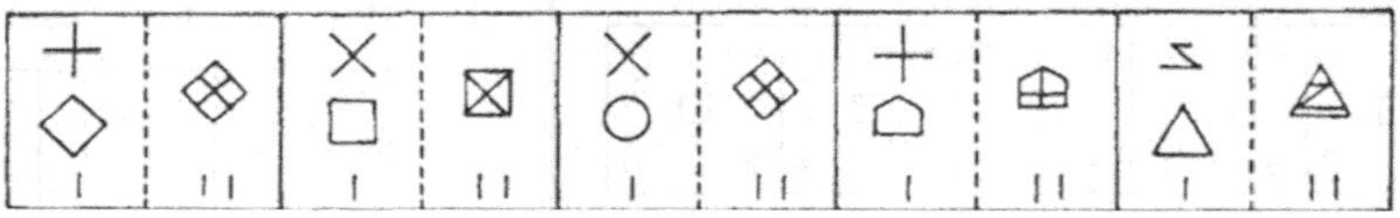

17. I II | A B C D E

18. I II | A B C D E

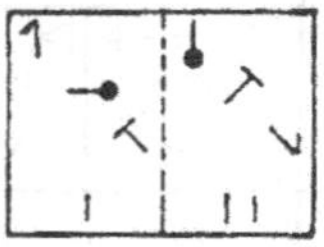

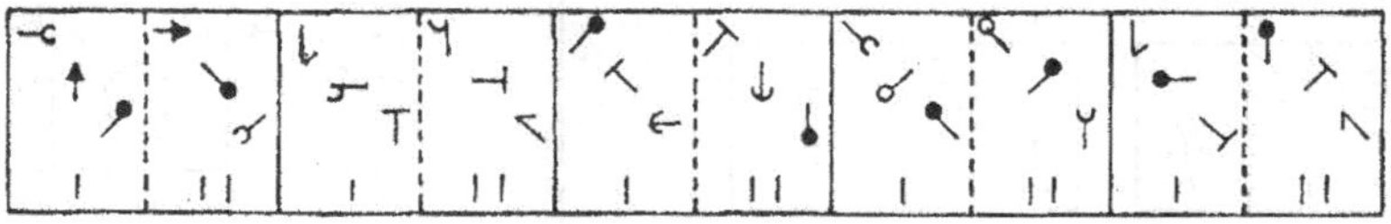

19. I II | A B C D E

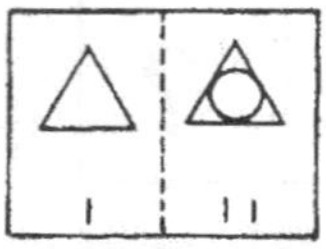

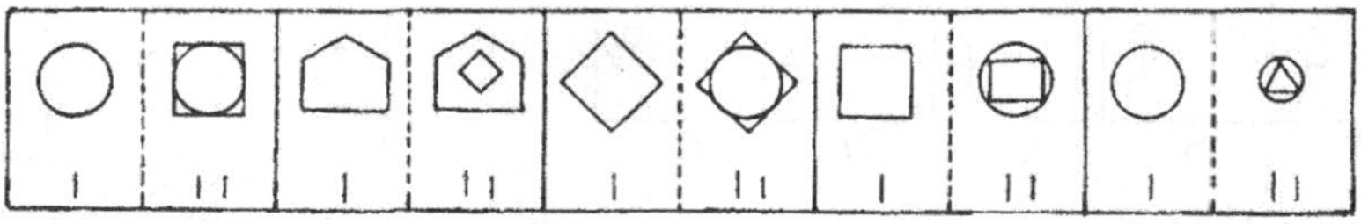

20. I II | A B C D E

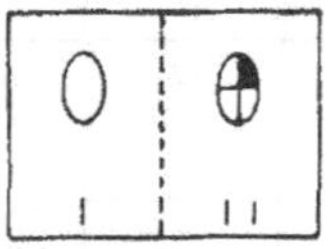

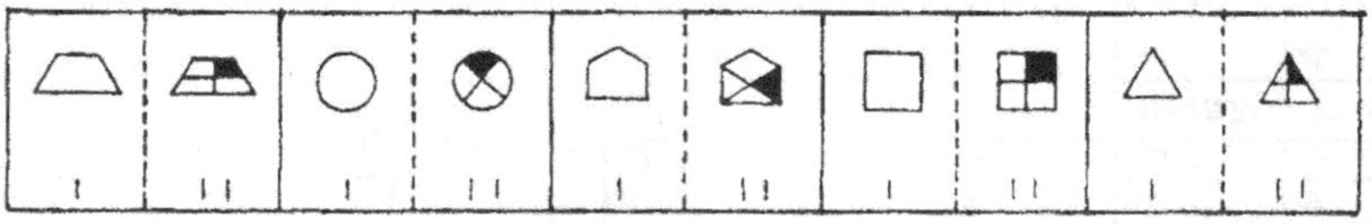

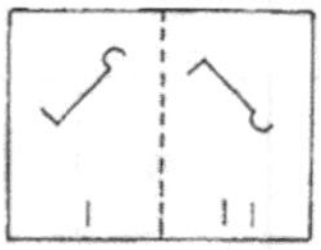

ANSWERS

1	2	3	4	5	6	7	8	9	10
B	C	B	A	E	D	A	E	A	B
11	**12**	**13**	**14**	**15**	**16**	**17**	**18**	**19**	**20**
B	B	A	E	D	B	A	E	D	E

SOME SELECTED EXPLANATORY ANSWERS

2. The element in the top left corner is turned 90° anticlockwise and moved to the centre, the element in the centre is turned 90° clockwise and moved to the bottom left corner position, the element in the bottom left corner is laterally inverted and moved to the top right corner position, and the element in the top right corner is laterally inverted and moved to the bottom right corner position.

4. The first figure is turned 135° clockwise, the inner element is moved out towards the base, the blank circle is shaded and a circle is added on its opposite side to get the second figure.

5. All arcs in the first figure except the left are below the line segment are turned to the other side to get the second figure.

7. The human sketch is moved to the right side and its hands and legs are extended and shortened respectively in a particular manner. The other two elements are turned upside down, the smaller one is enclosed within the larger one and then the two together are moved to the left and rotated 45° anticlockwise.

9. The left most element is made new and then the two corner elements are moved inbetween the two middle elements.

11. The triangle inside the circle is moved one and a half steps clockwise and turned outside. The elements on the side arc moved one step anticlockwise, the arrow and the triangle are turned 90° clockwise, and 90° anticlockwise respectively.

12. The first figure is turned 90° anticlockwise, one arc is turned to the other side to be in front of the line with a dot to get the second figure.

13. The petals in first figure are turned 135° anticlockwise to get the second figure.

14. Of the three elements the right most element is moved to the left, the design is turned 135° anticlockwise, the arrow is turned to the other side and the lines making the arrowhead are turned inwards.

15. The blank and shaded petals in first figure are turned 90° and 135° anticlockwise respectively to get the second figure.

16. The uppermost design enters into innerside side of the lower design from Ist figure to the IInd figure.

17. In element I to II upper left design comes at lower right rotating 135° C.W. Middle design goes to upper left and rotates 90° CW. While lower right design goes to middle and it also rotates 90° C.W. The same changes occur in option A.

18. In element I to II and ellipse is put in the triangle. Similarly in option E a triangle is put in the ellipse.

19. From first figure to IInd figure, design is divided into four equal parts and right side of the upper portion becomes shaded.

20. From Ist figure to IInd figure, design is reversed after moving 90° anticlockwise direction.

❀ ❀ ❀

21 Classification or Odd-One Out

Classification means arranging the given content in groups or classes having qualities of same kind. In classification type questions, the figures or items are sorted out in groups on the basis of their similarities in qualities in shapes, size, pattern, structure, genus, order, species, grade, style, constituents and other specifications, and thus the answer is found out.

Example

Which one of the following figures is different from the rest. Spot the figure.

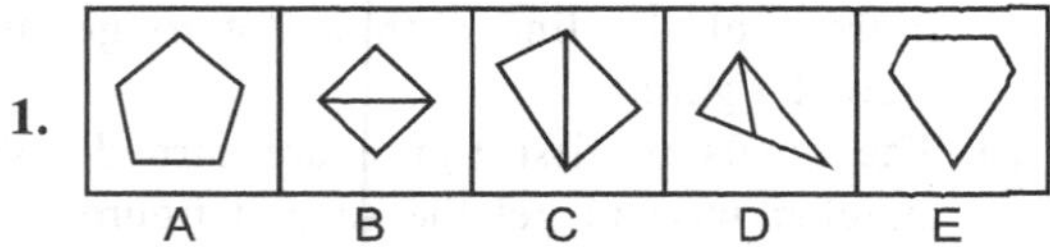

Answer D : Figures A, B, C and E are made of 5 straight lines, while D has only four straight lines. Thus A, B, C and E have a common characteristic (they have 5 straight lines each), but D does not have this characteristic. Therefore, D is different from the other four figures.

EXERCISE

Directions : *In each of the following questions one of the figures is different from the rest. Spot the figure.*

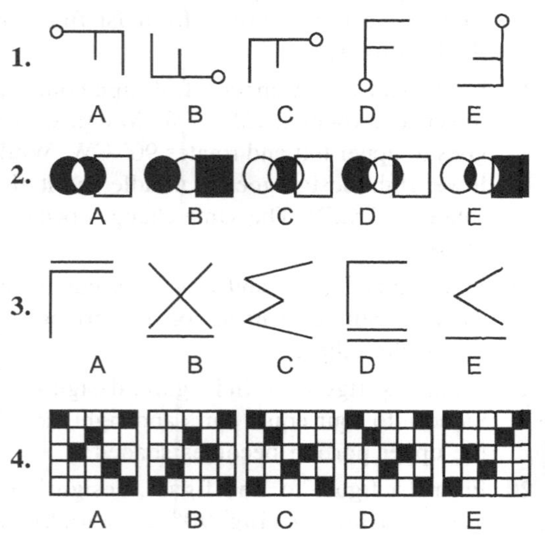

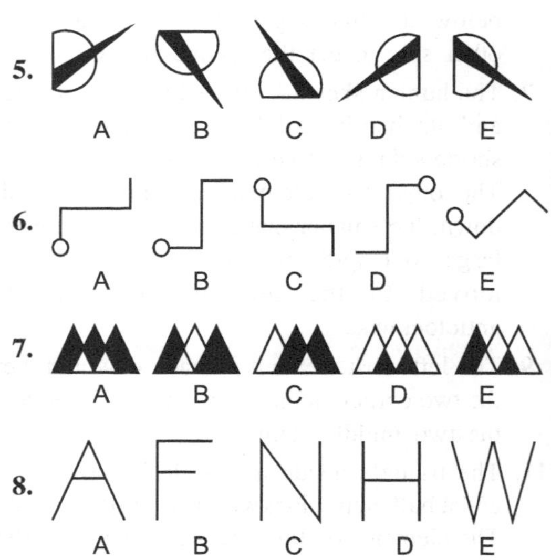

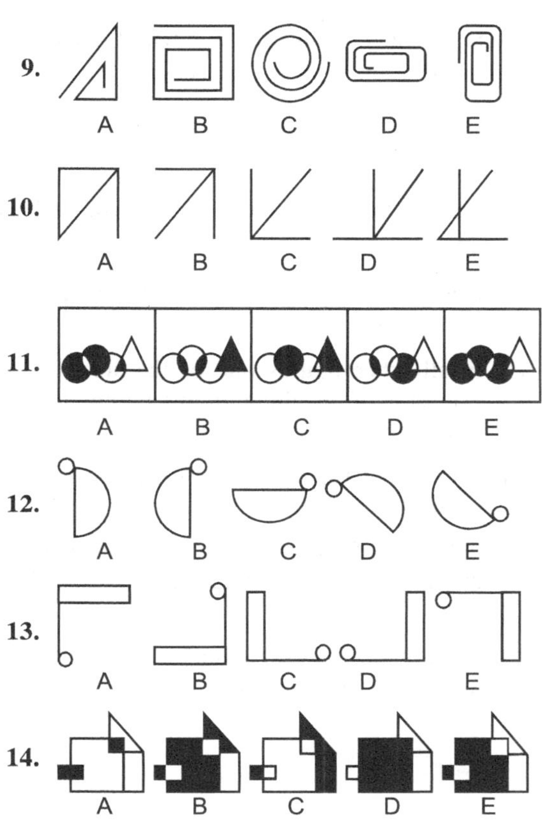

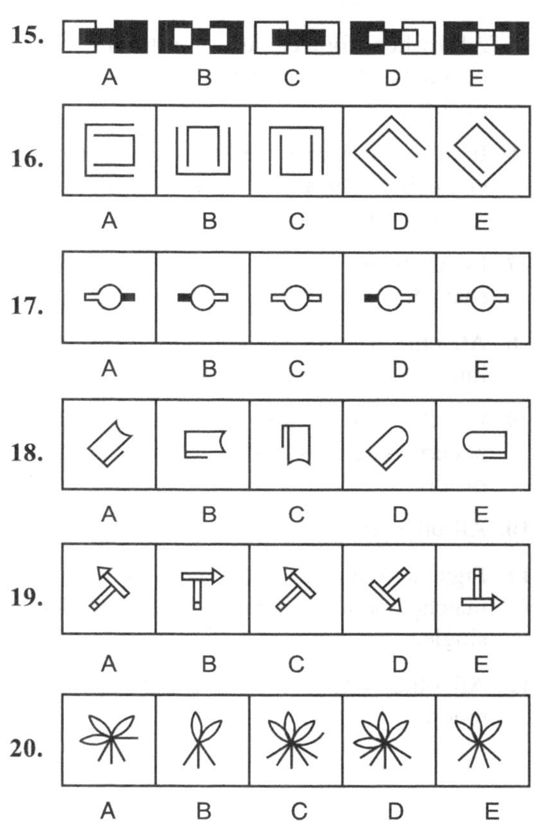

ANSWERS

1	2	3	4	5	6	7	8	9	10
C	D	C	D	E	A	A	E	D	A
11	**12**	**13**	**14**	**15**	**16**	**17**	**18**	**19**	**20**
C	B	D	E	E	D	D	E	B	C

SOME SELECTED EXPLANATORY ANSWERS

1. All other figures are identical. The two line segments are to the left of the line with a circle in this option.

2. Figures A and E and figures B and C form opposite pairs. Only figure D is left single.

3. All other figures are Roman Numerals rotated 90° anticlockwise.

4. All other figures have identical squares shaded. In this option one shaded square is on the diagonally opposite corner.

5. All other figures are identical. In this option the shaded part is rising from the left of the base.

6. In all other figures the line segment with the circle is to the right of the straight line. In this option it is on the left side.

7. In all other figures only two sections are shaded.

8. All other figures are made of three straight lines.

9. In all other figures the line forming the pattern is drawn clockwise from outside to inside.

10. All other figures contain three straight lines.

11. Figures A and D and figures B and E are matched opposite pairs. Only figure C is left single.

12. All other figures can be rotated into each other.

13. In all other figures the line with the circle is to the right side at the rectangle base.

14. Only this figure has two segments shaded, all others have three.

15. This is the only figure with a white/blank middle square.

16. Only in this figure the two shapes are not facing each other.

17. In all other figures one of the sides is the extension of the circle. In this figure both the side parts are seperated.

18. Only in this figure the line segment is parallel to the left side of the design.

19. All other figures have the arrowhead on the left side. In this figure it is on the right side.

20. In all other figures the number of lines is one more than the number of petals.

BANKING AWARENESS

BANKING INDUSTRIES

MEANING OF MONEY

Money is an important and indispensable element of modern civilization. In ordinary usage, what we use to pay for things is called money. To a layman, thus, in India, the rupee is the money, in England the pound is the money while in America the dollar is the money. But to an economist, these represent merely different units of money.

Traditionally, money has been defined on the basis of its general acceptability and its functional aspects. Thus, any thing which performed the following three functions:

(*i*) served as medium of exchange

(*ii*) served as a common measure of value and

(*iii*) served as a store of values, was termed as money.

To modern economists or empiricists, however, the crucial function of money is that it serves as a store of value.

It thus includes, not only currencies and demand deposits of banks, but also includes a host of financial assets such as bonds, government securities, time deposits with banks and equity shares which serve as a store of value. Some economists categorise these financial assets as near money, distinct from pure money which refers to cash and chequable deposits with commercial banks. The empiricists argue that whether a financial asset should be included in money should be decided on the basis of empirical investigation of the financial asset.

To them, money is what money does. While clustering financial assets as money they have laid down certain criteria :

(*i*) stability of the demand function

(*ii*) high degree of substitutability, and

(*iii*) feasibility of measuring statistical variations in real economic factors influenced by the monetary policy.

FUNCTIONS OF MONEY

In a ***static sense***, money serves :

(i) As a medium of exchange

The fundamental role of money in an economic system is to serve as a medium of exchange or as a means of payment. In the barter system goods are exchanged for other goods. This system prevailed throughout the world in the olden times. This system suffered from many shortcomings, the prominent being that it necessitated double coincidence of wants. For exchange of goods, persons desiring to exchange goods must specifically want those goods what others offered in exchange. Money has removed this difficulty. Now a person A can sell his goods (say clothes) to another person B for money and then can use to buy goods (say Mobile phone) he wants from others who have these goods.

(ii) As a unit of account

Money is a common measure or common denominator of value. The value in exchange of all goods and services can be expressed in terms of money. We can say that it is the general language we use to quote prices and compare them. It would be possible to use any good as a unit of account (say) mobile phones. This would mean that the prices of tables, chairs, books and groceries would all be quoted in terms of the number of mobile phones required to buy them.

In theory it sounds possible, but in practice who would want to carry around mobile phones to pay for everything they buy? Moreover, since there are different types of mobile phones which are available, the problem of developing an exchange rate relationship where the purchasing power of one phone would be quoted relative to another will arise. Even if prices are quoted in more basic unit, say gold, the problem of carrying gold will still remain. Moreover, some dishonest persons may shave off some of the gold from the gold coins and thus devalue them. Since we are generally not willing to accept commodities such as gold or phones as units of accounts, we require another alternative. This alternative is Fiat money.

Fiat Money : Fiat money exists where paper with no intrinsic value itself fulfils the functions of money, and government legislation ensures that it must be accepted for transaction.

For example in India, rupee is the fiat money. A hundred rupee note is capable of buying goods and services worth 100 rupees, although as such the note of hundred rupees is nothing but a piece of paper. In fact, it acts as a means of calculating the relative prices of goods and services.

(iii) As standard of deferred payments

Money is a unit in terms of which debts and future transactions can be settled. Thus loans are made and future contracts are settled in terms of money.

(iv) As store of value

Money being a permanent abode of purchasing power holds command over goods and services all the times-present and future. Money is a convenient means of keeping any income which is surplus to immediate spending needs and it can be exchanged for the required goods and services at any time. Thus it acts as a store of value.

In dynamic sense, money serves the following functions :

(v) Directs economic trends

Money directs idle resources into productive channels and there by affects output, employment, consumption and consequently economic welfare of the community at large.

(vi) As encouragement to division of labour

In a money economy, different people tend to specialise in the different goods and through the marketing process, these goods are bought and sold for the satisfaction of multiple wants. In this way, occupational specialisation and division of labour are encouraged by the use of money.

(vii) Smoothens transformation of savings into investments

In a modern economy, savings and investments are done by two different sets of people—households and firms. Households save and firms invest. Households can lend their savings to firms. The mobilisation of savings can be done through the working of various financial institutions such as banks. Money so borrowed by the investors when used for buying raw materials, labour, factory plant, etc. becomes investment. Saved money thus can be channelised into any productive investment.

MONEY STOCK IN INDIA

In 1979 the RBI classified money stock in India in the following four categories.

M_1 = Currency with the public *i.e.,* coins and currency notes + Demand deposits of the public known as narrow money.

M_2 = M_1 + Post office saving deposits.

M_3 = M_1 + Time deposits of the pubic with banks called broad money.

M_4 = M_3 + Total post office deposits. (excluding National Saving Certificates).

The basic distinction between narrow money (M_1) and broad money (M_3) is in the treatment of time deposits with banks. Narrow money excludes time deposits of the public with the banking system while broad money includes it. Not much significance is attached to M_2 and M_4 by the RBI. The third RBI working group (1998) redefined its parameters for measuring money supply and introduced new monetary aggregates (NM).

NM_1 = Currency + Demand deposits + Other deposits with RBI.

NM_2= NM_1 + Time liabilities portion of saving deposits with banks + Certificates of deposits issued by banks + Term deposits maturing within a year excluding FCNR (Foreign Currency now Residential Bank) Deposits.

NM_3= NM_2 + Term deposits with banks with maturity over one year + Call/term borrowings of the banking system.

NM_4 has been excluded from the scheme of new monetary aggregates. Three liquidity aggregates L_1, L_2 and L_3 have also been introduced.

It may, however be noted that the measures M_1, and M_3 are still used as measures of money supply in India.

PUBLIC BUDGET

A budget is the statement of the financial plan of a government. It indicates the revenue and expenditure of the last completed financial year, the probable revenue and expenditure estimates for the current year, *i.e.,* not completed and the estimates of the anticipated revenue and proposed expenditure for the next financial year.

In the constitution of India, a budget has been referred to as the annual financial statement of the estimated receipts and expenditure of the government of India or of a state government, in respect of a financial year. Article 112 of the constitution of India states that "an annual financial statement" will be placed before both Lok Sabha, and Rajya Sabha, while Article 202 of the constitution states that a similar financial statement for each state will be placed before the Legislature of that state.

Revenue and Capital Budgets

In many countries, the budget is divided into revenue and capital accounts. Revenue account covers those items which are of recurring nature; while capital account covers those items which are in the nature of the acquiring and disposing of capital assets.

In India, the constitution demands that the budget must distinguish expenditure on Revenue Accounts from other expenditure. Accordingly, the budget is necessarily presented into two parts, namely, **Revenue Budget** and **Capital Budget.** Revenue Budget consists of the revenue receipts—both tax revenue and non-tax revenue—and the expenditure met out of revenue receipts. The non-tax-revenue receipts include revenue from currency, coinage and mint, interest receipts, dividends, profits revenue from general services (such as police, jails, public works, etc.), revenue from social and community services (such as education, health, housing, broadcasting and so on), and revenue from economic services (such as agriculture and allied services, industry and mines, transport and communications, etc.)

Capital Account receipts, on the other hand, include market loans, borrowings from the RBI, etc., through the sale of Treasury Bills, loans from foreign governments and institutions, and repayment of loans by state governments and others to the central government. Capital disbursements would include expenditure on acquisition of various physical assets like land, buildings, machinery and equipment, investments in shares and debentures and loans to state governments and other bodies.

Zero-Base Budgeting

Zero-base budgeting (ZBB) is an innovative technique to guard against wastage in public expenditure. The technique works not through auditing which is a post-operative check, but through an examination of the very rational of an expenditure item under consideration. In a more practical way, ZBB means the evaluation and prioritisation of all programmes at different levels of efforts. To be more simple, each department is required to justify its budget requests from the bottom up, evaluating alternative programme packages and ranking programmes so as to select the best alternative and allocate resources accordingly. Thus, no consideration is given to the post or existing at present, any programme may be included or excluded. The Budget is considered as a whole and a fresh, *i.e.,* from zero-Base.

In the sphere of public budgeting, ZBB was first tried by **Mr. Jimmy Carter** in 1973 when he was the Governer of Georgia, with proper remoulding. Later on its was adopted by a number of states in the U.S.A.

Performance Budgeting

Performance Budgeting is generally under-stood as a system of presentation of public expenditure in terms of functions, programmes, performance units, viz., activities, projects, etc., reflecting primarily the government out-put and its cost.

The U.S. Bureau of the Budget defines a performance budget in these words, "As performance budget in one which presents the purpose and objectives for which funds are required, the cost of the programmes proposed for achieving those objective and quantitative data measuring the accomplishment and work performed under each programme."

Under Performance Budgeting System the over all budget is divided into functions based on the major purpose of government and then subdivided into programme and activities, funds are granted for doing a specific quantity of work.

Performance budgeting implies that the budget statement should indicate the actual achievement expected by a Ministry over a period of time from certain amount of expenditure.

Thus, the process of performance budgeting is not merely a technique, it constitutes a new approach to budget formation and execution. Since the cost and benefits indicated side by side, this technique helps in the decision-making regarding allocations of funds.

Types of Deficits

1. **Revenue Deficits:** Revenue Deficit = Revenue Expenditure – Revenue Receipts
   Current revenue expenditure of the central government is composed of plan and non-plan expanditure, and current-revenue receipts include net tax revenue and non-tax revenue of the central government.
2. **Budget Deficit:** Budget Deficit = Total Expenditure – Total Receipts
   The total expenditure of the central governments always exceeded its total revenue which is known as budget deficit or overall budgetary deficit.
3. **Fiscal Deficit:** In simple terms, fiscal deficit is budgetary deficit plus market borrowings and other liabilities of the government of India.
   ∴ Fiscal Deficit = Revenue receipts (Net tax revenue + Non-tax revenue) + Capital receipts (only recoveries of loans and other receipts) – Total expenditure (Plan and non-plan).
4. **Primary Deficit:** The excess of fiscal deficit over payments of interest is called primary deficit.
5. **Monetised Deficit:** The increase in net RBI credit for central government is called monetised deficit. It includes:
   A. Net increase in holdings of treasury bills of RBI.
   B. Contribution of RBI in market borrowings of the govt.

TRENDS IN INDIA'S BUDGET AND FISCAL DEFICITS

Budgetary deficit which shows the difference between total revenue and total expenditure does not give a true picture of the financial health of the economy. It treats government borrowing from the market or raising the funds from the public such as national savings schemes, post office saving deposits, provident fund collections, etc. as receipts. Originally, budget deficit was calculated to show RBI lending to the government. In 1997, the practice of RBI lending to government through ad hoc Treasury Bills was given up. Thus the concept lost its relevance and now it is no longer shown in the budgetary statement. The government now taps 91 days treasury bills from the market and shows it as part of the capital receipts under the heading "borrowings and other liabilities".

Fiscal deficit is a more comprehensive measure of the imbalances. It focuses on/measures the total resource gap and as such fully reflects the impact of the fiscal operations of the indebtedness of government. It is the measure of excess expenditure over the government's own income.

Fiscal deficit in India have grown rapidly. In the fifteen year period of 1975-90, the fiscal deficit of the Central Government rose alarmingly from 4.1 per cent of GDP to 7.9 per cent of GDP. The then present fiscal malaise had been caused by unchecked growth of non- planned revenue expenditure. Non plan revenue expenditure particularly on defense, interest payments and food and fertiliser subsidies rose sharply during 1980s. In 1991, major steps were taken to correct the fiscal imbalances. Many expenditures were cut and controlled (e.g. subsidies).

Fiscal deficit was reduced to 4.1 per cent in 1996-97. Since 1997-98, fiscal deficit had again started increasing. To restore fiscal discipline, the **Fiscal Responsibility and Budget Management (FRBM) Bill** was introduced in 2000 and FRBM Act was passed in 2003. The Act aims at reducing gross fiscal deficit by 0.5 per cent of the GDP in each financial year (beginning on April 1, 2000). As a result of the efforts taken, the fiscal deficit as a proportion of GDP started declining.

BALANCE OF PAYMENTS

The Balance of Payments (BOP) is one of the oldest and most important statistical statements for any country. It is a systematic record of all economic transactions between the residents of one country and the residents of the rest of the world in a year.

Since we merely record all receipts and payments in international transactions using double entry system, the balance of payments always balance in an accounting sense.

Balance of Trade

Balance of Trade may be defined as the difference between the value of goods sold to foreigners by the residents and firms of the home country and the value of goods purchased by them from foreigners. If value of exports of goods is equal to the value of imports of goods, we say that there is balance of trade equilibrium and if the latter exceeds the former, then we say that there is balance of trade deficit. But if the former exceeds the latter, *i.e.*, if value of exports of goods is more than the value of imports of goods, we say there is surplus balance of trade.

Balance of Current Account

Balance of current account is a broader concept than the balance of trade. It includes balance of services and balance of unilateral transfers (*i.e.*, unrequited transfers) besides including balance of trade. Balance of services records all the services exported and imported by a country in a year. Unlike goods which are visible and tangible, services are invisible and are not tangible.

The services transactions basically include:

(*i*) transportation, banking and insurance receipts and payments from and to the foreign countries.

(*ii*) tourism, travel services and tourist purchases of goods and services received from foreign visitors to home country and paid out in foreign countries by home country citizens.

(*iii*) expense of diplomatic and military personnel from overseas as well as receipts from similar personnel from overseas who are stationed in the home country, and

(*iv*) interest, profits, dividends and royalties received and paid from and to the foreigners. Balance of services is the sum of all invisible service receipts and payments which could be zero, positive or negative. Balance of unrequited transfers includes all gifts, donations, grants and reparation, receipts and payments to foreign countries.

All these balances, *i.e.*, balance of trade, balance of services and balance of unrequited transfers constitute balance of current account. It could again be positive, negative or zero depending upon the values of these balances. It is worth noting that balance of payments on current account covers all receipts on account of earnings (as opposed to borrowings) and all the payments arising out of spending (as opposed to lending). Thus, while all earnings and expenditure by way of exports and imports of goods and services and transfers like remittances, donations, etc. form a part of the current account, foreign investments (direct and portfolio), commercial borrowings, external assistance, NRI deposits, etc. form a part of the capital account.

Balance of Payment on Capital Account

Balance of payments on capital account includes balances of private direct investments, private portfolio investments and government loans to foreign governments. Balance of capital account basically deals with debts and claims of the country in question or we say it deals with borrowings or lending of the country in question.

Balance of Payments

Overall balance of payments is the sum of balance of current account and balance of capital account. It includes all international monetary transactions of the reporting country vis-à-vis the rest of the world. The balance of payments must always balance in a book-keeping sense. This is because for any surplus (or deficit) in the overall balance of payments there must be a corresponding debit (or credit) entry in the net changes in external reserves. In other words, if there is a surplus it adds to external reserves of the country and if there is a deficit, it reduces down the external reserves of the country.

RESERVE BANK OF INDIA

The Reserve Bank of India is the apex financial institution of the country which is entrusted with the task of controlling, supervising, promoting, developing and planning the financial system. RBI is the queen bee of the Indian financial system which influences the commercial banks' management in more than one way.

The RBI influences the management of commercial banks through its various policies, directions and regulations. Its role in banking is quite unique. In fact, the RBI performs the four basic functions of management, viz., planning, organizing, directing and controlling in laying a strong foundation for the functioning of commercial banks.

RBI possesses special status in our country. It is the authority to regulate and control monetary system of our country. It controls money market and the entire banking system of our country.

The origins of the Reserve Bank of India can be traced to 1926, when the Royal Commission on Indian Currency and Finance —also known as the Hilton-Young Commission – recommended the creation of a Central Bank for India to separate the control of currency and credit from the Government and to augment banking facilities throughout the country. The Reserve Bank of India Act of 1934 established the Reserve Bank and set in motion a series of actions culminating in the start of operations in 1935. Since then, the Reserve Bank's role and functions have undergone numerous changes, as the nature of the Indian economy and financial sector changed.

Origins of the Reserve Bank of India

- **1926:** The Royal Commission on Indian Currency and Finance recommended creation of a Central Bank for India.
- **1927:** A bill to give effect to the above recommendation was introduced in the Legislative Assembly, but was later withdrawn due to lack of agreement among various sections of people.
- **1928:** The Hilton Young Commission (1928 AD), which laid the groundwork for the Reserve Bank of India Act, 1934, considered Dr. B.R. Ambedkar's recommendation.
- **1933:** The White Paper on Indian Constitutional Reforms recommended the creation of a Reserve Bank. A fresh bill was introduced in the Legislative Assembly.
- **1934:** The Bill was passed and received the Governor General's assent.
- **1935:** The Reserve Bank commenced operations as India's Central Bank on April 1 as a private shareholders' bank with a paid up capital of rupees five crore (rupees fifty million).
- **1942:** The Reserve Bank ceased to be the currency issuing authority of Burma (now Myanmar).
- **1947:** The Reserve Bank stopped acting as a banker to the Government of Burma.
- **1948:** The Reserve Bank stopped rendering central banking services to Pakistan.
- **1949:** The Government of India nationalised the Reserve Bank under the Reserve Bank (Transfer of Public Ownership) Act, 1948.

Starting as a private shareholders' bank, the Reserve Bank was nationalised in 1949. It then assumed the responsibility to meet the aspirations of a newly independent country and its people. The Reserve Bank's nationalisation aimed at achieving coordination between the policies of the government and those of the Central Bank.

The Preamble to the Reserve Bank of India Act, 1934 (the Act), under which it was constituted, specifies its objective as "to regulate the issue of Bank notes and the keeping of reserves with a view to securing monetary stability in India and generally to operate the currency and credit system of the country to its advantage".

The objectives outlined in the Preamble hold good even after 75 years. As evident from the multifaceted functions that the Reserve Bank performs today, its role and priorities have, in the span of 75 years, changed in tandem with changing national priorities and global developments. Essentially, the Reserve Bank has demonstrated dynamism and flexibility to meet the requirements of an evolving economy.

A core function of the Reserve Bank in the last 75 years has been the formulation and implementation of monetary policy with the objectives of maintaining price stability and ensuring adequate flow of credit to productive sectors of the economy. To these was added, in more recent times, the goal of maintaining financial stability. The objective of maintaining financial stability has spanned its role from external account management to oversight of banks and non-banking financial institutions as also of money, government securities and foreign exchange markets.

The Reserve Bank designs and implements the regulatory policy framework for banking and non-banking financial institutions with the aim of providing people access to the banking system, protecting depositors' interest, and maintaining the overall health of the financial system. Its function of regulating the commercial banking sector, which emerged with the enactment of the Banking Regulation Act, 1949, has over time, expanded to cover other entities. Thus, amendments to the Banking Regulation Act, 1949 brought cooperative banks and regional rural banks under the Reserve Bank's jurisdiction, while amendments to the Reserve Bank of India Act saw development finance institutions, non-banking financial companies and primary dealers coming under its regulation, as these entities became important players in the financial system and markets.

Objectives of RBI

Prior to the establishment of the Reserve Bank, the Indian financial system was totally inadequate on account of the inherent weakness of the dual control of currency by the Central Government and of credit by the Imperial Bank of India.

The Preamble to the Reserve Bank of India Act, 1934 spells out the objectives of the Reserve Bank as: "to regulate the issue of Bank notes and the keeping of reserves with a view to securing monetary stability in India and generally to operate the currency and credit system of the country to its advantage."

The important objectives are:

1. **To Act as Monetary Authority:** Formulates implements and monitors the monetary policy to maintain price stability and ensuring adequate flow of credit to productive sectors.
2. **To Regulate and Supervise the Financial System of the Country:** It prescribes broad parameters of banking operations within which the country's banking and financial system functions. It helps to maintain public confidence in the system, protect depositors' interest and provide cost-effective banking services to the public.
3. **To Manage the Exchange Control:** Manages the Foreign Exchange Management Act, 1999 to facilitate external trade and payment and promote orderly development and maintenance of foreign exchange market in India.
4. **To Issue Currency:** Issues and exchanges or destroys currency and coins not fit for circulation to give the public adequate quantity of supplies of currency notes and coins and in good quality.
5. **To Undertake Developmental Role:** RBI performs a wide range of promotional functions to support national objectives.
6. **To Undertake Related Functions by Acting as:**
   - *Banker to the Government:* Performs merchant banking function for the central and the state governments; also acts as their banker.
   - *Banker to Banks:* Maintains banking accounts of all scheduled banks.
   - Owner and operator of the depository (SGL-Subsidiary General Ledger account) and exchange (NDS).

Functions of RBI

RBI performs various traditional banking function as well as promotional and developmental measures to meet the dynamic requirements of the country. Main functions of RBI can be broadly classified into three.

These are:

I. Monetary functions or Central banking functions
II. Supervisory functions
III. Promotional and Developmental functions.

I. Monetary Functions Include

A. Issue of currency notes
B. Acting as banker to the Government
C. Serving as banker of other banks
D. Controlling credit
E. Controlling foreign exchange operations

A. Issue of Currency Notes

Under Section 22 of the Reserve Bank of India Act of 1934, the Reserve Bank of India is given the monopoly of note issue. Now, RBI is the sole authority for the issue of currency notes of all denominations except one rupee notes and coins in the country. One rupee notes and coins are issued by Ministry of Finance of GOI. The RBI has a separate department called the Issue Department for the issue of currency notes.

Since 1956, system of Note Issue changed from **Proportional Reserve System** to **Minimum Reserve System.**

Under Proportional reserve system of note issue, not less than 40% of the total volume of notes issue by the RBI was to be covered by gold coins, bullion and foreign securities. But under the Minimum reserve system of note issue, RBI is required to maintain a minimum reserve of gold or foreign securities or both against the notes issued. No maximum limit is fixed on the volume of notes. RBI maintains gold and foreign exchange reserves of ₹ 200 crores of which 115 crores is in gold and balance in foreign securities, Govt. of India securities, eligible commercial bills, Pro-notes of NABARD for any loans, etc.

This change from Proportional Reserve System to Minimum Reserve System is made because of two major reasons. Firstly, the planned economic development of the country called for an increased supply of money, which could not be had under the proportional reserve system. Secondly, the foreign exchange held as reserve by the Reserve Bank had to be released for financing the Five Year Plans. In short, this was to enable the expanding currency requirements of the economy.

B. Acting as Banker to Government

The Reserve Bank act as a banker to the Central and State Governments. As a banker to the—

Government RBI acts in three capacities, viz.,

(*a*) as a banker,
(*b*) as a financial agent, and
(*c*) as a financial advisor.

(*a*) As a banker: RBI renders the following services:

1. Accepts deposits from the Central and State Government.
2. Collects money on behalf of the Government.
3. Makes payments on behalf of the Governments, in accordance with their instructions.
4. Arranges for the transfer of funds from one place to another on behalf of the Governments.
5. Makes arrangements for the supply of foreign exchange to the Central and State Governments.
6. It maintains currency chests with treasuries and other agencies in places prescribed by the Government of India. These chests are supplied with sufficient currency notes to meet the requirements for the transactions of the Government.
7. Short-term advances are granted to Central and State Governments for a period not exceeding three months. These advances are granted up to a certain limit without any collateral securities.
8. In times of emergencies like war, extraordinary loans are also granted to the Governments by the RBI.

(*b*) **As a financial agent:** The services given are:

1. Acts as an agent of the Central and State Governments in the matter of floatation of loans. On account of Reserve Bank's intimate knowledge of the financial markets, it is able to obtain the best possible terms for the Government in this matter. Further by coordinating the borrowing programmers of the various Governments, it is able to minimize the adverse effects of Government borrowings on the money and securities market.
2. On behalf of Central Government RBI sells treasury bills of 90 days maturity at weekly auctions and secures short-term finance for the Central Government. Apart from that RBI also sells Adhoc Treasury Bills of 90 day's maturity to the State Governments, Semi-Government Departments and foreign Central Banks on behalf of the Central Government.
3. RBI manages and keeps the accounts of the public debts of the Central and State Governments. It arranges for the payment of interest and principal amount on the public debt on the due dates.
4. As an agent, RBI also represents Government of India in the International institutions like the IMF, the IBRD, etc.

The Reserve Bank is an agent of Central Government and of all State Governments in India except for that of Jammu and Kashmir and Sikkim.

(*c*) **As a financial adviser:** Renders following services:

1. It advices the Central and State Governments on all financial and economic matters such as the floating of loans, agricultural and industrial finance, etc.
2. Advice on matters of International finance is also given to Central Government.
3. It collects the recent information on current economic and financial developments in India and abroad, with the help of its Research and Statistics Department and keeps Government informed periodically.

C. Banker's Bank

RBI acts as banker to Scheduled banks. Scheduled Banks include commercial banks, foreign exchange banks, public sector banks, state co-operative banks and the regional rural banks. As a bankers' bank, it renders the following services:

1. **It holds a part of the cash balances of the commercial banks:** Every commercial bank in India is required to keep with the Reserve Bank a cash balance of not less than 6% of its demand and time liabilities. This rate can be increased up to 20%. The two main purposes of maintaining cash reserve by commercial banks are as follows. Firstly to protect the interest of the depositors, secondly to enable the Reserve Bank to accommodate the commercial banks on times of difficulties and thirdly the Reserve Bank can control the credit created by the commercial banks by varying the statutory cash reserve requirements.
2. **It acts as the clearing house:** By acting as clearing house, the Reserve bank helps the member banks in the settlement of the mutual indebtedness without physical transfer of cash.
3. **It provides cheap remittance facilities** to the commercial banks.
4. **It provides financial accommodation to the commercial banks:** At times of financial crisis, the RBI is **the lender of last resort** for the commercial banks. Financial assistance is given by the Reserve Bank either by rediscounting eligible bills or by granting loans against approved securities.

D. Control of Credit

RBI undertakes the responsibility of controlling credit in order to ensure internal price stability and promote sufficient credit for the economic growth of the country. Price stability is essential for economic development. To control credit, RBI makes use of both quantitative and qualitative weapons by virtue of the powers given to it by Reserve Bank of India Act of 1934 and the Indian Banking Regulation Act of 1949. These weapons are listed below.

(a) *Quantitative Weapons*

1. **Bank Rate Policy:** Bank rate is the lending rate of central bank. It is the official minimum rate at which central bank of a country rediscounts the eligible bills of exchange of the commercial banks and other financial institutions or grants short-term loans to them. By increasing bank rate, RBI can make bank credit costlier.
2. **Open Market Operations:** RBI Act authorizes the RBI to engage in the purchase of securities of Central and State Government and such other securities as specified by Central Govt. But by and large, its open market operations are confined to Central Government Securities and to a very limited extend to State Government Securities. RBI uses this weapon to offset the seasonal fluctuations in money market. When there is an excessive supply of money, RBI sells the securities in the open market. In that way RBI is able to withdraw the excess money from circulation. But when there is shortage of money supply in the market, it purchases securities from the open market and as a result, more money is arrived at for circulation.
3. **Variable Cash Reserve Ratio:** Under the RBI Act of 1934, every scheduled and non-scheduled bank is required to maintain a fixed percentage of total time and demand liabilities as cash reserve with RBI. It is called statutory Cash Reserve Ratio (CRR). An increase in CRR reduces lending capacity of the bank and a decrease in CRR increases the lending capacity. RBI can prescribe a CRR ranging up to 15%.
4. **Variable Statutory Liquidity Ratio:** According to Sec 24 of BRA 1949, every commercial bank is required to maintain a certain percentage of its total deposits in liquid assets such as cash in hand, excess reserve with RBI, balances with other banks, gold and approved Government and other securities. This proportion of liquid assets to total deposits is called SLR. BRA empowers RBI to fix the SLR up to 40%. The variation of the SLR is intended to reduce the lendable funds in the hands of the commercial banks and to check the expansion of bank credit. An increase in SLR will decrease the lendable funds in the hands of commercial banks and vice versa.
5. **Repo Rate and Reverse Repo Rate:** Repo rate is the rate at which RBI lends to commercial banks generally against government securities. Reduction in Repo rate helps the commercial banks to get money at a cheaper rate and increase in Repo rate discourages the commercial banks to get money as the rate increases and becomes expensive. Reverse Repo rate is the rate at which RBI borrows money from the commercial banks. The increase in the Repo rate will increase the cost of borrowing and lending of the banks which will discourage the public to borrow money and will encourage them to deposit. As the rates are high the availability of credit and demand decreases resulting to decrease in inflation. This increase in Repo Rate and Reverse Repo Rate is a symbol of tightening of the policy.

(b) *Selective Credit Controls (Qualitative Weapons)*

1. **Credit Ceiling:** In this operation, RBI issues prior information or direction that loans to the commercial banks will be given up to a certain limit. In this case commercial bank will be tight in advancing loans to the public. They will allocate loans to limited sectors. Few example of ceiling are agriculture sector advances, priority sector lending.
2. **Credit Authorization Scheme:** Credit Authorization Scheme was introduced in November, 1965 when P.C. Bhattacharya was the chairman of RBI. Under this instrument of credit, the commercial banks are required to obtain the RBI's prior authorization for sanctioning any fresh credit beyond the authorized limits.

3. **Moral Suasion:** Moral Suasion is just as a request by the RBI to the commercial banks to follow a particular line of action. RBI may request commercial banks not to give loans for unproductive purpose which does not add to economic growth but increases inflation.
4. **Regulation of Margin Requirements:** Margin refers to the difference between loan amount and the market value of collateral placed to raise the loan. RBI fixes a lower margin to borrowers whose need is urgent. For example, if RBI believes that farmers should be financed urgently, RBI would direct to lower the margin requirement on agricultural commodities. RBI has used this weapon for a number of times.
5. **Issuing of Directives:** BRA empowers RBI to issue directives to banks and banks are bound to comply with such directives. RBI directives may relate to:
   - Purpose for which advance may or may not be made
   - Margins requirement
   - Maximum amount of loan that can be sanctioned to any company, firm or individual
   - Rate of interest and other terms and conditions on which loans may be given.

E. Control of Foreign Exchange Operations

One of the central banking functions of the RBI is the control of foreign exchange operations. For the control of foreign exchange business, the RBI has set up a separate department called the Exchange Control Department in September, 1939. This Department has been granted wide powers to regulate the foreign exchange business of the country. As the Central Bank of India, it is the responsibility of the RBI to maintain the external value of the Indian rupee stable. India being member of the IMF, the RBI is required to maintain stable exchange rates between the Indian rupee and the currencies of all other member countries of the I.M.F. Besides maintaining stable exchange rates, RBI also acts as the custodian of the foreign exchange reserves of the country. The foreign exchange reserves of the country held by RBI includes Euro, U.S. dollars, Japanese yen etc.

RBI also acts as the administrator of exchange control. It ensures that the foreign exchange reserves of the country are utilised only for approved purposes and the limited foreign exchange reserves of the country are conserved for the future.

II. Supervisory Functions

RBI has been given several supervisory powers over the different banking institutions in the country. The supervisory functions relate to licensing and establishment, branch expansion, liquidity of assets, amalgamation, reconstruction and liquiditation of commercial banks and cooperative banks.

III. Promotional and Developmental Functions

RBI is also performing promotional and developmental functions. These functions includes the following:

(*a*) Provision of Agricultural Credit

(*b*) Provision for Industrial Finance

(*c*) Development of Bill Market

(*d*) Collection and Publication of Statistics on Financial and Economic Matters

COMMERCIAL BANKS

The Banks which perform all kinds of banking business and generally finance trade and commerce are called commercial banks. Since, their deposits are for a short period, these banks normally advance short-term loans to businessmen and traders and avoid medium and long term lending. However, recently. Commercial banks have also extended their areas of operation to medium-term and long-term finance:

- A commercial bank is a financial intermediary.
- Its central objective is commercial that is, profit making.
- It takes money from a surplus unit by paying a low rate of interest and lends the same

fund to a deficit unit at a higher rate of interest and thus makes profit.

- It is said to be a dealer in credit.
- It may be organized privately or by the Government.

Functions of Commercial Banks

The Commercial Banks perform a variety of functions which can be divided in the following three categories:

1. Basic Functions
2. Agency Functions
3. General Utility Functions

Basic Functions

The basic functions of bank are those functions without performing which an institution cannot be called a banking institution at all. That is why these functions are also called primary or acid test function of a bank. The basic/primary/acid test function of a bank are:

(*a*) Accepting Deposits
(*b*) Advancing of Loans
(*c*) Credit Creation.

(a) Accepting Deposits

The first and the most important function of a bank is to accept deposits from those people who can save and spare for the safe custody with the bankers. It serves two purposes for the customers. On one hand their money is safe with the bank without any fear of theft and on the other hand they also earn interest as per the kind of saving they have made. For this purpose, the banks have different kinds of deposit accounts to attract the people which are as under:

(*i*) Saving Deposit Account
(*ii*) Fixed Deposit Account
(*iii*) Current Deposit Account
(*iv*) Recurring Deposit Account
(*v*) Home Loan Account

(*i*) **Saving Deposit Account:** The Saving Bank Account is the most common bank account being utilized by the general public. The basic purpose of this account is to mobilise the small savings of the general public. Certain restrictions are imposed on the depositors regarding the number of withdrawals and amount to be withdrawn in a given period of time. Generally, the rate of interest paid by the bank on these deposits is low as compared to recurring or fixed deposit account. Cheque facility is also provided to the depositors with certain extra restrictions on the depositors. One of the conditions is that the depositor shall have to maintain a minimum balance in the account say ₹ 1,000 in urban areas and ₹ 500 for rural areas. Some service charges are also imposed if the depositor uses the cheque facility at large levels.

(*ii*) **Fixed Deposit Account:** This is an account where money can be deposited for a fixed period of time say one year or two years or three years of five years and so on. Once the money is deposited for a fixed period of time, the depositor is prohibited from withdrawal of money from the bank before the expiry of the stipulated period of time. The basic advantage to be customer is that he is offered interest at the higher rate of interest and the banker is free to utilize the money for that fixed period.

But where a customer is in need of money in any contingency or emergency, the bank also has the facility to provide loan against the fixed deposit receipt at liberal terms and conditions. Even if a customer insist on the withdrawal of his money the fixed deposit receipt can also be encashed before the expiry of the stipulated period of time with the condition that the customer shall not be entitled to higher rate of interest, but the customer is allowed that rate of interest which is applicable on the saving deposit account as if the amount was deposited in the savings account.

(*iii*) **Current Deposit Account:** In the savings bank account, there are restrictions on the number of withdrawals that can be made in a day or a week or a month. Therefore, it does not suit to the needs of traders and businessmen who has to make several payments daily and deposits money in a similar manner. Therefore, there is a facility for them in the shape of another account called Current Deposit Account. These accounts are generally maintained by the traders and businessmen who have to make a number of payments every day. Money from this account can be withdrawn by the account holder as many times as desired by the customer. Normally, bank does not pay any interest on these current accounts, rather some incidental charges are charged by the banker as service charges. These accounts are also called demand deposits or demand liabilities.

The facility of Over Drafts is provided to the traders through these current accounts for which the banks charge interest on the outstanding balance of the customers. A limit is fixed by the bankers for withdrawal of over drafts and the customer is not allowed to withdraw more than that limit from his O/D current account. Say if a trader has an O/D limit of ₹ 1,00,000 with a bank, he can withdraw money upto ₹ 1,00,000 from the bank without depositing any money with the bank. But he cannot withdraw more than ₹ 1,00,000. He shall have to pay interest on such with-drawals.

(iv) **Recurring Deposit Account:** To encourage regular savings by the general public, another account is opened in the banks called Recurring Deposit Account. This account is preferred by the fixed income group, because a particular amount fixed at the time of opening the account has to be deposited in the account every month for a stipulated period of time. Say ₹ 500 per month for a period of three years. In this case the customer is bound to deposit ₹ 500 per month regularly for a period of three years. Generally the bank pays rate of interest higher than that of a saving account and just equal to the fixed deposit account on such recurring deposit accounts.

The withdrawal of money is allowed only after the stipulated period of time along with the interest. Rather the account stands closed at the end of the stipulated period of time. In this case also the bank provide a facility to withdraw the money before the stipulated period of time in the case of any emergency. The bank shall allow rate of interest which is applicable on saving bank account in case the customer want to close the account before the stipulated period of time.

(v) **Home Loan Account:** Home loan account facility has been introduced in some scheduled commercial banks to encourage savings for the purchasing of or construction of a house to live. In this account, the customer is required to deposit a particular amount per month or half yearly or even yearly for a period of five years. After the stipulated period bank provide three to five times of the deposited amount a loan to the subscribers to purchase or construct a house. Rate of interest is also very attractive on this account nearly equal to that of the fixed deposit account. Even the rebate of Income Tax is also available on the amount contributed in this account under Section 88 of the Income Tax Act, 1961. Facility to close the account after the stipulated period of time is also allowed.

(b) Advancing of Loans

Advancing of loans is the second acid test function of the commercial banks. After keeping certain cash reserves, the banks lend their deposits to the needy borrowers. It is one of the primary functions without which an institution can not be called a bank. The bank lends a certain percentage of the cash lying in the deposits on a higher rate of interest than it pays on such deposits. The longer the period for which the loan is required the higher is the rate of interest. Similarly, higher the amount of loan, the higher shall be the rate of interest. Before advancing the loans the bank satisfy themselves about the credit worthiness of the borrowers. This is how a bank earns profits and carries on its banking business.

There are various types of loans which are provided by the banks to the borrowers. Some of the important ways of advancing loans are as under:

(*i*) Call Money Advances
(*ii*) Cash Credits
(*iii*) Overdrafts
(*iv*) Discounting Bills of Exchange
(*v*) Term Loans

(*i*) **Call Money Advances:** The Call Money Market which is also known as inter-bank call money market deals with very short period loans called call loans. The Call Money Market is a very important constituent of the organized money market which functions as an immediate source of very short-term loans. The major suppliers of the funds in the call money market are All Commercial Banks, State Bank of India (SBI), Life Insurance Corporation of India (LIC), General Insurance Corporation (GIC), Unit Trust of India (UTI) and Industrial Development Bank of India (IDBI) and the major borrowers are the scheduled Commercial Banks. No collateral securities are required against these call money market loans.

As the participants are mostly banks, it is also called inter-bank call money market. The Scheduled Commercial Banks use their surplus funds to lend for very short period to the bill brokers. The bill brokers and dealers in the stock exchanges generally borrow money at call from the commercial banks. The bill brokers in turn use them to discount or purchase the bills. Such funds are borrowed at the call rate which varies with the volume of funds lent by the commercial banks. When the brokers are asked to pay off the loans immediately, then they borrow from SBI, LIC, GIC, and UTI, etc. These loans are granted by the commercial banks for a very short period, not exceeding seven days in any case. The borrowers have to repay the loan immediately when ever the lender bank call them back.

(*ii*) **Cash Credits:** This is a type of loan which is provided to the businessmen against their current assets such as shares, stocks, bonds, etc. These loans are not based on credit worthiness or personal security of the customers. The bank provides this loan through opening an account in the name of the customer and allows them to withdraw borrowed amount of loan from time to time upto the limit fixed by the bank which is determined by the value of security provided by the borrowers. Interest is charge only on the amount of money actually withdrawn from the banks and not on the amount of the sanctioned amount of loan.

In some other cases, certain banks follow a different procedure for cash credits. The whole amount of loan is credited to the current account of the borrower. In case of new customer, a separate account is opened and amount of loan is transferred to it. The borrower is free to withdraw the money through cheques as and when required by the borrower. But in this case the borrower has to pay the interest on the whole amount credited in their accounts.

(*iii*) **Over drafts:** The facility of Over Drafts is provided to the traders and businessmen through current accounts for which the banks charge interest on the outstanding balance of the customers. A limit is fixed by the bankers for withdrawal of over drafts and the customer is not allowed to withdraw more than that limit from his Over Draft Current Account. This facility is required by the traders and businessmen because they issue several cheques in a day and similarly deposits. So, many cheques daily go in their current accounts. They may not be knowing at a particular day that whether there is a balance in the account or not and their issued cheques are not dishonored so they are provided with the facility of overdrafts. Say it a trader has an Over Draft limit of ₹ 2,00,000 with a bank, he can withdraw money upto ₹ 2,00,000 from the bank without depositing any money with the bank. But he cannot withdraw more than ₹ 2,00,000. He shall have to pay interest on such withdrawals.

(*iv*) **Discounting Bills of Exchange:** This is another popular type of lending by the commercial banks. A holder of a bill of exchange can get it discounted with a commercial bank. Bills of Exchange are also called the Commercial Bills and the market dealing with these bills is also called commercial bill market. Bills of exchange are those bills which are issued by the businessmen or firms in exchange of goods sold or purchased.

The bill of exchange is a written unconditional order signed by the drawer (seller) requiring the drawee (buyer) to pay on demand or at a fixed future date, (usually three months after date written on the bill of exchange), a definite sum of money.

After the bill has been drawn by the drawer (seller), it is accepted by the drawee (buyer) by countersigning the bill. Once the buyer puts his acceptance on the bill by signing it, it becomes a legal document. They are like post dated cheques issued by the buyers of goods for the goods received. The bill holder can get this bill discounted in the bill market if he wants the amount of the bill before its actual maturity.

These bills of exchange are discounted and re-discounted by the commercial banks for lending credit to the bill brokers or for borrowing from the central bank. The bill of exchange market is not properly developed in India.

The Reserve Bank of India introduced the bill market scheme in 1952. Its main aim was to provide finance against bills of exchange for 90 days. The scheduled commercial banks were allowed to convert a part of their advances into promissory notes for 90 days for lodging as collateral security for advances from Reserve Bank of India.

Term Loan

Earlier the commercial banks were advancing only short-term loans. The commercial banks have also started advancing medium-term and long-term loans. Now, the maturity period of term loans is more than one year. The amount of the loan sanctioned is either paid to the borrower or it is credited to the account of the borrower in the bank. The interest is charged on the whole amount of loan sanctioned irrespective of the amount withdrawn by the borrower from his account. Repayment of the loan is accepted in lump sum or in the installments.

(c) Credit Creation

Credit Creation is one of the basic functions of a commercial bank. A bank differ from the other financial institutions because it can create credit. Like other financial institutions, the commercial banks also aim at earning profits. For this purpose, they accept deposits and advance loans by keeping a small cash in reserve for day-to-day transactions. In the layman's language when a bank advances a loan, the bank creates credit or deposit. Every bank loan creates an equivalent deposit in the bank. Therefore, the credit creation means multiple expansion of bank deposits. The word creation refers to the ability of the bank to expand deposits as a multiple of its reserves.

The credit creation refers to the unique power of the banks to multiply loans and advances, the hence deposits. With a little cash in hand, the banks can create additional purchasing power to a considerable extent. It is because of this multiple credit creation power that the commercial banks have been named the "factories of creating credit" or manufacturers of money.

REGIONAL RURAL BANKS (RRBS)

The Regional Rural Banks (RRBs) came into being under the 20-Point Economic Programme launched in 1975. Earlier, the Banking Commission, appointed by the Government to study the structure of banking development in India, mooted the idea of setting up RRBs in its report in 1972. The Government reviewed the recommendations of the

Banking Commission, and appointed the Narasimham Study Group on July 1, 1975. It submitted the report in just 30 days and favoured the setting up of RRBs.

The Government of India promulgated the RRBs ordinance dated 26th September, 1975 which was subsequently replaced by the Regional Rural Banks Act, 1976. On October 2, 1975, five RRBs were established in four states : 2 in Uttar Pradesh, one at Moradabad by the Syndicate Bank and the other at Gorakhpur by the State Bank of India; one in Rajasthan by the United Commercial Bank; one in Bhiwani (Haryana) by the Punjab National Bank and one in Malda (West Bengal) by the United Bank of India.

Prathama Bank is the first Regional Rural Bank of India, sponsored by Syndicate Bank established on 2nd October, 1975, with its Head office at Moradabad in accordance with Regional Rural Bank Ordinance 1975 issued on 25 September 1975.

In setting up RRBs, certain norms have to be observed. These are:

- Areas should be relatively backward or tribal
- RRBs are to be set-up in areas where the co-operative banks are not active
- There should not be any commercial bank in the area
- The area should have a real potentiality for development break through with the flow of credit.

While recommending the setting up of RRBs, the Working Group on Rural Banks appointed by the Government in 1975 opined that each RRB combines in itself the "local feel and familiarity with rural problems which the co-operative possessed and the degree of business organization, ability to mobilize deposits, access to central money markets and a modernized outlook which the commercial banks have".

Objectives of Regional Rural Banks

The importance of the rural banking in the economic development of a country cannot be overlooked. As Gandhiji said "Real India lies in Villages," and village economy is the backbone of Indian economy. Without the upliftment of the rural economy as well as the rural people of our country, the objectives of economic planning cannot be achieved.

In fact, the real growth of Indian economy lied in the freeing of rural masses from acute poverty, unemployment, and socio-economic backwardness.

Regional Rural Banks (RRBs) are oriented towards meeting the needs of the weaker sections of the rural population consisting of:

- Small and marginal farmers
- Agricultural labourers
- Artisans
- Small entrepreneurs
- Mobilise deposits from rural households.

RRBs are expected to make credit available to rural households besides inspiring carefulness. Put it simple to ensure sufficient institutional credit for agriculture and other rural sectors.

Functions of RRBs

A rural bank was described as "a primary banking institution set-up to serve a compact group of villages generally working as a co-operative bank, or as a subsidiary of a commercial bank", and its object would be "to provide at one place the special type of credit and banking facilities and related services needed by agriculturists and other rural producers".

The functions of RRBs are:

(*i*) To mobilize local savings.

(*ii*) To provide short-term and medium-term credit for agricultural and other purposes on its own and long-term credit as agents of the Land Development Banks.

(*iii*) To implement programmes of super-vised credit tailored to the needs of individual farmers.

(*iv*) To provide various ancilliary banking services to local people.

(*v*) To set-up a medium godowns.

The Operational Area of RRB

The area of operation of RRBs is limited to the area as notified by Government of India covering one or more districts in the State.

Structure of Regional Rural Banks

In RRBs, there are three share holder namely Government of India (50% share), Sponsor Bank (35% share), and State Government (15% share). Thus, we can say RRBs are jointly owned by Government of India, Sponsor Bank and respective State Government.

Role of RRBs/Gramin Bank

The role of RRBs can not be ignored in present day banking as these gramin banks have played a major role in implementation of central and state government sponsored various programme of poverty alleviation like SGSRY, PMRGP, Antyabasai. Payment to aganwadi, old age pension, mid-day meal, scholarship to student, Indira Awas Yojana, labour payment to NAREGA beneficiary has effectively been carried by these RRBs.

Regulatory Control

NABARD is the regulatory authority of Regional Rural Banks.

Organizational Structure : Organizational Structure for RRB's varies from branch to branch and depends upon the nature and size of business done by the branch. The Head Office of an RRB normally had three to seven departments.

The following is the decision making hierarchy of officials in a Regional Rural Bank.

- Board of Directors
- Chairman & Managing Director
- General Manager
- Chief Manager/Regional Managers
- Senior Manager
- Manager
- Officer/Assistant Manager
- Assistants.

One State-One RRB

The Finance Ministry has kicked off a 'One State-One RRB (Regional Rural Bank)' drive in 11 states-Andhra Pradesh, Karnataka, Gujarat, West Bengal, Rajasthan, Bihar, Maharashtra, Madhya Pradesh, Odisha, Uttar Pradesh and Jammu & Kashmir by amalgamating various RRBs into one. The scheme came into effect from May 1, 2025.

Amalgamation of RRBs

GoI was forced to start the reform process as several RRBs suffered humongous losses and had become unviable. During a review carried out by GoI in the year 2009 it was found that the Capital Risk Weighted Assets Ratio (CRAR) of the RRBs were too low. Therefore, Dr. K.C. Chakraborty Committee suggested bringing the CRAR of RRBs to at least 9 per cent in a sustainable manner. The Committee inter alia recommended recapitalisation support to the extent of ₹ 2,200 crore, to 40 RRBs.

As several Committees suggested for creation of viable RRBs by amalgamation of unviable RRBs, finally it was decided to amalgamate some of them on grounds of contiguity in a particular region. As on March 31, 2025; 43 RRBs with more than 22,000 branches are working in 26 States and 2 Union Territories.

NABARD

NABARD is an apex development bank in India, having headquarters in Mumbai (Maharashtra) and other branches are all over the country. The committee to review arrangements for institutional credit for agriculture and rural development (CRAFICARD), set up by the Reserve Bank of India (RBI) under the chairmanship of Shri B. Sivaraman, conceived and recommended the establishment of National Bank for Agriculture and Rural Development (NABARD).

It was established on 12 July 1982 by a special Act of parliament and its main focus was on upliftment of rural India by increasing the credit flow for elevation of agriculture & rural non farm sector.

RBI sold its stake in NABARD to the Government of India, which now holds 99% stake. NABARD is active in developing financial inclusion policy and is a member of the Alliance for Financial Inclusion.

Historical Background

Reserve Bank of India (RBI) established in 1934, inter alia, with a mandate to setup a special

Agricultural Credit Department (ACD) with expert staff. Agricultural Credit Department of RBI initiated different measures to develop a healthy rural credit structure and provided guidance to the State Government and Cooperative Credit structure.

Agricultural Refinance Corporation (ARC) was established in 1963 to support investment credit for agricultural development. Consequent to the undertaking, development and promotional functions, the ARC was renamed as Agricultural Refinance and Development Corporation (ARDC) in 1972.

Reserve Bank of India, at the instance of the Government of India (GOI), appointed a Committee to Review Arrangement for Institutional Credit for Agriculture and Rural Development (CRAFICARD) in 1979 under the Chairmanship of Shri B. Sivaraman, former member of the Planning Commission.

The Committee sought to review/examine the structure and operations of the ARDC in the light of the growing need for term loans for agricultural and allied purposes and the need for and the feasibility of integrating short-term and medium-term credit structure with long-term credit structure at the national, state, district and village levels.

CRAFICARD felt that the ARDC was not able to provide integrated credit services to its clientele on account of limitations in its statute and the Agricultural Credit Department (ACD) of RBI was not able to provide requisite attention to all the issues connected with rural credit. Further, the development role assigned to the ARDC was inadequate to take care of institution building, training and research. All these factors led to the recommendation for the establishment of NABARD, as the apex institution for integrated rural development through credit and development initiatives, to provide undivided attention, pointed focus and forceful direction to all matters and issues connected with rural credit.

But the committee, however, felt that it would be necessary for the new institution to maintain organic links with the RBI so that its continued guidance in financial assistance were accessible to it.

The Committee, in its report submitted in Jan 1981, recommended favourably among other things the setting up of a National Bank for Agriculture and Rural Development. The Government of India and the Reserve Bank of India approved the proposal of CRAFICARD. The parliament approved the setting up of NABARD through the Act 61 of 1981. The NABARD Act was passed in the parliament on 1st December 1981. It came into existence on 12th July 1982 and was dedicated to the service of the nation by the then Hon'ble Prime Minister, Smt. Indira Gandhi on November 2, 1982.

NABARD was established with the major objective of, as stated in the preamble to the Act, providing credit for the promotion of agriculture, small scale industries, cottage and village industries, handicrafts and other rural crafts and other allied economic activities in rural areas with a view to promote integrated rural development and securing prosperity of rural areas and matters connected therewith or incidental thereto.

Accordingly the NABARD took over the functions of the erstwhile Agricultural Credit Department (ACD), Rural Planning and Credit Cell (RPCC) of the RBI and ARDC. After, the establishment of NABARD, the entire property, liabilities, rights, interest, privileges and other things of ARDC have been transferred to and vested with the National Bank.

Objectives

The National Bank has been set up as an apex refinance agency for institutions providing investment and production credit for promoting various development activities in the rural areas.

The bank combines the developmental and financial role by undertaking the functions of agriculture and allied activities such as marketing, processing, storage and rural enterprises.

The main objectives of the National Banks are:

1. To provide refinance to eligible institutions, viz., State Cooperative Agriculture and Rural Development Banks (SCARDBs), State Cooperative Banks (SCBs), Commercial Banks (CBs), Regional Rural Banks (RRBs), and Scheduled Primary Urban Cooperative

Banks for supporting production and investment credit for development activities in the rural areas.

2. To take measures towards institution building for improving absorption capacity of credit delivery system including monitoring, formulation of rehabilitation schemes, restructuring of credit institutions, training of personnel, and other related matters.
3. To co-ordinate rural refinancing activities of all institutions engaged in the development work at the field level and to maintain liaison with the Central and State Governments and also the Reserve Bank of India.
4. To undertake monitoring and evaluation of projects refinanced by it.
5. To promote research in agriculture and rural development.

Role of NABARD

NABARD is the apex institution in the country which looks after the development of the cottage industry, small industry and village industry, and other rural industries. NABARD also reaches out to allied economies and supports and promotes integrated development. NABARD discharge its duty by undertaking the following roles:

1. Serves as an apex financing agency for the institutions providing investment and production credit for promoting the various developmental activities in rural areas.
2. Takes measures towards institution building for improving absorptive capacity of the credit delivery system, including monitoring, formulation of rehabilitation schemes, restructuring of credit institutions, training of personnel, etc.
3. Co-ordinates the rural financing activities of all institutions engaged in developmental work at the field level and maintains liaison with Government of India, state governments, Reserve Bank of India (RBI) and other national level institutions concerned with policy formulation. Undertakes monitoring and evaluation of projects refinanced by it.
4. NABARD refinances the financial institutions which finances the rural sector.
5. NABARD partakes in development of institutions which help the rural economy.
6. NABARD also keeps a check on its client institutes.
7. It regulates the institutions which provide financial help to the rural economy.
8. It provides training facilities to the institutions working in the field of rural upliftment.
9. It regulates the cooperative banks and the RRB's, and manages talent acquisition through IBPS CWE.
10. NABARD's refinance is available to state co-operative agriculture and rural development banks (SCARDBs), State Co-operative Banks (SCBs), Regional Rural Banks (RRBs), Commercial Banks (CBs) and other financial institutions approved by RBI. While the ultimate beneficiaries of investment credit can be individuals, partnership concerns, companies, State-owned corporations or co-operative societies, production credit is generally given to individuals. NABARD has its head office at Mumbai, India.
11. NABARD Regional Office [RO] has a Chief General Manager [CGMs] as its head, and the Head office has several top executives viz the Executive Directors [ED], Managing Directors [MD], and the Chairperson. It has 336 District Offices across the country, one special cell at Srinagar. It also has 6 training establishments.
12. NABARD is also known for its 'SHG Bank Linkage Programme' which encourages India's banks to lend to self-help groups (SHGs). Largely because SHGs are composed mainly of poor women, this has evolved into an important Indian tool for microfinance. By March 2006, 22 lakh SHGs representing 3.3 crore members had to be linked to credit through this programme.

13. NABARD also has a portfolio of Natural Resource Management Programmes involving diverse fields like Watershed Development, Tribal Development and Farm Innovation through dedicated funds set up for the purpose.

Functions

The functions of NABARD can be classified into four broad categories.

1. Credit Functions
2. Promotional and Development Func-tions
3. Institutional Development and Super-visory Functions, and
4. Statutory and Other Functions

Rural Infrastructure Development Fund (RIDF)

Good infrastructure is essential for better productivity of capital and labour. In India where more than 60% of the population lives in rural areas and nearly two-thirds of the work force derives their livelihood from agriculture, the rural infrastructure assumes crucial importance.

The direct effect of infrastructure via, technological improvement on poverty reduction relates to the increase in the demand for labour and thus wage rates. The increase in productive capacity of a labour reduces indirectly the incidence of poverty.

The Government of India announced in the Union Finance Budget for the year 1995-96, the scheme for setting up of "Rural Infrastructure Development Fund" (RIDF) in the NABARD for financing of ongoing rural infrastructure projects with a corpus of ₹ 2000 crores with the contribution from the Commercial Banks to the extent of short-fall in agricultural lending subject to a maximum of 1.5 per cent of net bank credit. The cumulative corpus from RIDF I to VIII aggregated to ₹ 28,500 crores.

The eligible purposes for financing under the RIDF include rural roads and bridges, major/ medium irrigation projects, soil conservation, watershed development, drainage improvement, flood protection, forest management, rural drinking water supply, systems improvement in power sector, building for primary health centres and primary and secondary schools, anganwadis, sishusiksha kendra's and other areas.

SIDBI

Banking scenario has been changed rapidly since 1990. The decade of nineties has witnessed a grass root changes in the way banking business carried out in India. Anywhere banking and anytime banking has become a reality. The financial sector now operates in a more competitive environment than before and intermediates relatively range volume of international financial flows.

On the contrary, most banks have been required to provide for the decline in the market value of their investments portfolio. Thankfully one, off setting factor has been the strong pick up in the credit take off due to buoyant demand in the economy and revival of industrial activity which have resulted in substantial increase in banks core interest income.

With a view to ensuring larger flow of financial and non-financial assistance to Small Scale Industries (S.S.I.) the Small Industries Development Bank of India (SIDBI) was set up by the Government of India under special Act passed by Parliament in October 1989 but SIDBI has been starting the work since April 2, 1990. It is the wholly-owned subsidiary of Industrial Development Bank of India (IDBI). SIDBI became operational on April 2, 1990. SIDBI has taken over the outstanding portfolio of IDBI relating to Small Scale Sector worth over ₹ 4,000 Crore. The authorized capital of SIDBI is ₹ 250 Crore which could be increased to ₹ 1,000 Crore.

SIDBI's headquarter is situated at Lucknow. It have five regional offices, 5 zones and 21 branch offices when it was started in different parts of India but now SIDBI has 73 Branches, 5 Regional Offices across the country.

After the establishment of Small Industries Development Bank of India (SIDBI), all duties related to small scale enterprises which are performed by Industrial Development Bank of India (IDBI) have been shifted to SIDBI.

Domain of Service

The Small Scale Industries (SSIs) sector is a vibrant and dynamic sector of the Indian economy. The sector presently occupies an important place and its contribution in terms of generation of employment, output and exports is quite significant. The Small Scale Industries sector including tiny units comprises the domain of SIDBI's business. Besides, the projects in the services sector with total cost up to ₹ 250 million are also taken within the area of SIDBI's operations. The Bank also finances industrial infrastructure projects for the development of SSI sector. The objectives of Government policy have been to impart vitality and growth impetus to the sector by removing bottlenecks that affect the growth potential. In the liberalized era and emerging economic scenario, the sector is assured of continued support.

SIDBI and the others banks have embraced technology right from the inception of their operation and therefore they have adapted themselves to the changes into the changes in the technology easily. Whereas the public sector banks (PSBs) and the old private sector banks have not been able to keep pace with these developments.

SIDBI which is the subsidiary bank of the IDBI, has also adopted the same strategy, and SIDBI already transformed itself into a universal bank. Now, the process of progeny IDBI bank merging itself with the parent IDBI is underway and is likely to be completed soon. This trend may lead logically to promote the concept of financial super market chain and making available all types of credit and non-fund facilities under one roof or specialized subsidiaries which is under one umbrella organization. There is a need to review our regulatory framework not only in the light of the global developments that have been mentioned, but also due to domestic compulsions.

SIDBI (Small Industries Development Bank of India) is now the principal financial institution and for the purpose of promotion, financing and development of small scale industries in the country. It co-ordinates the functions of existing institution on engaged in similar activities.

According to SIDBI, it has taken over the responsibility of administering Small Industries Development Fund (SIDF) and National equity fund (NEF) which were earlier administered by IDBI.

Function of SIDBI

SIDBI has a certain function.

The important function of SIDBI are as follows:

(*i*) SIDBI re-finance loans and advances extended by the primary lending institutions to small scale industrial units and also provide sources support to them.

(*ii*) SIDBI discounts and rediscounts bills arising from sale of machinery to or manufactured by industrial units in the small scale sector.

(*iii*) SIDBI extends seeds capital/soft loan assistance under National Equity Fund, Mahila Udyam Nidhi and Mahila Vikas Nidhi and seed capital scheme through specified lending agencies.

(*iv*) SIDBI grant direct assistance as well as re-finance loan extended by primary lending Institution for financing export of products manufactured by industrial concerns in the small scale sector.

(*v*) SIDBI provides services like leasing, factoring, etc. to industrial concerns in small scale sector.

(*vi*) SIDBI extends financial support to State Small Industries Development Corpora-tion (SSIDCs) for providing source raw materials to and marketing the end products of industrial units in small scale units.

(*vii*) SIDBI provides support to National Small Industries Corporation (NSICs) for providing leasing, hire-purchase, and marketing support to industrial units in the small scale sector.

(*viii*) Re-financing of loans & advances extended by the primary lending institution to small scale industrial unit concern and also providing resources support.

(*ix*) Discounting and re-discounting of bills arising from scale of machinery to or manufactured by industrial units in the small scale sector.

(*x*) Extension of seed capital/soft loan assistance under National Equity fund. **Mahila Udyam Nidhi** and **Mahila Vikas Nidhi** and seed capital schemes through specified lending agencies,

(*xi*) Granting direct assistance as well as re-financing of loans extended by primary lending institution for financing export of products manufactured by industrial concern in the small scale sector.

(*xii*) Providing services like learning factoring, etc. to industrial concerns in the small scale sector.

In setting up SIDBI, the intention of the Govt. of India was to ensure larger flow of financial assistance to small scale sector, SIDBI has already initiated step for technological upgradation and modernization of existing units. It is expanding the channels for marketing of products of SSI sector in internal and International market. It is promoting in a big way employment—oriented industries especially in semi-urban areas to credit more employment opportunities and thereby checking migration of rural population to urban and cosmopolitan areas.

Role of SIDBI

Since in inception, SIDBI has been endeavouring to meet the diverse needs of the Small and Medium Enterprises (SME) sectors through various tailor-made schemes and fulfill its vision, *i.e.,* "To emerge as a single window for meeting the financial and developmental needs of the Micro Small Medium Enterprises (MSME) sector to make it strong, vibrant and globally competitive, to position SIDBI Brand as the preferred and customer-friendly institution and for enhancement of share-holder wealth and highest corporate values through modern technology platform.

While extending financial assistance to the small units all over the country SIDBI makes use of the existing banking and financial institutions, such as the commercial banks, co-operative banks and RRBs, SFCs and SIDCs which have vast network of branches all over the country. As many as 870 institutions are eligible for assistance from SIDBI.

Objectives of SIDBI

Mandatory Objectives

Four basic objectives are set out in the SIDBI Charter. They are:

1. Financing
2. Promotion
3. Development
4. Co-ordination

The Charter has provided SIDBI consi-derable flexibility in adopting appropriate operational strategies to meet these objectives. The activities of SIDBI, as they have evolved over the period of time, now meet almost all the requirements of small scale industries which fall into a wide spectrum constituting modem and technologically superior units at one end and traditional units at the other.

Other Objectives

- To empower the Micro, Small and Medium Enterprises (MSME) sector with a view to contributing to the process of economic growth, employment genera-tion and balanced regional development.
- To emerge as a single window for meeting the financial and developmental needs of the MSME sector to make it strong, vibrant and globally competitive, to position SIDBI Brand as the preferred and customer-friendly institution and for enhancement of share-holder wealth and highest corporate values through modern technology platform.

SIDBI's charter includes Financing, Promotion, Development and Co-ordination for orderly growth of Small and Medium Enterprises. The Charter has provided SIDBI considerable flexibility in adopting appropriate operational strategies to meet these objectives. The activities of SIDBI, as they have evolved over the period of time, now meet almost all the requirements of SMEs which fall into a wide spectrum constituting modern and technologically superior units at one end and traditional units at the other.

SIDBI is committed to developing a strong, vibrant and responsive small scale sector. This commitment is to be achieved through a variety of means. Principal amongst them is finance. Alongside finance, SIDBI provides appropriate support in the form of promotional and developmental services. SIDBI has been built up as a financially sound, vibrant, forward looking and technically oriented institution and, it intends to sustain this orientation in future.

Features of SIDBI

Since 1992-93 SIDBI liberalized its term of assistance and amplified procedure with a view to widen its scope for large coverage of schemes. Some of salient features of SIDBI can be listed as follows.

(*a*) SIDBI has been operating **Single Window Scheme (SWS)** which is enlarged to cover units in identified area. The extent of refinance against cash credit sanctioned by banks under SWS was raised from 50 to 70 per cent.

(*b*) SIDBI provide refinance facilities under **Automatic Refinance Scheme (ARS).** The limit of term loans under ARS was initially fixed at ₹ 10 lakhs but was raised later to ₹ 50 lakh and the extent of refinance has been raised from 75 to 90 per cent.

(*c*) SIDBI has introduced equipment financing for assistance to existing well-run small-scale units for technology upgradation modernization.

(*d*) SIDBI has introduced refinance scheme for resettlement of voluntary retired worker of **National Textile Corporation (NTC)** and help them to buy up to four looms.

(*e*) SIDBI has set up a venture capital found to assist entrepreneurs within a short span of time; SIDBI has emerged as a major player in the field of finance for the small scale sector.

RECENT TRENDS IN BANKING

E-Banking

Electronic banking (E-banking) is a method of banking in which the customer conducts transactions electronically via the Internet. It is a system that allows the individuals to perform banking activities at their convenient place, via the internet. It is the automated delivery of banking products and services directly to customers through electronic, interactive communication channels. Online banking enables the customers to perform all routine transactions anytime, day or night, and can be done from anywhere. E-banking is also referred as online banking, internet banking, virtual banking, etc.

To access a financial institution's online banking facility, a customer would need to register with the institution for the service, and set up some password for customer verification. The online banking facilities offered by various financial institutions have many features and capabilities in common. The common features include:

1. Bank customers can perform non-transactional tasks through online banking including: (*a*) viewing account balances, (*b*) viewing recent transactions, (*c*) ordering cheque books, and (*d*) download periodic account statements.
2. Bank customers can transact banking tasks through online banking including: (*a*) fund transfers between the customer's linked accounts, (*b*) paying third parties, including bill payments, (*c*) investment purchase or sale, (*d*) loan applications and transactions, (*e*) credit card applications, and (*f*) register utility billers and make bill payments.

Today, many banks are internet only banks. Unlike their predecessors, these internet only banks do not maintain brick and mortar bank branches. Instead, they typically differentiate themselves by offering better and more extensive online banking features. Security of customers' financial information is very important without which, online banking could not operate. The use of a secure website has become almost universally adopted to reduce the risk of unauthorised online access to a customer's records.

Tele Banking

Telephone banking (Tele banking) is a service provided by a bank or other financial institution that enables the customers to perform their financial transactions over the telephone, without the need to visit a bank branch. It refers to the use of a system to allow customers of a bank to process various banking procedures over the telephone.

All the transactions can be done in the comfort of one's home using only a touch-tone telephone. The ease of access for services is one of the major advantages that telephone banking can provide for customers.

The types of financial transactions which a customer may transact through telephone banking include obtaining account balances and list of latest transactions, electronic bill payments, and funds transfers between a customer's or another's accounts. Cash withdrawals and deposits require the customer to visit a bank branch or an Automated Teller Machine (ATM). Banking over a telephone system can often be more convenient than banking in person, since some functions can be accessed even when a bank is closed.

M-Banking

Mobile banking (M-banking) is a system that allows customers of a financial institution to conduct a number of financial transactions through a mobile device such as a mobile phone or tablet through specifically designed Mobile Banking Apps. It is the most convenient and easy way to stay connected with the bank. It refers to provision and availing of banking and financial services with the help of mobile telecommunication devices. The scope of offered services may include facilities to conduct bank and stock market transactions, to administer accounts and to access customised information. Mobile banking has until 2010 most often been performed via SMS, known as SMS Banking.

The typical mobile banking services may include: (1) Mini-statements and checking of account history, (2) Funds transfers between the customer's linked accounts, (3) Paying third parties, including bill payments and third party fund transfers, (4) Alerts on account activity or passing of set thresholds, (5) Cheque book and card requests, (6) Access to loan statements, (7) Access to card statements, (8) Status of requests for credit, including mortgage approval, and insurance coverage, (9) Mutual funds/equity statements, (10) Real-time stock quotes, (11) Personalised alerts and notifications on security prices, (12) Monitoring of term deposits (13) Portfolio management services, (14) ATM Location, etc.

UPI (Unified Payments Interface)

UPI is a system that powers multiple bank accounts into a single mobile application, merging several banking features, seamless fund routing and merchant payments into one hood. This fastest and secure payments gateway was developed by NPCI (National Payments Corporations of India). The pilot launch was done by RBI at Mumbai. Through this system immediate money transfer can be done round the clock 24×7 and 365 days. This system played a significant role in post-demonetization period.

Cloud Banking

This technology will improve and organize banking and financial activities. Use of cloud-based technology will improve flexibility, efficiency, easier integration of new technologies and applications, faster services and solutions and improved data security.

Electronic Clearing Service (ECS)

ECS is an electronic mode of funds transfer from one bank to another. It can be used by different institutions for making payments such as distribution of dividend interest, salary, and pension among others. It can also be used to pay bill and other charges such as telephone, electricity, monthly installment payments on loan and sip investments. ECS can be used for both Debit and Credit purposes.

Consortium Banking

Consortium is an association or group of independent members with the objective of participating in a common activity or joint venture by pooling their resources for achieving a common goal and mutual benefit. *Consortium* is a Latin word, meaning 'partnership' or 'association' where the members co-operate with one another and conduct the operations that they would not be able to do individually. Consortium banking implies the collaboration of a group of banks to make a loan.

It is created to fund a specific project or to execute a specific deal. It is also known as 'loan syndication' where two or more banks come together to finance big projects requiring huge amount of money.

The consortium leverages individual banks' assets to achieve its objectives. All member banks have equal ownership shares – no one member has a controlling interest. It shares the security interest in common. After the bank's objective is met the consortium typically dissolves. Consortium lending is usually done by smaller banks to reap an opportunity to be a part of a big project financing by distributing the risks among the collaborator banks. By resorting to consortium lending, the banks not only saves their prospective customers but also builds good relations with other banks.

There is little bit difference between consortium banking and multiple banking. Under consortium banking, several banks or financial institutions finance a single borrower with common appraisal, common documen-tation, joint supervision and follow-up exercise. But in multiple banking, different banks provide finance and different banking facilities to a single borrower without having a common arrangement and understanding between the lenders.

Social Banking

Social banking is rightly defined by Roland Benediktar as "banking with a conscience." It calls for a move towards a more social and environmental responsibility in the financial sector beyond the principles of conventional business management. It is also known as ethical/alternative/civic/sustainable banking. Social banking policies were made to shift the focus of commercial banks from 'selective banking' to 'mass banking.' In their financing, it deals with sustainable and socially responsible projects which have particular dimensions of environmental assumptions and notions like justice and equality. Social or ethical banks do share a common set of principles, the most prominent being transparency and social or environmental aims of the projects they finance.

Social Banking describes the provision of banking and financial services that consequently pursue, as their main objective, a positive contribution to the potential of all human beings to develop, today and in the future. In Social Banking, the focus is on satisfying existing needs in the real economy and the society whilst simultaneously taking into account their social, cultural, ecological and economic sustainability. Social banking focuses on investing in community, providing opportunities for the disadvantaged, and supporting social, environmental and ethical concerns.

Social Banking describes a process, not a steady state. It is about jointly identifying and testing creative new ways to create social and environmental screens. The kind of analysis that conventional banks generally partake is a 'single bottom line analysis' which only considers the financial performance. But, social or sustainable banks consider a 'triple bottom line analysis' that takes into account the environmental, social, and financial perfor-mance.

Debit Cards

A debit card is a plastic payment card that provides the cardholder electronic access to their bank account at a financial institution. Most cards relay a message to the cardholder's bank to withdraw funds from a payer's designated bank account. Debit cards usually allow for instant withdrawal of cash, acting as the ATM card for withdrawing cash. The card, where accepted, can be used instead of cash when making purchases. Unlike credit and charge cards, payments using a debit card are immediately transferred from the cardholder's designated bank account, instead of them paying the money back at a later date.

There are currently three ways that debit card transactions are processed, namely, (*i*) *Online debit* or *PIN debit*, (*ii*) Offline debit or *signature debit*, and (*iii*) The Electronic Purse System. One physical card can include the functions of all three types, so that it can be used in a number of different circumstances. In many countries, the use of debit cards has become so widespread that their volume has overtaken or entirely replaced cheques and, in some instances, cash transactions. Although many debit cards are of the Visa or Master Card brand, there are many other types of debit card, each accepted only within a particular country or region. The National Payments Corporation of India (NPCI) has launched a new card called RuPay.

Debit cards may also be used on the Internet. Internet purchases can be authenticated by the consumer entering their PIN. The online debit cards require electronic authorization of every transaction and the debits are reflected in the user's account immediately. The transaction may be additionally secured with the personal identification number (PIN) authentication system.

Credit Cards

A credit card is a payment card issued to users as a system of payment. It allows the cardholder to pay for goods and services based on the holder's promise to pay for them. The issuer of the card creates a revolving account and grants a line of credit to the user from which he can borrow money for payment to a merchant or as a cash advance to the user. Credit cards may be treated as 'convenient credit' that allow the consumers a continuing balance of debt, subject to interest being charged. It can be used like currency by the owner of the card. It typically involves a third-party entity that pays the seller and is reimbursed by the buyer.

Credit cards may simply serve as a form of revolving credit. The main benefit to the cardholder is convenience. Compared to debit cards and checks, a credit card allows small short-term loans to be quickly made to a cardholder who need not calculate a balance remaining before every transaction, provided the total charges do not exceed the maximum credit line for the card. A credit card issuing company, such as a bank or credit union, would enter into agreements with merchants for them to accept their credit cards. Each month, the cardholder is sent a statement indicating the purchases made with the card, any outstanding fees, and the total amount owed.

Electronic verification systems allow merchants to verify in a few seconds that the card is valid and the cardholder has sufficient credit to cover the purchase, allowing the verification to happen at time of purchase. The verification is performed using a credit card payment terminal or point-of-sale (POS) system with a communications link to the merchant's acquiring bank. Credit card issuers usually waive interest charges if the balance is paid in full each month, but typically will charge full interest on the entire outstanding balance from the date of each purchase if the total balance is not paid.

Credit Card Vs Debit Card

Credit Card	Debit Card
1. It is a "pay later product".	It is "pay now product".
2. The card holder can avail of credit for 30-45 days	Customers account is debited immediately
3. No sophisticated communication system is required for credit card operation	Sophisticated communication network/ system is required for debit card operation (*e.g.*, ATM)
4. Opening bank account and maintaining required amount are not essential	Opening bank account and maintaining required amount are essential
5. Possibility of risk of fraud is high	Risk is minimised through using PIN

Credit cards are accepted in larger establishments in almost all countries, and are available with a variety of credit limits and repayment arrangements. Many credit cards offer rewards and benefits packages, such as enhanced product warranties at no cost, free loss/damage coverage on new purchases and various insurance protections. Credit cards can also offer a loyalty program, where each purchase is rewarded with points, which may be redeemed for further goods and services or cash back.

NEFT

National Electronic Funds Transfer (NEFT) is a nation-wide payment system facilitating one-to-one funds transfer. Under this Scheme, individuals, firms and corporates can electronically transfer funds from any bank branch to any individual, firm or corporate having an account with any other bank branch in the country participating in the Scheme. NEFT is a creditpush system *i.e.,* transactions can be originated by the payer or remitter.

The NEFT system takes advantage of the core banking system in banks. Accordingly, the settlement of funds between originating and receiving banks takes places centrally at Mumbai, whereas the branches participating in NEFT can be located anywhere across the length and breadth of the country. For being part of the NEFT funds transfer network, a bank branch has to be NEFT-enabled. Indian Financial System Code (IFSC) is an alpha-numeric code that uniquely identifies a bank-branch participating in the NEFT system. This is an 11 digit code with the first 4 alpha characters representing the bank, and the last 6 characters representing the branch. The 5th character is 0 (zero). IFSC is used by the NEFT system to identify the originating/destination banks/branches and also to route the messages appropriately to the concerned banks/branches.

RTGS

Real Time Gross Settlement (RTGS) can be defined as the continuous (real-time) settlement of funds transfers individually on an order by order basis (without netting). 'Real Time' means the processing of instructions at the time they are received rather than at some later time and 'Gross Settlement' means the settlement of funds transfer instructions occurs individually (on an instruction by instruction basis). The RTGS system is primarily meant for large value transactions. The minimum amount to be remitted through RTGS is ₹ 2 lakh. There is no upper ceiling for RTGS transactions.

Under normal circumstances the bene-ficiary branches are expected to receive the funds in real time as soon as funds are transferred by the remitting bank. The beneficiary bank has to credit the beneficiary's account within 30 minutes of receiving the funds transfer message. The RTGS service window for customer's transactions is available to banks from 9.00 hours to 16.30 hours on week days and from 9.00 hours to 14:00 hours on Saturdays for settlement at the RBI end. However, the timings that the banks follow may vary depending on the customer timings of the bank branches.

There is a fundamental difference between NEFT and RTGS. NEFT is an electronic fund transfer system that operates on a Deferred Net Settlement (DNS) basis which settles transactions in batches. In DNS, the settlement takes place with all transactions received till the particular cut-off time. These transactions are netted (payable and receivables) in NEFT whereas in RTGS the transactions are settled individually. For example, currently, NEFT operates in hourly batches. Any transaction initiated after a designated settlement time would have to wait till the next designated settlement time. Contrary to this, in the RTGS transactions are processed continuously throughout the RTGS business hours.

NPA

A Non-performing asset (NPA) is defined as a credit facility in respect of which the interest and/or instalment of principal has remained 'past due' for a specified period of time. NPAs refer to the loans that are in jeopardy of default. Once the borrower has failed to make interest or principal payments for 90 days, the loan is considered to be a non-performing asset. Nonperforming assets are problematic for financial institutions since they depend on interest payments for income. The account remains 'out of order' for a period of more than 90 days, in respect of an Overdraft/Cash Credit. NPAs result from defaults or the failure to meet financial obligations, say non-payment of a loan instalment.

NPAs do not just reflect badly in a bank's account books, they adversely impact the national economy. When bank do not get loan repayment or interest payments, liquidity problems may ensue. NPAs decrease profitability, reduce capital assets and lending limits, and increase the loan loss reserves. NPAs affect the credit ratings and goodwill of an organisation. Banks classify non-performing assets further into the following three categories based on the period for which the asset has remained non-performing and the realisability of the dues:

1. **Sub-standard Assets:** A sub-standard asset is one which has been classified as NPA for a period not exceeding 12 months.
2. **Doubtful Assets:** A doubtful asset is one which has remained NPA for a period exceeding 12 months.
3. **Loss Assets:** A loss asset is one which cannot be recovered and loss has been identified by the bank. But the amount has not been written off, wholly or partly.

Capital Adequacy Ratio

For the smooth flow of credit in an economy, it is essential that banks should be financially sound so as to meet its various requirements. Banks encounter various types of risks while carrying the business of financial inter-mediation as it is the highly leveraged sector of an economy. Capital adequacy ratio (CAR) is one of the measures which ensure the financial soundness of banks in absorbing a reasonable amount of loss. Regulation of capital assumes significant importance so as to reduce bank failures, to promote stability, safety and soundness of the banking system, to prevent systemic disaster and to ultimately reduce losses to the bank depositors. Capital Adequacy Ratio is the ratio which protects banks against excess leverage, insolvency and keeps them out of difficulty. It is defined as the ratio of banks capital in relation to its current liabilities and risk weighted assets.

Risk weighted assets is a measure of amount of banks assets, adjusted for risks. CAR = (Bank's Capital/Risk Weighted Assets). As per RBI norms, Indian Scheduled Commercial Banks should have a CAR of 9% *i.e.,* 1% more than stipulated Basel Norms while Public Sector Banks are emphasized to keep this ratio at 12%. Capital adequacy is an important para-meter for judging the strength and soundness of the banking system. An appropriate level of capital adequacy ensures that the bank has sufficient capital to expand its business, while at the same time its net worth is enough to absorb any financial downturns without becoming insolvent. CAR is the ratio which determines banks capacity to meet the time liabilities and other risks such as credit risk, market risk, operational risk, etc.

Demat Account

A DeMat account is one that allows you to buy, sell as well as transact without the need of any paperwork. DeMat accounts are very safe, convenient and secure. DeMat is nothing but a dematerialized account. If one has to save money or make cheque payments, then he/she needs to open a bank account. Similarly, one needs to open a DeMat account if he/she wants to buy or sell stocks. Thus, DeMat account is similar to a bank account wherein the actual money is being replaced by shares. In order to open a DeMat account, one needs to approach the Depository Participants [DPs]. This account is very popular in India. Physically only 500 shares can be traded as per the provision given by SEBI. From April 2006, it has become mandatory for any person holding a DeMat account to possess a Permanent Account Number (PAN).

Mutual Funds

Mutual funds are investment vehicles that pool funds from multiple investors to purchase various securities, such as stocks, bonds, and other assets, to generate returns for the investors. With the abundance of investment options available, understanding the basics of mutual funds is crucial for making informed investment decisions. In simple terms, a mutual fund is an investment vehicle that pools funds from multiple investors to invest in various financial assets. This pooling of funds allows individual investors to access a diversified portfolio of stocks, bonds, or other securities managed by professional fund managers.

Know Your Customer (KYC)

The Reserve Bank of India (RBI) has advised banks to follow "KYC guidelines", wherein certain personal information of the account-opening prospect or the customer is obtained. The objective of doing so is to enable the Bank to have positive identification of its customers. This is also in the interest of customers to safeguard their hard earned money.

The KYC guidelines of RBI mandate banks to collect three proofs from their customers. They are—

1. Photograph
2. Proof of identity
3. Proof of address

What is KYC?

Know Your Customer—KYC enables banks to know/understand their customers and their financial dealings to be able to serve them better.

Who is a Customer of the Bank?

For the purpose of KYC Policy, a Customer is defined as:

- A person or entity that maintains an account and/or has a business relationship with the Bank.
- One on whose behalf the account is maintained (*i.e.* the beneficial owner).
- Beneficiaries of transactions conducted by professional intermediaries, such as Stock Brokers, Chartered Accountants, Solicitors, etc. as permitted under the law, and
- Any person or entity connected with a financial transaction, which can pose significant reputation or other risks to the Bank, say, a wire transfer or issue of a high value demand draft as a single transaction.

Camel Rating of Banks

CAMEL model of rating was first developed in the 1970s by the 3 federal banking supervisors of the U.S (the Federal Reserve, the FDIC and the OCC) as part of the Regulators. "Uniform Financial Institutions Rating System", to provide a convenient summary of bank condition at the tirfie of its on-site examination.

C - Capital Adequacy
A - Asset Quality
M - Management Quality
E - Earnings
L - Liquidity
S - Sensitivity to Market Risk/System and control

RBI plans to change system in order to make the process more forward-looking. Indian financial sector would be evaluated under a dynamic risk-based mechanism, an aspect the present CAMELS rating system lacked.

RBI proposes to replace CAMELS with INROADS (Indian Risk-Oriented and Dynamic Rating System) from the next round of annual financial inspection.

For foreign banks in INDIA the rating model is a modified version called CACS , CACS means

C - Capital Adequacy
A - Asset Quality
C - Compliance
S - System and control

Core Banking Solution (CBS)

This word is more often used by bankers and now-a-days postal officials are also using it. CBS is an acronym of Core Banking Solutions. Again one will wonder what the meaning of core is, core is also an acronym.

It stands for ***"Centralized On-line Real-time Exchange".***

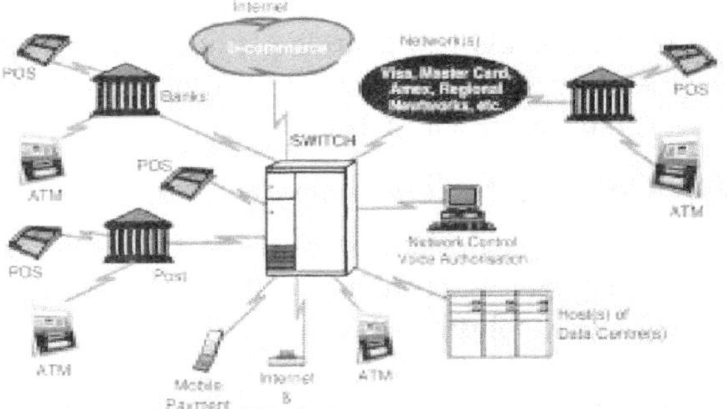

Definition

Core Banking Solution (CBS) is networking of branches, which enables Customers to operate their accounts, and avail banking services from any branch of the Bank on CBS network, regardless of where he maintains his account. The customer is no more the customer of a Branch. He becomes the Bank's Customer.

Another interesting fact regarding CBS is that all CBS branches are inter-connected with each other. Therefore, Customers of CBS branches can avail various banking facilities from any other CBS branch located anywhere in the world.

What it offers to a customer?

It offers invariably all information that a bank's customer would need if he/she visits a bank branch in person.

These are as herein follows:

1. To make enquiries about the balance or debit or credit entries in the account.
2. To obtain cash payment out of his account by tendering a cheque.
3. To deposit a cheque for credit into his account.
4. To deposit cash into the account.
5. To deposit cheques/cash into account of some other person who has account in a CBS branch.
6. To get statement of account.
7. To transfer funds from his account to some other account—his own or of third party, provided both accounts are in CBS branches.
8. To obtain Demand Drafts or Banker's Cheques from any branch on CBS—amount shall be online debited to his account.
9. Customers can continue to use ATMs and other Delivery Channels, which are also interfaced with CBS platform.

Top CBS Application Software Providers

1. Infosys Technologies Ltd. **Finnacle** is the universal banking solution from Infosys.
2. **I-flex solutions Ltd**. since late 2005 it is owned by Oracle.
3. **TCS FNS (Financial Network Services Limited)** is an Australian developer and supplier of banking application software, operating in world markets. Now owned and managed by TCS.

Thus, CBS is a step towards enhancing customer convenience through anywhere and anytime banking.

Bandhan Bank

Recently, there is a buzz about **BANDHAN BANK,** Lets know about it:

- **Bandhan Bank** was set up in **2001** to handle dual objective of **poverty alleviation** and **women empowerment.**
- It was previously a **Non-Banking Financial Company (NBFC)** but **Bandhan Bank** received its universal banking licence from **Reserve Bank of India.**
- The bank rolled out its services on **23rd August, 2015 (Founded).**
- The bank started with **501 branches** in all most **22 states** in India which is highest branches of any private bank on the **first day.**
- The bank will provide funds to help and develop the **Small and Medium Enterprises (SME).**
- The saving interest rates have been fixed at **4.25% below ₹ 1,00,000** and **5% above ₹ 1,00,000.**
- It is interesting to know that **Bandhan** was the only micro-finance institution that applied for a banking licence.
- **Headquarters** is located at **Kolkata, West Bengal.**
- **Slogan** of bank is **"Aapka Bhala, Sabki Bhalai".**
- Incidentally, Bandhan is the **first bank** to be **set up in eastern part of India after Independence.**

PAYMENT BANKS AND SMALL FINANCE BANKS

Payment banks can receive deposits and remittances, but cannot lend, focusing on migrant labour and low income households.

Small banks will lend to "unserved and under-served sections", including small business units, small and marginal farmers, and micro and small industries.

Payment Banks

On 19 August 2015, RBI approved "in-principle" licenses to 11 entities to start payment banks, these 11 entities are:

- Aditya Birla Nuvo
- Airtel M Commerce Services

- Cholamandalam Distribution Services
- Department of Posts
- FINO PayTech
- National Securities Depository
- Reliance Industries
- Dilip Shanghvi, founder of Sun Pharmaceuticals
- Vijay Shekhar Sharma, CEO of Paytm
- Tech Mahindra
- Vodafone M-Pesa

Mudra Bank

What is Mudra Bank?

- MUDRA means Micro Units Development and Refinance Agency (known as the MUDRA Bank)
- Mudra Bank is being set up through a statutory enactment and will be responsible for developing and refinancing through a Pradhan Mantri Mudra Yojna.
- It is first set up as a subsidiary of the **Small Industries Develpoment Bank of India (SIDBI)**. It will later be converted into full-fledged bank through an act of the parliament.
- **MUDRA** Bank is a public sector financial institution in India, It provides loan at low rates to small entrepreneurs.

Objective

- It was launched in 8th April 2015 with the objective of regulating micro and small enterprise financing business, and supporting them particularly those members who belongs from scheduled castes and scheduled tribes.
- MUDRA Bank will also register **MFIs (Micro Finance Institutions)** and will be responsible for accreditation and rating of MFI.
- It will also make proper last mile practices to be followed by MFI to provide proper client protection and to prevent from indebtedness.

Aim

- The finance ministry said measures to be taken up by the MUDRA are targeted mainly on young, educated or skilled workers and entrepreneurs including women entrepreneurs.
- Basically small entrepreneurs and small businessman are often cut from banking system because of limited branch presence, so MUDRA Bank will partner with local coordinators and provide finance to small and micro businesses.

Important Figures About Mudra Bank

- The bank will be set up with the initial corpus of ₹ 20000 cr and a credit guarantee corpus of ₹ 3000 cr.
- The bank have categorized the amount of loan to be given in three different categories.
- **SHISHU:** This is the first stage and in it the loan will be given for upto ₹ 50000.
- **KISHOR:** In the second stage a loan amount will be ranging from ₹ 50,000 to ₹ 5 lakh.
- **TARUN:** This is last category which will provide upto ₹ 10 lakh.
- The bank will cater to 5.77 crore small business units that spread all across India who currently find it difficult to access credit from the regular banking system.
- According to Mr NARENDRA MODI the bank would help over 6 cr families out of which 65% of them belongs to scheduled caste and scheduled tribes.

MONETARY POLICY

Monetary policy is the process by which monetary authority of a country, generally a central bank controls the supply of money in the economy by its control over interest rates in order to maintain price stability and achieve high economic growth.

In India, the central monetary authority is the Reserve Bank of India (RBI). It is so designed as to maintain the price stability in the economy.

Other objectives of the monetary policy of India, as stated by RBI, are:

- **Price Stability:** Price Stability implies promoting economic development with considerable emphasis on price stability. The centre of focus is to facilitate the environment which is favourable to the architecture that enables the develop-mental projects to run swiftly while also maintaining reasonable price stability.
- **Controlled Expansion of Bank Credit:** One of the important functions of RBI is the controlled expansion of bank credit and money supply with special attention to seasonal requirement for credit without affecting the output.
- **Promotion of Fixed Investment :** The aim here is to increase the productivity of investment by restraining non essential fixed investment.
- **Restriction of Inventories and stocks :** Overfilling of stocks and products becoming outdated due to excess of stock often results in sickness of the unit. To avoid this problem the central monetary authority carries out this essential function of restricting the ors of the economy and all social and economic class of people.
- **To Promote Efficiency:** It is another essential aspect where the central banks pay a lot of attention. It tries to increase the efficiency in the financial system and tries to incorporate structural changes such as deregulating interest rates, ease operational constraints in the credit delivery system, to introduce new money market instruments, etc.
- **Reducing the Rigidity :** RBI tries to bring about the flexibilities in the operations which provide a considerable autonomy.

  It encourages more competi-tive environ-ment and diversification. It maintains its control over financial system whenever and wherever necessary to maintain the discipline and prudence in operations of the financial system.

VARIOUS INSTRUMENTS OF MONETARY POLICY

These instruments are as below:

1. **Open market operations (OMO):** These refer to the purchase and sale of govt. securities by the RBI from/to the public and banks on its own account.
2. **Variations in Reserve Requirements:** This refers to the variations in cash reserve ratio (CRR), which all banks are statutorily required to hold with RBI as per cent of their net demand and time deposits.
3. **Bank Rate:** Traditionally called redis-count rate and refinance rate, the bank rate is the lending rate of RBI and if used, influences the cost and availability of Reserve bank credit to the banks.
4. **Statutory Liquidity Ratio (SLR):** This is a kind of directed investment norm imposed on banks in India. Under this, every bank is statutorily compelled to invest a certain portion of its total demand and time liabilities in the designated liquid assets. Any alternation in SLR changes the allocation of bank credit between the govt. and the commercial sector and influences the capacity of banks to lend.
5. **Moral Suasion:** It is both persuasion and pressure which is used by the RBI on banks in general and errant banks in particular. This is exercised through discussions, letters, speeches and hints thrown on banks and signals them to fall in line with the RBI policy.
6. **Selective Credit Controls:** As against the general credit controls discussed above (1 to 5), which influence the total volume of credit and cost of credit, selective credit controls are operated to alter the distribution of credit among various sectors of the economy. These have been used in India mainly to prevent speculative hoarding of essential commodities like food articles and agricultural raw materials to prevent any undue rise in their prices.

Following are the various forms of selective credit controls used by RBI.

(*a*) Minimum margin for lending against securities. These vary from a low of 20% to the high of 85%.

(*b*) Ceilings on maximum advances to individual borrowers against stocks of certain commodities.

(*c*) Prescription of minimum discriminatory rates of interest for certain kinds.

(*d*) Prohibition of clean advances to finance hoarding of sensitive commodities.

(*e*) Prohibition of the discounting of bills covering sale of sensitive commodities.

(*f*) Credit Monitoring Arrangement (CMA): This replaced, in October 1988, the earlier Credit Authorization Scheme (CAS), which required banks to obtain RBI's authorization before sanctioning any fresh credit in excess of prescribed limit.
Under CMA, RBI performs post-sanction scrutiny of large credit proposals sanctioned by the banks.
The main object is to prevent pre-emption of credit by large borrowers and ensure its fair distribution among all.

FISCAL POLICY

The term 'Fisc' in English means 'treasury'. Hence policy concerning treasury or Govern-ment exchequer is known as 'Fiscal Policy'.

Fiscal policy is that part of Government policy which is concerned with raising revenues through taxation and other means deciding on the level and pattern of expenditure it operates through budget. However, generally the expenditure exceeds the revenue income of the Government.

In order to meet this situation, the Government imposes new taxes or increases rates of taxes, takes internal or external loans or resorts to deficit financing by issuing fresh currency.

Thus, the collective form of policies of imposing taxation, taking loans or deficit financing is known as fiscal policy. The authors have defined it as follows:

By fiscal policy is meant the use of public finance or expenditure, taxes, borrowing and financial administration to further our national income objective. –**Buchler**

Changes in Government expenditure and taxation designed to influence the pattern and level of activity. – **J. Harry and Johnson**

"Fiscal policy is a policy under which the Government uses its expenditure and revenue programmes to produce desirable effects and avoid undesirable effects on national income, production and employment." - **Arthur Smithies**

There are mainly three constituents of the fiscal policy; these are:

(*i*) taxation policy,
(*ii*) public expenditure policy, and
(*iii*) public debt policy.

All these constituents must work together to make the fiscal policy sound and effective.

Objectives of fiscal policy

1. Development by effective Mobilization of Resources
2. Efficient allocation of Financial Resources
3. Reduction in inequalities of Income and Wealth
4. Price Stability and Control of Inflation
5. Employment Generation
6. Balanced Regional Development
7. Capital Formation
8. Reducing the Deficit in the Balance of Payment
9. Foreign Exchange Earnings

Significance of Fiscal Policy

1. Capital formation
2. Mobilization of resources
3. Incentives to savings
4. Inducement to private sector
5. Alleviation of poverty and unemploy-ment
6. Reduction in inequality

SECURITIES EXCHANGE BOARD OF INDIA (SEBI)

The Government has set up the Securities & Exchange Board of India (SEBI) in April, 1988. For more than three years, it has no statutory powers. Its interim functions during the period were

(*i*) To collect information and advice the Government on matters relating to Stock and Capital Markets

(*ii*) Licensing and regulation of merchant banks, mutual funds, etc.

(*iii*) To prepare the legal drafts for regulatory and development role of SEBI and

(*iv*) To perform any other functions as may be entrusted to it by the Government.

The need for setting up independent Govt. agency to regulate and develop the Stock and Capital Market in India as in many developed countries was recognised since the Sixty Five Year Plan was launched (1985) when some major industrial policy changes like opening up of the economy to outside world and greater role to the Private Sector were initiated. The rampant malpractices noticed in the Stock and Capital Market stood in the way of infusing confidence of investors which is necessary for mobilisation of larger quantity of funds from the public and help the growth of the industry.

The malpractices were noticed in the case of companies, merchants bankers and brokers who are all operating in the Capital Market. The need to curb these malpractices and to promote healthy Capital Market in India was felt. The security industry in India has to develop on the right lines for which a competent Govt. agency as in U.K. (SIB) or in U.S.A. (SEC) is needed.

As referred to earlier, malpractices have been reported in both the primary market and secondary market. A few examples of malpractices in the primary market are as follows:

(*a*) Too many self style Investment Advisors and Consultants.

(*b*) Grey Market or unofficial premiums on the new issues.

(*c*) Manipulation of market prices before new issues are floated.

(*d*) Delay in allotment letters or refund orders or in despatch of share certificates.

(*e*) Delay in listing and commencement of trading in shares.

A few examples of malpractices in the secondary Market are as follows:

(*a*) Lack of transperancy in the trading operations and prices charged to clients.

(*b*) Poor services due to delay in passing contract notes or not passing contract notes, at all.

(*c*) Delay in making payments to clients or in giving delivery of shares.

(*d*) Persistence of odd lots and refusal of companies to stop this practice of allotting shares in odd lots.

(*e*) Insider trading by agents of companies or brokers rigging and manipulating prices.

(*f*) Take over bids to destabilise manage-ment.

Objectives

The SEBI has been entrusted with both the regulatory and developmental functions. The objectives of SEBI are as follows:

(*a*) Investor protection, so that there is a steady flow of savings into the Capital Market.

(*b*) Ensuring the fair practices by the issuers of securities, namely, companies so that they can raise resources at least cost.

(*c*) Promotion of efficient services by brokers, merchant bankers and other intermediaries so that they become competitive and professional.

Pending the legislative sanction to SEBI it carried out the functions of supervisory and advisory body of the Govt.

It has initiated the basis for control and regulation of the market, arranged for the licensing of merchant banks, mutual funds, etc. and performed the advisory functions to the Govt.

The legislation giving powers to SEBI was passed on 4th April 1992 in the form of the Securities & Exchange Board of India Act to protect the interests of investors in securities and to promote the development of and to regulate the securities market and for matters connected therewith or incidental thereto.

Multiple Choice Questions

1. Second nationalisation of commercial banks (6 banks) was held in the year:
   A. 1979 B. 1980
   C. 1984 D. 1976
   E. None of these
2. Bank of England was established in the year:
   A. 1586 B. 1612
   C. 1694 D. 1656
   E. None of these
3. The first development bank in India is:
   A. IDBI B. IFCI
   C. ICICI D. SIDBI
   E. None of these
4. Central Land Mortgage Bank was started in Madras in:
   A. 1920 B. 1921
   C. 1922 D. 1928
   E. 1929
5. The first bank of India was:
   A. RBI
   B. SBI
   C. Bank of Hindustan
   D. HDFC
   E. None of these
6. The first nationalization of banks in India was held in the year:
   A. 1969 B. 1980
   C. 1991 D. 1985
   E. None of these
7. The first joint stock bank in India is ....
   A. IDBI B. ICICI
   C. Imperial Bank D. Allahabad Bank
   E. None of these
8. The first chartered bank was established at ....
   A. Japan B. Philadelphia
   C. India D. France
   E. None of these
9. REPO rate was introduced in:
   A. 1990 B. 1992
   C. 1982 D. 1980
   E. None of these
10. Bank of Hindustan was established at ....
    A. Bombay B. Chennai
    C. Kolkata D. Bengaluru
    E. None of these
11. General Bank of India was established in ....
    A. 1771 B. 1775
    C. 1786 D. 1780
    E. None of these
12. Second phase of Indian banks were nationalized in:
    A. 1960 B. 1969
    C. 1970 D. 1869
    E. None of these
13. The statutory definition of the term ''banking'' is given in:
    A. The Negotiable Instruments Act, 1881
    B. The Reserve Bank of India Act, 1934
    C. The Companies Act, 1956
    D. The Banking Regulation Act, 1949
14. Allahabad Bank was founded on .... by a group of Europeans at Allahabad.
    A. July 19, 1865 B. October 2, 1865
    C. April 24, 1865 D. October 7, 1961
    E. None of these
15. In 1923, the Head Office of the Allahabad Bank was shifted to .... on business considerations:
    A. Calcutta B. Chennai
    C. Darjeeling D. Patna
    E. None of these
16. Allahabad Bank was nationalized on:
    A. 5 November, 1980
    B. 19 July, 1969
    C. 15 January, 1971
    D. 1 October, 1969
    E. None of these

17. In October 1989 .... bank was merged with Allahabad Bank.
A. United Industrial Bank Limited
B. Unit Trust of India Bank Limited
C. New India Bank Limited
D. HDFC Bank Ltd.
E. None of these

18. Headquarter of Allahabad Bank is situated at:
A. New Delhi
B. Allahabad, Uttar Pradesh
C. Kolkata, West Bengal
D. Bhagalpur, Bihar
E. None of these

19. Slogan of Allahabad Bank is:
A. Together We Prosper
B. A Tradition of Trust
C. A Long Tradition of Trust
D. Come with Me
E. None of these

20. In ...., Allahabad Bank has implemented CBS in all its branches.
A. March, 2011 B. March, 2012
C. March, 2013 D. March, 2015
E. None of these

21. Syndicate Bank was established in .... in Udupi.
A. 1926 B. 1900
C. 1925 D. 1902
E. None of these

22. Udupi is related to abode of Lord ....
A. Hanuman B. Shiva
C. Krishna D. Ganesha
E. None of these

23. The Logo of Syndicate Bank contains picture of:
A. Elephant B. Lion
C. Dog D. Puma
E. None of these

24. Headquarter of Syndicate Bank is now situated at:
A. Shimla, Himachal Pradesh
B. Dispur, Assam
C. Manipal, Karnataka
D. Bhopal, Madhya Pradesh
E. None of these

25. The Syndicate Bank was nationalized on:
A. 14 November, 1969
B. 19 July, 1969
C. 2 October, 1969
D. 24 May, 1968
E. None of these

26. Which of the following is correct?
A. Reserve Bank of India Act, 1935
B. Reserve Bank of India Act, 1934
C. Reserve Bank of India Act, 1930
D. Reserve Bank of India Act, 1937
E. None of these

27. The Central Office of the Reserve Bank was initially established in ....
A. Indore B. Delhi
C. Calcutta D. Mumbai
E. None of these

28. The Central Office of the Reserve Bank was permanently moved to Mumbai in ....
A. 1934 B. 1937
C. 1935 D. 1938
E. None of these

29. Which among the following is correct about The Central Office of RBI?
A. Where Governor sits
B. Where only Policies are formulated
C. Both of above
D. Where Governor doesn't sit
E. None of these

30. Reserve Bank is fully owned by the Government of India since nationalization in:
A. 1950 B. 1949
C. 1965 D. 1947
E. None of these

31. The BFS was constituted in:
A. December, 1994 B. November, 1994
C. September, 1994 D. May, 1994
E. None of these

32. The Deputy Governor in charge of banking regulation and supervision, is nominated as the .... of the (BFS) board.
A. Head B. Vice-Chairman
C. President D. Vice-President
E. None of these

33. Which state government's business is not transacted by RBI?
A. Himachal Pradesh B. Jammu and Kashmir
C. Manipur D. Bihar
E. None of these

34. Where are four regional centres of RBI located?
A. Mumbai, Kolkata, Chennai and Delhi
B. Kolkata, Chennai, Mumbai, Bengaluru
C. Patna, Mumbai, Kolkata, Delhi
D. Either B or C
E. None of these

35. "INDIA's Central Bank" is a slogan of:
A. Reserve Bank of India
B. State Bank of India
C. IDBI
D. Bank of India
E. None of these

36. SLR stands for:
A. Special Liquidity Ratio
B. Special Lending Rate
C. Statutory Liquidity Ratio
D. Either A or B
E. None of these

37. Reserve Bank of India was set up on the recommendations of which of the following commission/committee?
A. D.R. Mehta Commission
B. Basel Committee
C. Royal Commission on Indian Currency and Finance
D. K. Santhanam Committee
E. None of these

38. Head Office of SBI is situated at:
A. Mumbai, Maharashtra
B. Kolkata, West Bengal
C. New Delhi
D. Chennai, Tamil Nadu
E. None of the above

39. Two new Savings Bank products for children namely 'Pehla Kadam and Pehli Udaan' introduced by:
A. State Bank of India
B. United Bank of India
C. Axis Bank
D. ICICI Bank
E. None of these

40. Original name of the State Bank of India was:
A. Bank of Calcutta B. Bank of Bengal
C. Both the Above D. Bank of Madras
E. None of these

41. State Bank of India comes in to existence in the year:
A. 1947 B. 1955
C. 1959 D. 1949
E. None of these

42. State Bank of India was formulated under:
A. SBI Act, 1957 B. SBI Act, 1959
C. SBI Act, 1955 D. SBI Act, 1949
E. None of these

43. Which is the first Bank to launch the Mutual Fund:
A. SBI B. PNB
C. RBI D. HDFC
E. None of these

44. What is tag line of SBI?
A. With you all the way, Pure Banking Nothing Else, The Nation's banks on us
B. The name you can bank upon
C. India's International Bank
D. Badhti Ka Naam Zindagi
E. None of these

45. "Imperial Bank of India" is the former name of which of the following bank:
A. SBI B. IndusInd Bank
C. RBI D. Axis Bank
E. None of these

46. State Bank of India started the Merchant Banking division in:
A. 1970 B. 1972
C. 1974 D. 1975
E. None of These

47. Name of the first bank to receive approval for getting full bank licence in Singapore is:
A. Punjab National Bank
B. Syndicate Bank
C. State Bank of India
D. Axis Bank
E. None of these

48. PIN stands for:
A. Portable Identification Number
B. Permanent Identification Number
C. Personal Identification Number
D. Private Identification Number
E. None of the above

49. The prepaid bank card is also called:
A. Convenience Gift Card
B. Bank Gift Card
C. Suitable Gift Card
D. Unsuitable Gift Card
E. None of the above

50. .... also provides a unified "Kisan Card" issued by banks across the country under Kisan Credit Card, enabling farmers to transact business on ATMs and POS terminals:
A. Maestro Card B. RuPay Card
C. Forex Card D. Visa Card
E. None of the above

51. Which was the first bank to set up talking ATM in India?
A. Union Bank B. Dena Bank
C. ICICI Bank D. SBI
E. None of these

52. "Overdrafts" covered under which of following function?
A. Accepting Deposits
B. Advancing of Loans
C. Both of Above
D. Rejecting Deposits
E. None of these

53. The account that allows you to buy, sell as well as transact without the need of any paperwork is:
A. Simple Account
B. Demat Account
C. Current Account
D. Saving Account
E. None of these

54. KYC is:
A. Know Your Customer
B. Know Your Cheque
C. Keep Your Cash
D. Know Your Balance
E. None of these

55. When ATM machine installed in the bank is out of order, it is called:
A. Operational Risk
B. Electronic Default
C. ATM Auto Default
D. ATM Normal Default
E. None of these

56. When the loans are not repaid in time, it is called:
A. Loan Defaulter
B. Credit Risk
C. Weak Creditworthiness
D. Payment Risk
E. None of these

57. IFSC denotes:
A. Branch Location of any Bank
B. Branch Code of any Bank
C. District Code of any Bank
D. State Code of any Bank
E. None of these

58. Rate of interest is determined by:
A. Commercial Bank B. Public Bank
C. Private Bank D. RBI
E. None of these

59. In MICR cheque, first six numbers indicates:
A. Branch Code and Location
B. City Location
C. Cheque Number
D. Account Number
E. None of these

60. Inventor John Shepherd Barron installed the worlds's first automatic cash dispenser at a .... near London.
A. London Bank Branch
B. Barclays Bank Branch
C. Royal Grand Federal Bank Branch
D. Bank of Britain Branch
E. None of these

61. The Banking Ombudsman Scheme was introduced under:
A. Banking Regulation Act, 1935
B. Banking Regulation Act, 1949
C. Banking Regulation Act, 1985
D. Banking Regulation Act, 1987
E. None of the above

62. The Banking Ombudsman Scheme was introduced under Section 35 A of the Banking Regulation Act, 1949 by RBI with effect from ....
A. 1992 B. 1993
C. 1995 D. 1994
E. None of the above

63. CBS stands for:
A. Central Banking Solutions
B. Core Banking Solution
C. Code Banking Solutions
D. Cross Banking System
E. None of these

64. First Bank in India to launch EMI facility on debit cards:
A. SBI B. Axis Bank
C. ICICI Bank D. HDFC Bank
E. None of these

65. Obtaining cash from an ATM is similar to:
A. Writing a Cheque
B. Open any Account
C. Any banking transaction
D. Close any Account
E. None of these

66. E-Banking covers both Computer banking and ....
A. Merchant Banking
B. Telephone Banking
C. Standard Banking
D. Choice Banking
E. None of these

67. Banking Ombudsman is a ....
A. Collateral Judicial Authority
B. Bi-Lateral Judicial Authority
C. Quasi Judicial Authority
D. Both A and B
E. None of these

68. In order to facilitate faster collection of outstanding cheques, the Reserve Bank of India commenced a special clearing facility called ....
A. Speed Clearing B. High Clearing
C. Standard Clearing D. Ultra Clearing
E. None of these

69. Which of the following cheque is not honored by the bank:
A. Self Cheque B. Stale Cheque
C. Cross Cheque D. All of the above
E. None of these

70. Social Control of the banks introduced during the year:
A. 1967 B. 1969
C. 1970 D. 1972
E. None of these

71. Local Area Banks were registered as public limited companies under which act:
A. Companies Act, 1956
B. SEBI Act, 1885
C. Limited Liability Partnership Act
D. Both B and C

72. RRB Act was enacted in the year:
A. 1974 B. 1979
C. 1975 D. 1976
E. None of these

73. Custodian of National Rural Credit Stabilisation Fund is:
A. RBI B. SBI
C. NABARD D. ARBI
E. None of these

74. Regional Rural Banks are classified as:
A. subsidiaries of NABARD
B. subsidiaries of the sponsor banks
C. scheduled commercial banks
D. All of the above
E. None of the above

75. Regional Rural Banks are empowered to transact the business of banking as defined under:
A. Regional Rural Banks Act, 1976
B. Negotiable Instruments Act, 1881
C. Banking Regulation Act, 1949
D. The Banking Companies (Acquisition and Transfer of Undertakings) Act, 1970
E. None of the above

76. Regional Rural Banks are managed by:
A. Reserve Bank of India
B. the State Government
C. the sponsor bank
D. a board of directors
E. All of these

77. Under which category will you classify Regional Rural Banks?
A. Scheduled Commercial Banks
B. Co-operative banks
C. Private sector banks
D. Development banks
E. None of these

78. All regional rural banks (RRBs) are required to maintain their entire statutory liquidity ratio (SLR) in:
A. current accounts with sponsor banks
B. time deposits with sponsor banks
C. government and other approved securities
D. gold holdings only
E. All of the above

79. Which of the following has become the first Regional Rural Bank issuing debit card in the country?
A. Punjab Gramin Bank
B. Nainital/Almora Bank
C. Kashi Gomti Sanyukta Gramin Bank
D. Baroda RRB
E. None of these

80. Through which of the following the funds to the projects aided by the World Bank and the International Monetary Fund (IMF) are distributed?
A. Regional Branches of RBI
B. NABARD
C. Integrated Rural Development Programme
D. Agriculture Corporation Refinance and Development
E. Ministry of Finance

81. All regional rural banks (RRBs) are required to maintain their entire statutory liquidity ratio (SLR) in
A. current accounts with sponsor banks
B. time deposits with sponsor banks
C. government and other approved securities
D. gold holdings only
E. All of the above

82. Co-operative enterprises entered into two or more business entities, known as:
A. Mergers B. Amalgamation
C. Joint Venture D. Either A or B
E. None of these

83. The Urban Credit Co-operatives are also commonly known as ....
A. Urban Co-operative Banks
B. Co-operative Banks
C. National Banks
D. Private Banks
E. None of the above

84. The .... controls the co-operative banks that falls under the Banking regulation Act of 1949.
A. Reserve Bank of India
B. NABARD
C. National Co-operative Union of India
D. State Bank of India
E. None of the above

85. Under the Banking Regulation Act, 1949, which of following is not qualified to be called as banks in the co-operative sector?
A. Urban Co-operative Banks
B. Primary Agricultural Credit Societies
C. State Co-operative Banks
D. Central Co-operative Banks
E. All of the above

86. A .... also acts as a balancing center and clearing house for the central co-operative banks.
A. State Co-operative Bank
B. District Central Co-operative Banks
C. Primary Agricultural Credit Societies
D. All the above
E. None of these

87. In India, the first co-operative land mortgage bank was established in 1920 at ....
A. Mumbai in Maharashtra
B. Jhang in Punjab
C. Chennai in Tamil Nadu
D. Ajmer in Rajasthan
E. None of these

88. The .... are organized in 3 tiers namely; state, central, and primary level and they meet the long-term credit requirements of the farmers for developmental purposes.
A. Land Development Banks
B. Primary Banks
C. Urban Co-operative Banks
D. NABARD
E. None of these

89. The Registered Office of NAFCUB is at .... and the area of operation is whole of the country.

A. Mumbai
B. Agra
C. Kolkata
D. Delhi
E. None of these

90. The Co-operative Credit Societies Act was passed in ....

A. 1901
B. 1902
C. 1903
D. 1904
E. 1905

91. The .... Committee constituted to Review the Arrangements for Institutional Credit for Agriculture and Rural Development in 1981, recommended the establishment of NABARD.

A. Sivaraman
B. Sir Maclagan
C. Khusro
D. Brahm Prakash
E. None of these

92. NABARD stands for:

A. National Bank for Agriculture and Research Development
B. National Bank for Analysis of Rural Development
C. National Bank for Agriculture and Rural Development
D. National Bank for Affordable Research and Development
E. None of the above

93. 'NABARD' came into existence on:

A. 8th July, 1982
B. 19th July, 1982
C. 12th July, 1982
D. 15 July, 1984
E. None of the above

94. Headquarter of 'NABARD' is located at:

A. Mangalore, Karnataka
B. Mumbai, Maharashtra
C. New Delhi
D. Hyderabad, Andhra Pradesh
E. None of the above

95. NABARD was established on the recommendations of:

A. Shivaraman Committee
B. Malhotra Committee
C. Kumarmangalam Committee
D. Nambiar Committee
E. None of the above

96. NABARD was set up essentially as a development bank for promoting:

A. Agriculture Development only
B. Rural Development only
C. Urban Development only
D. Both A and B
E. None of the above

97. The main function of NABARD is to provide refinance for rural credit disburse by the .... and other financial institutions as may be approved by the Reserve Bank of India.

A. State Co-operative Banks
B. The Regional Rural Banks
C. State Bank of India
D. State Co-operative Banks and The Regional Rural Banks
E. None of the above

98. CSR stands for:

A. Customer Satisfaction Responsibility
B. Corporate Social Responsibility
C. Corporate Social Reforms
D. Cooperation for Social Research
E. None of the above

99. Which of the following organizations/agencies is specifically set up to boost overall rural development in India?

A. RBI
B. SIDBI
C. NABARD
D. SEBI
E. None of these

100. Which of the following organizations maintains the Rural Infrastructure Development Fund (RIDF)?

A. RBI
B. NABARD
C. SIDBI
D. LIC
E. None of these

101. 'NABARD' was dedicated to which among the following Prime Ministers:

A. Gulzari Lal Nanda
B. Indira Gandhi
C. Shri Lal Bahadur Shastri
D. I.K. Gujaral
E. None of the above

102. When was 'Small Industries Development Bank of India' (SIDBI) established?
A. 1st April 1986 B. 1st April 1990
C. 1st April 1994 D. 1st April 1998
E. 1st April 1999

103. Where is the Headquarter of SIDBI?
A. New Delhi B. Mumbai
C. Kolkata D. Lucknow
E. None of these

104. What is the Authorised Capital of SIDBI?
A. ₹ 250 crore B. ₹ 500 crore
C. ₹ 1000 crore D. ₹ 1200 crore
E. None of these

105. What is the Paid-up Capital of SIDBI?
A. ₹ 250 crore B. ₹ 350 crore
C. ₹ 450 crore D. ₹ 550 crore
E. None of these

106. What is the maximum number of vehicles that a borrower should have so that the financing bank may get refinance from SIDBI?
A. 6 B. 10
C. 20 D. 30
E. No limit

107. What is the maximum Project Cost under National Equity Fund Scheme of SIDBI?
A. ₹ 5 lac B. ₹ 10 lac
C. ₹ 25 lac D. ₹ 50 lac
E. ₹ 75 lac

108. Which of the following has largest stake in the capital of SIDBI?
A. IDBI
B. LIC
C. State Bank group
D. Either A or B
E. None of these

109. SIDBI has recently tied up with .... to provide loans and other financial products to Small and Medium Enterprises.
A. Yes Bank
B. Krishna Baldeo Bank
C. Dena Bank
D. Punjab National Bank
E. None of these

110. What is the name of Credit Rating Agency set up by SIDBI in Sept. 2005 for aggregate rating of SMEs?
A. SME Rating Agency
B. SME Investment Rating Agency
C. SME Credit Rating Agency
D. SME Overall Rating Agency
E. None of these

111. What is the Paid up Capital of SME Rating Agency, SMERA?
A. ₹ 1 crore B. ₹ 2 crore
C. ₹ 5 crore D. ₹ 10 crore
E. ₹ 12 crore

112. In which year IRDA was constituted?
A. 19 April, 2000
B. 19 April, 2001
C. 19 April, 2002
D. 19 April, 2003
E. 19 April, 2004

113. Headquarter of General Insurance's Public Sector Association of India (GIPSA) is situated in:
A. Delhi B. Mumbai
C. Kolkata D. Hyderabad
E. None of these

114. Which of the following is a General Insurance Company functioning in India?
A. Life Insurance Corporation of India
B. ICICI Prudential
C. Tata AIG
D. United India Insurance Company
E. None of these

115. Expand the term IFRS:
A. Indian Financial Reporting Standards
B. Indian Financial Reporting Systems
C. International Financial Reporting Standards
D. International Financial Reporting Systems
E. None of these

116. LIC of India was established in:
A. 1897 B. 1956
C. 1956 D. 1965
E. 1957

117. "Zindagi ke Saath bhi, Zindagi ke Baad bhi", the punchline of this advertisement is related to which organization?
A. New India Assurance Company
B. General Insurance Corporation
C. ICICI Prudential
D. Life Insurance Corporation
E. None of these

118. "Insurance is a matter of solicitation," which one of the following Insurance companies writes this punchline in their advertisement?
A. GIC B. LIC
C. ING Vysya D. Tata AIG
E. None of these

119. When was the LIC Housing Finance Limited established?
A. 29 June, 1979 B. 19 June, 1985
C. 1 June, 1980 D. 19 June, 1989
E. 10 August, 1992

120. Which of the following types of companies/ organizations issue 'ULIP'? (The ULIPs were recently in news)
A. Insurance companies
B. Banks
C. NABARD
D. RBI
E. None of these

121. Insurance business in India is regulated by which of the following authorities?
A NFCG B. IRDA
C. CII D. FICCI
E. LIC

122. What is the term of United Nations Secretary General?
A. 3 years B. 6 years
C. 4 years D. 5 years
E. 7 years

123. Who was the only Secretary General of the UNO to have died while in office?
A. U Thant
B. Dag Hammarskjöld
C. Trygve Lie
D. Kurt Waldhiem
E. None of these

124. In which year was the UNO awarded the Nobel Peace Prize?
A. 1975 B. 1999
C. 2001 D. 2006
E. 2010

125. UN Secretary General heads which principal organ of the United Nations Organisation?
A. General Assembly
B. Security Council
C. Economic and Social Council
D. The Secretariat
E. None of these

126. Which organ of the UNO functions from Peace Palace in The Hague, The Netherlands?
A. Security Council
B. General Assembly
C. Economic and Social Council
D. International Court of Justice
E. None of these

127. What is the term of a judge of the International Court of Justice?
A. 5 years B. 7 years
C. 8 years D. 9 years
E. 10 years

128. Which organ of the United Nations Organisation is responsible for coordinating the work of its specialised agencies?
A. General Assembly
B. Economic and Social Council
C. Security Council
D. Secretariat
E. None of these

129. When was the United Nations Organisation founded?
A. August 9, 1945 B. October 24, 1944
C. October 24, 1945 D. December 10, 1945
E. None of these

130. The United Nations agency concerned with the improvement of standards of education and strengthening international co-operation in this field is :
A. U. N. E. F. B. U. N. E. S. C. O.
C. U. N. I. C. E. F. D. U. N. E. D. O.
E. None of these

131. How many Judges are there in the International Court of Justice?
A. 9 B. 10
C. 11 D. 15
E. 16

132. The first Secretary General of the United Nations was:
A. Mrs. Vijai Lakshmi Pandit
B. Trygve Lie
C. Dag Hammarskjoeld
D. U. Thant
E. None of these

133. Who was the first Indian to be the President of U. N. General Assembly ?
A. Natwar Singh
B. V. K. Krishna Menon
C. Smt. Vijay Laxmi Pandit
D. Romesh Bhandari
E. None of these

134. Which of the following countries is not a permanent member of the UN Security Council ?
A. USA B. UK
C. France D. Spain
E. None of these

135. Which of the following is not one of the official languages of the U.N.O.?
A. French B. Spanish
C. Arabic D. Italian
E. None of these

136. On what date did the U. N. O. adopt the Universal Declaration of Human Rights?
A. 20th October, 1945
B. 24th October, 1945
C. 26th June, 1945
D. 10th December, 1948
E. None of these

137. Which specialized agency of UNO lists World Heritage Sites?
A. UNESCO
B. UNICEF
C. UNWTO
D. WWF
E. None of these

138. Who of the following was the U.N.O.'s first Secretary General from the African continent?
A. Kofi Anan
B. Boutros Boutros-Ghali
C. Javier Perez de Cuellar
D. Ban Ki-moon
E. None of these

139. Who coined the term United Nations?
A. Franklin D Roosevelt
B. Harry Truman
C. Winston Churchill
D. Joseph Stalin
E. None of these

140. Which among the following countries Bank of Baroda (BoB) has its branches?
A. Uganda
B. United Arab Emirates
C. Fiji Islands
D. United Kingdom
E. All of the above

141. Bank of Baroda was nationalized along with 13 other major commercial banks of India on:
A. 20 July, 1969 B. 19 July, 1969
C. 18 July, 1969 D. 1 May, 1969
E. None of these

142. Slogan of Bank of Baroda is:
A. Prosperity for all
B. India's International Bank
C. Together we prosper
D. Either A or C
E. None of these

143. Which among the following is incorrect about BoB's domestic associates?
A. Baroda Uttar Pradesh Gramin Bank
B. Baroda Rajasthan Gramin Bank
C. Baroda Gujarat Gramin Bank
D. Baroda Lakshadip Gramin Bank
E. None of these

144. The founder of Bank of Baroda, Maharaja Sayajirao Gaekwad belongs to:
A. Maratha Kingdom
B. Sikh Kingdom
C. Rajput Kingdom
D. Either A or B
E. None of these

145. Which among the following was the Bank of Baroda's first domestic acquisition?
A. New Citizen Bank of India
B. Hind Bank
C. Bank of Rajput
D. Either A or C
E. None of these

146. Headquarter of ICICI Bank is located at:
A. Mumbai B. Hyderabad
C. Mysore D. Delhi
E. None of these

147. ICICI bank was originally promoted in .... by ICICI Limited an Indian financial institution, and was its wholly owned subsidiary.
A. 1994 B. 1995
C. 1997 D. 1998
E. None of these

148. ICICI was formed in 1955 at the initiative of:
A. World Bank
B. The Government of India
C. Representatives of Indian Industry
D. All of the above
E. None of these

149. In ...., the Bank of Rajasthan (BOR) was acquired by the ICICI bank.
A. 2010 B. 2011
C. 2012 D. 2009
E. None of these

150. Punjab National Bank was actually born on ....
A. May 21, 1894 B. May 20, 1894
C. May 19, 1894 D. May 27, 1894
E. None of these

151. The 'PNB' open its doors to the general public on:
A. 12 April, 1895 B. 14 April, 1895
C. 16 April, 1895 D. 11 April, 1895
E. None of these

152. For issuing commercial papers:
A. Prior approval of RBI is not required
B. Prior approval of RBI is required
C. Prior approval of SEBI is required
D. Prior approval of SBI is required
E. None of these

153. Certificate of deposits are issued by:
A. RBI B. Commercial banks
C. SBI only D. All the above
E. None of these

154. .... control(s) the money supply in a country.
A. RBI or Central Bank
B. SEBI
C. Government
D. All of these
E. None of these

155. .... is the rate banks receive for depositing funds with the Central Bank.
A. Reverse repo rate B. Repo rate
C. Interest rate D. All of these
E. None of these

156. .... policy is taken by RBI.
A. Monetary B. Fiscal
C. Both of them D. All of these
E. None of these

157. Repo rate means:
A. rate at which Govt. borrows money
B. rate at which RBI lends to banks
C. rate at which RBI borrows money
D. rate at which SBI borrows money
E. None of these

158. Whose signature appears on Indian ₹ 100 note?
A. Finance Minister
B. RBI Governor
C. Finance Secretary
D. Chairman, Planning Commission
E. None of these

159. RBI stipulates a healthy mix of CASA in the business figures of banks. What is CASA?
A. Customer Analysis and Savings Pattern
B. Cost Appreciation and Selling Analysis
C. Current Account and Saving Account
D. Credit and Savings Aggregate
E. None of these

160. ....is automation of banks across multiple–delivery channels.
A. ANBC B. OBE
C. NABARD D. CBS
E. None of these

ANSWERS

1	2	3	4	5	6	7	8	9	10
B	C	B	E	C	A	C	B	B	C
11	**12**	**13**	**14**	**15**	**16**	**17**	**18**	**19**	**20**
C	B	D	C	A	B	A	C	B	B
21	**22**	**23**	**24**	**25**	**26**	**27**	**28**	**29**	**30**
C	C	C	C	B	B	C	B	C	B
31	**32**	**33**	**34**	**35**	**36**	**37**	**38**	**39**	**40**
B	B	B	A	A	C	C	A	A	C
41	**42**	**43**	**44**	**45**	**46**	**47**	**48**	**49**	**50**
B	C	A	A	A	B	C	C	B	B
51	**52**	**53**	**54**	**55**	**56**	**57**	**58**	**59**	**60**
A	B	B	A	A	B	B	A	C	B
61	**62**	**63**	**64**	**65**	**66**	**67**	**68**	**69**	**70**
B	C	B	C	A	B	C	A	B	A
71	**72**	**73**	**74**	**75**	**76**	**77**	**78**	**79**	**80**
A	C	C	C	C	D	A	C	C	D
81	**82**	**83**	**84**	**85**	**86**	**87**	**88**	**89**	**90**
C	C	A	A	B	A	B	A	D	D
91	**92**	**93**	**94**	**95**	**96**	**97**	**98**	**99**	**100**
A	C	C	B	A	D	D	B	C	B
101	**102**	**103**	**104**	**105**	**106**	**107**	**108**	**109**	**110**
B	B	D	C	C	C	D	C	A	A
111	**112**	**113**	**114**	**115**	**116**	**117**	**118**	**119**	**120**
C	A	A	D	C	B	D	B	D	A
121	**122**	**123**	**124**	**125**	**126**	**127**	**128**	**129**	**130**
B	D	B	C	D	D	D	B	C	B
131	**132**	**133**	**134**	**135**	**136**	**137**	**138**	**139**	**140**
D	B	C	D	D	D	A	B	A	E
141	**142**	**143**	**144**	**145**	**146**	**147**	**148**	**149**	**150**
B	B	D	A	B	A	A	D	A	C
151	**152**	**153**	**154**	**155**	**156**	**157**	**158**	**159**	**160**
A	A	B	A	A	A	B	B	C	D

●●●

GENERAL AWARENESS

NATIONAL SYMBOLS

STATE EMBLEM

State Emblem of India is an adaptation from the Sarnath Lion Capital of Ashoka. It was adopted by the Government of India on January 26, 1950. In the adapted form, only three lions are visible, the fourth being hidden from the view. The wheel (Dharma Chakra) appears in relief in the centre of the abacus with a bull on the right and a horse on the left.

The bell-shaped lotus has been omitted. The words ''Satyameva Jayate'' meaning ''Truth alone triumphs'' are inscribed below the Emblem in Devanagari script.

NATIONAL FLAG

The National Flag of India is a horizontal tricolour of deep saffron (Kesari), white and dark green in equal proportion. In the centre of the white band there is a wheel in navy blue colour. It has 24 spokes. The ratio of the length and the breadth of the flag is 3 : 2. Its design was adopted by the Constituent Assembly of India on July 22, 1947.

NATIONAL ANTHEM

Rabindranath Tagore's song 'Jana-gana-mana' was adopted by the Constituent Assembly as the National Anthem of India on January 24, 1950.

Jana-gan-mana-adhinayaka jaya he, Bharata-bhagya-vidhata
Punjab-Sindh-Gujarat-Maratha-Dravida-Utkala-Banga
Vindhya-Himachala-Yamuna-Ganga Uchhala-jaladhi-taranga.
Tava subha name jage, Tava subha asisa mange, Gahe tava jaya gatha,
Jana-gana-mangala-dayak, jaya he Bharata bhagya vidhata,
Jaya he, jaya he, jaya he, Jaya jaya jaya, jaya he.

NATIONAL SONG

Bankim Chandra Chatterji's 'Vande Mataram' which was a source of inspiration to the people in their struggle for freedom, has been adopted as National Song. It has an equal status with the National Anthem.

Vande Mataram
Sujalam, suphalam, malayaja-shitalam,
Shasya shyamalam, Mataram
Shubhrajyotsna,pulkita yaminim,
Phulla kusumita drumadalashobhinim,
Subhasinim sumadhura—bhashinim,
Sukhadam, Varadam, Mataram.

NATIONAL CALENDAR

It is based on the Saka era with Chaitra as its first month and a normal year of 365 days. It was adopted from March 22, 1957. Dates of the national calendar have a permanent correspondence with dates of Gregorian calendar as Chaitra I falls on March 22 in a normal year and March 21 in a leap year. In official communications, both Saka and Gregorian calendar dates are written. Months of the national calendar are Chaitra, Vaishakha, Jaishtha, Ashada, Shravan, Bhadra, Ashvina, Kartika, Margashirsha, Pausha, Magha and Phalguna.

NATIONAL ANIMAL

The magnificent tiger — Panthera tigris (Linnaeus) is the national animal of India. Tiger is found in several parts of the country and is known for its grace, strength, agility and enormous power. 'Project Tiger' was launched in 1973 to check their dwindling population in India.

NATIONAL BIRD

The Indian Peacock — Pavo Christatus (Linnaeus) is the national bird of India. It is a colourful, swan-sized bird with a fan-shaped crest of feathers on its head and a long-slander neck. The male species is more colourful with blue breast and a spectacular bronze-green train of around 200 elongated feathers.

National Flower—Lotus

National Tree—Banyan

National Fruit—Mango

National Currency—Rupee '₹'

(One Rupee = 100 Paise)

National Aquatic Animal—Dolphin

BOOKS AND AUTHORS

Name of Book	Author
Ain-e-Akbari	Abul Fazal
Anand Math	Bankim Chandra Chatterjee
An Unknown Indian	Nirad C. Chaudhuri
Arthshastra	Kautilya
Coolie	Mulk Raj Anand
Das Kapital	Karl Marx
Discovery of India	Jawaharlal Nehru
Eternal India	Mrs. Indira Gandhi
Godan	Prem Chand
Gitanjali	Rabindranath Tagore
Gora	Rabindranath Tagore
Geet Govinda	Jayadeva
Harsha Charit	Bana Bhatta
Hindu View of Life	Dr. S. Radhakrishnan
India Wins Freedom	Maulana Abul Kalam Azad
Jobs of Millions	V.V. Giri
Jungle Book	Rudyard Kipling
Kamayani	Jai Shankar Prasad
Kadambari	Bana Bhatta
Life Divine	Sri Aurobindo
Last days of Netaji	G.D. Khosla
Les Miserables	Victor Hugo
Mahabharat	Veda Vyas
Macbeth	William Shakespeare
Mein Kempf	Hitler
Meghduta	Kalidas

Name of Book	Author
Mother (Maa)	Maxim Gorky
Mother India	Katherine Mayo
My Experiments with Truth	Mahatma Gandhi
My Presidential Years	R. Venkataraman
Neeti Shatak	Bhartrihari
Nehru and His Vision	Dr. K.R. Narayanan
Old Man and the Sea	Ernest Hemingway
One World	Wendell Wilkie
Panchtantra	Vishnu Sharma
Paradise Lost	John Milton
Ramayana	Valmiki (in Sanskrit)
Raghuvansham	Kalidas
Rajtarangini	Kalhan
Ram Charit Manas	Tulsi Das
Abhijnan Shakuntalam	Kalidas
Satanic Verses	Salman Rushdie
Saket	Maithili Sharan Gupta
Speed Post	Shobha De
The God of Small Things	Arundhati Roy
Treasure Island	R.L. Stevenson
Twelfth Night	William Shakespeare
Train to Pakistan	Khuswant Singh
Uttara Ram Charitra	Bhava Bhuti
Vanity Fair	W.M. Thackeray
War and Peace	Leo Tolstoy
Wealth of Nations	Adam Smith
Wake up India	Annie Besant

INVENTIONS AND DISCOVERIES

Geographical Discoveries

Discovery	Discoverer
America	Columbus
Brazil	Cabral
North Pole	Robert Peary
Everest (Conquered)	Tabie Junko
Planetary Motion	Kepler
Hawaiian Islands	Captain Cook
South Pole	Amundsen
Solar System	Copernicus

Chemistry and Physics

Discovery	Discoverer
Atom Bomb	Otto Hahn
Atomic Theory	Dalton
Atomic Numbers	Moseley
Cosmic Rays	R.S. Millikan
Dynamite	Alfred Nobel
Electrons Theory	Bohr
Electricity (current)	Volta
Electric Telegraphy (Code)	S. Morse

Discovery	Discoverer
Gravitation	Newton
Gas Light	Murdock
Oxygen	J. Priestly
Photography	L. Daguerre
Printing for the blind	Louis Braille
Radium	Madame Curie
Telegraph	Samuel Morse
Television	J.L. Baird
Telephone	Graham Bell
Wireless	G. Marconi
X-rays	W.K. Roentgen
Mechanical	
Aeroplane	Wright Brothers
Bicycle	Macmillan
Computer	Charles Babbage
Dynamo	Michal Faraday
Diesel Engine	Rudolf Diesel
Engine (Railway)	Stephenson
Fountain Pen	Waterman
Gramophone	Edison
Locomotive Power of Steam	James Watt
Helicopter	Brequet
Life Boat	Henry Greathead

Discovery	Discoverer
Microscope	Z. Jansen
Printing Press	Gutenberg
Revolver	Colt
Sewing Machine	Elias Howe
Thermometer	Fahrenheit
Transistor	W. Shockley
Typewriter	Sholes
Telescope	Hans Lippershey
Tank (Military)	Swinton
Medical	
Antiseptic Surgery	Lord Joseph Lister
Bacteria	Leeuwenhock
Circulation of Blood	William Harvey
Homoeopathy (Discovered)	Hahnemann
Insulin	F. Banting
Penicillin	Alexander Flemming
Malaria Parasite	Dr. Ronald Ross
Stethoscope	Laennec
Vitamins	Funk
Anti-Rabies Treatment	Pasteur
General	
Nylon	Carouthers
Science of Geometry	Euclids

WORLD'S GEOGRAPHICAL SURNAMES

• City of Sky-scrapers—New York • City of Seven Hills—Rome • City of Dreaming Spires—Oxford • City of Golden Gate—San Francisco • City of Magnificent Buildings—Washington D.C. • City of Eternal Springs—Quito (S. America) • China's Sorrow—Hwang Ho • Cockpit of Europe—Belgium • Dark Continent—Africa • Emerald Isle—Ireland • Eternal City—Rome • Empire City—New York • Forbidden City—Lhasa (Tibet) • Garden City—Chicago • Gate of Tears—Strait of Bab-el-Mandeb • Gift of the Nile—Egypt • Granite City—Aberdeen (Scotland) • Hermit Kingdom—Korea • Herring Pond—Atlantic Ocean • Holy Land—Jerusalem • Island Continent—Australia • Islands of Cloves—Zanzibar • Isle of Pearls—Bahrein (Persian Gulf) • Key to the Mediterranean—Gibralter • Land of Cakes—Scotland • Land of Golden Fleece—Australia • Land of Maple Leaf—Canada • Land of Morning Calm—Korea • Land of Midnight Sun—Norway • Land of the Thousand Lakes—Finland • Land of the Thunderbolt—Bhutan • Land of White Elephant—Thailand • Land of Thousand Elephants—Laos • Land of Rising Sun—Japan • Loneliest Island—Tristan De Gunha (Mid-Atlantic) • Manchester of Japan—Osaka • Pillars of Hercules—Strait of Gibraltar • Pearl of the Antilles—Cuba • Playground of Europe—Switzerland • Quaker City—Philadelphia • Queen of the Adriatic—Venice • Roof of the World—The Pamirs, Central Asia • Sugar bowl of the world—Cuba • Venice of the North—Stockholm • Windy City—Chicago • Whiteman's grave—Guinea Coast of Africa • Yellow River—Huang Ho (China) • Sickman of Europe—Turkiye

CAPITALS AND CURRENCIES OF COUNTRIES

Country	Capital	Currency
Afghanistan	Kabul	Afghani
Algeria	Algiers	Dinar
Angola	Luanda	New Kwanza
Argentina	Buenos Aires	Peso
Armenia	Yeravan	Dram
Australia	Canberra	Dollar
Austria	Vienna	Euro
Azerbaijan	Baku	Manat
Bahrain	Manama	Dinar
Bangladesh	Dhaka	Taka
Barbados	Bridgetown	Dollar
Belgium	Brussels	Euro
Bhutan	Thimphu	Ngultrum
Bolivia	La paz	Boliviano
Brazil	Brasilia	Cruzeiro
Bulgaria	Sofia	Euro
Belarus	Minsk	Ruble
Cambodia	Phnom-Penh	Riel
Canada	Ottawa	Dollar
Chile	Santiago	Peso
China	Beijing	Yuan
Colombia	Bogota	Peso
Congo (Republic)	Brazzaville	Franc (CFA)
Croatia	Zagreb	Euro
Cuba	Havana	Peso
Cyprus	Nicosia	Euro
Czech Republic	Prague	Koruna
Denmark	Copenhagen	Krone
Egypt	Cairo	Pound
Estonia	Tallinn	Euro
Ethiopia	Addis Ababa	Birr
Fiji	Suva	Dollar
Finland	Helsinki	Euro
France	Paris	Euro
Georgia	Tbilisi	Lari
Germany	Berlin	Euro
Ghana	Accra	Cedi
Greece	Athens	Euro
Guatemala	Guatemala City	Quetzal
Hong Kong	Victoria	Dollar
Hungary	Budapest	Forints
Iceland	Reykjavik	Krona
India	New Delhi	Rupee

Country	Capital	Currency
Indonesia	Jakarta	Rupiah
Iran	Teheran	Rial
Iraq	Baghdad	Dinar
Ireland	Dublin	Euro
Israel	Jerusalem	Shekel
Italy	Rome	Euro
Jamaica	Kingston	Dollar
Japan	Tokyo	Yen
Jordan	Amman	Dinar
Kazakhstan	Astana	Tenge
Kenya	Nairobi	Shilling
Korea (S)	Seoul	Won
Korea (N)	Pyongyang	Won
Kyrgyzstan	Bishkek	Som
Kuwait	Kuwait City	Dinar
Laos	Vientiane	Kip
Latvia	Riga	Euro
Lebanon	Beirut	Pound
Libya	Tripoli	Dinar
Lithuania	Vilnius	Euro
Malaysia	Kuala Lumpur	Ringgit
Maldives	Male	Rufiyya
Mauritius	Port Louis	Rupee
Moldavia	Chisinau	Leu
Mexico	Mexico City	Peso
Morocco	Rabat	Dirham
Mozambique	Maputo	Metical
Myanmar	Nay Pyi Taw	Kyat
Nepal	Kathmandu	Rupee
Netherlands	Amsterdam	Euro
New Zealand	Wellington	Dollar
Nigeria	Abuja	Naira
Norway	Oslo	Krone
Oman	Muscat	Rial
Pakistan	Islamabad	Rupee
Philippines	Manila	Peso
Poland	Warsaw	Zloty
Portugal	Lisbon	Euro
Qatar	Doha	Riyal
Romania	Bucharest	Leu
Russia	Moscow	Ruble
Saudi Arabia	Riyadh	Rial

Country	*Capital*	*Currency*
Slovakia	Bratislava	Euro
Spain	Madrid	Euro
Sri Lanka	Colombo	Rupee
Sudan	Khartoum	Dinar
Sweden	Stockholm	Krona
Switzerland	Berne	Swiss Francs
Syria	Damascus	Pound
South Africa	Capetown (Legislative) Pretoria (Administrative)	Rand
Tajikistan	Dushanbe	Somoni
Taiwan	Taipei	Dollar
Tanzania	Dodoma	Shilling
Thailand	Bangkok	Baht
Turkiye	Ankara	Turkish Lira
Turkmenistan	Ashgabat	Manat
Uganda	Kampala	Shilling
Ukraine	Kiev	Hryvna
United Arab Emirates	Abu Dhabi	Dirham
U.K.	London	Pound Sterling
U.S.A.	Washington	Dollar
Uzbekistan	Tashkent	Som
Vietnam	Hanoi	Dong
Yemen	Sana'a	Rial/Dinar
Zimbabwe	Harare	Dollar
Congo (Democratic Republic)	Kinshasa	Franc (CDF)
Zambia	Lusaka	Kwacha

INDIAN CITIES AND THEIR RIVERS

City	**State**	**River**
Agra	U.P.	Yamuna
Ahmedabad	Gujarat	Sabarmati
Alwaye	Keralam	Periyar
Kolkata	West Bengal	Hooghly
Cuttack	Odisha	Mahanadi
Delhi	Delhi	Yamuna
Haridwar	Uttarakhand	Ganga
Kanpur	Uttar Pradesh	Ganga
Ludhiana	Punjab	Sutlej
Lucknow	Uttar Pradesh	Gomati
Nasik	Maharashtra	Godavari
Patna	Bihar	Ganga
Prayagraj	U.P.	Confluence of the Ganga, Yamuna, and invisible Saraswati
Srinagar	J & K	Jhelum
Surat	Gujarat	Tapti
Tiruchirapally	Tamil Nadu	Kaveri
Ujjain	Madhya Pradesh	Shipra
Vijayawada	Andhra Pradesh	Krishna
Varanasi	Uttar Pradesh	Ganga

WONDERS OF THE WORLD

Seven Wonders of the Ancient World: (1) the Pyramids of Egypt, built in approximately 2700 BC; (2) the Hanging Gardens at Babylon; (3) the temple of Artemis at Emphesus; (4) the statue of Zeus at Olympia; (5) the tomb of Mausolus at Halicarnassus, built in nearly 350 BC; (6) the Colossus of Rhodes, built in nearly 280 BC; (7) the Pharos Lighthouse at Alexandria.

Seven Wonders of the Medieval World: (1) the Colosseum of Rome; (2) the Great Wall of China; (3) the Porcelain Tower of Nanking; (4) the Mosque at St. Sophia (Constantinople); (5) Stonehenge; (6) the Catacombs of Rome; (7) the Leaning Tower of Pisa.

Seven New Wonders of the World: (1) Taj Mahal of Agra (India); (2) Pyramid at Chichen Itza (Mexico); (3) Machu Picchu (Peru); (4) Statue of Christ The Redeemer (Brazil); (5) Great Wall of China; (6) Roman Colosseum, Italy; (7) Ruins of Petra, Jordan.

STATES & UNION TERRITORIES OF INDIA (CAPITALS, PRINCIPAL LANGUAGES)

States & Union Territories	Capitals	Principal Languages
■ Andhra Pradesh	Amravati	*Telgu and Urdu*
■ Arunachal Pradesh	Itanagar	*Monpa, Adi, Nissi etc.*
■ Assam	Dispur	*Assamese and Bengali*
■ Bihar	Patna	*Hindi and Maithili*
■ Chhattishgarh	Raipur	*Hindi*
■ Goa	Panaji	*Konkani*
■ Gujarat	Gandhinagar	*Gujarati*
■ Haryana	Chandigarh	*Hindi*
■ Himachal Pradesh	Shimla	*Hindi and Pahari*
■ Jharkhand	Ranchi	*Hindi*
■ Keralam	Thiruvananthpuram	*Malyalam*
■ Karnataka	Bengaluru	*Kannada*
■ Madhya Pradesh	Bhopal	*Hindi*
■ Maharashtra	Mumbai	*Marathi*
■ Meghalaya	Shillong	*Khashi, Jayantia and Garo*
■ Manipur	Imphal	*Manipuri*
■ Mizoram	Aizawl	*Mizo and English*
■ Nagaland	Kohima	*Naga, Assamese and English*
■ Odisha	Bhubaneshwar	*Odia*
■ Punjab	Chandigarh	*Punjabi*
■ Rajasthan	Jaipur	*Hindi, Rajasthani*
■ Sikkim	Gangtok	*Sikkimese and Gorkhali*
■ Tamil Nadu	Chennai	*Tamil*
■ Tripura	Agartala	*Bengali, Tripuri*
■ Uttar Pradesh	Lucknow	*Hindi*
■ Uttarakhand	Dehradun	*Hindi*
■ West Bengal	Kolkata	*Bengali*
■ Telangana	Hyderabad	*Telgu and Urdu*
■ Jammu & Kashmir	Srinagar/Jammu	*Kashmiri, Dongri, Urdu, Dardi and Pahari*
■ Andaman and Nicobar Islands	Shri Vijaya Puram	*Hindi, Nicobarese, Bengali, Malayalam, Tamil, Telugu*
■ Chandigarh	Chandigarh	*Hindi, Punjabi, English*
■ Dadar and Nagar Haveli and Daman and Diu	Daman	*Gujarati, Hindi*
■ Delhi	Delhi	*Hindi, Punjabi*
■ Lakshadweep	Kavaratti	*Malayalam*
■ Puducherry	Puducherry	*Tamil, Telugu, Malayalam, English and French*
■ Ladakh	Leh	*Ladakhi*

HIGH COURTS IN INDIA

Name	*Territorial Jurisdiction*	*Seat*
Allahabad	Uttar Pradesh	Prayagraj (Bench at Lucknow)
Andhra Pradesh	Andhra Pradesh	Amaravati
Bombay	Maharashtra, Goa, Dadar and Nagar Haveli and Daman and Diu	Mumbai (Benches at Nagpur, Panaji, and Aurangabad)
Calcutta	West Bengal and Andaman & Nicobar Islands	Kolkata (Circuit Benches at Port Blair and Jalpaiguri)
Chhattisgarh	Chhattisgarh	Bilaspur
Delhi	New Delhi	NCT of Delhi
Gauhati	Assam, Nagaland, Mizoram and Arunachal Pradesh	Guwahati (Benches at Kohima, Aizawl and Itanagar)
Gujarat	Gujarat	Sola (Ahmedabad)
Himachal Pradesh	Himachal Pradesh	Shimla
Jammu & Kashmir and Ladakh	Jammu & Kashmir/Ladakh	Srinagar and Jammu
Jharkhand	Jharkhand	Ranchi
Karnataka	Karnataka	Bengaluru (Circuit Benches at Dharwar and Gulbarga)
Kerala	Keralam & Lakshadweep	Kochi
Madhya Pradesh	Madhya Pradesh	Jabalpur (Benches at Gwalior and Indore)
Madras	Tamil Nadu & Puducherry	Chennai (Bench at Madurai)
Orissa	Odisha	Cuttack
Patna	Bihar	Patna
Punjab and Haryana	Punjab, Haryana and Chandigarh	Chandigarh
Rajasthan	Rajasthan	Jodhpur (Bench at Jaipur)
Sikkim	Sikkim	Gangtok
Uttarakhand	Uttarakhand	Nainital
Tripura	Tripura	Agartala
Meghalaya	Meghalaya	Shillong
Manipur	Manipur	Imphal
Telangana	Telangana	Hyderabad

FAMOUS HILL STATIONS

Hill Station	State/UT
1. Almora, Mussoorie, Nainital	: Uttarakhand
2. Cherrapunji (Shillong), Khasi Hills (Shillong)	: Meghalaya
3. Ooty, Kodaikanal, Yercaud	: Tamil Nadu
4. Dalhousie, Kassauli	: Himachal Pradesh
5. Darjeeling	: West Bengal
6. Gulmarg, Srinagar	: Jammu and Kashmir
7. Mahabaleshwar	: Maharashtra
8. Mt. Abu	: Rajasthan
9. Pachmarhi	: Madhya Pradesh

FAMOUS NATIONAL PARKS

1. Corbett National Park : Nainital, Uttarakhand
2. Dudhwa National Park : Lakhimpur Kheri, Uttar Pradesh
3. Kaziranga National Park : Jorhat, Assam
4. Kanha National Park : Jabalpur, Bhedaghat
5. Gir National Park : Rajkot, Junagarh, Gujarat
6. Guindy National Park : Guindy, Chennai, Tamil Nadu
7. Nagairhole National Park : Coorg, Karnataka
8. Bandipur National Park : Mysore, Karnataka

FAMOUS NATIONAL WILDLIFE SANCTUARIES

1. Dachigam Wildlife Sanctuary : Srinagar, Jammu and Kashmir
2. Sariska : Alwar, Rajasthan
3. Hazaribagh Wildlife Sanctuary : Hazaribagh, Jharkhand
4. Tiger Project : Sawai Madhopur, Rajasthan
5. Mudhumali Wildlife Sanctuary : Mudhumalia, Nilgiri, Tamil Nadu
6. Periyar Wildlife Sanctuary : Idukki, Kottayam, Keralam

HOLY PLACES IN INDIA

1.	Amarnath	Jammu and Kashmir
2.	Ayodhya	Uttar Pradesh
3.	Badrinath	Uttarakhand
4.	Dwarka	Gujarat
5.	Haridwar	Uttarakhand
6.	Kancheepuram	Tamil Nadu
7.	Kedarnath	Uttarakhand
8.	Mathura	Uttar Pradesh
9.	Puri	Odisha
10.	Rameswaram	Tamil Nadu
11.	Tirupati	Andhra Pradesh
12.	Ujjain	Madhya Pradesh
13.	Varanasi	Uttar Pradesh
14.	Bodh Gaya	Bihar

SPORTS

Terms Associated With Sports :

Cricket : Ashes, Bye, Bodyline, Bowling, Break, Cover-point, Creases, Chinaman, Chucker, Drive, Duck, Follow on, Googly, Hit-Wicket, Hat-trick, Leg-before-wicket, Leg break, Leg-bye, Maiden over, No ball, Night-watchman, Runner, Run-out, Stumped, Silly-point, Slip.

Football : Handball, Corner kick, Dribble, Free Kick, Hat-trick, Off-side, Penalty Kick, Try, Throw in, Wembley.

Hockey : Bully, Carry, Corner kick, Corner, Penalty stroke, Off-side, Penalty, Roll in scoop, Sticks, Sudden death, Striking circle, Short Corner, Scoop, Tie-breaker, Under-cutting, Hat-trick.

Tennis : Backhand drive, Deuce, Fault, Half-volley, Net, Let, Volley, Smash, Service.

Billiards : Break, Cannons, Cue, Pot, Jigger, Scratch, In Bauk, In, Off.

Bridge : Dummy, Finesse, Grand-slam, Little Slam, Revoke, Ruff slam, Trump, Tricks, Vulnerable.

Volley Ball : Booster, Love, Service, Volley, Smasher.

Badminton : Smash, Drop, Let.

Chess : Check, Checkmate, Gambit, State-mate.

Golf : Bogy, Caddie, Hole, Links, Stymie, Tee, Put.

Polo : Chukker, Mallet, Bunder.

Baseball : Bunting, Diamond, Pitcher, Put-out, Strike, Home.

Boxing : Knockout, Punch, Upper-cut, Jab, Hook.

FAMOUS TROPHIES

Agha Khan Cup	Hockey
Beighton Cup	Hockey
Corbillion Cup	World Table Tennis (Women)
Davis Cup	Lawn Tennis
Duleep Trophy	Cricket
Durand Cup	Football
Ezra Cup	Polo
I.F.A. Shield	Football
Irani Cup	Cricket (India)
Jayalaxmi Cup	Table Tennis (Women)
Lady Rattan Tata Trophy	Hockey (Women)
Nehru Cup	Hockey (India)
Obaidullah Cup	Hockey
Ranji Trophy	Cricket (India)
Rangaswamy Cup	Hockey (India)
Rovers Cup	Football (India)
Santosh Trophy	Football (India)
Subroto Cup	Football
Thomas Cup	Badminton
Uber Cup	Badminton (Women)
Wellington Trophy	Rowing (India)

BIGGEST, LARGEST, TALLEST OF THE WORLD

Airport, *Largest*—King Fahd International Airport, Dammon (Saudi Arabia)

Animal, *Tallest*—Giraffe (Average height 6.09 m); *Largest and Heaviest*—Blue Whale (190 tonnes)

Longest recorded Animal—Boot lace Worm (55 m); *Fastest*—Cheetah (Approximately 100 km/hr)

Bay, *Largest*—Bay of Bengal

Continent, *biggest*—Asia (31,845,872 km^2); *Smallest*—Australia Mainland (Area 76,17,930 km^2)

Desert, *Largest*—Sahara (N. Africa; maximum length 5,150 km EW; maximum width 3,200 km NS)

Dome, *Largest*—Singapore National Stadium (310 m)

Fish, *Largest fresh water*—Plabeuk (China, Laos and Thailand); *Most abundant*—Bristle mouth; *Most venomous*—Stone Fish (Indo-Pacific Waters)

Fountain, *Tallest*—King Fahd's Fountain (Jeddah, Saudi Arabia)

Gulf, *Largest*—Gulf of Mexico (1,544,000 sq. km)

Island, *Biggest*—Greenland (Kalaatdlit Nunaat-2,175,000 sq km)

Lake, *Largest*—Caspian Sea (Azerbaijan, Russia, Iran border: 37.18 lakh km^2); *Deepest*—Baikal (Siberia); *Largest (fresh water)*—Superior Lake (USA---Canada border: 82,350 km^2)

Mountain, *Highest peak*—Mt. Everest (8848 m; Nepal); *Highest range*—Himalayas, Asia (upto 4200 m); *Greatest mountain range*—Himalaya-Karakoram (96 out of 109 peaks over 7315 m are here)

Museum, *Largest*—American Museum of Natural History, New York

Ocean, *Largest and Deepest*—The Pacific (Area: 166,240,000 km^2; Depth: 10,924 m)

Platform, *Longest (rail)*—Shri Siddharoodha Swamiji Railway Station, Hubballi (Karnataka; India, 1507 m. long)

Railway Station, *Largest*—Grand Central Terminal (New York City; 19 hc)

Rivers, *Longest*—(i) Nile (6650 km) (ii) Amazon (6437 km)

Sea, *Largest*—Philippine Sea (5,695,000 sq. km)

Star, *Brightest*—Sirius A (also called Dog Star)

Temple, *Largest*—Angkor Vat (Cambodia: 402 acres)

Tunnel, *Longest (railway)*—Gotthard Base Rail Tunnel (Switzerland; 57.1 km); *Largest (road)*—Laerdal, Norway (24.51 km)

FIRST IN INDIA

Governor General of Independent India — Lord Mountbatten

Cosmonaut — Sq. Ldr. Rakesh Sharma

Field Marshal — S.H.F.J. Manekshaw

Indian Governor General of Indian Union — C. Rajagopalachari

Indian I.C.S. Officer — Satyendra Nath Tagore

Indian to swim across English Channel — Mihir Sen

Indian Women to swim across English Channel — Miss Arti Saha

Man to climb Mount Everest — Tenzing Norgay

Man to climb Mount Everest without Oxygen — Phu Dorjee

Man to climb Mount Everest twice — Nwang Gombu

Nobel Prize Winner — Rabindra Nath Tagore

President of Indian National Congress — W.C. Banerjee

President of Indian Republic — Dr. Rajendra Prasad

Talkie Film — Alam Ara (1931)

Test Tube Baby (Documented) — Indira

Viceroy of India — Lord Canning

Woman Minister of Indian Union — Rajkumari Amrit Kaur

Woman Governor — Mrs. Sarojini Naidu

Woman President of Indian National Congress — Dr. Annie Besant

Woman Prime Minister — Mrs. Indira Gandhi

Woman Speaker of a State Assembly — Mrs. Shanno Devi

Prime Minister of India — Pt. Jawaharlal Nehru

Muslim President of Indian Union — Dr. Zakir Hussain

Speaker of Lok Sabha — G.V. Mavlankar

Women to Climb Mount Everest — Bachhendri Pal

Woman Judge in Supreme Court — Mrs. Meera Sahib Fatima Biwi

Women Chief Justice of a High Court — Smt. Leela Seth

The First Indian Weightlifter to Win bronze medal in Olympics — Karnam Malleshwari (Sydney, in 2000)

Chief of Defence Staff (CDS) —General Bipin Rawat

World Chess Champion — Vishwanathan Anand

India's First Woman Merchant Navy Officer — Sonali Banerjee

The First Woman Air Vice-Marshal — P. Bandopadhyaya

The First Indian to be appointed as United Nations Civilian Police Advisor — Ms. Kiran Bedi

The First Women to be appointed Deputy Governor of Reserve Bank of India — K.J. Udeshi

The First Indian Lady to win a medal in World Athletic Championship — Anju Bobby George

The First Sikh Prime Minister of India — Dr. Manmohan Singh

IMPORTANT DAYS

15th January	—	Army Day
26th January	—	Republic Day
30th January	—	Leprosy Eradication Day/ Martyr's Day
28th February	—	National Science Day
8th march	—	International Women's Day
15th March	—	World Consumer's Day
21st March	—	World Disabled Day
5th April	—	National Marine Day
7th April	—	World Health Day
18th April	—	World Heritage Day
22nd April	—	International Earth Day
Ist May	—	Worker's Day
3rd May	—	International Sun Day
21st May	—	Anti-Terrorism Day
24th May	—	Commonwealth Day
31st May	—	World No Tobacco Day
5th June	—	World Environment Day
21st June	—	World Yoga Day
26th June	—	International Day against Drug Abuse
11th July	—	World Population Day
15th August	—	Independence Day
24th August	—	Sanskrit Day
5th September	—	Teacher's Day
8th September	—	World Literacy Day
27th September	—	World Tourism Day
1st October	—	World Elder's Day
4th October	—	World Animal Day
8th October	—	Air Force Day
10th October	—	National Solidarity Day
16th October	—	World Food Day
24th October	—	U.N. Day
14th November	—	World Diabetes Day
14th November	—	Children's Day
19th November	—	National Integration Day
26th November	—	Law Day
1st December	—	World AIDS Day
4th December	—	Navy Day
7th December	—	Flag Day
10th December	—	Human Rights Day

PARLIAMENTS OF IMPORTANT COUNTRIES

Afghanistan	—	Shora
Britain	—	Parliament House of Commons, House of Lords
Denmark	—	Folketing
The Netherlands	—	States General
India	—	Sansad
Israel	—	Knesset
Iran	—	Majlis
Ireland	—	Airetann
Iceland	—	Althing
Japan	—	Diet
Norway	—	Storting
Russia	—	Supreme Soviet
Spain	—	Cortes
Sweden	—	Riksdag
U.S.A.	—	Congress Senate
Germany	—	Bundestag

MINERAL RESOURCES OF THE WORLD

Mineral	Largest Producers
Iron Ore	China, Japan, Russia
Tin	China, Indonesia, Peru
Lead	China, Australia, U.S.A.
Zinc	China, Australia, Peru
Manganese	South Africa, Brazil, Australia
Aluminium	China, Russia, Canada
Petroleum	Saudi Arabia, Russia, USA
Silver	Peru, Mexico, China
Coal	China, USA, India

WORLD'S LARGEST PRODUCERS

Articles	Producers	Articles	Producers
Carpets	Iran	Cheese	USA
Cocoa	Cote d'Ivoire	Coffee	Brazil
Copper	Chile	Cotton	China
Diamonds	Russia	Jute	India
Rice	China	Rubber	Thailand
Silk	China	Steel	China
Sugar	Brazil	Tea	China
Tin	China	Wheat	China
Wool	Australia		

TEN LARGEST COUNTRIES BY AREAS

Rank by Area	Country	Area (sq. km.)
1.	Russia	17,075,400
2.	Canada	9,976,139
3.	China	9,561,000
4.	U.S.A.	9,363,123
5.	Brazil	8,511,965
6.	Australia	7,686,848
7.	India	3,287,263
8.	Argentina	2,776,889
9.	Kazakhstan	2,724,900
10.	Algeria	2,381,741

PRESIDENT OF INDIA

He is the constitutional head of the Republic but not the real executive.

Qualifications: (1) Indian citizen; (2) age not less than 35 years; (3) should have qualifications for election to Lok Sabha; (4) should not hold any office of profit; (5) should not be a Member of Parliament or State Legislature.

Election: He is elected by the elected Members of Parliament and State Legislative Assemblies in accordance with the system of proportional representation by means of single transferable vote.

Powers: He makes appointment to all the Constitutional posts. He can address either House of Parliament and send message to them. He can summon and prorogue either House of Parliament and dissolve Lok Sabha. All Bills passed by Parliament must receive his assent to become an Act. He issues Ordinance when Parliament is not in session. No money Bill can be introduced in Lok Sabha without his recommendation. He can grant pardon, reprieve or remit punishment and he can commute death sentences. He can declare national emergency, state emergency and financial emergency.

VICE-PRESIDENT OF INDIA

The Vice-President acts as the ex-officio Chairman of Rajya Sabha and acts as the President when the latter is unable to discharge his functions due to illness, absence or any other reason, or till the election of a new President when a vacancy is caused by the death, resignation or removal of the President.

The Vice-President is elected by an electoral college consisting of the members of both Houses of Parliament in accordance with the system of proportional representation by means of the single transferable vote. He must be a citizen of India, not less than 35 years of age, and should be eligible for election as a member of the Council of States.

PRIME MINISTER OF INDIA

The Prime Minister is the leader of the majority party in the Parliament and the President cannot exercise his discretion in the appointment of the Prime Minister. He stays in office till the majority of the members of Lok Sabha has confidence in him. He occupies an important posi-tion in relation to the council of Ministers. He recommends the names of the persons to be included in the Council of Ministers. He allocates portfolios among them and can ask any minister to tender resignation. He can drop a minister while reshuffling the ministry. He coordinates the administration of various departments. He is the chief link between the President and the Council. He is the leader of the majority party and so, he has a great influence on the Parliament and the party. The Prime Minister enjoys such extensive powers as have been described as the virtual ruler of the country.

THE SOLAR SYSTEM: SOME FACTS

Number of Planets: 8—Mercury, Venus, Earth, Mars, Jupiter, Saturn, Uranus and Neptune.

Largest most

Massive planet .... Jupiter
Brightest planet .... Venus
Brightest star .... Sirius
Fastest orbiting planet .... Mercury
Longest (Synodic) day .... Mercury
Planet with largest moon .... Jupiter
Greatest average density .... Jupiter
Tallest mountain .... Earth
Strongest magnetic fields .... Jupiter
Most circular orbit .... Venus
Shortest (synodic) day .... Jupiter
Hottest planet .... Venus
No moons .... Mercury, Venus
Planet with moon with most eccentric orbit............... Neptune
Lowest average density .... Saturn
Deepest Oceans....................... Jupiter
Greatest amount of liquid on the surface .... Earth

THE EARTH: FACTS AND DATA

Composition of the Earth: Aluminium (0.4%), Sulphur (2.7%), Silicon (13%), Oxygen (28%), Calcium (1.2%), Nickel (2.7%), Magnesium (17%), Iron (35%)

Surface area	: 510100500 sq km
Land Surface (29.1%)	: 148950800 sq km
Ocean Surface (70.9%)	: 361149700 sq km
Type of water	: 97% salt, 3% fresh
Total area of water	: 382672000 sq km
Equatorial diameter	: 12753 km
Equatorial Circumference	: 40066 km
Polar Circumference	: 39992 km
Polar diameter	: 12710 km
Equatorial radius	: 6376 km
Polar radius	: 6335 km
Mass (estimated weight)	: 594×10^{19} metric tons
Mean distance from the Sun	: 149407000 km

Earth's orbit speed (around sun)	: 107320 kmph	Time of Rotation (on its axis)	: 23 hrs 56 min 4.09 seconds
Period of Revolution (round the sun)	: 365 days 5 hrs 48 min. 45.51 seconds	Inclination of the axis (to the plane of the ecliptic)	: 23°27'

PRINCIPAL MOUNTAIN PEAKS OF THE WORLD

Mountains	Height in Metres	Range	Date of First Ascent
1. Mount Everest	8,848	Himalayas	May 29, 1953
2. K-2 (Godwin Austen)	8,611	Karakoram	July 31, 1954
3. Kanchenjunga	8,597	Himalayas	May 25, 1955
4. Lhotse	8,511	Himalayas	May 18, 1956
5. Makalu I	8,481	Himalayas	May 15, 1955
6. Dhaulagiri I	8,167	Himalayas	May 13, 1960
7. Mansalu I	8,156	Himalayas	May 9, 1956
8. Chollyo	8,153	Himalayas	Oct. 19, 1954
9. Nanga Parbat	8,124	Himalayas	July 3, 1953
10. Annapurna I	8,091	Himalayas	June 3, 1950
11. Gasherbrum I	8,068	Karakoram	July 5, 1958
12. Broad Peak I	8,047	Karakoram	June 9, 1957
13. Gasherbrum II	8,034	Karakoram	July 7, 1956
14. Shisha Pangma (Gosainthan)	8,014	Himalayas	May 2, 1964
15. Gasherbrum III	7,952	Karakoram	Aug. 11, 1975

POPULAR NICK NAMES OF SOME FAMOUS PERSONALITIES

Andhra Kesari	T. Prakasam
Anna	C.N. Anna Durai
Bang Bandhu	Sheikh Mujibur Rehman
Bapu	Mahatma Gandhi
Bard of Avon	William Shakespeare
Chachaji	Jawaharlal Nehru
Desh Bandhu	C.R. Das
Frontier Gandhi	Khan Abdul Gaffar Khan
Fuhrer	Adolf Hitler
G.B.S.	George Bernard Shaw
Grand Old Man of India	Dadabhai Naoroji
Grand Old Man of Britain	Gladstone
Guru Dev	Rabindra Nath Tagore
Guruji	M.S. Golwalkar
Iron Man of India	Sardar Patel
Lok Nayak	Jayaprakash Narayan
Lady with the Lamp	Florence Nightingale
Lal, Bal, Pal	Lala Lajpat Rai, Bal Gangadhar Tilak, Bipin Chandra Pal
Little Corporal	Napoleon Bonaparte
Lokmanya	Bal Gangadhar Tilak
Mahamana	Pt. Madan Mohan Malaviya
Maid of Orleans	Joan of Arc
Maiden Queen	Queen Elizabeth I
Missile Man	A.P.J. Abdul Kalam
Man of Destiny	Napoleon Bonaparte
Netaji	Subhash Chandra Bose
Nightingale of India	Sarojini Naidu
Panditji	Jawaharlal Nehru
Punjab Kesari	Lala Lajpat Rai
Shastriji	Lal Bahadur Shastri
Uncle Ho	Ho Chi Minh
Wizard of the North	Walter Scott

FAMOUS INTERNATIONAL ORGANISATIONS, HEADQUARTERS	
International Organisations	***Headquarters***
United Nations Organisations (U.N.O.)	New York
International Monetary Fund (I.M.F.)	Washington D.C.
World Health Organisation (W.H.O.)	Geneva
Food & Agricultural Organisation (FAO)	Rome
International Labour Organisation (ILO)	Geneva
UNESCO	Paris
International Court of Justice	The Hague
Universal Postal Union (UPU)	Berne
International Civil Aviation Organisation (ICAO)	Montreal
UNIDO	Vienna
International Atomic Energy Agency (IAEA)	Vienna
International Finance Corporation (IFC)	Washington
United Nations Development Programme (UNDP)	New York
UNICEF	New York
International Maritime Organisation (IMO)	London
World Meteorological Organisation (WMO)	Geneva
International Telecommunication Union (ITU)	Geneva
Arab League	Cairo
Commonwealth of Nations	London
World Trade Organisation (WTO)	Geneva
International Development Association (IDA)	Washington D.C.
International Bank for Reconstruction and Development (IBRD)	Washington D.C.
World Intellectual Property Organisation (WIPO)	Geneva
Organisation of Islamic Conference (OIC)	Jeddah (Saudi Arabia)
European Union	Brussels
Red Cross	Geneva
Interpol	Lyons (France)
Asian Development Bank (ADB)	Manila
North Atlantic Treaty Organisation (NATO)	Brussels
Association of South East Asian Nations (ASEAN)	Jakarta

AWARDS

NOBEL PRIZES

- These Prizes were instituted in 1901 by a Swedish scientist, Dr. Alfred Nobel; the discoverer of Dynamite.
- Six prizes are awarded annually for (*i*) Chemistry, (*ii*) Physics, (*iii*) Medicine, (*iv*) Literature, (*v*) Peace and (*vi*) Economics —started since 1969.
- The following Indians so far have been awarded these prizes: (*i*) Dr. Rabindra Nath Tagore (1913) for his "Geetanjali". (*ii*) Dr. C.V. Raman for Physics in 1930, (*iii*) Mother Teresa for Peace in 1979, (*iv*) Prof. Amartya Sen in 1998 for Economics and (*v*) Kailash Satyarthi in 2014 for Peace.
- In addition, four non-resident Indians have also been awarded the Nobel Prize. They are: (*i*) Hargobind Khurana for Medicine in 1968, (*ii*) Subramanian Chandrasekhar for Physics in 1983, (*iii*) Venkatraman Ramkrishnan for Chemistry in 2009, (*iv*) Abhijit Vinayak Banerjee for Economics in 2019.

BHARAT RATNA

- Bharat Ratna is India's highest Civilian Award. It was first awarded in 1954.
- The actual award is designed in the shape of a *peepal* leaf with Bharat Ratna inscribed in Devanagri script in the Sun Figure.
- This is India's highest civilian award. It is given for exceptional work on art, literature, science and recognition of public service of the highest order.
- The emblem, the Sun and the rim are of platinum. The inscriptions are in burnished bronze.
- Government servants are not eligible for it.

ART AND CULTURE

☞ Classical Dances

Dance	*State*	*Famous Artists*
Bharat Natyam	Tamil Nadu	Yamini Krishnamurthy, Rukmini Devi Arundale, Swapna Sundari, Sonal Mansingh, Vaijanti Mala, Mrinalini Sarabhai, Chandralekha, Indrani, Ram Gopal, Bal Saraswati
Kathakali	Keralam	Gopinath, K.K. Nayar, Kunju-Kurup, T.K. Chandu
Kuchipudi	Andhra Pradesh/ Telangana	Sapna Sundari, Raja Reddy, Shobha Nayar, Radha Reddy, Vedantam Satyanarayan, Vimpanti Chinna Satyam.
Kathak	North India	Birju Maharaj, Gopi Krishna, Shambhu Maharaj, Sitara Devi, Vishnu Sharma, Durga Lal, Shobhana Narayan
Odissi	Odisha	Kelucharan Mahapatra, Indrani Rehman, Madhavi Mudgal, Pratima Bedi, Samyukta Panigrahi, Sonal Mansingh, Debudas
Manipuri	Manipur	Uday Shankar, Bipin Singh, Suryamukhi, Darohra Jhaveri

☞ Famous Folk Dances

State/UT	*Folk Dance*	*State/UT*	*Folk Dance*
Andhra Pradesh/ Telangana	Dandari, Banjara	Keralam	Mohini Attam, Padayuni
Assam	Bihu, Keli Gopal, Sataria	Madhya Pradesh	Lota Nritya, Jawara
Bihar	Chhau, Magahi, Durga dance	Maharashtra	Tamasha, Dahi Handi, Gof, Deepak Dindi
W. Bengal	Kirtan, Kalatri, Asweabadh, Brita, Kalidance	Manipur	Dhol Cholam
Chhattisgarh	Saila, Karama, Bhagoria	Meghalaya	Nongakarem
Gujarat	Garba, Rasalila, Tippani, Dandia,	Nagaland	Bamboo dance
		Odisha	Chhau, Maya Shabari, Dalachai
Haryana	Damyal, Lahoor	Punjab	Gidda, Bhangra, Panihari
Himachal Pradesh	Dussehra dance, Hikat, Notio	Rajasthan	Thumar, Kathaputali, Tera Tali
		Tamil Nadu	Terukalathu, Kabalatam, Kargam, Pulivesham
Jammu & Kashmir	Dumhal	Tripura	Hazagiri
Jharkhand	Jhau, Ghumakudia, Jadur, Sarhul, Soharai, Karama, Vaima, Loojhari, Jat-Jatin, Vidayat	Uttar Pradesh	Rasalila, Nautanki, Thali, Dhurang, Jhumela, Huraka, Bol.
		Uttarakhand	Kajari, Karan
Karnataka	Yakshagan, Dolu Kunitha	Goa	Dhode Modini

MUSIC

Main Schools of Classical Music

- There are two main schools of classical music, namely, the Hindustani and the Carnatic. The Hindustani school of classical music is in vogue in north-western India, eastern India and northern parts of the South India.

Musical Instruments

- ***They are:*** Tabla, Mridangam, Pakhawaj, Chandai, Dholak, Veena, Sitar, Sarod, Gootuvadhyam, Sarangi, Flute, Nadaswaram, Shehnai, Shringi and Turahi.

FAMOUS INTERNATIONAL AIR SERVICES

Air Service	*Name of Country*	*Air Service*	*Name of Country*
Air India	India	Lufthansa Airlines	Germany
British Overseas Airways Corporation	Britain	Iraqi Airways	Iraq
Trans World Airlines	America	National Airlines	Iran
Russian Airlines	Russia	Quantas Airlines	Australia
Japan Airlines	Japan	Hong-Kong Airlines	Hong-Kong
Pakistan International Airlines	Pakistan	Egypt Airlines	Egypt
Malaysia Airlines	Malaysia	Slovak Airlines	Slovakia
Royal Nepal Airlines	Nepal	S.I.A.	Singapore
Swiss Airways	Switzerland	Garuda Airways	Indonesia
Air France	France	Bangladesh Viman Sewa	Bangladesh
Kuwait Airways	Kuwait	Air Lanka	Sri Lanka
Pan American World Airways	America	Elitalia Airlines	Italy
K.L.M. Royal Airlines	The Netherlands (Holland)	Air Canada	Canada

FAMOUS RELIGIONS, FOUNDERS, HOLY BOOKS & PLACES OF WORSHIP

Religion	*Founder*	*Holy Books*	*Place of Worship*
Hinduism	Hinduism has no one Founder. (This religion is based upon the religion of original Aryan Settlers)	Ramayan, Vedas, Puranas and Geeta	Temple
Sikh	Guru Nanak Dev	Guru Grantha Sahib	Gurdwara
Christianity	Jesus Christ	Bible	Church
Islam	Prophet Mohammed	Koran (Quran)	Mosque
Parsi	Zoroaster	Zend Avesta	Fire Temple
Jainism	Adinath Rishavdev	Jain Granth	Jain Temple
Buddhism	Gautam Buddha	Tripitaka	Buddha Temple
Jew	Moosa	Torah	Synagogue

INTELLIGENCE AGENCIES OF SOME PROMINENT COUNTRIES

Country	*Intelligence Agency*	*Country*	*Intelligence Agency*
India	Research & Analysis Wing (RAW), Intelligence Bureau (I.B.), Central Bureau of Investigation (C.B.I.)	Russia	K.G.B. (Komitel Gosudarstvennoy Bezopasnosty) (Committee for State Security)
Pakistan	Inter Service Intelligence (I.S.I.)	Canada	Security Intelligence Service
U.S.A.	Central Intelligence Agency, Federal Bureau of Investigation	S. Africa	Bureau of State Security
		Iran	Sabak
Britain	Military Intelligence (M.I.)-5 and 6, Special Branch, Ultra, Joint Intelligence Organisation	Iraq	Al-Mukhabarat
		Australia	Australian Security and Intelligence Organisation
Israel	Mosad	France	S.D.E.C.E.
Egypt	Mukhabarat	Spain	C.E.S.I.D.
Japan	Nicho	Cuba	D.G.I.

SOME PROMINENT RACES OF THE WORLD

Races	Country/Area	Races	Country/Area	Races	Country/Area	Races	Country/Area
Veddas	Sri Lanka	Pygmy	Congo Basin	Eskimo	Canada, Tundra Region	Bushman	Kalahari Desert
Somaid	West Siberia	Bantu	Central and South Africa	Lapps	European Tundra	Red Indian	North America
Masai	East Africa	Tartars	Siberia	Hausa	Nigeria		
Muree	New Zealand	Baddu	Arab's Desert	Kirghiz	Steppes (Russia)		
Yakoot	Russian Tundra	Semang	Malaysia				
Papuans	New Guyana						

FAMOUS STRAITS OF THE WORLD

Strait	Between	Country
Malacca Strait	Andaman Sea and South China Sea	Indonesia
Palk Strait	Mannar and Bay of Bengal	India-Sri Lanka
Magellan Strait	Pacific and South Atlantic Ocean	Chile
Dover Strait	English Channel and North Sea	England-France
Berring Strait	Berring Sea and Chukasi Sea	Alaska-Russia
Sugaroo Strait	Japan Sea and Pacific Ocean	Japan
Sunda Strait	Java and Indian Ocean	Indonesia
Gibralter Strait	Mediterranean Sea and Atlantic Ocean	Spain
Harmuj Strait	Persia and Bay of Oman	Oman-Iran
Hudson Strait	Bay of Hudson and Atlantic Ocean	Canada

FAMOUS NEWSPAPERS OF THE WORLD

Newspaper	*Place of Publishing*	*Language*
Daily News	New York (America)	English
Guardian	London (Britain)	English
Pravada	Moscow (Russia)	Russian
Al-Ahram	Cairo (Egypt)	Arabic
Merdeca	Jakarta (Indonesia)	Indonesian
Times	London (Britain)	English
People's Daily	Beijing (China)	Chinese
New Statesman	Britain	English
Daily Mirror	Britain	English

Newspaper	*Place of Publishing*	*Language*
Hindu, Hindustan, Times of India, Tribune, Statesman, Indian Express, Economic Times	India	English
Hindustan, Nav Bharat Times, Dainik Bhaskar, Dainik Jagaran, Punjab Kesari	India	Hindi

IMPORTANT BOUNDARY LINES

Boundary Line	*Countries*
Durand Line	Pakistan and Afghanistan
Hindenberg Line	Germany-Poland
Maginot Line	France and Germany
Mannerhein Line	Russia-Finland
Mc Mahon Line	India-China
Order Niesse Line	Germany-Poland
Radcliff Line	India-Pakistan
Seigfrid Line	Germany-France
24th Parallel	India-Pakistan
17th Parallel	The line which defined the boundary between North Vietnam and South Vietnam before the two were united.
38th Parallel	North Korea and South Korea
49th Parallel	U.S.A. and Canada

SIGNALS/SIGNS AND MEANING

Signal/Sign	*Meaning*	*Signal/Sign*	*Meaning*
Red Triangle	Family Planning	White Flag	Treaty or Surrender
Red Cross	Medical Help	Yellow Flag	Vehicles with patients of contagious diseases
Red Light	Danger, 'Stop' for the movement of vehicles	Two Bones across with a Skull	Danger of electricity
Green Light	Go	Half mast flown Flag	National mourning
Olive Branch	Peace	Lotus and culture	Sign of civilization
White Pigeon or Dove	Peace	Wheel (Chakra)	Sign of Progress
Black Strip on Arm	(i) Opposition (ii) Sorrow	A blind folded woman with scale in hand	Sign of Justice
Black Flag	Opposition	Reversed flown	National calamity flag
Red Flag	(i) Danger (ii) Revolution		

NATIONAL EMBLEMS OF IMPORTANT COUNTRIES

Country	*National Emblem*	*Country*	*National Emblem*
America	Golden Rod	New Zealand	Kiwi, Fern Southern Cross
Australia	Kangaroo	Norway	Lion
Ireland	Shamrock	Nepal	Kukri
Italy	White Lily	Pakistan	Crescent
Israel	Candelabrum	Poland	Eagle
Iran	Rose	France	Lily
Canada	White Lily	Belgium	Lion
Great Britain	Rose	Bangladesh	Water Lily
Chile	Candor and Huemul	Mongolia	The Soyombo
Germany	Corn Flower	Russia	Double headed eagle
Japan	Chrysanthemum	Lebanon	Cedar Tree
Zimbabwe	Zimbabwe Bird	Sudan	Secretary Bird
Denmark	Beach	Syria	Eagle
Turkiye	Crescent and Star	India	Lioned Capital
The Netherlands	Lion		

THE CONTINENTS OF THE WORLD

Name	*Population (2021) (In million)*	*Per cent of the world's population*
Asia	4,584	59.1
Africa	1,375	17.4
Europe	747	9.8
North America	373	4.8
South America	651	8.4
Australia	41.66	0.5
Antarctica	NA	NA

COMPUTER

The computer is the system of that electronic device through which various informations are processed on the basis of a definite set of instructions called program and mathematical (numerical) and non-mathematical both types of informations are processed.

The first mechanical computer was composed or fabricated by Blaise Pascal in 1642 and it is called Pascalene. But in 1833, Charles Babbage first time conceived an automatic calculator or computer. Charles Babbage is called the father of modern computer. Herman made an electronic tabulating machine based on punch cards which operates automatically.

In 1937, first mechanical computer mark-I was fabricated by Howard Akeen. The most outstanding contribution in the development of modern computer goes to John Wan Newmaan who brought the 2nd revolution in the area of computer in 1951. He discovered EDVAC (Electronic Discrete Variable Automatic Computer) and utilised the stored program and the binary number system in the computer.

FUNCTIONS OF COMPUTER

1. Collection and composition (input) of datas;
2. Storage of datas.
3. Processing of datas.
4. Retrieval or output of the proccessed informations and datas.

UNITS OF COMPUTER

1. Input unit.
2. Central processing unit–CPU.
3. External Memory unit.
4. Output unit.

The CPU of the computer is called brain of the computer and sometimes CPU is also called Micro Processor of the computer. The data is entered through the input unit in the computer and through the central processing unit with the help of External Memory Unit datas are arranged and processed. Ultimately by the output unit these datas or informations are issued or released.

PARTS OF COMPUTER

- **Monitor :** The monitor of the computer is like a television in which the picture appears in the form of doted points on the screen and these are called pixcels.
- **Hard Disc and Floppy Disc :** The Hard Disc is the permanent disc in the computers while the Floppy Disc is the disc utilised when datas or informations are to be transferred from one computer to another.
- **Mouse :** The mouse of the computer is like the remote control of TV through which computer is directly regulated or controlled without utilising the key-board.
- **Printer :** The printer is a device which prints any documents or processed informations of the computer.

SOME HIGH LEVEL LANGUAGES

1. **FORTRAN :** This language was developed for solving the mathematical formulae very quickly and conveniently.
2. **COBOL :** This language was developed for the commerical purposes. For the processing of this language a group of sentences is selected called paragraph and all paragraphs composed are called a section, while all sections composed are called a division.
3. **BASIC :** In basic a definite part of the prescribed instruction is only inserted in the computer.
4. **ALGOL :** This was basically fabricated and designed for the complex algebraic calculations.
5. **PASCAL :** It is an amplified and modified form of ALGOL.
6. **COMAL :** This computer language is used for the students of secondary level.
7. **LOGO :** This language is used for children and kids for drawing Graphic line diagrams.
8. **PROLOG :** This language is developed in 1973 in France and this language is used for Artificial Intelligence which is capable and equivalent to the logical program.

9. **FORTH :** This language was invented by Charles Mure which is frequently used in all types of the works in the computer.

COMPUTER VIRUS

The computer virus is an electronic code which is used to abolish or erradicate the inclusive informations or programs of the computer. Some important computer viruses are Micheleanjalo, Dork Avangor, kilo, filip, Macmug, Scores, Casecade, Jeruslem, Date crime, Coloumbs crime, Internet virus, Pachcom, Pach EXE, COM-EXE, Marizuana, C-brain, bloody, Chenge Mungu and Desi etc.

COMPUTER NETWORKING

There are two types of networkings which are usually occur—Local Area Networking (LAN) and Wide Area Networking (WAN). By LAN all the computers of the same buildings are connected like the computers of university premises, computers of offices etc.

By WAN all the comptuers of a large area are connected like the computers of all the offices of a city or town etc. In India a very large computer network namely INDONET has been installing through which all the main towns and cities has to be interlinked.

COMPUTER TERMINOLOGY

- **Bit :** The bit is a unit of measurement of the electronic data. One bit is either 0 or 1 but not both. On composing 8 bits, 1 byte is formed.
- **Bug :** The Bug is the error in the computer program or system and its eradication is called Debug.
- **Byte :** Total eight bits compose a byte. Thus 8 bits = 1 byte.
- **CD-ROM :** A CD like of music CD in which data can be stored substantially called CD-ROM. In a CD with comparison to floppy extremely more datas can be stored but one problem in it is that one time recorded data can not be deleted or modified.
- **Chip :** It is a thin slice on which by a special mechanism a circuit is designed which is normally made from Silicon.
- **Memory System :** The place where computer data and program are temporarily kept is called Memory system. Usually memory is implied from RAM.
- **Modem :** The device which converts digital signals into analogue signals and vice-versa is called Modem.
- **RAM :** It is Random Access Memory (a place) where datas to be processed are kept temporarily and it is unstable memory.
- **ROM :** It is Read Only Memory and it is stable or Non-valatile memory which doesn't ended after power off.
- **Scanner :** It is a device through which graphic image is transformed to digital image and the scanners are of usually two types one desktop and another hand operating.

PROGRAMING

Computers perform phenomenal feats of calculation, but they do not do so in a complicated way. They actually carry out very simple operations, such as addition and subtraction. They achieve their fantastic computing power by carrying out these operations at incredible speed.

The programme, or set of instructions for operating the computer, is therefore written as a sequence of very simple steps. (See box below) Several computer languages have been developed for different applications, including BASIC, COBOL, FORTRAN and PASCAL. Writing programmes is very skilled and time-consuming work. But for most typical computer applications ready-written programmes are available, called "packages".

☞ How A Programme Works

Without a programme to tell it what to do and how to do it, a computer is unable to function. If, for example, you wanted to know how many times the word 'the' appears in this paragraph, or in the whole book, it would not be enough merely to put the text into a computer and then ask it how many times the word appears. For the computer to accomplish the calculations it has to be told what to do in simple steps. The instructions might be:

1. Scan the text until a space followed by 'T' or 't' is found.
2. If the next letter is not 'h', go back to step 1.
3. If the letter is 'h', is the next letter 'e'?
4. If not, go back to step 1. If it is, go to step 5.
5. If 'e' is followed by a space, add 1 to the total.
6. Go back to step 1.

A full computer programme for this operation would need to be broken down into even more simple steps, but a series of such programmes could enable a computer to analyse any amount of text in great detail.

DEFENCE

The Supreme Command of the Armed Forces is vested in the hands of the President of the Country. The responsibility for national defence, however, rests with the Cabinet. All important questions having a bearing on defence are decided by the Cabinet Committee on Political Affairs, which is presided over by the Prime Minister. The Defence Minister is responsible to Parliament for all matters concerning the Defence Services. All the administrative and operational control of Armed Forces are exercised by the Ministry of Defence. The three services – Army, Navy and Air Force function through their respective service headquarters headed by the chief of Staff.

COMMISSIONED RANKS IN DEFENCE SERVICES

Army	*Navy*	*Air Force*
General	Admiral	Air Chief Marshal
Lieutenant-General	Vice-Admiral	Air Marshal
Major-General	Rear-Admiral	Air Vice-Marshal
Brigadier	Commodor	Air Commodor
Colonel	Captain	Group Captain
Lieutenant-Colonel	Commander	Wing Commander
Major	Lt.Commander	Squadron Leader
Captain	Lieutenant	Flight Lieutenant
Lieutenant	Sub-Lieutenant	Flying Officer

INTERNAL SECURITY ORGANISATIONS OF INDIA

S. No	*Name of Organisation*	*Year of Creation*	*Headquarters*
1.	Assam Rifles (A.R.)	1835	Shillong
2.	Central Reserve Police Force (C.R.P.F.)	1939	New Delhi
3.	National Cadet Corps (N.C.C.)	1948	New Delhi
4.	Territorial Army	1948	In different States
5.	Indo-Tibetan Border Police	1962	New Delhi
6.	Home Guard	1962	In different States
7.	Coast Guard	1978	New Delhi
8.	Border Security Force (B.S.F.)	1965	New Delhi
9.	Central Industrial Security Force (C.I.S.F.)	1969	New Delhi
10.	National Security Guard	1984	New Delhi
11.	Police	—	In different States

COMMANDER-IN-CHIEFS OF INDIA

1. General Sir Rob Lockhart	Aug. 15, 1947 — Dec. 31, 1947
2. General Sir Roy Bucher	Jan. 1, 1948 — Jan. 14, 1949
3. General K. M. Kariappa	Jan. 15, 1949 — Jan. 14, 1953
4. General Maharaj Rajendra Sinhji	Jan. 15, 1953 — March 31, 1955

FIRST INDIAN CHIEFS OF STAFF OF INDIAN FORCES

1. General Maharaj Rajendra Sinhji (Army Staff)	April 1, 1955 — May 14, 1955
2. Vice Admiral R.D. Katari (Naval Staff)	April 22, 1958 — June 4, 1962
3. Air Marshal S. Mukherjee (Air Staff)	April 1, 1954 — Nov. 8, 1960

ARMY INSTITUTES

1. Sainik Schools upto +2 Level	33 places in India
2. Rashtriya Indian Military College (prepare for entrance to N.D.A)	Dehradun
3. National Defence Academy (three services)	Khadakwasla, Pune
4. Indian Military Academy (Army)	Dehradun
5. Officers Training Academy (3 services) Short Courses	Chennai
6. National Defence College	New Delhi
7. The College of Combat	Mhow
8. The College of Military Engineering	Kirkee
9. Military College of Telecommunication Engineering	Mhow
10. The armoured Corps Centre and School	Ahmed Nagar
11. The School Artillery	Deolali
12. The Infantry School	Mhow and Belgaum
13. College of Material Management	Jabalpur

AIR FORCE INSTITUTIONS

Air Force Academy	Hyderabad
Helicopter Training School	Hakimpet
Flying Instructors School	Tambaram, Chennai
The College of Air Warfare	Secunderabad
Air Force Administrative College	Coimbatore
Air Force Technical College	Jalahalli

DEFENCE PRODUCTION UNITS

1. Bharat Dynamites Ltd.	Hyderabad
2. Praga Tools	Hyderabad
3. Mishra Dattu Nigam	Hyderabad
4. Bharat Electronics Ltd.	Bangalore
5. Bharath Earthmovers Ltd.	Bangalore
6. Heavy Vehicles Ltd.	Avadi, Chennai
7. Garden Reach Ship Builders and Engineers Ltd.	Kolkata
8. Mazagaon Dock	Mumbai
9. Goa Shipyard	Marmugao
10. Hindustan Shipyard Ltd.	Vishakhapatnam
11. Hindustan Aeronautics Ltd.	Bangalore, Hyderabad, Nasik, Koraput, Kanpur, Lucknow

☞ Indian Army Commands

Command	HQ Location	Command	HQ Location
Eastern Command	Kolkata	Western Command	Chandigarh
Northern Command	Udhampur	Southern Command	Pune
Central Command	Lucknow	Training Command	Shimla
South-Western Command	Jaipur		

☞ Indian Air Force Commands

Command	HQ Location	Command	HQ Location
Western Air Command	New Delhi	South-Western Air Command	Gandhinagar
Central Air Command	Prayagraj	Eastern Air Command	Shillong
Southern Air Command	Thiruvananthapuram	Training Command	Bengaluru

☞ Indian Navy Commands

Command	HQ Location	Command	HQ Location
Eastern Naval Command	Vishakhapatnam	Western Naval Command	Mumbai
Southern Naval Command	Kochi		

☞ Missile and Other Weapons

Name	Class	Range
✶ Agni I	SRBM	850 km
✶ Agni II	MRBM	2500 km
✶ Agni III	IRBM	3500 km-5500 km
✶ Agni IV *or* Agni II Prime	IRBM	4000 km
✶ Agni V	ICBM	5000 km-6000 km
✶ Agni VI	ICBM	8000 km-10000 km
✶ Agni 3SL	ICBM	5200 km-11600 km
✶ Dhanush	SRBM	350 km
✶ Nirbhay	Subsonic Cruise Missile	1000 km

Name	Class	Range
✶ Brahmos	Supersonic Cruise Missile	290 km
✶ Brahmos 2	Hypersonic Cruise Missile	290 km
✶ Prithvi I	SRBM	150 km
✶ Prithvi III	SRBM	350 km
✶ Sagarika	SLBM	700 km-2200 km
✶ Shaurya	TBM	700 km-2200 km
✶ Astra	Air to Air Missile	80 km-100 km
✶ Barak-I	SRSAM	12 km
✶ Barak-8	SRSAM	90 km

☞ Chief of Defence Staff (CDS)

To bring in reform in higher defence management in the country, the post of Chief of Defence Staff (CDS) was created in the rank of a four-star General with salary and prerequisites equivalent to a Service Chief. The Chief of Defence Staff will also head the Department of Military Affairs (DMA), to be created within the Ministry of Defence and functions as its Secretary. Gen. Bipin Rawat was the first CDS of the country from January 1, 2020 to December 08, 2021.

MULTIPLE CHOICE QUESTIONS

1. Match List-I with List-II and select the correct answer from the codes given below the lists:

List-I

(*a*) Napoleon Bonaparte
(*b*) Jean Jacques Rousseau
(*c*) Croce
(*d*) Madame Roland

List-II

1. 'A history is contemporary history'
2. 'Liberty what crimes are committed in thy name'
3. 'Man is born free but everywhere he is in chains.'
4. 'I am the Child of Revolution'

Codes :

	(*a*)	(*b*)	(*c*)	(*d*)
A.	1	2	3	4
B.	4	3	1	2
C.	3	4	2	1
D.	3	4	1	2

2. Abraham Lincon was elected the President of United States in:
A. 1862 B. 1860
C. 1875 D. 1855

3. Who was known as the 'Prince of Humanists'?
A. Francisco Petrarch B. Dante
C. Boccacio D. Erasmus

4. D-Day is the day when:
A. Germany declared war on Britain
B. US dropped the atom bomb on Hiroshima.
C. Allied Troops landed in Normandy
D. Germany surrendered to the allies

5. Whose teachings inspired the French Revolution?
A. Locke
B. Rousseau
C. Hegel
D. Plato

6. At a time when empires in Europe were crumbling before the might of Napoleon which one of the following Governor-Generals kept the British flag flying high in India?
A. Warren Hastings B. Lord Cornwallis
C. Lord Wellesley D. Lord Hastings

7. Which one of the following statements regarding Fascism in Italy is *not* true?
A. The Fascists came to power as a result of popular uprising
B. In 1926, all political parties except Mussolini's party were banned
C. The Fascists suppressed the Socialist movement
D. The Fascists were hostile to the Communists

8. The fall of Czar Nicholas-II is known as:
A. Bloody Sunday
B. Bolshevik Revolution
C. February Revolution
D. October Revolution

9. Industrial Revolution took place first in:
A. France B. Germany
C. United Kingdom D. Japan

10. The British Prime Minister at the outbreak of World War II was :
A. Churchill B. Baldwin
C. Attlee D. Chemberlain

11. The 'Great Depression' (1929) economic crisis was met by adopting the policy of
A. Stimulus B. Marshall Plan
C. New Deal D. Open Door

12. The slogan "No taxation without representation" was raised during the:
A. American War of Independence
B. Russian Revolution
C. French Revolution
D. Indian Freedom struggle

1741 (GA)–4

13. In the nineteenth century the people of Europe started moving from the villages to the cities due to the impact of :
A. Epidemics
B. War
C. Industrialisation
D. Population explosion in villages

14. The important cause of the Civil War in America was:
A. Abolition of slavery
B. Quest for freedom
C. Industrialisation
D. Rebellion by the native Americans

15. Industrial Revolution could not have come about without:
A. Merchant capitalism
B. The Enclosure Movement
C. The services of the proletariat class
D. An agricultural revolution

16. Consider the following statements :
The French Revolution came about mainly due to the :
1. Extreme poverty of the people
2. Impact of the works of great writers
3. Cruelty of the rulers
4. Impact of impulsive reaction
Which of the above statements are correct?
A. 1, 2 and 4 B. 2 and 3
C. 1, 3 and 4 D. 1, 2, 3 and 4

17. Asia's oldest and largest Buddhist monastery is situated in :
A. Tawang (Arunachal Pardesh)
B. Lhasa (Tibet)
C. Trincomallee (Sri Lanka)
D. Ulan Bator (Mongolia)

18. Who was the main architect of the Russian Revolution?
A. Karl Marx B. Lenin
C. Stalin D. Tolstoy

19. V.I. Lenin is associated with :
A. Russian Revolution of 1917
B. Chinese Revolution of 1949
C. German Revolution
D. French Revolution of 1789

20. Which one of the following statements is *not* correct?
A. Voltaire believed in Natural Religion
B. Rousseau wrote *Social Contract*
C. Montesquieu authored *The Spirit of Laws*
D. Necker believed in 'General Will'

21. 6th April, 1930 is well known in the history of India because this date is associated with...........
A. Dandi March by Mahatma Gandhi
B. Quit India Movement
C. Partition of Bengal
D. Partition of India

22. Which ruler enforced the system of 'Price Control' in India?
A. Mohammad Tughlak
B. Razia Begum
C. Alauddin Khilji
D. Sher Shah Suri

23. The concept of 'Din-e-Elahi' was founded by which king?
A. Dara Shikoh B. Akbar
C. Sher Shah Suri D. Shahjahan

24. Who are supposed to be the earliest inhabitants of India? Where did they come from?
A. Aryans from Central Asia
B. Dravidians from Mediterranean
C. Negroids from Africa
D. Bhils and the Santhals from West Asia

25. The one chief characteristic of temple architecture of the Gupta Age was :
A. Absence of dome
B. Huge size
C. Beautiful carvings
D. absence of a covered courtyard for the gathering of worshippers

26. The Rigveda consists of :
A. 1000 hymns B. 2028 hymns
C. 1028 hymns D. 1038 hymns

27. The central point in Ashoka's dharma was :
A. royalty to kings
B. peace and non-violence
C. respect to elders
D. religious tolerance

28. The social evil which was conspicuously absent during ancient India was :
A. *Sati*-System B. *Devadasi*-System
C. Polygamy D. *Purdah*-System

29. Which, among the following, can be accepted as a novelty introduced by Mughal emperors to their buildings?
A. Domes B. Minarets
C. Arches D. Attached gardens

30. The first ruler of India who defeated Muhammud of Ghur was :
A. Mularaja II of Gujarat
B. Prithviraja Chauhan of Delhi
C. Jayachand of Kannauj
D. Parmaldeva of Bundelkhand

31. What important event happened in India in 1911?
A. Bengal was partitioned
B. Non-Cooperation movement was launched
C. India's capital was shifted from Calcutta to Delhi
D. Mahatma Gandhi presided over the Congress session

32. The first phase of the Congress Party (1885-1905) was characterized by its efforts to secure:
A. limited independence
B. complete freedom
C. Indianization of services
D. constitutional reforms

33. The Muslim League demanded a separate homeland for the Indian Muslims openly for the first time at its annual session held in Lahore in the year :
A. 1931 A.D. B. 1936 A.D.
C. 1940 A.D. D. 1941 A.D.

34. Under whose governorship did the East India Company secure the Diwani Rights in Bengal, Bihar and Odisha from Emperor Shah Alam?
A. Lord Cornwallis
B. Lord William Bentinck
C. Lord Clive
D. Lord Wellesley

35. The Simon Commission was generally boycotted by the Indian political parties. What was the reason for this general non-cooperation?
A. the Commission aimed at dividing the people
B. it was an 'all white' Commission
C. it came after the Jallianwala Bagh carnage
D. it was an eye wash

36. Aligarh Muslim University was founded by :
A. Dr. Saifuddin Kitchlu
B. Mohammad Ali Jinnah
C. Sir Syed Ahmed Khan
D. Maulana Mohammad Ali

37. Ibn Batutah was an African traveller visiting India during the time of :
A. Alivardi Khan
B. Ala-ud-din Khalji
C. Iltutmish
D. Mohammad-bin-Tughlaq

38. The battle of Wandiawash was fought in :
A. 1726 B. 1760
C. 1818 D. 1857

39. The abolition of *Sati* by government regulation was at the time of :
A. Warren Hastings B. Lord Wellesley
C. Lord Bentinck D. Lord Ahmerst

40. Pick out the wrong combination :
A. Dilwara Temple : Mt. Abu
B. Pashupati Temple : Kathmandu
C. Padmanabh Temple : Bangalore
D. Minakshi Temple : Madurai

41. Match the following:
(a) Chanhudaro *(b)* Kalibangan
(c) Lothal *(d)* Surkotada
1. Alleged discovery of the skeleton of horse.
2. Bead making.
3. Traces of a dock and ship on seal.
4. Evidence of ploughing the fields.

The Correct code is :

	(a)	*(b)*	*(c)*	*(d)*
A.	2	4	3	1
B.	2	1	3	4
C.	1	2	3	4
D.	2	1	4	3

42. Match the Harappan settlements with the banks of rivers on which they were located :

(*a*) Harappa	1. Ravi
(*b*) Mohenjodaro	2. Indus
(*c*) Ropar	3. Sutlej
(*d*) Kalibangan	4. Ghaggar
(*e*) Lothal	5. Bhogava

Codes :

	(*a*)	(*b*)	(*c*)	(*d*)	(*e*)
A.	1	2	3	4	5
B.	1	2	3	5	4
C.	2	1	3	5	4
D.	2	1	4	3	5

43. The Goddess 'Kannagi' whose many temples were erected during the 'Sangam Age' was the goddess of :

A. Chastity B. Love
C. Prowess D. Wisdom

44. The Jain goal of life is to attain deliverance from the fetters of mudane existence, the way to which lies through three jewels. Which one of the following was not included among the 'three jewels' of Jainism?

A. Right faith B. Right action
C. Right knowledge D. Right conduct

45. The most striking feature of the Ashokan pillar is polish. Name the Ashokan pillar which is considered to be the most graceful of all Ashokan pillars.

A. Sarnath
B. Rampurva
C. Laurya-Nandangarh
D. Rummindei

46. Which are the correct statements?

1. The land grants, started in Satavahana period, paved the way for feudal developments in India.
2. Silk and spices were the Chief Indian export articles of Indo-Roman trade.
3. The Guptas issued the largest number of gold coins in ancient India.
4. The first memorial of a 'SATI' dated 510 A.D. is found at Eran in Madhya Pradesh.

A. 1 and 2 B. 1, 3, and 4
C. 1 and 4 D. 1, 2, 3 and 4

47. Who among the following patronised the 'Gandhara' (Indo-Greek style) School of Art?

A. Ashoka, the Great
B. Harsha Vardhana
C. Kanishka
D. Chandragupta Vikramaditya

48. The Sultanate of Delhi had five ruling dynasties. The dynasty having longest and shortest period were :

A. Ilbari and Khalji
B. Tughlaq and Khalji
C. Tughlaq and Sayyid
D. Ilbari and Lodis

49. Which one of the following events took place at the last during reign of Muhammad-bin-Tughlaq?

A. Introduction of token currency
B. Increase of land-revenue in Doab
C. Transfer of Capital from Delhi to Devagiri.
D. Conquest of Khurasan and Iraq

50. The most learned medieval Muslim ruler who was well versed in various branches of learning including astronomy, mathematics and medicine was :

A. Jalaluddin Khilji
B. Sikander Lodi
C. Ghiyasuddin Tughlaq
D. Muhammad-bin-Tughlaq

51. The 'Sufis' had 12 silsilas. They propounded the idea of Union with God through:

A. Love B. Rituals
C. Fasts D. Prayers

52. Match the following:

(*a*) Peshwa	1. Foreign affairs
(*b*) Panditrao	2. Audit and accounts
(*c*) Amatya	3. Providing grants to scholars
(*d*) Sumant	4. General supervision
	5. Military affairs

Select the correct code :

	(*a*)	(*b*)	(*c*)	(*d*)
A.	2	3	4	5
B.	4	1	2	3
C.	4	3	2	1
D.	3	1	4	2

53. The Regulating Act of 1773 can be regarded as the first measure to :
A. assert the right of British Parliament to legislate for India
B. separate the legislature from the executive
C. separate the judiciary from the executive
D. centralise law-making

54. What was the exact constitutional status of the Indian Republic on 26th January, 1950?
A. A Democratic Republic
B. A Sovereign, Democratic Republic
C. A Sovereign, Secular, Democratic Republic
D. A Sovereign, Socialist, Secular, Democratic Republic

55. When the British obtained the grant of Diwani of Bengal, Bihar and Odisha they acquired the right to :
A. maintain law and order in these territories
B. administer civil justice and collect revenue in these territories
C. collect revenue and establish revenue administration in these territories
D. militarily defend these territories

56. Which of the following were responsible for the growth of nationalism in India during the British rule?
1. Economic exploitation of India.
2. Impact of western education.
3. Role of the Press.

Select the correct answer using the codes given below :

Codes:

A. 1, 2 and 3 B. 1 and 2
C. 2 and 3 D. 1 and 3

57. Which one of the following nationalist leaders has been described as being radical in politics but conservative on social issues?
A. G.K. Gokhale
B. B.G. Tilak
C. Lala Lajpat Rai
D. Madan Mohan Malviya

58. Provincial Autonomy in British India was envisaged by the :
A. Act of 1909 B. Act of 1919
C. Act of 1935 D. Act of 1947

59. Dyarchy means :
A. double government
B. a government in which the centre is very powerful
C. a government based on division of power between centre and provinces
D. None of the above

60. The Indian National Congress observed 'Independence Day' for the first time on 26th January in :
A. 1920 B. 1925
C. 1930 D. 1947

61. ....is situated near the banks of Sabarmati River
A. Bhavnagar B. Aurangabad
C. Ahmedabad D. Rajkot

62. Sericulture is:
A. science of the various kinds of serum
B. artificial rearing of fish
C. art of silkworm breeding
D. study of various cultures of a community

63. The most abundant constituents of earth's crust are:
A. Igneous rocks
B. Sedimentary rocks
C. Metamorphic rocks
D. Granite

64. Indian Standard Time is based on:
A. 80°E longitude B. 82½°E longitude
C. 110°E longitude D. 25°E longitude

65. Tides in the oceans are caused by :
A. Gravitational pull of the moon on the earth's surface including sea water
B. Gravitational pull of the sun on the earth's surface only and not on the sea water
C. Gravitational pull of the moon and the sun on the earth's surface including the sea water
D. None of these

66. Nagarjunasagar Project is situated on the river:
A. Tungabhadra
B. Cauvery
C. Krishna
D. Godavari

67. The difference between the Indian Standard Time and the Greenwich Mean Time is:
A. – 3½ hours B. + 3½ hours
C. – 5½ hours D. + 5½ hours

68. Which of the following dams is not on Narmada river?
A. Indira-Sagar Project
B. Maheshwar Hydel Power Project
C. Jobat Project
D. Koyna Power Project

69. Which of the following statements is **not true** about the availability of water on the earth, the crisis for which is going to increase in the years to come?
A. About 97.5 per cent of the total volume of water available on the earth is salty
B. 80 per cent of the water available to us for use comes in bursts as monsoons
C. About 2.5 per cent of the total water available on the earth is polluted water and cannot be used for human activities
D. Possibility is that some big glaciers will melt in the coming ten-fifteen years and sea level will rise by 3-4 metres all over the earth

70. Which of the following is **not** a cash crop?
A. Jute B. Paddy
C. Cashewnut D. Sugarcane

71. Through which States does Cauvery River flow?
A. Gujarat, M.P., Tamil Nadu
B. Karnataka, Keralam, Tamil Nadu
C. Karnataka, Keralam, Andhra Pradesh
D. M.P., Maharashtra, Tamil Nadu

72. Indian Standard Time is the local time of 82½°E which passes through :
A. Guntur B. Delhi
C. Prayagraj D. Kolkata

73. The 17th parallel defines the boundary between:
A. North and South Korea
B. USA and Canada
C. North and South Vietnam
D. China and Russia

74. During the period of south-west monsoon, Tamil Nadu remains dry because:
A. the winds do not reach this area
B. there are no mountains in this area
C. it lies in the rain shadow area
D. the temperature is too high to let the winds cool down

75. Which country does top in producing cocoa?
A. Cote d'Ivoire B. Brazil
C. Croatia D. Nigeria

76. The biggest reserves of thorium are in :
A. India B. China
C. The Soviet Union D. U.S.A.

77. The Girnar Hills are situated in which of the following states?
A. Gujarat B. Karnataka
C. Madhya Pradesh D. Maharashtra

78. During December 22nd the sun is vertically over:
A. Tropic of Cancer
B. Tropic of Capricorn
C. The Equator
D. None of the above

79. Photosphere is described as the :
A. Lower layer of atmosphere
B. Visible surface of the sun from which radiation emanates
C. Wavelength of solar spectrum
D. None of the above

80. Broadly, there are three layers of the earth of the crust, the mantle and the core. The crust forms what percentage of the volume of the earth?
A. 0.5% B. 2.5%
C. 7.5% D. 12.5%

81. The grassland of Argentina is known as :
A. Pampas B. Campos
C. Savanna D. None of the above

82. Different seasons are formed because :
A. Sun is moving around the earth
B. of revolution of the earth around the Sun on its orbit
C. of rotation of the earth around its axis
D. All of the above

83. Eskers and Drumlins are features formed by:
A. underground water
B. running water
C. the action of wind
D. glacial action

84. Match List-I and List-II and select the correct answer using the codes given below the Lists :

List-I *(Rivers)*	**List-II** *(Towns)*
(*a*) Ghaghara	1. Lucknow
(*b*) Brahmaputra	2. Hoshangabad
(*c*) Narmada	3. Ahmedabad
(*d*) Sabarmati	4. Guwahati
	5. Ayodhya

	(*a*)	(*b*)	(*c*)	(*d*)
A.	4	5	1	2
B.	5	4	2	3
C.	5	4	3	1
D.	3	5	2	1

85. Which of the statements as regards the consequences of the movement of the earth is not correct?
A. Revolution of the earth is the cause of the change of seasons.
B. Rotation of the earth is the cause of days and nights.
C. Rotation of the earth causes variation in the duration of days and nights.
D. Rotation of the earth effects the movement of winds and ocean currents.

86. The world is divided into :
A. 12 time zones
B. 20 time zones
C. 24 time zones
D. 36 time zones

87. The 'Kiel' canal links the :
A. Pacific and Atlantic Oceans
B. Mediterranean Sea and Red Sea
C. Mediterranean Sea and Black Sea
D. North Sea and Baltic Sea

88. Match the following :

List-I	**List-II**
(*a*) Himadri	1. Outer Himalayas
(*b*) Shivalik	2. Inner Himalayas
(*c*) Himanchal	3. Middle Himalayas
(*d*) Sahyadri	4. Western Ghats

Codes:

	(*a*)	(*b*)	(*c*)	(*d*)
A.	1	2	3	4
B.	4	2	3	1
C.	2	1	3	4
D.	1	2	3	4

89. The term 'Regur' refers to:
A. Laterite soils
B. Black Cotton soils
C. Red Soils
D. Deltaic Alluvial Soils

90. Location of sugar industry in India is shifting from north to south because of:
A. cheap labour
B. expanding regional market
C. cheap and abundant supply of power
D. high yield and high sugar content in sugarcane

91. Consider the following statements :
1. Ozone is found mostly in the Stratosphere.
2. Ozone layer lies 55-75 km above the surface of the earth.
3. Ozone absorbs ultraviolet radiation from the Sun.
4. Ozone layer has no significance for life on the earth.

Which of the above statements are correct?
A. 1 and 3 B. 2 and 4
C. 2 and 3 D. 1 and 4

92. Match List-I with List-II and select the correct answer using the codes given below the Lists :

List-I *(Crops)*	**List-II** *(Producer)*
(*a*) Banana	1. Brazil
(*b*) Cocoa	2. Cote d'Ivoire
(*c*) Coffee	3. India
(*d*) Tea	4. China

Codes :

	(*a*)	(*b*)	(*c*)	(*d*)
A.	2	3	1	4
B.	3	2	1	4
C.	3	2	4	1
D.	2	3	4	1

93. Darjeeling and Dharamsala would be the right places to visit if one wanted to get a clear view respectively of :
A. Kanchanjunga and Dhauladhar ranges
B. Nandadevi and Dhauladhar ranges
C. Kanchanjunga and Nandadevi ranges
D. Nandadevi and Nanga Parvat

94. Atmosphere exists because:
A. The Gravitational force of the Earth
B. Revolution of the Earth
C. Rotation of the Earth
D. Weight of the gases of atmosphere

95. Victoria lake is located in the continent:
A. Africa
B. Asia
C. North America
D. South America

96. The famous Lagoon Lake of India is :
A. Dal Lake B. Chilka Lake
C. Pulicat Lake D. Mansarover

97. Where are most of the earth's active volcanoes concentrated?
A. Indian Ocean B. Pacific Ocean
C. Aral Sea D. Atlantic Ocean

98. Through which of the following states does the river Chambal flow?
A. U.P., M.P., Rajasthan
B. M.P., Gujarat, U.P.
C. Rajasthan, M.P., Bihar
D. Gujarat, M.P., U.P.

99. Which country is called the sugar bowl of the world?
A. Cuba B. India
C. Argentina D. USA

100. The area covered by forest in India is about:
A. 46% B. 33%
C. 23% D. 21.76%

101. A closed economy is the one which :
A. does not permit emigration or immigration
B. permits emigration but no immigration
C. engages in no foreign trade
D. engages in no foreign and domestic trade or transit

102. In a developed economy the major share of employment originates in the :
A. primary sector B. tertiary sector
C. secondary sector D. any of the above

103. The Economic and Social Commission for Asia and Pacific (ESCAP) is located at :
A. Bangkok B. Kuala Lumpur
C. Manila D. Singapore

104. Commercial vehicles are not produced by which of the following companies in India?
A. TELCO B. Ashok Leyland
C. DCM Daewoo D. Birla Yamaha

105. In India, the Public Sector is most dominant in:
A. transport
B. steel production
C. commercial banking
D. organised term-lending financial institutions

106. The main argument advanced in favour of small scale and cottage industries in India is that:
A. cost of production is low
B. they require small capital investment
C. they advance the goal of equitable distribution of wealth
D. they generate a large volume of employment

107. The most serious economic problems of India are:
A. Poverty and unemployment
B. Stagnation, not poverty
C. Unemployment, not poverty
D. Underdevelopment, not poverty

108. Which of the following is not one of the three central problems of an economy?
A. What to produce
B. How to produce
C. When to produce
D. For whom to produce

109. If saving exceeds investment, the national income will:
A. fall B. rise
C. fluctuate D. remain constant

110. In which of the following industries in India are the maximum number of workers employed?
A. Sugar B. Jute
C. Textiles D. Iron and Steel

111. Terrace Cultivation is practiced mostly:
A. in urban areas
B. on slopes of mountains
C. on tops of hills
D. in undulating tracts

112. Which of the following is a Selective Credit Control method?
A. Bank Rate
B. RBI directives
C. Cash Reserve Ratio
D. Open market operations

113. Which of the following taxes is not shared by the Central Government with the States?
A. Union excise duties
B. Customs duty
C. Income tax
D. Estate duty

114. ICICI is the name of a:
A. Financial Institution
B. Chemical Industry
C. Cotton Industry
D. Chamber of Commerce and Industry

115. Structural Unemployment arises due to
A. Deflationary conditions
B. Heavy industry bias
C. Shortage of raw material
D. Inadequate productive capacity

116. Which Commission replaced the Planning Commission in 2015?
A. NIYAM Aayog
B. NAGRIK Aayog
C. NITI Aayog
D. Jan Aayog

117. The largest public sector bank in India is:
A. Central Bank of India
B. Punjab National Bank
C. State Bank of India
D. Indian Overseas Bank

118. Which of the following statements best explains the term contraband goods?
A. Goods produced only for exports
B. Goods produced in joint sector only
C. Goods for the trading of which licence is not required
D. Goods that are forbidden, from export, import or even possession, by law

119. Price in the market is fixed by:
A. Stock exchange rates
B. The demand and supply ruling in the market at a particular time
C. The Finance Minister
D. None of the above

120. Devaluation of currency helps to promote:
A. National Income
B. Savings
C. Imports at lower cost
D. Exports

121. Balanced economic growth can be achieved only if:
A. All the sectors of economy grow at the same rate
B. Population growth is arrested
C. All the inter dependent sectors grow in harmony
D. Basic and heavy industries are assigned highest priority

122. P.V. Sindhu is associated with which of the following sports?
A. Badminton
B. Weightlifting
C. Swimming
D. Tennis

123. 'MODVAT' stands for:
A. Modified Value Added Tax
B. Deduction of cost of inputs from the value of output
C. Reduction in import duties
D. Imposition of tax on professions

124. Who among the following is the first to receive 'Dada Saheb Phalke' award?
A. Shivaji Ganeson B. Devika Rani
C. Dr. Raj Kumar D. None of the above

125. The term 'devaluation' means:
A. Reducing the value of a currency in terms of another currency
B. Increasing the value of a currency
C. Revising the value of a currency
D. None of the above

126. Per capita net availability of pulses has shown a tendency of:
A. Increase over time
B. Decrease over time
C. Constant over time
D. First increase then decrease

127. National Income is the same as:
A. Net national product at market price
B. Net domestic product at market price
C. Net national product at factor cost
D. Net domestic product at factor cost

128. Which one of the following is not an example of indirect tax?
A. Sales tax B. Excise duty
C. Customs duty D. Expenditure tax

129. The major aim of devaluation is to:
A. encourage imports
B. encourage exports
C. encourage both exports and imports
D. discourage both exports and imports

130. Structural unemployment arises due to:
A. deflationary conditions
B. heavy industry bias
C. shortage of raw materials
D. inadequate productive capacity

131. When was the Family Planning Programme officially started in India?
A. 1950 B. 1952
C. 1956 D. 1962

132. When was the Reserve Bank of India nationalised?
A. 1947 B. 1949
C. 1950 D. 1951

133. Which of the following is *not* a feature of the Indian economy?
A. High rate of population growth
B. Disguised unemployment
C. Lowest rate of adult literacy
D. High rate of exports

134. The 'Relative Deprivation' approach for measuring poverty has been adopted by:
A. developing countries
B. developed countries
C. under-developed countries
D. None of the above

135. One of the main factors that led to rapid expansion of Indian exports is:
A. Imposition of import duties
B. Liberalisation of the economy
C. Recession in other countries
D. Diversification of exports

136. Sustainable economic development means an increase in the rate of growth of real:
A. total and per capita product
B. total and per capita product and level of literacy rate
C. total and per capita product and life expectancy at birth
D. total and per capita product, taking into account the cost of degradation of the quality of environment in this process

137. Functional unemployment occurs when:
A. unemployed have no qualification for job
B. people frequently change their job
C. people were thrown out from job due to recession
D. None of these

138. Which among the following does **not** have a 'free trade zone'?
A. Kandla B. Mumbai
C. Visakhapatnam D. Thiruvanantpuram

139. Sun Belt of USA is important for which one of the following industries?
A. Cotton textile
B. Petrochemicals
C. Hi-tech electronics
D. Food Processing

140. Commercial banking system in India is
A. unit banking B. branch banking
C. mixed banking D. None of the above

141. Who gives recognition to political parties in India?
A. Parliament

B. President
C. Supreme Court
D. Election Commission

142. The Quorum of the Legislative Council is :
A. one-fourth of its total membership
B. one-third of its membership
C. one-tenth of its membership
D. 25

143. The Indian Constitution is:
A. federal
B. unitary
C. a happy mixture of the federal and unitary
D. federal in normal times and unitary in times of emergency

144. Universal adult franchise implies a right to vote to all:
A. adult residents of the State
B. adult male citizens of the State
C. residents of the State
D. adult citizens of the State

145. When a resolution prefering a charge against the President has been passed by a specified majority in the House, it is sent to the other House for investigation. If, as a result of such an investigation, a resolution is passed through a specified majority by the other House, declaring that the charge has been sustained, the President shall leave his office. The specified special majority must not be less than :
A. two-third of the members present and voting
B. one-third of the members present and voting
C. three-fourth of the members present and voting and two-third of the total membership
D. two-third of the total membership

146. Which one of the following judicial powers of the President of India has been *wrongly* listed?
A. he appoints the Chief Justice and other judges of the Supreme Court
B. he can remove the judges of the Supreme Court on grounds of misconduct
C. he can consult the Supreme Court on any question of law or fact which is of public importance
D. he can grant pardon, reprieves and respites to persons punished under Union Law

147. The Vice-president of India can be removed from his office before the expiry of his term if :
A. the Rajya Sabha passes a resolution by a majority of its members and the Lok Sabha agrees with the resolution
B. if the Supreme Court of India recommends his removal
C. the President so desires
D. None of the above

148. The Chief Justice of a High Court in India is appointed by the :
A. Governor of the State
B. Prime Minister of India
C. Chief Justice of the Supreme Court
D. President of India

149. Which of the following statements is constitutionally not true about the passing of the Union Budgets, Railway Budgets and Finance Bill in India?
1. Under the law, Finance Bill should be adopted by both the Houses of the Parliament within 45 days of its introduction.
2. If the Finance Bill is not adopted within specified period, the government loses its authority to levy the taxes proposed in the budgets.
3. In the absence of full budget, a vote-on-account gives the power to the government to spend.
4. Government cannot raise revenues without a proper approval of the Finance Bill

A. Only 2 B. Only 3
C. Only 4 D. Only 1, 2 and 3

150. Normally, on whose advice the President's Rule is imposed in a State?
A. Chief Minister
B. Legislative Assembly
C. Governor
D. Chief Justice of High Court

151. Which Article of the Indian Constitution deals with Amendment procedure?
A. Article 368 B. Article 358
C. Article 367 D. All of these

152. Government is the agency through which the will of :
A. the state is expressed
B. the people is expressed
C. the head of the state is expressed
D. the majority is expressed

153. In a unitary system of government :
A. The centre is all powerful
B. The centre is weaker than the states
C. The centre and states stand at par
D. The states and centre are supreme in their respective spheres

154. In Cabinet System of Government the real executive authority rests with :
A. The Council of Ministers
B. The Prime Minister
C. The Constitution
D. The Parliament

155. The Head of the State under a parliamentary government:
A. is an elected representative
B. is a hereditary person
C. is a nominated person
D. may be any one of the above

156. In the event of a ministerial proposal being defeated on the floor of the legislature, under the parliamentary system :
A. the government waits for a general no-confidence motion
B. the minister concerned is taken to task by the Prime Minister
C. the minister is forced to resign
D. the whole Council of Ministers resign

157. The "due process of law" is an essential characteristic of the judicial system of:
A. UK B. France
C. USA D. India

158. Under the Constitution it is :
A. obligatory for the President to accept the advice of the Council of Ministers but is not obliged to follow it
B. obligatory for the President to accept the advice of the Council of Ministers
C. not obligatory for the President to seek or accept the advice of the Council of Ministers
D. obligatory for the President to seek the advice of the Council of Ministers if his own party is in power

159. Which one of the following statements is correct?
A. the Presiding Officer of Rajya Sabha is elected every year
B. the Presiding Officer of Rajya Sabha is elected for a term of two years at a time
C. the Presiding Officer of Rajya Sabha is elected for a term of six years
D. the Vice-President of India is the ex-officio Presiding Officer of Rajya Sabha

160. The introduction of "no confidence" motion in the Lok Sabha requires the support of at least:
A. 50 members B. 70 members
C. 60 members D. 80 members

161. The High Court comes under :
A. State List B. Union List
C. Concurrent List D. None of the above

162. Which one of the following has been wrongly listed as a Fundamental Duty of the Indian citizens?
A. to develop scientific temper, humanism and spirit of inquiry and reform
B. to work for raising the prestige of the country in the international sphere
C. to protect and improve the natural environment
D. to strive towards excellence in all spheres of individual and collective activity

163. Which one of the following is not a Fundamental Duty as outlined in Article 51A of the Constitution?
A. to abide by the Constitution and respect its ideals
B. to defend the country and render national service when called upon to do so

C. to work for the moral upliftment of the weaker sections of society
D. to preserve the rich heritage

164. The main characteristics of the Directive Principles of State Policy given in the Indian Constitution are :
A. not enforceable by any court
B. fundamental in the governance of the country
C. 'Like instruments, instructions, political manifesto and a code of moral precepts which have to guide governors of the country'
D. no law can be passed, which is opposed to these principles

165. Of the following which are true?
A. In a State, the Legislative Council is dominant with regard to non-financial bills and the Legislative Assembly with regard to financial (money) bills
B. Vidhan Parishad can virtually block legisla-tion even if the same is passed by the Vidhan Sabha
C. In case of a tie between the two Houses, the Governor is duty-bound to call a joint session of the two Houses to have the issue settled on a majority verdict
D. If a Bill is twice approved by the Vidhan Sabha, it becomes law even if rejected by the Vidhan Parishad

166. Which one of the following types of emergency can be declared by the President?
A. Emergency due to threat of war and external aggresion
B. Emergency due to break-down of constitu-tional machinery in a State
C. Financial emergency on account of threat to the financial credit of India
D. all the three emergencies

167. The chairman of which of the following parliamentary committees is invariably from the members of ruling party?
A. Committee on public undertakings
B. Public accounts committee
C. Estimates committee
D. Committee on delegated legislation

168. Which of the following is not a formally prescribed device available to the members of parliament?
A. Question hour
B. Zero hour
C. Half-an-hour discussion
D. Short duration discussion

169. Which of the following is not a tool of executive control over public administration?
A. Power of appointment and removal
B. Line agencies
C. Appeal to public opinion
D. Civil services code

170. If the Speaker of the State Legislative Assembly decides to resign, he should submit his resignation to the:
A. Judges of the High Court
B. Deputy Speaker
C. Chief Minister
D. Finance Minister

171. Who was the first Home Minister of Independent India?
A. Rajendra Prasad
B. Jawahar Lal Nehru
C. B.R. Ambedkar
D. Sardar Vallabh Bhai Patel

172. India is a Federal State because of:
A. dual judiciary
B. dual citizenship prevalent here
C. share of power between the Centre and the States
D. rigid Constitution

173. Residuary Subjects are those subjects which are:
A. contained in the State list
B. contained in the Union list
C. contained in the Concurrent list
D. not covered by any of the three lists

174. Which of the following writs can be issued, by the Supreme Court, to enforce Fundamental Rights?
A. Writ of Habeas Corpus
B. Writ of Mandamus
C. Writ of Quo Warranto
D. All of these

175. When the offices of both the President and the Vice-President of India are vacant, who will discharge their functions?
A. Prime Minister
B. Home Minister
C. Chief Justice of India
D. The Speaker

176. The Supreme Court tenders advice to the President of India on a matter of law or fact:
A. on its own
B. only when such advice is sought
C. only if the matter relates to some basic issue
D. only if the issue poses a threat to the unity and integrity of the country

177. Six months shall **not** intervene between two sessions of the Indian Parliament because :
A. it is the customary practice
B. it is the British convention followed in India
C. it is an obligation under the Constitution of India
D. None of the above

178. The States of the Indian Union can be recognised or their boundaries altered by:
A. the Union Parliament by a simple majority in the ordinary process of legislation
B. two-thirds majority of both the Houses of Parliament
C. two-thirds majority of both the Houses of Parliament and the consent of the legislatures of concerned States
D. an executive order of the Union government with the consent of the concerned State governments

179. The Basic Feature theory of the Constitution of India was propounded by the Supreme Court in the case of :
A. Minerva Mills Vs. Union of India
B. Golaknath Vs. State of Punjab
C. Maneka Gandhi Vs. Union of India
D. Keshavananda Vs. State of Kerala

180. Which one of the following writs is issued by a court in case of illegal detention of a person?
A. Habeas corpus B. Mandamus
C. Certiorari D. Quo-warranto

181. Name the instrument with the help of which a sailor in a submarine can see the objects on the surface of the sea.
A. Telescope B. Periscope
C. Gycroscope D. Stereoscope

182. 'HEMOPHILLIA' is the disease of ....
A. liver B. blood
C. brain D. bones

183. Vitamin A is abundantly found in ....
A. Brinjal B. Tomato
C. Carrot D. Cabbage

184. .... is not soluble in water.
A. Vitamin A B. Vitamin B
C. Vitamin C D. None of these

185. The blood vessels with the smallest diameter are called ....
A. capillaries B. arterioles
C. venules D. lymphatics

186. Out of the following .... has the greatest elasticity.
A. steel B. rubber
C. aluminium D. annealed copper

187. Cooking gas is a mixture of which of the following two gases?
A. Carbon Dioxide and Oxygen
B. Butane and Propane
C. Carbon Monoxide and Carbon Dioxide
D. Methane and Ethylene

188. The substance most commonly used as a food preservative is:
A. sodium carbonate B. tartaric acid
C. acetic acid D. benzoic acid

189. Normally, the substances that fight against diseases in human systems are known as:
A. dioxyribonucleic acids
B. carbohydrates
C. enzymes
D. antibodies

190. The SI unit of temperature is ....
A. Kelvin B. Celsius
C. Fahrenheit D. None of the above

191. One of the common fungal diseases of man is :
A. plague B. ringworm
C. cholera D. typhoid

192. A clear sky is blue because:
A. red light is scattered more than blue
B. ultraviolet light has been absorbed
C. blue light is scattered more than red
D. blue light has been absorbed

193. Jenner introduced the method of making people immune to :
A. small pox B. rabies
C. cholera D. polio

194. The largest cell in the human body is :
A. Nerve cell B. Live cell
C. Muscle cell D. Kidney cell

195. What is the device that steps up or steps down the voltage?
A. Dynamo B. Conductor
C. Inductor D. Transformer

196. The protein deficiency disease is known as :
A. Kwashiorker B. Cirrhosis
C. Eczema D. Clycoses

197. Iron deficiency causes :
A. rickets B. anaemia
C. cirrhosis D. goitre

198. Blood group of an individual is controlled by :
A. Haemoglobin B. Shape of RBC
C. Shape of WBC D. Genes

199. In a normal man the amount of blood pumped out by the heart per minute is about :
A. 1 litre B. 3 litres
C. 4 litres D. 5 litres

200. Red/green colour blindness in man is known as :
A. Protanopia
B. Deutetanopia
C. Both A and B above
D. Marfan's syndrome

201. The blue colour of the water in the sea is due to :
A. Reflection of the blue light by the impurities in sea water
B. Reflection of the blue sky by sea water and scattering of blue light by water molecules
C. Absorption of other colours by water molecules
D. None of the above

202. The image formed on the retina of the eye is:
A. upright and real
B. larger than the object
C. small and inverted
D. enlarged and real

203. Unit of loudness of sound is:
A. bel B. decibel
C. phon D. none of these

204. Oil rises up the wick in a lamp :
A. because oil is volatile
B. due to the capillary action phenomenon
C. due to the surface tension phenomenon
D. because oil is very light

205. The 'stones' formed in human kidney consist mostly of :
A. calcium oxalate
B. sodium acetate
C. magnesium sulphate
D. calcium

206. We hear the sound later, while the light is seen earlier:
A. because light's speed is more than that of sound
B. because lights travel in a straight direction while sound in a zigzag direction
C. because sound's frequency is lower than light
D. All of the above

207. Which part of an eye is transplanted?
A. Cornea B. Retina
C. Iris D. Sciera

208. The Universal donor group of blood is:
A. O B. A
C. B D. AB

209. The green colour of the leaf is due to :
A. Presence of Chloroplast
B. Presence of Chromium
C. Presence of Nicoplast
D. Presence of excess of oxygen

210. Voice of a child is more shrill than that of an elderly person because:
A. the pitch of the child's voice is higher than that of the person
B. the pitch is lower
C. the child is more energetic
D. None of the above

ANSWERS

1	2	3	4	5	6	7	8	9	10
B	C	D	C	B	C	A	C	C	D
11	**12**	**13**	**14**	**15**	**16**	**17**	**18**	**19**	**20**
C	A	C	A	A	D	A	B	A	D
21	**22**	**23**	**24**	**25**	**26**	**27**	**28**	**29**	**30**
A	C	B	C	D	C	B	D	D	B
31	**32**	**33**	**34**	**35**	**36**	**37**	**38**	**39**	**40**
C	D	C	C	B	C	D	B	C	C
41	**42**	**43**	**44**	**45**	**46**	**47**	**48**	**49**	**50**
A	A	A	B	C	D	C	B	B	D
51	**52**	**53**	**54**	**55**	**56**	**57**	**58**	**59**	**60**
A	C	A	B	B	A	B	C	A	C
61	**62**	**63**	**64**	**65**	**66**	**67**	**68**	**69**	**70**
C	C	B	B	C	C	D	D	D	B
71	**72**	**73**	**74**	**75**	**76**	**77**	**78**	**79**	**80**
B	C	C	C	A	A	A	B	B	A
81	**82**	**83**	**84**	**85**	**86**	**87**	**88**	**89**	**90**
A	B	D	B	C	C	D	C	B	D
91	**92**	**93**	**94**	**95**	**96**	**97**	**98**	**99**	**100**
A	B	A	A	A	B	B	A	A	D
101	**102**	**103**	**104**	**105**	**106**	**107**	**108**	**109**	**110**
C	B	A	D	D	D	A	C	D	C
111	**112**	**113**	**114**	**115**	**116**	**117**	**118**	**119**	**120**
B	B	B	A	D	C	C	D	B	D
121	**122**	**123**	**124**	**125**	**126**	**127**	**128**	**129**	**130**
C	A	A	B	A	D	C	D	B	D
131	**132**	**133**	**134**	**135**	**136**	**137**	**138**	**139**	**140**
B	B	D	A	B	D	B	D	D	C
141	**142**	**143**	**144**	**145**	**146**	**147**	**148**	**149**	**150**
D	C	D	D	D	B	A	D	C	C
151	**152**	**153**	**154**	**155**	**156**	**157**	**158**	**159**	**160**
A	B	A	A	A	D	C	B	D	A
161	**162**	**163**	**164**	**165**	**166**	**167**	**168**	**169**	**170**
B	B	C	B	D	D	C	B	B	B
171	**172**	**173**	**174**	**175**	**176**	**177**	**178**	**179**	**180**
D	C	D	D	C	B	C	A	D	A
181	**182**	**183**	**184**	**185**	**186**	**187**	**188**	**189**	**190**
B	B	C	A	A	A	B	D	D	A
191	**192**	**193**	**194**	**195**	**196**	**197**	**198**	**199**	**200**
B	C	A	A	D	A	B	D	D	A
201	**202**	**203**	**204**	**205**	**206**	**207**	**208**	**209**	**210**
B	B	B	B	A	A	A	A	A	A